Get More a... ...mies.com®

Start with **FREE** Cheat Sheets

And Other Good Stuff!

To access the Cheat Sheet created specifically for this book, go to

www.dummies.com/cheatsheet/alaska

Get Smart at Dummies.com

Dummies.com makes your life easier with 1,000s
of answers on everything from removing
wallpaper to using the latest version
of Windows.

Check out our

- Videos
- Illustrated Articles
- Step-by-Step Instructions

Plus, each month you can win valuable prizes
by entering our Dummies.com sweepstakes. *

Want a weekly dose of Dummies?
Sign up for Newsletters on

- Digital Photography
- Microsoft Windows & Office
- Personal Finance & Investing
- Health & Wellness
- Computing, iPods & Cell Phones
- eBay
- Internet
- Food, Home & Garden

Find out "HOW" at Dummies.com

*Sweepstakes not currently available in all countries; visit Dummies.com for official rules.

Alaska
FOR
DUMMIES®
5TH EDITION

by Charles Wohlforth

WILEY

Wiley Publishing, Inc.

Alaska For Dummies®, 5th Edition

Published by
Wiley Publishing, Inc.
111 River St.
Hoboken, NJ 07030-5774
www.wiley.com

Copyright © 2011 by Wiley Publishing, Inc., Indianapolis, Indiana

Published simultaneously in Canada

For general information on our other products and services, please contact our Customer Care Department within the U.S. at 877-762-2974, outside the U.S. at 317-572-3993, or fax 317-572-4002.

For technical support, please visit www.wiley.com/techsupport.

Wiley also publishes its books in a variety of electronic formats. Some content that appears in print may not be available in electronic books.

ISBN: 978-0-470-88871-1 (paper); 978-1-118-03048-6 (ebk); 978-1-118-03049-3 (ebk); 978-1-118-03050-9 (ebk);

Manufactured in the United States of America

10 9 8 7 6 5 4 3 2 1

WILEY

About the Author

Charles Wohlforth is a lifelong Alaskan who has written ten books about the state, its nature, its history, and its politics. His most recent book, *The Fate of Nature: Rediscovering Our Ability to Rescue the Earth* (Picador), uses the story of Alaska's coasts to explore the capacity of humanity to solve global environmental challenges. His previous book, *The Whale and the Supercomputer: On the Northern Front of Climate Change* (North Point Press), won the *Los Angeles Times* Book Prize for science and technology. Wohlforth lives in Anchorage with his wife, Barbara; sons, Robin and Joseph; and daughters, Julia and Rebecca. Learn more about his work at www.fateofnature.com.

Author's Acknowledgments

This fifth edition of *Alaska For Dummies* is again the product of teamwork. Over 15 years of writing about travel in Alaska, I've received help from more friends than I can ever thank. For this edition, Mara Hill did the heavy lifting of updating the text. Karen Datko was, once again, an invaluable researcher. Talented writers from around the state contributed as well, bringing expertise about their own areas of Alaska: Jessica Edwards, Charlotte Glover, Eric Troyer, Kris Capps, Martha Robinson, Jay Barrett, and Anne Hillman.

Publisher's Acknowledgments

We're proud of this book; please send us your comments through our Dummies online registration form located at www.dummies.com/register/.

Some of the people who helped bring this book to market include the following:

Editorial

Editors: Stephen Bassman,
Eric T. Schroeder

Copy Editor: Elizabeth Kuball

Cartographer: Guy Ruggiero

Editorial Assistant: Andrea Kahn

Senior Photo Editor: Richard Fox

Cover Photos:

Front cover: © Doug Demarest /
AlaskaStock / PhotoLibrary

Back cover: © Bruce
Lichtenberger / Peter Arnold
Images RF / PhotoLibrary

Cartoons: Rich Tennant (www.
the5thwave.com)

Composition Services

Project Coordinator:
Katherine Crocker

Layout and Graphics: Claudia Bell

Proofreader: Sossity R. Smith

Indexer: BIM Indexing & Proofreading
Services

Publishing and Editorial for Consumer Dummies

Diane Graves Steele, Vice President and Publisher, Consumer Dummies

Kristin Ferguson-Wagstaffe, Product Development Director, Consumer Dummies

Kelly Regan, Editorial Director, Travel

Publishing for Technology Dummies

Andy Cummings, Vice President and Publisher, Dummies Technology/ General User

Composition Services

Debbie Stailey, Director of Composition Services

Contents at a Glance

Introduction..1

Part I: Introducing Alaska 7
Chapter 1: Discovering the Best of Alaska....................................9
Chapter 2: Digging Deeper into Alaska.......................................15
Chapter 3: Deciding Where and When to Go 25
Chapter 4: Great Alaska Itineraries..35

Part II: Planning Your Trip to Alaska.................. 45
Chapter 5: Managing Your Money..47
Chapter 6: Getting to Alaska 58
Chapter 7: Getting Around Alaska...69
Chapter 8: Cruising Alaska's Coast 81
Chapter 9: Planning an Outdoor Adventure 110
Chapter 10: Booking Your Accommodations 134
Chapter 11: Catering to Special Travel Needs or Interests......140
Chapter 12: Taking Care of the Remaining Details..................146

Part III: Anchorage and Environs 161
Chapter 13: Settling Into Anchorage..163
Chapter 14: Exploring Anchorage 184
Chapter 15: Side Trips from Anchorage 205

Part IV: Road Trips from Anchorage 223
Chapter 16: The Kenai Peninsula: Seward, Kenai Fjords
National Park, Kenai, and Homer.......................................225
Chapter 17: Fairbanks..264
Chapter 18: Driving Alaska's Highways 286
Chapter 19: Denali National Park 300

Part V: Southeast Alaska.................................... 325
Chapter 20: Juneau..327
Chapter 21: Skagway...347
Chapter 22: Sitka 356

Part VI: The End of the Road and Beyond:
Bush Alaska 369
Chapter 23: The Arctic..371
Chapter 24: Bear Country: Katmai National Park
and Kodiak Island 382

Part VII: The Part of Tens *395*
    Chapter 25: Ten Great Walks and Hikes in Alaska 397
    Chapter 26: Ten Questions to Ask an Alaskan..........................401
    Chapter 27: Ten Ways to Be an Alaska Know-It-All..................405

Appendix: Quick Concierge *410*

Index.. *415*

Maps at a Glance

Alaska Wildlife..120
Anchorage 171
Downtown Anchorage..177
The Kenai Peninsula and Prince William Sound...............................227
Seward 231
Homer 253
Fairbanks..269
Downtown Fairbanks 273
Alaska Highways..289
Denali National Park..309
Greater Juneau..331
Downtown Juneau 333
Skagway 351
Sitka...359

Table of Contents

Introduction *1*

  About This Book 1
  Conventions Used in This Book 2
  Foolish Assumptions 3
  How This Book Is Organized 3
      Part I: Introducing Alaska 3
      Part II: Planning Your Trip to Alaska......................4
      Part III: Anchorage and Environs 4
      Part IV: Road Trips from Anchorage 4
      Part V: Southeast Alaska......................................4
      Part VI: The End of the Road and Beyond: Bush
        Alaska 4
      Part VII: The Part of Tens......................................4
  Icons Used in This Book...5
  Where to Go from Here 5

Part 1: Introducing Alaska *7*

  Chapter 1: Discovering the Best of Alaska...................**9**
    The Best Big Ice...10
    The Best Bear Viewing 11
    The Best Places to Encounter Indigenous Culture 11
    The Best Gold-Rush Towns.......................................12
    The Best Day Hikes 13
    The Best One-of-a-Kind Lodgings 13

  Chapter 2: Digging Deeper into Alaska.....................**15**
    Understanding Alaska's Native Cultures.......................15
      Treating Alaska's first people properly 17
      Finding Native culture.......................................17
    Alaska History: Not an Oxymoron 18
      Searching for Russian America (1741–1867) 18
      Rushing for gold (1867–1940)............................19
      Defending the United States (1940–1968) 19
      Discovering oil (1968 to the present).....................20
    Speaking Alaskan 21
    Ordering Dinner: Hope Ya Like Fish 22
    Background Check: Recommended Books, Movies,
      and TV Programs 24

Chapter 3: Deciding Where and When to Go 25

Narrowing Your Travel Options...25
    Anchorage...25
    The Kenai Peninsula..26
    Fairbanks and the Interior highways 27
    Denali National Park..27
    Southeast Alaska..27
    The Bush..28
Sorting out the Seasons...28
    The seasons from Anchorage north........................29
    The seasons in coastal Alaska 31
Perusing Alaska's Calendar of Events 32
    February..32
    March 33
    May 33
    June 33
    July...33
    August 34
    November 34
Keeping Your Trip on Track...34

Chapter 4: Great Alaska Itineraries 35

Touring Southeast Alaska in One Week without
    a Cruise Ship...36
Seeing the National Parks: Denali and Kenai Fjords
    in One Week...38
Covering a Lot of (Alaskan) Ground in Two Weeks.........39
Planning a Kid-Friendly Week in Alaska 41
Experiencing Alaska in White: A Week of Real Winter 43

Part II: Planning Your Trip to Alaska................ 45

Chapter 5: Managing Your Money...............................47

Planning Your Budget...47
    Transportation...48
    Lodging..49
    Dining 49
    Sightseeing and outdoor activities........................49
    Shopping 50
    Nightlife...52
Keeping an Eye on Hidden Expenses.................................52
Cutting Costs — But Not the Fun.......................................53

Handling Your Money......................................55
Using ATMs and carrying cash 55
Charging ahead with credit cards 55
Toting traveler's checks 56
Dealing with a Lost or Stolen Wallet................56

Chapter 6: Getting to Alaska..........................58

Flying to Alaska 58
Finding out which airlines fly there.........58
Getting the best deal on your airfare 59
Booking your flight online 60
Getting to Alaska by Road, Water, or Rail...........61
Driving to Alaska......................................61
Taking the ferry to Alaska...........................61
Riding the rails to Alaska — not! 62
Finding a Travel Agent 62
Joining an Escorted Tour.............................64
Finding out the basics 64
Shopping for an escorted tour 65
Selecting an escorted-tour company.............65
Choosing a Package Tour.............................66

Chapter 7: Getting Around Alaska 69

Flying Around Alaska..................................70
Flying around Southeast Alaska..................71
Flying around Southcentral Alaska and
the Interior...71
Flying to the Bush.....................................72
Riding the Rails 72
Sailing the Alaskan Coast 72
Reserving ferry passage...........................73
Making your ferry ride more enjoyable 74
Covering Ground by Bus..............................74
Driving Around Alaska 75
Renting a car..75
Renting an RV 78
Driving safely in Alaska...........................79

Chapter 8: Cruising Alaska's Coast...................81

Weighing Your Cruise Options......................81
Deciding when to go.................................82
Knowing where to go.................................83
Choosing between a big ship and a small ship.......84
Finding the best cruise-ship experience for you 86

Booking Your Cruise...91
    Booking a small-ship cruise...............................92
    Finding an agent who specializes in mainstream
        cruises 92
    Booking air travel through the cruise line..............95
    Choosing your cabin 95
    Speaking up about special health and dietary
        concerns..96
The Small-Ship Cruise Lines 96
The Big-Ship Cruise Lines 99

Chapter 9: Planning an Outdoor Adventure 110

Getting Active in the Alaska Summer 110
    Backpacking 111
    Biking off-road 111
    Biking on pavement...112
    Canoeing 112
    Day-hiking 113
    Fishing...113
    Rafting 114
    Sea-kayaking 116
Keeping Active in the Alaskan Winter.........................116
    Dog-mushing...117
    Skiing 117
    Snowmobiling...118
Viewing Alaska's Wildlife 118
    Bald eagle..122
    Black bear 122
    Brown bear (grizzly)..122
    Caribou..123
    Dall sheep 124
    Humpback whales...124
    Moose..125
    Musk ox...125
    Orca (killer whale)..125
    Polar bear 126
    Puffin (and other alcids)..................................126
    Sea otter 127
    Wolf...127
Choosing an Activity-Based Escorted Tour...................128
Nine Tragic Deaths to Avoid in Alaska's Outdoors 128
    Getting eaten by a bear (and such).......................129
    Drowning in freezing water 130
    Succumbing to exposure 130
    Getting eaten alive by bugs 131
    Getting lost 131

Drowning while crossing a river 132
Keeling over from bad clams.................................132
Getting seasick 132
Drinking tainted water 133

Chapter 10: Booking Your Accommodations............134

Choosing the Lodging Right for You 134
Bed-and-breakfasts 136
Hotels 136
Wilderness lodge look-alikes.................................136
Knowing When to Reserve.......................................137
Finding the Best Room at the Best Rate....................137
Shop early for peak times 137
Travel off-peak 137
Ask for discounts 138
Don't stop with the Internet 138
Book a package tour...138
Don't worry about it 138
Booking Rooms Online..139

Chapter 11: Catering to Special Travel Needs or Interests 140

Vacationing in Alaska with Children 140
Tackling the challenges 140
Finding a family-friendly package 141
Keeping kids happy on the road.............................142
Traveling as Senior Citizens 143
Accessing Alaska: Advice for Travelers
with Disabilities..144
Resources for Gays and Lesbians 145

Chapter 12: Taking Care of the Remaining Details ..146

Playing It Safe with Travel and Medical Insurance.........146
Trip-cancellation insurance...................................147
Medical insurance..147
Lost-luggage insurance 148
Staying Healthy When You Travel 148
Reserving Activities, Restaurants, and Shows 149
Booking your activities 150
Reserving a table at restaurants............................151
Getting performing-arts reservations....................151
Packing for the North 152
Summer clothing...152
Winter clothing 152
Dressing like a local...154

Communicating on the Road 154
Logging on to the Internet 154
Making a cellphone call..155
Keeping Up with Airline Security Measures 155
Flying with Bulky Outdoor Equipment............................157

Part III: Anchorage and Environs.....................161

Chapter 13: Settling Into Anchorage 163

Getting to Anchorage...164
Flying in...164
Getting into town from the airport 165
Arriving by car 165
Arriving by train...166
Orienting Yourself in Anchorage 166
Downtown..166
Midtown and the rest of the Anchorage Bowl 166
Beyond the Bowl...167
Finding Information After You Arrive..............................167
Getting Around Anchorage 167
Driving around town 168
Calling a cab 168
Waiting for the bus 169
Riding a bike 169
Using shoe leather 169
Where to Stay in Anchorage 169
The top hotels and B&Bs 170
Runner-up accommodations 175
Where to Dine in Anchorage...175
The top restaurants..176
Runner-up restaurants 182

Chapter 14: Exploring Anchorage...............................184

Hitting the Top Sights..185
Getting Outdoors: Summer and Winter in the City.........186
Summertime outdoor activities 188
Wintertime outdoor activities..................................194
Discovering More Cool Things to See and Do 195
Downtown..195
Beyond downtown..196
Seeing Anchorage by Guided Tour 197
Spending One, Two, or Three Days in Anchorage..........197
Day 1 in Anchorage..198
Day 2 in Anchorage..198
Day 3 in Anchorage..198

Saving Time for Alaska Shopping.......................................198
Finding the best shopping areas............................198
What to look for and where to find it....................200
Getting Out in the Evening..202
Attending the performing arts 202
Hitting the nightclubs and bars 202
Spending the evening at the movies 203
Fast Facts: Anchorage 203

Chapter 15: Side Trips from Anchorage 205
Driving Between Mountain and Sea on the Seward
Highway..205
Getting there..205
Seeing the sights 206
Enjoying the Slopes of Girdwood..............................210
Getting there..210
Seeing the sights 210
Getting outdoors in Girdwood 211
Where to stay 213
Where to dine..214
Embarking on Prince William Sound from Whittier 214
Getting there..215
Getting out on the sound 216
Where to dine..219
Taking a Side Trip to the Mat-Su Area........................219
Seeing the valley's highlights 220
Where to stay and dine...221

Part IV: Road Trips from Anchorage.................223
**Chapter 16: The Kenai Peninsula: Seward, Kenai
Fjords National Park, Kenai, and Homer 225**
Discovering the Kenai Peninsula and Its Major
Attractions 226
Seward...226
Kenai Fjords National Park....................................226
Kenai and Soldotna..226
Homer..228
Landing in Seward...228
Getting there..229
Getting around 229
Where to stay 230
Runner-up accommodations 232
Where to dine..232
Seward's top attractions..233
Getting outdoors in Seward...................................234
More cool things to do in Seward.........................236

Fast Facts: Seward 236
Enjoying Kenai Fjords National Park 237
    Getting there...237
    Getting park information 238
    Enjoying the park 238
    Deciding on a tour 238
    Checking out Exit Glacier 241
Kenai and Soldotna 242
    Getting there and getting around 243
    Where to stay 243
    Where to dine 244
    Fishing in Kenai and Soldotna 245
    Canoeing near Kenai and Soldotna 247
    More cool things to do in Kenai and Soldotna......248
Fast Facts: Kenai and Soldotna 249
Driving to the Sea in Homer 250
    Getting there 250
    Getting around Homer 251
    Where to stay 251
    Runner-up accommodations 254
    Where to dine 255
    Finding Homer's top attractions 257
    Getting outdoors in Homer 258
    More cool things to do in Homer 261
    Nightlife 262
Fast Facts: Homer 262

Chapter 17: Fairbanks 264

Getting There 265
    By car 265
    By air 265
    By train 265
Orienting Yourself in Fairbanks 265
    Getting around by car 266
    Getting around by bus 266
    Getting information 266
Where to Stay in Fairbanks 267
    Runner-up accommodations 271
Where to Dine in Fairbanks 272
    Runner-up restaurants 275
Exploring Fairbanks 275
    The top attractions 275
    Getting outdoors in Fairbanks 277
    More cool things to see and do 279
    Spending one, two, or three days in Fairbanks......280
    Shopping 281
    Nightlife 282

Fast Facts: Fairbanks 283
A Side Trip on Chena Hot Springs Road.......................283
    Getting there.............................284
    Where to stay and dine 284
    Getting outside on Chena Hot Springs Road.........285

Chapter 18: Driving Alaska's Highways 286

Understanding Alaska's Road Map 287
The Prince William Sound Loop: Anchorage to
  Whittier to Valdez to Glennallen 289
    Day 1: Anchorage to Valdez.............................289
    Day 2: A day in Valdez.............................290
    Day 3: Valdez to Glennallen.............................290
    Day 4: The road back to Anchorage 291
The Denali/Fairbanks Loop: Anchorage to
  Glennallen to Fairbanks to Denali 292
    Day 1: Anchorage to Glennallen.............................292
    Day 2: Glennallen to Fairbanks.............................293
    Day 3: A day in Fairbanks.............................293
    Day 4: Fairbanks to Denali 293
    Day 5: A day in Denali.............................294
    Day 6: Denali back to Anchorage 294
Linking Up the Loops.............................294
Driving to the Arctic and Other Extremes 295
    Dalton Highway (Route 11).............................296
    Denali Highway (Route 8) 297
    Edgerton Highway and McCarthy
      Road (Route 10) 297
    The Klondike Loop 298
    Steese Highway (Route 6).............................299

Chapter 19: Denali National Park 300

Planning Ahead 302
    Reserving shuttle seats and campsites
      in advance.............................302
    Reserving when you arrive.............................303
    Paying entrance fees 303
    Reserving rooms 303
    Packing for the park 304
Getting There.............................304
    Driving to the park.............................304
    Taking the train.............................304
    Taking the bus.............................305
    Flying to Denali 305
Getting the Lay of the Land 307

Arriving in the Park...307
    Arriving at the park's main entrance.....................308
    Arriving in Talkeetna.......................................308
Riding the Shuttle Bus...308
    Choosing your bus and destination......................311
    Getting ready...312
    Spotting wildlife on your way............................312
Hiking and Backpacking from the Shuttle Bus...............313
    Day hikes by bus...313
    Backpacking...314
Great Activities off the Bus....................................314
    Day-hiking near the park entrance......................315
    Flightseeing..315
    Rafting..316
    Ranger programs...316
    Visiting educational centers............................316
Where to Stay..317
    The top hotels and lodges...............................317
    Runner-up accommodations.............................320
    Campgrounds...320
Where to Dine..321

Part V: Southeast Alaska.....................**325**

Chapter 20: Juneau...**327**
Getting There..328
    Arriving by air...328
    Arriving by ferry..328
Getting Downtown...328
    Navigating by taxi...328
    Navigating by bus...328
    Navigating by rental car..................................329
Orienting Yourself in Juneau..................................330
    Getting around by car.....................................330
    Getting around by bicycle...............................330
Where to Stay in Juneau..330
    The top hotels and B&Bs.................................332
    Runner-up accommodations.............................335
Where to Dine in Juneau.......................................335
Exploring Juneau..337
    Exploring the top attractions...........................337
    More cool things to see and do.........................340
Shopping...340
Nightlife...341

Getting Outdoors in Juneau..............................341
    Bear-viewing..............................341
    Fishing and whale-watching..............................342
    Flightseeing and dog-mushing..............................342
    Hiking..............................343
    Sea-kayaking..............................344
Spending One, Two, or Three Days in Juneau..............................345
    Day 1 in Juneau..............................345
    Day 2 in Juneau..............................345
    Day 3 in Juneau..............................345
Fast Facts: Juneau..............................345

Chapter 21: Skagway 347

Getting There..............................349
    By boat..............................349
    By road..............................349
    By air..............................349
Orienting Yourself in Skagway..............................349
Where to Stay..............................350
Where to Dine..............................352
Exploring Skagway..............................353
    The top attractions..............................353
    Getting outdoors in Skagway..............................353
    Other cool things to see and do..............................354
    Nightlife..............................355
Fast Facts: Skagway..............................355

Chapter 22: Sitka..............................356

Getting There..............................356
    By ferry..............................356
    By air..............................357
Getting Around Sitka..............................357
    By bus..............................357
    By car..............................358
    By bike..............................358
Where to Stay..............................358
    Runner-up accommodations..............................360
Where to Dine..............................361
    The top restaurants..............................361
    Runner-up restaurants..............................362
Exploring Sitka..............................362
    Exploring the top attractions..............................362
    Getting outdoors in Sitka..............................364
    More cool things to see and do..............................366
    Shopping..............................367
Fast Facts: Sitka..............................367

Part VI: The End of the Road and Beyond: Bush Alaska 369

Chapter 23: The Arctic 371

Discovering the Arctic and
   Its Major Attractions...372
      Barrow...372
      Nome 372
   Going to the Top of the World: Barrow..................373
      Getting there...373
      Getting around 373
      Where to stay 374
      Where to dine..374
      Exploring Barrow 375
      Getting outdoors in Barrow..............................376
   Fast Facts: Barrow 376
   On Your Own in Nome...377
      Getting there...377
      Getting around 377
      Where to stay 378
      Where to dine..378
      Exploring Nome...379
      Driving the tundra 379
      Shopping 380
   Fast Facts: Nome 380

Chapter 24: Bear Country: Katmai National Park and Kodiak Island 382

Discovering Bear Country
   and Its Major Attractions 383
      Katmai National Park..383
      Kodiak Island..383
   Bear-Watching at Katmai National Park..................384
      Getting there...384
      Getting around 384
      Where to stay and dine 385
      Exploring Katmai National Park.......................385
   Fast Facts: Katmai National Park 386
   Crossing to Kodiak Island 386
      Getting there...387
      Getting around 387
      Where to stay 387

Where to dine..388
Exploring Kodiak....................................388
Getting outdoors in Kodiak 389
Fast Facts: Kodiak Island.......................392

Part VII: The Part of Tens *395*

Chapter 25: Ten Great Walks and Hikes in Alaska 397
Glen Alps: Stepping from City to Mountain 397
Tony Knowles Coastal Trail:
    Exploring Urban Wilds....................................398
Bird Ridge Trail: A Spectacular Cardiac Test.................398
Alaska Center for Coastal Studies:
    Tide-Pool Adventure......................................398
Granite Tors Trail: Nature-Carved Monuments 399
Denali National Park: Finding Your
    Measure in the Backcountry................................399
Outer Point Trail: Walking to Whale Waters 399
The Streets of Juneau: Finding
    the Charm of Old Alaska 400
Sitka National Historical Park:
    Picturing the War 400
Barrow's Arctic Ocean Beach:
    Standing at the World's Edge 400

Chapter 26: Ten Questions to Ask an Alaskan 401
Where Are You from Originally? 401
How Long Have You Lived Here?.......................402
Would You Tell Me about Your
    Gun/Boat/Snow Machine? 402
What Do You Think of This New
    Land-Management Plan? 402
Is the Legislature Doing a Good Job? 402
Why Is the Capital in a City
    You Can't Drive To? 403
Where Do You Like to Go in the Summer?.....................403
Have You Ever Encountered a Bear?...............................403
Here's My Itinerary — Do You Have Any Suggestions? ...404
Why Do You Live in Alaska? 404

Chapter 27: Ten Ways to Be an Alaska
Know-It-All..405
How Big Is It? 405
That's a Lot of Park.......................................406
Those Mountains Are Really Tall 406

And They're Getting Bigger 406
A Whole Lot of Shaking 407
. . . And a Whole Lot of Spewing....................................407
Free Money Just for Breathing 407
The Most Famous Alaskan..408
Catching Politically Correct Fish 408
Stating the Facts..408

Appendix: Quick Concierge **410**
Fast Facts 410
Where to Get More Information......................................413

Index..*415*

Introduction

*Y*ears ago, I was on Kodiak Island, a ten-hour ferry ride from the Alaskan mainland, when three chic Italian women walked into the visitor center, their fashionable black outfits wet, their manner confused. In beginner's English, they explained that they had boarded the boat in Homer thinking it would be an afternoon lark, a short ferry ride like those at home. Instead, the ship had plunged onward through the night in the stormy North Pacific, and here they were, a day later, marooned. The folks in Kodiak took care of the visitors, and they ended up having a good time. But before leaving, one of them asked me discreetly about what was missing: snow and ice. They had arrived looking for Jack London's Alaska, but that summer everything was green.

They could've used this book. It's an instruction manual for a place that's probably unlike anything you've ever experienced.

Alaska is a world apart from the rest of the United States, or, for that matter, most other peopled places. It is, quite simply, wild. Many stereotypes about Alaska do not hold. For example, during the summer, the weather is pleasant, and short sleeves get plenty of use. But other clichés are quite accurate: Wildlife roams freely across vast spaces, unfettered by fences or roads. Grand scenery, on equal footing with the most awesome sights on Earth, is within reach in every part of the state. Opportunities to experience real wilderness are plentiful.

Alaska isn't just what you expect. It's probably much better.

About This Book

You didn't pick up this book because you wanted to read; you got it because you want to go to Alaska. So, my job as a writer is to deliver the information you need in the most efficient and straightforward way possible.

Because itinerary planning is one of the primary challenges of an Alaska trip, I've organized some material according to the routes you're most likely to follow. However, you don't have to use the book that way: It's also designed as a handy reference for you to dip in and find the one piece of information you're looking for at the moment you need it. You can refer to a single chapter on a visit to a region, jump to the section about traveling with kids, or just grab the facts you need right now to find a good restaurant.

I don't expect you to end up knowing who Tagish Charlie was (if you want to know, check out the gold-rush primer in Chapter 21), and you won't be tested on anything after you're done reading. Forgetting everything between these pages is okay as long as your trip to Alaska is a memorable one.

Please be advised that travel information is subject to change at any time — and this is especially true of prices. So, I suggest that you write or call ahead for confirmation when making your travel plans. The authors, editors, and publisher cannot be held responsible for the experiences of readers while traveling. Your safety is important to us, however, so we encourage you to stay alert and be aware of your surroundings. Keep a close eye on cameras, purses, and wallets, all favorite targets of thieves and pickpockets.

Conventions Used in This Book

Think of this book as a reference. I've organized material to help you quickly find the information you need, without wading through extra information or secondary options. Use the table of contents and index to jump to the topic you want to read about.

In this book, I've included lists of hotels, restaurants, and attractions. As I describe each, I often include abbreviations for commonly accepted credit cards. Take a look at the following list for an explanation of each:

AE: American Express

DC: Diners Club

DISC: Discover

MC: MasterCard

V: Visa

I've divided hotels and restaurants into two categories — my personal favorites and those that don't quite make my preferred list but still get my hearty seal of approval. Don't be shy about considering these "runner-up" hotels and restaurants if you're unable to get a reservation at one of my favorites or if your preferences differ from mine — the amenities that the runners-up offer and the services that each provides make all these good choices to consider as you determine where to dine and rest your head at night.

I also include some general pricing information to help you as you decide where to unpack your bags or dine on the local cuisine. I've used a system of dollar signs to show a range of costs for one night in a hotel or a meal at a restaurant. Hotel prices are for a standard room for two people during the high season. (Off-season prices are as little as half the high-season prices.) For more information about high and off seasons, be sure to check out Chapter 3. Meal prices are for a dinner with a main course that constitutes a full meal and does not include appetizers, dessert, or alcohol. For restaurants that don't serve dinner, the prices are for lunch. The following table explains the dollar signs:

Cost	Hotel	Restaurant
$	$100 or less	$12 or less
$$	$101–$130	$13–$18
$$$	$131–$165	$19–$25
$$$$	$166–$210	$26–$35
$$$$$	$211 or more	$36 or more

Foolish Assumptions

As I wrote this book, I made some assumptions about you and what your needs may be as a traveler. Here's what I assumed about you:

- ✔ You may be an experienced traveler who hasn't been to Alaska and wants expert advice when you finally get a chance to go.

- ✔ You may be an inexperienced traveler looking for guidance when determining whether to take a trip to Alaska and how to plan for it.

- ✔ You're not looking for a book that provides all the information available about Alaska or that lists every hotel, restaurant, or attraction available to you. Instead, you're looking for a book that focuses on the places that will give you the best or most unique experiences.

If you fit any of these criteria, *Alaska For Dummies* has the information you're looking for.

How This Book Is Organized

With the straightforward organization of this book, finding what you're looking for should be intuitive. But just in case, here's the blueprint.

Part 1: Introducing Alaska

In this part, I introduce you to what Alaska has to offer. You'll find chapters listing some of Alaska's highlights; a bit of background on Alaska's natural history, culture, and history; and advice on where and when to go (including timing, weather, and special events). I also provide five great itineraries that touch on Alaska's best destinations.

Part II: Planning Your Trip to Alaska

This part gets into the details of setting up your trip. I begin by covering budgets and other money considerations. Next, I cover the issues of getting to Alaska and getting around the vast state — a bit more complicated than some other destinations, but also part of what makes Alaska interesting and exotic. One long chapter covers options for visiting by cruise ship, and another provides details for going to Alaska for an outdoor adventure. I get into finding the right accommodations at the right price and offer specialized information for families, seniors, travelers with disabilities, and gays and lesbians. Finally, this part provides you with less-fun details that you can't do without: health and safety, airline security, insurance, and so on.

Part III: Anchorage and Environs

Now you're into the meat of it! Anchorage is the gateway to Alaska, its largest and most diverse city. It also lies at the threshold of some excellent outdoor destinations, including Girdwood (for skiing), Whittier and Prince William Sound (for sea-kayaking, wildlife-watching, and glacier cruises), and the Mat-Su area (for hiking).

Part IV: Road Trips from Anchorage

The easiest way for most independent travelers to see the bulk of Alaska is by flying or taking a cruise ship to Anchorage and then driving a rented car in big loops from there. Adhering to this simple premise, I cover much of Alaska as road trips from Anchorage: the Kenai Peninsula, including Seward, Kenai Fjords National Park, Kenai, and Homer; Fairbanks and its environs; Alaska's long rural highways; and Denali National Park.

Part V: Southeast Alaska

Southeast Alaska is a mountainous strip of rain forest and narrow ocean channels full of islands and quaint, historic towns. In this part, I focus on Juneau, the area's travel hub, the state capital, and an outdoor gateway; on the gold-rush destinations at Skagway; and on the rich Russian and Alaska Native cultural history at Sitka.

Part VI: The End of the Road and Beyond: Bush Alaska

If you're ready to go *way* out to the end of the earth, here's how to do it. I cover remote and fascinating places in the Arctic, along with the giant bears of Kodiak Island and Katmai National Park.

Part VII: The Part of Tens

Skip the rest and jump here for ten Alaska experiences not to miss on walks and hikes, ten questions to ask an Alaskan, and ten ways to be an Alaska know-it-all.

In back of this book I've included an appendix — your Quick Concierge — containing lots of handy information you may need when traveling in Alaska, such as liquor laws, time zones, and weather reports. Many handy phone numbers and addresses are included, too. Just flip to the pages on yellow paper in the back of the book.

Icons Used in This Book

While skimming through these pages, the icons help attract your eyes to the information you're looking for. This section tells you what each icon means.

 I've placed this icon where I note special values and money-saving tips.

 The Best of the Best icon highlights my top picks in all categories — hotels, restaurants, attractions, activities, shopping, and nightlife. You'll find some of these picks described in more detail in Chapter 1.

 Watch for the Heads Up icon to identify potential rip-offs or annoyances, time-wasting errors, tourist traps, and other such travel pitfalls.

 These little nuggets of hard-won knowledge — information you probably wouldn't otherwise stumble upon — may make life easier or more interesting.

 I have four kids ages 9 to 19. Believe me, when you see this icon next to an attraction, hotel, restaurant, or activity, the place has passed a very rigorous test, indeed.

 Where you see this icon, be on the lookout for critters. I also use it to mark some of the best wildlife-viewing destinations.

Where to Go from Here

Be not afraid! True, you go to Alaska for adventure. True, the essence of Alaska is untamed wilderness, wild animals, and uncontrollable nature. But Alaska is a popular visitor destination with every comfort you're looking for, and no harm is likely to come to you that you wouldn't face on any other vacation.

My advice: Go bravely northward!

Part I
Introducing Alaska

The 5th Wave   By Rich Tennant

"This afternoon I want everyone to go online and find all you can about Tlingit culture, history of the gold rush, and discount airfares to Alaska for the two weeks I'll be on vacation."

In this part . . .

*T*his book is designed to make planning a trip more like putting together a jigsaw puzzle than painting a picture on a blank canvas. This part helps you get those all-important puzzle-edge pieces into place so that you can start to fill in the picture of what your journey to Alaska will look like. Before you decide where you want to go and what you want to do, figure out why you want to go to Alaska in the first place. Skip this step, and you risk getting lost in a search of stereotypical images from media mythology that don't have much to do with the reality of the place you're visiting. I aim to help by suggesting some of the best Alaskan experiences you can pursue; surveying the history and culture of the state; and explaining the places, times, and routes that make for a good trip.

Chapter 1

Discovering the Best of Alaska

In This Chapter

▶ Discovering the best spots to see glaciers and bears
▶ Exploring indigenous Alaskan culture and gold-rush history
▶ Hiking Alaska's most beautiful day trails
▶ Checking out Alaska's top one-of-a-kind lodgings

*S*atellite photographs taken at night show much of the populated world as a thick network of lights. Cities and highways stand out clearly. The same view of Alaska, however, reveals just a couple of bright spots; the rest of the land appears as a vast, velvety blackness. It's as though this great subcontinent were an undiscovered country that extends beyond the web of civilization. Indeed, although Alaska has been completely mapped, immense areas are still unexplored. Not only do thousands of mountains remain unclimbed, but most have never even been named. Just to give you an idea of the scope, Alaska has 100,000 glaciers and 10 million lakes.

So this chapter's goal is to pick out the best of all that? Uh-oh.

A trip to Alaska should not be like one to Paris or the San Diego Zoo. Don't come to see certain sites or objects. It's silly to focus on a particular mountain or glacier when a practically infinite number are available. You never know when you may encounter wildlife — these meetings can't be scheduled. Moreover, each of the regions you're likely to visit boasts fabulous mountains, glaciers, wildlife, hikes, boating, rafting, sea-kayaking — all of it.

As a travel writer, I've visited a majority of the nation's great, crowded national parks, yet every summer in Alaska I see vistas as impressive, or even grander, that have no special designation. After a lifetime of such travels, I'm not even close to exhausting this wonder of discovery. I don't think I ever will be. Those are my "bests."

Although this chapter can provide reference points, stepping-off places from which you can get your bearings, don't get too caught up in ticking off a list of "the best." Instead, focus on the experience. Launch your own exploration and open yourself to discovery. Get out into all that vastness on foot, in a boat or kayak, in a small aircraft, or in a car. Do whatever you can to experience Alaska's unlimited expanse for yourself, and in doing so you'll find your own unique "best" that belongs to no one else.

 I discuss each of the places and experiences described in this chapter in detail later in this book. You can find them marked with — what else? — a Best of the Best icon.

The Best Big Ice

A glacier is a strange and unfamiliar thing. It looks like land, but it flows like water. Glaciers can be larger than a city or even a state, and yet they move constantly, sometimes suddenly, and they can bulldoze straight through mountains. Nothing else looks like a glacier. They're white, gray, and fluorescent blue. They drape gracefully through the mountains, but they also crack in enormous shards.

✔ **Prince William Sound Glaciers (Whittier):** Less than two hours from Anchorage, the port town of Whittier provides access to northwestern Prince William Sound, one of Alaska's most beautiful and heavily glaciated waterways. Day cruises from Whittier, easy to do as a day trip from Anchorage, compete on price, food service onboard, and number of glaciers you see in a few hours (up to two dozen). See Chapter 15.

✔ **Kenai Fjords National Park (Seward):** Here you find Exit Glacier (one of the few glaciers you can walk right up to) and the magnificent glaciers still carving the fjords, reached only by boats from Seward. This forbidding and untouched area, where mountains shoot a mile high straight out of the sea, is also among the best for seeing marine mammals and birds. See Chapter 16.

✔ **Ruth Glacier (Denali National Park):** Forget the traditional image of glacier ice falling into the ocean — this is a chance to land on one of Mount McKinley's glaciers in a ski plane, get out, and look around. These flights, mostly going from Talkeetna, are among the most spectacular experiences a visitor to Alaska can have. See Chapter 19.

✔ **Juneau Ice Field (Juneau):** Helicopters from Juneau fly over the immense ice field that lies beyond the mountains bordering the town. Visitors can just look, or join guided hikes on the ice, or even get in a dog sled and go mushing on the glaciers. See Chapter 20.

✔ **Glacier Bay National Park (Juneau):** This park encompasses fjords released from the grip of ice over the last century. Passengers on cruise ships and tour boats going to the head of the bay often see humpback whales before arriving at huge walls of ice. Sea kayakers get a much closer and more intimate view of the land and wildlife. See Chapter 20.

The Best Bear Viewing

Bears can turn up almost anywhere in Alaska — even in a city park. Trails sometimes close in Anchorage's Far North Bicentennial Park because of the enormous brown (grizzly) bears that feed on salmon in a creek there, and black bears can show up almost anywhere in the state's largest city. Alaska's thriving populations of black, brown, and polar bears can be found reliably for viewing at the right places and times. See Chapter 9 for more details.

✔ **Denali National Park:** Even more remarkable than the scenery is Denali's status as the site of one of the greatest and least expensive wildlife safaris you can experience. Thanks to the limited-access bus system that is the only motorized way into the park, every shuttle passenger has an excellent chance of seeing brown bears. See Chapter 19.

✔ **Pack Creek (near Juneau):** For decades, the brown bears of Admiralty Island that converge here to feed on the salmon have nonchalantly allowed humans to watch them from nearby viewing areas. It's a short flight from Juneau, but a different world. See Chapter 20.

✔ **Mendenhall Glacier (Juneau):** For those who didn't budget for an expensive wilderness journey to see bears, the autumn gathering of black bears at a creek near Juneau's municipal glacier are almost as good. Visitors can get within yards of the feeding bears next to a handy parking lot. See Chapter 20.

✔ **Kodiak Island and Katmai National Park:** These remote lands host some of the biggest salmon runs and, therefore, the biggest and most plentiful brown-bear population anywhere on Earth. Catch the season right, and you could see large groups of enormous bears fishing and feeding. See Chapter 24.

✔ **Barrow:** Point Barrow, the farthest north you can go in the United States, is among the best places to see polar bears in the country; bears congregate to feed on waste from Eskimo whale-hunting. However, this choice is an adventurous one: Tours in four-wheel-drive vehicles, offered casually by locals, don't always see bears; indeed, they don't always operate. See Chapter 23.

The Best Places to Encounter Indigenous Culture

Alaska is home to many distinct peoples. The cultural heritage and ways of life of Alaska's indigenous people remain largely intact in many areas of the state, and Alaska Natives are often interested in sharing their traditions with visitors who bring needed economic support to their communities.

✔ **Alaska Native Heritage Center (Anchorage):** Native peoples from all over Alaska joined together to create this magnificent cultural center and living museum. Here you can taste many cultures at once, see live performances and exhibits, meet artisans, and walk through traditional dwellings. See Chapter 14.

✔ **Sitka:** Tlingit people who made Alaska's great totem poles and clan houses present their own culture at three venues in Sitka (see Chapter 22):

- The **Sitka National Historic Park,** where you can see extraordinary historic totem poles and meet today's carvers

- The **Sheldon Jackson Museum,** with a unique collection of Alaska Native art

- Sitka Tribe's magnificent **community hall,** where authentic dance performances take place in the summer

✔ **Iñupiat Heritage Center (Barrow):** Eskimo culture is alive and well, and in Barrow you often can see subsistence hunters preparing for or returning from hunts for whale, caribou, or polar bear. At the town's fascinating cultural center and living museum, you also can see exhibits and dance performances and meet craftsmen selling authentic Iñupiat artwork. See Chapter 23.

The Best Gold-Rush Towns

The Klondike Gold Rush of 1898, when the non-Native population arrived all at once in search of riches, is the biggest event in Alaska's short history. Many towns owe their existence to it, and some have made that lineage a major attraction (see Chapter 16).

✔ **Fairbanks:** These days, Fairbanks is a city, but it still acts like a town, with lots of fun and corny activities for visitors (and one of the state's best museums, at the University of Alaska Fairbanks). Gold-mining goes on today, and you can see it demonstrated and tour historic gold-mining museums. See Chapter 17.

✔ **Juneau:** The gold discoveries in Juneau predated the Klondike Gold Rush, and led to the construction of massive hard-rock mining works. Check out the remains on outdoor trails, at indoor museums, and even on a tunnel tour at an old mine. See Chapter 20.

✔ **Skagway:** This may be America's best preserved gold-rush boomtown, the scene of legendary Wild West times when Klondike stampeders got off the boat here bound for the gold fields. Although overrun with cruise-ship visitors, the town is well preserved by the National Park Service. See Chapter 21.

✔ **Nome:** Nome's gold-rush stories top all. Although most of the historic structures are gone, the town retains a free-wheeling frontier spirit, making it feel more like a gold-rush boomtown than other more tourist-oriented places. Small-time prospectors are still at work here, too. See Chapter 23.

The Best Day Hikes

Every town in Alaska is surrounded by wilderness, even Anchorage. That means every town in Alaska has routes into beautiful, wild places. Go a little farther — in the national parks, or along hundreds of miles of remote highways — and you can hike in some of the biggest open country in the world. For more walking ideas, see Chapter 25.

- ✔ **Glen Alps Trailhead (Anchorage):** Drive above Anchorage into the rocky Chugach Mountains, and park your car well above the tree line, where views extend far beyond the city, over the ocean waters of Cook Inlet, and to the mountain ranges beyond. From this point, a wide choice of trails leads up mountains or across valleys; or you can take off on your own over open tundra. See Chapter 14.

- ✔ **Caines Head (Seward):** Hike all the way from town or take a water taxi partway to a boulder-strewn beach; from there, climb gradually through the woods to the ruins of a mountaintop World War II artillery fort with weird underground corridors and stupendous views across Resurrection Bay and beyond. See Chapter 16.

- ✔ **Granite Tors (near Fairbanks):** This challenging hike east of Fairbanks leads beyond the forest to the broad, tundra-clad Plain of Monuments, where strange natural towers of solid granite poke the sky at apparently random spots, defying the eye to determine their size in the absence of scale or reference points. See Chapter 17.

- ✔ **Toklat River (Denali National Park):** In the heart of Denali National Park, few trails exist; the best of the park is discovered beyond trail's end. You'll find easy walking along the braided river channels, including the Toklat, where you can go far without struggling over tundra and see more wildlife than people. See Chapter 19.

- ✔ **Perseverance Trail (Juneau):** Hard-rock gold-mining built Juneau in the 1880s; at one time, it was one of the most industrially advanced cities on the West Coast. Although that's no longer the case, this historic mountain trail goes back in time to the Silverbow Basin, where much of it happened. Across from the trailhead is a fascinating gold-rush museum. See Chapter 20.

The Best One-of-a-Kind Lodgings

When I travel, I want to feel as though I've gone somewhere. I try to eat with the locals and stay in lodgings with local character. In Alaska, I've sought out these authentic places for visitors. This list includes some of the best (and most unique).

- ✔ **Oscar Gill House (Anchorage):** It's not grand, but this is the oldest house in Anchorage. In fact, it predates the city — it was moved here by one of the early mayors. Lovingly restored, yet retaining a homey, lived-in feel, the house now offers bargain bed-and-breakfast accommodations. See Chapter 13.

✔ **Hotel Alyeska (Girdwood):** Alaska's grandest luxury hotel, an hour from Anchorage, has a one-of-a-kind location in an unspoiled mountain valley among huge spruce trees. Skiers can go right from the door to Alaska's best slopes; in the summer, the aerial tram is an easy way for anyone to experience the crisp air and magnificent views of an Alaska mountaintop. See Chapter 15.

✔ **Land's End Resort (Homer):** The hotel is charming, but the location is what makes it unique. Land's End Resort sits at the very end of a 5-mile-long point of land into Kachemak Bay, one of Alaska's most beautiful and ecologically productive bodies of water. You can walk from your room to fish for salmon, or sit back and watch sea otters swim by. See Chapter 16.

✔ **Aurora Express Bed & Breakfast (Fairbanks):** A family hauled a collection of railroad cars — plus a locomotive and caboose — up a mountain south of Fairbanks and remodeled the interior into a collection of accommodations, some too cute for words, others heavily nostalgic for those who remember the golden age of rail. See Chapter 17.

✔ **Pearson's Pond Luxury Inn & Adventure Spa (Juneau):** This remarkable inn, tucked away in a residential subdivision near the Mendenhall Glacier, is so full of amenities and attractions, it would take pages to describe it all. But the essence of it is simple: a sensual retreat for romantic stays when your goal is to be utterly pampered. See Chapter 20.

Chapter 2

Digging Deeper into Alaska

- -

In This Chapter

▶ Understanding Alaska's Native cultures

▶ Catching the flow of Alaska's history

▶ Speaking Alaskan

▶ Ordering Alaskan seafood

▶ Finding Alaska in books and films

- -

*N*ews flash: There are people here. That's right, although the tourist come-ons mostly show pictures of mountains, glaciers, and wildlife, Alaska's cultural landscape is at least as diverse and exotic as its physical landscape, if far less extensive.

Scores of indigenous languages are spoken here by Native peoples adapted to climates and environments as different as the icy Arctic Ocean and the rain forest of Southeast Alaska. Their ways of life are largely intact, and they own much of their homeland.

Alaska's non-indigenous people, representing the majority of the population, all arrived within the last century, after the 1898 Klondike Gold Rush. They have a culture of their own — or at least an image and a way of doing things — reflecting youth, mobility, and links to Alaska's resources. If you take your eyes off the glaciers for a few minutes, you may find some interesting people around here.

 On the other hand, focusing purely on the landscape is perfectly reasonable. If you want to skip straight to the animals and outdoors, jump ahead to Chapter 9.

Understanding Alaska's Native Cultures

The indigenous people of North America and South America arrived about 15,000 years ago. They may have walked from Siberia over ground that's now the seabed beneath the Bering Sea, which was exposed at the time by the lower sea level of those Ice Age years — or maybe not. Archaeologists are less sure now than they have been in years about exactly how these indigenous people arrived. New theories keep cropping up, each with an apparent claim on the evidence.

Who moves to Alaska?

At the end of Vladimir Nabokov's novel *Lolita,* the title character breaks for good from her pedophile stepfather to move to Alaska. That's one classic reason for going to Alaska: getting away. Alaska is off the map (literally, most of the time), a place so far away you can reinvent yourself. This fact makes for an odd irony in Alaskans' attitudes about each other. We tend not to ask questions about where people came from — everyone is accepted when they arrive. (This has led to a series of scandals in which politicians turned out not to be who they said they were.) On the other hand, the length of time a person has lived in Alaska is a powerful point of pride. It's one of the first pieces of information acquaintances exchange, even before they ask, "What do you do?" (I've lived here since 1966; my family moved from Brooklyn when I was 3 years old.) I suppose they don't do that in places where more of the population is native born.

Fewer than four in ten Alaskans were born in Alaska, and two of those four are Alaska Natives. (Nationally, 60 percent of people live in the same state where they were born.) Alaskans are young, mobile, well-educated, high-paid, active, and outdoorsy. And also ethnic: Alaska is more diverse than the average state. Many military members who rotate through Alaska end up retiring here. Many others possessed of an adventurous spirit move to Alaska to take a job for a few years and stay long-term. And plenty of people who come on vacation fall in love with the place and never leave.

Maybe that will be you.

However they arrived, communication among Native peoples continued long after the Ice Age. For example, the Eskimo or Inuit people (the two words mean the same thing, with *Eskimo* the preferred term by most of those in Alaska) scattered across Siberia, Alaska, northern Canada, and Greenland share ties of language, legend, and lifestyle. Archeologists believe this connection was forged about a thousand years ago, when the climate was warmer for a few hundred years and travel and migration was easier. When the weather got colder, people lost track of each other, but upon being reunited in the 20th century, a millennium of separation had left their language, stories, and cultural patterns still recognizable to one another.

Alaska's Eskimos include two peoples: the **Iñupiat** of the Arctic coast and the **Yupik** of the west and southwest. These are the legendary marine mammal hunters and users of the sea ice. In addition to Eskimos, there are several Alaskan peoples more properly called *Indians:* the **Athabascan** of interior Alaska, who are river dwellers and hunters of caribou and moose, and the **Tlingit** of southeastern Alaska, who were the richest of the Native people, thanks to the plentiful salmon, game, and wood of their rain-forest home. The **Aleuts,** seafarers of the Aleutian Archipelago, are neither Eskimos nor Indians. Within these peoples, there are many villages, which are analogous to tribes elsewhere in the United States, each with its own dialect and traditions. Almost half of

America's federally recognized tribes are in Alaska — more than 220 of them. Altogether, Alaska's indigenous people are called **Alaska Natives** (always capitalized), not American Indians.

If all this seems complicated, don't worry about it. No one expects you to know the details. Visitors need only be respectful and willing to learn.

Treating Alaska's first people properly

It should come as no surprise that people from cultural traditions completely independent of Europe or Asia have different ways of behaving, but many visitors to rural Alaska assume that the manners they bring with them are automatically the right ones. It's a common mistake, and most Natives probably aren't offended by faux pas committed in this way.

But if you really want to get to know people, you should know something about how they relate to each other and how to show respect as they do. Here are some tips:

- **Slow down and listen.** If you talk fast, interrupt, or don't wait for an answer, you may never hear anyone else speak. In Native communities, people speak slowly and carefully; a long pause means the person is thinking about what has been said. It takes time to catch the nuances — for example, people speak indirectly to avoid contradiction or conflict.

- **Show respect.** Being demanding, pushy, or argumentative places you completely on the outside. Alaska Native culture calls for respect to be paid to every person: deferring to others' wishes, helping, listening, offering and accepting small gifts (such as a cup of coffee), and *always* avoiding conflict.

- **Don't be shy.** Native people you meet, especially in places that tourists frequent, will respond to friendly approaches, conversation, and respectful questions. Tell people about yourself and where you're from; family ties are of special interest — anything that will create a connection.

- **Think about how you would feel.** What if visitors came to your town from a foreign land? How would you want to be treated? When I see visitors treating Native people as if they were objects, I wonder if the tourists ever asked themselves that question.

Finding Native culture

Here are some terrific places to see Alaska Native art and artifacts or to meet Native people who want to teach about their culture:

- **Alaska Native Heritage Center (Anchorage):** Indigenous people from all cultures join together where visitors can discover more about their ways of life. See Chapter 14.

✔ **Anchorage Museum at Rasmuson Center:** An extraordinary exhibit occupies a building completed in 2010, showing treasures of Alaskan art brought back from the vaults of the Smithsonian in Washington, D.C. See Chapter 14.

✔ **UAF Museum of the North (Fairbanks):** Alaska's most interestingly presented museum features Native art and demonstrations. See Chapter 17.

✔ **Alaska State Museum (Juneau):** Stop here for an overview using some of Alaska's best examples of Native art. See Chapter 20.

✔ **Sitka National Historic Site and other sites (Sitka):** The historic site operated by the National Park Service contains the best collection of historic totem poles and offers a chance to see artists at work. Elsewhere in Sitka, you can see Tlingit dance. See Chapter 22.

✔ **Iñupiat Heritage Center (Barrow):** The northernmost community in the United States has its best living museum of Eskimo culture. See Chapter 23.

Alaska History: Not an Oxymoron

Alaska's population tends to be young and transient. People come and go, following a pattern originally set by the northward flow of gold-rush prospectors that first brought non-indigenous Americans. Everyone seems to assume history began with their own arrival, but it happens that many people came before the gold rush, and not only the Alaska Natives who arrived 15,000 years ago, but also the Russians, the first Europeans to come to Alaska, in 1741.

Searching for Russian America (1741–1867)

That first visitor to Alaska set the pattern for short visits. Vitus Bering claimed the region while on a mission for Czar Peter the Great. Bering crossed Asia, sailed to and crossed the Kamchatka Peninsula, built new ships, and sailed across the North Pacific (the part now known as the Bering Sea). He made the journey twice, in fact, before he actually found Alaska and landed a man there for a few hours. It turns out that Bering's goal was to say he had made it there, and he didn't stay long enough to do anything. (Don't you make the same mistake!) In the end, he didn't even accomplish that goal — he died before making it back home.

Russian fur traders followed, and what became known as Russian America survived as a sea-otter exporting colony until the czar sold Alaska to the United States in 1867. After the sale, all the Russians left, and their history in Alaska essentially stopped.

 To see the remains of Russian America, head to Sitka (see Chapter 22) and Kodiak (see Chapter 24). The site where Russia handed over Alaska to the United States is preserved in Sitka, the former Russian capital.

Rushing for gold (1867–1940)

I have a hilarious Thomas Nast cartoon dated 1877, showing the last American soldiers abandoning the wasteland of Alaska, being bid good-bye by a horde of polar bears. The caption notes that the government had taken the sensible cost-saving measure of withdrawing its small Alaska garrison, because there was nothing worth guarding. Americans believed for many years that the Alaska purchase was a fiasco after it was engineered at a cost of $7.2 million (less than 2¢ per acre) by Secretary of State William Seward in 1867.

Americans suddenly changed their minds about the value of their purchase one day in 1897, when a ship arrived in Seattle from Alaska carrying a bunch of brand-new millionaires with trunks and gunnysacks of gold. These penniless prospectors had found gold in the Yukon's Klondike River, reachable only through Alaska. The population of Seattle emptied out as people stampeded to get their own gold — even the mayor went. The find was large enough to affect the U.S. economy, and more than big enough to jump-start the nation's interest in Alaska. Although the latecomers to the gold fields found few riches of their own, they spread out to new gold strikes that were located every few years for the next two decades. By the time of World War I, gold-rush prospectors had established many of Alaska's existing towns and cities.

 To see the legacy of the gold rush, go to **Juneau, Skagway, Fairbanks,** or **Nome.** (See Chapter 1 for my list of gold-rush bests.)

The last major piece in the pattern of development we see on today's map of Alaska fell into place with the construction of the Alaska Railroad, built by the federal government between 1914 and 1923. The rail line runs from Seward, set on the water south of Anchorage, to Fairbanks, in the center of the state. To build it, the government set up a work camp on upper Cook Inlet, near the village of Knik, at the mouth of Ship Creek. The camp probably got its name from a notation on the nautical chart of the area: "Anchorage."

 The **Alaska Railroad** is still a great way to see the state. You can find more information in the sections on **Seward** (see Chapter 16) and **Denali National Park** (see Chapter 19).

Defending the United States (1940–1968)

With the start of World War II, Alaska became a key to the nation's defense, a role it still maintains. The military buildup in Alaska began even before the Japanese attacked the United States in 1941. Farsighted military planners realized that the state commanded a strategic polar and Pacific position in an age of aviation, and air bases were built as pilots ferried aircraft through Alaska to Russia and points west.

When the United States entered the war, Alaska became the site of some of its most bitter fighting. In 1942, the Japanese attacked and held Kiska and Attu, two islands in the outer Aleutian archipelago, the only portion of U.S. homeland ever held by a foreign power since the War of 1812. The invaders were dislodged only a year later after the 18-day Battle of Attu, one of the most ferocious and costly battles of the Pacific war. After the war, Alaska became a critical element of the nation's Cold War defenses, and large bases and advanced radar outposts were installed here.

Fighter aircraft from Alaska used to scramble to intercept Russian strategic bombers in a frequently repeated game of nuclear chicken that was still being played as recently as the 1980s. A missile defense system, intended to protect the United States from North Korea, was constructed more recently and operates at Fort Greely, southeast of Fairbanks.

Discovering oil (1968 to the present)

Although military spending remains an important component of Alaska's economy, it no longer sets the pace. Oil took that role in 1968, when the largest oil field in North America was found at Prudhoe Bay, at the northern edge of the state. Because the oil was found on state-owned land, Alaska's state government suddenly became fabulously wealthy. The spending of the oil industry — including for construction of the $9-billion trans-Alaska oil pipeline, completed in 1977 — supercharged the economy and put cities such as Anchorage and Fairbanks on a path of explosive growth.

During this period, the cities seemed to change at the pace of a DVD on fast-forward, with new roads and buildings sprouting up like weeds. These were the years that made cities such as Anchorage and Fairbanks look like the grubby outskirts of any prosperous western U.S. urban area, with the same kinds of chain stores and wide highways you would find throughout the country. More than 30 years later, the ugly boomtown development has only partly been softened by more gracious cityscapes.

One of the most exciting times in Alaska history is happening right now. The output of Alaska's oil fields is in decline, but rising oil prices have more than offset that for now, leading to big government surpluses. However, oil-industry influence took a big hit when the FBI uncovered widespread bribery of legislators and other political leaders to hold down oil taxes and win other favors. Amid the turmoil, Sarah Palin rocketed to prominence from small-town mayor to governor with an anti-corruption message. And then she became Senator John McCain's running mate, nominated for vice president by the Republican Party. Despite their defeat in 2008 and her resignation from her position as governor in 2009, the media continues to feature Palin frequently.

To find out more about Alaska's history, head for the:

- ✔ **Anchorage Museum at Rasmuson Center:** The Alaska gallery offers a survey of Alaska's history and culture, and the Smithsonian Arctic Studies Center contains an astounding display of Native art. See Chapter 14.

- ✔ **Alaska State Museum (Juneau):** The history galleries on the second floor contain some of the most precious of Alaska's historic artifacts. See Chapter 20.

Speaking Alaskan

Alaska has its own language — and I'm not talking about Native languages, of which there are dozens. Alaskan lingo has words for things that people don't necessarily need to talk about in other places. Here's a partial glossary:

- ✔ **Breakup:** When God set up the seasons in Alaska, He forgot one: spring. While the temperate United States enjoys new flowers and baseball, Alaskans are looking at melting snowbanks and mud. Then, in May, summer miraculously arrives. Breakup officially occurs when the ice goes out in the Interior's rivers, but it stands for the time period of winter's demise and summer's initiation.

- ✔ **Bunny boots:** If you see people wearing huge, bulbous, white rubber boots in Alaska's winter, it's not necessarily because they have enormous feet. Those are bunny boots, super-insulated footwear originally designed for Arctic air-force operations — and they're the warmest things in the world.

- ✔ **Bush:** A region defined not by boundaries but by a way of living, the Bush is that part of Alaska (actually, the great majority of the state) off the road network, where life is dominated by nature rather than civilization, and where the traditions of Alaska Native people remain strong.

- ✔ **Cheechako (chee-*cha*-ko):** A newcomer or greenhorn. Not used much anymore, because almost everyone is one.

- ✔ **Damp:** Used to describe a town or village that outlaws the sale of alcohol, but not the possession of it.

- ✔ **Dry:** Used to describe a town or village that outlaws alcohol completely.

- ✔ **Lower 48:** The contiguous United States (everything but Alaska and Hawaii).

- ✔ **Native:** When capitalized, the word refers to Alaska's indigenous people. The term *American Indian* isn't used much in Alaska, *Alaska Native* being the preferred term.

✔ **Native corporation:** In 1971, Congress settled land claims with Alaska's Natives by turning over land and money; corporations were set up, with the living Natives as shareholders receiving the property. Most of the corporations still thrive.

✔ **Oosik (*ooh*-sik):** The huge penile bone of a walrus. Knowing this word could save you from being the butt of any of a number of practical jokes people like to play on cheechakos.

✔ **Outside:** Anywhere that isn't Alaska. This term is widely used in print, and it's capitalized, like any other proper noun.

✔ **PFD:** No, not personal flotation device. It stands for Permanent Fund Dividend. When Alaska's oil riches started flowing in the late 1970s, the voters set up a savings account called the Permanent Fund. Half the interest is paid annually to every man, woman, and child in the state. With more than $35 billion in investments, the fund now yields roughly $2,000 in dividends to each Alaskan annually.

✔ **Pioneer:** A white settler of Alaska who has been here longer than most other people can remember — 25 or 30 years usually does it.

✔ **Southeast:** Most people don't bother to say "southeastern Alaska." The region may be to the northwest of everyone else in the country, but it's southeast of most Alaskans, and that's all they care about.

✔ **Tsunami:** Earthquake-caused sea waves are often called tidal waves, but that's a misnomer. The destructive waves of the 1964 Alaska earthquake were tsunamis caused by underwater landslides and such.

✔ **Village:** A small, Alaska Native settlement in the Bush, usually tightly bound by family and cultural tradition.

Ordering Dinner: Hope Ya Like Fish

Fresh Alaskan seafood is the best in the world. Period. Don't argue unless you're prepared to defend yourself.

Okay, that's established. Now, a legitimate question: Do you want to eat salmon and halibut for every meal? Many Alaskans would say, "Sure." After all, our seafood consumption, per capita, is vastly greater than other Americans. However, I've noticed a certain fatigue on the part of some visitors when I announce that I'm throwing a few salmon filets on the grill for dinner, thinking I'm offering a great treat. The cruise ship or landside restaurants where they've been eating for a week or two have given them plenty of it.

On the (likely dubious) theory that more information will solve this problem, here are some tips on dining on Alaska's wonderful seafood:

✔ **Try the seafood that is Alaskan, instead of ordering what's flown in from elsewhere.** Pacific salmon, halibut, cod, sablefish (black cod), rockfish, clams, oysters, mussels, shrimp, and crab are all Alaskan. Atlantic (farmed) salmon, lobster, tuna, swordfish, and so on are not.

✔ **Order what's in season.** Fresh, wild Alaska salmon is available all year, but it's much more plentiful in the summer and fall. In the winter and early spring, fresh troll-caught salmon is served in the best restaurants. Other restaurants may serve farmed salmon off-season in order to say it's fresh. That fish comes from somewhere else and lacks the taste, texture, and purity of wild Alaska salmon. Bottom fish, such as halibut, cod, and rockfish, are in season almost all year.

✔ **If you're ordering salmon, go for the best salmon varieties.** You can be as much a connoisseur of salmon as you can of wine. There are five species of Pacific salmon, each with two names. The rank of tastiness I would put them in, starting with the best, would be king (chinook), red (sockeye), silver (coho), pink (humpy), and chum (dog). You shouldn't find the last two in any good restaurant, except perhaps in a salad or burger, but any of the first three can be fantastic as a fresh filet. The best king and red salmon come from the Copper and Yukon rivers, which produce fish with lots of healthy fat — the stuff that makes the fish taste so good.

✔ **Consider the environment.** Generally, Alaska's fisheries are well managed and in good shape. Eating Alaska salmon is good for your health and good for the environment, because stocks are plentiful and need to be used. It's all good with halibut and cod, too. Rockfish is a long-lived fish and can be depleted but is being carefully managed. Shellfish mostly come from family-owned coastal farms. Crab is okay, too, although some species have been overfished. The major environmental controversy surrounding Alaska fishing relates to the big factory trawlers that produce fake crab or fish sticks for fast-food and other such restaurants nationally.

✔ **Know how salmon should be prepared.** The best chefs know that they can't improve much on good, fresh Alaska salmon. They grill filets over alder wood with just some soy sauce, pepper, and dill, serving it when it's barely done. Baking and poaching also can be delicious, and I've had some wonderful exotic preparations. It's a question of the chef's skill when he tries to get fancy. Blackened salmon? Why?

✔ **Know how halibut should be prepared.** Halibut and rockfish have a delicate flavor that's easily ruined by sauces. Grilled, pan-seared, or baked preparations are best. Deep-fried halibut, such as halibut and chips, is good with a thin tempura batter, but many places glob so much batter on that you can't tell fish is inside. The best restaurants use nuts, sesame seeds, or soy sauce to accent the flavor without burying it; the worst restaurants use cheese.

Background Check: Recommended Books, Movies, and TV Programs

You probably already have your favorite books and movies about Alaska. The state's mythical existence is more firmly entrenched in our collective consciousness than its reality. The fact that so much of this mythical knowledge is grossly inaccurate attests to the poor quality of much of what is put out about Alaska — because the place is exotic and far away, writers and directors don't feel a need to be accurate.

Here are some recommendations for getting the straight scoop:

- ✔ *Coming into the Country,* **by John McPhee (Farrar, Straus and Giroux):** A gifted nonfiction writer captures the spirit of Alaska during the years of transition that marked the end of the frontier. McPhee's vivid portraits of backcountry personalities portray the motivations of the odd people you may encounter.

- ✔ *The Fate of Nature,* **by Charles Wohlforth (Thomas Dunne/St. Martin's Press):** Yes, I'm recommending my own book, which traces the relationship of Alaska's people to the land and waters of the Gulf of Alaska to find the hopes and motivations for saving this magnificent place. It's history, science, and biography in a single story.

- ✔ *Ordinary Wolves,* **by Seth Kantner (Milkweed Editions):** Credibly called the best novel about Alaska since Jack London, this autobiographical tale of a boy coming to manhood in an Arctic sod hut is both harrowing and extraordinarily enlightening.

- ✔ *Grizzly Man* **(2005):** Probably the best movie yet made about Alaska, Werner Herzog's documentary explores humanity's relation to nature using film shot by Timothy Treadwell, a misguided animal lover who ultimately was eaten by the bears he befriended.

- ✔ *Into the Wild* **(2007):** Director Sean Penn's dramatization of the true story of Christopher McCandless, a young wanderer who died in the Alaska wilderness. The movie is packed with spectacular scenery and was filmed on location.

- ✔ *The Simpsons Movie* **(2007):** This summer blockbuster cut uncomfortably close to home with its portrayal of greedy Alaskans eager to destroy the environment. Homer seemed so darned at home here, a place where "you can never be too fat or too drunk."

- ✔ *Northern Exposure* **(1990–95):** Alaskans laughed about the silly inaccuracies in this popular TV series, which is available on DVD and is shown periodically in reruns on cable. In spirit, however, the show got it right, depicting the freedom and oddity of small-town Alaska life.

- ✔ *Deadliest Catch* **(2005 to the present):** This surprise hit on the Discovery Channel records the real-life hazards and conflicts of hard-driving crab fishermen as they battle the notoriously bad weather of the Bering Sea.

Chapter 3

Deciding Where and When to Go

In This Chapter

▶ Getting your bearings in Alaska
▶ Sorting out the seasons
▶ Reviewing a calendar of local events
▶ Focusing on the purpose of your trip

*F*iguring out where to go in Alaska doesn't have to be daunting. For one thing, you're not likely to go wrong with anywhere you choose to visit. For another, in this chapter, I lay out the options simply, along with the best times of year to visit, the most noteworthy events in the state, and some tips I've developed from a lifetime of traveling in Alaska and advising travelers who visit here.

Narrowing Your Travel Options

Did I mention that Alaska is large? Well, it is. (We Alaskans put down Texans by telling them that Alaska could split in half and make Texas only the third-largest state.) That being true, covering every town or even every region in the state in this book would be a hopeless task. Some parts of Alaska are so sparsely populated and rarely visited that telling each potential visitor about them, one by one, would take less time than writing a book covering it all. Other places receive a reasonable number of visitors but don't have as much to offer as other similar places. To simplify your choices, in this section, I focus on the best locations, where you'll find the full range of what Alaska offers.

Anchorage

They say that **Anchorage** isn't Alaska, but you can see it from there. They're wrong: Any city with moose, bears, and eagles in its parks and neighborhoods is part of Alaska. But what they're hinting at is true: With 40 percent of the state's population (283,000 out of 670,000 in the state), Anchorage dwarfs all other towns, has little in common with typical remote Alaskan communities, and serves as the overwhelming hub of

Alaskan activities, with services and an urban feel that you'd expect to find only in a much larger city.

As a visitor, taking advantage of these qualities can make your trip easier and less expensive. For example, plane fares to Anchorage are relatively inexpensive because of heavy competition, but flying to many other Alaskan towns costs a fortune. Many cruises end in Anchorage, too, after docking in Seward and taking a 124-mile bus or train ride into town, or docking in Whittier and riding the road or rail for less than two hours. Car and RV rentals are plentiful in Anchorage, and flight services fan out for day trips as far north as the **Arctic Ocean** and as far south as **Katmai National Park.**

Anchorage was built by the federal government in 1915 on a site chosen for its location along the best route for a rail line from the coast to Alaska's **Interior.** It grew because of its strategic location as an international crossroad for air travel and national defense. The city sits in Southcentral Alaska in a bowl of mountains at the head of **Cook Inlet,** handy to the **Kenai Peninsula** to the south and the entire **Interior** region to the north.

Because of its central location, I structured this book around the idea that your visit to the main part of the state (everything but the Southeast panhandle) should begin and end in **Anchorage.**

The city has much to offer, indoors and out, including the state's largest museum, the most extensive Native cultural center, and several other sites of interest. **Chugach State Park,** the city's backdrop, contains some of Alaska's best day hikes and backpacking routes, and in town, you find superb bike and cross-country ski trails.

Just outside of town, **Girdwood** is a hip little skiing town with beautiful, steep slopes overlooking the waters of Turnagain Arm, a glacier-carved fjord. A bit farther, and through a tunnel, **Whittier,** less than two hours from Anchorage, is the jumping-off point for day trips and longer voyages into **Prince William Sound** by ship, boat, or sea kayak.

For information on the city and all the locations listed in this section, see Part III of this book.

The Kenai Peninsula

The **Kenai Peninsula** is Anchorage's playground. It's a big area, a five-hour drive from one end to the other, with three distinct parts you should consider for a visit:

✔ **Seward and nearby Kenai Fjords National Park:** About 124 road miles from Anchorage, this is a prime area for sea-kayaking, whale- and bird-watching, and ocean salmon-fishing. Visiting the park as a day trip from Anchorage is possible, but staying a night or two is a better idea. In the fjords, you'll see some of the world's most extreme scenery: Rock mountains rise straight up from the sea a mile high.

> ✔ **Kenai and Soldotna:** A prime area for fishing, the king salmon in the Kenai River grow to world-record size. Silver and red salmon and enormous trout run in the river, too.

> ✔ **Homer:** Sitting on the edge of the panoramic and fish-rich **Kachemak Bay,** Homer offers some of Alaska's best opportunities for outdoor exploration, with a guide or on your own, using services that make it easy for beginners to get into the wilderness for the first time. The town and its satellite waterfront communities also are home to many of Alaska's best artists and several of its best restaurants.

To get the inside scoop on the Kenai Peninsula, check out Chapter 16.

Fairbanks and the Interior highways

Long rivers and two-lane highways connect the central part of Alaska. These highways are worth exploring, when you have the time. The center of the region is **Fairbanks,** Alaska's second-largest city, sitting on the banks of the muddy Chena River. It's known for its **gold-rush history;** river floating; hot-spring soaks; and, in winter, dog-mushing and the **Northern Lights** (the aurora borealis — see Chapter 17 for more on this phenomenon and the region in general).

Denali National Park

Partway between Anchorage and Fairbanks, **Denali National Park** (see Chapter 19) is home to North America's tallest mountain, **Mount McKinley,** and some of its most expansive **alpine scenery.** It's also the place for the least expensive **wildlife safari** you'll ever take, a $30 bus ride that usually encounters brown bears and other animals. While riding the park's buses, I've seen wolves, caribou, moose, Dall sheep, beavers, and much more.

Southeast Alaska

The **Panhandle,** as this relatively narrow strip of land is called, is an extension of the Pacific Northwest, a region of big spruce, hemlock, and cedar trees; deep fjords; crashing glaciers; and islands full of wildlife. Almost the entire region is part of **Tongass National Forest,** and the opportunities for sea-kayaking, ocean-fishing, whale-watching, bear-viewing, and hiking are almost limitless.

The best hubs to visit are **Juneau** and **Sitka,** cities with interesting museums and historic sites. **Skagway** is a center of gold-rush history. In planning your trip, however, choosing to visit *either* the Southeast *or* the balance of the state is wise, unless you have two weeks or more. No roads connect most Southeast towns, and the distances between Anchorage and other towns are so great that getting to those places costs as much as getting to Alaska in the first place.

For details on hotels, attractions, and dining in this region, head to Part V of this book.

The Bush

Many people come to Alaska with an itch to see the **Arctic,** or simply to get beyond the roads into deep wilderness full of wildlife. That describes most of the state, yet getting to the outlying areas takes extra money, planning, and time. In Part VI of this book, I discuss some of the best Bush destinations and details for making the trip.

Sorting out the Seasons

Although Alaska actually spans five time zones, its residents tell time squeezed into just two of them: Alaska time for most of the state, and Hawaii-Aleutian time for a few Aleutian Islands. Similarly, Alaska has at least five distinct climates, ranging from temperate in the Southeast, with precipitation as heavy as any in the world, to the frigid Arctic, with skies as dry as any desert. (The distance north to south is the same as the distance from Bangor, Maine, to Miami, Florida — a little over 1,700 miles.) The seasons aren't simple, and another factor weighs in on the calculation: light. In the state's middle latitudes, the sun rises for only a few hours in December, but in June, the sky is light all night. In the Arctic, one winter night can last two months.

To help plan, Tables 3-1, 3-2, and 3-3 show the average temperature highs and lows and the number of days per month with rain or snow for three major Alaska destinations (Anchorage, Fairbanks, and Juneau, respectively). These tables also offer the hours of daylight on the 21st day of every month.

Table 3-1 Anchorage's Average Temperatures, Days with Precipitation, and Daylight Hours

	Jan	Feb	Mar	Apr	May	June	July	Aug	Sep	Oct	Nov	Dec
Average high (°F)	21	26	33	44	55	62	65	63	55	40	28	22
Average high (°C)	–6	–3	1	7	13	17	18	17	13	4	–2	–6
Average low (°F)	8	11	17	29	39	47	51	49	41	28	16	10
Average low (°C)	–13	–12	–8	–2	4	8	11	9	5	–2	–9	–12
Days of precipitation	8	8	8	6	7	8	11	13	14	12	10	11
Daylight hours	6:53	9:41	12:22	15:20	18:00	19:22	18:00	15:15	12:19	9:29	6:46	5:27

Table 3-2   Fairbanks's Average Temperatures, Days with Precipitation, and Daylight Hours

	Jan	Feb	Mar	Apr	May	June	July	Aug	Sep	Oct	Nov	Dec
Average high (°F)	–2	7	24	42	60	71	73	66	55	32	11	1
Average high (°C)	–18	–13	–4	6	16	22	23	19	13	0	–12	–17
Average low (°F)	–19	–15	–2	20	38	52	52	47	36	17	–5	–16
Average low (°C)	–28	–26	–19	–7	3	11	11	8	2	–8	–21	–27
Days of precipitation	8	7	6	5	7	11	12	12	10	11	11	9
Daylight hours	5:46	9:14	12:22	15:54	19:22	21:48	19:26	15:52	12:24	9:04	5:39	3:43

Table 3-3   Juneau's Average Temperatures, Days with Precipitation, and Daylight Hours

	Jan	Feb	Mar	Apr	May	June	July	Aug	Sep	Oct	Nov	Dec
Average high (°F)	29	34	39	48	55	62	64	63	56	47	37	32
Average high (°C)	–2	1	4	9	13	17	18	17	13	8	3	0
Average low (°F)	18	3	27	32	39	45	48	48	43	37	28	23
Average low (°C)	–82	–5	–3	0	4	7	9	9	6	3	–2	–5
Days of precipitation	18	17	18	17	17	15	17	17	20	24	20	21
Daylight hours	7:31	9:55	12:18	14:55	17:11	18:17	17:13	14:54	12:20	9:49	7:27	6:22

The seasons from Anchorage north

The area of the state from **Anchorage** north, including **Fairbanks,** the **Interior,** and the **Arctic,** is significantly drier and colder in winter than areas nearer the Pacific Ocean, making it better than the state's coastal areas for winter and fall visits.

Summer is the peak season because:

✔ Temperatures are comfortable from mid-May through August, although fall rains usually start in mid-August.

✔ Salmon-fishing is strong from early June through mid-September.

✔ The visitor season is in full swing, so you'll find plenty to do and everything open. Traditionally, in fact, this is the only time of year when visitors come to Alaska.

Shedding light on all the light

You may have always wanted to know but were afraid to ask why summer days are so long in the north and winter days are so short. The short answer is geometry. Seasons are controlled by the way the Earth leans on its axis: toward the sun in summer and away from the sun in winter. (Seasons are opposite in the Northern and Southern hemispheres.) As the Earth spins, any particular spot on the globe, such as Anchorage, travels a certain circle every day. On a globe, that circle is depicted as a line of *latitude*. When the Northern Hemisphere leans closer to the sun in summer, light hits more of that circle, so daylight lasts longer at any point along that line. As you travel farther north, each circular line of latitude becomes smaller and is shadowed less by the top of the Earth, so summer daylight lasts longer each day.

Heading north, the **Arctic Circle** is the first latitude where the sun doesn't set at least one day of each year. During winter, the reverse is true: The sun doesn't rise at least one day each year at the Arctic Circle. By comparison, every day at the equator has 12 hours of light (and 12 hours of darkness) all year. The poles aren't affected by days, because they sit right on the Earth's axis. There, the sky is light all summer and dark all winter.

But keep in mind:

- ✔ Prices are highest, reservations are hardest to get, and crowds are most common from mid-June through mid-August (when weather is best).

- ✔ Alaska's mosquitoes are worst when the weather is best.

- ✔ Cool, rainy weather can occur at any time, but the driest summer months are June and July.

- ✔ As you travel north, the season shortens. Ice often doesn't leave the Arctic until July, and hiking trails can be wet and muddy through June almost everywhere in the state. At **Denali National Park,** frosty nights and fall colors start in late August.

Winter is paradise for outdoor enthusiasts because:

- ✔ Skiing, both downhill and cross-country, peaks in February and March, with plenty of light and snow.

- ✔ Dark winter skies mean the Northern Lights shine frequently.

- ✔ Sled-dog racing season peaks in February and March, great times for your own dog-mushing adventures.

- ✔ With a few exceptions, prices are as low as half-off and reservations are easy to make.

But keep in mind:

- ✔ Most tourist attractions and even some roads are closed for the season.

- ✔ A road trip requires special safety preparations in extreme cold conditions.

- ✔ Wildlife-viewing is generally impossible.

Spring and **fall** are promising because:

- ✔ Prices are low and weather, although chilly, is not extreme.

- ✔ Fall colors are spectacular on the Arctic tundra of northern Alaska and in the *boreal forests* (the relatively sparse northern woods of Alaska's Interior). Depending on latitude, colors peak from late August through early October.

- ✔ Spring weather can be dry and bright.

But keep in mind:

- ✔ Most summer and winter attractions are closed.

- ✔ Weather is unpredictable and can be bad; visits in April, October, and November are probably not worth the risk of potentially rotten conditions.

- ✔ Not much wildlife is visible in spring or late fall.

The seasons in coastal Alaska

The climate of **Southeast Alaska, Prince William Sound,** and the **Kenai Peninsula** — the entire arc of the southern Alaska coastline, in fact — is controlled by the warmth and dampness of air from the Pacific Ocean. That's why rain forests grow here, why winters stay warm and summers cool, and why a waterproof raincoat is never a bad idea.

Summer is *the* time to come because:

- ✔ The region comes alive with outdoor activities, attractions, events, fishing, and wildlife-viewing.

- ✔ Weather is never dry, but it's much drier than in fall or winter. Temperatures are comfortable.

But keep in mind:

- ✔ Crowds can close in; reservations are a necessity.

- ✔ Because of the season's popularity, prices are high.

Fall and **winter** are impractical because:

- Attractions close or post short hours, outdoor activities become difficult, and most fishing shuts down.

- Heavy precipitation and chilly temperatures prevail beginning in mid-September.

Spring is an intriguing possibility because:

- March, April, and May are the driest months of the year, and comfortable temperatures arrive at least a month earlier than farther north, with some nice days in late March or early April.

- In areas with heavy higher-elevation snow and developed skiing (Juneau for downhill or Homer for cross-country, for example), you can combine skiing with ocean-fishing and often pleasant, cool weather.

- The tourist season doesn't begin until mid-May or later, leaving more than a month of lower prices and friendly hosts eager to please; prices are low and reservations easy.

But keep in mind:

- Many attractions and guided outdoor activities don't start until mid-May.

- Most salmon fishing hasn't started yet.

Perusing Alaska's Calendar of Events

Something is always going on in Alaska, but I list only the cream of the crop here — the kind of events around which you can plan part of your trip. Many other events take place during the time of year when Alaska doesn't play host to as many visitors. In summer, when most tourists arrive, Alaskans are too busy fishing, getting outdoors, and serving visitors to be able to organize many community events. But check on what's going on if you arrive during the off season, and get involved in one of the truly local happenings — it can give you a special entrance into the heart of these communities.

February

The **Anchorage Fur Rendezvous Festival** (☎ 907-274-1177; www.furrondy.net) started in 1935 and was recently rejuvenated with creative, youthful events such as the exciting and funny Running of the Reindeer, an event like the Pamplona Running of the Bulls but far safer for all involved, as reindeer are notably gentle animals. The Multi-Tribal Gathering and Native Arts Market should not be missed, and there are many community events as well: a parade, fireworks, a carnival, craft fairs, snowshoe softball, dog-sled rides, and so on. The Rondy's traditional centerpiece (global warming permitting) is the speedy **World Champion Sled Dog Race,** a three-day sprint event of about 25 miles per heat. Late February through early March.

March

The **Iditarod Trail Sled Dog Race** (☎ 907-376-5155; www.iditarod. com) is Alaska's biggest cultural and sporting event, drawing throngs of visitors, especially from overseas. The 1,000-mile race starts with fanfare from Anchorage and follows the historic gold-rush trail to Nome. The city's largest community celebration accompanies the start of the race in Anchorage, with ski-racing, parades, fireworks, and the like. For the finish, the little town of Nome turns into one huge party with days of silly happenings, such as a golf tournament on the sea ice. The editors of this guide have noted that some animal-rights activists outside Alaska oppose the race on the grounds that it's cruel to the dogs. Race supporters maintain that sled dogs love running and thrive on cold, and they believe that rigorous dog-care rules have addressed the activists' concerns. The race begins the first Saturday in March.

May

The **Kachemak Bay Shorebird Festival** (☎ 907-235-7740; www.homer alaska.org) in Homer celebrates the annual influx of thousands of migrating birds with guided bird-watching hikes and boat excursions, natural-history workshops, art shows, performances, and other events. Early May.

June

The **Sitka Summer Music Festival** (☎ 907-747-6774; www.sitkamusic festival.org) offers chamber-music concerts and other musical events, presenting top performers from around the world. Three weeks in June.

The **Summer Solstice** is celebrated in many ways in communities around Alaska. In most of the state, the longest day of the year means the sky is never dark. The oldest continuously observed event is the **Midnight Sun Baseball Game,** hosted by the semipro Alaska Goldpanners of Fairbanks (☎ 907-451-0095; www.goldpanners.com), which begins at 10:30 p.m. on the solstice and is played without artificial lights. The game began with a pair of pickup teams in 1906. The 'Panners have hosted since 1960. June 21.

July

You've never experienced a small-town Fourth of July until you've joined the throngs on the streets of Seward for its **Independence Day** celebration. Besides the parade and many other festivities, the main attraction is the **Mount Marathon Race** (☎ 907-224-8051; www.sewardak.org), an insane 3¼-mile scramble from the middle of town straight up the rocky mountain that is the race's namesake to its 3,022-ft. peak and down again in less than an hour. July 4.

August

The **Alaska State Fair** (☎ 907-745-4827; www.alaskastatefair.org) is in the Anchorage suburb of Palmer. The region's biggest event of the year, it features rides, musical performances, and country competitions. The biggest news of each year's fair is the winning cabbage; the area's good soil and long days produce cabbages the size of beanbag chairs. Mere beach-ball-size cabbages are laughed off the stage. Stop here, too, to see a mammoth rutabaga or kohlrabi. World records are broken every year. Runs the 12 days leading up to and including Labor Day.

November

In Anchorage, the University of Alaska Anchorage Seawolves play host to the **Carrs/Safeway Great Alaska Shootout** (☎ 907-786-1250; www.goseawolves.com). The event features a roster of the nation's top-ranked NCAA Division I men's and women's basketball teams for a weekend-long tournament. Thanksgiving weekend.

Keeping Your Trip on Track

When you're planning a trip, it's easy to get lost in the details and forget the most important thing — such as why you want to go to Alaska in the first place. When you've forgotten that all-important fact on a trip, you find yourself thinking, "What am I doing here?" Because I see too many Alaska visitors with that thought on their faces, I've put together some ideas to keep you on track:

✔ If you're visiting Alaska for scenery and wildlife, plan plenty of time outdoors, rather than in towns at museums and such.

✔ If you're hoping to see the wilderness, remember that will take planning and time; be sure to contact guides and tour operators in advance and allow plenty of money in your budget and time on your schedule for these activities. (See Chapter 12 to find out how early you need to make reservations for each kind of activity.)

✔ Schedule plenty of extra time in your itinerary, not only for the unexpected things that make travel more fun, but also for bad weather, which frequently postpones activities, flights, and boat rides in Alaska. Flexibility is a must.

✔ Don't try to see widely separated regions of the state unless you have plenty of money and time to spend. Distances between regions are truly extraordinary, and you can see most of the same highlights in either the Southeast or Southcentral/Interior regions.

✔ Try not to get hung up on bagging the big-name sights. Alaska has incredible experiences and scenery in many lesser-known places where you can make your own discoveries. Besides, weather may not cooperate at headline attractions you're hoping to see, so you should be ready to enjoy what you *can* see.

Chapter 4

Great Alaska Itineraries

In This Chapter

▶ Spending a week in Southeast Alaska
▶ Visiting Denali and Kenai Fjords National Parks in one week
▶ Seeing Alaska in two weeks
▶ Enjoying a week in Alaska with the kids
▶ Experiencing real winter for a week in Alaska

*R*eality is such a drag. It dictates that you won't have unlimited time for a trip to Alaska. In fact, most people's reality requires negotiating with a boss or co-workers to be able to get a week or two off for a trip. (You really should consider being a travel writer!) With reality in mind, then, I've designed the itineraries in this chapter so that you can make the most of the time you spend in Alaska. I don't think you need to jet or drive around to the four corners of the state, the way some commission-hungry travel agents seem to think is best. Instead, these itineraries put you in some of the very best places, where you have a chance of seeing and doing a great deal without spending too much money or time on the road.

Don't take my word for it — simply use these itineraries as a basis for putting together *your* ideal trip with *your* own interests in mind. People often ask me, "What's the best way to spend a week in Alaska?" I generally respond by asking whether the travelers are interested in scenery, wildlife, or cultural attractions, and whether they're athletic, disabled, adventurous, or averse to discomfort.

You may be a sturdy backpacker, an inquiring elder, or a parent with kids in diapers. Without knowing anything about you, I can give you advice, but it's based on my own preferences and interests. I'm not a complete oddball, so most people will find something that interests them here. But we're all different, so use these itineraries as examples to consider as you tailor your own travel plans to fit your interests.

Cruising *and* being independent

The simplest way to build an Alaska itinerary is to cruise through Southeast Alaska's Inside Passage, and join an escorted tour offered by the cruise line to see land-based attractions by tour bus. If that's your goal, then the itineraries in this chapter won't be much help. (Choosing a cruise is more about the boat than the destinations.) Instead, see Chapter 6 to find out about choosing a package tour and Chapter 8 to review your choices for cruising.

Before you skip ahead, however, consider a third course: Many cruise-ship passengers decide to go it alone after getting off the boat. Cruising offers some significant advantages to visitors who want to explore Southeast Alaska but dislike public transportation and its inherent unpredictability — the only other option for travel in this region is by air and ferry. But after your cruise ship arrives in the Southcentral region — including Seward, Whittier, or Anchorage — you can tour by private car. If you wouldn't normally sign on for a package tour on a bus, don't do it here. Instead, link your cruise with the independent itineraries listed in this chapter. Driving your own car and finding your own way makes the trip yours, tailoring it to your spontaneity and pace, and gives you a greater chance to find your own unique Alaskan experiences.

These itineraries also show the complexity and diversity that await you when traveling among Alaska destinations. Alaska has trains, planes, boats, and automobiles, but not all go to each destination. Most communities in Alaska aren't even connected by roads — including the state capital, Juneau. (Of Alaska's ten largest cities, only five can be reached by driving.) As it happens, this isn't a bad thing, because authentic charm grows best in isolation. On the other hand, isolation makes trip planning a bit more complicated than jumping in the car. For a table that shows the modes of transportation you can use to access the state's major destinations, see Chapter 7.

Touring Southeast Alaska in One Week without a Cruise Ship

The overwhelming majority of tourists to Southeast Alaska come on cruise ships; plenty of prospective visitors ask me if it's possible to see the region any other way. Of course, it is! In fact, I wonder if it's possible to see the Southeast region — to *really* see it — from the deck of a cruise ship larger than the towns it visits.

It *is* true that Southeast Alaska is a part of the world where people travel from town to town mostly in boats rather than in cars and buses. Boating, to them, is no inconvenience, and it's what makes this itinerary so appealing. The lack of highways continues to keep towns in this area quaint and the wild lands surrounding them remote.

Everything on this itinerary is covered in Chapters 20 and 22.

Day 1 begins with a flight to Juneau, where you grab a cab to your hotel in the downtown area; you have no need for a rental car at this stage. After settling in, explore the charming downtown streets on foot, stopping at the **State Museum** for an overview and orientation to Alaska's history and culture. In the evening, relax with a low-key dinner at one of the casual restaurants downtown or, if you're in the mood for a celebration, at the classy **Zephyr Restaurant.**

If you're blessed with good weather on **Day 2,** hike the **Perseverance Trail,** visiting the **Last Chance Mining Museum** at the trailhead. If your preference is for a less strenuous outing, then ride the aerial tram up **Mount Roberts** for its amazing views and the nature walks you can take while up top. Consider filling out the day with a helicopter ride to the **Juneau Ice Field,** perhaps for a dog-sled ride or just a walk on the snow. In the evening (again, when the weather is good), attend the **Gold Creek Salmon Bake** for outdoor dining and folksy entertainment, or enjoy a fun and tasty indoor meal at the **Twisted Fish Company Alaskan Grill** on the waterfront.

Day 3 is good for a daylong boat ride to **Tracy Arm** to see glaciers, high fjord cliffs, and wildlife. If you're more interested in whale-watching, join one of the Juneau-based operators with virtually surefire voyages to see whales. Those who like to plan ahead may be able to obtain one of the scarce reservations to fly to the **Pack Creek Bear-Viewing Area** on Admiralty Island to see lots of feeding brown bears. After seeing the bears, you can dine at the **Hangar** for a jolly end to the day.

On **Day 4,** check out of your Juneau hotel for an early 40-minute flight to **Sitka** on Alaska Airlines. Settle in there for a couple of days of walking amid historic sites, making sure that you visit the **Sitka National Historic Park** with its Tlingit battlefield and totem poles, exquisite Native art in the **Sheldon Jackson Museum,** and Russian-American architecture and treasures at the **Russian Bishop's House** and **St. Michael's Cathedral.** In the evening, dine at **Ludvig's,** a charming restaurant run by a local gourmet, and attend a traditional **Sitka Tribal Dance Performance** at the community house, before turning in at your Sitka hotel.

Staying in the Sitka area for **Day 5,** you can join a sea-kayaking outing to see the wildlife of **Sitka Sound,** including sea otters, sea lions, eagles, and possibly even whales. Fishing charters are also popular; less active travelers can take one of the excellent boat tours offered on a variety of large or intimate vessels. Dine at the **Channel Club.**

Day 6 starts aboard an **Alaska Marine Highway System ferry** for the spectacular 150-mile ride back to Juneau, where you take a cab from the docks to the airport so that you can rent a car for 24 hours and drive to your accommodations, dining along the way at one of the outlying restaurants, such as **Chan's Thai Kitchen.**

On **Day 7,** before your evening flight back home, use the car you rented yesterday to see the **Mendenhall Glacier** and the **Shrine of St. Therese,** and to enjoy the scenery **"out the road"** (which is how locals refer to the lovely 40-mile drive on the Glacier Highway).

Seeing the National Parks: Denali and Kenai Fjords in One Week

This itinerary and its variations are probably the most popular in Alaska for independent travelers. Some arrive in Anchorage by air to see the parks while others disembark from cruise ships in Seward or Whittier before renting a car. What makes the trip great for first-time visitors is the opportunity to see the best of the state's outdoor highlights: the amazing scenery and abundant wildlife of inland Denali National Park and maritime Kenai Fjords National Park.

On **Day 1,** fly to Anchorage, where you spend your first night and rent a car. (Chapter 7 offers information about car rentals in Alaska.) If you arrive early enough, you can take in some of the city, with a visit to the **Anchorage Museum at Rasmuson Center** or the **Alaska Native Heritage Center.** Or, if the weather is good, rent a bike and ride along the **Tony Knowles Coastal Trail.** In the evening, eat at **Simon and Seafort's Saloon and Grill,** which overlooks the waters of Knik Arm. (Part III of this book offers much more detail about the greater Anchorage area.)

On **Day 2,** drive 124 miles south on the Seward Highway to the **Kenai Peninsula** and Seward, your overnight destination for the next couple nights. (For details about the sights and services available during this part of the itinerary, check out Chapter 16.) This drive is one of the world's most spectacular. Scope out some of the places you'd like to stop, but don't actually stop until your return trip. You need to arrive in Seward in time to board a reserved tour boat into **Kenai Fjords National Park,** where you'll see mountains jutting a mile out of the water, big blue glaciers, thousands of seabirds, and many marine mammals, often including humpback or orca whales. Dine tonight at **Ray's Waterfront.**

Remaining in Seward for **Day 3,** paddle a sea kayak into **Resurrection Bay** among sea otters and (possibly) spawning salmon, or join a fishing charter. You should still have time to see the charming downtown and visit the **Alaska SeaLife Center,** a research aquarium. If, on the other hand, you want to spend more time outdoors, make the short side trip to see **Exit Glacier,** just north of town. Try the **Apollo Restaurant** or **Christo's Palace** for dinner.

Driving back to Anchorage on the morning of **Day 4,** don't forget to stop at some of those beautiful or intriguing spots you noted on the way down along the Seward Highway, and don't miss the **Portage Glacier Visitor Center.** You can have lunch in **Girdwood** at **Chair 5** or the **Hotel**

Alyeska, and you may even want to take the aerial tram up to the top of **Mount Alyeska** for its mountaintop views or for a hike on one of the trails near here in **Chugach National Forest** or **Chugach State Park.** On the drive into Anchorage, keep your eyes open for **beluga whales** and **Dall sheep.** With plenty of time left, you have a good opportunity to try either the **Marx Brothers Cafe** or **Club Paris** in Anchorage, two of Alaska's best restaurants, yet still turn in early in preparation for a long day on the road.

Get an early start on **Day 5** for the 4½-hour drive north to **Denali National Park** (see Chapter 19). Stop in **Talkeetna** along the way for a flightseeing tour of **Mount McKinley** (preferably with a landing on the mountain itself) before continuing on to the park, where you still have time for a **hike** or **raft ride** in and around the park's entrance area. The best place to eat is **229 Parks Restaurant & Tavern,** south of the park. Check into a hotel in **Healy** or near the park entrance for tonight and tomorrow night.

 On **Day 6,** board a shuttle bus into Denali for **wildlife-viewing** and **day-hiking.** Try to make your shuttle bus reservations a month or more in advance; choose the earliest departure time that you can stand. Arriving back at your lodging after a very long day, eat at your hotel or one of the low-key places near the park.

Reserve **Day 7** to drive back to Anchorage and catch your plane home.

Covering a Lot of (Alaskan) Ground in Two Weeks

One option for a two-week trip to Alaska is simply linking the preceding two one-week itineraries. Although that's a good trip, you may end up spending more time looking at sea otters and glaciers than you need. A better plan is padding those one-week itineraries with more days, more activities, and more side trips within the regions you're already covering. Doing so saves time and gives you a better chance to dig in and really get a better feel for the destinations. I've designed this two-week itinerary to show you how to use your additional time to add on to the basics. Some days overlap with the "Seeing the National Parks" itinerary earlier, because I assume you'll still want to see some of those big-name attractions.

For **days 1 and 2,** follow the first two days of the "Seeing the National Parks" itinerary, earlier in this chapter.

On **Day 3,** from Seward, get back in the car and drive about four hours to **Homer.** That gives you plenty of time to visit the galleries and the **Pratt Museum** and to find out why Homer is the art center of Alaska. Dine on the water at **Land's End** (see Chapter 16).

Head outdoors on **Day 4** by paddling a sea kayak out into **Kachemak Bay** to view seabirds and otters and other marine mammals, and to land on a lovely pebble beach in the wilderness. Less active travelers can choose a wildlife boat tour through some of these same waters or join a fishing charter. Before heading back to your hotel for your second of three nights in Homer, have dinner at **The Homestead** (see Chapter 16).

Day 5 is for adventure on your own. Take a water taxi to **Kachemak Bay State Park** for a day of **self-guided hiking** far from any road or settlement; you'll be on your own on the beaches and in the woods until your water taxi picks you up in the evening. If that sounds too scary, consider a day trip for lunch or dinner to **Halibut Cove,** a roadless arts community built on docks and boardwalks with a restaurant that offers great sushi (see Chapter 16).

You leave Homer on **Day 6,** driving back toward Anchorage, stopping along the way at the places you spotted on the way down. Don't miss the **Portage Glacier Visitor Center.** Stop in **Girdwood,** a half-hour short of Anchorage, and check in at the wonderful **Hotel Alyeska.** Ride the aerial tram to the top of **Mount Alyeska** for the mountaintop views, or, if time permits, hike the **Glacier Creek/Winner Creek Trail.** Eat at the hotel or at **Chair 5** (see Chapter 15).

On **Day 7,** briefly retracing your steps, drive about 15 miles south, back to the **Whittier Tunnel,** wait your turn, and go through the 2-mile-long, single-lane tunnel to **Whittier,** where you can put your car on the **Alaska Marine Highway System ferry to Valdez** for passage through the sublime rain-forest scenery of **Prince William Sound.** With any time that's left, visit the fascinating **Valdez Museum** and its annex, which houses a scale model of the town as it existed before destruction by the 1964 earthquake and tsunami (see Chapter 18).

On **Day 8,** drive the **Richardson Highway** to Fairbanks (364 miles). A long haul, yes, but I suggest this drive on purpose because it's one of the most awesome rides I've ever experienced. For up to six hours, you pass through unpopulated wilderness, rising from tidewater steeply into rocky mountains, passing the face of a glacier, and climbing still higher into the vast, treeless country of the **Alaska Range.** The road is a paved two-lane highway, but you'll encounter little other traffic. Find your room in **Fairbanks,** and then relax as you dine at **Gambardella's** (see Chapter 17).

Day 9 is an indoor day, taking in the sights of Fairbanks, including the extraordinary **UAF Museum of the North** and other on-campus sites, the **historic riverboat at Pioneer Park,** and perhaps a tour aboard the *Riverboat Discovery.* Or, when the weather's right, go outside and rent a canoe to float down part of the **Chena River,** landing at the **Pump House Restaurant & Saloon** for dinner (see Chapter 17).

You head out for the Arctic on **Day 10.** Board an Alaska Airlines jet bound for **Barrow,** the northernmost community in North America, on the shores of the Arctic Ocean. Through the airline, you can join a guided tour that includes a bus tour, **Eskimo dancing,** and a visit to the **cultural center** (see Chapter 23). After your visit to Barrow, simply fly back to Fairbanks for the night or stay over and fly back in the morning, giving you more relaxed time for exploration.

You've been traveling hard, so **Day 11** is for relaxation. Drive an hour from Fairbanks to **Chena Hot Springs Resort** and spend the day soaking in the hot pond or indoor and outdoor pools. If you have the energy, you can enjoy a hike or one of the many other recreational activities. Spend the night here or back in Fairbanks (see Chapter 17).

For **days 12 and 13,** drive to **Denali National Park,** which is less than two hours south of Fairbanks on the George Parks Highway, and follow the suggestions for days 5 and 6 in the "Seeing the National Parks" itinerary, earlier in this chapter.

On **Day 14,** drive 4½ hours back to Anchorage to catch your plane home.

Planning a Kid-Friendly Week in Alaska

An adult-paced trip to Alaska isn't easy with kids. The distances are great ("Are we there yet?") and activities are expensive. Nevertheless, I have four children of my own, and we spend entire Alaskan summers having fun outdoors and reminding ourselves that this really *is* our life (it's often too wonderful to believe that it's real). The key for us is discarding the idea of set goals. We hope to see wildlife, but we never plan to. We set out for a long drive, but we're ready to stop — overnight, if necessary. When we're outdoors, usually on the water, we often abandon any plan at all. We give our extended family a general outline of where we're going, but after we're on our way, any of the kids can say, "Let's land here," and we do. These randomly chosen places have often inspired us to stay for days, and have turned out to be the highlight of our summer.

This sort of spur-of-the-moment travel is much easier when you live in a place and know it well than when you're visiting for the first time. Even first-timers, however, can design a less goal-oriented trip that favors more of an experiential itinerary. Here are some suggestions for a family trip that uses Anchorage as home base.

On **Day 1,** fly into **Anchorage.** After getting your bearings, explore the downtown area. Don't miss the **Imaginarium,** an extraordinary children's science exhibit located within the Anchorage Museum at Rasmuson Center and included in the price of admission to the museum. If you have time, rent bikes for a roll along the **Coastal Trail** (see Chapter 14). Try **The Greek Corner** or **City Diner** for dinner — both are kid-friendly (see Chapter 13).

Take a day trip by boat on **Day 2** to see the glaciers and wildlife of **Prince William Sound** from Whittier. The tour-boat company arranges your transfer from Anchorage, or you can drive a rented car or take the train. Every kid enjoys the 2-mile-long **tunnel to Whittier** and the weird town itself, where everyone lives in one huge, concrete building. If your kids are old enough (depending on the child, 9–12), you can instead choose a **guided sea-kayaking outing** from Whittier as a day trip (see Chapter 15). Back in Anchorage, try the **Lucky Wishbone** for a stress-free dinner (see Chapter 13).

On **Day 3,** go hiking in **Chugach State Park.** The mountains behind Anchorage comprise one of the nation's greatest alpine parks. For the easiest access to **doable mountain climbs, mountain-biking above the tree line,** and **tundra rambles beyond trails,** start at the Glen Alps parking lot. The **Alaska Zoo** is right on the way there, if you have energy left for it (see Chapter 14). Eat at the **Moose's Tooth Pub & Pizzeria,** with the best pies and brews in town and a noisy dining room where manners aren't required (see Chapter 13).

For **Day 4,** drive to **Talkeetna,** on the south side of **Mount McKinley.** Although it's 112 miles from Anchorage, that's still about 120 miles less than a trip to the mountain's main park entrance. From Talkeetna, you can take a flight with a real glacier pilot over the mountain and, in season, land on a glacier high on its flanks. Although expensive, the glacier flight unquestionably becomes the highlight of your trip. Eat and spend the night at the **Talkeetna Alaskan Lodge** (or, on a budget, choose a less expensive lodging and meal option in Chapter 19).

Leaving Talkeetna on **Day 5,** head for **Hatcher Pass,** exploring the old mine buildings in a high mountain valley and staying in one of the cozy A-frame cabins at the **Hatcher Pass Lodge.** It's just short of camping, and you can walk from your door across a wide expanse of tundra. The tiny lodge dining room serves good burgers (see Chapter 15).

Day 6 offers an opportunity for a **white-water raft ride.** A company called Nova Raft and Adventure Tours invites children as young as 5 on rides that start in front of the impressive **Matanuska Glacier** (see Chapter 14), located up the Glenn Highway about two hours north of Anchorage and about 90 minutes from Hatcher Pass. After your adventure, you can spend your last evening at the **Glacier Brewhouse,** a fun place for a final dinner in Anchorage (see Chapter 13).

On **Day 7,** rent bikes to use up energy on Anchorage's paved and dirt trails before boarding a flight for home.

Experiencing Alaska in White: A Week of Real Winter

If you enjoy winter and winter sports, few places compare to Alaska. Even if you don't, winter is when the state is most beautiful. The scenery is purified by snow, and the aurora borealis brightly illuminates velvety skies. Travel is a bit trickier, however, and most of the attractions that pack in people during the summer are closed for the season.

Here is a weeklong itinerary that assumes you have an interest in skiing. Two of the destinations on the schedule are resorts where skiers normally spend more time than I've listed, so adjust the schedule to your liking.

On **Day 1,** arrive in **Anchorage** in early March, in time for the **Fur Rendezvous Festival** or the **Iditarod Trail Sled Dog Race** (see Chapter 3). If you enjoy **cross-country skiing,** take advantage of one of the nation's best trail systems at Anchorage's **Kincaid Park.** Or, if you prefer skating, try one of the groomed lakes, the best of which is **Westchester Lagoon** (see Chapter 14).

On **Day 2,** go to the Alyeska Resort for **downhill skiing on Mount Alyeska** and stay in the resort's grand **Hotel Alyeska.** You can ski 1,400 acres of mostly steep terrain right from the hotel's back door and dine on either side of the mountain — or on top of it. If you don't want to ski, you can spend time in the magnificent pool (see Chapter 15).

Day 3 offers another day of skiing at Mount Alyeska, or you can go **back-country skiing** or join a **snowmobile** outing into the **Chugach Mountains** from the resort.

On **Day 4,** catch the Alaska Railroad's weekly, **one-car winter train from Anchorage to Fairbanks,** a 12-hour journey through Alaska's most spectacular scenery, with no sign of human activities. With any luck, you'll see plenty of moose and a stunning view of **Mount McKinley** (see Chapter 7).

In Fairbanks for **Day 5,** visit the **UAF Museum of the North.** Save time for a **dog-sled ride** in this, the world's center of mushing.

On **Day 6,** head out to **Chena Hot Springs Resort,** enjoying the **hot pond,** the **indoor and outdoor pools,** and the **aurora-viewing facility;** go **cross-country skiing, dog-mushing,** or **snowmobiling** to explore the surrounding wilderness (see Chapter 17).

Day 7 offers time for one last soak or ski before you head back to the airport in Fairbanks for the trip home.

Part II
Planning Your Trip to Alaska

The 5th Wave
By Rich Tennant

"Oh Ted, this Alaskan cruise is everything I'd ever imagined! The sweeping vista of the salad bar, the breathtaking dessert tray, the majesty of the carving station..."

In this part . . .

You've planned your trip in your daydreams; now it's time to plan it on paper. This is the challenging part. The same aspects of Alaska travel that make the state an exotic destination — the extremes of weather and distances, the lack of roads, and the remoteness of the greatest attractions — also complicate planning a trip here. Fortunately, you won't be the first to address these issues: All you have to do is make selections, not blaze trails.

This part covers the big choices, including critical decisions about picking a cruise ship, setting up an outdoor adventure, and traveling independently or with a group, as well as many of the smaller details about how to get where you're going, book your room, keep within your budget, and so on.

Chapter 5

Managing Your Money

. . . .

In This Chapter

▶ Estimating how much your trip will cost
▶ Keeping an eye on hidden expenses
▶ Picking up a few money-saving tips

. . . .

*A*laska is expensive. Hotels and meals cost more than comparable choices elsewhere in the United States, especially during the time when most visitors come to the state. The peak season is short and operators charge all that the market will bear during the three or four months of active business.

With careful planning and some compromises, you can keep costs under control — the trick is knowing where to economize. You can't cut the cost of getting outdoors to see and do the things that make Alaska a special place to visit. Unless you're an expert sea-kayaker, you can't get out on the water cheaply; you need a guide to find out where and how to fish; and without your own wings, you can't see what Alaska looks like from above.

In this chapter, I explain when to save and when to splurge so you can hold down costs without sacrificing the whole point of the trip.

Planning Your Budget

I know the impulse well. After adding up the costs of your vacation in your head, you shave a figure or two here, leave out a detail there, and convince yourself that you can't afford *not* to go! If you want to do that, skip this section and ask your boss for a raise. If you want to go in with your eyes open, however, use these pages to make sure that you don't miss accounting for any costs in your planning. (See Chapter 8 for the costs of traveling to Alaska by cruise ship.) Also, see the nearby "Creating a real budget" sidebar for how I calculate costs when I travel.

Creating a real budget

As a writer of travel books and a freelance journalist, I travel a lot, and how much money I take home at the end of a project depends in large part on how much I've spent on the road. Sometimes I travel rough, and certainly I go at a pace that wouldn't interest any vacationer. But the tools I use to figure out how much my trip will cost may help you with yours, if budget is a critical issue.

Many travelers try to figure the cost of the trip by coming up with a per-day budget that seems reasonable and then multiplying that by the length of the trip. But on a real trip, one day may cost three times as much as another — and that's as it should be, because you should save up to spend a lot on major activities.

When I plan a trip, I use a spreadsheet program on my computer (Microsoft Excel, but any other will work as well). Each row is an actual expenditure I expect on a trip — a certain day's lodging or rail ticket, for example. Wherever possible, I include the actual cost. Using this book, you can get exact prices for hotels and most activities, and you can get a good ballpark figure for meals and transportation; you can pinpoint these prices even more using the Internet. When you have an exact price, add 20 percent for taxes, tips, and price changes.

Use the spreadsheet's SUM function to add up the column of costs to come up with your total cost at the bottom. If you can afford that bottom line, go ahead and start booking. (You can use this same sheet as your itinerary by adding times, dates, and confirmation numbers in new columns and then printing it out.) If the bottom line is too large, start eliminating days or finding ways to cut costs on individual items.

Transportation

Airline competition makes getting from Seattle to Anchorage by far the cheapest way to travel to the main part of Alaska (even cheaper than driving). It's useless for me to predict what you'll pay because, in the age of high fuel prices, airfares change rapidly. Obtain current price listings by checking a travel Web site such as Travelocity (www.travelocity.com). Watching for sales can pay off. Summer sales sometimes hit in April. At press time, a round-trip ticket from Seattle purchased 14 days in advance was $600.

Flying within the state is substantially more expensive than flying into the state, because Alaska Airlines is the only jet carrier in these markets, and distances over the great expanse of the state are such that many routes are served only by jet. At times, flying from Anchorage to some Alaska Bush communities costs as much as flying from Anchorage to Europe. (An exception is the Anchorage–Fairbanks route, which is competitive and relatively cheap.)

Again, the Web is the best place to check for current prices; www.alaskaair.com is a good place to start. (For more information on getting to Alaska, see Chapter 6.)

The cheapest and most convenient way to travel within the part of the state that has roads is by rental car ($250–$300 per week in Anchorage). But in Southeast Alaska, where most towns aren't linked by highways, a car is usually just an inconvenience. In that part of the state, it makes more sense to rely on the Alaska Marine Highway System ferries (cheap travel at $45 for a nine-hour, 150-mile trip) or to fly short hops by jet or propeller aircraft (pricey, but more affordable than the high fares for longer hauls within the state). The Alaska Railroad runs from Seward, south of Anchorage, to Fairbanks. Trips along this line are beautiful and reminiscent of the golden days of rail, but they're priced as tours, not as transportation, and, as such, they cost far more than any other mode of travel. For many more details on getting around Alaska (including contact information), see Chapter 7.

Lodging

During the high season, lodging prices in Alaska's cities are comparable to high-price destinations such as New York City. A comfortable standard hotel room without luxuries goes for around $170 a night, while a room in a high-rise or resort runs over $250. In smaller towns, you can find more reasonable rates, but rarely is a decent room available in the high season for under $100. In the shoulder season, when most tourist attractions are still open but off the peak, rates drop by 25 percent or more. Off season, you'll often pay half the high-season rate, or even less. Some skiing and other winter destinations, however, have a winter peak when high prices return.

 You can reduce what you pay for lodging by staying in bed-and-breakfasts (B&Bs); most such accommodations have moved beyond the spare bedroom and now are like personal little inns. I prefer them anyway, because you meet real Alaskans. With a private bath, expect to pay $100 to $150 for a small room. The breakfast saves you time and money, too.

Dining

A couple can easily spend $120 for dinner in Alaska's best restaurants, and you should splurge at least once so that you can sample the great regional cuisine that's based on the state's wonderful seafood trade. Most of the time, however, it makes more sense to dine at midrange places where a main course costs under $20. Traveling that way, a couple can budget $20 for breakfast, $25 for lunch, and $55 for dinner, or an average of $100 per day.

Sightseeing and outdoor activities

Don't pinch your pennies when planning what to see and do in Alaska; otherwise, you may end up spending your time simply looking through museums or walking around towns. Although the towns are worth seeing, they don't contain the sights and experiences most visitors come to Alaska for — glaciers, mountains, whales, and more.

To estimate how much to budget for your Alaska adventures, here are some typical activities and prices (exact prices are in the destination chapters):

- ✔ **In-town attractions, such as museums and tours:** $10 to $40.

- ✔ **Boat tours:** $100 to $200.

- ✔ **A five-hour guided excursion by sea kayak or raft:** $90 to $180.

- ✔ **An extensive flightseeing tour:** $150 to $350; up to $450 by helicopter.

- ✔ **Wilderness lodges and multi-day all-inclusive outdoor adventures:** At least $125 per person per day (for a rough tent experience) and up to $500 per day (for the best). The typical outdoor adventure is $350 per day.

 The high cost of outdoor activities is one reason why Denali National Park is such a bargain; the bus ride there is one of the state's best wildlife safaris, for around $30 per person. For more on the park, see Chapter 19.

For more details on outdoor activities, see Chapter 9.

Shopping

Finally, a break after all those big numbers! You don't have to spend a penny shopping on your trip to Alaska. When you get home and you meet the expectant gaze of your family and friends, you can just tell them about all the money you saved by not buying gifts, and they'll, of course, be thrilled by your thriftiness.

If skipping the gift-buying part of the program won't work, here are some options:

- ✔ **T-shirt and gift shops:** They're everywhere, full of inexpensive tourist items from Taiwan and other foreign lands. You can find a plastic totem pole that may satisfy the less discriminating on your list, such as kids 5 and under, or a funny T-shirt, without spending much.

- ✔ **Shops that have real Alaskan gifts:** This is the next level of souvenir shopping. I mention these locations throughout the book. Expect to pay more for fabric, ceramic, or wooden crafts, but you can still find items for less than $75. Items that originate in Alaska cost more but mean more, too. A symbol of two bears that says made in alaska (www.madeinalaska.org) indicates that a state contractor has determined that the item was at least substantially made in Alaska.

Help Alaska Natives: Don't buy fakes

Much of the "Alaska Native art" sold in the shops that line tourist areas is, in fact, carved by low-wage workers in Asia and then deceptively labeled as having been made by indigenous people. Estimates vary regarding the amount of counterfeit Alaska Native art sold annually, but authorities have put it at close to $100 million. That's money taken from Alaska Bush villages, where jobs in the cash economy are virtually nonexistent and prices for essentials such as fuel and housing are astronomical. Buying fake Alaska Native art is cultural and financial theft from subsistence hunters and fishermen who can least afford it. Besides, who wants to go home with an Eskimo mask made in Bali?

Federal enforcement has proved ineffective and officials have instead turned to educating the consumer as the solution. Here's what you need to know to do your part:

✔ **Find out who made the piece.** Any reputable art dealer will provide you with a biography of the artist who created an expensive work. Ask specifically whether that artist actually carved the piece. Some Alaska Native artists have sold their names and designs to wholesalers who produce knockoffs. Even craftwork that is less expensive should have the name of the person who made it attached, and the shop owner should be able to tell you how he acquired the item.

✔ **Consider the cost.** Price is a key tip-off. An elaborate mask, if authentic, is more likely to cost $3,000 than $300.

✔ **Check the material.** Most soapstone carvings are not made in Alaska. Authentic materials include wood, ivory, bone, and animal furs and skin.

✔ **Look for the silver hand.** The **Alaska State Council on the Arts** (☎ **907-269-6610;** www.eed.state.ak.us/aksca) authenticates Native arts and crafts with a **silver-hand label,** which assures you that an item to which it is affixed was made by the hands of an Alaska Native with Alaskan materials. The program isn't universally used, however, so the absence of the label isn't necessarily proof of a fake. Other labels aren't worth much; an item can legitimately say alaska made even when only insignificant assembly work happened within the state.

✔ **Buy direct from the artist.** In Bush Alaska, and in some urban shops and craft fairs, you can buy authentic work direct from craftspeople. Buying in Native-owned co-ops also is safe.

✔ **Authentic Alaska Native arts and crafts shops:** If authenticity is what you seek, be ready to spend money. Small toys may be under $50, but authentic Native items such as handmade clothing, woven grass baskets, or jewelry usually sell for $150 to $500, and larger or more lasting pieces, such as masks or fine art, often are priced in the thousands of dollars. See the "Help Alaska Natives: Don't buy fakes" sidebar, for tips on identifying authentic crafts.

Nightlife

Nightlife in an Alaskan summer? Fly-casting for red salmon on the Russian River under the midnight sun! But that's certainly not *all* there is. In summer, many communities play host to tourist shows. Tickets are around $20; for dinner theater, $60. They're often fun but always corny, and I doubt you'll want to attend more than one. Otherwise, performing arts events, movies, and nightclubs cost about the same as they do in the Lower 48 or anywhere else.

Keeping an Eye on Hidden Expenses

 How is it that a final bill can be more than the sum of its parts? It may have something to do with the little surprises that creep up on you unawares. Add a contingency to your budget for the following extra costs:

- **Taxes:** Most towns in Alaska (Anchorage is a notable exception) have sales taxes, and all have bed taxes designed to soak the tourists; together, these taxes can add 10 percent or more to the cost of your room. Car-rental taxes and airport-concession fees can add up to 40 percent, so make sure you include them when you price your reservation.

- **Baggage fees:** Struggling airlines are imposing fees for everything they can think of, and the most costly of these are for checking bags. Alaska Airlines, the dominant carrier to and within Alaska, charges $20 for each of your first three bags, and $50 for each additional bag. Also, bags over 50 pounds or 62 inches (length plus height plus width) cost $50 to $75 more. These limits aren't generous, so plan what to pack well in advance to avoid getting dinged. If you plan on camping, you may find that renting sleeping bags and other equipment in Alaska is cheaper than bringing your own.

- **Tipping:** All the tipping rules with which you're familiar hold true in Alaska: 15 percent to 20 percent in restaurants, $1 per bag for bell service, and so on. When you get into the area of guides, fishing charters, tour boats, and wilderness lodges, tipping becomes a little trickier. As a general rule, tip guides and outfitters $10 to $20 per person per day. For outings of less than a day, adjust the tip accordingly; a $20 tip for a family of four on a half-day sea-kayaking outing is reasonable. At wilderness lodges, which normally have all-inclusive rates, adding the tip to your final payment when you leave often is best, because doing so allows the proprietor to distribute the gratuity to the staff instead of your trying to do it at each meal; a blanket tip of $15 per guest per day is acceptable. Tipping isn't necessary when you're on a big tour boat with dozens of other guests, unless you want to reward a particular crew member who helped you.

✔ **Taxis and transfers:** Alaskan towns, especially the larger ones, can be expensive to get around when you don't have your own car. Allow $10 to $20 per person for each of your airport transfers, unless you pick up a car at the airport or your lodging has a courtesy van. If you plan activities out of the center of town, check ahead of time how to get there to make sure that it isn't too expensive. (The listings in this book include descriptions of how to get to particular locations.)

Cutting Costs — But Not the Fun

 There are plenty of options for reducing the cost of your trip. Some are as easy as finding money and should be a regular habit wherever you travel; others require compromises that could mean you have to rethink what you want to get out of your trip. I list general suggestions here. The Bargain Alert icons scattered throughout this book mark other money-saving opportunities.

✔ **Travel at off-peak times.** Prices drop significantly during May and September, yet these months still offer plenty to do. (See Chapter 3 for a discussion of what you gain and give up by traveling during each of Alaska's seasons.)

✔ **Check out a package tour.** For many Alaska destinations, you can book airfare, hotel, ground transportation, and even some sightseeing just by making one call to a travel agent or packager, for a price much less than if you put the trip together yourself. (See the section on package tours in Chapter 6 for suggestions, specific companies to call, and the downside.)

✔ **Consider a cruise.** When you add it all up, cruising can be less expensive than independent travel in Alaska at the same comfort level, especially if you snag a last-minute bargain. Similarly, the all-inclusive price of a cruise protects against the budget creep that often sneaks up on you when you pay as you go. (See Chapter 8 for details on cruising.)

✔ **Avoid cruise-line activity charges.** Cruise lines usually add enormous hidden charges to shore activities they sell onboard. You can save 50 percent and get a better outing by booking shore activities directly using this book (while making sure to coordinate with your ship's schedule so you don't get left behind). Make arrangements before you leave home — doing so will probably be difficult when you're traveling.

✔ **Have some meals in your room.** Some hotel rooms are equipped with kitchenettes, giving you the comfortable and cheap option of eating in. Even when you get a room with just a fridge and a coffeemaker, you can save time and money on breakfast and snacks.

✔ **Always ask for discount rates.** Membership in AAA, frequent-flier programs, trade unions, AARP, or other groups may qualify you for savings on car rentals, plane tickets, hotel rooms, and even meals. Ask about everything — you may be pleasantly surprised.

✔ **Choose rooms large enough for your entire family.** A room with two double beds usually doesn't cost any more than one with a queen-size bed. And even if you pay 50 percent more for a bigger room or suite, it still saves you the difference of renting two rooms (and you have more control over your kids). Most hotels won't charge you the additional-person rate if the additional person is pint-size and related to you.

✔ **Try expensive restaurants at lunch instead of dinner.** Lunch tabs are usually a fraction of what dinner would cost at a top restaurant, and the menu often boasts many of the same specialties in smaller portions.

✔ **Know your telephone costs.** Hotels often charge unreasonable fees for using the phone, including fees for using the phone to make a call you charge to a card. Cellphone roaming and long-distance fees can add up quickly, too. If you have a nationwide roaming plan on your cellphone, and it includes Alaska, that will certainly be the cheapest way to go, but check before leaving home to make sure your phone will work and find out how much it will cost. The second-cheapest choice is to purchase a by-the-minute phone card at a grocery store after you get to Alaska.

✔ **Take the Alaska Marine Highway System.** The ferry system is a fun and inexpensive way to travel from town to town and see the scenery in coastal Alaska. (Chapter 7 includes more information about getting around Alaska by ferry.)

✔ **Go flightseeing on a commuter flight.** If you can't afford a spectacular mountain or glacier flight — and many travelers can't — consider planning a short leg of your trip on a scheduled flight on a small plane, and then let the pilot know you're hoping to see plenty of scenery.

✔ **Use pedal power.** In all but only a few Alaska towns, bicycles are a great form of transportation in the summer and are cheaper than renting a car or using taxis.

✔ **Buy a coupon book.** Although *The Great Alaskan TourSaver* (☎ **907-278-7600;** www.toursaver.com) costs $100, it's well worth the price when you plan to travel as a couple, especially in the Southcentral region. Among the more than 100 coupons, you'll find many two-for-one deals on some of the best activities and tours — valuable enough to pay for the book after only a couple uses.

Handling Your Money

Alaska is as modern as any place in the United States, so you don't have to worry about relying on the barter system. Instead, pack your plastic, and keep cash on hand for emergencies — or handle money whatever way you normally do. The only type of payment that won't be as available to you is your personal checkbook, although it, too, may come in handy for some big expenses, such as wilderness lodges or outfitters, some of which don't accept credit cards. (In those rare situations, you'll know in advance, because those businesses typically require cash deposits well before the trip.)

Using ATMs and carrying cash

The easiest and usually the best way to get cash away from home is from an ATM. ATMs are everywhere in Alaska, as elsewhere in the United States. In the Bush, you can find one somewhere in every town that has jet service at the airport. Be sure you know your personal identification number (PIN) and your daily withdrawal limit before you leave home.

The only national bank with branches all over Alaska is Wells Fargo. Key Bank also has branches, but not as many. If your own bank doesn't have branches in Alaska, you can call to find out whether it's affiliated with a bank that does business in the state. Doing so may save you a charge of $2 or more for using a nonaffiliated ATM. (On top of this, the bank from which you withdraw cash may charge its own fee.) You also can reduce your withdrawal fees by taking out plenty of cash every time you use the ATM, or by using your ATM card to buy something at the grocery store or drugstore and getting extra cash (with no extra fee).

Charging ahead with credit cards

Credit cards are a safe way to carry money. They also provide a convenient record of all your expenses, and they generally offer relatively good exchange rates. Many credit cards also give you some form of insurance against dishonest commercial behavior, and you can earn frequent-flier miles or get money back for every dollar you spend. As long as you don't get in over your head and run up a balance that you can't pay at the end of the month, using a credit card is free.

You also can withdraw cash advances from your credit cards at banks or ATMs, provided you know your PIN. If you've forgotten yours, or you didn't even know you had one, call the number on the back of your credit card and ask the bank to send it to you. Getting your PIN usually takes five to seven business days, though some banks will provide the number over the phone if you tell them your mother's maiden name or some other personal information.

Don't use a credit card to get cash from an ATM or from a bank teller except in emergencies. The special fees and interest rates for this service tend to be outrageous.

Virtually every Alaska business accepts a variety of credit cards, even small B&Bs, convenience stores, and guys selling tourist junk from card tables on the street. The only major exceptions are at the high end: Wilderness lodges may insist on being paid in advance by check when you reserve. Generally, you don't need cash except for taxis and incidentals too small to bother with a card.

Toting traveler's checks

With the near-universal acceptance of credit cards and wide availability of ATMs in Alaska, traveler's checks make little sense. They're inconvenient to use and not accepted by every merchant. And, although you'll avoid a fee for using an ATM belonging to a bank other than your own, you'll only save money by using traveler's checks if the checks are free and you don't want to use credit cards for some reason. If you want to use the checks anyway, you can get traveler's checks in a variety of denominations at almost any bank, where you'll pay a service charge.

If you choose to carry traveler's checks, be sure to keep a record of their serial numbers separate from your checks, in case they're lost or stolen. You'll get a refund faster if you know the numbers.

Dealing with a Lost or Stolen Wallet

Be sure to contact all your credit card companies the minute you discover that your wallet has been lost or stolen and file a report at the local police department. (Your credit card company or insurer may require a police-report number or record of the loss.) Card issuers have emergency toll-free numbers to call if your card is lost or stolen; they may be able to wire you a cash advance immediately or deliver an emergency credit card in a day or two. Visa's U.S. emergency numbers are ☎ 800-847-2911 and 410-581-9994. American Express cardholders and traveler's check holders should call ☎ 800-221-7282. MasterCard holders should call ☎ 800-307-7309 or 636-722-7111. For other credit cards, call the toll-free directory at ☎ 800-555-1212.

If you need emergency cash and have no ATM card or access to a bank, you can have money wired to you via **Western Union** (☎ **800-325-6000;** www.westernunion.com).

Identity theft and fraud are potential complications of losing your wallet, especially if you've lost your driver's license along with your cash and credit cards. Notify the major credit-reporting bureaus immediately; placing a fraud alert on your records may protect you against liability for criminal activity. The three major U.S. credit-reporting agencies are

Equifax (☎ **866-766-0008;** www.equifax.com), **Experian** (☎ **888-397-3742;** www.experian.com), and **TransUnion** (☎ **800-680-7289;** www.transunion.com).

Finally, if you've lost all forms of photo ID, call your airline and explain the situation. It may allow you to board the plane if you have a copy of your passport or birth certificate and a copy of the police report you've filed.

Chapter 6

Getting to Alaska

In This Chapter
- ▶ Flying to Alaska
- ▶ Going the long way: Alaska by land or by sea
- ▶ Booking a tour on your own or through a travel agent
- ▶ Getting the scoop on packages

*T*he moment I put down a credit card for a plane ticket is, to me, like the moment I leap off a diving board. That's when I realize I really am going. Getting to the edge of the board is hard, too, just like narrowing all your choices and taking the plunge on a trip. But delaying only means that you'll lose out on some of your best choices. When you buy the tickets, you nail down your dates. Then you can start filling in all the days in between and lining up all your other reservations.

I'm assuming you *will* buy a plane ticket (or passage on a cruise with a flight home). You can get to Alaska otherwise, but except for the ferry, they're not practical for a typical one- or two-week vacation. (For more information on cruising to Alaska, check out Chapter 8.) The real questions for you to examine, then, are how and from whom you should buy your plane ticket, and whether you want it as part of a package or escorted tour.

Flying to Alaska

Since the beginning of commercial aviation, Alaskans have used airplanes as a primary means of transportation. Flights to Alaska are frequent and sometimes cheap enough for Alaskans to take weekend trips outside the state. This is the easy part.

Finding out which airlines fly there

Anchorage is the main entry hub served by several major domestic carriers, and sometimes flights from Europe or Asia. You also can fly into Fairbanks or Southeast Alaska. Most passengers come into Anchorage through Seattle, but for a bit more, you can fly nonstop to Anchorage from various major U.S. cities. You have many more options in summer than in winter.

Alaska Airlines (☎ 800-252-7522; www.alaskaair.com) offers more flights than all other airlines combined, as many as 20 a day from Seattle in summer, as well as nonstop flights in summer from a scattering of cities across the country. Alaska Airlines is the only jet carrier with more than token coverage anywhere in Alaska other than Anchorage and has arrangements with commuter lines that fan out from its network to smaller communities.

The complete list of other carriers serving Anchorage has changed rapidly in recent years. Some airlines offer seasonal service, with different arrangements annually. Here are three that, in addition to Alaska Airlines, currently offer year-round service with more than one or two flights per day:

- ✔ **Continental Airlines** (☎ 800-523-3273; www.continental.com)
- ✔ **Delta Air Lines** (☎ 800-221-1212; www.delta.com)
- ✔ **US Airways** (☎ 800-428-4322; www.usairways.com)

You can fly by jet to Alaska cities other than Anchorage, but Alaska Airlines is the only carrier to most communities. It's a good airline, but the lack of competition and expensive operating conditions make for high prices. Fares from Seattle to Juneau are more than for the hour-longer run from Seattle to Anchorage. And getting almost anywhere else in Alaska by jet from Anchorage costs as much as or more than fares to Seattle. You'll have a difficult time saving on fares to smaller communities. The only ways to save are to buy your ticket well ahead of your trip, possibly catch a last-minute bargain on the Alaska Airlines Web site, or buy a package from Alaska Airlines Vacations (see "Choosing a Package Tour," later in this chapter).

Getting the best deal on your airfare

Competition among the major U.S. airlines is unlike that of any other industry. Every airline offers virtually the same product (basically, a coach seat is a coach seat is a . . .), yet prices can vary by hundreds of dollars.

With airfares, you pay for flexibility. If you buy a ticket at the last minute or choose to fly on premium days, such as Friday or Sunday, you often have to pay the premium rate, known as the *full fare*. If, however, you book your ticket far in advance, stay over Saturday night, or travel on a Tuesday, Wednesday, or Thursday, you can qualify for the least expensive price — usually a fraction of the full fare. Also, because Alaska is the end of the line for most flights, many planes leave from Anchorage very early in the morning. You save a lot by taking one of these red-eye flights that leave between midnight and 3 a.m.

The airlines serving Anchorage add to the unpredictability of pricing by engaging in fare wars. Alaskans fly so much that we talk about airfares the way New Yorkers talk about real estate, including bragging about outrageous bargains. Fares vary wildly, so watching for sales can pay off.

Changing planes in Seattle is almost always cheapest, due to the competition on the Seattle–Anchorage route. The competition also makes these fares more volatile than the stock market.

Summer sales sometimes hit in April (but some years, they never hit). To get a crazy fare, you have to book quickly and go along with sometimes weird restrictions about when you can fly and how long you have to stay. Wait for these fare wars and then act fast before the airlines change their prices (within a day or two for the best fares). If you can make a last-minute decision, look for Web specials on the Alaska Airlines Web site and other airline sites — often, there are bargains to be had that you can't get any other way.

Booking your flight online

Search the **Internet** for cheap fares. The most popular online travel agencies are **Expedia** (www.expedia.com), **Orbitz** (www.orbitz.com), and **Travelocity** (www.travelocity.com). In the United Kingdom, go to **Travelsupermarket** (☎ 0845-345-5708; www.travelsupermarket.com), a flight search engine that offers flight comparisons for the budget airlines whose seats often end up in bucket-shop sales. Other Web sites for booking airline tickets online include **Cheapflights** (www.cheapflights.com), **Opodo** (www.opodo.com), **Priceline** (www.priceline.com), and **Smarter Travel** (www.smartertravel.com).

Meta search sites (which find and then direct you to airline and hotel Web sites for booking) include **SideStep** (www.sidestep.com) and **Kayak** (www.kayak.com); the latter includes fares for budget carriers like JetBlue and Spirit Airlines, as well as the major airlines. In addition, most **airlines** offer online-only fares that even their phone agents know nothing about.

If you're really looking to save money, don't rely on a single Web site. For an Alaska trip, it's worthwhile to check a travel agency site, the site of the airline that shows as the lowest cost, and the **Alaska Airlines** site (www.alaskaair.com). Alaska's site is especially useful, because it shows the price of each leg of your flight separately.

Unless you really know what you're doing, don't use the Internet for a complicated itinerary or special circumstances. There are tricks to getting a good deal on multiple-layover or *open-jaw* itineraries (itineraries in which the departure city is different on the way out than on the return), and unless you know them, the Internet may not give you the cheapest fare. For example, a good travel agent may figure out how you can buy the tickets as pairs of round-trips and save money instead of putting all your stops on the same ticket. You can spend hours on the Internet figuring out something like that, but a good agent already knows. Likewise, if you're traveling with kids or using a combination of frequent-flier and paid-for tickets, you may miss companion fares or other savings that you don't know about. A skilled travel agent can beat the system in these circumstances in ways that just aren't obvious.

Getting to Alaska by Road, Water, or Rail

Cruise ships carry as many visitors to Alaska as any other means of transport. Choosing a cruise is a big decision that will affect your whole trip, so that option has its own chapter (see Chapter 8). You also can drive or take a ferry to Alaska. Look to these alternatives — cruise, ferry, or road — for the experience, not for savings. All of them take more time and cost more money than a competitive plane fare to Anchorage.

Driving to Alaska

Before you contemplate a drive to Alaska, you need to understand the distances involved. Driving from Seattle to Anchorage is 2,350 miles on two-lane highways. That's about the same as Seattle to Detroit. You'll put a lot of wear on your car and yourself, you'll spend a lot of money on gas and lodgings, and you'll burn a week of vacation time each way (more if you live in the eastern or southern states).

Crossing the U.S./Canadian border requires preparation even for U.S. citizens. U.S. citizens need **passports** to reenter the country over the road, and Canadians need passports but not visas. (Check `http://travel.state.gov` for the latest, because these requirements have changed frequently in the last few years.) If in doubt, call before you go, because the border is a long way from anywhere: **Canadian Customs** in Whitehorse (☎ 867-667-3943), or **U.S. Customs and Border Protection** on the highway (☎ 907-271-6855) or in Skagway (☎ 907-983-2325).

If you choose to drive to Alaska, get a mile-by-mile road guide called _The Milepost_ (www.milepost.com).

Taking the ferry to Alaska

If you plan to tour Southeast Alaska, take the **Alaska Marine Highway System ferry** (☎ 800-642-0066; www.ferryalaska.com) part of the way. From the south, embark at Bellingham, Washington, or Prince Rupert, British Columbia. Riding the ferry is fun, and you can stop over anywhere along the way without paying much extra for your tickets.

You're better off not bringing a car. The small towns of Southeast Alaska are easy to tour on foot or by bicycle; you can rent a car for a day when you want to go farther afield, which will likely cost less than the ferry passage for your own car. I include car-rental agency suggestions in the appropriate city chapters later in this book. If you do bring your car, you need to reserve your ferry space at least several months ahead.

If you're headed beyond Southeast Alaska, the best choice is to disembark the ferry at **Juneau** and fly onward to Anchorage or Fairbanks. If you're determined to make the trip without flying, get off the ferry in **Haines** or **Skagway**. From these cities, you'll need a car or RV to get to the rest of the state, and you'll have a lot of road ahead of you: Skagway to Anchorage is 832 miles. (Bus service from Skagway via Whitehorse is irregular and requires overnight changes — that option is so unattract-ive, I haven't included the details.) You can rent a car or RV and drive it one-way to Anchorage, but you'll have to pay a drop-off fee that will add hundreds of dollars to your rental cost. Car rentals in Skagway are avail-able from **Avis,** in the Westmark Hotel at 3rd and Spring streets (☎ **800-230-4898** or 907-983-2247; www.avis.com). **Alaska Motorhome Rentals** (☎ **800-323-5757;** www.bestofalaskatravel.com) rents RVs one-way to Anchorage with a drop-off fee of up to $995, plus the cost of the rental, mileage, and gas.

You also can take the ferry all the way across the Gulf of Alaska from Juneau to Whittier, less than a two-hour drive from Anchorage. This is a 40-hour voyage in open ocean, and the ferry only runs once or twice a month.

Riding the rails to Alaska — not!

You can't get to Alaska by train, but you can get close. From the West Coast of the U.S. you can take **Amtrak** (☎ **800-USA-RAIL [800-872-7245];** www.amtrak.com) to Bellingham, Washington; the dock for the Alaska ferry is quite close to the railroad station. From the eastern United States, using Canada's **Via Rail Canada** (☎ **888-VIA-RAIL [888-842-7245];** www.viarail.ca) makes more sense. The transcontinental route starts all the way back in Toronto; you change in Jasper to end up in Prince Rupert, British Columbia, where you can catch the Alaska ferry north.

Finding a Travel Agent

Finding a *good* travel agent can really be a feat. If you find one, tell every-one you know. They're as rare as trustworthy auto mechanics. The prob-lem is, the job is a very tough one, and the incentives — commissions on the trip's price — reward agents who make the trip cost *more,* not less. At the same time, agents working on commission are struggling as the airlines have eliminated the payments they used to receive. Add to these pressures the need to be universally knowledgeable about every place in the world that your client may want to go, and you have a virtually impossible job.

I've seen the results of some well-off travelers simply calling their local travel agent and asking for the perfect Alaska vacation. They end up flying back and forth across the state, going to expensive places in quick succession, with little consideration of their true interests. Even an agent who is scrupulously honest but knows little about Alaska will likely book visitors into only the best-advertised places. The defense against these pitfalls is knowledge: Go to the agent with a good idea of what *you* want to do (based on what you've discovered in reading this book), not asking for the agent to fill in a blank slate. A good agent can then take your preferences, shop for the best prices, and make your reservations, saving you a good deal of work and sometimes finding bargains you'd be hard-pressed to find on your own.

Some businesses in Alaska don't pay agents any commission, especially small operators such as bed-and-breakfasts and outdoors guides, while some big operations have cut agency commissions to the breaking point. So, expecting an agent — especially an Alaska expert — to work without charging you a fee is probably unreasonable these days. Some of the best Alaska experts — the ones you really can trust to plan your whole itinerary — charge clients $100 or more per person, on top of the commissions they receive from service providers. You get what you pay for, and if you're spending several thousand dollars on a trip, a couple hundred more to ensure the best trip is probably a good investment.

Here are some agencies that specialize in setting up Alaska trips:

- ✔ **Alaska Bound** (☎ 888-252-7527 or 231-439-3000; www.alaska bound.com) is the only one I know of in the Lower 48 that specializes in Alaska with a staff of former Alaskans. The company started as a cruise planner, working primarily with Holland America Line, but now plans many independent trips, too, charging fees based on the length of the trip ($100 per person would be typical).

- ✔ **Alaska.org** (☎ 888-252-7528) is a deep and well-built Web site that allows users to shop and customize package trips or design their own vacations in the Southcentral-to-Fairbanks region with as much or as little structure and guidance as they choose, and without a surcharge. When you've seen enough, call the toll-free number for questions and booking — or don't. Unique for this kind of site, you can use it just to get information and call the listed operators yourself.

- ✔ **Alaska Tour & Travel** (☎ 800-208-0200; www.alaskatravel. com) claims to be the largest custom vacation company in Alaska. The same folks operate the Park Connection shuttle between Denali and Kenai Fjords national parks, and that central part of the state is what they know best and cover deeply. The Web site is remarkable, including a search tool that brings up preset itineraries based on criteria you specify and a live availability-and-rate calendar for a range of Denali National Park hotels.

- ✔ **Sport Fishing Alaska** (☎ 888-552-8674; www.alaskatrip planners.com) is a good choice for a fishing vacation. The owner, former lodge owner Sheary Suiter, knows where the fish are from week to week. She'll also book the balance of your trip at fun and interesting places. Compensation begins with a $95 upfront fee, plus commission.

- ✔ **Viking Travel** (☎ 800-327-2571 or 907-772-3818; www.alaska ferry.com) plans trips around the whole state but specializes in Southeast Alaska trips, outdoor activities, and using the ferries of the Alaska Marine Highway System. It's a friendly small-town business with total knowledge of its own area.

Joining an Escorted Tour

Hundreds of thousands of visitors come to Alaska each year on escorted tours, leaving virtually all their travel arrangements in the hands of a single company that takes responsibility for ushering them through the state for a single, lump-sum fee. Most of these visitors arrive on a cruise ship and add a land-tour package with the same firm.

If you decide to go with an escorted tour, I strongly recommend purchasing travel insurance, especially if the tour operator asks you to pay upfront. But don't buy insurance from the tour operator! If the tour operator doesn't fulfill its obligation to provide you with the vacation you paid for, there's no reason to think that it'll fulfill its insurance obligations either. Get travel insurance through an independent agency. (I tell you more about the ins and outs of travel insurance in Chapter 12.)

Finding out the basics

If you can't relax and enjoy a trip knowing that unforeseen difficulties could happen, then take an escorted package tour. You know in advance how much everything costs, you don't have to worry about making hotel and ground-transportation reservations, you're guaranteed to see the highlights of each town you visit, and you always have a guide. Everything happens on schedule, and you rarely have to touch your baggage other than to unpack when it magically shows up in your room. Though you may sometimes feel like you're a member of a herd, you'll also meet new people — a big advantage if you're traveling on your own. Many passengers on these trips are retired, 65 or over.

Escorted packages have their disadvantages, too. They often travel at an exhausting pace. Passengers get up early and cover a lot of ground, with sights and activities scheduled solidly through the day. That may be good if you're short on time, but the stops last only long enough to get a taste of what the sight is about. You typically don't have time to dig in and learn about a place you're especially interested in.

Also, on an escorted trip, you meet few, if any, Alaska residents, because most tour companies hire college students from *Outside* (a term Alaskans use to refer to anyplace that's not in Alaska) to fill summer jobs. You stay in only the largest hotels and eat in the largest, tourist-oriented restaurants — no small, quaint places loaded with local character. Also, the big tour companies try to take visitors primarily to attractions they own, bypassing some terrific public attractions. For visiting the wilderness, such as Denali National Park, the quick and superficial approach can spoil the whole point of going to a destination that's about an experience, not just seeing a particular object or place.

Unfortunately, some people choose an escorted tour based on expectations that aren't valid. Studies by Alaska tourism experts have found that many visitors choose escorted packages to avoid risks that don't really exist. Alaska may still be untamed, but that doesn't mean it's a dangerous or uncomfortable place to travel. Visitors who sign up for a tour to avoid having to spend the night in an igloo or use an outhouse may wish they'd been a bit more adventurous when they arrive and find that Alaska has the same facilities found in any other state. Except for tiny Bush villages that you're unlikely to visit anyway, you'll come across the standard American hotel room almost anywhere you go.

Shopping for an escorted tour

When choosing an escorted tour, in addition to finding out whether you have to put down a deposit and when final payment is due, ask a few simple questions before you buy:

✓ **What is the cancellation policy?** Can the tour operator cancel the trip if it doesn't get enough people? How late can you cancel if you're unable to go? Do you get a refund if you cancel? Do you get a refund if the tour operator cancels?

✓ **How jam-packed is the schedule?** Does the tour schedule try to fit 25 hours into a 24-hour day, or does it give you ample time to relax or shop? I sometimes see visitors sleeping through spectacular scenery because they're exhausted from early departures and super-busy days.

✓ **How large is the group?** The smaller the group, the less time you spend waiting for people to get on and off the bus. Tour operators may be evasive about this, because they may not know the exact size of the group until everybody has made reservations, but they should be able to give you a rough estimate, and they certainly know the maximum they'll take. Likewise, if the tour has a minimum group size, the operator may cancel if it doesn't book enough people; ask how close the tour operator is to reaching any minimum.

✓ **What exactly is included?** Don't assume anything. You may have to pay to get yourself to and from the airport. A box lunch may be included in an excursion, but drinks may be extra. How much flexibility do you have? Are all your meals planned in advance? Can you choose your entree at dinner, or does everybody get the same chicken cutlet?

✓ **Can I go off on my own?** Can you ditch the group at times and do your own thing? Often, the answer is no, because a big group with a fast pace has to stick together. But you can look for a tour with more on-your-own time.

Selecting an escorted-tour company

Two major tour and cruise-ship companies, both owned by Carnival Cruise Lines, dominate the Alaska market with operations that allow them to take care of everything you do while in Alaska with tight quality control. Each also offers tours as short as a couple hours for independent travelers who want to combine their own exploring with a more structured experience. You can book all tours through any travel agent. *Note:* Outdoor-oriented escorted tours are covered in Chapter 9.

  ✔ **Holland America Line** (☎ 800-544-2206; www.graylineof alaska.com or www.hollandamerica.com), part of Holland America Line, is the giant of Alaska tourism. Thousands of visitors do business with no one else when they come. The Alaska/Yukon operation employs more than 2,100 workers operating 225 buses, 14 railcars, and two day boats. Most clients arrive in the state on one of the company's ships (see Chapter 8), but even within Alaska, chances are good that a tour you sign up for will put you on a Gray Line coach and exclusively in Westmark hotels, both owned by Holland America. Some of the Westmarks are among the best in town, including those in Juneau (called the Baranof) and Fairbanks, while others are unremarkable. But then, on a group tour, you don't spend much time in the room, because schedules generally are tightly planned and daily departures are early. The company's railcars on the Denali National Park run are like something from the Orient Express. Gray Line coaches are first-rate, too. And the company goes more places than any other, with a catalog that covers just about anything in the state that could possibly be done with a group. Some of the tour excursions — on the Yukon River between Dawson City and Eagle, for example — are entirely unique. Prices depend on a variety of factors, but a tour of a week is about $1,400 per person.

  ✔ **Princess Tours** (☎ 800-426-0550; www.princesslodges.com), now owned by Carnival, built its tour operation from the ground up, surpassing Holland America with the consistently outstanding quality of its smaller list of offerings. That advantage persists. Two hotels are near Denali National Park, and one each is in Fairbanks, Cooper Landing (on the Kenai Peninsula), and Copper Center, near Wrangell–St. Elias National Park. Princess operates its own coaches and has superb railcars on the Alaska Railroad route to Denali. Descriptions of each property can be found in the appropriate chapter. Most people on the tours come to Alaska on a cruise ship, but tours are for sale separately, too.

Choosing a Package Tour

Though most visitors choose to see Alaska by escorted tour, more and more people are cutting the apron strings and exploring Alaska on their own, either in whole or after a cruise, and in the process discovering a more relaxed, spontaneous experience.

The big reason to book a package tour is to save money. In many cases, a package tour that includes airfare, hotel, and transportation to and from the airport costs less than the hotel alone on a tour you book yourself. That's because packages are sold in bulk to tour operators, who resell them to the public. It's kind of like buying your vacation at a buy-in-bulk store — except the tour operator is the one who buys the 1,000-count box of garbage bags and resells them ten at a time at a cost that undercuts the local supermarket. Package tours can vary as much as those garbage bags, too. Some offer a better class of hotels than others; others provide the same hotels for lower prices. Some book flights on scheduled airlines; others sell charter flights. In some packages, your choice of accommodations and travel days may be limited.

Do some comparison-shopping before you commit to a package, however, because you may be able to undercut all package-tour prices using my money-saving tips about airfare (earlier in this chapter) and lodging (see Chapter 10). For more information on package tours and for tips on booking your trip, see www.frommers.com/planning.

Airlines often package their flights with accommodations. To find a bargain, you may need to be flexible. Prices vary significantly depending on the time you travel and the kinds of hotels you pick. Several big **online travel agencies** — Expedia, lastminute.com, Orbitz, and Travelocity — also highlight packages. If you're unsure about the pedigree of a smaller packager, check with the Better Business Bureau (BBB) in the city where the company is based, or go to www.bbb.org. If a packager won't tell you where it's based, don't fly with that packager. Several large-scale scams have ripped off visitors to Alaska, so caution is well advised.

Within Alaska, certain hotels and destinations that are priced reasonably as package tours cost much more if you book them separately. If you go to Barrow or Nome, the package-tour price offered by **Alaska Airlines Vacations** (☎ 800-468-2248; www.alaskaair.com/vacations) is sometimes less than the cost of the plane ticket by itself. (Compare current prices on the Web site.) This pricing doesn't make much sense, but you may as well take advantage of it. These packages are for day trips with a tour, or for the tour and an overnight stay. If you're not the escorted-tour type, you can still take advantage of the bargain, stick around for as much of the tour as you want, and then do your own thing, as long as you catch the return flight.

Traveling on the **Alaska Railroad** (☎ 800-544-0552 or 907-265-2494; www.alaskarailroad.com) is also cheaper as a package. The railroad sells a wide variety of its own packages, which it calls "Rail Tours," specializing in the area that the train reaches, from Anchorage to Fairbanks and Seward. Check out the choices on the Web site — you can choose from vacation packages, design your own, or buy the railroad's excellent day trips a la carte. Some selections are designed as continuations of cruises. Part of the appeal: This hybrid, independent/package approach is the chance to have a trip with plenty of guided activities but without having your hand held every minute. Prices are reasonable, too.

Alaska Highway Cruises (☎ 800-323-5757; www.bestofalaskatravel.com) offers the unique option of traveling one-way on a Holland America cruise ship, and then picking up an RV for a land tour. You can choose a package that ends up back in Seattle by road or by air. The tours follow set itineraries with reservations along the way — the service is designed for first-time Alaska travelers and RV drivers who don't want to worry about the details — so some spontaneity is sacrificed. You get the security and simplicity of a package without being marched around in a group or cooped up in hotels.

Several travel agencies offer packages that resemble preplanned custom tours, with details you can adjust but a basic plan with a standard total price. **Alaska Tour & Travel** and **Alaska.org** (both of which are listed in the "Finding a Travel Agent" section, earlier in this chapter) are two reputable firms using this model. The concept is to start with a template itinerary that covers what most people want to do, and then change it to fit your particular interests and needs. This approach makes sense, especially for visitors making their first trip to Alaska, because it prevents travelers from being overwhelmed with choices at the start of the process.

Chapter 7

Getting Around Alaska

In This Chapter

▶ Flying around Alaska
▶ Traveling by train, ferry, or bus
▶ Driving around Alaska

*A*s I may have mentioned elsewhere, Alaska is big — and it's rugged and sparsely developed. So, even in this modern age, some areas are accessible only by certain methods of transportation. Airplanes are the only means of transport that can take you everywhere (although, in some cases, flying makes no sense); you can get to the capital city of Juneau only by boat or air; and trains serve only a narrow region.

Almost every Alaska vacation combines at least two modes of transportation, with air and car or air and cruise ship being the most common. But in Southeast Alaska, you're likely to need three: air, boat, and car. Adding a little rail is a tasty seasoning to the mixture, because the Alaska Railroad is quite luxurious. And don't overlook the attractions of connecting to small towns by propeller-driven aircraft. Flying in one of these little planes is as Alaskan as dog-mushing and gives you a vivid, bird's-eye perspective of the countryside that you can't get any other way.

This chapter is irrelevant for travelers visiting Alaska by cruise only (with a flight at the beginning or end of the trip). Unless you'll add a land portion to your cruise vacation, you don't really need this information. (See Chapter 8 for cruise details.)

Table 7-1 lists the places I cover in this book and the ways to get there. I leave off choices that are possible but not advisable. The rest of this chapter provides you with the details of getting from here to there in Alaska.

Table 7-1	How to Get Around Alaska			
City	Air	Ferry	Rail	Road
Anchorage	Jet		X	X
Barrow	Jet			
Denali National Park	Prop		X	X
Girdwood			X	X
Homer	Prop	X		X
Juneau	Jet	X		
Katmai National Park	Prop			
Kenai	Prop			X
Kodiak Island	Jet	X		
Mat-Su				X
Nome	Jet			
Seward			X	X
Sitka	Jet	X		
Skagway	Prop	X		X
Whittier		X	X	X

Flying Around Alaska

Alaska has three levels of scheduled air service:

- ✔ **Alaska Airlines jets:** This airline (☎ 800-252-7522; www.alaska air.com) serves most communities of 1,000 residents or more that can't be reached by road. This includes most towns in Southeast Alaska and hubs around the Alaska Bush.

- ✔ **Commuter-class airlines:** Operating frequently scheduled service with larger propeller-driven planes to towns that may or may not have roads, these services fan out from Anchorage, Fairbanks, and Juneau to smaller communities.

- ✔ **Air services to the Bush:** With planes carrying as few as three passengers, these services fly from hubs to tiny communities, wilderness lodges, and fishing sites that can't be reached any other way. This mode of transportation serves more than 200 communities in Alaska.

Bush planes are scheduled, but operators don't always get hung up on strict definitions of time. I remember the surprise of some tourists who walked into a flight service for the 4 p.m. flight. A guy reading the newspaper behind the desk got up and said, "Okay, let's find a plane." He eventually found one and flew them where they were going.

I list the air services that go to each community in the appropriate chapters in this book, with sample airfares. Fares change frequently, so use these listings only as guidelines. Also, compare both the jet and the prop options, if both exist — either one may be cheaper. Taking a prop saves time on security. Sometimes, the larger commuter carriers have specials that you can find only on their Web sites, as does Alaska Airlines. These specials are usually last-minute deals, and they turn up less frequently in the high tourist season. Otherwise, you rarely can save much money over the regular, quoted fare when flying between Alaska communities.

Anyone who comes to Alaska should take at least one flight in a small plane. Only then can you see for yourself how little civilization exists in this vast place. Every part of the state has beautiful scenery, but the very best flights go around Denali National Park from Talkeetna or the park entrance, or fly over the glaciers and islands of Southeast Alaska from Skagway or Juneau. If a flightseeing outing doesn't fit into your budget, try to travel between two towns on a small plane.

Flying around Southeast Alaska

Ferries are the most relaxing way to enjoy Southeast Alaska, but if you don't have time for a boat ride, you can combine a ferry with air travel to make the most of your trip. For example, a ferry ride to Sitka from Juneau takes most of a day and the adult fare is around $45. For around $125, you can fly back in less than an hour and save a day that you would otherwise spend taking the same boat ride back.

Flying around Southcentral Alaska and the Interior

Driving usually makes the most sense for this highway-connected portion of the state, both because you save money and you get to see so much between towns. But for winter trips, or to save time, you can hop from town to town by plane and rent a car when you arrive. (I don't recommend long wintertime highway drives for folks not used to driving on ice; Alaska roads are icy all winter, help is often far away, and temperatures can be very cold.)

Flying from Anchorage to Fairbanks usually costs under $300 round-trip with advance purchase and is sometimes as low as $200. Flying saves a full day each way over driving or taking the train. (The lowest round-trip train fare is $420 in the high season.) You also can fly from Anchorage to towns such as Homer, Kenai, or Valdez, saving many hours of driving; using this strategy, you can make Anchorage a base for far-flung fishing or sightseeing day trips that would take two or three days by car.

Flying to the Bush

The only way to the great mass of Alaska is by air. **Alaska Airlines** flies jets to larger Bush hubs, such as Nome, Barrow, and Kodiak. Expect to pay $400 to $1,000 to Barrow or Nome with advance purchase and $400 or more to Kodiak. You usually can save by buying a package from Alaska Airlines Vacations (details are in the chapters on individual towns, later in this book). After you arrive in the Bush communities, small flight services carry passengers and cargo to the surrounding Alaska Native villages in prop-driven planes. Taking one of these planes, for a relatively inexpensive fare, gets you into very remote areas where you can see how Native people live — but don't go in bad weather.

Riding the Rails

Alaska has only one full-service rail line, running from Seward about 500 miles north, through Anchorage and Denali National Park and ending in Fairbanks. The **Alaska Railroad** (☎ 800-544-0552 or 907-265-2494; www.alaskarailroad.com) runs through unbelievably beautiful country. The trains are well appointed, recalling the golden days of rail, and you can ride in dome cars to soak in the views.

 The train is expensive and slow. For example, to get from Anchorage to Denali National Park takes 7½ hours each way and costs almost $300 round-trip in the high season. For the much more desirable Gold Star service, add another $160. (For around $250, you can rent a car for a week, and the drive is only 4½ hours.) And, after you arrive by train, you still need to find a way to get around. For these reasons, I advise most parties to drive; if you're traveling alone, or traveling as a couple and you don't like to drive, consider using the railroad. Also, check out the Alaska Railroad's money-saving packages on its Web site. (See Chapter 6 for information on package tours.)

The state's other railroad, the gold-rush-era **White Pass & Yukon Route,** is primarily an excursion train, as opposed to a people-moving service. It takes sightseeing runs from Skagway into the pass and back (see Chapter 21).

Sailing the Alaskan Coast

The state-run **Alaska Marine Highway System** (☎ 800-642-0066; www.ferryalaska.com) is a subsidized fleet of big, blue-hulled ferries the mission of which is to connect the roadless coastal towns of Alaska for roughly the same kind of cost you'd pay if the area had roads to drive on. The schedule is on the Web site.

 The system's strengths are its low cost, frequent summer sailings, inexpensive stopovers, exceptional safety, and the fact that kids love it. In the summer, U.S. Forest Service guides offer interpretive talks onboard.

The system's weaknesses are crowds during July peak season, occasional lengthy delays, and a shortage of cabins, which means that most people camp on deck or sleep in chairs during overnight passages.

You can ride the ferry to Alaska, starting off in Bellingham, Washington, or Prince Rupert, British Columbia, but you'll need to add a couple days to your itinerary. For most travelers, it makes more sense to fly to your starting point somewhere in the middle of Southeast Alaska. Flying saves time and reduces the chance of having to spend the night sleeping in a chair onboard. Long hauls on the ferry can be uncomfortable and don't save much money compared to flying, but the ferry is much less expensive and more appealing for connecting towns within the Southeast region.

Fly into Juneau or Sitka and plan a ferry trip from there, stopping at various places before returning to catch your plane home. The schedule has varied in recent years, but during the summer, you can count on the larger ships in the fleet stopping daily (although sometimes in the middle of the night) in Ketchikan, Wrangell, Petersburg, Juneau, Haines, and Skagway. Sitka currently receives daily service, but in the past, ships stopped there slightly less frequently. One high-speed catamaran, the *Fairweather,* saves about half the sailing time over the traditional vessels, but I can't predict which route it will be serving when you visit. The ferry *Kennicott* crosses the Gulf of Alaska once or twice a month in the summer, connecting Juneau to Whittier, near Anchorage, and points west. Other ferries link towns in Prince William Sound and between the Kenai Peninsula and Kodiak and even to the remote Aleutian Islands. Check out the map on the inside back cover of this book to find out where the Alaska ferries travel.

The ferry is quite economical. For example, the run from Juneau to Sitka takes nine hours on the regular ferry, five on the fast ferry, for a fare of $45, plus approximately $80 to bring your car along (though you have more flexibility and freedom if you don't — see the upcoming section, "Making your ferry ride more enjoyable"). Fares for kids 6 to 11 are half-price, and kids 5 and under ride free. A cabin with an outside window and private bath is only $58 on that route (although there are no cabins on the fast ferry).

Reserving ferry passage

The **Alaska Marine Highway System** (www.ferryalaska.com) has an online booking system that makes figuring out a trip far easier than using its inscrutable timetables. Just be sure to make vehicle and cabin reservations as early as possible. If you need to talk to a real person for advice or to change reservations, the system has a toll-free number (☎ **800-642-0066**). An alternative, without waiting on hold, is **Viking Travel,** in Petersburg (☎ **800-327-2571** or 907-772-3818; www.alaska ferry.com), which will accept your booking before the official reservation system opens, and then reserve it the first day the system becomes available. It can also take care of all your air and tour connections, lodgings, activities, and so on.

Making your ferry ride more enjoyable

You won't find anything difficult about riding the ferry — in fact, it's the most relaxing mode of transportation I know. But a few insider tips may make it even better:

- ✔ Buying ahead or booking round-trip tickets saves you nothing on the ferry, and stopovers of any length add little to the cost of your passage. Use the ferry system to explore the towns along the route, grabbing the next ferry through to continue your journey.

- ✔ If you travel without a vehicle, you generally don't need reservations (with the possible exceptions of the Bellingham sailings and passages across the Gulf of Alaska from Juneau to Whittier).

- ✔ Bring along a bike, or even a sea kayak, to have wonderful freedom in exploring Southeast Alaska. You can carry either quite cheaply.

- ✔ Don't count on *port calls* (the time your boat spends in port) to be long enough to see the towns. If the boat is running late, the staff may not let you off at all. Instead, get off and catch the next ferry through.

- ✔ In the summer, you need to make a reservation well in advance, often several months ahead, for any real chance of taking a vehicle on the ferry. It's expensive, too. Renting a car at your destination will probably save money and enhance your trip by allowing you more flexibility in your stopovers.

- ✔ Try to bring some of your own food on the ferry. Ferry food can get boring after several meals in a row, and during peak season, lines are sometimes unreasonably long. My family usually brings a cooler or picnic basket. Even if you're traveling light, you can pick up some bagels and deli sandwiches on a stopover or long port call.

- ✔ You can avoid some crowds on the boats by scheduling around them. Ferries are crowded northbound in June, southbound in August, and both ways in July. If you're planning to fly one way and take the ferry the other, go against the flow (southbound in June and northbound in Aug).

Covering Ground by Bus

If you don't want to rent a car, fly, or pay the outrageous fares on the Alaska Railroad, you can get around parts of Alaska by bus or van. When traveling alone, the bus can be a good way to meet other adventurous travelers. Most of the buses run only in the summer and mainly serve visitors. No single large bus company serves the entire state. Instead, mom-and-pop operations cover certain home routes. With some exceptions, the quality is below intercity coaches operated by the big bus lines. Here are some of the larger operations with the places they serve:

- ✔ **Alaska/Yukon Trails** (☎ 800-770-7275; www.alaskashuttle. com), a van and bus service, operates on the Parks Highway from Fairbanks to Anchorage and also serves the Alaska and Top of the World highways from Fairbanks to Dawson City. You can start or stop anywhere in between. The Anchorage to Denali fare is $75, a fraction of the train fare. The shuttle stops at hostels and is popular with backpackers.

- ✔ The **Park Connection** (☎ 800-208-0200 or 907-245-0200; www. alaskatravel.com/bus-lines) connects Seward with Anchorage and Denali National Park daily in the summer in each direction with big, comfortable coaches. Fares are competitive: $75 from Anchorage to Seward, $145 from Seward to Denali.

- ✔ **Stage Line** (☎ 907-868-3914) runs older-model vans from Homer to Anchorage and points in between. The fare is $78 one-way, $144 round-trip.

Driving Around Alaska

In the summer, driving is the most practical way to see the Interior and Southcentral Alaska. The road network is simple, with just a few two-lane highways connecting Anchorage, Fairbanks, and the towns in their orbits. Although few roads exist, you'll encounter little traffic on most of them (though around Anchorage, weekend drivers can clog the roads). The stunning, undeveloped scenery you'll pass through on your drive can be a highlight of your trip. Touring these highways with an RV is another classic way to see Alaska; I cover that in the following section. (Details on the best driving routes are in Chapter 18.)

Renting a car

Because I don't recommend driving to Alaska (unless you have lots of time on your hands), you should rent a car after you get here. You can find the major car-rental companies based at the Anchorage and Fairbanks airports, including **Alamo, Avis, Budget, Dollar, Hertz, National,** and **Payless** (national reservation numbers and Web addresses are listed in the Quick Concierge). I don't recommend renting a car in Southeast Alaska towns, except perhaps for a day to see the edges of town.

Checking road conditions

The **Alaska Department of Transportation** posts current information on driving conditions, accidents, and road closures around Alaska on its Web site, which you can search using detailed maps. You also can get much of this data over the phone through a hot line. In winter, checking highway conditions before heading out of town is an important safety measure. In summer, checking the road conditions helps you avoid drastic construction delays. Check out **511.Alaska.gov** (http://511.alaska.gov) or call ☎ **511**. For conditions on the Alaska Highway in Canada, check with the **Yukon Department of Highways** (☎ **867-456-7623** or 511 within the Yukon; www.511yukon.ca).

Some of Alaska's greatest drives are on gravel roads, but nearly every rental agency prohibits taking its cars off pavement, where broken windshields and flat tires are common. Driving a car on a gravel highway in violation of your rental contract exposes you to costs for damages that likely will not be covered by insurance. Some independent companies that permit their cars on the unpaved roads offer questionable older vehicles, but I've never received a complaint about the following outfits in Fairbanks and Anchorage, which cater to drivers who want to conquer the gravel rural roads. Note that you'll likely pay more for a vehicle you can drive on gravel, and you'll need insurance.

✔ In Fairbanks, **Arctic Outfitters** (☎ **907-474-3530;** www.arctic-outfitters.com) rents the Ford Escape. The vehicles are equipped with CB radios, maintenance kits, and two full-size spare tires. Drivers must be at least 30 years old.

✔ In both Anchorage and Fairbanks, **GoNorth** (☎ **866-236-7272** or 907-479-7272; www.gonorth-alaska.com) rents SUVs, trucks, and campers on four-wheel-drive pickups, as well as RVs for use on gravel highways.

✔ In Anchorage, **High Country Car & Truck Rental** (☎ **888-685-1155** or 907-562-8078; www.highcountryanchorage.com) rents vehicles for use on gravel highways (although not the Dalton Highway). It rents one-way to Seward and Whittier, too.

Finding the best deal

Car-rental rates vary widely and you can save a lot of money if you keep some of the following details in mind when you book:

✔ Weekend rates may be lower than weekday rates. Check if the rate is the same for pickup Friday morning as it is Thursday night. Also, weekly rates usually amount to the daily rate for five days, so it may not cost more to keep the car for a sixth or seventh day.

✔ In Alaska, you generally pay prohibitively high drop-off charges if you don't return the car to the rental location where you picked it up.

✔ Picking up your car is usually cheaper in town than at the airport, because airports charge concession fees, but the actual savings depends on the cost of getting to the car. In Anchorage, for example, the airport charges 11 percent plus a $6.50-per-day fee, which together could easily add $70 to a weekly rental (that's in addition to 18 percent in state and local taxes). If your hotel courtesy van takes you near a downtown rental site, you can save the airport fees; if you have to spend $40 on round-trip cab fare, it may not be worth it.

✔ A car-rental quote that doesn't include taxes and fees doesn't mean much. You pay the 10 percent state rental-car tax anywhere. But Anchorage and its airport add enough charges to bring the total add-ons to almost 40 percent in some cases. Depending on the length of the rental and the base cost, it may pay to rent in a lower-tax community, such as Kenai, Seward, or Fairbanks, flying or taking the train to the rental starting point (which also enhances your trip).

✔ Many car-rental companies add on a fee for drivers under 25; some don't rent to them at all.

✔ If you see an advertised price, ask for that specific rate. Don't forget to mention membership in AAA, AARP, and trade unions, which often entitle you to discounts ranging from 5 percent to 30 percent.

✔ Check your frequent-flier accounts. Not only are your most-used airlines likely to have sent you discount coupons, but most car rentals add at least 500 miles to your account.

✔ As with other aspects of planning your trip, using the Internet can make comparison-shopping for a car rental much easier. Major booking sites, such as **Expedia** (www.expedia.com), **Orbitz** (www.orbitz.com), and **Travelocity** (www.travelocity.com), have search engines that dig up discounted car-rental rates. After finding the companies with the best rates, go to their own sites and find out whether they have additional discounts or incentives available only to direct customers.

Knowing what to initial on the rental contract

In addition to the standard rental prices, taxes, and airport fees, optional charges apply to most car rentals. If you're not careful, you can lose all the savings you gained by shopping around if you impulsively initial the rental contract for one of these extras. Here are some key items:

✔ The car-rental contract generally makes you responsible for damage to the car and the company's associated costs in case of an accident, which may go well beyond the car's replacement cost. The car-rental companies let you out of that obligation, however, if you buy the **collision damage waiver** when you rent the car. The waiver is essentially insurance, but it's often unreasonably priced for as much as $20 a day. To get an idea how bad a deal that is, imagine paying $7,000 a year for collision insurance on your own car. Your own car insurance or your credit card probably covers you for most of this risk; check before you leave home.

✔ The car-rental companies also offer additional liability insurance (if you harm others in an accident), personal-accident insurance (if you harm yourself or your passengers), and personal-effects insurance (if someone steals your luggage from your car). Your insurance policy on your car at home probably covers most of these unlikely occurrences. However, if your own insurance doesn't cover you for rentals or if you don't have auto insurance, the rental company's liability coverage is a wise choice.

✔ How should you bet on the refueling gamble? Some companies try to sell you an initial full tank of gas with the agreement that you don't have to return it full. Then you spend the trip trying to run the car on empty to avoid giving gas back to the rental company, for which you get no credit. The better option is to buy the gas yourself and fill up the car before you return it, so you pay for only the gas you use. But if you're running late and don't fill up, the rental company zings you with astronomical refueling charges. If you often run late and a refueling stop may make you miss your plane, go ahead and buy the agency's gas; otherwise, buy your own. Check out the location of a gas station when you leave the airport at the start of your trip so you can refuel quickly before you drop off your car.

Renting an RV

An RV has obvious advantages in Alaska: It's warmer and more predictable than tent camping, yet more spontaneous and outdoorsy than staying in hotels. There are negatives, too: The vehicles are difficult to drive, you'll have to deal with the sewage, and it's not cheap (expect to pay at least $1,500 a week with limited mileage, plus high fuel costs, campground fees, food, and so on). When I tried this mode of travel, I didn't anticipate how the size of the vehicle would tie us down — after we parked, we didn't want to move. Rent the smallest vehicle you can fit into.

Many RV parks are not very attractive: They look like parking lots. You can use more-rustic public campgrounds, and then go to a commercial RV park every third day to wash up and drain your tanks. A map that lists all the public campgrounds is available from the Alaska Public Lands Information Centers (see the Quick Concierge) for a nominal cost. Or get *Traveler's Guide to Alaskan Camping,* by Mike and Terri Church (Rolling Homes Press), which contains detailed reviews of virtually every public and commercial campground in the state.

Several RV-rental agencies operate in Alaska. One reputable company that offers many one-way choices (with significant drop-off fees) is **Alaska Motorhome Rentals** (☎ 800-323-5757; www.bestofalaska travel.com). It also has packages, under the name Alaska Highway Cruises (see Chapter 6). You can find a company offering RVs that you can drive on Alaska's unpaved rural highways in the "Renting a car" section, earlier in this chapter.

Driving safely in Alaska

Driving in Alaska is definitely different from driving in other states. You don't have to worry about carjacking or purse snatching, but you do need to be prepared for immense distances between services and even, in winter, survival in extreme conditions.

Here are a few tips for **summer driving on *paved highways:***

✔ Keep your headlights on all the time for safety on these two-lane highways.

✔ The law requires that you pull over at the next pullout whenever five or more cars are trailing you on a two-lane highway, regardless of how fast you're going. You'll usually find these roadside parking areas, most of which are simply widened road shoulders, spaced every few miles. Pulling over saves the lives of people who otherwise will try to pass.

✔ Driving fast on an empty highway is tempting, but remember that these roads sometimes have violent dips and humps called *frost heaves.* Hitting a frost heave at high speed isn't fun and can be dangerous. Plus, wildlife, such as moose, caribou, or bears, sometimes wanders onto the road.

✔ Bring along sweaters and jackets, a picnic or some snacks, water or other beverages, CDs and tapes for the stereo, and mosquito repellent.

✔ Check your jack and spare tire before you leave.

✔ Bring a cellphone if you have one; you'll find coverage available in most of the state's populated regions.

✔ You usually can use a credit card wherever you go, but bring along at least $100 in cash just in case.

✔ Don't let your gas tank get low, because it may be a couple hours between gas stations — even on paved highways. Likewise, take advantage of your opportunities to use a toilet.

Not all Alaska roads are paved. Here are few tips for **summer driving on gravel highways:**

- ✔ If the vehicle is rented, verify you can drive it off pavement without violating the rental contract. A couple companies that do allow this are mentioned in the "Renting a car" section, earlier in this chapter.

- ✔ When passing a vehicle going the other way, slow down and pull as far as possible to the side of the road to avoid losing your windshield to a flying rock. Always think about the path of rocks that you're kicking up toward other vehicles.

- ✔ Make sure that you have a good, full-size spare tire and jack.

- ✔ Bring along a first-aid kit, emergency food, a towrope, and jumper cables, and keep your gas tank full. On some rural roads, it's a tank of gas between gas stations.

In **winter,** Alaska's roads are dark most of the time and always icy. Moose stand on or run into the road in the dark, causing potentially fatal accidents for the people in the car as well as the moose. Long periods can pass between each car, long enough for frostbite in extreme cold if you have a breakdown and don't plan ahead. For many people, flying makes more sense than driving for long trips, but if you choose to drive rural Alaska highways in winter, take precautions:

- ✔ Be prepared for cold-weather emergencies far from help. Take all the items previously listed for summer driving on gravel roads, plus a flashlight, matches and materials to light a fire, chains, a shovel, and an ice scraper. A camp stove to make hot beverages is also a good idea.

- ✔ If you're driving a remote highway (such as the Alaska Highway) between December and March, take along gear adequate to keep you safe from the cold in case you have to wait overnight with a dead car at –40°F (–40°C). (See the list of heavy winter gear in Chapter 12, and add warm sleeping bags.)

- ✔ Never drive a road marked closed or unmaintained in winter.

- ✔ Studded tires are a necessity; non-studded snow tires or so-called "all-weather" tires aren't adequate.

- ✔ Never leave your car's engine stopped for more than four hours in temperatures of –10°F (–23°C) or colder. Alaskans generally have electrical head-bolt heaters installed to keep the engine warm overnight. You can find electrical outlets everywhere you may park in cold, Interior Alaska areas.

Chapter 8

Cruising Alaska's Coast

by Fran Wenograd Golden and Gene Sloan

- -

In This Chapter

▶ Sorting out when and where to cruise in Alaska

▶ Choosing a big or small ship

▶ Finding the best cruise bargains

▶ Profiling Alaska's best cruise lines

- -

As you may expect from a state that offers a number of varied options for getting into and out of its communities, cruising in Alaska is big business. This chapter offers the details you need to help you decide whether cruising is the option for you to take to arrive in Alaska. You'll also find information to help you choose which type of cruise is best for you and to let you know what you can expect to pay for traveling to Alaska via cruise ship.

Waterway transportation is so critical to Alaskans that the state has its own ferry system, the Alaska Marine Highway System, which you can use to travel to and around Alaska. However, to make this option work, you must be willing to invest a considerable amount of time — for actual travel and for planning — and be willing to give up the comforts and diversions that a cruise ship offers. The Alaska Marine Highway System is covered in more detail in Chapter 7. This chapter is devoted to the cruise ship, focusing primarily on those cruise options that give a real in-depth experience. (If you want more information about cruising in Alaska, pick up a copy of *Frommer's Alaska Cruises & Ports of Call,* by Fran Wenograd Golden and Gene Sloan [Wiley Publishing].)

Weighing Your Cruise Options

Your three main questions in choosing a cruise in Alaska are "When should I go?," "Where do I want to go?," and "How big a ship?"

Cruise ships in Alaska: Angel or devil?

The 49th state is one of the top cruise destinations in the world, with about 750,000 people cruising there annually. That may not sound like much in the abstract — after all, Alaska's a huge state, right? — but two facts make it actually a pretty big figure:

✔ Even though Alaska has more coastline than the rest of the United States combined, cruise ships sail in only about 20 percent of that area (and really concentrate on about half that).

✔ The cruise season is incredibly short, lasting only from late May to mid-September.

This leads to crowding in the biggest ports of call, and also to some backlash, with local critics decrying excessive pedestrian traffic on their city streets, heavy bus traffic on outlying roads, and environmental damage to the air and seas.

Some towns, particularly Juneau, Ketchikan, and Skagway, really can get overwhelmed by cruise passengers at the height of high season, with a potential for more than 6,000 people floating in daily. The delicate balancing act between the resulting congestion and the plain fact that tourism provides the state's second-largest pool of jobs has led to debate in recent years over imposing head taxes on cruise passengers, with the proceeds going to infrastructure support, conservation efforts, and other initiatives. The latest effort, which would have slapped a $46 tax on every passenger sailing state waters, was defeated in the Alaska legislature in May 2005, but don't expect debate to end.

On the environmental front, several well-publicized cases of illegal dumping over the past decade have led the cruise industry to institute in-house and industry-wide compliance and monitoring — after all, they can't sell cruises to pristine Alaska if they're perceived as making it less pristine. State and local governments also have a hand in minimizing cruise ships' impact in some of Alaska's most famous wild places. Glacier Bay, for example, has a strict permit system that allows in only two large cruise ships and several smaller vessels on any given day.

Deciding when to go

Alaska is very much a seasonal, as opposed to a year-round, cruise destination, generally open to cruising from May through September (although some smaller ships start up in late Apr). May and September are considered the shoulder season, and lower brochure rates are offered during these months (and more aggressive discounts as well; watch your local newspaper and check the Internet).

Cruising in May is extremely pleasant; crowds have yet to arrive, and locals are friendlier than they are later in the season. May also is one of the driest months in the season. Late September, on the other hand, offers the advantage of fewer fellow cruise passengers clogging the ports.

The warmest months are June, July, and August, with temperatures generally around 50°F to 80°F (10°C–27°C) during the day and cooler at night. In the past couple years, the temperature has soared even higher. You may not need a parka, but you'll need to bring along some outerwear and rain gear. June 21 is the longest day of the year, with the sky lit almost all night. June tends to be drier than July and August. April and May are drier than September, although in early April you may encounter freezing rain and other vestiges of winter.

If you're considering traveling in a shoulder month, keep in mind that some shops don't open until Memorial Day, and the visitor season is generally considered over on Labor Day (although cruise lines operate well into Sept).

Knowing where to go

Many Alaskan cruises, particularly of the small-ship variety, combine transportation with activities after you arrive. Here's the lowdown on your primary options:

- **Inside Passage cruises:** One of two basic weeklong itineraries offered by the major cruise lines, Inside Passage cruises generally sail round-trip from Vancouver, British Columbia, visiting three or four port towns (typically Juneau, Skagway, Ketchikan, and either Sitka, Haines, or Victoria, British Columbia) along the Inside Passage, spending a day in Glacier Bay or one of the other glacier areas, and spending two days at sea (meaning they just cruise along, enabling you to relax and enjoy the scenery).

- **Gulf of Alaska cruises:** The second-most-popular cruise choice is a Gulf of Alaska cruise, which generally sails northbound and southbound between Vancouver and Seward (the port for Anchorage) in alternating weeks. These cruises visit many of the same towns and attractions that the Inside Passage cruises hit, but because they don't have to turn around and sail back to Vancouver, they tack on visits to Hubbard Glacier, College Fjord, or other gulf towns and natural attractions.

- **Small-ship cruises:** Although most of the major cruise operators stick pretty closely to these two basic routes, the small-ship cruise lines tend to offer more **small-port and wilderness-oriented itineraries,** some sailing round-trip between Juneau and Ketchikan, and one even sailing between Juneau and Glacier Bay. Although many of these ships visit major ports of call, they also may include visits to small ports that aren't accessible to the bigger ships — towns such as Petersberg, Wrangell, Gustavus, Elfin Cove, and possibly the Native village of Metlakatla. Some ships offer itineraries that enable passengers to explore waterways by kayak or hike inland trails.

✔ **Cruise tours:** Combining a cruise with a land tour, either before or after the cruise, typical cruise-tour packages link a cruise with a three- to five-day Anchorage-to-Denali-to-Fairbanks tour, a seven-day Yukon tour (which visits Anchorage, Denali, and Fairbanks on the way), or a five- to seven-day tour of the Canadian Rockies. Holland America and Princess are the two leaders in the cruise-tour market (Cruise West has folded). Even when you book with another cruise line, chances are, your land tour will be through one of these operators.

Choosing between a big ship and a small ship

Imagine an elephant. Now imagine your pet beagle, Sparky. That's the kind of size difference you can expect between your options in the Alaska cruise market: behemoth modern ships and small, more exploratory coastal vessels.

But your choice is more than just deciding between a bunch of or a little extra room for stowing your bags (although, truth be told, cabin size is pretty minimal in most cases, even on the largest ships). Your interest in the variety of activities and amenities also needs to play a role in your choice of which cruise ship to sail.

Cruising on bigger ships

The **big ships** in the Alaska market generally fall into two categories: midsize ships and megaships.

Carrying as many as 2,670 passengers, the **megaships** look and feel like floating resorts. Big on glitz, they offer loads of activities, attract many families and (especially in Alaska) seniors, offer many public rooms (including fancy casinos and fully equipped gyms), and provide a wide variety of meal and entertainment options. And although they may feature one or two formal nights per trip, the ambience is generally casual. The Alaska vessels of the Carnival, Celebrity, Princess, and Royal Caribbean fleets all fit in this category, as do Norwegian Cruise Line's *Star* and *Pearl,* Holland America's *Zuiderdam* and *Westerdam,* and the *Disney Wonder.*

Midsize ships in Alaska fall into two segments: the ultraluxurious, such as Regent Seven Seas' *Seven Seas Navigator,* Silversea's *Silver Shadow,* and Crystal's *Crystal Symphony,* and the modern midsize, such as Holland America's *Veendam, Amsterdam, Volendam, Zaandam,* and *Statendam,* and Oceania's *Regatta.*

In general, the sizes of these bigger ships are less significant than the general onboard atmosphere created by the companies that run them; therein lay the **advantages** of big-ship cruising:

✔ You have lots of opportunities to meet and greet (and meet and greet). With the many and varied meal and entertainment options, combined with the diversity of activities, you're bound to meet a passenger or ten who share your interests.

✔ The cruise ship is your oyster. Midsize ships and megaships offer a great range of facilities for passengers. You won't lack things to do and places to go on these ships.

✔ Big ships have room for every need, with or without a view. Cabins on these ships range from cubbyholes to large suites, depending on the ship and the type of cabin you book.

✔ You *will* eat well. Big dining rooms and a tremendous variety of cuisines will be the norm.

The sizes of these big ships also come with **four major drawbacks** for passengers:

✔ You have lots of opportunities to meet and greet (and meet and greet). These bigger ships carry many people and, as such, can at times feel crowded.

✔ Size limits access. The big ships just can't sail into narrow passages or shallow-water ports, limiting your in-port and sailing options.

✔ Size limits opportunity. The size and inflexible schedules of bigger ships limit their ability to stop or even slow down when wildlife is spotted.

✔ Alaska becomes lost in the crowd. When passengers on a big ship disembark in a town, they tend to overwhelm that town, thus limiting your ability to see the real Alaska. (For more info on the relationship between Alaska and the cruise industry, see the "Where there are ships, there are crowds" sidebar.)

Cruising on smaller ships

In the same way that big cruise ships are mostly for people who want every resort amenity, **small** or **alternative ships** are best suited for people who prefer a casual, crowd-free cruise experience that offers passengers a chance to get up close and personal with Alaska's natural surroundings and wildlife.

Smaller ships have a number of advantages:

✔ The sea becomes larger. Small ships can sail almost anywhere (including far into Misty Fjords, an area that no large ship can penetrate).

✔ You can take more time to smell the roses — or whatever may be swimming your way. Small ships tend to have more flexibility in their schedules than the large ships, and they usually take time to linger whenever whales or other wildlife are sighted nearby.

✔ Everything looks bigger. Smaller watercraft don't scare off wildlife as easily as the big ships, and the fact that you're at or near the waterline (as opposed to ten stories up on the large ships) means you get a more close-up view.

✔ **Land-based activities truly are land-based.** Many smaller cruise companies compensate for a lack of onboard activities by offering more active off-ship opportunities, such as hiking or kayaking.

✔ **You can discover Alaska's depth.** The alternative ships are also more likely to feature expert lectures on Alaska-specific topics, such as marine biology, history, and Native culture.

But, as with everything in life, small ships also have their drawbacks:

✔ **Small ships are, well, small.** Small ships usually have small cabins, only one lounge/bar and dining room, and no exercise facilities. They just don't have room for all the amenities.

✔ **Don't expect a smooth ride.** Most of these smaller ships have no stabilizers, so the ride can be bumpy in open water — which isn't much of a problem on Inside Passage itineraries, because most of the areas in which small ships cruise are protected from sea waves.

✔ **Accessibility is not always a given.** Smaller ships are difficult for travelers with disabilities — none of the ships in the market have elevators.

✔ **Face it — you'll pay more.** Despite all the disadvantages — at least from an amenity and activity standpoint — smaller ships are universally more expensive than their bigger counterparts, and the small-ship cruise lines offer fewer discounts.

Visitors aboard large ships may physically be in Alaska, but unless they're reminded of it, they may never know it — such is the disjunction between the glitzy modern ships and the real world outside. The experiences of visitors aboard small ships, however, are many times more intimate, which enables them to get in touch with the places they've come to see. For these reasons, our advice to anyone who wants to experience Alaska (rather than receive just a postcard impression of it) is to spend the extra money for a small-ship cruise. As is true of any product, you get what you pay for, and by paying extra in the short term for a more intimate cruise, you're almost always guaranteed to have an Alaskan experience that you can recall fondly for the rest of your life.

Finding the best cruise-ship experience for you

Cruise lines are in the business of providing a good time for their guests, so they all have something going for them. This section provides a brief rundown of some of Alaska's best cruise ships, in a few different categories (with more details near the end of this chapter under the individual cruise listings).

Where there are ships, there are crowds

Now for the bad news: All those cruise ships aren't necessarily good for Alaska and its residents. Alaskans, who are known for their hospitality, all have their limits. Imagine living in a coastal settlement and having the equivalent of an entire town full of new people arriving all at once — doubling the population, and then some. These one-day visitors crowd your streets and hiking trails, and their ships spew pollution into the air and water. Imagine this deluge happening every day, all summer. Suppose also that tacky souvenir stands and seasonal gift shops have driven out the old community businesses on the waterfront.

For years, the cruise-ship industry exploited the hospitality of Southeast Alaska as if it were an inexhaustible resource. Local residents took a stand, however, when two lines, Royal Caribbean and Holland America, were convicted of felonies for dumping pollution such as dry-cleaning fluid, photo chemicals, and used oil in the pristine waters of the Inside Passage, and then lying about it. A series of environmental scandals followed, leading to new state laws and a commitment by the cruise industry to clean up its act. Alaska now has the toughest cruise-ship legislation of any state.

Protecting the environment is easier, however, than restoring the experience of living in or visiting a small town. The presence of too many cruise-ship passengers has spoiled some of these quaint places. Once-charming streets are transformed into carnival midways jammed wall-to-wall with people from ships landing simultaneously. Some communities think the income generated by these "floating cities" isn't worth what they must sacrifice in their quality of life and, thus, they place limits on the number of ships that can dock or they levy new taxes based on the number of people each ship carries.

After years of fast growth, the industry also began talking of a *carrying capacity* (that is, determining just how much tourism is too much). And yet still more ships come, bringing ever more visitors. The terrorist attacks of September 11, 2001, aggravated the situation further, because cruise lines withdrew ships from certain foreign routes and brought them to Alaska. Although the increase in capacity produced some extraordinary bargains for cruise passengers, whether that will continues is anyone's guess.

Defining luxury

So, you think any type of cruise ship offers a certain measure of luxury? Well, although you're probably correct, these lines really know how to serve up the extravagance:

✔ Big-ship luxury in Alaska is defined in 2011 by **Regent Seven Seas, Silversea, and Crystal.** If you want a more casual kind of luxury (a really nice ship with a no-tie-required policy), the *Seven Seas Navigator* offers just that on an all-suite vessel (most cabins have private balconies) with excellent cuisine. **Silversea,** on the other hand, represents a slick, Italian-influenced, slightly more formal luxury experience with all the perks — big suite cabins and excellent food, linens, service, and companions. **Crystal** offers the glitz and glamour of a luxury experience on a bigger ship, complete with show productions and lively casino. Both Regent and Silversea include fine wine and booze in their cruise fares.

✔ For the ultimate Alaska experience in a small-ship setting, check out the yachts of **American Safari Cruises,** where soft adventure comes with luxury accouterments.

Being pampered in style

The following ships offer the crème de la crème of indulgences:

✔ Celebrity's *Infinity* and *Millennium* offer wonderful AquaSpas complete with thalassotherapy pools and a wealth of soothing and beautifying treatments.

✔ The solariums on Royal Caribbean's *Rhapsody of the Seas* and *Radiance of the Seas* offer relaxing indoor-pool retreats.

✔ **Regent Seven Seas** pampers you all-around.

✔ We're also fans of the thermal suite (complete with hydrotherapy pool) in the Greenhouse Spas on **Holland America's** *Zuiderdam* and *Westerdam.*

Finding the best meal

Regent Seven Seas and Oceania's Regatta, with culinary inspiration from celebrity chef Jacques Pepin, are tops in this category. And the expertly prepared and presented cuisine on **Silversea's** *Silver Shadow* must also come in for some props. Although this may surprise you, of the mainstream lines, we like the buffet and dining room offerings of **Carnival** — flavorful food, well prepared. The *Carnival Spirit* in Alaska also boasts the Nouveau Supper Club ($30 service charge per person), where you can enjoy just about as fine a meal as you're likely to find anywhere. The *Crystal Symphony* has a restaurant operated by top sushi chef Nobu (at no extra charge). And **Norwegian Cruise Line's** teppanyaki restaurant ($25 per person charge) is also an experience not to be missed — yummy food and a show by knife-wielding chefs.

Bringing along the family

All the major lines have well-established kids' programs, with **Carnival, Royal Caribbean,** and **Norwegian Cruise Line** leading the pack in terms of facilities and activities. **Princess** gets a nod for its National Park Service Junior Ranger program to teach kids about glaciers and Alaska wildlife (they can even earn a Junior Ranger badge); it recently increased shore excursions geared for families. But no one can beat **Disney** in 2011, with the *Disney Wonder* making its debut in the Alaska market.

Weighing the dining options on various cruises

Smaller ships usually serve dinner at a certain time, with open seating, allowing you to sit at any table you want. **Large ships** may offer only two fairly rigid set-seating times, especially for dinner. This means that your table will be pre-assigned and remain the same for the duration of the cruise. However, increasingly, there are some exceptions to the rule in the large-ship category. The ships of Norwegian Cruise Line and Regent Seven Seas now serve all meals with open seating — dine when you want and sit with whomever you want (within the restaurants' open hours). Princess has its own innovative version of this system, allowing guests to choose between traditional early or late seating, or open restaurant-style seating, before the cruise. Most large ships today also offer multiple **alternative-dining options,** featuring casual buffets and specialty restaurants, some with an additional charge (as a gratuity) of up to $30.

Participating in the best onboard activities

The ships operated by **Carnival** and **Royal Caribbean** offer a very full roster of onboard activities that range from the sublime (lectures) to the ridiculous (contests designed to get passengers to do or say outrageous things). **Princess**'s ScholarShip@Sea program is a real winner, with excitingly packaged classes in such diverse subjects as photography, personal computers, cooking, and even pottery. Crystal leads the luxury lines with such enrichment offerings as Berlitz language classes and Yamaha music lessons.

Cruising in style

Every line's most recent ships are beautiful, but **Celebrity's** *Infinity* is a true stunner, as is its sister ship, *Millennium.* These modern vessels, with their extensive art collections, cushy public rooms, and expanded spa areas, give Celebrity a formidable presence in Alaska. And the late-model *Sapphire Princess* and *Diamond Princess* have raised the art of building big ships to new heights.

Experiencing whale-watching at its best

If the whales come close enough, you can see them from all the ships in Alaska — Fran spotted a couple of orcas from her cabin balcony on a recent Holland America cruise, for instance. Smaller ships, though — such as those operated by **American Safari, InnerSea Discoveries,** and **Lindblad** — actually may change course to follow a whale. Get your cameras and binoculars ready!

Booking the best cruise tours

Princess, Holland America, and the twin-brand Royal Caribbean Cruises (which owns **Royal Caribbean International** and **Celebrity**) are the market leaders in getting you into the Interior of Alaska either before or after your cruise. They own their own deluxe motor coaches and rail-cars. Princess and Holland America also own lodges and hotels.

The strength of Holland America's cruise tour is its three- and four-night cruises combined with an Alaska/Yukon land package. Princess arguably is stronger in seven-day Gulf of Alaska cruises in conjunction with Denali/ Fairbanks or Kenai Peninsula land arrangements. Royal Caribbean is a comparative latecomer, but its land company, Royal Celebrity Tours, with some of the finest rolling stock (rail and road) around, has made huge strides.

Stopping at the best ports

Juneau, Sitka, and Skagway are our favorites, but Haines also is a winner:

✔ **Juneau** is one of the most visually pleasing small cities anywhere and certainly the prettiest capital city in the United States.

✔ **Sitka**'s Russian architecture, historic totem-pole park, and Raptor Rehabilitation Center earn it the nod here, not to mention the fact we've had very pleasant conversations with Sitka locals about topics ranging from the fishing season to local politics — when the first non-locally-owned T-shirt shop was railroaded in a few years ago, the whole town was abuzz.

✔ No town in Alaska is more historically significant than **Skagway.** The old buildings are so perfect, you may think you stepped into a Disney version of what a gold-rush town should look like.

✔ For a more low-key Alaska experience, take the ferry from Skagway to **Haines,** which reminds us of the folksy, frontier Alaska depicted on the TV show *Northern Exposure.* It's also a great place to spot eagles and other wildlife.

Discovering the best shore excursions

Most cruise lines offer some great shore-excursion options to include with your trip. Here are a few of the most recommended activities to ask about when booking your cruise:

✔ Flightseeing and helicopter trips in Alaska are unforgettable ways to check out the scenery if you can afford them. (They're pretty pricey.) A helicopter trip to a dog-sled camp at the top of a glacier (usually the priciest of the offerings) affords both incredibly pretty views and a chance to try your hand at the truly Alaskan sport of dog-sledding (earning you bragging rights with the folks back home).

Shore excursions:
The what, when, and why

Shore excursions offered by the cruise lines provide a chance for you to get off the ship and explore the sights close up, taking in the history, nature, and culture of the region — from exploring gold-rush-era streets to experiencing Native Alaskan traditions such as totem carving.

Some excursions are of the walking-tour or bus-tour variety, but many others are activity oriented: Cruise passengers have the opportunity to go sea-kayaking, mountain-biking, horseback-riding, salmon-fishing, and even rock-climbing or zip-lining through the treetops, and to see the sights by seaplane or helicopter — and maybe even to land on a glacier and go for a walk. Occasionally, with some of the smaller cruise lines, you'll find quirky excursions, such as a visit with local artists in their studios. Some lines even offer scuba diving and snorkeling. The cruise lines vet the operators, so you do get assurance that you're dealing with pros.

With some lines, select shore excursions are included in your cruise fare, but with most lines they're an added (though very worthwhile) expense.

> ✔ For a less extravagant excursion, nothing beats a ride (on a clear day) on the White Pass & Yukon Route railway out of Skagway to the Canadian border at Fraser — the route followed by the gold stampeders of '98.

> ✔ Active excursions, such as kayaking and mountain-biking, afford not only an opportunity to work off those shipboard calories, but also optimum opportunities for spotting eagles, bears, seals, and other wildlife.

Booking Your Cruise

 Almost every cruise line publishes brochure prices that are the travel equivalent of a new car's sticker price: wildly inflated, hoping that someone, somewhere, may take them at face value. In reality, you may be able to get the cruise for 40 percent or 50 percent off at the last minute. But here's the problem with waiting: Alaska right now is hot, hot, hot. Sure, you may be able to save by taking your chances, but if you don't reserve space early, you may be left out in the cold. (Cold in Alaska, get it?)

So how do you book your cruise? Traditionally (meaning over the past 30 years or so), people have booked their cruises through **travel agents.** But you may be wondering, hasn't the traditional travel agent gone the way of typewriters and eight-track tapes and been replaced by the Internet? Not exactly. Travel agents are alive and kicking, though the Internet has, indeed, staked its claim alongside them and knocked some of them out of business. In an effort to keep pace, most traditional travel agencies have created their own Web sites.

So, which is the better way to book a cruise these days? Good question. The answer can be both. If you're computer savvy, have a good handle on all the elements that go into a cruise, and have narrowed down the choices to a few cruise lines that appeal to you, Web sites are a great way to trawl the seas at your own pace and check out last-minute deals, which can be dramatic. On the other hand, you'll barely get a stitch of personalized service searching for and booking a cruise online. If you need help getting a refund or arranging special meals or other matters, or deciding which cabin to choose, you're on your own.

In this section, you find details for booking cruises on large and small ships. So, regardless of whether you're a veteran cruiser or a first-timer, the details and money-saving tips here can help you book an enjoyable and affordable cruise.

Booking a small-ship cruise

The small-ship companies in Alaska — **American Safari**, **Lindblad Expeditions**, and **InnerSea Discoveries** — all offer real niche-oriented cruise experiences, attracting passengers who have a very good idea of the kind of experience they want (usually educational and/or adventurous, and always casual and small scale). In many cases, a large percentage of passengers on any given cruise will have sailed with the line before. Because of all this, and because the passenger capacity of these small ships is so low, in general you're not going to find the kind of deep discounts you do with the large ships. Still, for the most part, these lines rely on agents to handle their bookings, taking very few reservations directly. All the lines have lists of agents with whom they do considerable business, and they can hook you up with an agent if you call or e-mail and ask for an agent near you.

Finding an agent who specializes in mainstream cruises

If you don't know a good travel agent already, try to find one through your friends, preferably those who have cruised before. For the most personal service, look for an agent in your area, and for the most knowledgeable service, look for an agent who has cruising experience. It's perfectly okay to ask an agent questions about his personal knowledge of the product, such as whether he has ever cruised in Alaska or with one of the lines you're considering. The easiest way to be sure the agent is experienced in booking cruises is to work with a **cruise-only agency** (meaning that the whole agency specializes in cruises), or to find somebody in a more conventional agency who is a **cruise specialist** (meaning he handles that agency's cruise business). If you're calling a full-service travel agency, ask for the **cruise desk**, which is where you'll find these specialists. If the agency doesn't have a cruise desk per se, it may be wise to check elsewhere.

A good and easy rule of thumb to maximize your chances of finding an agent who has cruise experience and who won't rip you off is to book with agencies that are members of the **Cruise Lines International Association** (CLIA; ☎ 754-224-2200; www.cruising.org), the main industry association. Membership in the **American Society of Travel Agents** (ASTA; ☎ 800-275-2782; www.asta.org) ensures that the agency is monitored for ethical practices, although it does not designate whether the agency has cruise experience.

You can visit the Web sites of these organizations for easy access to agents in your area.

Figuring out what's included in the cost

No matter how you arrange to buy your cruise vacation, what you basically have in hand at the end is a contract for transportation, lodging, dining, entertainment, housekeeping, and assorted other miscellaneous services that are provided for you during the course of your vacation. Remembering what extras are *not* included in your cruise fare, however, is just as important.

Aside from **airfare,** which usually isn't included in your cruise fare (see "Booking air travel through the cruise line," later in this chapter), the most pricey additions to your cruise fare are likely to be **shore excursions.** Ranging from about $30 for a bus tour to $299 and up for a helicopter or seaplane flightseeing excursion, these sightseeing tours are designed to help you make the most of your time at the ports that the ship visits, but they do add a hefty sum to your vacation costs.

Another item you'll want to add to your calculations is the amount of **tips you need to add for the ship's crew.** One exception in Alaska recently is Regent Seven Seas, the only line in the market to include tips in the cruise fare. Tips are given at the end of the cruise. Count on tipping at least $10 per passenger in your party, per day. That figure takes care of the room steward, waiter, and busboy. (In practice, most people tend to give a little more.) Additional tips to other personnel, such as the headwaiter or maitre d', are at your discretion. On the small ships, all tips often go into one pot, which the crew divides up after the cruise.

All but a few ships charge extra for **alcoholic beverages** (including wine at dinner) and for soda. Prices are comparable to what you'd pay at a bar or restaurant ashore. Non-bubbly soft drinks, such as lemonade and iced tea, are included in your cruise fare.

Port charges, taxes, and other fees are usually included in your cruise fare but not always, and these charges can add as much as $250 per person onto the price of a seven-day Alaska cruise. Make sure you know whether these fees are included in the cruise fare when you're comparing rates. Read the fine print!

Of course, the same as at a hotel, you also pay extra for such items as ship-to-shore phone calls or faxes, e-mails, spa treatments, and so on.

New cruisers

There is a saying in the industry that nobody should cruise just once. On any voyage, a ship could encounter bad weather. On any given day at sea, the only seat left in the show lounge may be behind an unforgiving pillar. Or a technical problem may affect the enjoyment of the onboard experience. Jerry vividly remembers one occasion on which the air-conditioning on his ship — which shall remain nameless — went out for half a day. It was an uncomfortable time and could have turned a neophyte off cruising forever. That would've been a mistake.

In travel, there is liable to be an occasional snafu. Your hotel room is not available, even though you have a valid confirmation number. Your flight is canceled. The luxury car you thought you rented is not on the lot, and all that's available is a mini-subcompact. But you don't stop flying, you don't refuse to stay in a hotel ever again, and you don't stop renting cars. Nor should one unforeseen problem on a cruise ship cause you to swear off cruising forever. Give it another go — on a different cruise line, if you prefer. If you still haven't had the enjoyable experience that millions of others have discovered, then, and only then, maybe it's time to abandon hope of becoming a cruise aficionado.

Booking early

The best way to save on an Alaska cruise is to **book in advance.** In a typical year, cruise lines offer early-bird rates, usually 25 percent or more off the brochure rate, to those who book their Alaska cruise by mid-February of the year of the cruise. If the cabins don't fill up by the cutoff date, the early-bird rate may be extended, but it may be lowered slightly — say, a 15 percent or 20 percent savings.

In the past couple of years, the cruise lines have been getting even more aggressive with early-booking discounts, hoping to encourage passengers to make their Alaska cruise plans months in advance. (Cruise-line executives like their ships filled up as early as possible.) If the cabins still aren't full as the cruise season begins, cruise lines typically start marketing special deals, usually through their top-producing travel agents. These last-minute discounts can run as high as 50 percent. And keep in mind that last-minute deals are usually for a very limited selection of cabins. Planning your Alaska cruise vacation well in advance and taking advantage of early-booking discounts is still the best way to go.

Traveling the shoulder season

Think of the Alaska cruise season as three distinct periods: **peak season** (late June, July, and early to mid-Aug), **value/standard season** (early June and late Aug), and **budget or economy Season** (May and Sept). You can save by booking a cruise during this last period, during the shoulder months of May and September. That's when cruise pricing is lower. Although the weather may be a little chillier — and September is known for rain — fewer people visit during these months, thus enabling your experience of Alaska to be a bit more pristine, especially when you're sailing on a small ship. A friend who recently took an early-May sail reported that he felt like he had the state all to himself.

Sharing a cabin or booking as a group

Most ships offer highly discounted rates for third and fourth passengers sharing a cabin with two "full-fare" passengers (even if those two have booked at a discounted rate). Although doing so may mean a tight squeeze, it nevertheless saves you a bundle. Some lines also offer **special rates for kids,** usually on a seasonal or select-sailing basis, that may include free or discounted airfare. Kids 1 and under generally cruise free.

One of the best ways to get a cruise deal is booking as a **group** of at least 16 people in at least eight cabins. The savings include a discounted rate, and at least the cruise portion of the 16th ticket will be free. A "group" in this case can be a real group of friends, relatives, and so on, or simply a block of passengers booked by a travel agency on the same cruise. You don't even have to pretend to know the other people — the savings are the same. Ask about any group deals your travel agent may offer.

Using age to your advantage

Seniors may be able to get extra savings on their cruise. Some lines take 5 percent off the top for those 55 and over, and the senior rate applies even if the second person in the cabin is younger. Membership in groups such as AARP is not required, but such membership may bring additional savings.

Booking air travel through the cruise line

Except during special promotions, airfare to the port of embarkation rarely is included in cruise rates, so you have to purchase airfare on your own or buy it as a package with your cruise through your travel agent or online cruise site. You usually can find information about these *air-sea programs* in the back of cruise-line brochures, along with prices.

The benefits of booking through the cruise line are that round-trip **transfers** are included, and the cruise line knows your airline schedule, so that in the event of delayed flights and other unavoidable snafus, it can do more to make sure that you and other people on your flight board the ship. When you book your air transportation separately, you're on your own.

On the downside, air add-ons may not be the best deals and booking your own airfare may be cheaper. Furthermore, you probably won't be able to use any frequent-flier miles that you've accumulated.

Choosing your cabin

Cruise-ship cabins range in size from tiny boxes with accordion doors and bunk beds to palatial multi-room suites with hot tubs on the balcony. Cabins are either **inside** (without a window or porthole) or **outside** (which do have a view), the latter being more expensive. On big ships, the more deluxe outside cabins also may come with private **verandas.** Cabins usually are described by price (highest to lowest), category (suite, deluxe, superior, standard, economy, and other types), and furniture configuration ("sitting area with two lower beds," for example). Which is right for you?

Price will likely be a big factor here, but so should the vacation style you prefer. If, for instance, you plan to spend a lot of quiet time in your cabin, you should probably consider booking the biggest room you can afford. If, conversely, you plan to be out on deck all the time checking out the glaciers and wildlife, you may be just as happy with a smaller (and cheaper) cabin to crash in at the end of the day.

Speaking up about special health and dietary concerns

The cruise line should be informed at the time you make your reservations about any special dietary requirements you have. Some lines offer kosher menus, and all will have vegetarian, low-fat, low-salt, and sugar-free options available.

The Small-Ship Cruise Lines

Small ships enable you to see Alaska from sea level, without the kind of distractions that you encounter aboard the big ships — no glitzy interiors, no big shows or loud music, no casinos, no spas, and no crowds, because the largest of these ships carries only 382 passengers. You're immersed in the 49th state from the minute you wake up to the minute you fall asleep, and for the most part, you're left alone to form your own opinions. These types of cruises usually cost more, but by far, they provide the better cruise experience for anyone who really wants to get the feel of Alaska.

Small-ship itineraries can be placed into one of the following categories:

- ✔ **Port-to-port:** These itineraries mimic larger ships simply by sailing between port towns.

- ✔ **Soft-adventure:** These itineraries provide some outdoor experiences such as hiking and kayaking, but they don't require participants to be trained athletes.

- ✔ **Active-adventure:** For the true adventurer, hiking and kayaking are the focus of the trip, and the experience may be strenuous.

On each of these types of cruises, the small-ship experience tends toward the educational rather than the glitzy. You'll likely listen to **informal and informative lectures** and sometimes watch video presentations about Alaska wildlife, history, and Native culture. Meals are served in open seatings, so you can sit where and with whom you like, and time spent huddled on the outside decks scanning for whales fosters great camaraderie among passengers.

 Cabins on these ships don't generally offer TVs or phones and tend to be small and sometimes spartan (see the individual reviews for exceptions).

American Safari Cruises

American Safari Cruises promises an intimate, all-inclusive yacht cruise to some of the more out-of-the-way stretches of the Inside Passage — and it succeeds admirably. The price is considerable — but so is the pampering. The company's three small vessels carry between 12 and 36 guests, guaranteeing unparalleled flexibility, intimacy, and privacy. When passenger interests become apparent, the expedition leader shapes the cruise around them. Black-bear aficionados can chug off in a Zodiac boat for a better look, active adventurers can explore the shoreline in one of the yacht's kayaks, and slacker travelers can relax aboard ship. A crew-to-passenger ratio of about one to two ensures that a cold drink, a good meal, or a sharp eagle-spotting eye is always nearby on the line's comfortable 120-ft. ships. In 2011, the yachts offer 7-night Discoverers' Glacier Bay itineraries and season-beginning and season-ending 14-night Inside Passage cruises as well. The core seven-night itinerary includes an unusual two full days in Glacier Bay National Park, in which passengers can hike on glaciers or in the rain forest with a park ranger, as well as stops in more off-the-beaten-path Alaskan areas such as Frederick Sound and Dawes Glacier.

Passengers, almost always couples, tend to be more than comfortably wealthy and range from 45 to 65 years of age. Most hope to get close to nature without sacrificing luxury. Dress is always casual, with comfort being the primary goal. Note that age requirements stipulate that "passengers under the age of 21 years must stay in the same stateroom and be accompanied by a parent, relative, or guardian 25 years or older."

More private yachts than cruise ships, the 22-passenger *Safari Quest,* the 12-passenger *Safari Spirit,* and the company's newest, the 36-passenger *Safari Explorer,* look like Ferraris — all sleek, contoured lines and dark glass. Cabins are comfortable, and sitting rooms are intimate and luxurious, almost as if they had been transported whole from a spacious suburban home. A big-screen TV in the main lounge forms a natural center for impromptu lectures during the day and movie-watching at night. A shipboard chef assails guests with multiple-course meals and clever snacks, barters with nearby fishing boats for the catch of the day, and raids local markets for the freshest fruits and vegetables — say, strawberries the size of a cub's paw and potent strains of basil and cilantro.

☎ **800-426-7702** *or 206-441-8687. Fax: 206-441-4757.* www.cruisewest.com. *Sample nightly rates per person: Lowest-price outside cabin from $699 for seven-night cruise on Safari Explorer. No inside cabins or suites.*

InnerSea Discoveries

Looking for an off-the-beaten-path adventure in Alaska? That's what it's all about at InnerSea Discoveries, a new line for 2011. As this book went to press, the two-ship operator had yet to sail its first cruise (scheduled for May 2011). But the company comes with a strong pedigree, and its focus — getting adventure-minded vacationers into the most beautiful and wildlife-filled corners of Southeast Alaska's Inside Passage — has many Alaska tourism watchers excited. InnerSea Discoveries is the brainchild of Dan Blanchard and Tim Jacox, who revolutionized luxury cruising in Alaska in 1997 with the launch of American Safari Cruises. This time around, the duo aims to offer a more affordable way for adventurers to explore the region. Operating as a sister brand to American Safari, InnerSea Discoveries will cost less than half as much as its sibling, with pricing starting around $300 per person per day (American Safari trips often start at $850 per person per day or more). The ships are a bit bigger than at American Safari, with room for 49 passengers; not everything is included in the price; and the crew-to-passenger ratio of about one to three is not quite as impressive. But, in many ways, the concept is similar. By foregoing calls in Southeast Alaskan towns such as Skagway and Haines, InnerSea's ships will have more time to explore the many remote (and little visited) bays, fjords, and glaciers of the region. The company says the voyages should appeal to adventurers who thrive on new experiences and want to push themselves physically, mentally and emotionally.

The company is anticipating a relatively young, outdoorsy type of customer — the kind of people who shop at outdoor store REI, says one manager. Most passengers will be in their mid-30s to mid-60s in age, with a smattering younger and older; multigenerational families are expected to be a solid market, because the line won't have the age restrictions imposed at sister American Safari Cruises.

Although the line is new, its two ships aren't. In fact, the ships will be quite familiar to some experienced Alaska cruisers. InnerSea Discoveries is launching with the 49-passenger **Wilderness Discoverer** and the 49-passenger **Wilderness Adventurer.** Parent company American Safari purchased the vessels in 2009 from a bank that had held them since the bankruptcy of Glacier Bay Cruise Lines in 2006. The two ships, originally built for 80 and 66 passengers, respectively, have gone through a top-to-bottom overhaul over the past year.

☎ **877-901-1009.** *Fax: 206-283-9322. www.innerseadiscoveries.com. Sample nightly rates per person: Lowest-price outside cabin from $300 for seven-night Inside Passage cruise on either ship.*

Lindblad Expeditions

Lindblad Expeditions specializes in environmentally sensitive, soft-adventure vacations that are explorative and informal in nature, what the company calls "respectful tourism." Its programs — operated since 2004 in partnership with the National Geographic Society — are designed to appeal to the intellectually curious traveler seeking a cruise that's ecologically friendly and educational as well as being relaxing. Days aboard are spent learning about life above and below the sea (from National Geographic experts and high-caliber expedition leaders trained in botany, anthropology, biology, and geology) and observing the world either from the ship or during shore excursions, which are included in the cruise package. Educational films and slide presentations aboard ship precede nature hikes and quick jaunts aboard Zodiac boats. Flexibility and spontaneity are keys to the experience, because the route may be altered at any time to follow a pod of whales or school of dolphins.

The Alaska program of its two ships, the nearly identical 62-passenger *Sea Lion* and *Sea Bird,* includes 7-night cruises between Juneau and Sitka from May through August, and an 11-night cruise between Seattle and Juneau (including the San Juan Islands and British Columbia) in April and September.

Lindblad Expeditions tends to attract well-traveled and well-educated, professional, 55-and-older couples who have "been there, done that" and are looking for something completely different in a cruise experience — and who share a belief in the need to preserve the environment.

The 62-passenger *National Geographic* Sea Lion and *National Geographic* Sea Bird (built in 1981 and 1982, respectively) are nearly identical. Both are well-appointed vessels built to get you to beautiful spots and feature a minimum of public rooms and conveniences: one dining room, one bar/lounge, and lots of deck space for wildlife and glacier viewing. They have the added advantage of being accompanied throughout by historians, anthropologists, scientists, and other such specialist lecturers chosen by the National Geographic Society. Cabins are small and functional, but not inexpensive.

☎ **800-397-3348** *or 212-765-7740. Fax: 212-265-3770.* www.expeditions.com. *Sample nightly rates per person: Lowest-price outside cabin $770 for seven-night cruise. No inside cabins or suites.*

The Big-Ship Cruise Lines

The ships featured in this section vary in size, age, and offerings but share the common thread of having more activities and entertainment options than any one person can possibly take in during the course of a cruise. You'll find swimming pools, health clubs, spas, nightclubs, movie theaters, shops, casinos, multiple restaurants, bars, and special kids' playrooms, and in some cases sports decks, virtual golf, computer rooms, martini bars, cigar clubs, and even quiet spaces where you can get away from it all. In most cases, you'll find an abundance of onboard activities, including games, contests, classes, and lectures, plus a variety of entertainment options and show productions, some very sophisticated.

Carnival Cruise Lines

Carnival is the ultimate fun-in-the-sun warm-weather line, and even in Alaska the Caribbean-focused operator retains its "Fun Ship" philosophy.

Sure, you'll be cruising past glaciers and on the lookout for whales, but you'll be doing it with people who like to take in the natural wonders with a multicolored party drink in hand. Drinking and R-rated comedians are part of the scene, as are "hairy-chest contests" and the like.

Entertainment is among the industry's best, with each ship boasting a dozen dancers, a ten-piece orchestra, comedians, jugglers, and numerous live bands, as well as a big casino. Activity is nonstop. Cocktails begin to flow before lunch, and through the course of the day you can learn to country-line-dance or ballroom-dance; take cooking lessons; learn to play bridge; watch first-run movies; practice your golf swing by smashing balls into a net; or just eat, drink, shop, and then eat again. Alaska-specific naturalist lectures are delivered daily. In port, Carnival offers more than **120 shore excursions,** divided into categories of easy, moderate, and adventure. For kids, the line offers Camp Carnival, an expertly run children's program with activities that include Native arts-and-crafts sessions, lectures conducted by wildlife experts, and special shore excursions for teens.

Carnival's ship in Alaska cruises the Inside Passage route with round-trip departures out of Seattle.

Overall, Carnival has some of the youngest demographics in the industry. But it's far more than age that defines the line's customers. Carnival executives are fond of using the word *spirited* to describe the typical Carnival passenger, and, indeed, the descriptor is right on target. The line's many fans increasingly come from a wide range of not just ages but occupations, backgrounds, and income levels, but what they share is an unpretentious, fun-loving, and outgoing demeanor. On Carnival, you'll find couples, a few singles, and a good share of families, but the bottom line is, this is not your average sedentary, bird-watching crowd. Passengers want to see whales and icebergs, but they also want to dance the Macarena.

The 2,124-passenger megaship *Carnival Spirit* returns to Alaska in 2011. It offers plenty of activities, great pool and hot-tub spaces (some covered for use in chillier weather), a big ocean-view gym and spa, and more dining options than your doctor would say are advisable.

☎ **800-227-6482.** *Fax: 305-471-4740. www.carnival.com. Sample nightly rates per person: Lowest-price inside cabin $125, lowest-price outside cabin $161, lowest-price suite $261 for seven-night Inside Passage cruise.*

Celebrity Cruises

Celebrity Cruises offers a great combination: a classy, tasteful, and luxurious cruise experience at a moderate price — it's definitely the best in the midrange category. The line's ships are real works of art; the cuisine is above the norm; the service is first-class, friendly, and unobtrusive; and the spa facilities are among the best in the business.

A typical day may offer bridge, darts, a culinary-art demonstration, a trap-shooting competition, a fitness-fashion show, an art auction, a volleyball tournament, and a not-too-shabby stage show. Resident experts give lectures on the various ports of call, the Alaskan environment, glaciers, and

Alaskan culture. For children, Celebrity ships employ a group of counselors who direct and supervise a camp-style children's program. Activities are geared toward different age groups. There's an impressive kids' play area and a lounge area for teens.

Celebrity, like sister company Royal Caribbean, visits the tiny port of Icy Strait Point between Juneau and Glacier Bay; the port offers a prime vantage point for whale- and wildlife-watching and easier access to the Alaskan wilderness. The company offers seven-night Inside Passage and seven-night Gulf of Alaska itineraries.

The typical Celebrity guest is one who prefers to pursue his R&R at a relatively relaxed pace, with a minimum of aggressively promoted group activities. The overall impression leans more toward sophistication and less toward the kind of orgiastic Technicolor whoopee that you'll find, say, aboard a Carnival ship. You'll find everyone from kids to retirees.

Sleek, modern, and stunningly designed, the 1,814-passenger *Century* and the larger 1,950-passenger *Infinity* and *Millennium* have a lot of open deck space and lots of large windows that provide access to the wide skies and the grand Alaskan vistas. All the ships (but especially *Century*) feature incredible spas with hydrotherapy pools, steam rooms, and saunas, plus health and beauty services and exceptionally large fitness areas.

☎ **800-437-3111** *or 305-262-8322. Fax: 800-437-5111.* www.celebritycruises. com. *Sample nightly rates per person: Lowest-price inside cabin $128, lowest-price outside cabin $150, lowest-price suite $757 for seven-night cruise.*

Crystal Cruises

Crystal's brand of luxury cruising appeals to a discerning clientele. Everything is first class, with fine attention paid to detail and to making guests feel comfortable. The line has been sailing for just over two decades and has received widespread recognition for providing a truly luxurious experience with the largest ships in the category. Its two vessels, which debuted in 1995 and 2003, have been beautifully refurbished and the line is always looking for ways to update and embellish the onboard experience. Crystal also recently has revamped its pricing policy, offering many two-for-one fares, onboard spending credits and a Price Guarantee program.

After many years of skipping Alaska, the line is returning in 2011 with a single ship, the *Crystal Symphony,* which will sail a 12-night Inside Passage itinerary round-trip from San Francisco.

Generally, the passengers aboard Crystal are people of some discernment — say, successful businesspeople who can afford to pay for the best. Whereas, at one time, that couple may have been closer to the average age on an Alaska cruise (meaning, fairly old), they no longer are. Probably thanks to Crystal's innovative shore-excursion program and its entertainment package, *Crystal Symphony* will attract a younger breed of cruiser, many under 50. The average age has, in fact, dropped considerably since the line's early days, making for a very sociable mix of age groups onboard. And, although the entire cruise industry, including the luxury segment, is more casual than it used to be, a "colder" weather destination such as Alaska does seem to attract those who, whatever their age, tend to like to dress up rather than down. Casual nights don't mean the same to Crystal guests as they do to some others.

Plush, streamlined, extravagantly comfortable, and not as overwhelmingly large as the megaships being launched by less glamorous lines, the 960-passenger *Crystal Symphony* (1995) offers a broad choice of onboard diversions and distractions, more than you'd expect on a luxury vessel. The ship underwent a major $25-million refurbishment to both public spaces and staterooms/suites in late 2009, really making the ship sparkly all over again with beautiful new features and fittings.

☎ **800-446-6620** *or 310-785-9300. Fax: 310-785-3891. www.crystalcruises. com. Sample nightly rates per person: Lowest-price deluxe cabins from $388, balcony cabins from $528, suites from $923 for 12-night cruise.*

Disney Cruise Line

When it comes to entertaining every member of a family — from the littlest children to parents and grandparents — no other cruise line has it down quite like Disney. The 12-year-old operator has famously focused on catering as much to adults as to kids, with a number of adults-only areas to balance an industry-leading array of kids' facilities and activities.

Entertainment, as you'd expect from a movie-studio-owning company, is among the industry's best, with family-oriented musicals featuring classic Disney characters. Dining, too, has a measure of Disney's trademark pixie dust, with an innovative system where passengers (along with their servers) rotate between three themed restaurants. And, of course, what other ship can boast Mickey, Donald, and the gang out and about to entertain passengers?

The summer of 2011 will mark the first time Disney has sent a ship to Alaska. The *Disney Wonder* will sail seven-night Inside Passage cruises out of Seattle.

Disney's ships attract a wide mix of passengers, from honeymooners to seniors, but as at the company's famous theme parks, the largest percentage is made up of young American families with children. Because of this, the average age of passengers tends to be younger than aboard many of the other mainstream ships, with many passengers in their 30s and 40s. The bulk of the line's passengers are first-time cruisers, and because the line attracts so many families, more than half of its bookings are for multiple cabins.

The 1,754-passenger **Disney Wonder** is the line's sole ship in Alaska in 2011. It offers plenty of activities, great pools (including one shaped like Mickey Mouse's head) and the family-friendliest cabins at sea (in addition to being larger than the industry average, all rooms come with pullout sofas or pull-down beds that allow, in many cases, for up to five people).

☎ **800-951-3532.** *Fax: 407-566-3541. www.disneycruise.com. Sample nightly rates per person: Lowest-price inside cabin $194, lowest-price outside cabin $261, lowest-price suite $739 for seven-night Inside Passage cruise.*

Weddings at sea

Lovers have long known that nothing is as romantic as cruising. Luxury cruise ships have been vastly popular honeymoon vehicles for decades. And recently, with the growing popularity of cruises, they've assumed new significance in the marriage business. Ship operators now make it easier to tie the knot either in a port of call during the voyage or onboard the vessel. Most lines will help you set it all up — if you give them enough advance notice. They'll provide the music, photographer, bouquets, champagne, hors d'oeuvres, cake, and other frills and fripperies. All you have to do is bring somebody to share your "I do" moment. The wedding package may cost you $1,000 or so over the price of your cabin.

Today in Alaska, Carnival, Celebrity, Norwegian Cruise Line, Royal Caribbean, and Holland America Line allow you to hold your marriage ceremony in a specially decorated lounge onboard while in port, officiated by a local clergyman or justice of the peace. Princess goes one better: Whereas before you could be married only on the *Diamond Princess, Sapphire Princess, Island Princess,* and *Coral Princess* — all of them equipped with wedding chapels in which the captain himself can conduct the ceremony — now you can be wed on any ship in the Princess fleet, including those in Alaska. It's all perfectly legal. The ships have been reflagged to Bermuda registry, the authority under which your nuptials will be certified. The captain of the *Carnival Spirit* also can marry couples at sea (including same-sex couples) in the waters off British Columbia (international waters).

If you want guests to attend your special onboard moment while in port, the ship line must be notified well in advance, and your guests will be required to produce valid ID and go through the same kind of screening process that passengers go through. Princess makes it easy for friends and family onshore to share the event by filming the entire process and then posting it on a special Webcam found on its Web site (www. princess.com/bridgecams). And, no, it's not really live. The images are there for all to see long after the rites are concluded.

No matter where you wed, you have to have a valid U.S. marriage license (or a Canadian license, if you want to bid farewell to the single life in one of the British Columbia ports). The cruise line's wedding planner will help you set that up. Just remember to plan in advance — these things take time.

Holland America Line

Holland America Line can be summed up in one word: *tradition.* The company was formed way back in 1873 as the Netherlands-America Steamship Company, and its ships today strive to present an aura of history and dignity, like a European hotel where they never let rock stars register. Thanks to its acquisition over the years of numerous land-based tour operators, Holland America also has positioned itself as Alaska's most experienced and comprehensive cruise company. The company has seven ships in the Alaska market in 2011.

Though most of Holland America's Alaskan fleet is relatively young, the ships are designed with a decidedly "classic" feel — no flashing neon lights here. Similarly, Holland America's ships are heavy on more mature, less frenetic kinds of activities. You'll find good bridge programs and music to dance (or just listen) to in the bars and lounges, plus health spas and the other amenities found on most large ships. Service is excellent, delivered by a crew mostly trained at the line's own schools in Indonesia and the Philippines. The line has improved its nightly show-lounge entertainment, adding magicians, comedians, and the like. Alaska Native guides are onboard most Glacier Bay–bound ships, offering their local insight. With fewer kids on these ships than some of the other mainstream lines, the Club HAL children's playrooms are small, but the program is nonetheless big on creative activities. A recently launched "as you wish" dining program allows guests to choose either a set time or anytime dining for dinner. Alaska itineraries include seven-night Inside Passage cruises and seven-night Gulf of Alaska cruises.

Holland America's passenger profile used to reflect a much older crowd. Now the average age is dropping, thanks to an increased emphasis on its Club HAL program for children and some updating of onboard entertainment. Still, Holland America's passengers in Alaska include a large percentage of middle-age-and-up vacationers.

The 1,266-passenger **Statendam** boasts cabins with sitting areas and lots of closet and drawer space, and even the least expensive inside cabins run almost 190 sq. ft., quite large by industry standards. Outside doubles have either picture windows or verandas. The striking dining rooms, two-tiered showrooms, and Crow's Nest forward bar/lounges are among these ships' best features. The somewhat newer, 1,440-passenger **Volendam, Zaandam,** and **Veendam,** and 1,380-passenger **Amsterdam,** are larger and fancier, with triple-decked oval atriums, nearly 200 suites and deluxe staterooms with private verandas, five showrooms and lounges, and an alternative restaurant designed as an artist's bistro, featuring drawings and etchings. The smallest cabin is a comfortable 190 sq. ft. The **Zuiderdam** and **Westerdam,** two of the newest vessels in the fleet, weigh 82,300 tons and carry 1,916 passengers. These are sophisticated, spacious, yet intimate ships, well equipped to support Holland America's position as a force in the Alaska market.

☎ **800-426-0327** or *206-281-3535. Fax: 206-286-7110.* www.hollandamerica. com. *Sample nightly rates per person: Lowest-price inside cabin $128, lowest-price outside cabin $157, lowest-price suite $343 for seven-night cruise.*

Norwegian Cruise Line

Very contemporary Norwegian Cruise Line offers an informal and upbeat onboard atmosphere on two large ships, the *Norwegian Pearl* and *Norwegian Star,* both sailing from Seattle. The line excels at activities, and its recreational and fitness programs are among the best in the industry. Norwegian recently launched a food-upgrade program — the best food is at venues where you pay an extra fee — and has what has become a very popular "freestyle" casual-dining policy that allows passengers to have dinner pretty much whenever they want, with whomever they want, dressed however they want.

In Alaska, Norwegian offers an Alaskan lecturer, wine tastings, art auctions, cooking demonstrations, craft and dance classes, an incentive fitness program, and bingo, among other activities. Passengers can choose from a good selection of soft-adventure shore excursions, including hiking, biking, and kayaking. Entertainment is generally strong and includes Vegas-style musical productions. The top-notch kids' program includes an activity room, video games, an ice cream bar, and guaranteed baby-sitting aboard, plus sessions with park rangers and escorted shore excursions. Norwegian offers seven-night Inside Passage cruises.

In Alaska, the demographic tends more toward retirees than on Norwegian's warmer-climate sailings, but you'll find families as well, including grandparents bringing along the grandkids.

One of the first ships built with Norwegian's trademark "freestyle" cruising in mind, the 2,240-passenger *Norwegian Star* has no fewer than 14 places where people can eat — depending on the time of day. The *Norwegian Star* also is well-equipped for the sports-minded and active vacationer — in addition to the fitness center, there are three heated pools, a jogging/walking track, and a wide array of sports facilities. The 2,394-passenger *Norwegian Pearl* is the line's newest ship in Alaska and has the most bells and whistles (including one of the only bowling alleys at sea!), providing a fun and lively Alaska cruise experience.

☎ **800-327-7030** or *305-436-4000. Fax: 305-436-4120. www.ncl.com. Sample nightly rates per person: Lowest-price inside cabin $114, lowest-price outside cabin $136, lowest-price suite from $271 for seven-night cruise.*

Oceania Cruises

Oceania Cruises entered the cruise industry in late 2003 when it launched *Regatta,* formerly the *R2* from Renaissance Cruises, which went belly-up after 9/11. It was an interesting beginning for *Regatta,* along with its sister ship, *Insignia,* formerly the *R1,* as the ships were being positioned above the premium lines and below the luxury lines. It was essentially a new category they called "deluxe," and it's been very successful, with Oceania adding a third ship to the fleet in 2005 (*Nautica,* formerly the *R5*). The line has its first newly built vessel, *Marina,* arriving in January 2011. Oceania is now a sister line to luxury operator Regent Seven Seas, with the two comprising Prestige Cruise Holdings, a cruise division of the Apollo Management investment firm, which also owns a big portion of Norwegian Cruise Line.

Oceania truly offers a deluxe, upscale experience. There's little glitz or hoopla onboard and the hallmarks are dining, service, and itineraries. The two no-charge alternative restaurants are way above the norm. But one of the biggest strengths is the size of its first three vessels. At 30,277 tons and carrying 684 guests, they're notably small to midsize by today's standards. It's an informal setting (Oceania calls it country-club-casual) without crowds and lines. The summer of 2011 will mark the first visit to Alaska by an Oceania ship, so it's a completely new experience for the ship and the cruise line. It likely will draw upon the experience of the Regent Seven Seas ships, which have been in the 49th state for more than a decade. And the ship size allows for docking right in downtown Anchorage, a very big convenience.

The basic profile is one of couples in their 40s and 50s, but it's a very comfortable ship for both younger and older cruisers. It's appropriate for those looking for a somewhat informal cruise, where dining and excellent service take a higher priority than glitz, glamour, and nonstop activity. Historically, Oceania's itineraries have been port-intensive, with few sea days, so a busy shipboard agenda has never been a priority to passengers.

The *Regatta*'s small size certainly has its advantages in a destination such as Alaska, allowing for easier navigation through the Inside Passage's narrow waterways. Carrying only 684 passengers, it's a more intimate alternative to the much larger mass-market ships that dominate cruising in the region, with plenty of upscale features at significantly lower fares than the luxury lines. At press time, *Regatta* is scheduled for major refurbishment in January 2011. All staterooms and suites and the two alternative restaurants will be redone. There will be new carpeting and artwork throughout the ship.

☎ **800-531-5658.** *www.oceaniacruises.com. Sample nightly rates per person: Lowest-price inside cabin $350, lowest-price outside cabin $400, lowest-price suite $600 for ten, twelve, and fourteen-night cruises.*

Princess Cruises

Bringing on several new vessels in recent years, Princess has impressively maintained consistency. Aboard Princess, you get a lot of bang for your buck, attractively packaged and well executed. Although its ships serve every corner of the globe, nowhere is the Princess presence more visible than in Alaska, where it will have six ships in 2011 — almost as many as sister line Holland America. Through its affiliate, Princess Tours, it owns wilderness lodges, motor coaches, and railcars in the 49th state, making it one of the major players in the Alaska cruise market, alongside Holland America.

Princess passengers can expect enough onboard activities to keep them going morning to night, if they've a mind to, and enough nooks and crannies to allow them to do absolutely nothing if that's their thing. Kids are well taken care of, with especially large playrooms. On shore, the line's shore-excursion staff gets big points for efficiency. Passengers have the option of eating dinner at a set time (early and late seating) or dining in the "anytime dining" room, at any time.

Princess offers the standard seven-night Inside Passage cruises and seven-night Gulf of Alaska cruises, as well as ten-night Inside Passages cruises from San Francisco.

Typical Princess passengers are likely to be between 50 and 65, and are experienced cruisers who know what they want and are prepared to pay for it. Recent additional emphasis on its youth and children's facilities has begun to attract a bigger share of the family market.

Princess's diverse fleet in Alaska comprises six ships, five of which are new since the millennium. The fleet includes the **Diamond Princess** and **Sapphire Princess,** which were completed in 2004; the **Coral Princess** and **Island Princess,** of 2003 vintage; the **Golden Princess** (2001); and the **Sea Princess,** which was built in 1998 and served in the British P&O Cruises fleet until joining Princess after a major refit in 2005. The ships generally are pretty but not stunning, bright but not gaudy, spacious but not overwhelmingly so, and decorated in a comfortable, restrained style that's a combination of classic and modern. They're a great choice when you want a step up from Carnival, Royal Caribbean, and Norwegian but aren't interested in the slightly more chic ambience of Celebrity or the luxury of Regent Seven Seas.

☎ **800-568-3262** or 661-753-0000. Fax: 661-753-1535. www.princess.com. Sample nightly rates per person: Lowest-price inside cabin $109, lowest-price outside cabin $139, lowest-price suite $185 for seven-night cruise.

Regent Seven Seas Cruises

Regent's guests travel in style and extreme comfort. Its brand of luxury is casually elegant and subtle, its cuisine among the best in the industry. That goes for the Seven Seas Navigator, which is sailing in Alaska this year for a second season. The line assumes, for the most part, that passengers want to entertain themselves onboard, so organized activities are limited, but they do include lectures by local experts, well-known authors, and the like, plus facilities for card and board games, blackjack and Ping-Pong tournaments, bingo, big-screen movies with popcorn, and instruction in the fine arts of pompom making, juggling, and such. Bridge instructors are onboard on select sailings. The line has a no-tipping policy and offers creative shore excursions. Room service is about the best you'll find on any ship, and the cuisine is excellent. Regent recently switched to a fleet-wide liquor-inclusive policy on all departures. **Seven Seas Navigator** now sails primarily a 7-night Gulf of Alaska itinerary between late May and August, with two interesting 12-day itineraries between San Francisco and Vancouver, British Columbia, at the beginning and end of the season.

Regent tends to attract passengers in their 40s, 50s, and 60s who have an annual household income of more than $200,000 and don't like to flaunt their wealth. The typical passenger is well-educated, well-traveled, and inquisitive.

Cabins on the 490-passenger **Seven Seas Navigator** are all ocean-view suites, all but a handful of which have private verandas. The standard suite is a roomy 301 sq. ft.; some suites can interconnect if you want to book two for additional space. The Seven Seas Lounge is a comfortable, two-tiered showroom that, despite the space limitations imposed by the ship's small size, succeeds in presenting a high level of cabaret, Broadway revue, classical music, and comedian/magic shows. Elsewhere on the ship, Star's Lounge offers dancing to the music of a DJ, from which the less hectic piano bar, Galileo's, is a welcome alternative. The Connoisseur Club is a cushy venue for pre-dinner drinks and after-dinner fine brandy and cigars, and a smallish casino allows guests to indulge their taste for blackjack, roulette, stud poker, craps, and slot machines. The ship's Carita Paris spa, though not as extensive as those of its larger Alaska rivals, is nevertheless well-equipped to provide a variety of services using a variety of herbal and water-based therapies.

☎ **800-285-1835.** www.rssc.com. *Sample nightly rates per person: Lowest-price suites start at $575 for seven-night cruise.*

Royal Caribbean International

Royal Caribbean sells a mass-market style of cruising that's reasonably priced and offered aboard informal, well-run ships with nearly every diversion imaginable — craft classes, horse racing, bingo, shuffleboard, deck games, line-dancing lessons, wine-and-cheese tastings, cooking demonstrations, art auctions, and the like — plus elaborate health clubs and spas; covered swimming pools; large, open sun-deck areas; and innumerable bars, lounges, and other entertainment centers. The Viking Crown Lounge and other glassed-in areas make excellent observation rooms from which to see the Alaska sights. Royal Caribbean spends big bucks on entertainment, which includes high-tech show productions. Headliners are often featured. Port lectures are offered on topics such as Alaska wildlife, and the line offers dozens of adventurous shore excursions. Royal Caribbean's children's activities are some of the most extensive afloat. The line offers seven-night Inside Passage and Gulf of Alaska cruises.

The crowd on Royal Caribbean ships, like the décor, rates pretty high on the party scale, though not quite at the Carnival level. Passengers represent an age mix from 30 to 60, and a good number of families are attracted by the line's well-established and fine-tuned kids' programs (Royal Caribbean's ships are a particularly good bet for tweens and teens, who love such trademark Royal Caribbean decktop offerings as climbing walls and miniature golf).

Royal Caribbean owns the largest ships in the world, including the much-ballyhooed, 225,282-ton *Oasis of the Seas,* which set a new record for size when it debuted in December 2009. Although this groundbreaking 5,400-passenger ship — which includes such innovative design features as an open-air Central Park with live trees, an outdoor AquaTheater for water shows, and onboard zip-lining — is not in Alaska this year, Royal Caribbean does offer the very up-to-date 90,000-ton, 2,112-passenger **Radiance of the Seas** sailing Gulf of Alaska cruises between Vancouver, British Columbia, and Seward. Also returning to Alaska in 2011 is the older (1997) but still up-to-date 1,998-passenger **Rhapsody of the Seas,** a Vision-class ship cruising out of Seattle.

☎ **800-327-6700** or *305-379-2601.* www.royalcaribbean.com. *Sample nightly rates per person: Lowest-price inside cabin $78, lowest-price outside cabin $157, lowest-price suite $264 for seven-night cruise on the Rhapsody, Royal Caribbean's least-expensive ship.*

Silversea

Silversea is one of the most luxurious — and pricey — cruise lines in the business, and it's known for exquisite service, gourmet cuisine, and spacious and elegant all-suite accommodations. The line offers an impressive enrichment program with naturalists, well-known authors, and even celebrity chefs mingling with passengers nightly. A cooking-school program allows for cooking lessons at sea. Entertainment is more low-key than on the bigger big-ship lines, but the passengers seem to enjoy the cabaret-type acts. The company offers niceties including free alcohol and a fine selection of complimentary wines at lunch and dinner — and probably at breakfast as well, if you're really interested. A friend of Fran's is fond of telling about the time he ordered a late-night hot dog from room service and it came elaborately presented on a silver tray. For Alaska, the line offers seven- to ten-night Gulf of Alaska cruises between Vancouver and Seward, Alaska.

Look for the 60-something set, well heeled, well educated, and knowing what to look for when they lay out the kind of money it takes to get a place on one of this company's ships.

Silversea has a growing fleet of six ships, but it sends just one to Alaska, the 382-passenger **Silver Shadow.** There are no rock-climbing facilities, but there are two alternative restaurants, one of which doubles as the breakfast and lunch buffet room, and there's a small casino — there is no children's program; it's not a ship for kids.

☎ **800-774-9966.** *Fax: 954-356-5881.* www.silversea.com. *Sample nightly rates per person: Least-expensive suite $508 for seven-night cruise.*

Chapter 9

Planning an Outdoor Adventure

In This Chapter

▶ Joining outdoor activities — summer and winter
▶ Viewing Alaska's wildlife
▶ Choosing an outdoor escorted tour
▶ Assessing outdoor health and safety

You wouldn't go to Paris and view the Louvre only through the window of a bus, but many visitors to Alaska *do* see the wilderness only through glass. They miss the detail in the flowers, the scent of the forest, the feeling of the air on their skin, and the tundra under their feet. They miss the irreplaceable feeling of being a small part of the overwhelming power of nature.

For some very elderly or frail travelers, surveying the scenery from a vehicle is better than missing out entirely. But most visitors, including those with disabilities, can get outdoors in Alaska in some way. Experienced hikers, anglers, sea-kayakers, canoeists, and other nature lovers will be in heaven. But you don't have to know anything or have any experience in the outdoors; someone is always available to help and to introduce you to Alaska's wild lands at your own level.

Getting Active in the Alaska Summer

Summer in Alaska is a time to get outside; on a sunny weekend, you're hard-pressed to find an Alaskan in town. Here's a mini-directory to help you figure out which activities are best for you, where you can do them, and who you can get to take you. I also provide information to help you decide whether to participate in these activities on your own or with a guide. I suggest a few guides here to get you started; the destination chapters in this book include alternative guides, as well as information on renting equipment in each town.

Backpacking

I can't imagine a more beautiful or exciting place for a backpacking expedition than Alaska. You can have immense swaths of tundra or mountain to yourself, places with more wildlife than people.

- ✔ **Difficulty level:** Take an overnight hike near home before you invest in a backpacking trek in Alaska to hone your skills and make sure you enjoy carrying a pack. Even Alaska's trail hikes tend to be remote, with potentially tough weather; the most dramatic hiking routes are challenging, far beyond the trails.

- ✔ **Best places:** For self-guided trail hikes, pick the pathways of Chugach National Forest and Chugach State Park near Anchorage (see Chapter 14). For self-guided, off-trail hiking, try Denali National Park (see Chapter 19). For guided, off-trail hikes, consider St. Elias Alpine Guides at Wrangell–St. Elias National Park (see the last item in this list).

- ✔ **Guided or on your own:** To set up your own trip, you need to buy trail guidebooks and maps, bring or rent equipment, and arrange for transportation at your starting and ending points. You can start with the outfitters that I recommend throughout this book. This takes a lot of planning, but it's doable if you're motivated. A guided trek takes out the guesswork but costs many times more.

- ✔ **Who to go with: St. Elias Alpine Guides** (☎ 888-933-5427; www. steliasguides.com) specializes in trekking and climbing the rugged and spectacular Wrangell–St. Elias National Park, some of the most remote wilderness on the planet. A four-day trek starts at around $900 per person.

Biking off-road

Mountain-biking is allowed off-road almost everywhere in Alaska except in the national parks. Literally thousands of miles of dirt roads and tracks reach through the coastal forests. In the cities, excellent cross-country ski trails become excellent mountain-biking trails in the summer.

- ✔ **Difficulty level:** Mountain-biking rough terrain is a real skill, but novices can enjoy fat-tire bikes on dirt roads and ski trails around many communities without difficulty.

- ✔ **Best places:** Many places in Alaska have superb mountain-biking. The remote roads across Kachemak Bay from Homer are among the best: They're not connected to the highway network, they're easy to reach by boat, and the town has good bike shops (see Chapter 16).

- ✔ **Guided or on your own:** Some areas do have guided mountain-biking day trips, but mostly it's a self-guided activity — you rent the bike and go. Plan ahead by contacting a bike shop in the area where you plan to ride (see the appropriate chapter in this book for suggestions), getting advice on the area, and reserving your equipment.

✔ **Who to go with:** Bike-rental agencies are listed with each destination in this book.

Biking on pavement

In Alaska's smaller communities, especially in the Southeast, a bicycle is a visitor's most efficient way of getting around. Vigorous cyclists also can use a bike to see natural places on the edge of town on day trips. Some vigorous cyclists tour the state's scenic highways on bikes.

✔ **Difficulty level:** Almost anyone with physical mobility can get on a bike and coast along the coastal trail in Anchorage. Highway trips are for physically fit riders who can handle traffic.

✔ **Best places:** The bike paths of Anchorage (see Chapter 14) allow casual rides into the woods, where you can frequently spot moose and eagles. There are good trails in Juneau, too, and in Seward, Skagway, and Sitka the quiet streets are fine for riding (see Chapters 16, 20, 21, and 22).

✔ **Guided or on your own:** You don't need a guide to rent a bike and explore a quaint town or wooded bike trail. You may want to join a group for a bike expedition.

✔ **Who to go with:** I list bike-rental agencies with each town in this book. **Alaskabike** (☎ 907-245-2175; www.alaskabike.com) offers vacations for avid cyclists. An eight-day tour over the spectacular Richardson Highway costs around $3,000, inclusive. The schedule includes tours with kayaking, too.

Canoeing

Gliding down a gently flowing stream or across the mirrored surface of a pristine lake may be the most serene way to get into the true Alaska. Wild land unfolds around you as if you were the first person to float on the waterway.

✔ **Difficulty level:** Anyone can get out for a paddle on Fairbanks's gentle Chena River. Expert canoeists find a paradise of thousands of miles of little-used routes in many locations.

✔ **Best places:** Fairbanks is a canoeing center, with accessible river routes for every ability level or journey length (see Chapter 17). The Swan Lake Canoe Route, near Kenai, is a good self-guided backcountry trip for novices (see Chapter 16).

✔ **Guided or on your own:** If you're confident paddling a canoe, you can manage the easier routes that I mention in this book. Always check water levels and stream conditions with local authorities. To get deeper into the wilderness, where emergency help is unavailable, go with a guide.

✔ **Who to go with:** River guide and author Karen Jettmar leads long floats by canoe or raft on exotic wilderness rivers for small groups all summer through her firm, **Equinox Wilderness Expeditions** (☎ 206-462-5246; www.equinoxexpeditions.com). A ten-day float costs $4,200.

Day-hiking

Part of Alaska's magic is that no place is so urban that it's more than an hour from big, unspoiled natural areas. Anyone who can should make a point of getting off on the trails that lead out from every town.

✔ **Difficulty level:** You set the level of difficulty. Hike a half-mile up a level seaside trail or conquer a mountain on an all-day hike.

✔ **Best places:** You find great day hikes everywhere you go in Alaska. The best trails are near towns in coastal Alaska, including Anchorage (see Chapter 14), the Kenai Peninsula (see Chapter 16), and every town in Southeast Alaska (three of which are covered in Part V). You can hike on tundra, off trails, at Denali National Park (see Chapter 19), and many other places.

✔ **Guided or on your own:** All you need are walking shoes and directions to the trailhead. I mention some of the best hikes throughout this book. If you're uncomfortable on your own, the national parks lead guided hikes.

✔ **Who to go with:** The best guided day hikes are at Denali National Park, where rangers lead daily Discovery Hikes off trails deep inside the park (see Chapter 19).

Fishing

Alaska's legendary salmon- and halibut-fishing drive the rhythm of life in coastal communities. Just *try* not to get excited when you haul in a fish bigger than you up from the sea floor, or hook a mass of fighting muscle in a remote stream. The best all-around source of information about fishing in Alaska is the Web site of the **Alaska Department of Fish & Game Sport Fish Division** (www.sf.adfg.state.ak.us). The site includes guides on where, how, and when to fish; fishing reports updated weekly; and the option to purchase licenses online. Nonresident sport-fishing licenses start at $20 for a one-day license and go up to $80 for a two-week license. You also can get a license on the spot from sporting-goods stores, grocery stores, and guides.

✔ **Difficulty level:** Just about anyone can enjoy guided fishing on a boat in the Kenai River or on the ocean in Southeast or Southcentral Alaska. Avid anglers can schedule time at a remote fishing lodge or on a guided or unguided floatplane fly-in, or just fish streamside on one of Alaska's highways.

✔ **Best places:** For halibut (from a boat), go to Homer, Juneau, or Sitka (see Chapters 16, 20, and 22). For salmon in the ocean (from a boat), head to Seward, Juneau, or Sitka (see Chapters 16, 20, and 22). And for salmon in a stream (on a boat or on the bank), try the Anchorage environs and Kenai (see Chapters 14 and 16).

✔ **Guided or do-it-yourself:** Fishing is easy; catching a fish is what takes some skill. Unless you have plenty of time for research and trial and error, take at least your first fishing trip with a guide to learn the unique skills required for salmon-fishing. (You must have a guide for halibut, because you need a boat.)

✔ **Who to go with:** If fishing is the primary reason you're going to Alaska, contact **Sport Fishing Alaska** (☎ 907-344-8674; www. alaskatripplanners.com), a fee-based booking agency that gets anglers to Alaska's hottest fishing spots. If fishing is just one of your goals, check with the fishing resources I list in the chapters specific to the towns you plan to visit.

Rafting

River-rafting comes in different flavors: half-day white-water thrill rides or multi-day journeys across great swaths of Alaska wilderness that you can't reach any other way — or a combination of the two.

✔ **Difficulty level:** Sitting in a raft is easy. But floating through violent rapids in cold water is inherently hazardous and definitely not for everyone. A guided raft expedition is the most comfortable way to see remote wilderness, but you must be ready to sleep in a tent and endure the bugs, and you have no way to quit before the end.

✔ **Best places:** For day trips, the Nenana Canyon outside Denali National Park (see Chapter 19) and the fast rivers around Anchorage (see Chapter 14) are among the best options. For expeditions, the rivers of the Arctic may be best for their broad scenery and wildlife-viewing.

✔ **Guided or on your own:** Unless you're an expert, putting together your own raft trip is probably impractical. Guided expeditions should be planned and booked three months in advance, to reserve a spot and to make sure you know what you're getting into. You can take day trips on a next-day basis.

✔ **Who to go with:** For day trips near Anchorage, try **Nova** (☎ 800-746-5753 or 907-745-5753; www.novalaska.com). At Denali National Park, contact **Denali Outdoor Center** (☎ 888-303-1925 or 907-683-1925; www.denalioutdoorcenter.com). For expeditions, check out **Equinox Wilderness Expeditions** (☎ 206-462-5246; www.equinoxexpeditions.com) or **Mountain Travel Sobek** (☎ 800-586-1911; www.mtsobek.com).

Secrets of Alaska Salmon

In Alaska, it's not so much where you wet your line, but when. The primary catch, Pacific salmon, lives in salt water but spawns in fresh water, with each fish returning to the stream of its birth during a certain, narrow window of time called a "run." When the salmon are running, fishing is hot; when they're not running, it's dead. And the runs change from day to day, typically lasting only a few weeks. (Halibut, on the other hand, are bottom-dwelling ocean fish; you can fish them from a boat every day when the tide is right.) You can fish salmon all over the state in fresh and salt water, but the closer you are to the ocean, the better the fish are. Salmon flesh softens in fresh water and the skin turns dull and red. Salmon right from salt water that haven't started their spawning cycle are called silver bright—when you see one, you'll understand why. No Pacific salmon feeds in fresh water, but kings and silvers, meat eaters at sea, strike out of habit even in the river.

There are five species of Pacific salmon, each preferring its own habitat, and, even when the habitat overlaps, each timing its run differently. Each species has two names.

King (or **chinook**) is the most coveted, best fighting fish, commonly growing to 30 pounds in 5 to 7 years at sea (the sport record, from the Kenai River, was 97 pounds, and the largest ever, taken by commercial fishermen near Petersburg, was 126 pounds). It takes a lot of effort to hook and land a big king, but it's the ultimate in Alaska fishing. You also need a special king stamp on your fishing license from the Alaska Department of Fish and Game, which you can buy at the same time you buy your license. King runs come mostly from late May to early July.

The **silver** (or **coho**) is smaller than the king, typically 6 to 9 pounds, but it fights and jumps ferociously, making it nearly as big a prize. Silvers run mostly in the fall, beginning in August and lasting into October in some streams.

Red (or **sockeye**) salmon, so named for their tasty red flesh, are the trickiest to catch. They usually weigh 4 to 8 pounds and can run in any of the summer months, depending on the region and stream. Reds feed primarily on plankton at sea, and when they strike a fly, it's out of an instinct that no one really understands; you need perfect river conditions to catch reds legally, because snagging anywhere but the mouth generally is not allowed in fresh water.

Pinks (or **humpies**) grow to only a few pounds and aren't as tasty as the other three species; their flesh lacks the fat that makes salmon so meaty in flavor, and it deteriorates quickly once the fish enter fresh water. Pinks are so plentiful that Alaska anglers usually view them as a nuisance to get off the line, but visitors often enjoy catching them: There's nothing wrong with a hard-fighting 4-pound fish, especially if you use light tackle, and a sliver-bright pink salmon is tasty if cooked right.

Chum (or **dog**) salmon return plentifully to streams over much of the state but are rarely targeted by anglers. Yet a typical 5- to 10-pound chum hits and fights hard. Chums aren't prized for the table and are mostly used for subsistence by Alaska Natives, who smoke or dry the fish for winter use or freeze it to feed dog teams.

(continued)

(continued)

The gear you use depends on the species you are after and the regulations for the area you're fishing. You have to catch the fish in the mouth; snagging is allowed only in special circumstances. On salt water, boats troll for kings and silvers with herring bait and gear to hold it down. Lures, salmon eggs, or flies will work on silvers and kings in the rivers, but regulations vary. Flies work best with reds. Most Alaska fishermen use spinning gear on the larger salmon species — landing such a large fish is iffy with a fly rod.

Sea-kayaking

A sea kayak is a uniquely intimate way to see the abundance of the marine world. Rich seafloor life glides by inches below you in clear water, sea otters and birds let you approach, and whales take no notice. You enter into their universe.

- ✔ **Difficulty level:** Almost any adult or teen can safely handle a guided sea-kayaking outing, but you can get into serious danger quickly without a guide or the proper skills. People with joint or back problems may not be comfortable, and young children must be able to sit perfectly still.

- ✔ **Best places:** Virtually every coastal community has a sea-kayaking guide and someplace beautiful to take guests for day trips, so there is no need to tailor your itinerary to taking a day paddle. Expeditions are available in many places, too; some of the best waters for extended paddling are in Southeast Alaska, accessed from Juneau (see Chapter 20).

- ✔ **Guided or on your own:** Experienced kayakers can easily rent what they need for a wonderful trip. You also can find operators who rent sea kayaks to raw beginners — a life-and-death gamble I don't recommend. You're better off going with one of the guides always found in Alaska's coastal towns. Reserve expeditions well in advance and book day trips a day or two ahead.

- ✔ **Who to go with:** I recommend kayak guides for day trips in every coastal town covered in this book. For a sea-kayaking expedition, try **Mountain Travel Sobek** (☎ **800-586-1911;** www.mtsobek. com), with trips into Glacier Bay National Park, a whale-watching paddle from a base camp, and even cushy inn-to-inn journeys. A five-day trip, with four days of kayaking, three days of camping, and one day at an inn, costs around $2,390.

Keeping Active in the Alaskan Winter

For people who live in Alaska, getting outdoors in winter is a matter of maintaining sanity: Winter lasts from October through April, and you just can't stay inside that long. For visitors, the winter holds a magnificent opportunity for winter sports. In many ways, this is when Alaska is at its best.

The following sections cover the variety of winter activities you can try, including their difficulty level, some suggestions for the best places to go, and whether to try them on your own or with a guide. As with the preceding section on summer activities, I also suggest a few outfitters for you to consider; you can find more options, as well as rental providers, in the destination chapters in this book.

Dog-mushing

No one should come to Alaska in the winter and not take at least a quick spin in a dog sled. You simply can't believe the speed, joy, and intelligence of the dogs running ahead of you as you ride quietly through the trees.

- ✔ **Difficulty level:** Anyone can ride in a sled driven by an experienced musher, although few folks will want to do it for more than an hour or so. You can certainly learn to drive a well-trained team, but you need to be confident around dogs and agile enough to handle situations that arise.

- ✔ **Best places:** The Fairbanks area is the state's center for mushing, with plenty of dogs, snow, and land for running — all the necessary ingredients (see Chapter 17).

- ✔ **Guided or on your own:** If you don't own a dozen trained dogs and a sled, doing it yourself isn't an option. The choice is in the basket or on the runners (riding or driving); learning to drive a sled is great, but it takes time and money. You usually can arrange day-trip rides a day or two in advance, or a few weeks for peak race periods.

- ✔ **Who to go with:** In Fairbanks, **Sun Dog Express Dog Sled Tours** (☎ **907-479-6983;** www.mosquitonet.com/~sleddog) charges as little as $15 for a quick spin, up to $325 to learn to drive a team in a half-day.

Skiing

Alaska has outstanding downhill skiing and snow that you can count on. Even better, because of the distance from population centers, lift lines are a rarity even at the busiest ski resorts. Cross-country skiers will find great trails without fees and unlimited backcountry to explore.

- ✔ **Difficulty level:** Going all the way to Alaska to ski makes sense mostly for those who already know how, but you can still find easy slopes to learn on. Expert skiers find no limit to challenges.

- ✔ **Best places:** Alaska's best ski resort is Alyeska Resort in Girdwood, just south of Anchorage (see Chapter 15). The best cross-country trails, more than 30 miles of them, are at Kincaid Park in Anchorage (see Chapter 14). Turnagain Pass, near Girdwood, is prime country for backcountry skiing.

✔ **Guided or on your own:** Planning a skiing vacation is relatively easy, because you only need to deal with one place. For Christmas or spring-break reservations, call well ahead.

✔ **Who to go with: Alyeska Resort** (☎ 800-880-3880; www.alyeska resort.com) offers inexpensive learn-to-ski and advanced lesson packages; you can set many other activities through them, too.

Snowmobiling

In most of Alaska, snowmobiles are like cars are in other places: They're simply the most practical way to get from place to place in a frozen landscape. Recreationists also use them for thrill-riding, but for visitors, their primary value lies in the ability to get to beautiful places without using more muscle than you may have.

✔ **Difficulty level:** Riding is simple to pick up, but you can quickly get stuck or tip over in powder snow. The sport is hazardous: The machines are fast, your body is unprotected, and you can find yourself far away in cold, dangerous places in minutes. Take it easy.

✔ **Best places:** The snowy mountains and glaciers south of Anchorage offer plenty of room to ride and scenery to enjoy, and the area has a professional guide service (see the last item in this list).

✔ **Guided or on your own:** Before setting out on their own, even experienced riders should go with a guide, to get the lay of the land and learn about the special hazards of extreme terrain.

✔ **Who to go with:** Based in Girdwood, near Anchorage, **Glacier City Snowmobile Tours** (☎ 877-783-5566; www.snowtours.net) guides groups on outings of up to 5½ hours for $240.

Viewing Alaska's Wildlife

Ask visitors to Alaska, "How was your trip?," and they usually respond by telling you what kind of animals they saw, such as "We saw two bears and a whale." I've found this rule holds true even for lifelong residents who've been traveling in the state.

The corollary to the rule is the reaction of travelers who've seen no wildlife: They complain about the weather.

If seeing wildlife is important to you, why not plan your trip to maximize the number of animals you see? Don't count on just tripping over a moose here or there. Pick the very best places to see bears or whales, and go. Even then, you still may not see anything. Part of the electricity of encountering wild animals is the sheer unpredictability of the experience. But you stand a much better chance of giving one of those positive trip reports than you do if you don't plan for it.

Getting Your Fish Home

An angler can easily come back from a halibut charter with 60 pounds of fish that, when cleaned, will yield 30 pounds of filets. A serving is around half a pound of halibut. Eat as much fresh as you can, as it will never be better, but be prepared for how you will deal with the rest of your bounty, which, if bought in a grocery store, would cost as much as $500 (it's illegal to sell sport-caught fish). If it is properly and quickly frozen, it will retain much of its quality well into the winter; if not, you waste this superb food. If you're lucky enough to catch that much salmon, the problem is even more immediate, as salmon is more sensitive to proper handling.

Most fishing towns have a sport processor who can vacuum-pack and flash-freeze your catch for $1 to $1.25 a pound. You can get it home conveniently as checked baggage; depending on your airline baggage fees, that may or may not be a cost-effective option. The processor can provide sturdy fish boxes and cold packs. If you aren't leaving right away, processors may be willing to hold the fish, and many hotels have freezer facilities. If you have to ship it, use an overnight service and make sure someone is there to put it in the freezer on the other end. Above all, keep the fish *hard frozen;* thawing and refreezing diminishes the quality off any fish and can turn salmon into mush.

Consider having some of your salmon smoked, if possible, making it a ready-to-eat delicacy very welcome as a homecoming gift. Halibut can be smoked, too, but because of its low fat content and delicate flavor and texture doesn't come out as well as salmon.

In Homer, **Coal Point Trading Co.**, 4306 Homer Spit (☎ **907/235-3877**; www.welovefish. com), will process and pack your catch as ordered. Ask your charter captain and they will come and get the fish directly from the boat.

Like so many of the better things in life, getting to good wildlife-viewing areas in Alaska is expensive. Wild animals stay away from highways, which are noisy and dangerous for them. During a one-week trip, you may see moose or caribou or some other creature from a road (or on a hike or while snowmobiling), or you may not. It's a matter of probabilities. With one very significant exception, you'll need a boat, a small plane, or some other means of traveling into large-mammal habitat. The significant exception is **Denali National Park** (see Chapter 19), where a bus ride on a road that's closed to private vehicles leads to superb wildlife-viewing at a reasonable price.

I've seen every animal in this section more than once, but that's after a lifetime of traveling in Alaska. On a short trip, you need to make an investment of time and money, you need luck, and you may need to be satisfied with seeing animals at a distance with binoculars. But if you try, you're very likely to see some exciting wildlife in Alaska.

The following sections cover the varieties of wildlife you may see, including some distinguishing features, where they're found, how easy or difficult they are to find, and whether you need help getting there. For

Alaska Wildlife

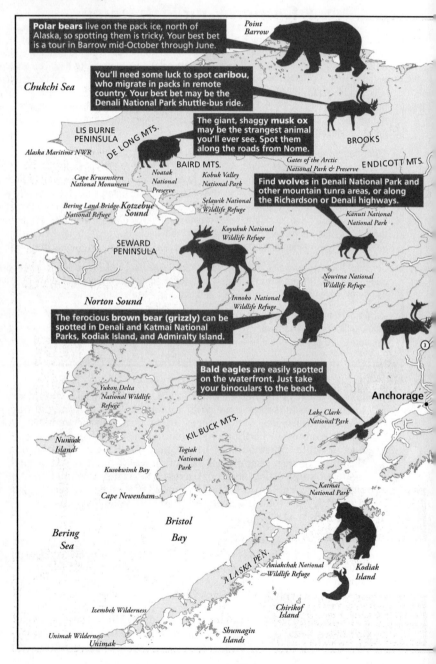

Polar bears live on the pack ice, north of Alaska, so spotting them is tricky. Your best bet is a tour in Barrow mid-October through June.

Point Barrow

You'll need some luck to spot **caribou**, who migrate in packs in remote country. Your best bet may be the Denali National Park shuttle-bus ride.

Chukchi Sea

The giant, shaggy **musk ox** may be the strangest animal you'll ever see. Spot them along the roads from Nome.

LIS BURNE PENINSULA

DE LONG MTS.

Alaska Maritime NWR

BAIRD MTS.

BROOKS

Gates of the Arctic National Park & Preserve

ENDICOTT MTS.

Cape Krusenstern National Monument

Noatak National Preserve

Kobuk Valley National Park

Find **wolves** in Denali National Park and other mountain tunra areas, or along the Richardson or Denali highways.

Bering Land Bridge National Refuge

Kotzebue Sound

Selawik National Wildlife Refuge

Kanuti National National Park

SEWARD PENINSULA

Koyukuk National Wildlife Refuge

Nowitna National Wildlife Refuge

Norton Sound

Innoko National Wildlife Refuge

The ferocious **brown bear (grizzly)** can be spotted in Denali and Katmai National Parks, Kodiak Island, and Admiralty Island.

Bald eagles are easily spotted on the waterfront. Just take your binoculars to the beach.

Yukon Delta National Wildlife Refuge

Lake Clark National Park

Anchorage

Nunivak Island

KIL BUCK MTS.

Togiak National Park

Kusokwimk Bay

Katmai National Park

Cape Newenham

Bristol Bay

Bering Sea

Aniakchak National Wildlife Refuge

Kodiak Island

ALASKA PEN.

Chirikof Island

Izembek Wilderness

Unimak Wilderness Unimak

Shumagin Islands

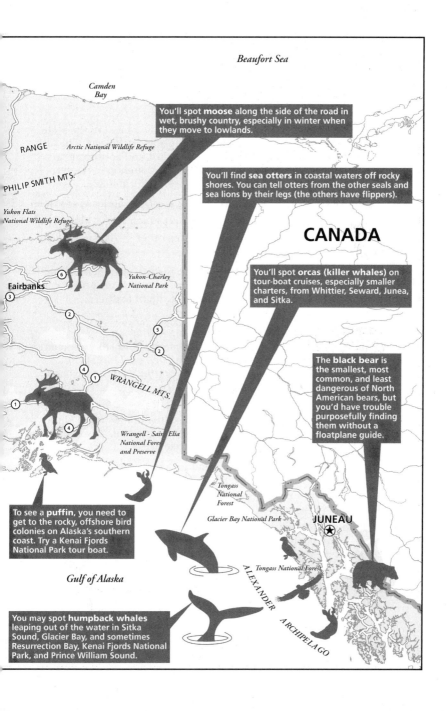

Beaufort Sea

Camden Bay

RANGE   Arctic National Wildlife Refuge

PHILIP SMITH MTS.

Yukon Flats National Wildlife Refuge

You'll spot **moose** along the side of the road in wet, brushy country, especially in winter when they move to lowlands.

You'll find **sea otters** in coastal waters off rocky shores. You can tell otters from the other seals and sea lions by their legs (the others have flippers).

CANADA

Yukon-Charley National Park

Fairbanks

You'll spot **orcas (killer whales)** on tour-boat cruises, especially smaller charters, from Whittier, Seward, Junea, and Sitka.

WRANGELL MTS.

The **black bear** is the smallest, most common, and least dangerous of North American bears, but you'd have trouble purposefully finding them without a floatplane guide.

Wrangell - Saint Elia National Forest and Preserve

Tongass National Forest

Glacier Bay National Park

JUNEAU

To see a **puffin**, you need to get to the rocky, offshore bird colonies on Alaska's southern coast. Try a Kenai Fjords National Park tour boat.

Gulf of Alaska

Tongass National Forest

ALEXANDER ARCHIPELAGO

You may spot **humpback whales** leaping out of the water in Sitka Sound, Glacier Bay, and sometimes Resurrection Bay, Kenai Fjords National Park, and Prince William Sound.

general safety tips in bear and moose country, see "Getting eaten by a bear (and such)," later in this chapter.

Bald eagle

The bald eagle, the symbol of the United States, is a huge bird of prey that has always been quite common and easy to find in Alaska.

- ✔ **Size:** 6- to 7½-ft. wing span; 8 to 14 pounds.

- ✔ **Where to find them:** Bald eagles show up over most of the state, even wheeling around the high-rise hotels in Anchorage. They're most common in coastal towns in Southeast and Southcentral Alaska, where they feed on fish. Eagles are common in Homer, Seward, Juneau, and Sitka (see Chapters 16, 20, and 22).

- ✔ **Easy or hard to spot:** Easy. Go to the waterfront and you see them.

- ✔ **Guided or on your own:** You can just take your binoculars to the beach. If you take a tour-boat ride to see other birds and animals, you're likely to see eagles, too.

- ✔ **ID notes:** Bald eagles take five years to mature into their distinctive white head; younger birds have mottled brown plumage but can be recognized by their size, shape, and long flight feathers.

Black bear

The smallest, most common, and least dangerous of North American bears, black bears show up in most of Alaska's coastal forests; in Southeast Alaska towns, they're often pests getting into the garbage.

- ✔ **Size:** 5 ft., nose to tail; 200 pounds.

- ✔ **Where to find them:** Locals in coastal communities often know salmon-spawning streams where bears congregate, or you can simply stumble over them, even in urban areas.

- ✔ **Easy or hard to spot:** Hard. Without chartering a floatplane to certain hot spots at certain times, you can't count on finding black bears (although you have a decent chance of encountering one unexpectedly).

- ✔ **Guided or on your own:** Most people don't focus on black bears. If you do, you need a knowledgeable floatplane guide to find them reliably (see the list in the following section).

- ✔ **ID notes:** Black bears are usually pure black, but they can come in many other colors (even blue or white); you can be sure of distinguishing a black bear from a brown bear by noting its smoother back, bigger ears, and long, straight nose.

Brown bear (grizzly)

Also known as the grizzly bear when found inland, brown bears are among the largest and most ferocious of all land mammals, and among the most exciting to see. More than 98 percent of the U.S. brown bear population is in Alaska.

 ✔ **Size:** Up to 9 ft. tall when standing; normally 250 to 900 pounds, with a maximum of 1,400 pounds.

 ✔ **Where to find them:** Denali National Park (see Chapter 19), Katmai National Park (see Chapter 24), Kodiak Island (see Chapter 24), near Homer (see Chapter 16), and Admiralty Island near Juneau (see Chapter 20).

 ✔ **Easy or hard to spot:** Can be easy. Certain surefire spots on salmon streams predictably gather many huge bears, but all are expensive to get to ($400 per person and up). Grizzly sightings are common but not assured on Denali National Park bus rides for much less money; these animals are the smaller inland ones, under 500 pounds.

 ✔ **Guided or on your own:** Denali and Katmai national parks are the on-your-own options (see Chapters 19 and 24). Other choices are with fly-in guides — in Anchorage, **Rust's Flying Service** (☎ 800-544-2299; www.flyrusts.com); in Kodiak, **Sea Hawk Air** (☎ 800-770-4295; www.seahawkair.com); in Juneau, **Alaska Fly 'N' Fish Charters** (☎ 907-790-2120; www.alaskabyair.com).

 ✔ **ID notes:** Brown bears are generally larger than black bears and have a humped back and smaller ears.

Caribou

Alaska's barren-ground caribou are genetically identical to reindeer but were never domesticated as reindeer were in Europe. For many Alaska Natives, their huge herds remain an essential source of food and hides.

 ✔ **Size:** 4 ft. tall; 200 to 600 pounds.

 ✔ **Where to find them:** On broad tundra areas where you can see a long way, for example, along northern Interior highways, such as the Richardson, Dalton, or Denali (see Chapter 18); in Denali National Park (see Chapter 19); and in the Arctic (see Chapter 23).

 ✔ **Easy or hard to spot:** Hard. Migrations of tens of thousands of animals take place in remote country that few visitors reach. Near the road system, caribou are more scattered and they're shy of humans. You need some luck.

 ✔ **Guided or on your own:** Backcountry treks sometimes observe caribou migrations in remote regions of Alaska, but that's for the highly committed; for most of us, the best chance is the Denali National Park shuttle-bus ride.

 ✔ **ID notes:** Unlike other Alaska deer (including moose), caribou prefer open country and travel in groups, sometimes in herds of many thousands.

Dall sheep

These sheep, which look like smaller versions of bighorn, stay in high, rocky places, where their incredible agility keeps them safe from predators.

- ✔ **Size:** 3 ft. tall at the shoulder; 150 to 300 pounds.

- ✔ **Where to find them:** Dall sheep live in high, craggy mountains over much of Alaska, but they're usually difficult to spot. The notable exception is on the cliffs along the Seward Highway near Anchorage (see Chapter 15), where they often venture near the road.

- ✔ **Easy or hard to spot:** Generally hard, but often easy on the Seward Highway near Anchorage.

- ✔ **Guided or on your own:** Just keep your eyes on the high cliffs and keep checking white spots you see with your binoculars; no guided option is available.

- ✔ **ID notes:** Mountain goats use the same habitat as Dall sheep; the goats have straighter horns and shaggier bodies.

Humpback whales

Behaviors such as feeding by lunging through the surface and leaping completely out of the water make the huge humpback among the most spectacular of whales to watch. I've seen leaping humpbacks many times from a sea kayak, from a small boat, and from shore. In Alaska, you can find them reliably, in beautiful settings, and without many other boats around.

- ✔ **Size:** 45 ft. long; 45 tons.

- ✔ **Where to find them:** Whales usually show up in Sitka Sound near Sitka and in Glacier Bay (see Chapter 22), and less reliably in Resurrection Bay and Kenai Fjords National Park near Seward (see Chapter 16) and in Prince William Sound near Whittier (see Chapter 15).

- ✔ **Easy or hard to spot:** Easy, if you're willing to invest some time and money. For your best chance of success on any particular day, you have to spend some money on a tour-boat ride; budget $90 to $175 per person. Seeing humpbacks from a sea kayak requires a bigger commitment of time and money, plus a little of your own effort. Spotting them from shore is hit or miss.

- ✔ **Guided or on your own:** Booking a whale-watching boat ride a few days ahead is easy, and it's even possible the day of the outing. For tours from Whittier, Seward, Juneau, or Sitka, see Chapters 15, 16, 20, and 22.

- ✔ **ID notes:** The shape of the humpback's back and small dorsal fin are a giveaway when you're familiar with the sight. The whales also have white fins up to 14 ft. long that they use to slap the water.

Moose

In winter, when they move to the lowlands, Alaska's abundant moose can be pests, blocking roadways and eating expensive shrubbery. In the summer, they're a little more elusive, often standing in forest ponds eating the weeds from the bottom or pruning willows from stream banks or disturbed roadsides.

- ✓ **Size:** Length 7 to 10 ft.; 800 to 1,600 pounds.

- ✓ **Where to find them:** Moose live over much of Alaska but show up most reliably in the Interior and Southcentral regions. Your best chance of seeing one is along a road in wet, brushy country.

- ✓ **Easy or hard to spot:** Seeing a moose by design is hard, but it's a rare week that goes by at our home in Anchorage when we don't run across at least one.

- ✓ **Guided or on your own:** Guided viewing is not available, but you never know when you may see a moose.

- ✓ **ID notes:** Alaska moose can grow larger than horses, with brown, shaggy hides; bulbous noses; and heavy antlers.

Musk ox

The musk ox may be the strangest animal you'll ever see: a big, shaggy mop of a thing that seems to glide slowly over the tundra. The wool, said to be one of Earth's warmest fibers, is gathered from the tundra and knitted by Alaska Native women into exquisite garments.

- ✓ **Size:** 4 to 5 ft. tall at the shoulder; 400 to 800 pounds.

- ✓ **Where to find them:** Along the roads that radiate across the tundra from Nome (see Chapter 23).

- ✓ **Easy or hard to spot:** Getting to Nome is expensive; after you're there, finding a musk ox by car isn't too difficult.

- ✓ **Guided or on your own:** You can rent a car in Nome to explore the surrounding roads. Private guided tours often can be arranged; ask at the visitor center.

- ✓ **ID notes:** If you see an animal that looks like it wandered out of a science-fiction movie, you're probably observing a musk ox.

Orca (killer whale)

The starkly defined black-and-white patches of the orca seem painted by their creator to reflect the speed, agility, and fierceness of the ocean's top predator. You can easily feel envy when a well-organized family pod of orcas passes by your boat in calm procession.

✔ **Size:** 23 to 27 ft. long; 10 tons.

✔ **Where to find them:** Resurrection Bay from Seward (see Chapter 16), Prince William Sound from Whittier (see Chapter 15), and waters near Juneau and Sitka (see Chapter 20).

✔ **Easy or hard to spot:** Moderate. Orcas aren't as predictable in their feeding locations as humpbacks, but good tour-boat captains often know where to find the resident pod.

✔ **Guided or on your own:** You'll need to join a tour-boat cruise from Whittier, Seward, Juneau, or Sitka. If seeing killer whales is your priority, choose a smaller charter to focus on that goal.

✔ **ID notes:** Look for the tall, black dorsal fin.

Polar bear

The polar bear is among the scariest and most dramatic of all animals. Seeing one is a rare and unforgettable experience shared by few Alaskans and even fewer visitors. Polar bears, classified as marine mammals, live on the pack ice, north of Alaska, venturing ashore only at certain times.

✔ **Size:** 8 to 10 ft. tall when standing on hind legs; 400 to 1,200 pounds, with a maximum of 1,500 pounds.

✔ **Where to find them:** The only places for visitors to see polar bears are the villages on the Arctic Ocean coast, the largest of which is Barrow (see Chapter 23). With luck, you may find them feeding on bones left by Eskimos after whale hunts.

✔ **Easy or hard to spot:** Hard. Going to Barrow is expensive, and you must arrive at the right time (mid-Oct through June); even then, you need good luck to see a bear. The tour operators are casual businesses (see Chapter 23).

✔ **Guided or on your own:** You'd better hope you don't see a polar bear on your own! **Arctic Air Expeditions** (☎ **907-694-4294;** www. alaskapolarbeartours.com) takes visitors to arctic viewing sites from Fairbanks by plane starting at $2,423 per person for an overnight, based on a group of five.

✔ **ID notes:** The polar bear is unmistakable.

Puffin (and other alcids)

The horned and tufted puffin are the most delightful of seabirds to encounter, with their large, brightly colored beaks and comedic movements. When you enter their habitat of seaside cliffs, you also find many other *alcids,* fascinating birds that live only at sea.

✔ **Size:** 14 in. long; 1¼ pounds.

✔ **Where to find them:** Kenai Fjords National Park and Homer (see Chapter 16), and Sitka (see Chapter 22).

✔ **Easy or hard to spot:** Easy during the summer season on a boat tour to the bird colonies.

✔ **Guided or on your own:** For a good chance of seeing puffins, you need to get to the rocky, offshore bird colonies on Alaska's southern coast. A tour boat is the best opportunity, with Kenai Fjords National Park leading the list (see Chapter 16). You also can see puffins on a sea-kayaking tour (see "Sea-kayaking," earlier in this chapter), with less certainty of success.

✔ **ID notes:** If you see a bird that looks like a small penguin with a toucan's beak, you've probably found a puffin. Horned puffins are the more familiar kind; tufted puffins have tufts of feathers curling back from their heads.

Sea otter

The charming sea otter is quite common in coastal Alaska, rarely warranting a second glance from locals. Otters usually put up with close inspection as they float on their backs, using their tummies as tables for shellfish or to carry their young.

✔ **Size:** Up to 4 ft. long; 40 to 90 pounds.

✔ **Where to find them:** All coastal waters off rocky shores; most common in Prince William Sound (see Chapter 15) and near Sitka (see Chapter 22), Juneau (see Chapter 20), Seward (see Chapter 16), Homer (see Chapter 16), Kodiak (see Chapter 24), and other shoreside communities.

✔ **Easy or hard to spot:** Easy. Often you don't even need to leave the dock, and you can expect a good look on a tour boat or sea-kayak ride.

✔ **Guided or on your own:** Otters live in the ocean, where you need help to get to them. Any of the tour boats or sea-kayaking guides in this book can help you spot them.

✔ **ID notes:** You can tell otters from the seals and sea lions that are common in the same waters by their legs (the others have flippers); even when the legs aren't showing, more of the otter shows above the surface.

Wolf

Unlike other parts of the United States, wild wolf populations in Alaska are plentiful, yet the animals are shy around humans, and sightings are a rare treat.

✔ **Size:** 3½ to 6½ ft. long; 75 to 145 pounds.

✔ **Where to find them:** Denali National Park (see Chapter 19) and other mountain tundra areas with long views, such as along the

Richardson or Denali highways (see Chapter 18). Wolves live all over Alaska, but they're hard to see in brush or trees.

✔ **Easy or hard to spot:** Very hard. Wolves don't like to show themselves. You need to be able to see a long way to have any chance of sighting a pack.

✔ **Guided or on your own:** Any wolf sightings are likely to be fleeting, lucky glimpses. Although wolf numbers are low in Denali National Park, conditions on the shuttle-bus rides are good for sightings.

✔ **ID notes:** I've seen wolves, yes, but I've heard them more often; listen for the howl during quiet outings in the evening, such as while hiking or cross-country skiing.

Choosing an Activity-Based Escorted Tour

If scheduling an outdoor vacation in Alaska on your own seems intimidating, an easier way is available: Book an outdoor escorted tour, a group exploration of some of the state's best activities and wildlife-viewing with a guide to take care of all the details. These trips are escorted samplers of places and activities, with everything included except your travel to the starting point. The companies that offer them know that the itineraries work and have polished the outings along the way to appeal to the majority of their guests. On the downside, you don't get to choose each stop or linger longer than the group. (For more on escorted tours, see Chapter 6.)

✔ **Alaska Wildland Adventures** (☎ 800-334-8730; www.alaska wildland.com) pioneered the "Alaska safari," a highway tour from lodge to lodge, with fishing, rafting, wildlife-viewing, and the like scheduled along the way. Alaska Wildland owns an outstanding fishing lodge on the Kenai River and another on a remote lake, in addition to other high-quality facilities. Trips concentrate on Southcentral Alaska and Denali. Guides tend to be young and enthusiastic. Packages include choices for varying interests, as well as tours aimed at families with teens and even children as young as 6. It's not a cheap way to travel, however; an 11-day safari costs about $6,000 per person, although shorter trips cost less.

✔ **Mountain Travel Sobek** (☎ 800-586-1911; www.mtsobek.com) offers trips in Southeast Alaska similar to those offered by Alaska Wildland Adventures for comparable per-day prices. Mountain Travel Sobek calls them "Inn-to-Inn Tours." The company is best known for more rigorous outdoor adventures and has superb guides for activities.

Nine Tragic Deaths to Avoid in Alaska's Outdoors

Violent death is the first thing that some urbanites think of when they contemplate going out into nature. As it happens, some rural Alaskans share the same thoughts when they contemplate going to a big city. (I remember as a child being told by friends, and believing, that New York City had "blocks of death" — normal-looking blocks where, if you set foot there, immediate assassination was virtually guaranteed.)

 In Alaska, we have no blocks of death, or trails of death (or whatever the wilderness version would be). Some activities are inherently hazardous, such as white-water rafting or snowmobiling. (Any time you have to sign a release, it probably means you're taking a risk.) Other than those obvious exceptions, however, you encounter danger mainly if you behave foolishly or get in over your head. Consider this safety rule number one: If you don't know what you're doing, you need to be with someone who does, such as the experienced guides I recommend earlier in this chapter.

I feel safer in the Alaska wilderness than anywhere else, but in the spirit of the paranoia I remember from those "blocks of death," here's a list of safety tips, arranged to begin with everyone's worst fantasies of disaster and work down from there.

Getting eaten by a bear (and such)

Bear-mauling is probably the least likely way for your vacation to end. Deaths from dog bites are much more common, for example. (Don't worry: It's an example. I'm almost certain you won't die from a dog bite either.) But you still need to be prepared for bears and know how to avoid being trampled by moose.

 The first rule of defense is simple: *Don't attract bears.* It's not that hard:

- ✔ Keep your food and trash in airtight containers when you're camping. (When car-camping, the vehicle's trunk works.)

- ✔ Keep a clean camp, avoiding fish odors or other food residue near where you're staying.

- ✔ Never keep food, pungent items, or clothing that smells like fish in your tent.

- ✔ Clean fish away from your campsite.

When walking through brush or thick trees or hiking at night, make lots of noise to avoid surprising a bear or moose. You can sing, carry on a loud conversation, or periodically holler, "Hey, bear!" At all costs, avoid coming between a bear and its cubs or a bear and food. Here's one safety tip that's the same in New York as in Alaska: If a mugger wants your wallet, give it to him; if a bear wants the fish you just caught, consider it his. Moose also are strongly defensive of their young and can attack if they feel you're getting too close.

 Most people hurt by moose are in urban settings — they're quite common in Anchorage — so don't assume that because you meet a moose on a paved path he's going to step politely aside. Wait at a safe distance for the moose to move, or go around or return the way you came. Don't approach the moose for a picture. Human contact stresses moose and they can snap and attack someone.

 If you see a bear, stop, wave your arms, and make noise. If you're with others, group together so that you look larger to the bear. Don't run, tempting the bear to chase; depart by slowly backing away, at an angle if possible, so that you're not going directly away from the bear. If the bear follows, stop and begin making noise again.

We sometimes carry a shotgun loaded with slugs for protection in bear country, but that's not practical for most visitors. A good alternative is a bear-deterrent spray, available in a canister for about $45. Buy the holster, too, because the spray is useless unless you can quickly get at it. You shoot the spray to produce a burning fog of capsaicin pepper between you and a threatening bear. Transportation Security Administration (TSA) regulations essentially prohibit the product on the airlines, even in checked baggage. (Ironically, you can check guns and ammunition.) Unless you can borrow one, you'll have to buy it here and give it away before you leave. They're available in all sporting goods stores. You can research and order pepper spray direct from **Counter Assault** (☎ **800-695-3394;** www.counterassault.com).

Drowning in freezing water

Because of the cool temperatures, unpredictable weather, and cold water, going out on the ocean or floating down a fast river is more hazardous in Alaska than in most other places. You should go only with an experienced, licensed operator unless you really know what you're doing.

 There's little margin for error if you fall into the water or capsize. The cold water can cause sudden shock, which leads to drowning. If you make it past the first couple of minutes without panic or shock, you have limited time to get out and get warm before the onset of *hypothermia* (a cooling of the body that can lead to death). A life jacket can keep you afloat during the period of shock, but it won't keep you alive in 40°F (4°C) water. If you're sea-kayaking or canoeing, stay close to shore and take dry bags (also called *float bags*) with everything you need to quickly warm a person who gets wet (see the following section).

Succumbing to exposure

Hypothermia, also called exposure, is a potentially fatal lowering of core body temperature. It's most dangerous when it sneaks up on you, perhaps in 50°F (10°C) weather on a damp mountain hike or rainy boating trip. Dress in material (whether wool or synthetic) that keeps its warmth when wet, choosing layers to avoid chilling perspiration. Make sure you eat well and avoid exhaustion. Keep chocolates or other energy foods in reserve.

Hypothermia's symptoms include

✔ Having cold extremities

✔ Being uncommunicative

✔ Displaying poor judgment or coordination

✔ Fighting sleepiness

A shivering victim still has the ability to warm up if better dressed. A lack of shivering means the body has gone beyond that point and you need to add warmth from the outside and from warm drinks. Get indoors; force down hot liquids (except in cases of shock, when the victim could choke); and, if shelter is unavailable, apply body heat from another person, skin on skin, in a sleeping bag.

Getting eaten alive by bugs

Actually, you can't die this way. Alaska has no snakes, poisonous spiders, or (at this writing) West Nile virus. But you may wish you were dead when the mosquitoes or black flies swarm during warmer weather. The bugs can be too intense for anyone to stand. As a reporter, I once covered the story of a man who threw a rock through a bank's plate-glass window so that he could get arrested and get away from the mosquitoes.

Effective insect repellent is a necessity, as is having a refuge from the bugs, such as a tent or cabin. Mosquitoes can bite through light fabric. In the Interior and the Arctic, where mosquitoes are worst, we use jackets of tightly woven fabric with net hoods, which you can buy in Alaska. Benadryl tablets or other antihistamines often relieve swelling caused by mosquito bites.

Getting lost

Even experienced people get lost. Hiking off-trail or voyaging in a canoe, raft, or kayak, you quickly find that one mountain looks a lot like another. If you're unsure of your navigational skills, maps, or equipment, don't go. Beyond those basics, the most important safety precautions are to go with another person and to make sure someone knows where to look for you if you don't come back. For extended trips (more than a day hike on a trail), leave a written trip plan with a person who will call rescuers if you're late. At the very least, leave a note in your car indicating where you're bound. Cellphones sometimes work near towns and some highways, but not reliably, and there is no coverage beyond populated areas.

Iridium satellite phones work outdoors anywhere on Earth. You can rent them from **Roadpost** (☎ **888-290-1616** or 905-272-5665; www.road post.com), starting at $9 a day, plus $1.80 a minute, and a $35 delivery fee — cheap if it saves your life, but not as good as knowing where you are and what you're doing. Roadpost sends you the phone by overnight express, and customer service is excellent. However, the phones are finicky, and they only work outdoors.

Drowning while crossing a river

Hiking off trails in Alaska's backcountry, such as at Denali, can require crossing rivers without bridges. Wading a small stream may be safe, but use great caution in substantial flows: You can easily get in trouble. Often, the water is glacial melt, barely above freezing and heavy with silt that makes it opaque. The silt can fill your pockets and drag you down. If in doubt, don't do it.

If you do decide to cross, unbuckle your pack, keep your shoes on, face upstream, use a heavy walking stick if possible, and rig a safety line. Carry children or have them follow next to an adult who breaks the full force of the current.

Keeling over from bad clams

Don't eat mussels, clams, or scallops you pick or dig from the seashore unless you know they're safe to eat. Generally, that means you need some specific and reliable local knowledge. There is a government program to assure shellfish safety, but the only easily accessible beaches it affects are on the eastern shore of Kachemak Bay. The risk is paralytic shellfish poisoning (PSP), a potentially fatal malady caused by a naturally occurring toxin. It causes total paralysis that includes your breathing. A victim may be kept alive with mouth-to-mouth resuscitation until medical help is obtained. For more information, check the Web site of the **Alaska Department of Environmental Conservation** (www.alaska.gov/dec/eh/fss/seafood/psphome.htm, or go to www.alaska.gov and search for "PSP").

Getting seasick

Seasickness sometimes feels like it will be fatal, and it always kills the fun of a boat trip. Here are tips that will work in Alaska or anywhere else your stomach can't keep up with you:

- ✔ Abstain from alcohol the night before, eat a light breakfast, and limit coffee.

- ✔ Sit low and near the middle of the boat, away from odors and with your eyes on the horizon — and no reading.

- ✔ Alternative-medicine cures, such as ginger or acupressure, have no proven benefits but work for many of those who believe in them. (A placebo, such as a sugar pill, is 40 percent effective with seasickness if the patient has faith.)

- ✔ The very best cure is the scopolamine skin patch, available only by prescription, which lasts up to three days.

✔ The main choices for over-the-counter drugs are meclizine (brand names Bonine, Antivert, or Dramamine II) and dimenhydrinate (Dramamine Original). Both are drowsiness-inducing antihistamines, but there's less of that side-effect with the newer meclizine.

To be effective, the drugs need at least two hours to get through your digestive system, so you must take the pill well before you get on the boat. For best effectiveness, take a tablet before bed and another on the morning of the outing.

If you've taken nothing and you feel yourself getting seasick, there is a last-minute cure that sometimes works: Chew up the tablets but don't swallow them, holding the mush under your tongue or against your cheek. The drug is partly absorbed through the lining of the mouth.

Drinking tainted water

Unpurified river or lake water may not be safe to drink (although it won't kill you). Hand-pumped filters (available from sporting-goods stores for about $75) are the most practical way of dealing with the problem on long backcountry trips. Iodine kits and boiling also work. The danger is a protozoan cyst called *giardia lamblia,* which causes diarrhea and has been spread to thousands of water bodies all over the United States by animal droppings. You may not experience the diarrhea for a couple weeks after exposure, and then it could become chronic. If symptoms show up after you get home, tell your doctor you may have been exposed so that he can test and treat you.

Chapter 10

Booking Your Accommodations

In This Chapter

▶ Finding your lodging options

▶ Reserving in plenty of time

▶ Getting a good rate

▶ Booking online

*T*he room you sleep in isn't the most important factor in determining how much you enjoy your trip, but it certainly is close to the top of the list. Relaxing can be difficult unless you are comfortable, feel safe and clean, and have at least the amenities you're used to at home. Beyond those minimums, a room can add something to your vacation, giving you some insight into why living in Alaska is so worthwhile.

Alaska offers plenty of places that meet the first set of needs: It has all the chain hotels you already know, with the comfort and predictability that make them reassuring. But those places are guaranteed to miss on the second criteria, so I recommend very few of them. Instead, I've looked hard for lodging that can add to your experience of Alaska, and perhaps become one of its most memorable parts.

Choosing the Lodging Right for You

Authentically Alaskan accommodations come in different flavors. **Wilderness lodges** are the best, but they cost a lot ($300 or more per person, per night, all-inclusive), they're often expensive to get to, and they usually have minimum stays of three days or more (which you probably won't mind, given the investment you put into getting to the lodge). Unfortunately, most of us can't afford $2,000 or more for three nights. However, many **inns** and **bed-and-breakfasts (B&Bs)** and some **specialty hotels** also can add to your feel for Alaska, and save money over strictly anonymous accommodations. I've also included lodgings with **suites** and **cooking facilities,** even when they don't have loads of character: These can be a godsend for families or large parties. In all cases, except as noted for the wilderness lodges, the rates I quote are for a standard room with two people in it during the high season.

 Like other destinations in the United States, Alaska is going smoke-free. Some hotels still offer some smoking rooms, especially in small towns, where smoking is still common, but many B&Bs and lodges have no-smoking policies. Finding lodgings that take pets is difficult; often, those that do aren't places I would recommend.

Table 10-1 explains the price ranges I've assigned to the lodgings reviewed in this book, and what you can expect in each category.

Table 10-1	Key to Hotel Dollar Signs	
Dollar Sign(s)	*Price Range*	*What to Expect*
$	$100 or less	Stay here if saving money is your overriding concern. Expect a small hotel room in an old building, or a simple B&B room with a shared bathroom.
$$	$101–$130	In smaller Alaska towns, this rate will buy you a basic but attractive room or a good B&B room with its own bathroom. In the large cities, rooms at this price are still in the budget category.
$$$	$131–$165	You sacrifice nothing to stay here. Hotel rooms will have all the usual conveniences, perhaps in a smaller, independent establishment. B&B rooms should be well-appointed.
$$$$	$166–$210	Falling in this price range are the larger, full-service hotels, often with extra amenities and central locations. Also expect to pay this much for a luxury B&B with some special attraction or lots of extras.
$$$$$	$211 or more	The best luxury hotels charge more than this amount, as do all wilderness lodges that include meals or guiding in a single price. At elite wilderness lodges, prices can top $500 per person per night (so far beyond most travelers' reach that I haven't included any in this book).

Bed-and-breakfasts

I can offer some sensible reasons for staying at B&Bs but few reasons for avoiding them.

You don't have to worry about being stuck in Junior's room in an otherwise ordinary family home. Although you can still find some places like that, I don't list them in this book, and they're easy to steer clear of. Most B&Bs do have hosts who live there, but the rooms usually have the amenities (and twice the charm) of an ordinary hotel room, with a smaller bathroom and perhaps a small TV. These hosts are great assets when visiting a place like Alaska. They have stories to tell about bear and moose encounters (everyone has plenty of these), and they can provide lots of advice for your trip. At best, they'll make you feel like you have friends in Alaska.

The other important benefit of staying at a B&B is the significant money you'll save. Rates are often $30 to $50 less than for a comparable room in a hotel, and the inclusion of breakfast saves you another $20 (for a couple). Expect to pay about $130 per night.

If you're vacationing with kids or you have a disability, don't choose a B&B unless you first question the proprietor about whether you'll be comfortable in the rooms. B&Bs often have narrow stairs or small rooms that may not be suitable for you.

Hotels

Good, inexpensive hotel rooms can be found in Alaska's cities, but not easily and not with many choices. Instead, you'll find a variety of standard hotel rooms (with an interior hallway and the expected amenities) with a wide range of prices. At the top of the list are the luxury hotels in the larger cities, which are often found in the town's tallest buildings. These rooms usually cost more than $200 per night. The next tier down consists of good, comfortable places that are often found in smaller buildings. Some of these establishments are operated by particular owners who keep the quality top-notch. These rooms rent for $165 to $185 per night. Next are the budget lodgings, which are usually found in older buildings, with small rooms and perhaps less-desirable addresses. I've found the good ones, where dedicated people offer decent rooms for a reasonable price. They charge $120 to $140 per night.

Wilderness lodge look-alikes

Another category of hotels, which may be unique to Alaska, includes hotels impersonating wilderness lodges. A real Alaskan wilderness lodge, even a very expensive one, generally has plenty of rough edges that add to the authentic frontier atmosphere. Operating way out in the boonies, with difficult transportation, a short season, and a staff that has to live on-site, wilderness lodges have to charge enough to make it. But in recent years, some beautifully built midsize hotels and inns that are situated on the road system have taken on a wilderness-lodge persona, with good results. They cost much less than a remote lodge, although they still aren't cheap ($200–$250 double).

Knowing When to Reserve

Recent, extensive hotel construction has made rooms easier to find in Alaska cities, but not the special ones that I aim to put you into. The new rooms are all in chain hotels; if that's what you're after, your favorite brand is probably here, and you can probably book it fairly easily on the Internet or through the hotel's toll-free number a week or two ahead (see the Quick Concierge for contact information).

If you want something interesting or unique, coming to Alaska in the high season without your rooms booked a month or two in advance is unwise. You'll get a place to sleep somewhere, but you may go through plenty of trouble to find it — and it won't be anyone's first choice.

Lodgings that I recommend often book earliest because they're the best, so it makes sense to start reserving the minute you set the dates for your trip (six months should be adequate). Before June or after August, rooms are much easier to reserve; you usually can have your choice with little advance notice. The exceptions are around the Iditarod Trail Sled Dog Race, in early March, and through the winter at a pair of resorts — Alyeska Resort and Chena Hot Springs Resort (see Chapters 15 and 17, respectively) — which have wintertime peak seasons.

Finding the Best Room at the Best Rate

Some hotels publish *rack rates* (the public rates that are really their maximums) without intending to charge anyone that price. I've run into hotel managers who try to keep the rack rate a secret, because they know it's outrageous and nobody pays it anyway: Everyone who comes in the door qualifies for a discount. But other lodgings, especially smaller establishments and budget places, really mean the rates they publish. Here are some tips on requesting a better rate and knowing when not to try.

Shop early for peak times

As your date nears and rooms book up, you have fewer choices, and that means you have to pay more. If you're coming to Alaska between mid-June and mid-August, January is not too early to be on the phone shopping among lodgings for the best prices and accommodations. Proprietors love early bookings and may be willing to compete for your business, especially when you let them know you're shopping around for the best price.

Travel off-peak

Rates crash like a bear stock market when the season starts winding down; big, luxury hotels often charge less than half their peak rates during the off season, putting them in competition with the cheapest budget lodgings. Rooms stand empty, so you can show up at the desk and ask for their best deal, ready to walk next door if they don't go low enough. You can sometimes use these same tactics to get killer deals at the big, package-tour hotels at Denali and elsewhere on the day of your stay, even during high season, because gaps between groups sometimes leave them with blocks of empty rooms. But you'll be gambling if you count on this happening.

Ask for discounts

Hotels (but not usually B&Bs and small inns) usually offer various discounts for people with travel-club or other memberships, and some offer automatic discounts to anyone who asks. I've tried telling reservationists that I want the corporate or AAA discount, even though I don't qualify; sometimes they laugh and say, "Sure," and other times I just get a "No." It never hurts to ask. You're more likely to be able to dicker this way with a small hotel where the person you're talking to actually has some authority rather than with a large chain where you're talking to someone at a call center. Some small places don't have discount programs, but you still can ask for a discount, especially if the rate isn't already low. For example, B&Bs sometimes will knock something off the price when you stay more than one night or when you offer to pay cash. But don't count on it, and don't push it when they say no, because you can sour your relationship from the start.

Don't stop with the Internet

Using Web sites to shop for prices is great, but you may be able to do better if you follow up on the establishment's own Web site or call directly. Sometimes you can get a Web special, extra airline mileage, or other deals by contacting a hotel yourself (this works for rental cars and airline tickets, too). Check out the "Booking Rooms Online" section, later in this chapter, for more helpful info.

Book a package tour

Package tours, whether escorted or unescorted, often offer significant savings over the a la carte approach to booking hotels. The big hotels at Denali National Park have set their rates very high to accentuate the value they give customers on their escorted packages, because these customers make up virtually the entire clientele. (See Chapter 6 for more about booking packages.)

Don't worry about it

If the thought of all this checking and calling and dickering makes you tired, don't fret over it. Some people ruin their vacations worrying about how much they've paid for things (I know — I get letters from some of them). The point is: Did you have a good time? Did you stay within your budget? If so, you got a good deal.

Booking Rooms Online

The Internet is a great way to find out about a hotel or B&B and to check availability and going rates. Virtually every hotel and B&B has its own Web site, and you can discover a lot about an establishment from what you see there (and from what you don't). But making a choice without knowing more than what the proprietor wants to tell you can lead to disappointment. I've checked out all the accommodations listed in this book, but if you want to find other choices with guidance from people who've actually been there, use a travel Web site that offers user ratings. The sites are agents for many hotels at once, listing many more options than any travel book can, and sometimes you can even get a better rate from a third-party Web site than from the establishment itself.

Because travel Web sites are not discriminating in the accommodations they list, you can easily book yourself into a dive if you don't read the user comments. The sites also have had problems in Alaska with listing places together that are geographically unreasonable alternatives, although they seem to be improving on that point. To spot-check them, I reviewed Expedia (www.expedia.com), Hotels.com, Orbitz (www.orbitz.com), and Travelocity (www.travelocity.com), searching for hotel rooms in Anchorage for the same span of nights. As always with these sites, the choices and rates that came up were similar but not identical, with one or two great deals that you could find only on one or two sites. All four sites have user ratings, which flagged the bad choices and seemed accurate for the good ones, too, but Orbitz didn't have enough ratings for that system to work well. Don't book a room without recent, authentic user ratings to back up your choice, unless the hotel is part of a chain that you already trust. Few of the best B&Bs and interesting small inns were listed on any of the sites.

For those places with local color, try an Alaska-based Web site. Before discussing lodging choices in cities and regions covered elsewhere in the book, I provide Web sites that link with associations or bookers of local B&Bs or small inns. The best site for these places on a statewide basis is **Alaska.org.**

Chapter 11

Catering to Special Travel Needs or Interests

In This Chapter

▶ Bringing the kids with you to Alaska

▶ Going to Alaska as a senior citizen

▶ Accessing Alaska if you're a traveler with disabilities

▶ Finding gay-friendly resources

A lot of visitors have been going to Alaska for a long time. By now, the place is pretty much ready with services that cater to just about everyone. This chapter offers some advice on finding and using those services.

Vacationing in Alaska with Children

Even though my name appears on the title page, I think of my travel books as a family project. When I researched my first Alaska travel book, my son, Robin, was 3, and my daughter, Julia, was 6 months. Today, Robin is 19, Julia is 15, Joseph is 11, and Becky is 9. You may run into us at a campground or on a boat dock anywhere in Alaska as we travel to research our next guidebook. (If we see you carrying the book, we'll introduce ourselves.) Yes, it's a great job, and bringing the family along is the best part.

Alaska's magnificent scenery is something that even young children can understand and appreciate. Also, an Alaska vacation is largely spent outdoors, which is where kids like to be. Children never get enough ferry-riding, boating, or camping, and the older ones especially enjoy hiking, canoeing, sea-kayaking, skiing, and dog-mushing. Alaska makes good sense for families if you do your homework.

Tackling the challenges

Alaska does have drawbacks as a family destination. It's expensive. Some activities, such as flightseeing and tour-boat cruises, tend to have less-than-generous children's discounts and cost too much for most families. Hotel rooms and restaurant meals in Alaska cost a lot for a sizable family (though I include some family-friendly listings through-out this book and mark them with a Kid Friendly icon). Often, bed-and-breakfast rooms are too small for a family. Although camping solves many of these problems, getting your camping gear to Alaska is a logisti-cal challenge. For tips on doing so, see Chapter 12. (I don't review camp-grounds in this book. A book that covers all of Alaska's campgrounds in detail is *Traveler's Guide to Alaskan Camping,* by Mike and Terri Church [Rolling Homes Press].)

Most parents know to plan the necessities, such as food and lodging, when traveling with kids, but for an Alaska trip you also should think carefully about your itinerary and activities. Alaska's highways are long, and children require a gradual approach to covering a lot of ground. They also need time to play, explore, and rest. Children often don't enjoy wildlife-watching. Searching for the animals takes a long time, and when you do find them, they're usually off in the distance. Kids 7 and under often don't have the visual skills or patience to pick out the ani-mals from the landscape and can get bored quickly, even when they can see the animals. The "Keeping kids happy on the road" section, later in this chapter, includes some ideas that I've picked up over years of trav-eling the state with my kids that may help keep your kids engaged during your trip.

Though your kids will likely love the outdoors as much as you will, don't overtax them with excessively long walks and hiking trips. Keep track of the longest hike you've managed without excessive whining, and then try to extend that record just a little bit each time out. If your kids aren't accustomed to hiking, try taking them on a few hikes at home to help them (and you) build stamina for the trip. Short sea-kayaking excur-sions, on the other hand, are great for children who are old enough, riding in the front of a double-seat boat with a parent in back. In prac-tice, the age limit depends on the outfitter and your child's level of responsibility.

If you're like most families, you'll be getting on each other's nerves after a few weeks on the road. Our family makes it through those tough moments by leaving time for low-key kid activities monitored by one adult, such as beachcombing and playing in the park, while the other adult splits off for a museum visit, shopping, or a special, more expen-sive activity. Of course, if you want to preserve your relationship, you'll have to be scrupulously fair about who gets to go flightseeing and who has to stay behind and change diapers, because you won't have my all-purpose excuse: research.

Finding a family-friendly package

I wouldn't recommend a typical escorted package trip for a family with young children. A scripted tour on a motor coach will bore any child who needs activity and spontaneity to be happy. Better to get the kids outdoors — which is possible with a specially designed package.

Alaska Wildland Adventures (☎ 800-334-8730; www.alaskawildland. com) has various trips for kids as young as 12, and can take children as young as 6 for a package of day activities based at its Kenai Riverside Lodge. The package, called the "Kenai Explorer," is flexible in length and geared to families, offering games and kid-oriented guides. The shortest, two-night, three-day version is $995 adults, $900 kids 7 and over. **Mountain Travel Sobek** (☎ 800-586-1911; www.mtsobek.com) takes children as young as 12 on some of its extended Southeast Alaska sea-kayaking trips, which start at $995 for three days and two nights, and welcomes younger children on its non-camping trips.

In addition, the cruise-ship industry is courting families, and many ships offer fun activities for children. Some cruise lines even have programs that take the kids off your hands for a while — something that both children and parents enjoy. (See Chapter 8 for cruise lines that offer kid-oriented programs.)

Keeping kids happy on the road

My wife and I have taken trips with our children that no sane person would attempt — all over Alaska and all over the United States, for as long as seven weeks at a time; we've even spent two weeks all alone in the remote wilderness with three kids and a baby. We've enjoyed all our trips. One reason, besides having great kids, is that we've learned the importance of adjusting our plans and our behavior to our children's needs. Here are some of our discoveries:

✔ **Keep consistent mealtimes.** This is the most important factor to keeping your crew happy. Carry food with you in case you can't make it to a restaurant when your regular lunch, dinner, or afternoon snack time arrives. Make no exceptions. Hungry people get grumpy and irrational, and then everything falls apart.

✔ **Don't compromise on nutrition when you're traveling.** If you normally eat junk all the time, okay. But if you have a healthy diet at home, don't stop now. With the stress of traveling, your kids need good food more than ever. Pass on the burger in a box in favor of a healthy, real restaurant meal or a picnic.

✔ **Choose rooms with cooking facilities.** You'll go crazy if you eat three meals a day in restaurants with children for your whole trip. You can save money and time — *and* reduce stress — by staying in for breakfast and an occasional lunch or dinner.

✔ **Remember Alaska's long summer days.** We don't sweat bedtime in the summer, and neither do most of the Alaskan parents we know. The Alaskan sky stays light late at night and everyone is energized. Getting to bed early is hard for kids and adults.

✔ **Leave time for fun and spontaneity.** Often, when driving a highway in Alaska, you may see a place where you're tempted to just jump out of the car and romp in the heather. What a shame if you're in a rush to get somewhere and can't stop.

✔ **Don't overdo it.** One big activity a day is enough.

✔ **Bring toys and activities** — but just a few — and then buy more as you go. Hold back some fresh toys for tough times. New toys are a lot more fun than old ones. Your toy bag also can include crayons, pencils, pads of paper, stickers, pipe cleaners, cards, magnetic checkers, picture books, coloring books, activity books, and maps. Bring little prizes to make car games more exciting. If you're careful, you can fit all this in one small backpack a child can carry.

✔ **Consider entertainment.** Bring an inexpensive personal music player with headphones for each child with a collection of music or recorded stories. Kids enjoy listening to something that no one else can hear. Buy some new audiobooks to break out on the way when the going gets rough. What about video entertainment? Our kids do watch iPods and occasionally DVDs on long, routine drives, but I don't think I'd do that on a scenic drive where looking out the window is a big reason you're traveling.

✔ **Craft a family journal.** Make a journal of your trip by buying postcards everywhere you go (even gas stations) for your children to put in a cheap photo album or otherwise make into a book. They can write on the back of the postcards, or draw pictures, and put them in the album. Rearranging, editing, and showing off the book uses up a lot of time. And when you get home, it's a good souvenir.

✔ **Create a personal journal.** Our children have always kept journals every night when traveling or at our summer cabin, even when they were too young to write. (They drew pictures and dictated words.) At the beginning of the summer, each child picks out a good bound journal that they really value. Journal time is a wonderfully quiet evening ritual and a good prelude to bedtime. My wife and I are always surprised at which experiences the children think are important enough to mention, and their teachers are pleased at how their writing skills improve over the summer. In the fall, the kids proudly show off their work to their grandparents and classes at school. For us, the old journals have become treasured keepsakes.

✔ **Take this time to get to know your kids again.** Talk to them, read to them, and take advantage of learning about a new place together.

Traveling as Senior Citizens

People 65 and over make up 25 percent of all visitors to Alaska. Most of the people coming over the road or by ferry are retired, presumably because they have the time to make the trip. So, there's nothing "special" about an older visitor to Alaska; indeed, whatever way you come, you'll often find yourself with people your own age. Consequently, facilities are used to dealing with senior citizens, and they won't be surprised to hear your request for reduced-admission prices for seniors, which many Alaska attractions offer.

The National Park Service offers a senior free admission and discount program to those 62 and over under the ungainly name **America the Beautiful–National Parks and Federal Recreational Lands Pass–Senior Pass** (formerly called the **Golden Age Passport**). The pass is good for lifetime free entrance to national parks, monuments, historic sites, recreation areas, and national wildlife refuges for a one-time processing fee of $10. If you have a pass, make sure to mention it when making shuttle or camping reservations at Denali National Park, because otherwise park attendants will automatically add the entrance fee to your bill. The pass does not give a discount on concession-offered services such as the Denali shuttle. Buy the pass in person at any park that charges an entrance fee. For more information, go to www.nps.gov/fees_passes.htm or call the **U.S. Geological Survey (☎ 888-275-8747)**, which issues the passes.

Most towns have a senior center where you'll find activities and help with any special needs. The **Anchorage Senior Activity Center,** 1300 E. 19th Ave. (☎ **907-258-7823;** www.anchorageseniorcenter.org), offers guidance for visitors, as well as use of the restaurant and fitness room, a gift shop, and a chance to meet locals. Dances are held most Friday nights.

Many reliable agencies and organizations target the 50-plus market. **Road Scholar (☎ 800-454-5768;** www.roadscholar.org), formerly called Elderhostel, operates many weeklong Alaska learning vacations for groups of people 55 and over. A catalog of tour and program options is available on the Web site. **ElderTreks (☎ 800-741-7956;** www.elder treks.com) offers small-group yacht cruises in Alaska to off-the-beaten-path ports, with sea-kayaking and hiking in remote spots, as well as adventure travel to many destinations around the world for travelers 50 and over.

Accessing Alaska: Advice for Travelers with Disabilities

Today, finding a hotel without rooms accessible for people with disabilities is rare, and even some B&Bs have made the necessary adjustments. The results often are the best rooms in the house. Make sure to ask for the special rooms when making reservations, and question smaller establishments closely about exactly what *accessible* means to them.

People with permanent disabilities can get a free lifetime pass to national parks and many other federal public lands and a 50 percent discount on some camping fees and the like. Apply in person at any facility (such as a park that charges an entrance fee). You'll need to show proof of a medically determined disability. Other details (including the program's absurdly long name) are the same as those listed for the senior pass in the previous section (except this one ends with "Access Pass," instead of "Senior Pass").

Resources for Gays and Lesbians

Anchorage, Juneau, and Fairbanks have active gay and lesbian communities. In Anchorage, **Identity** (www.identityinc.org) offers referrals, publishes a newsletter called *Northview,* sponsors activities throughout the year, and operates a gay and lesbian helpline (☎ **888-901-9876**). The June Pridefest includes a parade and picnic, among other events. The **Gay and Lesbian Community Center** of Anchorage is at 336 E. 5th Ave. (☎ **907-929-4528**).

Gays and lesbians can find some Alaska B&Bs and tours specifically marketing to them. For example, **Olivia Travel** (☎ **800-631-6277**; www.olivia.com) typically brings a lesbian cruise to Alaska each summer, with well-known entertainers onboard. In Fairbanks, **Out in Alaska** (☎ **877-347-9958**; www.outinalaska.com) is a small company specializing in outdoor tours and backcountry trips for gays and lesbians.

Chapter 12

Taking Care of the Remaining Details

In This Chapter

▶ Buying travel and medical insurance

▶ Reserving popular activities in advance

▶ Knowing what to pack

▶ Getting your outdoor stuff to Alaska

▶ Staying in touch by Internet and cellphone

▶ Keeping abreast of airline security

Ready to go? Have you asked someone to feed the cat?

The little details can be the ones that trip you up. For example, I've created a conundrum by suggesting throughout this book that you do a lot outdoors in Alaska but also recommending that most visitors fly. So how do you get your gear to Alaska on a plane when it won't fit in the overhead bin or under the seat? I have some handy solutions to this problem, along with some other practical information to help you out.

Playing It Safe with Travel and Medical Insurance

Several kinds of travel insurance are available, ranging in value from essential to rip-off; I cover the differences in the following sections. Buying any sort of travel insurance is easy: Go to www.insuremytrip. com; the site allows travelers to get quotes from many insurance companies at once by providing the dates of the trip, the amount and type of coverage, and the age of the travelers. To contact a firm directly, try one of the following: **Access America** (☎ 866-807-3982; www.access america.com), **Travel Guard** (☎ 800-826-1300; www.travelguard. com), **Travel Insured International** (☎ 800-243-3174; www.travel insured.com), or **Travelex Insurance Services** (☎ 888-457-4602; www. travelex-insurance.com).

Trip-cancellation insurance

If you've already made many of your reservations, you've probably put down a lot of money in deposits. Alaska tour operators, guides, lodges, and bed-and-breakfasts all make this demand, and often with more rigorous refund requirements than you may be used to. These deposits are nonrefundable after a certain date. The reasons are understandable: Alaskans in the tourism industry have only two or three months to make a year's income, so they can't afford a significant number of no-shows that leave them with empty rooms or seats. But what if you get sick or bad weather intervenes and you can't get there? Or what if your airline goes bankrupt or a catastrophe prevents travel? You lose your deposits and your vacation. Trip-cancellation insurance protects you against that dreadful possibility for around 5 percent to 7 percent of the cost of the trip. Given the uncertainty of Alaska travel, I think this insurance is worth the price.

The Alaska travel-planning industry has been hit by several large fraud cases and many smaller incidents in recent years. Being cautious about whom you do business with is always wise, but in one case a large, mainstream operator turned out to be a fraudulent house of cards. Besides insurance, you can protect yourself by paying for everything — including the insurance — with a credit card. You can get your money back on goods and services not received if you report the loss within 60 days after the charge is listed on your credit card statement.

Note: Many tour operators, particularly those offering trips to remote or high-risk areas, include insurance in the cost of the trip or can arrange insurance policies through a partnering provider, a convenient and often cost-effective way for the traveler to obtain insurance. But this option entails higher risk than buying the insurance yourself from a third party. If the company you've bought your trip from fails, you'll have a harder time recovering your money if it's also your insurer. In addition, I've encountered policies that exclude coverage of trips by a referring company. As always, it pays to read the fine print. For the greatest security, buy your insurance independently of buying your trip.

Medical insurance

Medical insurance for travelers from outside the United States is a worthwhile investment, but it probably doesn't make sense for most travelers from the United States, who likely are already covered under their regular health insurance. However, if you're heading into remote areas on your own, check to make sure you're covered for medical evacuation should you get sick or be injured. A medevac flight can easily exceed $10,000.

Also, if you belong to an HMO, check to see whether you're fully covered while away from home.

International visitors should make health-insurance arrangements before traveling to the United States. Good policies will cover the costs of an accident, repatriation, or death. Packages such as **Europ Assistance's Worldwide Healthcare Plan** are sold by European automobile clubs and travel agencies at attractive rates. Try **Europ Assistance USA** (☎ **240-330-1000;** www.worldwideassistance.com).

Lost-luggage insurance

Insurance on your baggage is included in most travel-insurance plans. If not, consider the pros and cons of a separate policy. Your baggage is often covered under your homeowner's policy or credit card benefits, but that coverage may expose you to high deductibles or sneaky exclusions, so read the fine print carefully and, if relying on a card, make sure to use that card for everything relevant to the coverage. If an airline loses or damages your bags, it's usually responsible for up to $2,500 per passenger on domestic flights or, on international flights, up to approximately $635 per checked bag, excluding expensive items such as jewelry and cameras. Good luck getting the airline to actually pay in a reasonable period of time, however — it's notoriously difficult. The simplest course is to leave valuables at home or carry them with you, insuring your baggage only if justified by the worth that you can prove. You need to establish the value of your lost clothing and such with bills of sale or similar documentation for each item.

If your luggage is lost, immediately file a lost-luggage claim at the airport, detailing the luggage contents. For most airlines, you must report delayed, damaged, or lost baggage within four hours of arrival. The airlines are required to deliver luggage, once found, directly to your house or destination free of charge.

Staying Healthy When You Travel

Getting sick will ruin your vacation, so I *strongly* advise against it. Some readers, however, refuse to follow this advice. (In fact, I've been known to pick up a bug on a trip now and then.)

The obvious things you do at home to avoid getting sick are even more important on a trip, because you'll be exposed to many more pathways to pick up germs. Passing through airports, eating in restaurants, and visiting attractions all put you in contact with more people than a normal day at home. Washing your hands frequently is the most important defense, especially before eating anything at all. The Centers for Disease Control (CDC) recommends carrying a waterless hand sanitizer such as Purell and using it as you travel. It's also important to avoid getting exhausted by jet lag and over-filled days under the midnight sun — tired people get sick more easily.

Visitors who come to Alaska on cruise ships or spend time on escorted bus tours should be especially careful. These closely contained groups are ripe breeding grounds for the spread of infectious disease, especially the miserable *Norovirus,* which causes vomiting for a day or two but remains contagious long after the symptoms have passed. You can pick up the bug from a doorknob or railing, and hand-washing is the only defense. The CDC offers a health Web site for travelers, which includes sanitation ratings for the ships and a lot of other useful information, at wwwnc.cdc.gov/travel.

You'll find modern, full-service hospitals in each of Alaska's larger cities, and even in some small towns that act as regional centers. There's some kind of clinic even in the smallest towns, although they often are staffed by physicians' assistants rather than medical doctors. I've listed the addresses and phone numbers for medical facilities in each destination under "Fast Facts." Call those numbers, too, for referrals to a dentist or other health professional. In an emergency, call ☎ **911.**

For domestic trips, most healthcare plans provide coverage if you get sick away from home. For information on purchasing additional medical insurance for your trip, see the "Medical insurance" section, earlier in this chapter.

If health is a particular concern, consider joining **MedicAlert** (☎ **888-432-5378;** www.medicalert.org) and wearing their engraved bracelet, which will inform emergency medical personnel of a primary preexisting medical condition and provide them with access to the organization's response center for your information on file, such as medications, physician, and family contacts. The cost is $40 for the first year, and then $30 per year after that.

For information on safety during Alaskan outdoor activities, see Chapter 9.

Reserving Activities, Restaurants, and Shows

After you've reserved your flight, car, and room, you're finished planning your vacation — if you plan to spend the trip sitting in a room and a car, that is. The highlights of an Alaska trip are the activities: fishing, wildlife-watching, flightseeing, and the like. Make reservations for most of these activities at least a few days in advance; for others (such as the Denali National Park bus tour), you should make reservations as soon as you know your vacation schedule. I let you know which activities need more advanced reservations in the destination chapters in this book. A few of the best restaurants also require advance reservations, and if you want to catch a popular performing-arts event, you should check schedules before you leave home.

Booking your activities

As a general rule, the larger your party is relative to the size of the entire group on the outing, the more important reservations become. If you want to fish, sea-kayak, or take a bear-viewing flight on a certain day — all activities that involve four to ten people per outing — reserve at least a few days ahead, and preferably a few weeks ahead, to make sure you get to do what you want on the day you're ready to do it. If your party is larger than three, make reservations even further in advance.

Likewise, if your vacation is short, reserve everything ahead. On a quick trip, you don't have flexibility in your schedule to adjust for booked-up activities. Besides, spending valuable vacation time on the phone trying to line things up at the last minute is a real drag.

When you call to reserve, always check for cancellation policies in case of bad weather so that you aren't faced with the choice between losing a deposit and going on a seasickness-inducing or scary ride.

If possible, set up your itinerary so that it includes an extra day after each weather-dependent activity. Even in summertime, weather often stops or disrupts outdoor activities, especially on the water. Guides, boat captains, and pilots won't endanger you by going out in bad weather, but they may make you miserable on a tossing boat or bumpy aircraft, with reduced visibility due to driving rain. Suppose you don't want to go out in such marginal weather, but the tour is going anyway. Despite your (reasonable) decision, the operator may decline to give you your money back, because the tour hasn't been cancelled. However, most operators will rebook you for the next day, because they still get paid that way. Having that extra day available means you get to go, and it saves your deposit.

Certain activities are so difficult to book and so important to a great trip that you should, if possible, plan your trip around them. Make the hard-to-get reservation first so that you have flexibility to accept any available dates. Then fill in your itinerary with that one date locked in. If you can adjust the dates of your entire vacation, you'll have an even better chance of doing the most popular activities.

Here are the main activities ranked by how quickly you need to act. I don't list activities included in package tours or multi-day adventures, which are also integral to setting up your trip. (For activities without chapter references, see area-specific chapters for more information.)

✔ **Reserve as early as possible:**

- Permit-limited bear-viewing hot spots, including Brooks Camp at Katmai National Park (see Chapter 24) and Pack Creek on Admiralty Island in Tongass National Forest (see Chapter 20)

- Early-morning Denali National Park shuttle-bus rides (see Chapter 19)

- White Pass & Yukon Route rail tickets (see Chapter 21)
- Guided river-fishing during run peaks (the only time you should fish for salmon)

✓ **Reserve a week or two ahead:**

- Sea-kayaking and ocean charter fishing
- Fly-in fishing
- Mount McKinley flightseeing from Talkeetna (see Chapter 19)
- Helicopter flightseeing in Juneau (see Chapter 20)
- Dog-mushing and snowmobiling during peak periods (Feb–Mar)

✓ **Reserve a few days ahead:**

- Whale-watching and tour-boat outings (on large boats)
- Most flightseeing outings
- River-rafting
- Rental equipment such as bikes and canoes
- Town tours and other bus tours

✓ **No need to reserve:**

- Museums and other public facilities
- Hiking and self-guided outdoor activities
- Skiing

Reserving a table at restaurants

Just a few of the best restaurants in Anchorage fill up all reasonable dining hours on weekends several days in advance. If you plan on some special meals, read the listings in this book and call ahead to make sure that you can get a table at any that say, "Reservations recommended."

Getting performing-arts reservations

Some events are aimed specifically at tourists, including gold-rush melodramas, dramatic Robert Service poetry recitations, and films about wildlife or the aurora. You generally don't need to reserve these activities ahead, unless I note otherwise in my descriptions in each chapter.

If you're interested in something a bit more sophisticated, consider attending a performance with the locals. Although winter is the busy season for concerts and theater, you can catch shows in the summer, too. Make your evenings more interesting by checking out what will be showing and arranging your schedule to attend a live performance. Check Chapter 3 for major happenings such as the Sitka Summer Music Festival. The Web site or phone number of the festival itself is the best place to find event times and tickets.

For complete listings of performing-arts, spectator sports, community activities, and the like, local Web sites are the best source. Here are the best of these for Alaska's three largest towns:

- **Anchorage:** The *Anchorage Daily News* produces an extensive entertainment section in the Friday edition; the calendar is exhaustive (www.adn.com/play).

- **Fairbanks:** The Fairbanks Convention and Visitors Bureau offers a very informative calendar at www.explorefairbanks.com/calendar.

- **Juneau:** Check www.traveljuneau.com/events, operated by the Juneau Convention & Visitors Bureau.

Packing for the North

"What should I pack?" is among the most frequent questions of visitors to Alaska. Although most travelers know they aren't headed into a scene from *Nanook of the North,* they also don't know exactly what they *are* headed into. You won't need mukluks and you won't need a necktie, but you will need to prepare for swings in temperatures broader than you may be used to. And you'll need binoculars and mosquito repellent.

Summer clothing

You're not going to the North Pole; for a summer visit, don't weigh down your luggage with a down parka or winter boots. But you should be ready for swings from sunny 80°F (27°C) days to windy, rainy 45°F (7°C) outings on the water. The way Alaskans prepare for such a range is with layers. The content of the layers depends on what you're doing, but everyone should bring at least the following:

- Warm-weather clothes (shorts and T-shirts)
- Heavy long-sleeved shirts and pants
- A wool sweater
- A warm jacket
- A waterproof raincoat and rain pants

Gloves and wool hats are a good idea, too, especially for boating trips. If you're camping, add synthetic thermal long underwear and wool socks to the list and make your jacket thick synthetic fleece. Combine these items, and you're ready for any summer conditions. For hiking, bring sturdy shoes or cross-trainers.

Winter clothing

You can be comfortable no matter how cold it is. When you know how to dress warmly, the world of snow opens up to you. But first, what not to wear: People don't wear heavy Arctic gear in town, even in the Arctic. To make the dash from car to heated building, you can get by with a heavy overcoat, sweater, hat, gloves, wool socks, and long underwear.

For vigorous winter activities

For outdoor pursuits, what you wear depends on how active you are. The key to warmth and safety during vigorous outdoor activities is to wear layers of breathable clothing that stay warm when wet, such as wool or synthetics. With the following layers, you're ready for temperatures well below 0°F (18°C), at which point you won't want to ski or skate anyway:

- Synthetic thermal long underwear
- Synthetic fleece pants and coat
- Wool sweater
- Wind-resistant pants and jacket
- Wool socks and hat
- Warm boots with liners or covers
- Lined mittens

Strip off these layers for warmer temperatures.

For sedate winter activities

For more sedentary outdoor activities, such as watching the aurora or riding a snowmobile or dog sled, you need warmer clothing. Likewise, drives on rural highways in winter require warm clothing in case of breakdowns. On guided trips or at cold-weather resorts, they either tell you what to bring or provide or rent the gear. If you need to get your own, a full outfit includes the following:

- Synthetic thermal long underwear
- The stoutest Sorel-style or Air Force bunny boots
- Insulated snow pants
- A heavy down parka with a hood
- Thick, insulated mittens (not gloves)
- A wool hat
- A face-insulating mask
- Ski goggles or quality sunglasses

You don't want any skin showing while riding a snowmobile or standing in a strong wind in temperatures below 0°F (18°C). Such a getup costs more than $500. You can buy what you need in Anchorage at **Army Navy Store**, 320 W. 4th Ave. (☎ **888-836-3535** or 907-279-2401; www.army-navy-store.com), or in Fairbanks at **Big Ray's Store**, 507 2nd Ave. (☎ **800-478-3458** or 907-452-3458; www.bigrays.com).

Dressing like a local

One of the most dramatic examples of a culture clash I ever witnessed was during the *Exxon Valdez* oil spill, which I covered as a newspaper reporter. Suddenly, Texan oil executives in sharp suits flooded into little Alaskan fishing towns where, previously, a man in any kind of a business suit was enough to cause a double take. The Exxon executives took only a few days to figure out just how out of place they looked and how poorly that served their PR aims, and soon they all started wearing flannel shirts and blue jeans — crisply pressed flannel shirts and blue jeans. They stood out just as much as ever!

The uniform of coastal Alaska is simple: rubber boots, T-shirts or flannel shirts, and blue jeans or Carhart canvas pants. (Carhart-brand clothes are those stiff, loose-fitting, rough-woven work clothes that you may have seen on your auto mechanic. They're for sale all over Alaska, especially at the shops listed at the end of the preceding section.) In inclement weather, add a fleece or lined Carhart canvas jacket and rubber rain gear. Fish blood on the clothing is a mark of pride. Away from the coast, the rubber boots may be replaced by leather work boots, and the Carharts become a permanent fixture: Mosquitoes can't bite through them.

 If you don't want to dress like a local, you won't go wrong with sturdy casual clothing. The great thing about Alaska is that no one really cares what you wear.

Communicating on the Road

Alaska's telecommunications network is world-renowned. Even tiny villages without indoor plumbing have TV, telephone, and Internet connections. Adventurers crossing trackless Arctic terrain can check their e-mail by satellite. The question is, how connected do you want to be when you're seeking nature?

Logging on to the Internet

Taking a laptop on vacation isn't just for losers anymore. You can watch DVDs on the plane, listen to music, and write home. These days even most B&Bs offer Internet access through wireless networks. On the other hand, you'll be lugging a computer around, worrying about it being stolen, and you'll face the constant temptation to keep up with the office — and that *is* for losers!

 The very reasonable alternative is to rely on public Web access. Even tiny Alaska towns offer access to travelers; most have an Internet cafe, while in others you can log on at the public library. Internet access for each Alaska community is listed in the appropriate sections of the book under "Fast Facts." Typically, you can find the information you want for less than $5.

To retrieve your e-mail from a public computer, ask your **Internet service provider (ISP)** if it has a Web-based interface tied to your existing e-mail account. If your ISP doesn't have such an interface, you can use the free **mail2web** service (`www.mail2web.com`) to view and reply to your home e-mail (click Secure Login to protect your privacy).

Making a cellphone call

Bringing your cellphone to Alaska makes good sense. It doesn't take up much space, and you may need it. Your BlackBerry or iPhone will work in populated areas. However, using your phone extensively could get expensive if you don't have a plan that covers the state. It's wise to check about roaming charges before you start making a lot of calls. Alaska's main providers are AT&T and local companies called ACS and GCI. The most densely populated portion of the state and most of the paved highways have cellular coverage. Don't bet your life on being able to make a call anywhere beyond the end of pavement, though.

To be sure you're always in touch, you can rent a satellite phone; that's more expensive, and the phones are not at all handy to use. I cover that option in Chapter 9.

Keeping Up with Airline Security Measures

Security measures at airports get tighter all the time, often with little warning. One threat meant everyone had to begin taking shoes off before getting on an airplane; another meant no liquids could go onboard with passengers. There's not much you can do except be patient, allow extra time, and check the Web sites that keep up-to-date information on the latest rules at `www.tsa.gov`. Here are a few obvious tips to save you time and trouble:

- ✔ **Arrive early.** Usually, being at the airport two hours before your flight is not necessary, but every once in a while you run into horrendous security or check-in delays at major airports. At Alaska's small airports, an hour is generally adequate. You should be in the boarding area for Alaska Airlines flights 30 minutes before departure.

- ✔ **Be sure to carry plenty of documentation.** A government-issued photo ID (federal, state, or local) is required. Bring paper backup for your electronic ticket, just in case. And be sure that your ID is up-to-date: An expired driver's license, for example, may keep you from boarding the plane. (Kids 17 and under don't need government-issued photo IDs for domestic flights.) Each traveler should have possession of his own ID and boarding pass before entering the security area.

- ✔ **Use E-tickets to help beat the lines.** Avoid using paper tickets. Passengers with E-tickets can beat ticket-counter lines by using airport electronic kiosks or even online check-in from a home computer. Online check-in involves logging on to your airline's Web site, accessing your reservation, and printing your boarding pass — and the airline may even offer you bonus miles to do so! If you're using a kiosk at the airport, bring the credit card you used to book the ticket or your frequent-flier card. Print your boarding pass at the kiosk and simply proceed to the security checkpoint with your pass and a photo ID. If you're checking bags or looking to snag an exit-row seat, you'll be able to do so using most airline kiosks. **Curbside check-in** is also a good way to avoid lines where it's available.

✔ **Prepare for special needs.** If you have trouble standing for a long time, tell an airline employee; the airline will provide a wheelchair. Only ticketed passengers are allowed past security, except for folks escorting children or disabled passengers; those helpers will need documentation from the airline before approaching security.

✔ **Speed up security by not wearing metal objects** such as big belt buckles. If you have metallic body parts, a note from your doctor can prevent a long chat with the security screeners.

✔ **Know what you can carry on and what you can't.** The Transportation Security Administration (TSA) publishes a list of items prohibited in carry-on or checked baggage; the list changes frequently, and TSA agents are empowered to ignore it and confiscate anything they find suspicious. The general rule is that sharp things and liquids are out. For the latest detailed list, check the TSA Web site at www.tsa.gov. See the "Camping and airline security" sidebar in this chapter for advice on bringing outdoor supplies on a plane.

✔ **Prepare to be searched.** Take out your laptop and put it in a separate tray. Try to send it through last so it'll be exposed to theft for less time on the other end. (The same goes for cellphones, iPods, and the like.) Be ready to remove your shoes and jacket for X-ray. Remove anything metal from your pockets and take off your belt if it has anything but a small buckle. Don't complain about being searched; the security people have the power to ruin your day on a whim if you irritate them.

✔ **Prepare to have your checked bags searched.** Checked baggage is subjected to powerful X-rays and often inspected by hand as well. Don't leave film in your bag, because the X-rays will ruin it. If you lock your bag, use an approved lock that allows screeners to open and relock it; otherwise, a TSA agent will likely cut your lock or force your bag open. Look for Travel Sentry–certified locks. Many brands are certified and available virtually anywhere you buy luggage. Also, don't overstuff your luggage — screeners may not be able to get it back together after a search.

✔ **Don't joke.** A physician who made a stupid joke at one Alaska airport after September 11 was barred permanently from flying on Alaska Airlines. Because no other airline flies to the town he was in and it can't be reached by road, he was stuck there for some time — and humiliated in the media to boot.

Camping and airline security

Security baggage screening makes life tough for all outdoors people. Critical survival gear can be confiscated without the passenger's knowledge: One party found themselves in the Alaska wilderness without matches to build a fire or glue to fix their rafts because a screener had intercepted those items on the flight out. I list some advice here, but the rules change (and sometimes even allowed items are confiscated — screeners have complete discretion). For the latest regulations, check www.tsa.gov and search using the keyword *camping*. That should bring up a list of camping equipment and how to handle each item. The best solution for many of these issues is to buy what you need on arrival; but allow time to responsibly dispose of anything you buy in Alaska and can't take on the plane ride home.

✔ **Camp stoves:** Camp stoves are not allowed onboard with even the slightest odor of fuel. Effectively, that means you can't bring a stove with an attached fuel tank on your trip. Indeed, even stoves without attached fuel tanks often are barred. Don't try — you'll either lose your stove or miss the plane. Rent a stove in Alaska, buy an inexpensive stove you can get rid of when you're done, or mail your detached-tank stove ahead and buy a tank on arrival.

✔ **Bear-deterrent spray:** It isn't allowed even as checked baggage, so you'll have to buy this item in Alaska or do without (see Chapter 9).

✔ **Matches and lighters:** Lighters generally are not allowed in checked baggage, but you can bring common pocket lighters and one book of safety matches on your person or as carry-on luggage.

✔ **Insect repellent:** You can take repellent in checked baggage, but I find the rules about bringing it in aerosol cans unclear. Just in case, stick with the pump or lotion variety in your checked luggage.

✔ **Flares:** These are not allowed at all. You can take an unloaded flare gun in checked baggage in a hard-sided case, declaring it at the counter, but you'll have to buy flares on arrival.

Remember: When you arrive, inventory your survival equipment to make sure it's all still there. If anything is missing, replace it before you set out for your adventure.

Flying with Bulky Outdoor Equipment

Two issues make flying and camping tough. One is the bulkiness of the gear, and the other is getting it past security screeners. (The latter is addressed in the "Camping and airline security" sidebar in this chapter.)

Backpackers don't have to worry about bulky equipment, because their stuff is already compact: They can simply check the pack with the airline. Family camping entails a lot more gear than backpacking, and that adds challenges. Just the bedding for our family of six could fill the belly of a 747.

Baggage fees can make it expensive to send your gear. Check airline Web sites before you begin packing. Currently, Alaska Airlines charges $20 per bag for each of your first three checked bags, and $50 per bag for each additional bag. Size and weight restrictions also affect campers: No longer can you just stuff a huge duffle. Anything over 62 inches in length plus width plus height or weighing over 50 pounds carries a $50 to $75 fee.

Services such as **Sports Express Luggage Delivery** (☎ 800-357-4174 or 617-482-1100; www.sportsexpress.com) can take care of all this for you, including sending ahead items like bikes and kayaks. Parcel services like FedEx and UPS can deliver you luggage, too, but that generally costs even more than excess baggage charges.

Here are some tips for family camping without the family car:

- **Start with a list.** A list keeps you from forgetting things and makes it easier to decide what *not* to take.

- **Find out how much baggage is allowed.** Airlines charge stiff fees for extra baggage. Most campers won't be able to stay within the limits. Before you start, check airline Web sites so you can balance baggage costs against renting what you need on arrival.

- **Figure out how much you can handle.** Will you need to tote everything yourself to get on a train or boat, for example? If so, figure out who carries what, and make sure each person can really carry his assigned items. If you rent a car at the airport, you don't have to carry everything at once, but it does have to fit in the car's trunk. Consider the bulk of whatever you plan to rent, too.

- **Start packing early.** You won't believe how much space all your stuff takes until you see it all together. If you start early enough, you'll have more time for alternatives, such as buying smaller gear or arranging to rent gear at your destination.

- **Bring an extra collapsible bag.** A spare duffel can be great for items you pick up on the way, for dirty clothes, or for segregating stuff you don't need so that you can stash it somewhere.

- **Mail back the extras.** You don't have to haul around souvenirs you buy or items you aren't using. Have shops mail them home for you. If you brought along something that's hanging around your neck like a millstone (a friend told me a hilarious story of a trip weighed down by an old manual typewriter), stop in at a post office, buy a box, and mail it home. I list the location of the local post office in the "Fast Facts" section for each town in this book.

- **Stow gear at your hotel.** Many lodgings are willing to hold onto extra luggage for a few days, especially if you're coming back to stay there again. Keep camping gear with you only for the outdoor excursion, and then store it until you're ready to head home.

- **Don't bring what you can buy cheaply.** For example, water bottles are sold in every convenience store.

✔ **Arrange to rent as much as you can.** I list outdoor rental agencies in Anchorage, Fairbanks, and Juneau, Alaska's key gateways, in Chapters 13, 17, and 20, respectively. Make sure to call ahead and reserve what you need. You can rent camping equipment as well as large items such as bikes, canoes, and sea kayaks.

Part III
Anchorage and Environs

The 5ᵗʰ Wave   By Rich Tennant

"Okay, I've got room for five in my plane. Who wants to go fishing this afternoon?"

In this part . . .

I've given Anchorage and the easy day trips around the city an entire three-chapter part in this book, and not just because it's my hometown. Anchorage is a fun city to visit and a perfect base of operations for a survey of the largest part of Alaska. You can do and see most of what you've come for within a half-day's drive of Anchorage, and you can be in spectacular wild country less than an hour from the largest downtown hotel. With all its transportation options, in addition to its big stores and offices, the city serves as Alaska's heart.

These chapters provide information on what to do, where to stay and eat, and how to get around Anchorage and the surrounding area, including the nearby Seward Highway, the ski resort at Girdwood, Prince William Sound, and the Mat-Su area.

Chapter 13

Settling Into Anchorage

. . . .

In This Chapter

▶ Getting to Anchorage
▶ Orienting yourself in Anchorage
▶ Making your way around Anchorage
▶ Finding accommodations
▶ Finding a good meal

. . . .

*A*nchorage isn't a beautiful city, but it's in a beautiful place, and that's good enough. The main part of the city lies in the Anchorage Bowl, which is rimmed by the Chugach Mountains and the broad mud flats and swirling gray water of Cook Inlet. Wilderness is only minutes away in either direction — by air over the water to the west or on foot or bicycle into the mountains to the east. Yet the town itself is quite civilized and firmly linked to the rest of the United States in its culture and in the way it looks. On a city street, if you keep your eyes off the mountains, you could be almost anywhere. But a few steps off the street, and you're into a greenbelt or a big natural park, ready to encounter moose, eagles, or beluga whales.

I wouldn't recommend that anyone spend an entire vacation in Anchorage (well, maybe a skiing vacation), but you can and should use the city as a base. As I discuss in earlier chapters, Anchorage is the cheapest gateway into the largest part of the state, with the state's most complete services and transportation network. The city is a world transportation hub; the airport here sees as much air cargo pass through as any in the United States and has the world's busiest floatplane base at Lake Hood. The Alaska Railroad is based here, and the three busiest highways meet close by. You need Anchorage, just as Alaskans do.

But the city is more than a jumping-off point; it has its own attractions, including several options for rainy-day activities. The state's biggest museum, an extraordinary Native cultural center, and Alaska's only zoo are here. And some of the state's best outdoor activities are found within the (quite large) city limits or on easy day trips to Prince William Sound or to the mountains and rivers north and south of town. Anchorage also has a thriving performing-arts scene, a choice of superb restaurants, and plenty of places to shop for art or schlock.

In this chapter, I cover the practical advice about how to get to Anchorage and where to stay and eat. In Chapters 14 and 15, I go into the attractions and activities that make this a great city to visit.

Getting to Anchorage

Most visitors to Alaska pass through Anchorage at some point. It's a simple gateway, much like other midsize American cities, but knowing a few details can ease your way.

Flying in

You'll probably fly into Anchorage at the start of your trip, because it has the most flights linking Alaska to the rest of the world. The **Ted Stevens Anchorage International Airport** is a major hub. Seattle has the most frequent flights to Alaska, with numerous domestic carriers flying nonstop all day (see Chapter 6). Within Alaska, many flights route through Anchorage, even for communities much closer to each other than either is to Anchorage. **Alaska Airlines** (☎ 800-252-7522; www. alaskaair.com) is the dominant carrier for Alaska destinations and the only jet operator to most Alaska cities (see Chapter 7).

Various commuter carriers link Anchorage to rural destinations not served by jet. **Era Alaska** (☎ 800-866-8394 or 907-266-8394; www. flyera.com) is the largest and can be booked directly or through Alaska Airlines.

Here are some tips for getting oriented at the airport; for more, check www.anchorageairport.com:

- ✔ The **South Terminal** is the main terminal and hosts Alaska Airlines, other domestic airlines and all commuter airlines. The **North Terminal** receives international flights.

- ✔ **Baggage claim** in the South Terminal is downstairs next to the lower ramp, where you'll also find taxis, airport courtesy vans, a tunnel to the railroad station (used only for cruise-line charters) and airport shuttles.

- ✔ **Rental-car counters** are connected to the main terminal, which accesses the parking garage. The closest gas stations are at the intersection of Spenard Road and Minnesota Drive.

- ✔ **ATMs** are within a few steps everywhere in the airport, on either side of the security barriers.

- ✔ The airport offers **free Wi-Fi,** which seems to work all over the buildings.

- ✔ **Visitor information desks** at the airport are in the baggage-claim area in the South Terminal's C concourse and in the North Terminal.

Getting into town from the airport

The airport is right in the city, an easy trip from downtown. However, Anchorage is big and spread out, so getting around beyond downtown can be expensive without a car.

Renting a car

The most practical way to tour this part of Alaska is to rent a car. Even if you're just staying in Anchorage, taxis are expensive to use because of the spread-out urban design. On an ideal visit, you'll travel to sites beyond downtown at least once a day for hiking, skiing, sightseeing, dining, or accommodations. Chapter 7 covers tips on renting a car or RV in Anchorage. Pick up your baggage and head under the lower ramp to where the car-rental desks are located.

As you leave the airport, a divided highway leads east (toward the mountains); this is International Airport Road. At the first major intersection, Spenard Road leads to the left, toward the main area of airport hotels. The next intersection on International is a large interchange. Follow the signs to head north on Minnesota Drive, which leads downtown.

Catching a cab or shuttle

Some hotels have free courtesy vans. That's the cheapest way to get to your hotel, and it allows you to postpone renting a car until you really need it. Find out the arrangement for getting the van when you reserve your room. If your hotel doesn't have a courtesy van, a taxi is the easiest way to get to your accommodations and costs only a little more than taking a shuttle, even for a person traveling alone. The ride downtown from the airport costs $18 to $20 (plus a tip of around $3) and takes 15 to 30 minutes, depending on traffic. Try **Alaska Yellow Cab** (☎ 907-222-2222).

Various airport shuttles have operated from time to time. Ask at the visitor information desk for the current options. If you don't have much luggage, you can consider taking the **People Mover** city bus, which connects the airport and the downtown transit center hourly. Take Spenard Route 7A (every other Route 7 bus on weekdays). For finding schedules and other details on using the People Mover see "Getting Around Anchorage," later in this chapter.

Arriving by car

Only one road connects Anchorage to the rest of the world: the **Glenn Highway.** The Glenn starts 330 miles from Anchorage in Tok, at the intersection with the Alaska Highway, and runs through Glennallen and the Mat-Su area before entering downtown Anchorage and becoming 5th and 6th avenues. From Fairbanks or Denali National Park, the Parks Highway leads south through Mat-Su, where it merges with the Glenn Highway 30 miles out of Anchorage. (Alaska's highways are covered in Chapter 18. The Mat-Su area is in Chapter 15.)

The only other road entering town, the Seward Highway, connects the city to the Kenai Peninsula, to the south (see Chapters 15 and 16). If you arrive in the region by cruise ship or ferry, you'll probably land in Seward (124 miles south of Anchorage) or Whittier (50 miles south of Anchorage). Cruise lines take care of the bus or rail transfer to Anchorage. The highway becomes Ingra and Gambell streets in downtown Anchorage, where it meets the origin of the Glenn Highway.

Arriving by train

Some cruise-ship passengers arrive in Anchorage by rail from Seward or Whittier. Some trains go straight to the airport, others to the main depot downtown on 2nd Avenue, a short bus ride from downtown hotels.

Orienting Yourself in Anchorage

Navigating Anchorage is easy if you just remember that the mountains are to the east. Use them as your compass. The "Anchorage" map, later in this chapter, familiarizes you with the major streets, but to find a particular address, you need to pick up a more detailed map at one of the visitor centers I mention in "Finding Information after You Arrive," later in this chapter.

Downtown

Many visitors here for only a day never make it beyond the **downtown area,** the old-fashioned grid of streets at the northwest corner of the city where the large hotels and gift shops are located. Street numbers and letters work on a simple pattern. Numbered avenues run east–west. Lettered streets run north–south. East of A Street, north–south streets have the alphabetized names of Alaska places (Barrow, Cordova, Denali, Eagle, and so on). Check out the "Downtown Anchorage" map in this chapter for a detailed look at this easy-to-navigate area.

Midtown and the rest of the Anchorage Bowl

Most of Anchorage beyond the compact downtown area is a newer creation, built in the western U.S. model of commercial strips along big roads. **Midtown,** just south of downtown, is the main added-on commercial center. **South Anchorage** is roughly everything south of Dimond Boulevard and includes **Hillside,** the district east of the Seward Highway in the foothills and mountainsides of the Chugach Range. Learning the names of most other neighborhoods isn't important.

Three major north–south thoroughfares run from downtown, through Midtown, to the shopping malls and residential districts of South Anchorage. These are **Minnesota Drive,** which becomes I and L streets downtown; **C Street** and **A Street;** and the **New Seward Highway,** which is Ingra and Gambell streets downtown and heads out of town to the south. Major east–west roads in the grid are 5th and 6th avenues, becoming the **Glenn Highway** and leading out of town to the north; **Northern Lights Boulevard** and **Benson Boulevard,** running across the city in Midtown; and **Dimond Boulevard,** in South Anchorage.

Beyond the Bowl

Some parts of Anchorage are outside the Bowl defined by the Chugach Mountains. The communities of **Eagle River** and **Eklutna** are northeast of Anchorage on the Glenn Highway; go a little farther that way and you reach the **Mat-Su area. Girdwood** and the **Portage Glacier** are on the Seward Highway, to the south. A tunnel near the glacier leads to **Whittier** and **Prince William Sound.**

Finding Information After You Arrive

Besides the information desks at the airport, you can get questions answered at the **Log Cabin Visitor Information Center,** downtown at 4th Avenue and F Street (☎ 907-274-3531). It's open June through August daily 7:30 a.m. to 7 p.m., May and September daily 8 a.m. to 6 p.m., and October through April daily 9 a.m. to 4 p.m. The **Anchorage Convention & Visitors Bureau** (☎ 907-276-4118; www.anchorage.net) operates the information center.

Diagonally across the street is an indispensable stop for anyone planning an outdoors trip: the **Alaska Public Lands Information Center,** 605 W. 4th Ave. (☎ 866-869-6887; www.nps.gov/anch). It's open in the summer daily 9 a.m. to 5 p.m., in winter Monday through Friday 10 a.m. to 5 p.m. It's not just a place to get advice and information, it's also an outdoors museum. Located in a 1930s post office and federal court-house, the center houses exhibits in a grand room with high ceilings. All the land agencies are represented and the bookstore has an excellent selection of trail and field guides available. Rangers are on hand with advice based on personal experience. Employees also offer talks, films, and children's programs. A visit is well worth the brief inconvenience of going through federal security screening.

Getting Around Anchorage

The population of Anchorage roughly doubled during the oil-boom years of the 1970s and early 1980s. Large sections of forest and swamp suddenly became city. It achieved its current form and size by 1985. Maybe there wasn't enough time to do it right. In any event, Anchorage ended up as one big sprawl.

If you plan to break out of the older, pedestrian-friendly downtown area, you're almost forced to rent a car. Taxis often cost as much or more, and they're much less convenient. The People Mover city bus will work if your aim is to save money, but you pay the price in time — buses come only every 30 minutes at best, a poor use of valuable vacation time. Bus tours are available; they're good for orientation or to get to the Alaska Native Heritage Center, but otherwise they aren't recommended for getting around. (Find out more about guided tours in Chapter 14.)

Driving around town

Driving in the city is simple, at least in the warm months. The roads are wide and straight, turning right at a red light is permitted, finding your way with a map is easy (just remember the mountains are east), and parking is not a problem (half the town is parking lots). If you have trouble finding a space downtown, just duck into one of the many pay-to-park public lots or garages. The fees won't break you at any of these places, but you pay cheaper fees farther east.

 The allowable blood alcohol level in Alaska is low: 0.08 percent. Penalties for driving while intoxicated are extremely stiff: Besides mandatory jail time, big fines, and fees, Anchorage police can take away your car on the spot and sell it.

Winter driving can be a challenge. The roads are slick and the lines between lanes become invisible under snow and ice. Driving under these conditions is a skill, but the principles are simple: Go slowly, accelerate gradually, and plan ahead so that you're prepared to stop safely. When starting from a stop, apply as little gas as possible; avoid spinning your wheels. Renting a four-wheel-drive vehicle is probably worth the money. Avoid a car with rear-wheel-drive; front-wheel-drive handles much better on ice.

For winter drives to outlying areas, such as the ski resort in Girdwood, check on road conditions with the **Alaska Department of Transportation & Public Facilities** hot line or Web site (☎ **511;** http://511.alaska.gov). Occasionally, the road to Girdwood, the Seward Highway, is closed by avalanche conditions or is undrivable because of wet ice. (See "Arriving by car," earlier in this chapter, as well as Chapter 7, for more information on driving in Alaska.)

Calling a cab

 If you can't drive, taking a taxi may be your second-best choice. Because of the size of the city, taxis are an expensive way to get around, but if you plan your trips carefully and don't go too far — like the zoo, Chugach State Park, or Eklutna — you can make it work. I've had the best luck with **Alaska Yellow Cab** (☎ **907-222-2222**).

Hailing a cab usually isn't possible, so you need to call. Normally, a cab comes within ten minutes of being called, but if you need one around the time the bars close (2 a.m.) or near the start of the workday, and you want to be on time, allow at least half an hour. If you leave something in a cab, call the cab company. To file a complaint, call the city's **Transportation Inspection Division** (☎ **907-786-8525**).

Waiting for the bus

It takes patience to go a long way on the **People Mover** buses (☎ 907-343-6543; www.peoplemover.org), but the system is convenient and inexpensive for destinations such as the Alaska Native Heritage Center that are served by direct routes from downtown. Anchorage buses are safe and well-maintained and cover most of the city. Bus fares all over town are $1.75 adults; $1 kids 5 to 18; 50¢ seniors 60 and over, people with disabilities, or those with a valid Medicare card; free for kids 4 and under. The transit center bus depot is at 6th Avenue and G Street. Buses generally come every half-hour (hourly on weekends), but to use the system conveniently, go online and figure out your route and timing in advance.

Riding a bike

The network of bike trails is a great way to see the best side of Anchorage but not a practical means of transportation for most people. The city is just too large. The **Tony Knowles Coastal Trail** comes right downtown, linking to trails that weave along greenbelts all over town. The trails and bike rental are covered in Chapter 14.

Using shoe leather

In the downtown area, the simplest way to get around is on foot. If you're spending only a day in Anchorage before heading off to activities elsewhere in the state, you don't need to go any farther than downtown for an interesting visit, so you don't need transportation.

Where to Stay in Anchorage

Find a place in Anchorage you can use as a handy base for your trip. If you're using the airport frequently for getting around the state, staying in that part of the city makes sense. If you don't plan to rent a car, renting a room downtown gives you foot and bike access to the greatest number of attractions. If you're renting a car, you can stay anywhere in the city. If you reserve at the same establishment for each time you pass through the city, you can stow extra baggage there and, when you come back for your subsequent stay, receive an extra level of hospitality.

Anchorage is a good place to consider staying in a bed-and-breakfast or small inn for two reasons:

✔ Compared to a similar room in a hotel, you can save $50 a day with the lower rate and the breakfast that's included.

✔ It offers a chance to make a personal link with a local, your host, who can give you insider advice and regale you with stories of Alaskan adventure. (The visitor bureau gives all residents an annual exam to make sure we have enough bear stories.)

I've searched for some of the best small places, choosing those with character and reasonable prices. Anchorage has hundreds more, many of them just as good. Dozens link through a Web site maintained by the cooperative **Anchorage Alaska Bed & Breakfast Association** (www. anchorage-bnb.com). Browse through or search by amenities or location. Links go the B&Bs' own sites, which often have online availability calendars. Without a computer, call their hot line (☎ **888-584-5147** or 907-272-5909), which is answered by hosts at member properties to offer referrals to places that meet callers' requirements.

The top hotels and B&Bs

Anchorage Grand Hotel
$$$$ **Downtown**

This all-suite hotel has a rare combination of advantages: a superb, central location; solid, quiet rooms; fully equipped kitchens in every unit full of housewares and with dishwashers and automatic ice makers; generous amenities; and rates competitive for this area of town. The hotel lacks much of a lobby, as the main entrance and handicap entrance lead directly into a stairway or hallway; that's because it's a reincarnation of an old, concrete apartment building. But the immaculate rooms and tile bathrooms are quite large, decorated in a trim, subdued style with fine cabinetry. Despite the full kitchens, I've never noticed odors in the many rooms I've checked on several occasions, which is remarkable. Also, despite the kitchen, they serve a free continental breakfast in the morning (and deliver the newspaper). Every unit has a bedroom and a queen-size sofa sleeper in the living room.

See map p. 177. 505 W. 2nd Ave., Anchorage. ☎ *888-800-0640 or 907-929-8888. Fax: 907-929-8899. www.anchoragegrandhotel.com. Rack rates: Summer $199 double, winter $99 double; extra person 14 and over $20. Rates include continental breakfast. AE, DISC, MC, V.*

Copper Whale Inn
$$$$ **Downtown**

A pair of clapboard houses overlook the water and Elderberry Park right on the Coastal Trail downtown, with attractive rooms of various shapes and sizes, all done in fashionable tans and browns, with comfortable new beds, huge nature photographs and Alaskan art on the walls, and granite countertops in the bathrooms and common areas. The small upstairs rooms in the main building have wonderful views and funny angles; two of those share a bathroom. Lower-level rooms open on a patio. The rooms in the newer building, nearer the water, have high ceilings on the upper level and are larger, although none is very large. The staff is more than hospitable, creating the homey feeling of a country inn right in the urban core. They serve a large continental breakfast in the common area, which is comfortable for relaxing but not well suited for meals.

Anchorage

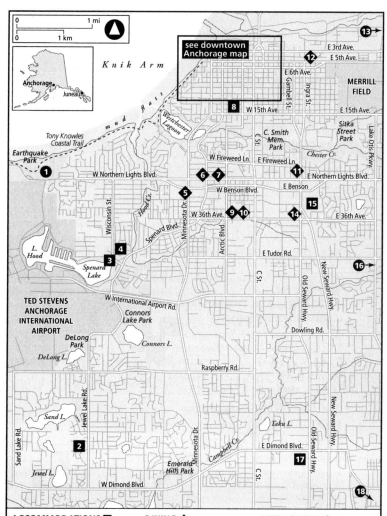

ACCOMMODATIONS ■
Dimond Center Hotel **10**
Earth B&B **8**
Elderberry B&B **2**
Lake Hood Inn **3**
Lakeshore Motor Inn **4**
Residence Inn by Marriott **14**

DINING ◆
Bear Tooth Theatrepub & Grill **6**
Campobello Bistro **9**
City Diner **5**
The Greek Corner **10**
Jens' Restaurant **8**
The Lucky Wishbone **11**
The Moose's Tooth Pub & Pizzeria **13**
Spenard Roadhouse **7**

ATTRACTIONS ●
Alaska Botanical Garden **15**
Alaska Native Heritage Center **12**
The Alaska Zoo **17**
Earthquake Park **1**

See map p. 177. 440 L St., Anchorage. ☎ **866-258-7999** *or 907-258-7999. Fax: 907-258-6213.* www.copperwhale.com. *Rack rates: High season $185 double with shared bathroom, $210 double with private bathroom; off season $85 double with shared bathroom, $110 double with private bathroom; extra person $20. Rates include continental breakfast. AE, DISC, MC, V.*

Dimond Center Hotel
$$$$$ **South Anchorage**

This hotel is unique in several ways. Owned by the Seldovia Native Association, its primary clientele is rural Alaska residents coming to the big city for shopping and entertainment. That explains the location, on the south side of town, far from downtown sites, in the parking between a Wal-Mart store and a large shopping mall. Strange as it sounds, however, the location makes sense for many visitors: Chugach State Park, the zoo, and the Seward Highway and its many attractions are closer than anywhere else you could stay. Since the owners built the hotel for themselves, the attention to comfort and detail are impressive. The common areas are stylish and decorated with Native art, and the rooms are grand: high ceilings, granite counters, attractive modern furniture, 42-inch flat-screen TVs, and pillow-top beds with comforters. The bathrooms are elaborate, with large shower areas and separate soaking tubs that can connect to the bedroom by opening wooden shutters. Amenities are exhaustive. *Note:* A car is essential at this location, and you'll have to drive if you want to eat anything but fast food.

See map p. 171. 700 E. Dimond Blvd., Anchorage. ☎ **866-770-5002** *or 907-770-5000. Fax: 907-770-5001.* www.dimondcenterhotel.com. *Rack rates: Summer $181–$300, winter $99–$179; extra person $25. Rates include continental breakfast. AE, DC, DISC, MC, V.*

The Historic Anchorage Hotel
$$$$ **Downtown**

This inn at the center of the tourist area is among the city's oldest businesses. The existing concrete building dates to 1936 and has the smaller scale of that period. Standing above a corner full of pedestrians, its facade is topped with little triangular turrets. The historic theme carries through the building, with furniture in Queen Anne style, brocade, and the familiar warm patterns once favored by hotels. The walls are decorated by Alaska landscapes. Rooms are average in size and equipped in modern fashion. None has a view, and those on the street side can suffer from noise, which is addressed with white-noise machines. The friendliness of the staff adds to the intimate feeling of being in a small building just steps from the sights and best restaurants. Breakfast is served in the attractively appointed lounge.

See map p. 177. 330 E St., Anchorage. ☎ **800-544-0988** *or 907-272-4553. Fax: 907-277-4483.* www.historicanchoragehotel.com. *Rack rates: High season $189–$209 double, $239–$259 suite; off season $89–$159 double, $159–$189 suite; extra person 13 and over $10. AE, DC, DISC, MC, V.*

The Hotel Captain Cook
$$$$$ **Downtown**

This is Alaska's great, grand hotel, where royalty and rock stars stay. (For a mere $1,500 per night, you can stay in the same suites they do.) The late Governor Wally Hickel built the first of the three towers after the 1964 earthquake, and now the hotel fills a city block and anchors the downtown skyline. Inside, the earth tones and dark-wood décor contribute to a fully realized (maybe a little excessive) nautical theme, with art memorializing Cook's voyages and enough teak to build a square-rigger. The regularly renewed rooms are decorated in a rich, sumptuous style using exquisite fabrics, unique pieces of custom-built furniture, and lots of varnished trim. Rooms are comfortable in size, but not as large as those in modern upscale chains, and all have a choice only of a king or two twin beds. Lots of custom tile, mirrors, and granite make up for the relatively small size of the bathrooms. There are great views from all sides and you don't pay more to be on a higher floor. The pool, spa, and fitness facilities in the below-ground lower lobby are among the best in town.

Sophisticated food and superb service justify the high prices at the **Crow's Nest,** the city's most traditional fine-dining restaurant, on the hotel's top floor. Most tables have stupendous views, and high-backed booths lend intimacy for a romantic dinner. The cuisine draws on many influences without being trendy and looks wonderful on the plate. Main courses range from $28 to $55. The wine list is voluminous, with few bottles under $40. **Fletcher's,** off the lobby, is an English pub serving good Italian-style pizza, pasta, and seafood. **The Pantry** is an above-average hotel cafe, with interesting entrees in moderate serving sizes. The **Whale's Tail** serves light meals, coffee, and cocktails amid overstuffed chairs and big TVs; it's a good place for a drink without feeling like you're in a bar.

See map p. 177. 939 W. 5th Ave., Anchorage. ☎ **800-843-1950** *or 907-276-6000. Fax: 907-343-2298.* www.captaincook.com. *Rack rates: High season $255–$265 double, $270–$1,500 suite; off season $155–$165 double, $170–$1,500 suite; extra person $20. AE, DISC, MC, V.*

Lake Hood Inn
$$$$ **Airport**

Pilot Bill Floyd built this place right next to his floatplane slip (he flies a Cessna 180) and filled it with fascinating aviation stuff: photographs, propellers, and even rows of seats from a Russian airliner. The guestbook is an aircraft logbook. On the comfortable balconies, headphones are at the ready to listen to radio traffic between the tower and the aircraft you can see taxiing on the lake in front of you. Floyd invested in commercial-quality construction and the rooms have the feel of a solid, upscale hotel room, not a family B&B; they're decorated in cool, muted shades with Berber carpet, light flooding in through big windows. The bathrooms have large shower stalls. Beds can be configured as two twins or as one king. Two front rooms have their own balconies and cost $20 more; the two backrooms have access to a shared balcony and are smaller. All four rooms are up a flight of stairs.

See map p. 171. 4702 Lake Spenard Dr., Anchorage. ☎ **866-663-9322** or 907-258-9321.
www.lakehoodinn.com. Rack rates: $169–$189 double; extra person 17 and over
$20. Rates include continental breakfast. AE, DISC, MC, V.

The Oscar Gill House
$$ **Downtown**

On the Delaney Park strip, just a few blocks from downtown, this is truly
the oldest house in Anchorage — it was built in 1913, in Knik, before
Anchorage was founded, and moved here on a barge a few years later.
Oscar Gill was an early civic leader. The house was to be torn down in
1982 but was moved to storage by a historic preservation group; Mark and
Susan Lutz saved it in 1993, transferring it to its present location and, with
their own labor, restoring it authentically as a cozy bed-and-breakfast.
Now it's on the National Register of Historic Places. Appropriate antiques
sit on plank floors in rooms sized in those more modest times. With the
period decoration it's like visiting your grandmother's house when it was
brand-new. The outgoing Lutzes create a warm, social setting. Book early,
because they fill up; you can check availability and even select a room on
their Web site.

See map p. 177. 1344 W. 10th Ave., Anchorage. ☎/Fax: **907-279-1344**. www.oscar
gill.com. Rack rates: High season $115 double with shared bathroom,
$135 double with private bathroom; off season $80 double with shared bathroom,
$95 double with private bathroom; extra person $25. Rates include full breakfast.
AE, MC, V.

Susitna Place
$$ **Downtown**

Just a few blocks from the downtown core, where a narrow residential
street reaches a quiet end, a nondescript door under a carport leads into
a rambling house of rooms ranging from comfortable and inexpensive to
grand. It turns out that the street side is really the back of the house,
which sits at the top of a high bluff facing an unobstructed view of Cook
Inlet and Mount Susitna beyond, a view so unlike most urban vistas that
it's easy to forget you're right in town. A large, gracious common room
and breakfast area and an adjoining balcony command this extraordinary
view. The suite is quite luxurious, but the four rooms that share two bathrooms are the rarer find: Cozy and very clean, sharing this prime location,
they allow travelers to save money without compromise. A good, simple
room with two double beds and its own bathroom rents for $135 double.
The hosts, successful journalists, are hospitable Alaskans.

See map p. 177. 727 N St., Anchorage. ☎ **907-274-3344**. Fax: 907-272-4141. www.
susitnaplace.com. Rack rates: High season $105–$110 double with shared
bathroom, $135–$140 double with private bathroom, $165–$195 suite; off season
$65–$70 double with shared bathroom, $80–$85 double with private bathroom, $95–
$115 suite; extra person $15. Rates include continental breakfast. AE, DISC, MC, V.

Runner-up accommodations

Anchorage Marriott Downtown

$$$$$ **Downtown** This is a high-rise with a nice pool and fabulous views from rooms with wall-size picture windows. *See map p. 177. 820 W. 7th Ave., Anchorage.* ☎ *888-228-9290 or 907-279-8000.* www.marriott.com/ancdt.

Earth Bed & Breakfast

$$–$$$ **Downtown** These five bedrooms are comfortable and quite clean, but basic; all share bathrooms. Guests eat a deluxe self-served continental breakfast in the large and immaculate common rooms. *See map p. 171. 1001 W. 12th Ave., Anchorage.* ☎ *907-279-9907.* www.earthbb.com.

Elderberry Bed & Breakfast

$$ **Airport** If you enjoy staying in a family home, this one has hosts who socialize with guests and describe their Alaska experiences. *See map p. 171. 8340 Elderberry St., Anchorage.* ☎ *907-243-6968.* www.elderberrybb.com.

Lakeshore Motor Inn

$$$ **Airport** At $159 for a double in the peak season, this place has the lowest-priced, consistently acceptable standard hotel rooms I've found near the airport. *See map p. 171. 3009 Lakeshore Dr., Anchorage.* ☎ *800-770-3000 or 907-248-3485.* www.lakeshoremotorinn.com.

Residence Inn by Marriott Anchorage Midtown

$$$$$ **Midtown** The units here are all suites with cooking facilities, big enough to provide family members with privacy and sanity breaks, and loaded with amenities. *See map p. 171. 1025 35th Ave., Anchorage.* ☎ *800-314-0781 or 907-563-9844.* www.marriott.com/ancri.

A Wildflower Inn

$$ **Downtown** A warm, cozy house behind a picket fence across from a gourmet grocery and casual eatery. *See map p. 177. 1239 I St., Anchorage.* ☎ *877-693-1239 or 907-274-1239.* www.alaska-wildflower-inn.com.

Where to Dine in Anchorage

Anchorage offers some great dining experiences. The regional cuisine of fresh salmon, halibut, shellfish, and game dominates all fine-dining establishments, and as long as they don't overcook the fish or keep it frozen for too long, you can't go wrong. The very best restaurants, however, use these ingredients creatively, combining various international styles in exciting and unexpected ways. (And you can always get a steak, too.)

But dining in style is expensive and takes a long time. Most people can't afford to do it every night. Moreover, some of our family and friends who have come to Alaska get tired of salmon. So, I include plenty of other, less expensive places, too. If I list them here, they're good — but read on to discover which restaurants offer a unique Alaskan experience and which just serve satisfying meals.

The top restaurants

Bear Tooth Grill
$ Midtown   SOUTHWESTERN

You can't find food of this quality for prices this low anywhere else in Anchorage. Dishes such as the soy grilled halibut are sophisticated and nicely done, but they make up only a small part of a menu that goes on and on with Mexican choices, sandwiches, and other selections inexpensive enough to make the restaurant fit for an after-work impulse — most main courses are under $14. The partners who own the restaurant started in business by making beer and then opened a pizzeria to sell the beer (see Moose's Tooth, later in this section); next they opened a theater/pub (see Chapter 14); the grill, in the same building, was the final addition. Eat tacos, wraps, or pizza while watching a movie or at tables in the movie-theater lobby, a loud, free-flowing setting perfect for kids and open for lunch daily at 11 a.m. The grill is in a separate, calmer, and more confined dining room, best for couples and parties of four or fewer, and opens at 4 p.m. The food comes more slowly, as befits the atmosphere. Tables are more comfortable than booths, but at peak times you have to take what you can get, often with a wait, so try to dine here early or late. Besides the beer, they have a full bar serving many margaritas and 20 wines by the glass.

See map p. 171. 1230 W. 27th Ave., Anchorage. ☎ **907-276-4200.** *Main courses: $6–$20. AE, DC, DISC, MC, V. Open: Daily 11 a.m.–11:30 p.m.*

Campobello Bistro
$$$ Midtown   NORTHERN ITALIAN BISTRO

Arriving at this quiet little Midtown restaurant is like stepping into northern Italy, except for the Alaska seafood. Even the service has the quality of jocular professionalism I remember from Italy. The same priceless pair of waiters has developed a following over a decade in the restaurant. Unlike most of Anchorage's best restaurants, the bistro doesn't try to reinvent the cookbook. Most of the menu consists of recognizable dishes, such as veal Marsala or Italian sausage and polenta. Meals are bold, highly flavored, and entirely satisfying. The seafood crepe is fantastic. Those seeking the bland tomatoes and cheese of a typical Italian family restaurant should go elsewhere. The wine and food are reasonably priced.

See map p. 171. 601 W. 36th, Suite 10, Anchorage. ☎ **907-563-2040.** *Main courses: $10–$13 lunch, $15–$25 dinner. DC, MC, V. Open: Mon–Fri 11 a.m.–2:30 p.m. and 5–9 p.m., Sat 5–9 p.m.*

Downtown Anchorage

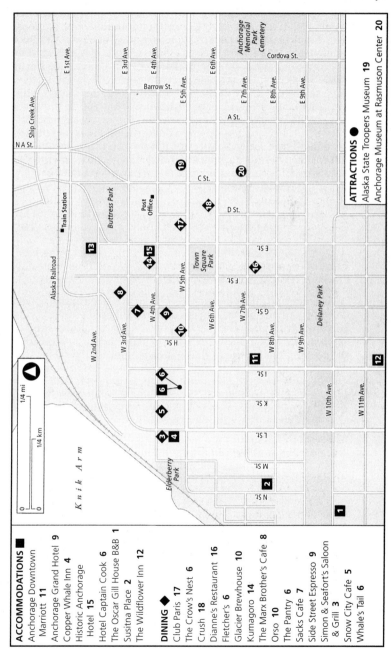

ACCOMMODATIONS ■
Anchorage Downtown
  Marriott **11**
Anchorage Grand Hotel **9**
Copper Whale Inn **4**
Historic Anchorage
  Hotel **15**
Hotel Captain Cook **6**
The Oscar Gill House B&B **1**
Susitna Place **2**
The Wildflower Inn **12**

DINING ◆
Club Paris **17**
The Crow's Nest **6**
Crush **18**
Dianne's Restaurant **16**
Fletcher's **6**
Glacier Brewhouse **10**
Kumagoro **14**
The Marx Brother's Cafe **8**
Orso **10**
The Pantry **6**
Sacks Cafe **7**
Side Street Espresso **9**
Simon & Seafort's Saloon
  & Grill **3**
Snow City Cafe **5**
Whale's Tail **6**

ATTRACTIONS ●
Alaska State Troopers Museum **19**
Anchorage Museum at Rasmuson Center **20**

Club Paris
$$$$ Downtown STEAK

Coming from a bright spring afternoon into midnight darkness, under a neon Eiffel Tower and past the bar, I sat down at a secretive booth for two, and felt as if I should lean across the table and plot a shady 1950s oil deal with my companion. And I would probably not have been the first. In contrast to Sullivan's Steakhouse, across the street, which contrives a masculine, retro feel, Club Paris is the real·thing, decorated with mounted swordfish and other cocktail-era décor. The club is the essence of old Anchorage boomtown years, when the streets were dusty and an oilman needed a classy joint in which to do business. Steak, of course, is what to order, and rare really means rare. It's consistently voted the best in town. Ask for the blue-cheese stuffing; the stuffed filet is worth the years it probably takes off your coronary arteries. They have a full bar.

See map p. 177. 417 W. 5th Ave., Anchorage. ☎ **907-277-6332.** *www.clubparis restaurant.com. Reservations recommended. Main courses: $7–$15 lunch, $18–$44 dinner. AE, DC, DISC, MC, V. Open: Mon–Thurs 11:30 a.m.–2:30 p.m. and 5–10 p.m., Fri–Sat 11:30 a.m.–2:30 p.m. and 5–11 p.m., Sun 4–9 p.m.*

Glacier BrewHouse
$$–$$$$ Downtown BREW PUB

An eclectic and changing menu is served in a large dining room with lodge décor, where the pleasant scent of the wood-fired grill hangs in the air. It's a lively place to see others and be seen. A glass wall shows off the brewing equipment, which produces eight or more hearty beers, and also turns out spent grain for bread that's then set out on the tables with olive oil. An advantage for travelers is the wide price range — a pizza with feta cheese, sun-dried tomatoes, pesto, and garlic is $11; crab legs are $37. The food is usually quite good. Choose this place for a boisterous meal with quick, casual service that will get you out in time to do something else with the evening. Do reserve ahead, however, as waits can be long.

See map p. 177. 737 W. 5th Ave., Anchorage. ☎ **907-274-2739.** *www.glacierbrew house.com. Reservations recommended. Main courses; $8–$15 lunch, $9–$34 dinner. AE, DC, DISC, MC, V. Open: High season daily 11 a.m.–11 p.m.; off season Mon 11 a.m. 0:30 p.m., Tues–Thurs 11 a.m.–10 p.m., Fri–Sat 11 a.m.–11 p.m., Sun 4–9:30 p.m.*

Jens' Restaurant
$$$$ Midtown INTERNATIONAL

Chef Jens Hansen is truly gifted. His restaurant is for the kind of diner who loves exciting food, surprises, and beautiful plates of new tastes and textures. The meals are about the food, sharing bites, and saying "Wow" and "How did he do that?" The cuisine is highly eclectic, but I won't call it experimental, despite the raw kangaroo I tried on one visit, because these dishes work far more often than any experimentalist has a right to expect. There's often only one item on the changing menu that isn't unusual or challenging: the superb pepper steak. Like everything, even that dish has a sauce, and it's complex and memorable. The wine list is exceptional but manageable and reasonably priced, and you can sip your selection while dining inexpensively on appetizers in a pleasant bar area; try the incredible spinach ravioli with Gorgonzola, for example. Desserts are sublime. The dining room is uncluttered and decorated with modern art. Service is highly professional, with each formally attired waiter assigned to just a few tables; they earn their keep as well by helping diners learn about food and wine they've probably never tried.

See map p. 171. 701 W. 36th Ave., Anchorage. ☎ *907-561-5367.* www.jens restaurant.com. *Reservations recommended. Main courses: $9–$34 lunch, $18–$39 dinner. AE, DC, DISC, MC, V. Open: Mon 11:30 a.m.–2 p.m., Tues–Fri 11:30 a.m.–2 p.m. and 6–10 p.m., Sat 6–10 p.m.; wine bar serves appetizers starting at 4 p.m. Closed Jan.*

The Marx Bros. Cafe
$$$$$ Downtown   NEW AMERICAN

A restaurant started by three friends back when gourmet food was an exotic hobby in Anchorage long ago became the standard of excellence in the state. Treatments of Alaska seafood that began here as cutting-edge creative cuisine now turn up in many of the best restaurants, yet Chef Jack Amon's signature macadamia-nut-encrusted halibut is nowhere done better. He still presides in the kitchen of the cottage downtown, one of the city's first houses, while maitre d' Van Hale manages the front, preparing his famous Caesar salad at tableside, a ritual that allows him to schmooze with anyone he chooses in the tiny dining rooms. His attitude mirrors the casual elegance of the entire evening, where those wearing ties are in the minority. I've labeled the cuisine "New American" because I had to choose from a list, but the cuisine is eclectic, ranging from Asian to Italian to uncategorizable, and always turned out flawlessly. The changing menu is not long, but the wine list is the size of a dictionary, winner of many awards, but potentially intimidating. A meal is an experience that takes much of the evening and at this writing all entrees are over $35. Save room for the exceptional desserts.

See map p. 177. 627 W. 3rd Ave. ☎ **907-278-2133.** www.marxcafe.com. *Reservations required. Main courses: $36–$38. AE, DC, MC, V. Open: Summer Tues– Sat 5:30–10 p.m.; winter Tues–Thurs 6–9:30 p.m., Fri–Sat 5:30–10 p.m.*

Moose's Tooth Pub & Pizzeria
$ Midtown PIZZA

The best pizza and beer in Anchorage undoubtedly come from this fun and friendly place. The microbrewery came first, but the pizza really is the greater accomplishment. It has a soft, light crust like Italian pizza but the oomph of American pie. They offer many ingenious toppings, but not just to dump on: The combinations really work. The ambience is youthful, casual, and loud; the high energy means kids aren't out of place. The dining room, although handsomely rebuilt, still looks from top to bottom like a college-town pizzeria. Service is quick and friendly. The only drawback is the restaurant's popularity, which can make for long waits at peak times.

See map p. 171. 3300 Old Seward Hwy., Anchorage. ☎ **907-258-2537.** www. moosestooth.net. *Main courses: Large pizza $13–$25. AE, DC, DISC, MC, V. Open: Summer Sun 11 a.m. to midnight, Mon–Thurs 10:30 a.m. to midnight, Fri 10:30 a.m.–1 a.m., Sat 11 a.m.–1 a.m.; winter Sun 11 a.m.–11 p.m., Mon 10:30 a.m.–11 p.m., Tues–Thurs 10:30 a.m. to midnight, Fri 10:30 a.m.–1 a.m., Sat 11 a.m.–1 a.m.*

Orso
$$–$$$$ Downtown   MEDITERRANEAN

This restaurant is unique in Anchorage for serving interesting food even though it's large and oriented to the downtown tourist trade. The warm colors of the ornate dining room are lightened with big modern paintings. Bold flavors amp up a long menu full of surprises. The mushroom ravioli, with a generous dose of smoked salmon, was rich and strongly flavored. Service is professional but not stuffy, and the food comes fast enough not to use up the entire evening. Generally, the prices are reasonable for this kind of food, and the bar offers "Bear Bites" discounts on appetizers before 6 p.m. and after 9 p.m. We also enjoy the bar later in the evening for a drink and dessert at the end of an evening out. (It's open an hour later than the dining room.) Saturday and Sunday brunch is served 11 a.m. to 3 p.m.

See map p. 177. 737 W. 5th Ave. ☎ **907-222-3232.** www.orsoalaska.com. *Reservations recommended. Main courses: $10–$15 lunch, $12–$33 dinner. AE, MC, V. Open: Summer Sun–Thurs 11:30 a.m.–4 p.m. and 5–10 p.m., Fri–Sat 11:30 a.m.– 4 p.m. and 5–11 p.m.; winter Tues 11:30 a.m.–2:30 p.m. and 5–9:30 p.m., Wed–Thurs 11:30 a.m.–2:30 p.m. and 5–10 p.m., Fri 11:30 a.m.–2:30 p.m. and 5–11 p.m., Sat 11 a.m.– 3 p.m. and 5–11 p.m., Sun 11 a.m.–3 p.m. and 5–9:30 p.m.*

Sacks Cafe & Restaurant
$$$–$$$$ Downtown   INTERNATIONAL

Long a favorite of my wife's and mine, this stylish cafe presents terrific food with a style of service that's both crisply professional and relaxingly casual. The storefront dining room, in warm Southwest colors and sharp angles, resembles a showcase for the food and diners, who can sit at tables or at a *tapas* bar. The cuisine defies categorization but is consistently interesting and creative, often fusing Asian influences with European or regional styles, including plenty of local seafood. Vegetarians do as well as meat eaters. For lunch, the sandwiches are unforgettable, with choices such as shrimp and avocado with herb cream cheese on sourdough. Don't miss the tomato soup with Gorgonzola. The beer and wine list is extensive and reasonably priced. Brunch is served Saturday 11 a.m. to 3 p.m., Sunday 10 a.m. to 3 p.m.

See map p. 177. 328 G St., Anchorage. ☎ **907-274-4022.** www.sackscafe.com. *Reservations recommended for dinner (reserve a day ahead for weekend nights). Main courses: $5–$15 lunch, $18–$34 dinner. AE, MC, V. Open: Mon–Thurs 11 a.m.– 2:30 p.m. and 5–9:30 p.m., Fri 5–10:30 p.m., Sat 11 a.m.–3 p.m. and 5–10:30 p.m., Sun 10 a.m.–3 p.m. and 5–9:30 p.m.*

Simon & Seafort's Saloon & Grill
$$$$ Downtown   GRILL

Simon's, as it's known, is a jolly beef and seafood grill where voices boom off the high ceilings. On sunny summer evenings, the rooms, fitted with brass turn-of-the-20th-century saloon décor, fill with light off Cook Inlet, down below the bluff; the views are magnificent. The food is consistently good. A nightly list of specials covers any gustatory adventures, but most of the cuisine is simpler — prime rib, for example. Service is warm and professional and quick enough to allow time for other evening activities. Children are treated well. To enjoy the place on a budget, come early for a $25 three-course *prix fixe* menu, or order a sandwich and soup or appetizer at the well-stocked bar; it's open until 11 p.m. every night. Getting a table in the restaurant at a reasonable hour requires advance planning in peak season or on off-season weekends; call a couple days ahead.

See map p. 177. 420 L St., Anchorage. ☎ 907-274-3502. www.simonand seaforts.com. Reservations recommended (make dinner reservations a couple of days in advance in summer). Main courses: $7.50–$18 lunch, $16–$42 dinner. AE, DISC, MC, V. Open: Summer Mon–Fri 11 a.m.–2:30 p.m. and 4:30–10 p.m., Sat–Sun 4:30–10 p.m.; winter Mon–Thurs 11 a.m.–2:30 p.m. and 5–9:30 p.m., Fri 5–10 p.m., Sat 4:30–10 p.m., Sun 4:30–9 p.m.

Snow City Cafe
$ Downtown   CAFE

This is the happening spot downtown for breakfast or lunch. What started as a smaller, granola-crowd place grew on the basis of hearty, tasty food and a friendly young waitstaff into a large, busy restaurant with lots of life and energy and a diverse clientele. It's especially popular in the morning, when you'll rarely do better than the salmon cakes and eggs, omelets, or five kinds of eggs Benedict. Breakfast is served all day. Lunch, starting at 11 a.m., includes comfort food such as mac and cheese or meatloaf, but also unusual sandwiches, such as roast beef and blue cheese or grilled veggie and chèvre panini. The dining room is light and colorful, with a clean feel, and with tables out in the open amid lots of movement. The restaurant offers free Wi-Fi. Small monthly art shows begin with artist receptions every first Friday, a pattern shared with all the downtown galleries. They serve beer and wine.

See map p. 177. 1034 W. 4th Ave., Anchorage. ☎ 907-272-2489. www.snowcity cafe.com. Main courses: $8–$12. AE, DISC, MC, V. Open: Daily 7 a.m.–4 p.m. (Mon–Fri after 3 p.m. espresso counter only).

Spenard Roadhouse
$ Midtown   AMERICAN

Anchorage has grown up enough to have a restaurant that celebrates the kitschy frontier culture of the 1970s with loving irony, displaying old license plates on the wall and offering TV dinners as specials. But the owners, a team who started two of the city's coolest restaurants individually (Sacks and Snow City Cafe), know that the younger clientele who have made this part of Spenard newly hip don't mainly want the chocolate milk and macaroni and cheese on the menu, so they serve a broad range of choices, including a sumptuous blackened Ahi tuna with yellow Thai curry, rice noodles, and pineapple salsa, as well as steaks, chops, sandwiches, pizza, and lots of small plates to share. The full bar makes good strong drinks and specializes in small-batch and single-barrel bourbons. It's a fun, social place to eat.

See map p. 171. 1049 W. Northern Lights Blvd. ☎ **907-770-7623.** www.spenard roadhouse.com. *Main courses: $9–$23. AE, DISC, MC, V. Open: Mon–Fri 11 a.m.– 11 p.m., Sat–Sun 9 a.m.–11 p.m.*

Runner-up restaurants

City Diner

$$ Midtown DINER With all the chrome and neon of the movie set of a classic diner, this fun place was founded by chefs who bring professional skill to classic eats. *See map p. 171. 3000 Minnesota Dr., Anchorage.* ☎ **907-277-2489.** *Main courses: $7–$19. AE, DISC, MC, V. Open: Daily 6 a.m.–11 p.m.*

Crush

$–$$ Downtown BISTRO An elegant place situated in the city's small upscale shopping area, Crush offers inexpensive plates of noshes and delicacies to pass around the table, as well as wonderful salads or sandwiches for lunch and coffee and pastries in the morning. *See map p. 177. 343 W. 6th Ave., Anchorage.* ☎ **907-865-9198.** *Main courses: $8–$14. AE, DC, MC, V. Open: Mon–Thurs 8 a.m.–11 p.m., Fri 8 a.m. to midnight, Sat 5 p.m. to midnight.*

Dianne's Restaurant

$ Downtown SOUP/SANDWICH A perfect choice for a quick, healthful, and inexpensive bite downtown is this cafeteria serving freshly baked bread, soups, sandwiches, and lunchtime specials. *See map p. 177. 550 W. 7th Ave., Suite 110, Anchorage.* ☎ **907-279-7243.** *Main courses: $4.75–$10. AE, DISC, MC, V. Open: Mon–Fri 7 a.m.–4 p.m.*

The Greek Corner

$$ Midtown GREEK/ITALIAN The sunny, spacious, and informal dining room and the restaurant's warm hospitality and quick, inexpensive food make it a great choice for families. *See map p. 171. 201 E. Northern Lights Blvd., Anchorage.* ☎ **907-276-2820.** *Main courses: $5.50–$10 lunch, $10–$20 dinner. MC, V. Open: Mon–Fri 11 a.m.–10 p.m., Sat noon to 10 p.m., Sun 4–10 p.m.*

Kumagoro

$$$ Downtown JAPANESE This good, authentic Japanese restaurant is right on the main tourist street downtown. Try the box lunch ($16), a large sampler that includes sushi and sashimi. The dining room is pleasantly low-key, with tables in narrow rows. They have a beer and wine license. *See map p. 177. 533 W. 4th Ave., Anchorage.* ☎ **907-272-9905.** *Main courses: $8–$16 lunch, $16–$42 dinner. AE, DC, DISC, MC, V. Open: Summer daily 11 a.m.–10:30 p.m., winter daily 11 a.m.–10 p.m.*

The Lucky Wishbone

$ Downtown DINER This Anchorage institution is where families go out for a delicious, not-too-greasy, fried-chicken dinner and famous milkshakes. You'll see few other tourists, because the location is too far to walk to from the hotels. They have a drive-through window. *See map p. 171. 1033 E. 5th Ave., Anchorage.* ☎ *907-272-3454. Main courses: $3.50–$12. MC, V. Open: Summer Mon–Thurs 10 a.m.–10 p.m., Fri–Sat 10 a.m.–11 p.m., winter daily 10 a.m.–10 p.m.*

Chapter 14

Exploring Anchorage

In This Chapter

▶ Discovering the top sights
▶ Getting outside and finding more to do
▶ Planning an Anchorage itinerary
▶ Shopping for Alaskan gifts and souvenirs
▶ Going out at night

*Y*ou can find plenty to do for a few days in Anchorage, but not all of it is indoors. As good as the museum is, it can't compare to flying over Mount McKinley or climbing to the top of a rocky peak above the city. No museum can beat a sunny day in the world's most spectacular places. An easy rule helps set priorities: If the sun is out, stay outside; if it rains, check out the indoor attractions until it stops. That's how Alaskans do it, with one exception: They stay outside in the rain, too.

Now, a quick note on definitions. I define anything that involves the world out of doors as *outdoors,* not just bear-wrasslin' or rock-climbing with your fingernails. Driving to a fabulous mountain overlook or riding in a small aircraft over a wildly rugged terrain counts as outdoors in this book, too. So, you don't have to be active to see the good stuff. You *do,* however, need an interest in nature, for participation or observation.

Two essential indoor attractions in Anchorage are worth anyone's time: the Alaska Native Heritage Center and the Anchorage Museum. These are places where you can put your Alaskan experiences in context, adding layers of meaning beyond the sheer beauty. The zoo is fun, too, but it's mostly outdoors.

This chapter helps you plan your Anchorage explorations, and it includes two maps to help you chart your course.

Hitting the Top Sights

Alaska Native Heritage Center
Glenn Highway (East of Downtown)

Alaska Natives built this extraordinary center to bring their cultures to visitors. It's Alaska's best Native cultural attraction. What makes it so is not the graceful building or the professional and informative displays, but the Native people themselves — real village people, who often make a personal connection with visitors and rarely come across as practiced or distant.

The three main parts of the center take much of a day to absorb; allow three hours, not for the exhibits, but to have time to interact with the people. First, storytellers, dancers, and Native athletes perform in a hall with three 30-minute programs rotating through the day. The second part features a gallery of educational displays, and a series of workshops, where artisans practice and show off traditional crafts, often teaching visitors. Finally, don't miss the pond surrounded by traditional Native dwellings, each representing a cultural group, and each with a Native host. The center has a snack bar and grill serving soup, sandwiches, and other meals. The gift shop has inexpensive items mixed in with real Native arts and crafts for sale by the center or on consignment from Native artisans.

The center is about the same distance from downtown as the airport, but to the east. It's a 10- to 20-minute drive, depending on traffic. The center offers a free shuttle from various places in town; call for details. Depending on the size of your party, you may prefer to rent a car on the day you visit the center, using it later for further explorations or to go out in the evening. Also, ask for discounts, including family admission or a joint admission with the Anchorage Museum.

See map p. 171. 800 Heritage Center Dr. From the Glenn Highway (6th Avenue downtown), take the North Muldoon exit. ☎ **800-315-6608** *or 907-330-8000.* www.alaska native.net. *Open: Summer daily 9 a.m.–5 p.m.; winter call for hours and discounts. Admission: $25 adults ($10 Alaska residents), $21 seniors and military, $17 kids 7–16 ($7 Alaska residents), free for kids 6 and under. AE, MC, V.*

The Alaska Zoo
Hillside

Alaskan animals are the zoo's best attraction. I enjoy watching polar bears Ahpun and Lyutyik play and swim underwater. Gravel paths meander through the woods past large enclosures with natural flora for bears, seals, otters, musk oxen, Dall sheep, moose, caribou, waterfowl — all the animals you were supposed to see in Alaska but may have missed. You can see a few exotic species, such as Bactrian camels and snow leopards, from beyond Alaska, too. You can easily spend half a day at the zoo, but if it's raining, you may not want to, because there is little shelter. Two-hour naturalist tours take place every day at noon, and include some backstage stops; the cost is $25 adults, $15 kids 12 and under. A snack bar serves basic meals, and there is a gift shop. The zoo is a 20-minute drive from downtown, without traffic. If you don't have a car, it's possible in the summer to catch the zoo's free shuttle, which picks up from several downtown locations daily; call for details.

See map p. 171. 4731 O'Malley Rd., Anchorage. ☎ **907-346-3242.** *www.alaska zoo.org. Open: May–Aug daily 9 a.m.–6 p.m. (until 9 p.m. Tues and Fri), summer educational programs most Tues at 7 p.m., live music most Fri at 7 p.m.; Sept–Apr open daily 10 a.m. to sunset. Admission: $12 adults, $9 seniors, $6 kids 3–17, free for kids 2 and under. MC, V.*

Anchorage Museum at Rasmuson Center
Downtown

The museum completed a $106-million expansion project in 2010, and the new galleries are extraordinary. The Smithsonian Arctic Studies Center, upstairs, contains the world's ultimate treasures of traditional Alaska Native Art, 600 pieces, most of which were collected a century ago but were never displayed. I was astounded by the quality of this exhibit. Multimedia screens allow you to zoom in on the objects and learn more, and an unequalled collection of contemporary Alaska Native art is nearby. A science museum called the Imaginarium resides within the museum, included in the price; it's aimed at young children, but any curious adult will be enchanted by the ingenious and well-made interactive exhibits, including a planetarium and large touch tanks of creatures. The museum's traditional attraction, the Alaska Gallery, is a popular introduction to Alaska's history and anthropology, although it's grown a bit stodgy compared to the other attractions in the building. You can spend most of a day here; plan at least two hours.

A new restaurant, **Muse,** occupies a space off the entry lobby. It's operated by the locally famous gourmets who own The Marx Bros. Cafe (see Chapter 13), and produces excellent food in a relaxed, modern setting, in reasonable portions and for reasonable prices. The restaurant has a large dining room and a patio.

See map p. 177. 625 C St., Anchorage. ☎ **907-929-9200.** *www.anchorage museum.org. Open: May 15–Sept 15 daily 9 a.m.–6 p.m.; Sept 16–May 14 Tues–Sat 10 a.m.–6 p.m., Sun noon to 5 p.m. Admission: $15 adults ($10 Alaska residents), $8 seniors 66 and over, $7 kids 3–12, free for kids 2 and under.*

Getting Outdoors: Summer and Winter in the City

In most cities, you have to go somewhere else for a natural outdoor experience. In Anchorage, you may be able to do it right from your hotel. The city is a shallow scratch of civilization on a vast wilderness. You find big parks with plenty of wildlife mixed in among the cars and strip malls. Just beyond the last houses, but still within the city limits, is **Chugach State Park,** one of the largest and most beautiful in the nation (indeed, many *national* parks don't come close). You can drive right to some of its most impressive views.

Gearing up in Anchorage

You can rent almost anything you need for outdoor activities in Anchorage. The city also may be the best place to stock up and gear up before heading out on the next leg of your trip, renting a canoe, bike, skis or camping equipment here to carry with your rental car.

✔ **Backcountry gear and Nordic skis:** You can get advice and rent cross-country skis, snowshoes, bear-proof containers, and mountaineering equipment at **Alaska Mountaineering & Hiking,** 2633 Spenard Rd. (☎ 907-272-1811; www.alaska mountaineering.com). It's a small shop where the staff takes the time to help you plan a trip. A block away, at 1200 W. Northern Lights Blvd., **REI** has a much larger store (☎ **907-272-4565;** www.rei.com) that rents a wide range of gear, including lightweight canoes and touring kayaks with car-top carriers, camping gear, tents, packs, sleeping bags, and cross-country skis (but not bikes or ice-climbing gear); it also carries the town's best stock of outdoor athletic clothing.

✔ **Bikes:** Try **Downtown Bicycle Rental,** at 4th Avenue and C Street (☎ **907-279-5293;** www.alaska-bike-rentals.com). Rates start at $16 for three hours, $4 per additional hour, with a maximum of $32 per day. The shop also carries tandems, kids' bikes, and trailers.

✔ **Downhill skis:** Each of the downhill ski areas listed in the "Wintertime outdoor activities" section, later in this chapter, has a full rental operation.

✔ **Ice skates:** Skates rent for $10 per day at **Champions Choice,** in the University Center Mall at Old Seward Highway and 36th Avenue (☎ 907-563-3503).

If you miss the outdoors, you're missing the whole point of Anchorage.

I cover some indispensable outdoor day trips in Chapter 15. Although you can't do them all, you should do at least one. Here, I cover the top outdoor places and activities right in town, including activities that take place far afield but begin and end at the airport here (such as flightseeing and fly-in fishing).

In town, the city's **bike trails** connect through greenbelts whose soothing, creekside woods span the noisy, asphalt urban core. **Kincaid Park** and **Far North Bicentennial Park** are both on the trail system within the city and encompass scores of miles of trails for Nordic skiing, mountainbiking, and horseback-riding. The **Chugach Mountains,** which form the backdrop to the town, offer tundra-hiking, backpacking, mountainbiking, and climbs that range from easy to technical. Or you can just drive up and take a look at the view.

Summertime outdoor activities

Don't be overwhelmed by the length of this section. I can only boil down warm-weather activities so far while still offering something for every ability level. Use the alphabetized listing here to jump to what you're interested in doing, and then choose a place to match your interests and energy level.

Biking and walking on pavement

Anchorage has an award-winning network of paved **bike trails** spanning the city along wooded greenbelts. You rarely see a building and almost always cross roads and rail lines through tunnels and over bridges, so you're never in traffic. Here are two of the best:

 ✔ **Tony Knowles Coastal Trail:** Leading 10 miles from the western end of 2nd Avenue along the shore to **Kincaid Park,** the coastal trail is a unique pathway to the natural environment from the heart of downtown and is among my favorite things about Anchorage. I've been stopped by moose so many times on the trail between Earthquake Park and Kincaid that it's become a darned nuisance; closer to downtown, I've ridden parallel to beluga whales swimming along the trail at high tide (just once). The most popular entry is at **Elderberry Park,** at the western end of 5th Avenue. **Westchester Lagoon,** a large dammed pond, is ten blocks south of Elderberry Park, making for a lovely stroll. It's an equally enjoyable destination for a picnic or to feed the ducks and geese. A couple miles farther, the trail arrives at Earthquake Park and Point Woronzof, mentioned in the upcoming section, "Driving to beautiful places."

 ✔ **Lanie Fleischer Chester Creek Trail:** Starting at an intersection with the Coastal Trail at Westchester Lagoon, the trail runs about 4 miles east along the greenbelt to **Goose Lake,** where you can swim in a cool woodland pond at the end of a hot bike ride — still, improbably enough, in the middle of the city. In the summer, you'll often find snacks for sale and boats for rent there, too. South from the lake, a wooded trail leads partway through the University of Alaska Anchorage campus and, with some navigation, to miles more riding.

Driving to beautiful places

If you're not up to muscle-powered sports, and you don't want to spend the money it takes to go flightseeing, you can still get a taste of Anchorage's beauty behind the wheel of a rental car. Here are directions to some lovely places in town (don't miss the day trips mentioned in Chapter 15, either):

 ✔ **Glen Alps Overlook:** High in the mountains above Anchorage, the popular trailhead also has a short, easy trail to a spectacular overlook with interpretive signs. For directions, see "Hiking and mountain-biking," later in this chapter.

✔ **Point Woronzof:** A parking lot here sits atop a bluff over the edge of Cook Inlet with the best sunset views in town and a clear view of Mount McKinley in good weather. A short walk on a pathway down the bluff leads to a broad sand and pebble beach. Drive west on Northern Lights Boulevard, past Earthquake Park (see the "Discovering More Cool Things to See and Do" section, later in this chapter). You'll have to pass by an airport security booth, which is normally unoccupied. After the road makes a sharp left above the water, look for the sign on the right.

✔ **Potters Marsh:** A boardwalk leads into an enormous wetland rich in waterfowl and other bird life. Take the New Seward Highway south, turning left just past the Rabbit Creek exit.

Fishing

Hatchery salmon run in many of Anchorage's streams, and stocked trout, salmon, or char in more than 28 lakes, so you don't need to leave town to catch a fish. The **Alaska Department of Fish & Game,** 333 Raspberry Rd., Anchorage (☎ 907-267-2218; www.sf.adfg.state. ak.us), publishes informative booklets on the Web and on paper, as well as an online fishing report updated weekly in season. There's also a recorded information line (☎ **907-267-2503**) with what's hot and lots of other advice.

✔ **Fly-in fishing:** Use Anchorage as a base from which to fly to a remote lake or river with a lot of fish and not many other people. Even folks who are unenthusiastic about fishing may find such a flight an unforgettable experience. The plane lifts off from Anchorage's Lake Hood floatplane base and within half an hour smoothly lands on a remote lake or river. You climb out and watch as the plane lifts off and disappears, leaving behind the kind of silence unique to true wilderness. Taking a guided outing is a good opportunity to learn how to hook a salmon. I've heard people complain about how sore their arms got from pulling in too many. It's on such trips that avid anglers are made — or spoiled.

Several companies offer fly-in trips; among the largest is **Rust's Flying Service** (☎ **800-544-2299** or 907-243-1595; www.flyrusts. com). They can take you out guided or on your own, for the day or for a longer stay in a cabin or lodge. If you fly to a lake, they'll provide a boat. They can't make fish appear if the fish aren't running, but they will try to take you to the hot spots. You can bring your own gear, or they can provide it. Prices for an unguided day trip start at around $250 per person, with a two-person minimum; guided, $495. Pickup from your hotel is included, but fishing licenses are extra.

✔ **Roadside fishing (unguided):** Although the setting (under a high-way bridge in an industrial area) may not be the wilderness experience you've dreamed about, the 25- to 40-pound king salmon you pull from **Ship Creek** may make up for it. From downtown, just walk down the hill to the railroad yard. At present there is no gear rental on the creek, so you have to bring your own. Fishing for kings is best in June; for silvers, in August and September. Fish only on the rising tide, when the fish come into the creek. Fishing near the end of the rising tide will mean crossing less mud, but one successful angler I know insists it's the start of the tide that's best. Either way, you need rubber boots, preferably neoprene chest waders, for the muddy banks, but don't go too far out — the mud flats are dangerous, and several times every summer the fire department has to rescue stuck fishermen. **Bird Creek,** 25 miles south of Anchorage on the Seward Highway (see Chapter 15), carries a strong hatchery run of silver salmon, peaking in August. When silver fishing is hot, it gets crowded. Pink salmon run from late June through early August in even-numbered years. Other creeks along this stretch of highway have similar but smaller runs.

Flightseeing and bear-viewing

If Anchorage is the heart of Alaska's transportation system, small planes are the blood cells. Anchorage hosts several busy airports and, of these, **Lake Hood** is the world's busiest floatplane base. Many providers offer flightseeing tours. If you're planning to travel to Talkeetna or Denali National Park (see Chapter 19) or Juneau or Glacier Bay National Park (see Chapter 20), it may be wise to save your flightseeing splurge for those extraordinary places. Likewise, for bear-viewing flights, Juneau (see Chapter 20) and Katmai National Park and Kodiak (see Chapter 24) are closer to the action. On the other hand, plenty of spectacular territory is near Anchorage, and, if time is short, you can see bears or Denali in an afternoon. I recommend Rust's Flying Service (see the preceding section), a reliable operator that has designed a menu of choices around visitors' most common interests. They can take you on a floatplane ride for as little as $100. A flight to see Mount McKinley (without landing) is $375 and takes three hours. An all-day bear-viewing tour from Anchorage is $595 to $785 per person. The exact destination — Lake Clark, Katmai National Park, or somewhere else — depends on where bears are active when you're traveling.

Hiking and mountain-biking

The following choices of where to hike or mountain-bike are arranged in order of convenience to downtown, but all are best reached by rental car:

✔ **Kincaid Park:** Covered in more detail later in this chapter, under "Skiing," Kincaid Park is an idyllic summer setting for mountain-biking and day hikes. Moose are sighted daily on the wide dirt and grass trails that snake for about 40 miles through the birch and white spruce of the park's hilly 1,500 acres of boreal forest. You get many views of the sea and mountains beyond. Within the park, wooded Little Campbell Lake is a picturesque swimming hole, and a fun spot for family canoeing and fishing for stocked trout, salmon, and char; however, it has no lifeguard. The park also has an 18-hole Frisbee golf course. To get here from downtown, take Minnesota Drive (I Street) south beyond the airport interchange to Raspberry Road, which leads to the park. Be sure to park outside the park if you plan on staying late — the gates are locked at 10 p.m.

✔ **Far North Bicentennial Park:** The 4,000-acre park, on the east side of town (also known as the Campbell Tract), is a unique patch of urban wilderness, a habitat for bear, moose, and spawning salmon. People use it for dog-mushing and skiing in winter, and for day-hiking and exceptional mountain-biking in summer. The **Alaska Botanical Garden** and **Hilltop Ski Area** are both within the park's boundaries. A good place to start a hike or ride through the woods is the **Campbell Creek Science Center** (☎ **907-267-1247;** www. blm.gov/ak/sciencecenter), an educational facility where staff are often on hand to answer questions and you can consult books and maps and admire a big aquarium of native fish. To get there from downtown, take Gambell Street (which becomes New Seward Highway) south to Dowling Road, go east (toward the mountains), and turn right on Lake Otis Road and left on 68th Avenue, following it to the end, and then left at the BLM Campbell Tract entrance sign. Note that the park is home to potentially dangerous brown bears that fish from the creek; observe signs closing trails, and stick to daylight hours for hiking or biking.

✔ **Glen Alps Trailhead and Flattop Mountain:** You can find many ways to reach the alpine tundra, intoxicating fresh air, and cinematic views of the Chugach Mountains behind Anchorage, but the easiest and best developed are at Chugach State Park's **Glen Alps Trailhead.** Even if you're not up to hiking, a drive and a walk on a short, paved overlook loop with incredible views and good interpretive signs is well worth the effort. (Payment of the $5 day-use fee is not required for those visiting only the overlook.) If you're ready for a hike, you can start at the trailhead for trips of up to several days, following the network of trails or taking off across dry, alpine tundra by yourself, but largely within cellphone range. Camping is permitted anywhere off the trails.

Flattop Mountain is the most popular hike from the Glen Alps Trailhead, so it can be a bit crowded on weekends. It's a steep afternoon hike, easy for fit adults and doable for school-age kids. Watch out for a bit of a scramble near the summit and be sure to stick to the painted markers on the rocks. Also, don't forget to dress warmly and don't go in the rain, when slick rocks can be hazardous. For a longer or less steep hike or a mountain-biking trip, follow the broad gravel trail that leads up the valley from the Glen Alps Trailhead to several other great routes. Trails lead all the way over the mountains to Indian or Bird Creek, on Turnagain Arm, up some of the mountains along the way, or to round alpine lakes in high, rocky valleys. You're always above the tree line, so you don't need to follow a trail if you have a good map. The area is wonderful backpacking country.

To get to the Glen Alps trailhead, take New Seward Highway to O'Malley Road, head east toward the mountains, then turn right on Hillside Drive and left onto Upper Huffman Road. Finally, turn right on the narrow, twisting Toilsome Hill Drive. Don't forget to bring cash for a self-service day-use fee of $5.

✔ **Eagle River Valley and Crow Pass:** The **Eagle River Nature Center,** at the end of Eagle River Road, 12 miles up Eagle River Valley from the Glenn Highway exit (☎ **907-694-2108;** www.ernc.org), is like a public wilderness lodge, with hands-on naturalist displays about the area and guided nature walks or talks daily in the summer and weekends year-round (2 p.m. weekends; call for other times). Operated by a nonprofit concessionaire for Chugach State Park, it's open June through August daily 10 a.m. to 5 p.m.; May and September Tuesday through Sunday 10 a.m. to 5 p.m.; October through April Friday through Sunday 10 a.m. to 5 p.m. There's a $5 parking fee. Outside the center, the ¾-mile **Rodak Nature Trail,** with interpretive signs, leads to a viewing platform over a beaver pond. The **Albert Loop Trail** is a 3-mile route; a geology guide from the center matches with numbered posts on the way. Both trails have good bird- and wildlife-watching. The 25-mile **Crow Pass Trail,** a portion of the historic Iditarod Trail, continues as a backpacking route up the valley and across the mountains to Girdwood (see Chapter 15). To use it for a day hike of around 6 miles, loop back to the starting point on the **Dew Mound Trail.**

✔ **Thunderbird Falls and Eklutna Lake:** The hike to Thunderbird Falls is an easy, 1-mile forest walk with a good reward at the end: a view of the falls (possible without making the steep final descent to their base). The trail is easy to find: Take Glenn Highway north to the Thunderbird Falls exit, 25 miles from Anchorage. You can visit Eklutna Lake on the same outing. From the falls, continue 10 miles up the Eklutna Lake Road until you come to the glacial lake, a place for canoeing, hiking, and exceptional mountain-biking. The Lakeside Trail leads 14 miles to Eklutna Glacier, with lake views along the way. (Doing the whole thing and back is too much for a day trip; you can camp on the way or stay at the state park's communal Serenity Falls hut at 13 miles. Reserve in person only at the **Department of Natural Resources Public Information Center,** 550 W. 7th Ave., Suite 1260, Anchorage; it's open Monday through Friday from 10 a.m. to 5 p.m.) Rental bikes, kayaks, and other equipment, as well as guided kayak tours, are available through **Lifetime Adventures,** with a booth at the trailhead (☎ **907-746-4644;** www.lifetimeadventures.net). For $75, you can kayak 8 miles to the other end of the lake and pick up a bike there to ride back. This glacial melt is also where Anchorage gets most of its city water. People bottle it and sell it as "glacier water."

Answering outdoors questions

The **Alaska Public Lands Information Center**, 605 W. 4th Ave., Anchorage (☎ 866-869-6887 or 907-644-3661; www.alaskacenters.gov), offers guidance for outdoor activities all over the state, especially around Anchorage. For information on the bike trails, cross-country skiing parks, and other city recreation, contact **Anchorage Parks & Recreation** (☎ 907-343-4355; www.muni.org/parks). Cross-country skiers can get information from the **Nordic Skiing Association of Anchorage** (☎ 907-276-7609; www.anchoragenordicski.com). Get advice about **Chugach State Park** from the Public Lands Information Center or directly from the park (☎ 907-345-5014; www.dnr.state.ak.us/parks/units/chugach/index.htm). Their *Ridgelines* newspaper is packed with useful information about the park, including a map adequate for most day-hikers, and is available for download at www.alaskageographic.org. The best trail guide to the entire region is Helen Nienhueser and John Wolfe, Jr.'s *55 Ways to the Wilderness* (The Mountaineers), which is available in any bookstore in the area. An excellent **trail map** is the Chugach State Park map published by Imus Geographics and sold at either of the sporting-goods stores mentioned in the "Gearing up in Anchorage" sidebar, earlier in this chapter.

Rafting

Several whitewater rivers are within a 90-minute drive of Anchorage. **NOVA** (☎ 800-746-5753 or 907-745-5753; www.novalaska.com) has more than 30 years of experience offering multi-day trips all over the state, and five different half-day floats in the Anchorage area. Various rafting trips are available, ranging from the relatively easygoing Matanuska and Kings rivers to the class IV and V white water of Six-Mile Creek, which begins with a required instructional swim and includes fun optional swims. That wild white water is about 90 minutes south of Anchorage on the Seward Highway. White-water rafting always entails risk, but NOVA's schedule allows you to calibrate how wild you want to get, and the company offers add-ons for self-paddling, helicopter flight-seeing, or glacier hiking. The half-day trips range in price from $75 to $135. Kids 5 to 11 can go on the calmer Matanuska River float for $45. Other trips are suitable only for older kids and adults. You'll need your own transportation to the river, and you may need to bring your own lunch. **Chugach Outdoor Center** (☎ 866-277-7238 or 907-277-7238; www.chugachoutdoorcenter.com) also offers several rafting options south of Anchorage. The company has two daily choices on Six-Mile Creek, and trips in nearby Turnagain Pass that allow your party to split up, with some doing the crazy Six-Mile white water and others having a leisurely float in the pass. They also raft Seward's Resurrection River.

Sea-kayaking

Except at Eklutna Lake (see "Hiking and mountain-biking," earlier), kayaking day trips from Anchorage go through Whittier, on Prince William Sound (see Chapter 15).

Wintertime outdoor activities

If you don't enjoy winter sports, Anchorage during the snowy months (usually Nov–Mar) probably isn't for you. Less-active summer activities such as fishing, walking, or driving are difficult, impossible, or chilly. But cold weather doesn't feel so cold when you're active. Skiers and snow-mobilers pray for snow. And around here, their prayers get answered pretty consistently.

Ice-skating

Westchester Lagoon, just ten blocks from downtown (see "Biking and walking on pavement," earlier in this chapter), is a skating paradise in the winter. When the ice gets thick enough, usually by mid-December, the city clears a large rink and over a mile of wide paths that wind across the pond, mopping the ice regularly for a smooth surface. Skaters gather around burn barrels, to socialize and warm their hands, and on weekends, vendors often sell hot chocolate and coffee.

Skiing

Kincaid Park is one of the best **cross-country skiing** areas in the country, with the first World Cup–certified trails in the United States. National Championships and Olympic trials were held here in 2010. More than 40 miles of trails are geared to every ability level, with the majority intermediate and expert. Superb trails aside, Kincaid is a beautiful place to ski, with rolling hills of open birch and spruce and views of the mountains and ocean. Trails are groomed for skating and classical techniques. Ten miles are lighted (important on short winter days). The **Kincaid Park Outdoor Center** (☎ **907-343-6397**) is open daily from noon to 9 p.m., with shorter hours on holidays. The gate closes at 10 p.m., so park outside it if you plan on skiing later. Skiing usually lasts through March. Big races occur in February and early March.

Far North Bicentennial Park also has some excellent trails — 20 miles total, 4⅓ miles lighted — and a slightly longer season because of its hill-side location. Start at Hilltop Ski Area (see the end of this section).

Many other parks and bike trails have lengthy skiing routes, too, many of them lighted. You can ski right from downtown on the Tony Knowles Coastal Trail. (See the "Gearing up in Anchorage" sidebar, earlier in this chapter, for ski rentals.)

Anchorage has several **downhill ski areas.** The best, **Alyeska Resort,** is described in the Girdwood section of Chapter 15. **Hilltop Ski Area,** 7015 Abbott Rd. (☎ **907-346-2167;** www.hilltopskiarea.org), in Bicentennial Park in town, is a great place to learn to ski, with one long beginner slope. One-day lift tickets are $22 to $30, and ski-package rentals are around the same price.

Snowmobiling

Glacier City Snowmobile Tours (☎ **877-783-5566** or 907-783-5566; www.snowtours.net) operates out of the Great Alaskan Tourist Trap gift shop in the shopping center on the Seward Highway. Guides suit up clients — most of whom have never been on a snowmobile — and drive them to a promising site, determined according to snow conditions. At best, the winter tours make it all the way to Spencer Glacier. Groups are no larger than six and the attitude is casual: After a brief introduction, you're driving your own machine, using your own judgment. A 5½-hour outing is $240 per person; a 3-hour outing, $190 per person.

Discovering More Cool Things to See and Do

These ideas can be part of a fun visit to Anchorage.

Downtown

Here are options you can reach on foot downtown:

✔ **Visit Old City Hall.** Built in 1936, the building is on the right side of 4th Avenue as you approach E Street. The lobby contains a fun and illuminating free display on city history, including dioramas of the early streetscape, old photographs, and the fire bell and fire pole that once were used in this building. Crossing E Street, notice on the left side of 4th Avenue that all the buildings are modern — everything on that side from E Street east for several blocks collapsed in the 1964 earthquake. The street split in half, lengthwise, with the left side ending up a dozen feet lower than the right.

✔ **Visit a quirky little museum.** Downtown at 245 W. 5th Ave., the free **Alaska Law Enforcement Museum** (☎ 800-770-5050 or 907-279-5050; www.alaskatroopermuseum.com) is a prideful trove of law-enforcement insignia, police equipment, a 1952 Hudson Hornet, photographs, and other memorabilia.

✔ **Entertain the kids with science.** Admission to the **Imaginarium,** located inside the Anchorage Museum (☎ 907-929-9200; www.anchoragemuseum.org), is included in the price of admission. Displays are aimed at young children, but the ingenious interactive exhibits will enchant many adults. There are over 80 exhibits included in the 9,000-sq.-ft. area, including a planetarium, large touch tanks of marine animals, and a bubble space. Admission is $15 adults ($10 Alaska residents), $7 kids 3 to 12, free for kids 2 and under. (For more on the Anchorage Museum, see "Hitting the Top Sights," earlier in this chapter.)

✔ **Walk at the speed of light.** A scale model of the solar system begins with the sun in the plaza at 5th Avenue and G Street, with the planets spread clear across town. Walking pace equals the speed of light, so Earth, a few blocks west, is eight minutes away, just as it takes the sun's energy eight minutes to reach us. The model is beautifully made and informative. The route between planets (and out the coastal trail up to Pluto in Kincaid Park, more than five hours away) is the best walk in Anchorage.

Beyond downtown

You need wheels to reach the following attractions:

- ✔ **Walk a wooded garden trail.** The **Alaska Botanical Garden** (☎ 907-770-3692; www.alaskabg.org) is a pleasant place to learn about native flora and some of the garden flowers and herbs that grow in Alaska. The plantings are in a few small clearings connected by gravel paths on thickly wooded grounds at the edge of a large wildland park. The Lowenfels Family Nature Trail is a 1-mile loop with a guide brochure that is pitched at an unusually thoughtful level. Along the walk is a chance to see salmon in Campbell Creek. Those without a strong interest in gardening or native plants may find other attractions more deserving of limited time, however, especially considering the drive from downtown, which is 20 minutes without traffic, and possibly twice that at rush hour. Take New Seward Highway (Gambell Street) to Tudor Road, exit to the east (left), turn right off Tudor onto Campbell Airstrip Road, and park at the Benny Benson School. A $5 donation is requested, $10 per family; the garden is open in summer during daylight hours.

- ✔ **See the remains of the continent's biggest earthquake.** On Good Friday in 1964, the biggest earthquake ever recorded in North America hit Southcentral Alaska, registering 9.2 on the Richter scale, killing 131 people, and flattening much of the region. **Earthquake Park** preserves some of the landscape that was thrown into a chaos of slides, cracks, and wave-like humps, and a sculpture and interpretive signs have been added to commemorate and explain the event. Anyone can get to the interpretive area, but the land devastated by the earthquake is overgrown and requires climbing through the brush on an unmaintained trail. From near the memorial, walk downward on the paved Coastal Trail, and then choose one of the informal trails that make off into the woods. Earthquake Park is a good access point to the Coastal Trail. To drive to the park from downtown, take L Street (which becomes Minnesota Drive) to Northern Lights Boulevard, and turn right. The park is on your right after you pass the last houses.

- ✔ **See a mysterious Native cemetery.** The Athabascan village of Eklutna has a fascinating old cemetery, still in use, in which a highly decorated spirit house, the size of a large dollhouse, encloses each grave. These little shelters excite the imagination in a way no ordinary marker can. Two small **Russian Orthodox churches** are also on the tribal Eklutna Historic Site (☎ 907-688-6026), including one built of logs sometime before 1870, making it among the oldest buildings in the state. Guides give an introductory talk and then lead a tour through the site and churches. Admission is $5 adults, $2.50 kids 10 to 18, free for kids 9 and under. The site is open in summer Monday through Saturday 10 a.m. to 4 p.m.,; it's closed in the off season. Wear mosquito repellent. To find the site, drive the Glenn Highway 26 miles to the Eklutna exit, and then go left over the overpass. If you come out

this far, don't miss **Thunderbird Falls,** described earlier in this
chapter under "Hiking and mountain-biking."

✔ **Attend a summer-league baseball game.** Perhaps the best way to
spend a fresh June or July evening in Anchorage is at **Mulcahy
Stadium,** watching the Anchorage Glacier Pilots (☎ **907-274-3627;**
www.glacierpilots.com) or the Anchorage Bucs (☎ **907-561-
2827;** www.anchoragebucs.com). You hear, smell, and feel the
rhythm of the game when you sit in the tiny park. The teams are
made up of college players spending their summer in the six-team
Alaska League. Among famed alumni are Mark McGwire, Rick
Aguilera, Tom Seaver, Dave Winfield, Barry Bonds, Wally Joyner,
Randy Johnson, and Jason Giambi. Check the *Anchorage Daily News*
or the team Web sites for game times. Mulcahy is at 16th Avenue
and A Street, a long walk or a short drive from downtown. Tickets
are around $5. Dress warmly for evening; a blanket is rarely out of
order.

Seeing Anchorage by Guided Tour

Gray Line of Alaska's Anchorage Highlights Tour (☎ **800-544-2206;**
www.graylineofalaska.com) takes three hours to visit the Ship
Creek area below downtown, the Anchorage Museum, and the Alaska
Native Heritage Center. It spends an hour at the center, not as long as I
like to stay. The tour costs $49 adults and is half-price for kids 12 and
under; the fee includes admission to the Native Heritage Center. The
company's bus tours to Portage Glacier are covered in the next chapter.

Spending One, Two, or Three
Days in Anchorage

If I had a nickel for every time I've been asked, "What should I do in just
one day in Anchorage?" I'd have a big bag of nickels. I long ago gave up
asking people to read over all the options I've written about and make
choices based on their own interests. So, here are ideas for how to
spend one, two, or three days in Anchorage, with my standard dis-
claimer: I think Alaska is about nature and the outdoors, even in the
state's biggest city. So, if you ask my advice, I'm going to send you out
under the sky. Also, consider the day trips from Anchorage that I cover
in Chapter 15.

For simplicity's sake, I've set up these itineraries with the assumption
that you're staying downtown, but they work from anywhere in
Anchorage. Also, I don't list these days in order of priority: Choose any
of the three for a great one-day itinerary, or pair them up in any combination. You can find more information throughout this chapter about
the attractions mentioned in the itineraries. For details on lodging and
dining recommendations, check out Chapter 13.

Day 1 in Anchorage

In the morning, head out to the **Alaska Native Heritage Center** to meet Alaska's indigenous people and discover their culture. Arrive there close to the 9 a.m. opening time so that you can get back downtown for lunch. Eat casually but well at the **Glacier BrewHouse,** and then check out the shops in the area, including the string of galleries and offbeat businesses along G Street. When you're done shopping, walk five blocks west on 5th Avenue to **Elderberry Park,** where you'll find the **Tony Knowles Coastal Trail** and the sea. Walk the coastal trail to see the ocean, mud flats, and wildlife, or **rent bikes** at a nearby booth at 5th Avenue and L Street and ride the trail. The ducks of **West Chester Lagoon** make a good, close destination; in less than an hour, you can bike to **Earthquake Park** and **Point Woronzof.** If you're a hard-core bicyclist, you can ride 10 miles (one-way) all the way through the woods to **Kincaid Park.** At the end of your coastal-trail sojourn, back at Elderberry Park, you'll be a block from one of the best restaurants in town, **Simon & Seafort's** (but you must reserve a table a day or two ahead).

Day 2 in Anchorage

This morning, gather sweaters, jackets, and a picnic, and drive to the **Glen Alps Trailhead** for a hike (or mountain-bike) above the tree line with wonderful views and clear, crisp air. You can stay the whole day, or spend the afternoon at the **Alaska Zoo,** on the drive back. Afterward, go for a special dinner at **Jens',** which takes up the evening.

Day 3 in Anchorage

Start the day at the **Anchorage Museum at Rasmuson Center.** See the Smithsonian Arctic Studies Center and the Alaska Gallery for a survey of Alaska's history and culture and explore the Imaginarium, located inside the Museum. Have lunch at Muse at the museum. Now drive out the Glenn Highway to the **Eagle River Valley** and the nature center and trails there, perhaps joining a naturalist program. If time remains, drive a bit farther to see **Thunderbird Falls** and the **Eklutna Historical Park.** Back in town, catch a **summer-league baseball game** at Mulcahy Stadium and enjoy hot dogs and beer under the midnight sun.

Saving Time for Alaska Shopping

You can buy any of Alaska's unique creations in Anchorage — Alaska Native arts and crafts, furs, and fine art. The city has some of the state's best galleries and all its largest fur shops, and it's big enough to have a few quirky, offbeat shops, too.

Finding the best shopping areas

Most of the shopping choices that interest visitors are downtown, and all are within walking distance of one another. I've identified two clusters of the best shops.

4th Avenue Market Place (and nearby)

Fourth Avenue is Anchorage's old-time main street. Although mostly flattened by the 1964 earthquake, it remains an active center of street life in the summertime. The centerpiece is a small shopping mall on the north side between C and D streets, which houses a Native arts-and-crafts mall and entertainment center, collecting together Alaska Native businesses. The **Two Spirits Gallery,** owned by the Cook Inlet Tribal Council, presents carvers and artists working on-site every day. Alaska Natives cultural groups are scheduled to perform in the common area daily during the summer. On the eastern end of the building, take in large, interesting graphics about the 1964 earthquake and other historic topics. The Alaska Experience Theater shows a dizzying large-format film on Alaska ($10) and an interactive earthquake exhibit ($6), which has been popular for a quarter century at another location. Call ☎ 907-272-9076 for show times.

Here are a few other highlights of the area:

- ✔ **The Rusty Harpoon,** 411 W. 4th Ave., just west of the Market Place (☎ 907-278-9011; www.rustyharpoongifts.com), carries authentic Native crafts, handmade jewelry, and distinctive gifts, and is staffed by reliable long-time proprietors.

- ✔ The **International Gallery of Contemporary Art,** half a block south of 4th Avenue at 427 D St. (☎ 907-279-1116; www.igcaalaska. org), is a nonprofit space dedicated to in-depth exploration of just a few artists' work at a time. Because it's run by volunteers, hours are short and vary; currently, they're Tuesday through Sunday noon to 4 p.m., plus 5:30 to 7:30 p.m. on the first Friday of every month.

- ✔ If you're in the market for gear to keep you warm at –40°F (–40°C), or if you're just curious, check out the **Army Navy Store,** 320 W. 4th Ave. (☎ 888-836-3535 or 907-279-2401; www.army-navy-store.com).

- ✔ The **5th Avenue Mall,** between 5th and 6th avenues and C and E streets, is Alaska's largest upscale shopping center, anchored by Nordstrom and JCPenney, with a large food court on the top level and scores of shops arrayed around a tall atrium. Most of the stores are national chains.

A walk down G Street

G Street from 5th to 3rd avenues has a concentration of interesting and unusual shops. Here are some highlights, starting on 6th Avenue and working north:

- ✔ **Aurora Fine Arts,** 737 W. 5th Ave. (☎ 907-274-0234), contains fine art and more affordable items: prints, crafts, gifts, and other creations in a pleasingly cluttered environment.

- ✔ A good spot to meet people for booze is **Darwin's Theory,** 426 G St. (☎ 907-277-5322); for java, **Side Street Espresso,** 412 G St. (☎ 907-258-9055).

- ✔ **Suzi's Woollies,** 420 G. St. (☎ **907-277-9660;** www.suziswoollies. net), is a Celtic shop carrying imported sweaters, jewelry, and CDs, with live Irish music on Saturday afternoons.

- ✔ Across the street is **Cabin Fever,** 650 W. 4th Ave. (☎ **907-278-3522**), one of the classier gift shops in town.

- ✔ And finally, the next block north contains **Artique,** 314 G St. (**800-848-1312** or 907-277-1663; www.artiqueltd.com), a high-end gallery of popular work that also has a large print collection.

Anchorage Market

If you can be in town on a weekend during the summer, be sure to visit the **Anchorage Market** (www.anchoragemarkets.com), held all day Saturday and Sunday from mid-May through mid-September in the parking lot at 3rd Avenue and E Street. It's a huge street fair with food, music, and hundreds of miscellaneous booths.

What to look for and where to find it

Shoppers are hunters or gatherers. If you're looking for something in particular, you're a hunter, and this section is for you.

Alaska Native arts and crafts

Many stores in Anchorage carry Native Alaskan arts and crafts. Before making major purchases, know what you're buying. You can read up on this subject in Chapter 5. In the Bush, you'll find lower prices but a smaller selection.

Nowhere else can you find a business like the **Oomingmak Musk Ox Producers' Co-operative** (☎ **888-360-9665** outside Alaska, or 907-272-9225; www.qiviut.com), located in the house with the musk ox on the side at 6th Avenue and H Street. Owned by 250 Alaska Native women in villages across the state, the co-op sells only scarves and other items they knit of *qiviut* (*ki*-vee-oot), the light, warm, silky underhair of the musk ox, which is collected from shedding animals. Each village has its own knitting pattern. They're expensive — adult caps cost $130 to $180 — but the quality is extraordinary.

The **Alaska Native Arts Foundation Gallery,** at 6th Avenue and E Street (www.alaskanativearts.org), is a nonprofit promoting the best work of indigenous artists, both in traditional and contemporary forms. The gallery hosts shows dedicated to individual artists in a light, open space; another area shows a mix of pieces. The Web site is well worth a visit and has an online shopping function.

The shop at the Anchorage Museum at Rasmuson Center has superb Native art. The Alaska Native Heritage Center shows original work, too, mostly crafts. **The Rusty Harpoon,** 411 W. 4th Ave. (☎ **907-278-9011;** www.rustyharpoongifts.com), has authentic Native items, less-expensive crafts, and reliable proprietors. Likewise, the tiny **Yankee Whaler,** in the lobby of the Hotel Captain Cook, at 5th Avenue and I Street (☎ 907-272-9071), is a well-regarded shop carrying Native arts.

Probably the best place for Native crafts in Anchorage is the **Hospital Auxiliary Craft Shop,** in the Alaska Native Medical Center, off Tudor east of Bragaw (☎ 907-729-1122), where everything is made by Alaska Natives who alone are eligible to use the hospital. The work you find here is all authentic and entirely traditional. The shop is open Monday through Friday from 10 a.m. to 2 p.m. and the first and third Saturday of the month from 11 a.m. to 2 p.m. It doesn't accept credit cards. You can see exceptional Native art on the walls of the hospital, too. Call for directions.

Furs

If you're in the market for a fur, Anchorage has a wide selection and no sales tax. **David Green Master Furrier,** 130 W. 4th Ave. (☎ 907-277-9595; www.davidgreenfurs.com), is an Anchorage institution. Others are nearby.

Gifts

You'll find lots of places to buy both mass-produced and inexpensive handmade crafts that aren't from the Bush. The **Anchorage Market** street fair, every summer weekend in the parking lot at 3rd Avenue and E Street, has hundreds of booths (see "Anchorage Market," earlier in this chapter). You won't have any trouble finding gift shops on 4th Avenue, including the ones I mention earlier in this chapter. The **Kobuk Coffee Company,** at 5th Avenue and E Street next to the town square (☎ 907-272-3626; www.kobukcoffee.com), occupies one of Anchorage's earliest commercial buildings; it's a cozy little candy, coffee, and collectibles shop with a tiny space to sit down for a hot cup in back. In midtown, on International Airport Road between the Old and New Seward highways, **Alaska Wild Berry Products** (☎ 800-280-2927 or 907-562-8858; www.alaskawildberryproducts.com) is a fun but touristy store to visit, where visitors come by the busload. Inside are a chocolate waterfall and a big window where you can watch the candy factory at work. Outside, they've built an area like a little theme park in the woods where you can stroll, as well as a theater hosting various live performances and several films about Alaska. The chocolate-covered-berry jellies sold here are addictive.

Fine art

Downtown has several galleries, the best of which I mention earlier under "4th Avenue Market Place (and nearby)" and "A walk down G Street." Openings at all the galleries happen on the first Friday of each month, allowing for an evening of party-hopping to meet artists and non-tourists of like interests.

Getting Out in the Evening

Anchorage isn't exactly a nightlife capital, but you always can find something to do in the evening.

Attending the performing arts

To find out what's happening, pick up the Friday edition of the *Anchorage Daily News* or check its exhaustive event and music scene calendar online, at http://play.adn.com. For the larger venues in town, the agency is **Ticketmaster** (☎ 800-745-3000; www.ticketmaster.com), which also sell through Fred Meyer grocery stores. The **Alaska Center for Performing Arts,** 631 W. 6th Ave. (www.myalaskacenter.com), operates its own ticket agency, **CenterTix** (☎ 907-263-2787; www.centertix.net). The call center and box office in the center are open Monday through Friday 9 a.m. to 5 p.m., Saturday noon to 5 p.m., and evenings prior to events.

The **Anchorage Concert Association** (☎ 907-272-1471; www.anchorageconcerts.org) offers a fall-through-spring schedule of classical music, theater, dance, and other performing arts. **Whistling Swan Productions** (www.whistlingswan.net) promotes folk and acoustic alternative performers in intimate venues. The **Anchorage Symphony Orchestra** (☎ 907-274-8668; www.anchoragesymphony.org) performs during the winter season.

Anchorage also has lots of community theater, opera, and limited professional theater, including the experimental **Out North Contemporary Art House,** 3800 DeBarr Rd. (☎ 907-279-3800; www.outnorth.org), which produces local shows and imports avant-garde performers. Downtown, **Cyrano's Off Center Playhouse,** at 4th Avenue and D Street (☎ 907-274-2599; www.cyranos.org), is a tiny theater with its own semiprofessional repertory company.

Hitting the nightclubs and bars

The hippest downtown club is **Bernie's Bungalow Lounge,** 626 D St. (☎ 907-276-8808), which grew from a little bungalow into a large, artsy playground with a backyard patio enclosed by a hedge. You can sometimes find foreign films, poetry readings, and similar cultural fare here, and, more often, you can socialize with people interested in such things. Also downtown: **Humpy's,** 610 W. 6th Ave. (☎ 907-276-2337), a popular tavern with a young crowd, decent food, and live music; **Darwin's Theory,** 426 G St. (☎ 907-277-5322), a friendly, elbows-on-the-table hangout; and the bar at **Simon & Seafort's,** 420 L St. (☎ 907-274-3502), an upscale after-work place for the professional set.

Note that downtown has some rough bars and nightclubs that are best avoided, mostly along 4th Avenue.

If you can get beyond the downtown area, you'll find more choices for music or dancing. **Blues Central/Chef's Inn,** 825 W. Northern Lights

Blvd. (☎ 907-272-1341), is a showcase of the best blues performers and presents imported rock acts, with live music virtually every night. Major blues names and up-and-coming national performers come through on a regular basis. Shows start at 9:30 p.m. They're also known for their beef.

The most famous bar in Anchorage, with the slogan, "We cheat the other guy and pass the savings on to you," is the huge **Chilkoot Charlie's,** at Spenard Road and Fireweed Lane (☎ 907-272-1010; www.koots.com). It has two stages, three dance floors, and ten bars on different themes, including a historic old dive from the Seward Highway called the Bird House that was picked up and moved into the building. The place is huge and full of entertainment, like an adult Disneyland, but I find it claustrophobic when crowded, with its low ceilings and confusing layout. It's open every day of the year from 10:30 a.m. until after 2 a.m. If you do go there late, avoid conflict and use caution when leaving — it can be a wild crowd and a rough neighborhood.

Spending the evening at the movies

A movie at the **Bear Tooth Theatre Pub,** 1230 W. 27th Ave. (☎ 907-276-4200; www.beartooththeatre.net), is a chance to sit back with a big glass of craft-brewed beer and a plate of nachos or a full dinner — it feels a lot like watching at home except for the big screen and the other people around you in the dark. (Well, our home is usually a bit cleaner, but our cooking isn't as good.) The films tend to be independent or second run; Monday is art-house night, and film festivals and special events often come through. The dining choices include gourmet tacos, pizzas, and other hand-held selections. Everything is quite good. They also put on concerts monthly; check the Web site. And now the fine print: Even bad movies sell out and there's often a crush. You must arrive quite early to find parking, get your ticket and seat, order your food and beer, and finish waiting in various lines before the movie starts. The staff brings the meal to you in the theater.

There are several multiplexes in Anchorage playing all the current Hollywood output; check the sources at the beginning of this section for listings and reviews. **Century 16,** 301 E. 36th Ave. (☎ 907-770-2602; www.cinemark.com), is an attractive, modern multiplex a reasonable cab ride from downtown.

Fast Facts: Anchorage

Area Code
The area code is **907**.

ATMs
A bank is rarely far away, and grocery stores also have ATMs.

Emergencies
Dial ☎ **911** for all emergency services.

Hospitals
Alaska Regional Hospital is at 2801 DeBarr Rd. (☎ **907-276-1131**), and Providence Alaska Medical Center is at 3200 Providence Dr. (☎ **907-562-2211**).

Information

Contact the Anchorage Convention & Visitors Bureau (☎ **907-276-4118;** www.anchorage.net), or drop by its Log Cabin Visitor Information Center, downtown at 4th Avenue and F Street (☎ **907-274-3531**). The center is open June through August daily 7:30 a.m. to 7 p.m., May and September daily 8 a.m. to 6 p.m., and October through April daily 9 a.m. to 4 p.m.

Internet Access

Downtown, try The UPS Store, 645 G St., next to City Hall (☎ **907-276-7888**).

Maps

Ordinary street maps are available at the visitor center or any grocery store. Outdoors maps and guidebooks are for sale at the Alaska Public Lands Information Center at 4th Avenue and F Street (☎ **907-644-3661;** www.alaskacenters.gov).

Newspapers/Magazines

Barnes & Noble is in midtown, at the corner of Northern Lights Boulevard and A Street (☎ **907-279-7323**).

Pharmacies

Try the large pharmacy in the Fred Meyer grocery store at 1000 E. Northern Lights Blvd. (☎ **907-264-9633**).

Police

For emergencies, dial ☎ **911**. The Anchorage Police Department has main offices at 4501 Elmore Rd., south of Tudor Road; for a non-emergency, call ☎ **907-786-8500**. For non-emergency police business outside the city, call the Alaska State Troopers, 5700 E. Tudor Rd. (☎ **907-269-5511**).

Post Office

The downtown post office is in the lower level of the brown building at 4th Avenue and D Street.

Restrooms

The public restrooms in hotel lobbies and public buildings are your best bet. Most businesses serving food are also required to have public restrooms; this includes grocery stores.

Safety

Muggings are rare in Anchorage, but sexual assault is not. Women need to be careful, especially around the rough downtown bars or in lonely places at night. Just because the sun is up at night doesn't mean it's safe. Most women I know don't walk the bike trails alone at night.

Smoking

Anchorage outlaws smoking in virtually all indoor public places, including bars. Many accommodations don't allow smoking in any rooms, and some small places don't even allow smoking outside. Check when you reserve.

Taxes

Anchorage has no sales tax. Room tax is 12 percent.

Taxis

See Chapter 13 for a discussion of using taxis in Anchorage. One operator is Alaska Yellow Cab (☎ **907-222-2222**).

Transit Info

The bus system is called the People Mover (☎ **907-343-6543;** www.peoplemover.org). See Chapter 13 for advice on using it.

Weather Updates

The National Weather Service has an Alaska Weather Line at ☎ **907-266-5145** from Anchorage or from outside Alaska, or ☎ **800-472-0391** toll-free anywhere within Alaska. Or check www.arh.noaa.gov.

Chapter 15

Side Trips from Anchorage

In This Chapter

▷ Enjoying the vertical landscape of the Seward Highway
▷ Taking in some winter (and summer) activities in Girdwood
▷ Cruising Prince William Sound
▷ Breaking away in the Mat-Su Valley

A base in Anchorage puts you close enough to some of Alaska's most appealing destinations for you to experience them as day trips. Few days that you spend in town can compare with what you'll see on some of the outings discussed in this chapter.

Driving Between Mountain and Sea on the Seward Highway

One of the world's great drives starts in Anchorage and leads roughly 50 miles south on the Seward Highway to Portage Glacier. The journey, not the destination, is what makes the drive worthwhile. The two-lane highway is chipped from the foot of the rocky Chugach Mountains along the waters of Turnagain Arm, providing a platform to see a magnificent, ever-changing, mostly untouched landscape full of wildlife.

I list the sights in the style of a highway log because you'll find interesting stops all along the road. This route also leads to several other great places: Girdwood's ski slopes, Whittier and Prince William Sound (covered later in this chapter), and the Kenai Peninsula (see Chapter 16).

Getting there

Getting lost on the Seward Highway is hard to do. It leaves downtown Anchorage under the name Gambell Street, becomes a limited-access freeway through the rest of the city, and then narrows to two lanes at Potter Marsh as it leaves the developed part of Anchorage (even though you remain within the enormous city limits almost all the way on this drive). From the marsh, the highway traces the edge of Turnagain Arm.

Taking a tour

If you don't want to drive, bus tours follow this route and visit Portage Glacier. **Gray Line of Alaska** (☎ 800-544-2206; www.graylineofalaska.com) offers a seven-hour trip that includes a stop in Girdwood and a boat ride on Portage Lake for $72 adults, $36 kids 12 and under. Even better, go on the **Alaska Railroad** (☎ 800-544-0552 or 907-265-2494; www.alaskarailroad.com), which sends excursion trains along the same route as the highway, and then climbing up into the mountains through glaciated terrain that can't be reached any other way. Remote stops in Chugach National Forest offer the opportunity for guided or on-your-own hiking or for river-rafting before an evening return to Anchorage. The basic tour is $110 adults, about half-price for kids.

A sightseeing drive takes at least half a day round-trip, and you can find plenty to do if you want to make it an all-day excursion. Use your head-lights for safety even during daylight and be patient whenever you get stuck behind a summertime line of cars. If you pass, you'll soon come up behind another line ahead once again. You simply can't make good time when the roads are full of summer travelers — and, with the scenery, there's little reason to try.

If you're taking the train to Seward or driving elsewhere on the Kenai Peninsula later in your trip, don't take this day trip, because you'll be covering the same ground.

Seeing the sights

The sights described in the following list are in order of the highway mileage markers that you'll encounter on the way from Anchorage:

✔ **Potter Marsh (mile 117):** Heading south from Anchorage, the Seward Highway descends a bluff to cross a broad marsh formed by water impounded behind the tracks of the Alaska Railroad. Beside the marsh is a boardwalk from which you can watch a huge variety of birds. Salad-green grasses grow from sparkling, pond-green water.

✔ **Potter Section House (mile 115):** At the south end of Potter Marsh, the section house was an early maintenance station for the Alaska Railroad. Today it contains offices of Chugach State Park, open during normal business hours, and outside features a few old train cars and interpretive displays. Across the road is the trailhead for the **Turnagain Arm Trail,** a mostly level path running down the arm well above the highway with great views breaking now and then through the trees. Hike as far as you like and then backtrack to your car; or, if you can arrange a one-way walk with a ride back from the other end, continue 4 miles to the McHugh Creek picnic area and trailhead, or 9 miles to Windy Corner.

✔ **McHugh Creek (mile 111):** Four miles south of Potter is an excellent state park picnic area and a challenging day hike with a 3,000-ft. elevation gain to **Rabbit Lake,** which sits in a tundra mountain bowl, or a 4,301-ft. ascent to the top of **McHugh Peak.** You don't have to climb all the way; spectacular views are to be had within an hour of the road. Take the Turnagain Arm Trail to the left, west; the trailhead is on the right.

From this point onward, most of the sights are on the right or ocean side of the road: Plan your stops for the outbound trip, not on the return (when you would have to make left turns across traffic).

✔ **Beluga Point (mile 110):** The state highway department didn't really need to put up scenic overlook signs at this spectacular pullout, 1½ miles south of McHugh Creek, because you'd probably have figured it out on your own. The terrain is simply awesome, as the highway traces the edge of Turnagain Arm below the towering cliffs of the Chugach Mountains. If the tide and salmon runs are right, you may see beluga whales, which chase the fish toward fresh water. Sometimes they overextend their pursuit, stranding themselves by the dozens in the receding tide, but they usually aren't harmed. The pullout has spotting scopes to improve the viewing. The right-hand pullouts for the next few miles ahead have interpretive signs about the 1895 gold rush in this area and other topics.

✔ **Windy Point (mile 106):** Be on the lookout on the mountain side of the road for Dall sheep picking their way along the cliffs. It's a unique spot, because the sheep get much closer to people here than is usual in the wild; apparently, they believe they're safe. Windy Point is the prime spot, but you also have a good chance of seeing sheep virtually anywhere along this stretch of road. If cars are stopped, that's probably why; get well off the road and pay attention to traffic, which will still be passing at high speeds.

✔ **Bird Ridge Trail (mile 102):** This trail is a lung-busting climb of 3,000 ft. in a little more than a mile. It starts as an easy, accessible trail but then rises steeply to views that start at impressive and become ever more amazing as you climb.

✔ **Bird Creek (mile 100):** A parking lot carved from a cliff side and pathways provide safe access to the creek, a popular silver and pink salmon stream (for details, see Chapter 14). Non-anglers can enjoy a short trail, interpretive signs, and an overlook.

✔ **Bird Point (mile 96):** The remarkable wayside here is not to be missed. A paved pathway rises up to a bedrock outcropping with a simply wonderful view — all the severity of the Turnagain Arm, but framed by the soft green of a freshwater wetland with a beaver lodge. Take a look at the fascinating interpretive signs on many subjects. Bike trails that run parallel to the highway are accessed here, too. A $5 day-use fee is charged for each vehicle at a self-service kiosk.

✔ **The flats (miles 96–90):** At Bird Point, the highway descends from the mountainside to the mud flats. Several pullouts on the right side of the highway have interpretive signs. At high tide, water comes right up to the road. At low tide, the whole arm narrows to a thin, winding channel through the mud. The arm is not practical to navigate, and navigational charts are not even available. Few have ever tried to navigate it other than gold prospectors in rowboats a century ago or today's occasional death-defying canoeist or kayaker. The first to try was Captain James Cook, in 1778, as he was searching for the Northwest Passage on his final, fatal voyage of discovery. (He was killed by Hawaiians later that year.) He named this branch of Cook Inlet Turnagain Arm because the shoals and the strength of the currents defeated his efforts to explore.

✔ **Turnoff to Girdwood (mile 90):** The attractions of Girdwood, which I cover later in this chapter (see "Enjoying the Slopes of Girdwood"), are worth a visit, but the shopping center here at the intersection is not chief among them. Stop for a simple meal or a restroom break (the convenience store has large public restrooms), or to fill your gas tank for the last time for many a mile.

✔ **Twentymile River (mile 80):** Three species of salmon and a small smelt, the eulachon, known locally as the hooligan, spawn in this river. In the spring you can see Native people dip-netting the hooligan.

There is good bird-watching here and from turnouts farther on, but venturing out on Turnagain Arm's tidal mud carries the real risk of getting stuck in quicksand-like mud and drowning in the tide. Don't do it.

✔ **Old Portage (mile 80):** All along the flats at the head of Turnagain Arm are large marshes full of what looks like standing driftwood. These are trees killed by salt water that flowed in when the 1964 quake lowered the land as much as 10 ft. On the right, ¾ mile past the Twentymile River and across from the rail depot, a few ruins of the abandoned town of Portage are still visible, more than 40 years after the great earthquake.

✔ **Alaska Wildlife Conservation Center (mile 79):** The nonprofit center (☎ 907-783-2025; www.awcc.org), developed with visitors in mind, gives homes to injured and orphaned deer, moose, owls, elk, bison, musk ox, bear, fox, and caribou. Visitors drive through the 200-acre compound to see the animals in fenced enclosures as large as 110 acres — you often can get a close look at the animals, but the larger enclosures give them natural vegetation and the ability to get away from view if they want to. There's no need to visit both here and The Alaska Zoo (see Chapter 14). The zoo has more kinds of animals and it's a fun place to stroll, but the cages there are much smaller and often seem constricting. Here, the animals' settings are more natural and perhaps more humane, but viewing is car-based. A big, log gift shop and outdoor snack bar are at the end of the tour. Admission is $10 for adults and $7.50 for military, seniors, and kids 4 to 12 (with a maximum of $30 per vehicle). In summer, it's open daily 8 a.m. to 8 p.m. (last admission 7:30 p.m.); in winter, daily 10 a.m. to 5 p.m. (last admission 4:30 p.m.).

🖊 **Portage Glacier (take the 5½-mile spur road at mile 78):** The named attraction has largely melted, receding out of sight of the visitor center. (The glacier that you can see is Burns Glacier.) When the center was built in 1985, Portage Glacier was predicted to keep floating on its 800-ft.-deep lake until the year 2020. Instead, it withdrew to the far edge of the lake in 1995. Today, the exhibits in the lakeside **Begich-Boggs Visitor Center** focus on the Chugach National Forest as a whole, rather than just the glacier; these informative displays are well worth an hour or two to become oriented with the area's nature, history, and lifestyles. Children and adults alike will be interested.

Several short trails start near the center. Rangers lead nature walks on the ¼-mile, paved Moraine Trail. Another trail leads less than a mile to Byron Glacier, in case you're interested in getting up close to some ice. Always dress warmly, because cold winds are the rule in this funnel-like valley.

A **day boat** operated by **Gray Line of Alaska** (☎ **800-478-6388** or 907-277-5581 for reservations, 907-783-2983 at the lake; www.gray lineofalaska.com) traverses the lake to get within a few hundred yards of Portage Glacier on hour-long tours, ice conditions permitting. It costs $29 adults, $15 kids 12 and under; it operates five times daily in summer, every 90 minutes starting at 10:30 a.m. If this is your only chance to see a glacier in Alaska, the tour is probably worth your time, but if your itinerary includes any of the great glaciers in Prince William Sound, Kenai Fjords National Park, or the like, you won't be as impressed by Portage.

Family history

The **Begich-Boggs Visitor Center** at Portage Glacier is named for Hale Boggs, who was U.S. House majority leader, and Rep. Nick Begich, then Alaska's lone congressman, who disappeared together in a small plane during Begich's 1972 reelection bid. The most likely theory is that the wings iced up in Portage Pass, causing a crash into Prince William Sound just beyond the mountains. No trace was ever found—as with many other Alaskan planes that have simply flown off into oblivion. Begich was reelected anyway. His opponent, Republican Don Young, later won a special election and continued, 38 years and counting, as Alaska's only congressman. He won re-election in 2008 even after both houses of Congress voted to ask the FBI to investigate him for corruption. In 2010, after the FBI dropped the investigation, he was reelected again, becoming the second most senior Republican member of Congress. Boggs' wife, Lindy, served out her husband's term and was elected to eight more. Boggs' daughter, Cokie Roberts, is the famous broadcast journalist. Begich's son, Mark, served as mayor of Anchorage from 2003 to 2008, when he was elected to the U.S. Senate.

Enjoying the Slopes of Girdwood

Girdwood, 37 miles south of Anchorage, is proof that a charming little town can coexist with a major ski resort, as long as the resort goes undiscovered by the world's skiers. Girdwood still has a sleepy, offbeat character. Retired hippies, ski bums, and a few old-timers live in the houses and cabins among the big spruce trees in the valley below the Mount Alyeska lifts. Everyone expected a development explosion to follow the construction of an international resort here a number of years ago, but it hasn't happened. Although that may not be good news for the investors in the resort, it's great for skiers and other visitors who discover this paradise. They find varied, uncrowded skiing through long winters, superb accommodations, and an authentically funky community.

The primary summer attractions are the hiking trails, the tram to the top of **Mount Alyeska,** and the **Crow Creek Mine,** described later in this chapter. In winter, it's skiing. Mount Alyeska isn't as big as the famous resorts in the Rockies, but it's large and steep enough. Better still, there's room for everyone, half the mountain is above the tree line, and the snow lasts a long time. Olympian Tommy Moe trained here, and the Alpine national championships raced down these slopes many times, most recently in 2009. The national extreme skiing and snowboarding competition used Alyeska's lifts in 2008. Skiers who are used to tamer, busier slopes rave about the skiing here, with long, challenging downhills, few lift lines, and stunning views of the Chugach Mountains above and glistening Turnagain Arm below.

Getting there

A **rental car** is the most practical way to reach Girdwood. The preceding section ("Seeing the sights") gives directions for driving from Anchorage to Girdwood. In summer, you can come down for the sights and hikes; in winter, you can make it a day trip for winter sports. If you plan to stay at the resort for skiing, however, you may not need a car. Call the **Alyeska Resort** (see "Where to stay," later in this chapter) to find out about current shuttle arrangements. The **Girdwood Chamber of Commerce** also maintains a Web site (www.girdwoodalaska.com).

Seeing the sights

Here I cover sights and activities specific to Girdwood, but you also can use Girdwood as a base for a large area south of Anchorage, including the wildlife cruises and sea-kayaking from Whittier (covered in the "Embarking on Prince William Sound from Whittier" section, later in this chapter), and the river-rafting and snowmobiling farther down the highway (see Chapter 14).

Crow Creek Mine
Girdwood

This mine, opened in 1898, is still operated in a small way by the Toohey family, but mostly they use the paths and eight small original buildings as a charming tourist attraction. You can see the frontier lifestyle and watch rabbits and ducks wandering around. A bag of dirt, guaranteed to have some gold in it, is provided for gold panning, and you can dig and pan to get more if you have the patience for it.

Crow Creek Road (off the Alyeska Highway), Girdwood. ☎ **907-278-8060.** www.crowcreekmine.com. *Open: May 15–Sept 15 daily 9 a.m.–6 p.m. Admission: With gold panning $15 adults, $10 seniors and active military, $5 kids 7 and under; without gold panning $5 adults, free for kids 7 and under.*

Mount Alyeska Tram
Girdwood

The tram isn't cheap, but it's worth the price if you otherwise may not make it to high alpine tundra during an Alaska trip. (In winter, ride on your lift ticket; in summer, ride free while taking in a meal at the Seven Glaciers Restaurant at the top — covered in the "Where to stay" section, later in this chapter.) The tram takes seven minutes in summer to rise to the 2,300-ft. level, where it stops at a station with the Seven Glaciers and an attractive cafeteria with a limited selection, the Glacier Express. The tram presents an opportunity for everyone, no matter how young, old, or infirm, to experience the pure light, limitless views, and crystalline quiet of an Alaska mountaintop. Take the opportunity to walk around and enjoy it. Dress very warmly.

At the Alyeska Prince Hotel (see "Where to stay," later in this chapter), Girdwood. Open: Summer daily 9 a.m.–9 p.m., winter when lifts operate (call as hours vary). Admission: $18 adults, $15 seniors 60 and over, $15 kids 8–17, $9 kids 4–7, free for kids 3 and under.

Getting outdoors in Girdwood

For additional information about activities in this area, contact the **Alyeska Resort.** For snowmobiling, see Chapter 14.

Skiing

Mount Alyeska, at 3,939 ft., has 1,400 acres of skiing, operated by Alyeska Resort (☎ **907-754-1111;** www.alyeskaresort.com), beginning from a base elevation of only 250 ft. and rising 2,500 ft. The normal season is from early November through April, and it's a rare year when there isn't plenty of snow all winter (although the warming climate has brought some poor ski seasons). Skiing on the upper mountain usually lasts through Memorial Day weekend (not for beginners). The average yearly snowfall is 721 in., or 61 ft. Because it's near the water, the weather is rarely very cold. Light is more of an issue, with the short days in midwinter. There are 27 lighted trails covering 2,000 vertical feet on Thursday, Friday, and Saturday evenings from mid-December through late-March, but the best Alaska skiing is when the days get longer and warmer in the spring. Besides, the lighted trails are only for more-accomplished skiers.

Alyeska has nine lifts, including the tram. Two chairs serve beginners, with a vertical drop of around 300 ft. The other 89 percent of the mountain is geared toward intermediate to expert skiers. The biggest drawback for less experienced skiers is a lack of runs in the low to inter-mediate ability range. After graduating from the primary beginners' lift, Chair 3, skiers must jump to significantly more challenging slopes. That explains the long lines in busy periods on Chair 3. (It's the only lift on the mountain with real waits.) More confident skiers like the mountain best. Most of it is steep and the expert slopes are extreme. Helicopter and snowcat skiing goes right from the resort's hotel as well.

An all-day lift ticket costs $60 adults, $45 seniors 60 to 69 and kids 14 to 17, $40 kids 8 to 13, and $15 seniors 70 and over and kids 7 and under. Private and group instruction is available. You can save a lot of money by buying your lessons, lift ticket, and equipment rental at the same time. The day lodge rents basic gear and the hotel rents high-performance gear. A basic rental package costs $35 per day for adults, $27 for seniors 60 and over and kids 13 and under; high-performance and demo pack-ages costs $45 to $75. The resort also has groomed **cross-country trails** and gear for rent, but the best Nordic skiing is in Anchorage (see Chapter 14).

The utilitarian **day lodge** is a large, noisy building with snack and rental counters, located at the front of the mountain. The **Sitzmark Bar** is a more comfortable place for a meal. The hotel is on the other side of the mountain, connected to the front by the tram to the top and beginner-level Chair 7 — you can ski right from the door. The hotel is a quieter and more genteel starting point for day-trippers and guests, because it has its own rental counter with better equipment (and higher rates) and day lockers. The hotel has several dining choices, two at the top of the tram (see "Where to dine," later in this chapter).

A center operated by **Challenge Alaska** (☎ **907-344-7399**) enables skiers with disabilities to use the mountain, skiing down to the lift to start and back to the center at day's end.

Hiking

A couple of great hiking trails begin in Girdwood. Among the best trails in the region for a family hike is the **Winner Creek Trail,** which begins behind the Hotel Alyeska and leads to a roaring gorge where Winner

Creek and Glacier Creek meet; a hand-operated tram crosses the water. The trail is essentially level and a good length for an afternoon: the round-trip to the gorge is about 4½ miles. The **Crow Pass Trail** is more ambitious. The route rises into the mountains and continues all the way over to Eagle River, after a 26-mile hike that can take a couple days. But with less expenditure of time, you can make a strenuous day hike of it going just up to the pass, where you can see the glaciers, wildflower meadows, and old mining equipment. The trail head is up Crow Creek Road, off the Alyeska Highway.

Where to stay

Besides the resort hotel, plenty of condos and B&Bs are in town. **Alyeska Accommodations,** 203 Olympic Mountain Loop (☎ **888-783-2001** or 907-783-2000; www.alyeskaaccommodations.com), offers condos, cabins, and luxurious houses.

Hotel Alyeska
$$$$$ Girdwood

The Alyeska Resort's hotel is among Alaska's best. The beauty of the building alone separates it from the competition, as does its location in an unspoiled mountain valley among huge spruce trees. Studded with dormers and turrets, it's an impressive sight. Inside, sumptuous cherrywood and rich colors unite the welcoming common rooms and elegant guest rooms. Although not large, rooms have every convenience. The saltwater swimming pool is magnificent, with a cathedral ceiling and windows by the whirlpool overlooking the mountain. A few days spent here skiing and swimming can make daily reality seem drab.

Now for the bad news: On weekends and school holidays in the winter, the hotel is overrun by partying families from Anchorage who overtax the facilities and destroy the peaceful ambience. Children run wild, the pool becomes impossibly crowded, and service deteriorates to an unacceptable level. If you're coming for a skiing vacation, avoid these times.

Six dining options vie for attention. The **Seven Glaciers,** 2,300 ft. above the lobby by tram on Mount Alyeska, serves trendy and beautifully presented dinners in a sumptuous dining room floating above the clouds. Service is warm and highly professional, but slow. Meals are expensive. The restaurant opens only on the weekends in the winter. A mountaintop cafeteria is right next door (great views, limited choices). At the base level, choices include a *teppanyaki* and sushi place, a hotel cafe, a bar and grill, and a casual cafe.

1000 Arlberg Ave., Girdwood. ☎ *800-880-3880 or 907-754-1111. Fax: 907-754-2200. www.alyeskaresort.com. Rack rates: Summer and Christmas $275–$360 double, $400–$1,500 suite; winter $145–$240 double, $300–$1,500 suite; extra adult $25; kids stay free in parent's room. AE, DC, MC, V.*

Where to dine

The six dining options at the Alyeska Prince Hotel are described in the preceding section. Two excellent independent restaurants follow.

Chair 5
$$$ Girdwood   AMERICAN

This is where Girdwood locals meet their friends and take their families for dinner, and it's also one of our favorites after skiing. One afternoon, Bob Dylan music accompanied a friendly game of pool, while men with ponytails and beards sipped microbrews. Another evening, a guy in the entryway entertained the children with magic tricks and the waitress asked them to draw pictures to enter into a contest. The menu offers choices pleasing to each family member, including pizza, burgers, fresh fish, and steaks.

5 Linblad St., in the New Girdwood Town Square, Girdwood. ☎ **907-783-2500.** www. chairfive.com. *Main courses: $9–$13 lunch, $18–$28 dinner, $18–$28 large pizza. AE, DC, DISC, MC, V. Open: Daily 11 a.m.–11 p.m.*

Double Musky Inn
$$$–$$$$ Girdwood   CAJUN

The ski-bum-casual atmosphere and rambling, cluttered dining room among the trees match the wonderful Cajun and New Orleans food in a way that couldn't have been contrived — it's at once too improbable and too authentic. Service is relaxed to a fault, and food takes a long time to arrive, but when it does, every dish is flawless. I love the jambalaya and the steaks, which are famous (by which I mean, really famous — Food Network chose this as one of the ten best restaurants in the United States). Dining with two couples, each item on our plates — from appetizers through dessert — was remarkable; because I love talking about the food over dinner, I love this place. The Double Musky isn't to everyone's taste, however; your senses can feel raw after the extreme noise, highly spiced food, and crowds. Parking also can be difficult. Loud groups will enjoy it more than couples, and families don't really fit. Because the restaurant doesn't take reservations, here's an important tip: Grab seats in the bar and dive into your meal there with appetizers and drinks instead of simply waiting.

Mile 3, Crow Creek Rd., Girdwood. ☎ **907-783-2822.** www.doublemuskyinn. com. *Main courses: $18–$37. AE, DC, DISC, MC, V. Open: Tues–Thurs 5–10 p.m., Fri–Sun 4:30–10 p.m. Closed Nov.*

Embarking on Prince William Sound from Whittier

Almost all of Prince William Sound is in Chugach National Forest, the nation's second largest. The sound is a world to itself, one largely free of people, with 3,500 miles of shoreline enfolded within its islands and deeply penetrating fjords and passages. Glaciers loom on the mountains at the northwestern part of the sound, and on the way to see them it's commonplace to encounter humpback and orca whales, dolphins, seals, otters, and a variety of birds.

Whittier is Anchorage's portal to this vast wildness. Although Anchorage itself is on Upper Cook Inlet, that muddy, fast-moving waterway is little used for recreational boating. Whittier, on the other hand, stands on the edge of a long fjord in the northwest corner of the sound, where clear waters are full of salmon, orcas, and otters, and bounded by rocky shores, rain forests, and glaciers. The water also is calmer here than on excursions to Kenai Fjords National Park (see Chapter 16), so seasickness is rare and the glaciers are more numerous.

Whittier, in itself, is not a destination. Passengers on many Princess cruises arrive here to board trains to Anchorage, but they see no more of the town than the road they walk across from the dock to the rails. There's no reason for them to stay, nor for land-based visitors to spend the night. Other than activities on the water, which are easy as a day trip from Anchorage or Girdwood, there's nothing to do. Whittier is an odd town where most of the tiny population lives in a single, 14-story concrete building. I don't recommend a visit other than to go out on Prince William Sound.

Getting there

If you plan to take a day trip on the sound from a base in Anchorage — the way most people use Whittier — you can leave the car behind and take a train or bus all the way. Tour-boat operators (listed in "Getting out on the sound," later in this chapter) will book the transportation from Anchorage for you, simplifying the process and assuring that you'll be on time for the boat. On the other hand, if you have more than two in your group, a car may save you money and give you flexibility to make other stops on the way. Likewise, drive if you plan to continue through the sound by ferry or to make Whittier a stop on the way down the Kenai Peninsula to Seward or Homer.

If you plan to drive, carefully read "By car," a few sections later in this chapter, to find out about the unusual process of getting through the tunnel to Whittier.

By bus

Tour-boat operators put visitors on buses and vans from Anchorage that are less expensive than riding the train. The bus ride is included in the cost of the tour-boat ticket, adding around $50 per adult to the fare. Children's fares tend to be half-price.

By train

The **Alaska Railroad** (☎ 800-544-0552 or 907-265-2494; www.alaska railroad.com) runs a daily train timed to match the schedules of

Prince William Sound tour boats. The large tour operators will book it for you when you buy your boat ticket, potentially with a substantial savings over booking with the railroad directly. The round-trip train fare from Anchorage to Whittier is $80 adults, $40 kids 2 to 11, free for kids 1 and under. The train ride is scenic and fun, but extends an 8-hour trip from Anchorage to more than 11 hours and costs more than a rental car even for a single traveler.

By car

Take the Seward Highway, as described in "Driving between Mountain and Sea on the Seward Highway," earlier in this chapter, to the Portage Glacier Road, at mile 78.9 (48 miles from Anchorage). Allow at least an hour from Anchorage to the Portage Glacier area, without stops. From there, the road goes through a 2¾-mile-long World War II–era rail tunnel to Whittier; the single lane is also used to accommodate trains, so you'll probably have to wait your turn. Get the schedule through the tunnel's Web site (www.tunnel.alaska.gov), through its phone recording (☎ 877-611-2586 or 907-566-2244), or by tuning your radio to 1610 AM in Portage or 530 AM in Whittier. Checking the schedule can help you avoid a wait of an hour or more caused by missing the opening for your particular direction of travel.

In summer, the first opening from Whittier is at 5:30 a.m. and the last to Whittier is at 11:15 p.m. Winter hours are shorter and changeable, so check ahead. The toll ($12 for cars; $20 for RVs, cars with trailers, or large vans) is charged only for travel toward Whittier. Special permits are required for really huge vehicles (over 14 ft. high or 10 ft. wide). Parking in Whittier costs $10 per day.

By ferry

The fast ferry *Chenega* of the **Alaska Marine Highway System** (☎ 800-642-0066; www.ferryalaska.com) connects Whittier to the other two towns in Prince William Sound, Cordova and Valdez. From Valdez, you can drive north on the beautiful Richardson Highway, making a complete circle back to Anchorage in two days or more (see Chapter 18). The *Kennicott* runs a two-week-long loop several times a summer from Prince Rupert, British Columbia, to Juneau, Whittier, and then westward to Homer and Kodiak. It's the only practical public transportation connecting this part of Alaska to the outside world without flying.

Getting out on the sound

Whittier is the entrance to western Prince William Sound, at the end of one of many long, deep fjords where marine mammals and eagles are common. You can ride one of the tour boats that cruise these waters from Whittier, viewing glaciers at the heads of many of the fjords.

Large tour boats

Several companies with offices in Anchorage compete for your business for day-trip tours to the sound's western glaciers. Besides having incredible scenery, the water is calm, making seasickness unlikely — for the queasy, this is a much better choice than Kenai Fjords National Park. Each operator times departures to coordinate with the daily Alaska Railroad train from Anchorage (see the "By train" section, earlier), which means they have up to six hours for the trip. Some try to see as much as possible, while others take it slower to savor the scenery and wildlife sightings. Between the train and boat fare, expect to spend around $250 per person for this day's outing, leaving Anchorage at 10 a.m. and returning at 9:30 p.m.

 You can save around $30 per person and up to three hours by taking a bus that the tour-boat company arranges instead of the train. With two or more people, you can save over the bus by renting a car and driving. You'll be able to buy meals onboard or meals will be provided.

Note that, although all the prices in this book are subject to change, those listed here are especially shaky because of changing fuel costs.

Phillips Cruises & Tours

The 26-glacier cruise travels the sound on a fast three-deck catamaran, allowing it to cover many miles of scenery and count the glaciers as it goes, more territory than competitors reach. The boat ride is five hours, so if you use their bus, your total time from Anchorage is less than 8½ hours. The tour now includes narrow Esther Passage and a visit to a sea lion haul-out. As a pioneer of these tours, Phillips has many years of experience and does a professional job. The boat has a snack bar, and a hot lunch is included in the fare.

519 W. 4th Ave., Anchorage. ☎ **800-544-0529.** *www.26glaciers.com. Price: $139 adults, $79 kids 11 and under; fuel surcharge $17 per passenger.*

Major Marine Tours

This company operates a smaller, 149-passenger vessel at a slower pace than Phillips — they visit a mere ten glaciers, but spend more time waiting for ice to fall from glaciers. Another important feature: The tour is narrated by a Chugach National Forest ranger, not the company. The route goes up Blackstone Bay. The boat is comfortable, with reserved table seating. They emphasize their food, which costs extra; the salmon and prime-rib buffet is $19 adults, $9 kids — it's quite good. Time on the water is five hours. Prices are expected to change, so check beforehand.

411 W. 4th Ave., Anchorage. ☎ **800-764-7300.** *www.majormarine.com. Price: $107 adults, $53 kids 11 and under.*

Prince William Sound Glacier Cruises

The emphasis of this Native-owned firm is on the indigenous culture and natural history of the sound, while also showing off the area's glaciers and wildlife. Cruises last four or six hours. The shorter cruise goes to Blackstone Bay only, where crew members gather plankton for guests to observe through microscopes; the six-hour trip travels to the more impressive Surprise Glacier, and includes Esther Passage and a stop at a salmon hatchery. Interpretation is by the captain and crew. Crab cakes are served for the meal (included in the price).

☎ **877-777-4054** *or 907-277-2131.* www.princewilliamsound.com. *Price: $109 four-hour cruise, $139 six-hour cruise; half-price for kids 2–11, free for kids 1 and under.*

Small tour boats

Instead of getting on a giant tour boat with a mob of people, you can go on a small boat with a local whom you'll get to know as he shows off favorite places and lands on beaches for picnics and walks. If you see a whale or other point of interest, you can stay as long as you like, and in a small boat you can get closer. What you give up are the comforts of a larger, tour-bus-like vessel, and most small boats have a four-person minimum.

Honey Charters

Family-run Honey Charters has three sturdy aluminum boats built for these waters, specializing in personal tours, water transportation, and kayaker drop-offs. They operate with a minimum of four passengers; by paying the four-person minimum, you can have a boat to yourself. Their *Qayaq Spirit* boat carries up to 30 passengers for kayaking and sightseeing cruises. Bring your own food.

On the waterfront, Whittier. ☎ **888-477-2493.** www.honeycharters.com. *Price: Three-hour cruise $125 per person, six-hour cruise $175 per person.*

Sound Eco Adventures

Gerry Sanger is a retired wildlife biologist who spent years researching the waterfowl and ecology of Prince William Sound. A few times a week he carries up to six passengers on whale, wildlife, and glacier sightseeing and photography tours from his speedy 30-ft. aluminum boat. Fares include snacks, but bring your own lunch.

Whittier. ☎ **888-471-2312.** www.soundecoadventure.com. *Price: Eight-hour glacier and wildlife tour $190 per person, five-hour sightseeing cruise $155 per person.*

Fishing

About 30 charter fishing boats operate out of Whittier, the closest salt-water fishing to Anchorage. Most target halibut but some also go after salmon during hot runs. The **Greater Whittier Chamber of Commerce**

(☎ **907-677-9448**; www.whittieralaskachamber.org) can help find an operator and has links to several on its Web site. **Bread-n-Butter Charters** (☎ **888-472-2396** or 907-472-2396; www.breadnbutter charters.com) has been around for many years. They charge $285 per person for a day of halibut fishing and have an office on the waterfront. **Honey Charters** (listed in the "Small tour boats" section, earlier in this chapter) has a similar service.

Sea-kayaking

Whittier is a popular starting point for kayak trips to beautiful and protected western Prince William Sound. Day trips for beginners paddle along the shore near Whittier, often visiting a cliff-side bird colony, or you can take a boat 5 miles from the harbor to Shotgun Cove and paddle back. Longer multi-day trips go by boat to even more interesting waters, where you can visit glaciated fjords and paddle narrow passages. Here are a couple kayaking businesses competing in Whittier:

- ✔ **Alaska Sea-Kayakers** (☎ **877-472-2534** or 907-472-2534; www. alaskaseakayakers.com) offers three- and five-hour day trips for $79 and $220, respectively. Paddles at Blackstone Glacier, which begin with a charter-boat ride, cost $330. Guides are well trained and occasionally offer weekend instructional clinics (check the Web site for times). Offices are at each end of Whittier Harbor. They rent to experienced paddlers, too.

- ✔ The **Prince William Sound Kayak Center** (☎ **877-472-2452** or 907-472-2452; www.pwskayakcenter.com) offers guided half-day trips starting at $80, as well as full days and other options; it also rents kayaks. It's been in business since 1981.

Where to dine

Most meals served in Whittier are for people grabbing a sandwich while waiting for a boat or otherwise passing through. Several such restaurants are in the triangle at the east end of the harbor where you can conveniently check them all out before making a choice.

Taking a Side Trip to the Mat-Su Area

Here are some highlights of the **Matanuska and Susitna valleys,** the suburbs to the north of Anchorage commonly referred to as Mat-Su. Reached by the Glenn Highway about 40 miles from Anchorage, the Mat-Su area is both a bedroom community for the city and a former frontier-farming region with a quirky identity (but marred by road frontage commercial development). Among the towns is the once obscure Wasilla, now famous as the hometown of Sarah Palin. Just because you've heard of the place, however, doesn't make it worth visiting (unless you want to see just how little there is to see). Most travelers pass through on a drive north, perhaps taking advantage of some of the area's attractions for a break along the way.

In this summary, I discuss a few attractions in the central area of the valley. Other places of interest in the Matanuska-Susitna Borough, which covers an area the size of West Virginia, are elsewhere in the book where they fit better with the itineraries I recommend: Talkeetna, in the northern Susitna Valley along the Parks Highway, is grouped with Denali National Park in Chapter 19; rafting the Matanuska River, a good Anchorage day activity, is included in Chapter 14; and the skiing and mountain lodges near the Matanuska Glacier on the Glenn Highway are covered in Chapter 18. The region's biggest annual event, the **Alaska State Fair,** is covered in the calendar of events in Chapter 3.

Seeing the valley's highlights

The only way to travel the Mat-Su area is by car. Here are some stops to make if you're passing through or exploring the area.

Hatcher Pass

Heading north to Denali National Park or Fairbanks, the rough, winding gravel road through Hatcher Pass to Willow makes a glorious alpine detour around what otherwise would be the least attractive part of your drive (it bypasses the traffic and blight of Wasilla). Past the mine and skiing area, the road is open only in summer and is not suitable for large RVs. Just after the Parks Highway branches from the Glenn Highway, exit to the right on the Trunk Road and keep going north on Palmer-Fishhook Road. From the Glenn Highway near Palmer, take Palmer-Fishhook just north of town.

Even if you're not headed north, a trip to Hatcher Pass combines one of the area's most beautiful drives, access to great hiking and Nordic skiing, and interesting old buildings to look at. The **Independence Mine State Historical Park** (☎ 907-745-2827 or 907-745-3975; http://dnr. alaska.gov/parks/units/indmine.htm) takes in the remains of a hard-rock gold mine that operated from 1938 to 1951. Some buildings have been restored, including an assay office that's a museum and the manager's house that's a welcoming visitor center, while a big old mill, towering on the hillside, sags and leans as a picturesque ruin. A visit is interesting even if you don't go inside, using the interpretive panels and map on a self-guided tour. The paved trails are easily navigable by anyone, and the rugged, half-mile Mill Trail leads up to that building's ruins. The setting, in a bowl of rock and alpine tundra, is spectacular. The day-use fee is $5 per vehicle. The visitor center is open from 10 a.m. to 7 p.m. daily in the summer; it's closed in the off season.

The valley high in the **Talkeetna Mountains** that the site occupies is ideal for a summer ramble in the heather or for Nordic or Telemark skiing in winter, with several miles of groomed trails for cross-country skis and limitless alpine terrain for exploration on backcountry skis. There are four hiking trails and two mountain-biking routes in the area — ask at the visitor center. The **Gold Cord Lake Trail** is less than a mile. The **Reed Lakes Trail** is spectacular for its mountain scenery and waterfalls; starting from the Archangel Road, it gains 3,000 ft. over 4½ miles to Upper Reed Lake. Another challenging hike is the **Gold Mint Trail,** which starts across the road from the Motherlode Lodge on Hatcher Pass Road and leads 8 miles to the Mint Valley.

Along the Parks Highway

Driving north on the Parks Highway from Anchorage to Denali National Park or Fairbanks takes you through the populated central part of the valley. Although this stretch of the road is unattractive, like unplanned highway development anywhere, you may want to stop at the **Museum of Alaska Transportation & Industry,** off the Parks Highway at mile 47, on Museum Drive, west of Wasilla (☎ **907-376-1211;** www.museumof alaska.org). Volunteers have gathered every conceivable machine and conveyance — 14 airplanes, 13 fire trucks, 7 locomotives, and 2 steam cranes, for example — and fixed up as many as they could to running condition. An indoor museum displays the finished masterpieces, while the 20 acres outside are crammed with deteriorated treasures — trains, aircraft, tractors, fishing boats, and mining equipment — all grist for memories and imagination. The museum is open May through September daily from 10 a.m. to 5 p.m., October through April Tuesday from 10 a.m. to 2 p.m. Admission is $8 for adults, $5 for seniors and military, $18 for families.

Along the Glenn Highway

The Glenn Highway, north of the Parks Highway intersection and onward north of Palmer, is one of Alaska's prettiest drives. The road traces the edge of a rugged canyon over the Matanuska River and Matanuska Glacier (see Chapter 18). Nearer Anchorage, the main attraction is the **Alaska State Fair** in Palmer, which takes place the week before Labor Day (see Chapter 3 for details).

Where to stay and dine

There are unlimited fast-food spots and roadhouse burger places in the Mat-Su area. Here are some choices with a little local flavor: **Vagabond Blues,** 642 S. Alaska St., Palmer (☎ **907-745-2233;** www.vagblues.com), a coffeehouse and cafe offering sandwiches, wraps, baked goods, homemade bread, and soup, and which is also the region's outstanding music venue; and the **Windbreak Cafe,** located on the Parks Highway in Wasilla (☎ **907-376-4484;** www.windbreakalaska.com), which serves good diner food with prices ranging from $5 to $30.

Best Western Lake Lucille Inn
$$$–$$$$$ **Wasilla**

This attractive lakeside hotel in Wasilla shares a lake with former Governor Palin's house. It offers large and well appointed rooms, and those facing the lake have balconies and a grand, peaceful view. In-room amenities are numerous, including both wired and wireless broadband Internet. The hotel helps with activities and offers discounts. Flightseeing trips take off from the dock below the lawn.

1300 W. Lucille Dr., Wasilla. ☎ **800-528-1234** *or 907-373-1776. Fax: 907-376-6199.* www.bestwesternlakelucilleinn.com. *Rack rates: High season $169–$224 double, $299 suite; off season $89 double, $175 suite; extra person $20. AE, DC, DISC, MC, V.*

Hatcher Pass Lodge
$$$ **Hatcher Pass**

A charming family presides over this tiny mountain lodge 3,000 ft. high in a treeless alpine bowl near the Independence Mine State Historic Park. Out on the open snowfield in winter, or the heather in summer, the nine cabins and A-frame lodge seem far more remote than they really are, just 90 minutes from Anchorage. There is a phone in the main lodge for emergencies but no TV. The cabins are clean and nicely set up, with no rustic edge except chemical toilets and the lack of running water. Guests go to the main lodge for showers, meals, and drinks; the family produces surprisingly professional meals there. Stay in summer for a taste of the real Alaska, with doorstep access to wonderful alpine hiking.

North of Palmer. ☎ **907-745-5897.** www.hatcherpasslodge.com. *Rack rates: $150 cabin for two, lodge rooms $100 double; extra person $15. AE, DC, DISC, MC, V.*

Part IV
Road Trips from Anchorage

The 5th Wave   By Rich Tennant

"The guests are getting hungry. You'd better push over another garbage dumpster."

In this part . . .

The easiest way to many of Alaska's best destinations is along the two-lane highways that wind through the mountains from the Southcentral coast into the Interior and beyond, all the way to the Arctic Ocean. With a car that you rent in Anchorage, you can get to the forests and ocean shores of the Kenai Peninsula, including Seward, Kenai Fjords National Park, Kenai, and Homer. You can drive to Fairbanks and explore the long Interior highways. And you can see the wildlife and scenery of Denali National Park.

Chapter 16

The Kenai Peninsula: Seward, Kenai Fjords National Park, Kenai, and Homer

In This Chapter

▶ Anticipating the highlights in the Kenai Peninsula
▶ Discovering Seward
▶ Cruising Kenai Fjords National Park
▶ Fishing in Kenai and Soldotna
▶ Experiencing Homer

*T*he Kenai (*keen*-eye) Peninsula is a microcosm of what's most appealing about Alaska, and you can get to it without the expense and distances that can make traveling much of the state difficult. South of Anchorage, between Cook Inlet and Prince William Sound, the peninsula is a large enough landmass to show up on any globe, but unlike much of Alaska, it's not unimaginably vast and intimidating. And it's accessible, with roads, rails, and frequent air service. Traveling here is a bit more like traveling anywhere else in the United States (if you leave aside the amazing beauty and huge undeveloped areas). You have no need for guides or tour buses; on the Kenai Peninsula, you can discover Alaska on your own.

Most of what you're looking for — glaciers, whales, legendary sportfishing, spectacular hiking trails, interesting little fishing towns and art colonies, bears, moose, and high mountains — lies along a few hundred miles of blacktop, within reach with a rental car and perhaps a tour boat. People from Anchorage go to the peninsula for the weekend to fish, hike, dig clams, and paddle kayaks. Certain places can become crowded, but it's easy to get past the humanity into places where you'll see few, if any, other people. You can easily and inexpensively get beyond the road network altogether.

Discovering the Kenai Peninsula and Its Major Attractions

Set aside enough time to visit Kenai Fjords National Park from Seward, at least one overnight from Anchorage. For Homer or Kenai, allow two or more nights. Driving around that area takes time when you consider how tempting it is to stop along the way to view all the open and beautiful public land. The following sections contain a few of the highlights to be aware of while planning.

Seward

The attractive small town of Seward, situated at the head of a large fjord opening on the Pacific Ocean called Resurrection Bay, is a threshold to the ocean and marine-oriented Kenai Fjords National Park. The town lies 124 miles by road or rail from Anchorage on the southeastern side of the peninsula. While in Seward, you may want to:

✔ **Visit the Alaska SeaLife Center,** a research aquarium where you can see marine mammals and birds up close.

✔ **Fish salmon or halibut** in the ocean from charter boats.

✔ **Sea-kayak** among sea otters and along rocky shores and streams where salmon spawn.

Kenai Fjords National Park

At this **marine park,** mile-high mountains jut straight from the sea. Glaciers burst over the mountains' shoulders, dumping big chunks of blue ice in the water. Craggy islands poke out of the ocean, hosting thousands of nesting seabirds; whales and other marine mammals cruise through regularly. Visitors arrive at the park on day-tour boats from Seward. The park also has a back door, **Exit Glacier,** accessible by land from Seward. A short drive from town, that area's nature trails allow visitors to walk up for a closer look at ancient ice.

Kenai and Soldotna

The towns of Kenai and Soldotna sit on the banks of a supremely productive salmon stream, the **Kenai River,** which produces the world's biggest king salmon and many other species of fish. Visitors come to fish, but non-fishing members of the family can easily find some sightseeing to interest them, too. Alaska's most easily accessible canoe route is close at hand in the **Kenai National Wildlife Refuge** (which is *not* part of Kenai Fjords National Park). Kenai is about a three-hour drive from

The Kenai Peninsula and Prince William Sound

Anchorage on the peninsula's west side. While you're there, consider these activities:

- ✔ **Salmon-fishing in the Kenai River** — one of Alaska's top attractions — for a chance to catch enormous, hard-fighting fish.

- ✔ **Walking through Russian heritage and contemporary art** for an afternoon in the town of Kenai.

- ✔ **Paddling a canoe in wilderness** on an overnight in Kenai National Wildlife Refuge.

Homer

This hip, artsy, and vigorous little town is on the shore of **Kachemak Bay,** which stretches out across the community's front yard like an outdoor smorgasbord. After seeing the galleries in town, take the opportunity to experience Alaska directly by getting across the water and beyond the road network. Spend at least a couple days to get a feel for the land and to justify the 4½-hour drive down from Anchorage to the end of the road. While in Homer, you can

- ✔ **Visit the galleries and the Pratt Museum.** View the output of Alaska's most active art colony and learn about the area's natural history.

- ✔ **Go tide-pooling and take a nature walk.** A nature center teaches about the area, with several options for guided nature walks in forest or tide pools.

- ✔ **Hook into a monstrous halibut.** The state's biggest fleet of charter boats goes after fish that can top 300 pounds.

- ✔ **Sea-kayak among tiny islands.** The waters of Kachemak Bay are also home to some fascinating wildlife, including sea otters and puffins.

- ✔ **Mountain-bike and hike beyond the reach of cars.** A water taxi can take you for a day to wonderful paths and byways off the road network.

- ✔ **Dine at a watery art colony.** Boats are the only vehicles in the village of Halibut Cove, near Homer.

Landing in Seward

This agreeable little town started life as a place to get off the boat to Alaska. Later, it became a place for Alaskans and visitors to get *on* boats to see the bay, to fish, and to visit Kenai Fjords National Park (described in the "Enjoying Kenai Fjords National Park" section, later in this chapter). With the growth of the cruise industry, Seward is once again a place to get *off* the boat. Many cruises that cross the Gulf of Alaska begin or end here, with their passengers taking a bus or train to or from the airport in Anchorage.

Located by the broad fjord of Resurrection Bay, Seward is a mountain-side grid of streets lined with old wood-frame houses (see the "Seward" map, later in this chapter). It's long been the sort of place where pedestrians casually wander across the road, hardly glancing for cars, because there likely won't be any. Or, if there are, they're ready to stop. The growing tourism industry brought more traffic, but most of what's new has been good for the town. The **Alaska SeaLife Center** is a research aquarium that's open to the public. Combined with the excellent ocean fishing, the national park, the wonderful hiking trails, and the unique and attractive town itself, Seward is well worth a two-day visit (although if you don't want to go out on the water, one day is plenty).

Getting there

The least expensive and most convenient way to Seward is by car from Anchorage, but the train is an appealing option.

By car

The 127-mile drive down from Anchorage on the Seward Highway is easy and particularly scenic. It takes under 2½ hours without stops, but allow an additional hour to get out and look at the scenery, a highlight of any trip to Seward. The first 48 miles of this drive are described in detail in Chapter 15. For tips on renting a car, see Chapters 7 and 13.

By train

The **Alaska Railroad** (☎ **800-544-0552** or 907-544-0552; www.alaska railroad.com) offers passenger service from Anchorage to Seward and back daily during summer. The route is even prettier than the highway, passing close to glaciers and following a ledge halfway up the narrow, vertical Placer River gorge, where it ducks into tunnels and pops out at bends in the river. The landscape still looks as it did when the first person beheld it. The fare is $75 one-way, $119 round-trip; kids ages 2 to 11 ride for half-price. The railroad also offers money-saving lodging and sightseeing packages through its Web site. Don't do Seward as a day trip by rail — it's too tiring.

 Here's a fluke of pricing and taxation that could save money: Rental car taxes are so high in Anchorage that, depending on how long you'll keep your car, you may find it makes financial sense to take the train to Seward, rent a car from there from the local office of **Hertz** (☎ **800-654-4378**; www.rentacaralaska.com), and return the car in Anchorage when your trip is over.

Getting around

You can easily cover downtown Seward on foot, although a little help is handy to get back and forth from the boat harbor. If it's not raining, a bike may be the best way. **Seward Bike Shop** (☎ **907-224-2448**), in a railcar near the depot at the harbor, rents high-performance mountain bikes and models good for just getting around town, plus accessory equipment. A cruiser is $12 for a half-day, $19 for a full-day. **PJ's Taxi** (☎ **907-224-5555**) is one of the cab companies in Seward.

Where to stay

Alaska's Point of View Reservation Service (☎ **907-224-2323;** www. alaskasview.com) is a Seward lodging and tour-booking agency. The Web site has a search function for lodging, including B&Bs and hotels that are otherwise hard to find on the Internet.

Breeze Inn
$$$–$$$$$ Boat Harbor

Located right at the busy boat harbor, a block back from the water, this three-story hotel completed a large expansion in 2008 that added many spacious rooms in earth tones, all with good amenities and a polished feel. The original wing is a bargain: older motel rooms, but clean and well maintained. In whole, the setup lets visitors choose the level of luxury they want and the cost they want to pay, and the property is consistently well run. The location is the most convenient in town for a fishing charter or Kenai Fjords boat trip, which means that the building occupies a busy harbor parking lot near the highway and isn't landscaped. A courtesy van helps guests get around town.

See map p. 231. 1306 Seward Hwy., Seward. ☎ **888-224-5237** *or 907-224-5237. Fax: 907-224-7024.* www.breezeinn.com. *Rack rates: High season $139–$269 double, off season $49–$119 double; extra person $10. AE, DC, DISC, MC, V.*

Seward Windsong Lodge
$$$$$ North of Seward

This hotel is the only one at Kenai Fjords National Park with a national park atmosphere. The big lobby, with its high ceiling, huge wood beams, fireplace, and cedar shingles could be at Yellowstone. Moreover, the posh, solidly finished quality of the place puts it in first place among Seward's hotels. The location is out of town, among spruce trees on the broad valley of the Resurrection River, and the collection of buildings goes on and on. Rooms are in separate lodges with entry from exterior porches. They have a crisp feel, all with two queen-size beds and rustic-style furniture and good amenities. Family suites are available with TVs and video games in the kids' room. The hotel restaurant, the Resurrection Roadhouse, is reviewed later, under "Where to Dine."

Mile 0.5, Exit Glacier Road (also known as Herman Leirer Road), Seward. ☎ **888-959-9590** *or 907-777-2800.* www.sewardwindsong.com. *Rack rates: High season $249–$299 double, off season $149–$199 double; extra person 12 and older $15. AE, DISC, MC, V. Closed Oct–Apr.*

The Van Gilder Hotel
$$$ Downtown Seward

This 1916 building on the National Register of Historic Places was restored with authentic period details and decorated in a Victorian style

Seward

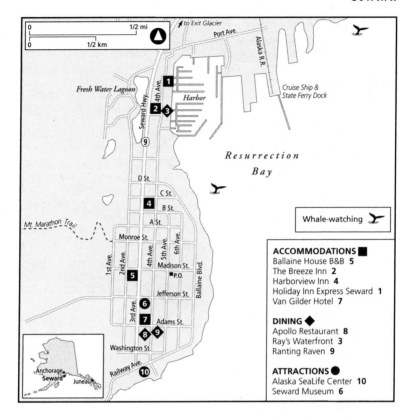

that complements the woodwork and stained glass. Old hotels have small bedrooms, and some of the bathrooms that were added are tiny (all but one with shower stalls, not tubs), but that's all easy to forgive in a place that feels very cozy and very real. The atmosphere is conducive to a fun social visit. A community kitchen on the main floor allows guests to stop for a free hot drink any time, or even cook their own meals. In Seward's high-priced lodging market, the hotel is a good value, and yet it would be the first choice of many visitors who want to experience an authentic part of this interesting town. All rooms have queen-size beds and some also have a fold-down Murphy bed for a third person. The location is right downtown.

See map p. 231. 308 Adams St., Seward. ☎ **800-204-6835** *or 907-224-3079. Fax: 907-224-3689.* www.vangilderhotel.com. *Rack rates: High season $119 double with shared bath, $159–$179 double with private bath, $219 suite; off season $59 double with shared bath, $69–$89 double with private bath, $159 suite; additional person $10. AE, DISC, MC, V.*

Runner-up accommodations

Ballaine House B&B

$ **Downtown Seward** The hostess offers gear for outings, cooks breakfast to order, and even does laundry. She can book your activities and boats in Seward and some other towns, giving you the booking commission, which can save as much as 20 percent. The B&B does not take kids 7 and under. *See map p. 231. 437 3rd Ave., Seward.* ☎ *907-224-2362.* www.superpage.com/ballaine. *Rack rates: $99 double. Rates include full breakfast cooked to order. No credit cards.*

Harborview Inn

$$$$ **Near the Small-Boat Harbor** The location, midway between the small-boat harbor and downtown, puts both within long walking distance. Families and large groups may enjoy the four-bedroom family suite with the features and size of a house. *See map p. 231. 804 3rd Ave., Seward.* ☎ *888-324-3217* or *907-224-3217.* www.sewardhotel.com.

Holiday Inn Express Seward Harbor

$$$$–$$$$$ **Boat Harbor** Standing above the harbor wall close to the railroad depot, the hotel has excellent amenities (including a pool) and superb views. *See map p. 231. 1412 4th Ave., Seward.* ☎ *888-465-4329* or *907-224-2550.* www.hiexpress.com/sewardak.

Where to dine

You can find various places at the harbor to grab a sandwich or a quick meal on the way out to sea; they change too frequently for me to include here. Downtown, the **Ranting Raven,** 228 4th Ave. (☎ **907-224-2228**), is a great little gift and coffee shop serving pastries, sandwiches, and light lunches. It's open April through Christmas.

Apollo Restaurant

$$ **Downtown Seward** **MEDITERRANEAN/SEAFOOD**

Seward families come back for a menu that includes anything they might want: Greek and southern Italian cuisine, steaks, seafood, pizza, and much more. They'll even cook your own day's catch. The service is fast, skilled, and flexible — great for families with kids. The dining room, with many booths, takes the Greek theme as far as it'll go — I especially enjoy the miniature Doric columns. They serve beer and wine.

See map p. 231. 229 4th Ave., Seward. ☎ *907-224-3092.* www.apollorestaurant ak.com. *Main courses: $10–$24. AE, MC, V. Open: Daily 11 a.m.–11 p.m.*

Christo's Palace

$$$–$$$$ **Downtown Seward** **SEAFOOD/ITALIAN/MEXICAN**

I was skeptical of a restaurant with faux 1890s décor and Formica tables serving a family-friendly menu of pizza, pasta, tacos, burgers, subs, fried fish, steaks, and much finer dining, such as rack of lamb or stuffed halibut. I quickly became a believer; the friendly and efficient service, children's menu that met my kids' needs perfectly, and seafood platter prepared won me over. Everything was served quickly.

133 4th Ave., Seward. ☎ **907-224-5255.** www.christospalace.com. *Main courses: $9–$38. AE, DC, DISC, MC, V. Open: Daily 11 a.m.–11 p.m.*

Ray's Waterfront
$$$–$$$$ Boat Harbor   STEAK/SEAFOOD

The lively, noisy dining room looks out from big windows across the small-boat harbor, with tables on terraces so everyone can see. The atmosphere is fun and the consistently good food is just right after a day on the water. Though not perfect, it's more nuanced than the typical harborside place; the seafood chowder is great. Most important, they don't overcook the fresh local fish — and that's really all you can ask. On a busy summer weekend, however, the place can be overrun, with long waits and harried servers. They have a full bar.

See map p. 231. At the small-boat harbor, Seward. ☎ **907-224-5606.** *Reservations recommended. Main courses: $9–$16 lunch, $19–$35 dinner. AE, DISC, MC, V. 18 percent gratuity added for parties of six or more. Open: Daily 11 a.m.–11 p.m. Closed Oct to mid-Apr.*

Seward's top attractions

Seward has only one *top* attraction. I cover other in-town pastimes later in this chapter under "More cool things to do in Seward."

Alaska SeaLife Center
Downtown Seward

The center's role as an important research institution makes it an especially vibrant and fascinating aquarium in which to see creatures from nearby Alaska waters. There's always something happening. You may have seen puffins diving into the water from a tour boat; here you can see what they look like flying *under* the water. Seabirds, harbor seals, octopus, and sea lions reside in three spectacular exhibits viewed from above or below — you can get within a few feet of the birds without glass. There are smaller tanks with fish, crab, and other creatures; a touch tank where you can handle starfish and other tide-pool animals; and exhibits on current ocean changes and hot research issues. An exhibit traces the life cycle of salmon; the staff hatches salmon eggs on a schedule so fish at each stage of development will always be present in their realistic habitats. I don't want to oversell the place, however: The center is not as large as a big-city aquarium, and you'll likely spend no more than a couple hours here, unless you sign up for one of the lectures or special behind-the-scenes programs for adults and children that happen all day.

See map p. 231. 301 Railway Ave., Seward. ☎ **888-378-2525** *or 907-224-6300.* www. alaskasealife.org. *Admission: $20 adults, $15 students 12–17 or with student ID, $10 kids 4–11, free for kids 3 and under. Open: May 14–Sept 14 Mon–Thurs 9 a.m.–6:30 p.m., Sept 15–May 13 daily 10 a.m.–5 p.m.*

Getting outdoors in Seward

In this section, I describe things to do outdoors in Seward other than the main event, the national park, with its fjords and road-accessible Exit Glacier. For that information, see "Enjoying Kenai Fjords National Park," later in this chapter.

Sea-kayaking

Sunny Cove Sea Kayaking (☎ **800-770-9119** or 907-224-4426; www.sunny cove.com) has earned a good reputation for guided kayaking in Resurrection Bay and beyond. Its day trips suitable for beginners are offered as part of the Kenai Fjords Tours trips to its Fox Island lodge. More ambitious day trips and multi-day trips venture into the fjords themselves (see the "Kenai Fjords National Park" section, later in this chapter). On a budget, you can take one of Sunny Cove's tours right from Seward. They launch from Lowell Point, following the shore toward Caines Head State Recreation Area, where you can see sea otters, sea-birds, intertidal creatures, and the salmon in Tonsina Creek. Three-hour paddles are $65; eight-hour trips, $130. A trip to Fox Island is more expensive but comes with a fjords boat tour and salmon bake, so the cost of the kayaking comes out roughly the same.

Fishing

Seward is renowned for its saltwater silver-salmon fishing. The silvers start showing up in the bay in mid-July and last through September. You can catch the fish from shore, from Lowell Point south of town, or even near the boat harbor, but your chances for success are far greater from a boat. I prefer small, six-passenger boats, because you can get to know the skipper better and learn more about fishing. (If seasickness is a concern, choose a large boat — it'll bob less in the waves.) When your party has the entire boat, you can control where it goes, perhaps adding whale-watching or sightseeing to the day. The going rate for a guided charter, with everything provided, is about $199 per person, or $299 to fish for salmon and halibut on the same day. You can choose from among many charter services, either using a central booking agency or engaging a charter directly. Here are two choices:

✔ Andrew Mezirow, a marine biologist and maritime instructor, operates two boats. Besides day-fishing, he takes guests on multi-day fishing expeditions to extremely remote and beautiful places. His business is **Crackerjack Sportfishing Charters** (☎ **800-566-3192** or 907-224-2606; www.crackerjackcharters.com).

✔ To choose among a variety of boats, contact **The Fish House,** located at the small boat harbor (☎ **800-257-7760** or 907-224-3674; www.thefishhouse.net). They operate their own boats, book charters with other skippers, sell and rent ocean-fishing and spin-casting gear, and carry some fly-fishing supplies. If you want to be on a small vessel, make sure to ask for a "six-pack," as the six-passenger boats are known. For charters, reserve ahead.

Hiking

You'll find some excellent hiking trails near Seward. You can obtain a complete list and directions at the Kenai Fjords National Park Visitor Center (see the upcoming section about the park).

✔ The **Mount Marathon Trail** is a challenging hike to the top of a 3,022-ft. mountain, with a couple trails of varying difficulty levels. The route of the famous Mount Marathon footrace is the more strenuous choice, basically going straight up from the end of Jefferson Street; the hikers' route starts at the corner of 1st Avenue and Monroe Street. Either trail rises steeply to the top of the rocky pinnacle, which has incredible views. Allow an entire day, unless you're a racer; in that case, expect to make it up and back in less than 45 minutes.

✔ The **Caines Head State Recreation Area** (http://dnr.alaska. gov/parks/units/caineshd.htm) has a 7-mile coastal trail south of town. Parts of the trail are accessible only at low tide, so it's best done either as an overnight or with someone picking you up or dropping you off in a boat at the far end; the **Miller's Landing water taxi** (☎ 866-541-5739 or 907-224-5739; www.millers landingak.com) offers this service for $48 round-trip. The trail has some gorgeous views, rocky shores, and a fascinating destina-tion at the end: a towering cliff with the concrete remains of Fort McGilvray, a World War II defensive emplacement. Take flashlights and you can poke around in the spooky, pitch-dark underground corridors and rooms and imagine what each was used for. (Going in without lights would be foolhardy.) The trailhead from town is just south of Seward on Lowell Point Road; pull off in the lot right after the sewage plant, and then cross the road through the gate and follow the dirt road a bit until it becomes the actual trail. Stop at the Kenai Fjords National Park Visitor Center at the boat harbor for tide conditions and advice.

If you take a boat both ways to North Beach, 4½ miles in, you cut the hike to the fort down to a size any family can manage. We had a wonderful day with grandparents and little ones that way.

Sled-dog mushing

When Mitch Seavey won the Iditarod Trail Sled Dog Race in 2004, many agreed it couldn't have happened to a nicer guy. He's made a lot of friends over the years offering rides with his dogs. It's a family business, including his four boys (one is a Junior Iditarod champ), making use of their kennel on Old Exit Glacier Road off Herman Leirer Road. They offer summer rides in Seward and in winter in Sterling (near Soldotna). The summer ride uses a wheeled sled and a full, 12-dog team — not the real thing (no snow), but you'll get a feeling for the dogs' power and intelligence. Husky puppies are available for cuddling, too. The 90-minute tour costs $59 for adults, $29 for kids 11 and under. They call their company **IdidaRide** (☎ **800-478-3139** or 907-224-8607; www.ididaride.com).

Those willing to spend much more should consider mushing on snow at the height of summer by joining a helicopter tour to Godwin Glacier from the Seward Airport with **Godwin Glacier Dog Sled Tours** (☎ **888-989-8239** or 907-224-8239; www.alaskadogsled.com). A chopper lands at a camp of 100 dogs, where guests take a ride in the dog sled, or even drive it themselves. The company also offers glacier hikes and overnight camping on the ice. They charge $450 for adults, $430 for kids 12 and under.

More cool things to do in Seward

Most of Seward's attractions are of the modest, small-town variety and involve exploring downtown and the waterfront on foot:

✔ **Walk along the beach** on Ballaine Avenue. The broken concrete and twisted metal you see are the last ruins of the Seward waterfront that was destroyed by a tsunami wave that resulted from the 1964 earthquake. Sometimes you can see sea otters swimming just offshore.

✔ **Visit the Seward Museum** at 3rd and Jefferson (☎ **907-224-3902**). It's a charming grandma's attic of a place, with clippings, memorabilia, and curiosities recalling the history of the town and of the Iditarod Trail, painter Rockwell Kent, and the ways of the past. Admission is $3 adults, 50¢ kids 17 and under. The museum is open in the summer daily from 10 a.m. to 5 p.m.; in the winter, it's usually open weekends noon to 4 p.m., but call ahead to be sure. Evening slide programs take place during the summer months.

Fast Facts: Seward

ATMs

Wells Fargo, at 908 3rd Ave., has an ATM. You also can find an ATM at the Safeway grocery store at 1907 Seward Hwy., among other places.

Emergencies

Dial ☎ 911.

Hospital

Providence Seward Medical Center is at 417 1st Ave. (☎ 907-224-5205).

Information

Contact the Seward Chamber of Commerce and Conference & Visitors Bureau, 2001 Seward Hwy. (☎ 907-224-8051; www.seward.com).

Internet Access

You can access the Internet for free at the Seward Public Library, 5th and Adams (☎ 907-224-4082).

Police

For non-emergency situations, call the Seward Police Department (☎ 907-224-3338) or, outside the city limits, the Alaska State Troopers (☎ 907-224-3346).

Post Office

The post office is at 5th Avenue and Madison Street.

Taxes

Sales tax is 7 percent. The room tax totals 11 percent.

Enjoying Kenai Fjords National Park

Kenai Fjords National Park is all about remote rocks, mountains, and ice that meet the ocean, and the animals that live there. The park comprises 670,000 acres of the south coast and impassible highlands of the Kenai Peninsula. The shore here is exposed to the Gulf of Alaska, where wild, recurrent storms beat against the mountainous shore unbuffered by any landmasses from the vast expanses of the Pacific to the south. Wildlife thrives, but humans have never made a mark.

The majority of the area, in the impossibly rugged interior of the Kenai Peninsula, was likely first seen by human eyes only in 1968, when mountain climbers initially crossed the **Harding Ice Field,** which covers most of the national park (Alaska Natives had no use for that area). **Exit Glacier** and all the glaciers of Kenai Fjords flow from this Ice Age leftover, which may be a mile thick. The ice field lies in a high bowl of mountains that jut straight out of the ocean to heights of 3,000 to 5,000 ft.

Visitors travel the park's marine periphery, seeing the glaciers that dip into the sea, the shore's razor-sharp mountains, and the abundant wildlife that lives in the water, on the rocks, and in the air. A large vessel, such as a tour boat operating out of Seward, is the only practical way for most people to do this, and that takes time and money. Better destinations are available for people who get seasick (for example, Prince William Sound; see Chapter 15). But if you go, you'll experience a ride into primeval wilderness that's pretty much unequaled.

Getting there

Seward is the threshold to the park. Exit Glacier is 13 miles from the town by road. The Kenai Fjords National Park Visitor Center is at the Seward small-boat harbor; tour boats that visit the park also leave from the harbor.

Don't try to see the park in a day (coming from Anchorage by train or road, touring the park by boat, and then returning that evening). To see the best of the park, you need to take an all-day boat trip — most half-day trips barely leave Resurrection Bay and see hardly any of the park proper. Besides, the trip down from Anchorage and back in one day, especially by train, is too tiring, amounting to 16 hours of near-constant boat and train rides. A better plan is to spend a night or two in Seward, taking in the full Kenai Fjords boat trip and visiting Exit Glacier.

Getting park information

At the **Kenai Fjords National Park Visitor Center,** at the small-boat harbor, Seward (☎ 907-224-7500; www.nps.gov/kefj), rangers answer questions about the park, provide information on the all-important tour boats, and operate a small bookstore. The center is open late May through early September daily from 8:30 a.m. to 7 p.m., the balance of May and September daily 9 a.m. to 5 p.m.; it's closed October through April.

Note that the park is pure wilderness, with no commercial facilities of any kind. Seward is the place to stay, eat, and do any non-wilderness activities.

Enjoying the park

Kenai Fjords is essentially a marine park. On a boat tour, you'll see its mountains, glaciers, and wildlife. On any of the tours, you're sure to see sea otters and sea lions, and you have a good chance of seeing humpback whales, orcas, mountain goats, and black bears. I saw all that wildlife on one trip to Aialik Bay. Gray whales come in the early spring and huge fin whales show up sometimes, too, but they're hard to see. Birdwatchers may see bald eagles, puffins (both tufted and horned), murrelets (marbled, ancient, and Kittlitz's), cormorants (red-faced, pelagic, and double-crested), murres (common and thick-billed), auklets (rhinoceros and parakeet), and various other sea ducks, alcids, and gulls.

The farther you go into the park, the more you'll see. If you really want to see Kenai Fjords National Park and glaciers that drop ice into the water, the boat has to go at least into **Aialik Bay** to **Holgate Glacier** or **Aialik Glacier. Northwestern Glacier** is even deeper in the park. Half-day **Resurrection Bay** cruises offer plenty of impressive scenery but pass only one glacier, and that at a distance. Passengers also have fewer opportunities for seeing whales and puffins and other birds. The longest trips into the heart of the park encounter the greatest variety and number of birds and animals. If you're lucky with the weather, you can make it to the exposed **Chiswell Islands,** which are home to some of the greatest bird colonies in Alaska, supporting more than 50,000 seabirds of 18 species. I've seen clouds of puffins swarm here. The daylong trips also provide more time to linger and really witness the behavior of the wildlife. Whatever your choice, binoculars are a necessity; you may be able to rent them onboard.

Deciding on a tour

Prices are about $170 to go to **Northwestern Glacier** in Northwestern Fjord off Harris Bay, a 10- to 12-hour trip; $140 to $160 to go to **Holgate**

Glacier or **Aialik Glacier** in Aialik Bay, which takes six to eight hours; and $60 to $90 for a three- to five-hour **Resurrection Bay** tour, which doesn't go to the national park at all. Children's prices are usually about half off. I've seen misleading publicity material from the tour operators, so ask exactly where the boat goes or get a map of the route.

Bear Glacier, on the edge of the park, is unimpressive, because boats can't get anywhere near it. Go at least to Holgate Glacier for a noteworthy glacier sighting.

The season begins in April with tours to see the gray whale migration, mostly within Resurrection Bay. That's done by mid-May, when the regular schedule of tours begins, which lasts into September. Although you can sometimes obtain early-season or Web specials, fares with each operator differ little. Instead, shop for the destination, length of trip, food service, interpretation, and size or intimacy of the boat. Ask how much deck space is outside so that you can really see. What is the seating arrangement? How many passengers will be onboard and how many crew members can answer questions? Is lunch provided, and what does it consist of? Another important point of comparison is whether you have a ranger providing the commentary, or only the captain — some captains don't know when to shut up and can give inaccurate information.

Try to schedule loosely so that if the weather is bad on the day you choose for your boat trip, you can wait and go the next day. In bad weather, you'll be uncomfortable and the animals and birds won't be as evident, or the boat may not go out at all. If you pay upfront to hold a reservation on a boat — probably a good idea in the busiest months — find out the company's policies regarding refunds and rescheduling.

Most operators offer packages with the Alaska Railroad and the Alaska SeaLife Center, which may save you money, but make sure you have enough time to do everything you want to do in Seward. All have offices at the small-boat harbor in Seward.

Kenai Fjords Tours

This is the dominant tour operator, with the most daily sailings and choices of destination. The main part of the operation uses 90- to 150-passenger vessels, many of which have forward-facing seats, like an airplane's. They're professionally staffed. The whole operation runs remarkably smoothly, and we found the crew extremely attentive. When the ships are crowded, however, the experience becomes more impersonal. Onboard, the captain primarily narrates with other employees sometimes helping.

The same company also owns **Mariah Tours,** which operates more-intimate 16-passenger vessels. Their trips are more spontaneous and go to Northwestern Fjord every day, weather permitting; the downside is that the smaller boats move more in the waves.

Beware of seasickness

A critical factor in choosing your boat tour is your susceptibility to **seasickness**. To reach the heart of the park, vessels must venture into the unprotected waters of the North Pacific. Large, rolling waves are inevitable on the passage from Resurrection Bay to the fjords themselves, although once you're in the fjords the water is calm. On a rough day, most boats will turn back for the comfort of the passengers and change the full-day trip into a Resurrection Bay cruise, refunding the difference in fare. Of course, they'd rather not do that, and the decision often isn't made until the vessel is out there and some people are sick. This has happened to us more than once. On one trip, about 80 percent of the passengers were already vomiting when the boat turned around. (Even for those who don't lose it, being around that much puke isn't fun.) If you get seasick easily, my advice is to stick to the Resurrection Bay cruise or take a boat tour in protected Prince William Sound out of Whittier (see Chapter 15), where the water is smooth. Details on avoiding and treating seasickness are in Chapter 9. In any event, when you book, ask about the tour company's policy on turning back and refunds.

Most of the large Kenai Fjords vessels visit a day lodge that the company owns on Fox Island, in Resurrection Bay, for lunch and National Park Service ranger talks. The lodge sits on a long cobble beach near Sunny Cove, where painter Rockwell Kent lived in seclusion with his son in 1918 and 1919 and produced the art that made him famous; it's an inspiring spot. The lodge itself stands on a narrow strip of land between the beach and a pond, which visitors overlook from large wooden decks. Lunch is grilled Alaska salmon and prime rib with an option of adding king crab. Some passengers spend the night at the company's Kenai Fjords Wilderness Lodge on all-inclusive packages. Half-day sea-kayaking paddles from the island are offered for day-trippers or overnight guests: $89 to $100 per person as an add-on for overnighters; or $89 to $169, including a Resurrection Bay tour-boat ride, for day-trippers.

At the small-boat harbor, Seward. ☎ **800-478-8068** *or 907-276-6249.* www.kenai fjords.com.

Major Marine Tours

This company pioneered first-class onboard dining and commentary by park rangers, who go on every trip. Their boats are slower than some of the competitors', so they don't make the long trip to Northwest Glacier; they either go to Holgate Glacier or tour Resurrection Bay around Seward. Instead of bringing sandwiches or stopping for a meal, they serve a buffet of salmon and prime rib onboard ($19 adults, $9 kids). The food is surprisingly good. I also like their table seating arrangement with forward-facing seats. Your seat is assigned, so there's no need to rush aboard or try to stake out your spot.

At the small-boat harbor, Seward. ☎ **800-764-7300,** *or 907-274-7300 or 907-224-8030 in Seward.* www.majormarine.com.

Sunny Cove Sea Kayaking

Seeing the fjords from a sea kayak is quieter and more intimate than a big boat with too many people. Even beginners can do it on a guided day trip. Sunny Cove Kayaking takes guests for a wildlife tour to Aialik Bay on a small charter boat, and then launches kayaks for a paddle in front of the glacier. At $399 per person, it's more than double the cost of a regular tour-boat ride, but this is the best of the best. If you're sure you like kayaking and camping, spend a couple days; a two-night kayak camping trip costs $1,199.

Point Lowell, Seward. ☎ **800-770-9119** *or 907-224-4426.* www.sunnycove.com.

Checking out Exit Glacier

The only land-accessible part of the park is the engaging **Exit Glacier,** one of the few glaciers in Alaska that you can stroll near to. Approaching the glacier, you can see the pattern of vegetation reclaiming the land that the melting ice has uncovered, a process well explained by interpretive signs and a nature trail. At its face, cold, dense spires of ice loom over you, breathing chilled air like an open freezer door. A National Park Service nature center adds to the comfort and educational content of a visit. You can easily spend a couple hours on a casual, pleasant visit to the glacier (longer if you do a hike).

A safety note: Big chunks fall off the glacier ever more frequently as Alaska's climate warms. Stay behind the signs or you stand a good chance of being crushed.

The easiest way to get to the glacier is to drive. Take the Seward Highway 3⅔ miles north of town to the clearly marked 9-mile route to the glacier. In winter, the road is closed to vehicles. If you don't have a car, a shuttle may be available; check with the Kenai Fjords National Park Visitor Center (see the "Getting park information" section, earlier in this chapter) to see who currently offers this service.

Following the road along the broad bed of the wandering Resurrection River, you can observe, in reverse order, the succession of vegetation, from mature Sitka spruce and cottonwood trees down to smaller alders and shrubs. It takes time for nature to replace the soil on sterile ground left behind by a receding glacier. As you get closer, watch for signs with dates starting a couple of centuries in the past; they mark the retreat of the glacier through time. At the glacier itself, nothing grows at all.

The Exit Glacier Nature Center is open sporadically in May, Memorial Day weekend through Labor Day daily 9 a.m. to 8 p.m., and September 9 a.m. to 5 p.m. Ranger-led nature walks start daily at 10 a.m., 2 p.m., and 4 p.m. on the short trail to the glacier. However, no guide is needed — the trails are simple.

Spending the night on an island

Fox Island stands with high, rocky pinnacles like a castle over Resurrection Bay, a seductive destination for anyone exploring those waters. For a price, you can spend a night or two there. Sea-kayaking outings among the sea otters, puffins, and sheer rocks are an essential add-on, priced at $80 to $100 per person for lodge guests. An overnight package on the island costs $379 per person, including meals and a full-day cruise in the national park. Contact **Kenai Fjords Tours** (☎ **800-478-8068** or 907-224-8068; www. kenaifjords.com) to make a reservation.

One of the glacier's striking features is a high berm of gravel that fits around its leading edge like a necklace. This is a *moraine,* the glacier's refuse pile. The glacier gouges out the mountains with its immense, moving weight as new ice flows down from the ice field above and melts here. It carries along the rock and gravel torn from the mountain like a conveyor belt. This moraine is where the conveyor belt ends and the melting ice leaves the debris behind in a big pile. Probably without knowing it, you've seen hundreds of moraines all over North America, where the glaciers of the last Ice Age piled debris into hills, but this is the most obvious moraine I've ever seen, and it helps you understand how they work.

An all-day hike, 8 miles round-trip, climbs along the right side of the glacier to the **Harding Ice Field** — Exit Glacier gets its name for being an exit from that massive sheet. The walk is a challenging 3,000-ft. elevation gain, but it's the easiest access I'm aware of to visit an ice field on foot. Because of snow, the trail doesn't open until late June or early July. The ice field itself is cold and dangerous.

Kenai and Soldotna

The largest sport-caught king salmon in the world, almost 100 pounds, came from the Kenai River. That's why people come here. The Kenai's kings run so large that the river has a different trophy class. Everywhere else in the state, the Alaska Department of Fish & Game certifies a 50-pounder as a trophy, but, on the Kenai, your catch has to be at least 75 pounds. That's because kings in the 60-pound class — with enough wild muscle to fight ferociously for hours — are just too common here. Anglers prepared to pay for a charter will be in their element on the river when the fish are running hot. Catching a big king isn't easy or quick, however, and success rates vary greatly year to year and week to week.

Visitors who aren't interested in fishing find less than a day's sightseeing in these towns. Instead, they can use the towns as bases for the outdoors. Kenai has a strangely beautiful ocean beach and the Kenai River mouth offers exceptional bird-watching during migrations. Best of all, wonderful canoeing waters lie north of town in the lake-dotted **Kenai National Wildlife Refuge,** which has headquarters in Soldotna.

Getting there and getting around

The drive on the Seward and Sterling highways to the Kenai/Soldotna area from Anchorage is 147 miles and takes a good three hours without stops. In summer, traffic slows you down, and in winter, speeds are limited by ice and the fear of hitting moose. (The first 48 miles of this trip are covered in Chapter 15.) Bear right onto the Sterling Highway about 90 miles from Anchorage. Car rental in Anchorage is covered in Chapters 7 and 13.

Kenai receives frequent flights from Anchorage via **Era Alaska** (☎ 800-866-8394; www.flyera.com). Four car-rental companies operate at the Kenai airport: **Avis, Budget, Hertz,** and **Payless.**

The area is too spread out to walk and has no public transportation. You can get by without a car if you do nothing but fish and you eat at your lodgings; in that case, you can get the rides you need from your guide, your host, or a taxi. One of the cab companies in the area is **Alaska Cab** (☎ **907-283-6000** in Kenai, ☎ **907-262-1555** in Soldotna).

Where to stay

Rates at all the hotels in the area are on seasonal schedules with three, four, or even more levels linked to the salmon runs. When I list high-season and off-season rates in this section, I'm talking about the highest and lowest rates of the year.

Aspen Hotel Soldotna
$$$$ Soldotna

Try here for accommodations with high-end amenities in an up-to-date corporate style. The building is a rectangle without much personality, visible from the Sterling Highway as you drive through town, but inside it has high ceilings and a solid feeling of quality. Rooms, newly outfitted in 2009, include family suites with bunk beds, privacy between parents and kids, and PlayStation video games. Suites with cooking facilities are available, too, as well as other handy configurations. All rooms are decked out with lots of amenities. The hotel is near Arby's on the commercial strip, but offset from traffic and with a view out the back of a settling pond and the river, where a walkway provides access to fishing.

326 Binkley Circle, Soldotna. ☎ **888-308-7848** *or 907-260-7736. Fax: 907-260-7786.* www.aspenhotelsak.com. *Rack rates: High season $169–$179 double, $199 suite; off season $99 double, $119 suite; extra person 18 and over $10. Rates include continental breakfast. AE, DC, DISC, MC, V.*

Great Alaska Adventure Lodge
$$$$$ Sterling

For anglers, it's the location that counts, and for that, this lodge is hard to top, with a third of a mile of river frontage where the Moose and Kenai rivers converge, a hot fishing spot since time immemorial, as an ancient

Native site attests. In the evening, the lodge keeps a guide and campfire on the beach so you can keep casting in the midnight sun. Lodge rooms overlooking the river are spacious and have gas fireplaces and private bathrooms. Unfortunately, the site suffers from vehicle noise from the adjacent Sterling Highway. The lodge offers a wide variety of guided fishing activities, including fly-fishing and halibut outings. For guests interested in seeing wildlife, the lodge offers trips to its own backcountry tent camps, including one across Cook Inlet with good brown-bear-viewing. Check the lodge's Web site for information on the many tours and wilderness safaris that they offer, as well as rates, which are too extensive to itemize here.

33881 Sterling Hwy., Sterling. ☎ **800-544-2261** *or 907-262-4515. Fax: 907-262-8797 in summer, 360-697-7850 in winter. www.greatalaska.com. Rack rates: $295–$550 day trip without lodging, $1,195–$5,495 packages of two to ten days. Rates include all meals, guide service, transfers, and travel from Anchorage. AE, MC, V. Closed Oct to mid-May.*

Harborside Cottages Bed and Breakfast
$$$$ **Kenai**

On a grassy compound at the top of the bluff over the mouth of the Kenai River in Old Town, these little white cottages make the most of a perfect site. The view and quiet can keep you in a peaceful reverie all day. Inside, the cottages are clean and trim, each with its own light country decoration. They have either king-size beds or pairs of twin beds. There are no tubs, just shower stalls. The hostess stocks a self-serve breakfast the night before. Outside is a patio with a picnic table and gas barbecue.

13 Riverview Dr., Kenai. ☎ **888-283-6162** *or 907-283-6162. www.harborside cottages.com. Rack rates: High season $185 double, off season $150 double. AE, DISC, MC, V. Closed winter.*

Where to dine

Fast-food franchises and burger-steak-seafood places dominate in Kenai and Soldotna. Here are some good choices that aren't familiar brands.

Charlotte's Bakery, Café, Espresso
$ **Kenai** **CAFE**

Some of the best sandwiches I've ever tasted came from this little strip-mall restaurant in Kenai. They're anchored by rich-textured bread and enlivened by unique combinations — for example, a sub with olive tapenade, or a turkey sandwich with cranberry cream cheese. The salads, soup, and chili are memorable, too, and the desserts are amazing — ten selections, all baked in-house, were on the tray on a typical day when I last visited. Besides the food, the dining experience is a delight, with service by women who seem to know all their customers and work efficiently in a bright, clean room with cheerful, feminine décor.

115 S. Willow, Kenai. ☎ **907-283-2777.** *Main courses: $5–$12. MC, V. Open: High season Mon–Fri 7 a.m.–4 p.m., Sat 8 a.m.–3 p.m.; off season Mon–Fri 7 a.m.–3 p.m. Sat 8 a.m.–3 p.m.*

Mykel's Restaurant
$$$–$$$$ Soldotna SEAFOOD

This is a traditional fine-dining restaurant for a date or an especially relaxing evening, located in the Soldotna Inn, near the intersection of the Sterling and Kenai Spur highways. The cuisine is exceptional; the service, professional and more than friendly. Nothing else in the area even plays in the same league, and Mykel's is only a half-step below Alaska's best. The dinner menu contains many familiar beef and chicken dishes done just right. When they "borrowed" the pepper steak created by Jens Hansen at his restaurant in Anchorage, they admitted it on the menu — classy. In addition, the restaurant offers various ways of having local seafood in creative ways. Servings are large, even for the exceptional desserts, so don't order extra courses. The full bar serves 18 wines by the glass and 6 local microbrews. At lunchtime, there are lots of salads to choose from besides the expected sandwiches.

35041 Kenai Spur Hwy., Soldotna. ☎ **907-262-4305.** *www.mykels.com. Reservations recommended. Main courses: $9–$18 lunch, $15–$35 dinner. AE, DISC, V. Open: High season daily 11 a.m.–10 p.m.; off season Tues–Thurs and Sun 11 a.m.–9 p.m., Fri–Sat 11 a.m.–10 p.m.*

Suzie's Cafe
$–$$ Sterling DINER

If you're traveling the Sterling Highway and you want a pleasant and filling lunch or dinner, you'll do no better than this local favorite on the east side of the road in the town of Sterling itself. Cheerful, efficient servers bring big plates of comfort food and hearty sandwiches. The dining room, heavily decorated in burly country style, has only eight tables and a small lunch counter, and no room for waiting. It's kept bright and immaculate. They offer meals to go, too.

Mile 87.2, Sterling Highway, Sterling. ☎ **907-260-5751.** *Main courses: $7–$25. MC, V. Open: Summer daily 11:30 a.m.–9 p.m. Closed mid-Sept to May.*

Fishing in Kenai and Soldotna

Fishing the Kenai River is the point of coming to the area for most visitors. Check at the visitor centers (see "Fast Facts: Kenai and Soldotna," later in this chapter) for information and regulation booklets. Or contact the **Alaska Department of Fish & Game,** 43961 Kalifornsky Beach Rd., Soldotna (☎ **907-262-9368,** or 907-262-2737 for a recorded fishing report; www.alaska.gov/adfg). Serious anglers shouldn't miss that Web site, which includes daily sonar counts of salmon in the river and information on biology and fishing techniques; click the "Sport Fish" link, and then click the Southcentral region on the map. Licenses are for sale on the site, as well as in any sporting-goods store in Alaska and many grocery stores.

The Kenai River has more than two dozen public-access points along its 80-mile length. A **guide brochure** with a map is available from the state **Division of Parks and Outdoor Recreation (☎ 907-262-5581;**

www.alaskastateparks.org); you also can pick up a copy at one of the town visitor centers.

Fishing for king salmon

King salmon, the monsters of the river, come in two runs. The early run comes from mid-May to the end of June, peaking in mid-June. On average, less plentiful and smaller — in the 20- to 40-pound range — the run did also produce the sport-caught world record (97 lbs., 4 oz.). The second run comes during the month of July and includes more of the massive fish. Most people fish kings from a boat, fishing certain holes. Boats hold stationary or back slowly down the river; or fishermen drift downriver. Your chances from the bank are low; on average, with or without a boat, it takes 29 hours of fishing time to land a king. (You'll likely get at least a dozen strikes for every fish that makes it into the boat.) With a guide, the average time to land a fish is cut in half, but that still means that if you fish for only one day, chances are good that you'll get skunked. A boat of three anglers on a half-day guided charter has roughly a 50 percent chance of landing a king between them.

A guided charter averages $150 to $170 for a six-hour trip, $250 to $265 full-day. There are dozens of guides. Contact the visitor center in Kenai or Soldotna for a referral (see "Fast Facts: Kenai and Soldotna," later in this chapter), or book through your lodgings — many have their own boats and guides. The **Sports Den,** 44176 Sterling Hwy., Soldotna (☎ **907-262-7491;** www.alaskasportsden.com), is one charter operator that offers river and ocean trips, fly-in fishing, and hunting, and that also has lodging packages. I've found them friendly and helpful.

Fishing for red salmon

The area really goes crazy when the red (or sockeye) salmon join the kings in the river, from mid-July through early August. Reds are plankton eaters; some say they won't strike a lure and others say they do. In some popular fishing areas, regulations allow only the use of flies; check the regulations or contact Fish & Game for details. The best approach is to fish from the bank with coho or streamer flies with small weights 18 to 36 in. from the fly. Flip the rig upstream, allowing the fly to drift down with the current, near the bank. This can be done with a bait, spinning, or fly rod, as you aren't really casting — just pull out 15 ft. of line, flip upstream, let the fly drift by in front of you, and repeat. While waiting for a strike, debate whether the fish really attack the flies, or if they get caught when they instinctively move their mouths in an eating motion, which they do in quick-moving water.

Fishing for silver salmon

Silvers first arrive in late July, peaking during August, but continuing to be in the river through September and even in October. They're easiest to catch anchored in a boat, but you can also do well from shore. Lures (such as spinners, spoons, and plugs) work well, as does sinking bait (such as salmon eggs).

Fishing for other species

Trophy-size rainbow trout and Dolly Varden char also come out of the river, catch-and-release only. Anglers using light tackle also may enjoy catching pink salmon, which are plentiful in the Kenai during even-numbered years, arriving in late July and lasting until mid-September. Use spinning gear and lures. Most Alaskans turn up their noses at this easy-to-catch 4-pound fish; just smile and keep hauling them in. Fresh, bright pinks taste great over a campfire.

Canoeing near Kenai and Soldotna

Floating through the Kenai National Wildlife Refuge in a canoe narrows the world into a circle of green water, spruce, and birch. You can paddle and hike for days without encountering more than a few other people. Your only expenses are the costs of your canoe and the vehicle that carried you to the trailhead. Most of the western half of the Kenai Peninsula lies within the 2 million acres of the refuge — it's almost as large as Yellowstone National Park — and much of that is impossibly remote and truly dedicated to wildlife. Canoeists use the lowlands on the west side, west of the Sterling Highway and north of Kenai and Soldotna. The region is a maze of lakes connected by trails. You can reach more than 70 lakes on canoe routes that stretch more than 150 miles. It's the easiest way to real Alaska wilderness that I know.

Stop in at the **Kenai National Wildlife Refuge Visitor Center,** Ski Hill Road, Soldotna (☎ **907-262-7021;** http://kenai.fws.gov), for guidance before plunging into the wilderness. The U.S. Fish & Wildlife Service, which manages the refuge, exhibits natural history displays here, shows a film each hour in the afternoon in the summer, and maintains a 3-mile nature trail. The staff offers advice and sells books and maps that you'll definitely need for a successful backcountry trip. To find the center, turn left just south of the Kenai River Bridge, taking a right turn in front of the building-supply store uphill on the unpaved road. It's open in summer, Monday through Friday 8 a.m. to 5 p.m., Saturday and Sunday 9 a.m. to 5 p.m.; in winter, Monday through Friday 8 a.m. to 4:30 p.m., Saturday and Sunday 10 a.m. to 5 p.m. The Web site also contains detailed trip-planning information for the canoe routes.

I haven't provided detailed driving instructions because you'll need detailed maps to go at all. You can order a good one printed on plastic from **Trails Illustrated** (☎ **800-962-1643;** www.natgeomaps.com). A serviceable free map is distributed by the refuge visitor center. I also recommend the book *The Kenai Canoe Trails,* by Daniel L. Quick (Northlite Publishing), an extraordinary guide with super-detailed maps and directions.

You can find a guide or prepare for an unguided trip with the help of **Alaska Canoe & Campground** (☎ **907-262-2331;** www.alaskacanoe trips.com), where the Finch family rents canoes and everything else you need for a wilderness trip, near the intersection of Swanson River

Road and the Sterling Highway in Sterling. Lightweight canoes rent for $53 for 24 hours. They offer a shuttle service to carry canoeists from one entrance to another so you don't have to double back on your trip, and they can give valuable expert advice. They also rent a lot of other outdoor stuff: kayaks, mountain bikes, rafts, and so on. Call ahead to check on equipment and to reserve. Their campground is fully equipped, too — a good base where you can return for showers and laundry—and they offer a couple large cabins for rent.

The refuge has two main canoe routes, both reached from Swanson River and Swan Lake roads, north of the Sterling Highway from the town of Sterling. Many dozens of remote campsites are along the shores — just lakeside areas of cleared ground with fire rings — and most of the paths between lakes are well marked and maintained with wooden planking over wet areas.

- ✔ The **Swan Lake Canoe Route** is a 60-mile network of 30 lakes connected sometimes by channels but more often by *portages* (paths on which you carry your boat and gear from one point of water to another). It meets Swan Lake Road twice, allowing a loop of several days, although most people explore a few lakes before returning to the starting point. You can penetrate deep into the wilderness, visiting remote lakes that you'll have all to yourself. Canoeing through to the Moose River and riding its current 17 miles over a long day back to the Sterling Highway also is possible. However, getting anywhere requires frequent portages of a quarter-mile or so, and more ambitious routes have mile-long portages.

- ✔ You can skip the portaging by floating two days down the **Swanson River** to its mouth, at the Captain Cook State Recreation Area north of Kenai. Join the river at a landing at Mile 17.5, Swanson River Road. The water is slow and easy all the way.

More cool things to do in Kenai and Soldotna

Here are some of the things to do in Kenai and Soldotna that don't require a fishing rod or canoe paddle:

- ✔ **See the museum at the Kenai Visitors & Cultural Center.** Located at 11471 Kenai Spur Hwy. (☎ **907-283-1991;** www.visitkenai. com), the permanent exhibits cover the area's history and a little natural history. A highlight is the "King of Snags" — an immense conglomeration of lost fishing lures and sticks from the bottom of the river. In the summer, good temporary art exhibitions are mounted, too. Summer admission to the museum is $5, free for students through high school; off season, admission is free. The center is open in the summer Monday through Friday 9 a.m. to 7 p.m., Saturday and Sunday 10 a.m. to 6 p.m.; off-season, Monday through Friday 9 a.m. to 5 p.m., Saturday 11 a.m. to 4 p.m.

- ✔ **Walk Kenai's historic area.** Start at the visitor and cultural center mentioned in the preceding paragraph and get a copy of the *Old*

Town Kenai Walking Map; follow the numbered markers. Not many of the simple, weathered buildings remain from Kenai's life before it became an oil boomtown, but those that do are interesting and lie only a few blocks down Main Street from the center, along the Cook Inlet bluff. These include the 1895 **Holy Assumption Russian Orthodox Church,** a quaint, onion-domed church, brightly kept but with old icons. A donation is requested.

✔ **Watch fishing boats and whales in the river mouth.** The best vantage point is from Erik Hansen Scout Park, at Cook and Mission avenues, near the church mentioned in the preceding paragraph. When the salmon are running, you can occasionally see white beluga whales chasing them from here, sometimes in great numbers, competing with the transiting fishing boats and personal-use dip-net fishermen.

✔ **Walk the sandy beach.** From the Kenai Spur Highway, turn left on South Spruce Street, where you'll find a simple beach park and a place to begin a walk. A $10 fee applies while the dip-net fishery is in progress in July, when the parking is in demand. Alaska residents (only residents are permitted) line up with long-handled nets to grab salmon from the river. On quieter days, with calm water, the beach sand, the mudflats, and the inlet's gray, glacial water seem to meld together into one vast shimmering plain. Walking south, the beach wraps around and becomes the shore of the Kenai River. It's too cold for swimming.

✔ **Swim in a great public pool.** The magnificent **North Peninsula Recreation Area Nikiski Pool** (☎ **907-776-8472**), 10 miles north of Kenai on the Kenai Spur Road, occupies a large gold dome and has a 136-ft. water slide, mushroom fountains of water, and a raised hot tub from which parents can watch their children play in the pool below. The water slide is open in the summer Tuesday through Sunday 1 to 5 p.m. and 6 to 9 p.m. (swimming without the slide opens those days at 7 a.m.); the winter hours are complicated, so call for details. Pool admission is $4, or $7 to use the slide and pool. Weekends can be crowded.

Fast Facts: Kenai and Soldotna

ATMs

Banks are on the Kenai Spur Highway in the middle of town; in Soldotna, they're on the Sterling Highway commercial strip. In addition, ATMs are in grocery stores all across the area.

Emergencies

Dial ☎ **911.**

Hospital

Central Peninsula General is in Soldotna at 250 Hospital Place (☎ 907-262-4404); from the Sterling Highway, take Binkley Street to Marydale Avenue.

Information

The Kenai Convention & Visitors Bureau is at 11471 Kenai Spur Hwy. (☎ 907-283-1991;

www.visitkenai.com). It's open summer Monday through Friday 9 a.m. to 7 p.m. and Saturday to Sunday 10 a.m. to 6 p.m., winter Monday through Friday 9 a.m. to 5 p.m. and Saturday to Sunday 11 a.m. to 4 p.m. The Soldotna Visitor Information Center, 44790 Sterling Hwy. (☎ 907-262-9814 or 907-262-1337; www.visitsoldotna.com), is located on the south side of town; drive through the commercial strip and turn right after the Kenai River Bridge. It's open in summer daily 9 a.m. to 7 p.m.; in winter, Monday through Friday 9 a.m. to 5 p.m.

Internet Access

Connect to the Web for free at the Kenai Public Library, 163 Main St. Loop

(☎ 907-283-4378), or at the Soldotna Public Library, 235 Binkley St. (☎ 907-262-4227).

Police

For non-emergencies in Kenai, call the Kenai Police Department (☎ 907-283-7879); in Soldotna, call the Soldotna Police Department (☎ 907-262-4455); outside city limits, call the Alaska State Troopers (☎ 907-262-4453).

Taxes

In Kenai and Soldotna, there is a 6 percent sales tax. Sales tax is 2 percent outside city limits.

Driving to the Sea in Homer

Homer is at the end of the road. The nation's paved highway system comes to an abrupt conclusion at the tip of the Homer Spit, a narrow strip of land almost 5 miles out in the middle of Kachemak Bay. That geography has brought together a wonderfully odd collection of artists and retirees, fundamentalist preachers and New Age healers, wealthy North Slope oil workers and land-poor settlers with no visible means of support. They all live here simply because they choose to. The choice is understandable. Homer lies on the north side of Kachemak Bay, a branch of lower Cook Inlet of extraordinary biological productivity. The halibut fishing is especially good. The town has a breathtaking setting on the spit and on a wildflower-covered bench high above the bay. Outdoor opportunities here are among Alaska's best, and the arts community has developed into an attraction of its own.

You'll be disappointed, however, if you expect a charming little fishing town. Poor community planning has created a town that doesn't live up to its setting. Homer Spit in summer is a traffic-choked jumble of cheap tourist development and RVs. Ignore that. It's where the spit goes that counts. At its tip, out in the middle of the bay, you can feel like you're at sea. The town depends on that unique finger stretching out into the ocean — an exceptional launching point to one of the world's great marine recreation areas.

Getting there
Most visitors drive, but you can save time by flying from Anchorage.

By car
The scenic 235-mile drive from Anchorage to Homer takes roughly 4½ hours by car, if you don't stop at any of the many interesting or beautiful

places along the way. Follow the Seward Highway south from Anchorage (the first hour of the drive is detailed in Chapter 15), and then join the Sterling Highway at the Tern Lake junction (about 90 miles from Anchorage). You'll pass Soldotna and Kenai on your way to Homer. Save time for the view from Baycrest Hill as you enter town. Car rental in Anchorage is covered in Chapters 7 and 13.

By air

Era Alaska (☎ 800-866-8394; www.flyera.com) serves Homer from Anchorage several times a day. Small air-taxi operators use Homer as a hub for outlying villages and the outdoors.

By ferry

The **Alaska Marine Highway System** (☎ 800-642-0066; www.ferry alaska.com) connects Homer to Seldovia, Kodiak, and points west along the Alaska Peninsula and Aleutian Archipelago. The run to Kodiak takes ten hours and costs $74 for an adult walk-on passenger (kids 6–11 are half off).

Getting around Homer

Homer is spread out and has no public transportation, so the best way to get around is by car. If you fly or arrive by ferry, you can rent a car at the airport from **Hertz** (☎ 800-654-3131 or 907-235-0734; www.hertz. com) or three local firms.

For a taxi, one company is **Kostas Taxi Service** (☎ 907-399-8008).

Where to stay

Homer has many good B&Bs. The Web site of the Homer Chamber of Commerce (www.homeralaska.org) has links to scores of them.

Driftwood Inn
$–$$$$$ Downtown Homer

This is a rare find, a hotel appropriate for either a budget-minded back-packer or a well-off family seeking lovely beachfront lodgings. The original part of the inn is a historic building a block from Bishop's Beach and across from the Bunnell Gallery, which resembles a lodge or B&B with its large fireplace of beach rock, the hot coffee pot and inexpensive self-serve breakfast in the lobby, and a friendly attitude. Next door, the upscale rooms are in newer buildings, with spectacular views and fresh, charming seaside décor. A cottage that sleeps eight has its own deck and lawn over the beach. The original building has rooms like Pullman compartments in size and configuration — besides being inexpensive, they're cute and clean and have some real style. Nine of those units share two bathrooms. In the old building the upstairs walls are thin, so there's a no-noise policy during evening hours. The lodge also has an appealing 22-site RV park and a fenced playground, a fish-cleaning station and freezing facility, and year-round fishing charters.

See map p. 253. 135 W. Bunnell Ave., Homer. ☎ **800-478-8019** *or 907-235-8019.* www.thedriftwoodinn.com. *Rack rates: High season $80–$245 double, off season $49–$129 double; extra person $10. MC, V.*

Land's End Resort
$$$–$$$$$ **Homer Spit**

Traditionally *the* place to stay in Homer, Land's End would be popular no matter what it was like inside because of its location at the tip of Homer Spit, the best spot in Homer and possibly the best spot for a hotel in all of Alaska. It's composed of a line of weathered buildings that fittingly straggle along the beach crest like driftwood logs. The hotel is near the boat harbor, and some people fish right from the beach in front. Inside, the local owners keep high standards and make constant improvements. Rooms range from cute ship-like compartments with fold-down Murphy beds to big, two-story suites. The front desk also rents a series of privately owned town-house condos next door; for groups or couples on extended visits, these are the best accommodations in the region, with stylish furniture, lots of space and light, and a beachfront location second to none. The condos rent for $325 to $450 a night, with a two-night minimum stay.

The **Chart Room** restaurant makes good use of its wonderful location, looking out over the beach and bay from big windows. There's a casual, relaxing atmosphere in the long, wood-trimmed dining room. The deck outside has glass windshields, making it a warm, satisfying place to sit over coffee on a sunny day. You can watch otters, eagles, and fishing boats while you eat. The selection of main courses ($16–$38) is fairly typical of a seaside fine-dining restaurant, and the food is good if not memorable. The appetizer menu, however, is much more extensive and interesting, and the appetizer portions are easily large enough to make a full meal.

See map p. 253. 4786 Homer Spit Rd., Homer. ☎ **800-478-0400** *or 907-235-0400. Fax: 907-235-0420.* www.lands-end-resort.com. *Rack rates: High season $125–$245 double, off season $85–$145 double; extra person $10. AE, DC, DISC, MC, V.*

The Ocean Shores
$–$$$$ **Downtown Homer**

Buildings on a grassy compound have a commanding view of Kachemak Bay, with a path leading down to Bishop's Beach, yet the location is right off the Sterling Highway as you enter town, within walking distance of downtown Homer. Rooms are fresh and bright, most with private balconies, refrigerators, and microwaves; four have full kitchens. The less expensive rooms lack the views and are older, but are still modern and have cute touches. The place is decorated with photographs and art collected over a family's five generations in Alaska.

Homer

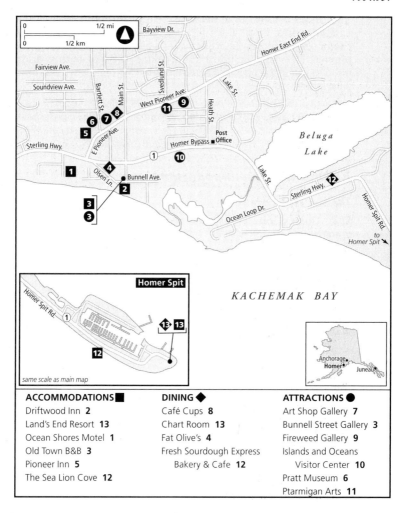

ACCOMMODATIONS ■
Driftwood Inn **2**
Land's End Resort **13**
Ocean Shores Motel **1**
Old Town B&B **3**
Pioneer Inn **5**
The Sea Lion Cove **12**

DINING ◆
Café Cups **8**
Chart Room **13**
Fat Olive's **4**
Fresh Sourdough Express
  Bakery & Cafe **12**

ATTRACTIONS ●
Art Shop Gallery **7**
Bunnell Street Gallery **3**
Fireweed Gallery **9**
Islands and Oceans
  Visitor Center **10**
Pratt Museum **6**
Ptarmigan Arts **11**

See map p. 253. 451 Sterling Hwy. no. 1, Homer. ☎ **800-770-7775** or *907-235-7775. Fax: 907-235-8639. www.oceanshoresalaska.com. Rack rates: High season $129– $204 double, off season $79–$109 double; extra person $5. AE, DISC, MC, V.*

Old Town Bed & Breakfast
$–$$ **Downtown Homer**

These rooms combine the artiness of the excellent Bunnell Street Gallery downstairs and the funky, historic feel of the old trading post/hardware store that the building used to house. The wood floors undulate with age and settling, their imperfections picked out by light from tall, double-hung windows that look out at Bishop's Beach. The antiques, handmade quilts, and wonderful original art fit in as if they've always been there, yet the rooms are comfortable, fresh, and clean. The B&B has no TVs or in-room phones. The rates include a hot breakfast at 8 a.m. in the parlor and afternoon tea. This place is not a good choice for people who have any trouble with stairs.

See map p. 253. 106-D W. Bunnell St., Homer. ☎ *907-299-1492.. www.oldtownbed andbreakfast.com. Rack rates: High season $95 double with shared bath, $115 double with private bath; off season $56 double with shared bath, $75 double with private bath; extra person $15. Rates include breakfast. MC, V.*

Runner-up accommodations

The Sea Lion Cove

$$$ **Homer Spit** Above the Sea Lion Gallery on Homer Spit are two comfortable rooms with kitchens and a deck right over the beach. *See map p. 253. 4241 Homer Spit Rd., Homer.* ☎ *907-235-3400 in summer, 907-235-8767 in winter. www.sealiongallery.com/cove.*

Pioneer Inn

$–$$ **Downtown** Apartment-style lodgings and simple rooms right in the middle of town are offered by a friendly family at a bargain rate. *See map p. 253. 244 W. Pioneer Ave., Homer.* ☎ *800-782-9655 or 907-235-5670. www. pioneerinnhomerak.com.*

Calling a water taxi

To enjoy the best of the Homer area, get on and across Kachemak Bay. Using a system of water taxis that run from the small boat harbor on Homer Spit to beaches and docks that are half an hour and a world away is easy. Go for hiking, mountain-biking, or self-guided sea-kayaking. Many operators are available, and rates vary little, about $75 to get to Kachemak Bay State Park, plus a $4 park fee, for example. Here are two of the best:

✔ **Mako's Water Taxi** (☎ 907-235-9055; www.makoswatertaxi.com) is owned by Mako Haggerty, who is experienced and has a good reputation. Besides carrying passengers, Mako's rents sea kayaks and drops them off for experienced paddlers. Using Mako's advice, kayakers can plan a one-way paddle, with the water taxi providing a lift at each end.

✔ Karl Stolzfus's **Bay Excursions Water Taxi & Tours** (☎ 907-235-7525; www. bayexcursions.com) offers simple transportation but also specializes in hosting serious birders. He rents sea kayaks, too.

Where to dine

Besides being a center of art in Alaska, Homer has some of the state's best restaurants. In addition to those I list here, try the **Chart Room,** at Land's End Resort, described earlier under "Where to stay."

Café Cups
$$$ **Downtown   SEAFOOD**

The facade of the yellow house on Pioneer Avenue is unmistakable with its elaborate bas-relief sculpture. The small dining room is a work of art, too, a masterpiece of wood, light, and space. Jennifer Olsen seats guests, and her husband, David, is the chef. As the owners, they've combined a love for good food with practicality in a small town. The menu comes in two parts. The regular daily menu is mostly mainstream — aimed at local diners looking for something familiar — but they also have an extensive daily menu of orally described specials, usually including interesting choices based on local seafood. Don't make a choice before considering these, which are the heart of the experience. David has a terrific sense of the texture of food — the lamb chops are a sensual delight, crisply seared on the outside, tender and juicy inside, on rich mashed potatoes. Portions are large. They serve beer and wine.

See map p. 253. 162 W. Pioneer Ave., Homer. ☎ *907-235-8330. Reservations recommended. Main courses: $18–$30. MC, V. Open: Tues–Sat 4:30–10 p.m.*

Fat Olives
$$$ **Downtown   MEDITERRANEAN**

Built with great style in a former school-bus garage on the Sterling Highway near the visitor center, the restaurant is a wonder of warm Mediterranean colors, shiny metal, and primitive art — not the sort of place you expect to find in a small town in Alaska. The cuisine brings further surprises: bold flavors and textures, a little Tuscany, and plenty of Homer, too, including local seafood. The centerpiece is a wood-fired Italian brick oven that produces pizza, grilled sandwiches, steaks, and other delights. They serve local beers on tap and 30 wines by the glass. Although the restaurant is not oriented to children, my kids love it because of the big pieces of pizza available by the slice (which means adults can eat inexpensively, too). Note that at peak hours it can take a long time to get a table and they don't take reservations.

See map p. 253. 276 Olson Lane, Homer. ☎ *907-235-8488. Main courses: $7–$12 lunch, $16–$26 dinner. MC, V. Open: Daily 11 a.m.–10 p.m.*

Fresh Sourdough Express Bakery and Café
$$–$$$ **Near Homer Spit**   CAFE

Ebullient Donna and Kevin Maltz's organic eatery is quintessential Homer, starting with its motto: "Food for people and the planet." But there's no New Age dogma here. The Sourdough Express is fun and tasty, even as it grinds its own grain and recycles everything in sight. An inexpensive lunch menu includes many vegetarian choices as well as hearty sandwiches. The evening menu includes many specials, elaborate dishes (including huge portions of local seafood with rich sauces), and, perhaps more remarkably, simple, solid choices, too, for those who don't want to spend a lot. All-you-can-eat crab is served from 3 to 8 p.m. Families will enjoy the relaxed atmosphere, the big sandbox, and an old van out front where kids can play while you wait for your meal. Stop by on the way to the harbor for a brown-bag lunch that you'll need for a charter fishing trip. Don't miss dessert from the made-from-scratch bakery.

See map p. 253. 1316 Ocean Dr., Homer. ☎ **907-235-7571.** www.freshsourdough express.com. *Main courses: $6–$12 breakfast, $6.50–$15 lunch, $10–$25 dinner. MC, V. Open: High season daily 8 a.m.–8:30 p.m., low season daily 8 a.m.–3 p.m.*

The Homestead Restaurant
$$$$ **East of Homer**   SEAFOOD

The ambience is that of an old-fashioned Alaska roadhouse, in a large log building decorated with contemporary art and lots of summer light. After a day outdoors, it's a warm, exuberant place for dinner, but with polished edges: white table linens and professional service. The food is terrific and wonderfully executed. The many seafood choices are done many different ways — in some cases simply grilled to a turn, and in others with complex sauces and various international influences. The portions are generous. If you want a big piece of rare prime rib, go no further. We love this restaurant and have chosen it for our most important occasions. The wine list is well selected and arranged — not intimidating; plenty of bottles are in the $21 to $34 range. They also have a full bar with local beers on tap.

Mile 8.2, East End Road, Homer. ☎ **907-235-8723.** www.homesteadrestaurant. net. *Reservations recommended. Main courses: $21–$39. AE, MC, V. Open: June–Aug daily 5–10 p.m., Mar–May and Sept–Dec Wed–Sat 5–9 p.m. Closed Jan–Feb.*

Saltry
$$$$ **Halibut Cove**   SEAFOOD

What makes this restaurant unforgettable is the location and the trip to get there. It's about 5 miles across the water from the boat harbor on Homer Spit; going there is a wonderful day's outing to a remote art colony. A classic wooden boat, the *Danny J*, leaves Homer daily in the summer at noon for lunch and at 5 p.m. for dinner. (Seating on the *Danny J* is mostly outdoors; they provide rain gear, but you still may not want to go in bad weather.)

Each trip allows time to wander the charming boardwalks and galleries of Halibut Cove, a tiny seaside village without roads where boats take the place of cars. The restaurant itself sits on pilings above the edge of the smooth, deep green of the cove's main watery avenue. You can sit back in the deck gazebo; sip microbrews; and eat fresh-baked bread, mussels, sushi, and locally grown salads, followed by fresh fish grilled over charcoal. Those who don't eat seafood don't have wide choices, but there are several vegetarian and non-seafood items. In addition to the price of the meal, budget for the boat ride: The noon trip is $50 adults, $45 seniors, $30 kids; the dinner trip is $30 for everyone. Make meal and boat reservations at the same phone number; you typically need to book a few days ahead.

On the main channel, Halibut Cove, Homer. ☎ **907-296-2223.** www.halibut-cove-alaska.com/saltry.htm. *Reservations required. Main courses: $10–$18 lunch, $18–$20 dinner. MC, V. Open: Lunch and dinner seatings coordinate with daily Danny J schedule. Closed Labor Day to Memorial Day.*

Finding Homer's top attractions

Homer's outdoor attractions overwhelm anything you can do indoors, but there are a couple don't-miss spots that put nature in context and are worth a stop even on a sunny day. The town also is one of the best places in Alaska to shop for art. I provide guidance on spending a rainy day in the galleries in the "More cool things to do in Homer" section, later in this chapter.

Islands & Ocean Visitor Center
Downtown Homer

The term *visitor center* doesn't do justice to this magnificent building and the fascinating exhibits inside. Everyone coming to Homer should stop in to see the building, an architectural gem that perfectly reflects the rocky shores that the refuge takes in, and to experience exhibits, some added in 2010, that use technology and a deft sense of theater to re-create remote places in thought and feel. It is also the best place to stop for information if you plan to go outdoors anywhere in the area, or to learn about the Alaska Maritime National Wildlife Refuge and the Kachemak Bay Research Reserve, the co-sponsoring organizations. An easy nature trail descends to the salt marsh below the center.

See map p. 253. 95 Sterling Hwy. (on the right entering town), Homer. ☎ **907-235-6961.** www.islandsandoceans.org. *Admission: Free. Open: Summer daily 9 a.m.–6 p.m.; winter hours vary.*

Pratt Museum
Downtown Homer

The Homer Society of Natural History's award-winning museum is as good as any you'll find in a town of this size. The Pratt displays art and explains local history, too, but it's strongest in natural history. It helped pioneer technology that allows viewing of wildlife through live remote-control cameras without disturbing the animals. Visitors at the museum can watch puffins and other birds on Gull Island, and operate the camera's controls. Another remote camera focuses on the brown bears of Katmai National Park. There is a saltwater aquarium housing local marine life, and if you're curious about all the fishing boats down in the harbor, you can find out about the different types of gear as well as the fish they catch. In the small botanical garden outside, you can learn to identify all the local wildflowers, and a forest trail teaches about the area's ecology. There's much more to see, too, including a good gift shop.

See map p. 253. 3779 Bartlett St., at Pioneer Avenue, Homer. ☎ **907-235-8635.** *www. prattmuseum.org. Admission: $8 adults, $6 seniors, $4 kids 6–18, $25 families. Open: High season daily 10 a.m.–6 p.m., off season Tues–Sun noon to 5 p.m. Closed Jan.*

Getting outdoors in Homer

Homer is all about summer outdoor activities; it's almost a crime not to get out on that spectacular bay or up into those lovely hills and mountains. Here are some choices.

Driving or mountain-biking

Several gravel roads around Homer make for exquisite drives or bike rides. Mountain-bikers can use any of the hiking trails, too (see "Hiking," later in this section). Drive out **East End Road,** through lovely seaside pastures, a forest, and the village of Fritz Creek, and then follow the bluff line through meadows toward the head of the bay. The road eventually gets rough and steep, a good time to deploy a mountain bike. **Skyline Drive** has extraordinary views of high canyons and Kachemak Bay; drive up East Hill Road just east of the downtown area.

After a boat ride across Kachemak Bay, an incredible wealth of mountain-biking routes presents itself. This is a world accessible only by water. It has few cars but many long, remote dirt roads. Rent a bike in town and take it on a water taxi to the **Jakolof Bay Dock.** Supreme mountain-biking routes lead along the shore and right across the peninsula through forests and meadows for berry picking. A well-maintained 10-mile road west leads along the shore to the charming village of Seldovia. For a good boat operator, see the "Calling a water taxi" sidebar, earlier in this chapter.

Homer Saw and Cycle, 1532 Ocean Dr. (☎ **907-235-8406**) rents mountain bikes, street bikes, kids' bikes, and trailers. Bike rentals start at $25 per day. The shop keeps track of trail conditions and can offer good advice for your ride. It's open Monday through Friday 9 a.m. to 5:30 p.m., Saturday 11 a.m. to 5 p.m. Reserving bikes a day or two ahead of time is wise, especially when an outing depends on getting one.

Fishing

Homer is known for **halibut,** those huge, flat-bottom fish, and the harbor is full of charter boats that can take you out fishing for the day for about $275 per person in the high season. Every day, a few people catch fish that are larger than they are, and halibut weighing more than 50 pounds are common. You can even bet you'll catch an enormous fish. The summer-long Jackpot Halibut Derby has a prize that has topped $50,000 for the biggest fish of the summer, and smaller monthly prizes and tagged fish prizes. The grand-prize winner is generally more than 300 pounds. A ticket is $10 per day, and, of course, you have to buy it before you fish. Stop at a booth on the spit to get yours (☎ **907-235-7740;** www.homer halibutderby.com).

Getting out to where big halibut are plentiful requires an early start and a long ride to unprotected waters. People prone to seasickness shouldn't go, because the boat wallows on the waves while you're fishing. (See the tips in Chapter 9 on avoiding or curing seasickness.) One large, reliable operator is **Silver Fox Charters (☎ 800-478-8792** or 907-235-8792; www.silverfoxcharters.com). Half-day charters are less likely to get way out to the biggest fish, but they cost a lot less. **Rainbow Tours (☎ 907-235-7272)** operates a big boat for the shorter outings, charging $105 adults, $95 seniors, $85 kids. This choice makes good sense if you aren't a fishing fanatic or you're taking kids along — a full day of halibut fishing is exhausting and can be tedious. Other charter boats can be booked through Inlet Charters Across Alaska Adventures, listed in the "Booking your outing" sidebar, later in this chapter.

Hiking

The 7-mile **Homestead Trail** is an old wagon road used by Homer's early settlers. The largely informal trail is lovely and peaceful, tunneling through alders, crossing fields of wildflowers, and passing historic cabins with great views. From a hilltop meadow, you can see all the way to the inlet and the volcanoes beyond. The eastern trail head is at the reservoir on Skyline Drive — drive up West Hill Road from the Sterling Highway, turn right, and follow Skyline to the fourth left. The western trailhead is on Rogers Loop, which branches from the Sterling Highway just before it crests the last big hill before entering Homer. (That's also the place to join Homer's outstanding cross-country ski trails.) A map and guide produced by the Kachemak Heritage Land Trust is available at the visitor center.

If you're a bit more adventurous, one of Alaska's great outdoor opportunities awaits you in Homer: **a hike in Kachemak Bay State Park.** The park encompasses much of the land across the water that makes all those views from Homer so spectacular. For around $75, you can get a water taxi to take you (and the skipper can give you all the advice you need). Have the boat drop you off in the park after breakfast, walk the beach, hike in the woods, climb the mountains, and then meet your boat in time to be back in Homer for dinner. (See the "Calling a water taxi" sidebar, earlier in this chapter, for names of operators.)

The park has about 80 miles of trails, mostly linking near Halibut Cove. The most popular route, with water taxis landing through the day, is the easy Saddle Trail, which leads less than 2 miles from a seaside staircase to the lake in front of Grewingk Glacier. Many other choices allow hikers of varying ability levels to get as far from other people as they choose, climbing high peaks, finding secluded beaches, or even taking multi-day treks. A free trail guide is available at the town visitor center, the Islands & Ocean Visitor Center, and the ranger station in Halibut Cove Lagoon, and detailed maps are for sale in Homer. Bring mosquito repellent. For park information before you go, contact the **Kachemak Bay State Park District Office,** 4 miles from town, at mile 168.5, Sterling Highway (☎ **907-235-7024;** www.alaskastateparks.org). The office is usually open Monday through Friday 9 a.m. to 5 p.m.

Natural history tours

The nonprofit **Center for Alaskan Coastal Studies** (☎ **907-235-6667;** www.akcoastalstudies.org) is dedicated to educating the public about Homer's natural environment. Near town, its **Wynn Nature Center** offers a chance to discover the ecology of the area on easy guided or unguided walks across 140 acres of spruce forest and wildflower meadow off Skyline Drive, with an 800-ft. boardwalk accessible to people with disabilities. This is a lovely area, and the center has done a fine job of adding an educational component without diminishing it. It's open from mid-June through Labor Day daily 10 a.m. to 6 p.m., with guided walks twice a day. Fees are $7 adults, $6 seniors, $5 kids 17 and under. Call and ask about the interesting weekly programs.

For a more ambitious and truly memorable outing, take the center's daily trip across Kachemak Bay to its facility in the **Peterson Bay** area. At low tide, they lead guests on a fascinating guided tide-pool walk. The center also has access to lovely woodlands where nature walks cover forest ecology and geology and visit an archaeological site. Saltwater tanks at the lodge contain creatures from the intertidal zone and micro-scopes to inspect your finds. It's a relaxed and truly Alaskan outing. You can add on guided sea-kayaking or a reasonably priced overnight stay in a yurt so you're there, ready for an early-morning low tide. Reserve by calling the center at ☎ **907-235-6667.** The all-day tour is $105 adults, $73 kids 11 and under; it operates from Memorial Day through Labor Day daily. Pack your own lunch and bring footwear suitable for hiking and potentially wet beach walks and warm clothing for the boat ride.

Sea-kayaking

The protected waters, tiny islands, and remote settlements across Kachemak Bay are fascinating places to paddle. You'll probably see sea otters and puffins and other seabirds. Floating above the shore gives a great view of life in the intertidal zone — tide-pool creatures above or below the waterline. You have to take a boat ride first to go sea-kayaking in Homer, so it costs more than in some other places, but it's worth it to get away from town. **True North Kayak Adventures** (☎ 907-235-0708; www.truenorthkayak.com) offers an eight-hour beginner day trip for $150, including lunch and passage across the bay. True North also offers more challenging overnight and multi-day trips to remote waters in the area and a $245 package that includes the day tour, a night in the attractive Hesketh Island Cabins, and a second day of hiking. Various other companies offer Kachemak Bay kayak trips, too. See the nearby "Booking your outing" sidebar.

More cool things to do in Homer

Homer is known for its artists and galleries. Take an afternoon to check out some of these options:

- ✔ **Bunnell Street Arts Center,** 106 W. Bunnell Ave. (☎ 907-235-2662; www.bunnellstreetgallery.org), is a nonprofit gallery, in an old hardware store near Bishop's Beach at the lower end of Main Street. One of my favorite galleries in Alaska, Bunnell was made by and for artists and is a noncommercial, often surprising place. It's open in summer daily 10 a.m. to 6 p.m.; in winter Monday through Friday 10 a.m. to 5 p.m., Saturday noon to 4 p.m.

- ✔ **Norman Lowell Studio & Gallery** is on Sterling Highway at mile 160.9, near Anchor Point, about 12 miles from Homer (☎ 907-235-7344). Lowell built his own huge gallery on his homestead to show his life's work. The immense oils of Alaska landscapes, which are not for sale, hang in a building that counts as one of Alaska's largest art museums. Lowell or his wife, Libby, often serve as host to guests walking through and sell smaller paintings and prints from their shop. This sincere, dramatic, and expert work can be quite moving. Hours are Monday through Saturday 9 a.m. to 5 p.m., Sunday 1 to 5 p.m. They're closed mid-September through May 1.

- ✔ For some more **downtown gallery-hopping,** a widely distributed brochure lists most of the galleries in town, with a map. (You can find it online at http://fireweedgallery.com.) Many are close together on Pioneer Avenue. Among my favorites are **Ptarmigan Arts,** 471 E. Pioneer Ave. (☎ 907-235-5345; www.ptarmiganarts.com), an artists' co-op showing a cross-section of what the area offers; the **Fireweed Gallery,** 475 E. Pioneer Ave. (☎ 907-235-3411; http://fireweedgallery.com), right next door in an elegant, airy space; and the large, friendly **Art Shop Gallery,** 202 W. Pioneer Ave. (☎ 907-235-7076; www.artshopgallery.com).

Booking your outing

Setting up a day on or across the water in Homer is easy because one central booking agency represents many businesses. Call **Inlet Charters Across Alaska Adventures** (☎ 800-770-6126; www.halibutcharters.com) for advice and arrangements for water taxis and other outdoors booking arrangements.

Nightlife

The **Pier One Theatre** (☎ 907-235-7333; www.pieronetheatre.org) is a strong community theater group, housed in a square, red building on the spit, just short of the small-boat harbor on the left. It presents serious drama, musicals, comedy, dance, classical music, and youth theater events. There's generally something playing Thursday through Sunday nights in the summer. Check the *Homer News* or the Web site for current listings. They strongly recommend making reservations by phone; you can change or cancel your reservations if necessary. Tickets are sometimes also available at the door.

The landmark **Salty Dawg Saloon** is a small log cabin on the spit with a lighthouse on top — you can't miss it. This is the place to swap fish stories after a day on the water. Wherever you go to hoist a beer, order a draft from the **Homer Brewing Company** — Red Knot Ale is my favorite.

Fast Facts: Homer

ATMs

Wells Fargo, with an ATM, is on the Sterling Highway near Heath Street.

Emergencies

Dial ☎ 911.

Hospital

South Peninsula Hospital is at the top of Bartlett Street, off Pioneer Avenue (☎ 907-235-8101).

Information

The Homer Chamber of Commerce Visitor Information Center, 201 Sterling Hwy. (☎ 907-235-7740; www.homeralaska. org), is on the right as you enter town. It's open in the summer Monday through Friday 9 a.m. to 7 p.m., Saturday and Sunday 10 a.m. to 6 p.m.; winter hours are Monday through Friday 9 a.m. to 5 p.m.

Internet Access

Tech Connect Computer Sales and Services, 432 E. Pioneer Avenue, Suite C (☎ 907-235-5248), offers broadband access for $5 per hour on its computers or Wi-Fi on yours.

Police

For non-emergencies within the city limits, call the Homer Police Department (☎ 907-235-3150); outside the city, phone the Alaska State Troopers (☎ 907-235-8239).

Post Office

The post office is on the Sterling Highway at Heath Street.

Taxes

Sales tax in Homer is 7.5 percent. Outside the city, you pay 3 percent.

Chapter 17

Fairbanks

. . . .

In This Chapter

▶ Getting to Fairbanks
▶ Finding your way around town
▶ Dining and sleeping in Fairbanks
▶ Getting outdoors in and around Fairbanks
▶ Retreating to Chena Hot Springs

. . . .

*I*f you're expecting Fairbanks, Alaska's second-largest city and the site
of the University of Alaska's main campus, to be somewhat cosmopol-
itan, not only are you wrong, but you could hurt people's feelings.
Fairbanks doesn't pride itself on being at the center of things; it likes
being out on the edge. The city is the last outpost before the great,
unpeopled expanse of Alaska, a town with a self-image of being tougher
and more extreme than anyplace else. It's got a full range of eccentrics,
from granola-crunching university types who climb glaciers to bear-
eating gold prospectors who would like to see Alaska become its own
nation. And not many people are in the middle — most live here for a
reason, not because it's just where they happened to end up. Nothing
stops them, not even winter days that can drop to –40°F (–40°C). They
claim to like it.

Individualism and toughness are Alaskans' favorite qualities about themselves (whether in truth or in myth), and Fairbanks is the quintessential
Alaska town. But truth be told, individualism and toughness can have
their downside. Fairbanks is not pretty. The downtown area has been
sucked dry by its outskirts, which look like any other suburban commercial area in the United States: lots of malls and parking lots. Sightseeing
centers on sites beyond the urban core: the **university,** which has a
great museum and other sights, a big community park, and several commercial tourist attractions. Indeed, some visitors tell me Fairbanks was a
disappointment.

But I love going to Fairbanks, especially if I've got my kids along. The
Chena River runs through town and you can float right up to a restaurant for dinner. With its many accessible river floats, Fairbanks is
Alaska's canoeing capital. **Pioneer Park** (formerly called Alaskaland) has
charmed and amused my family for hours. And the outlying residential
areas and the roads out of town are lovely, with big rounded hills

clothed in birch and spruce trees. A little farther afield, **Chena Hot Springs Road** leads to wonderful day hikes and swimming at the springs.

If you can get into the lusty spirit of the place, Fairbanks can be a lot of fun.

Getting There

I think renting a car or RV in Anchorage and making Fairbanks the far point in a driving loop that includes the Richardson Highway and Denali National Park makes the most sense. The next chapter explains the highway layout and suggests some loop itineraries. But you can also save time and many miles of driving by flying, or, if time is not a concern, by taking the train to Fairbanks and renting a car there. The train is slow, taking 12 hours from Anchorage to Fairbanks. Driving takes under seven hours and flying takes about one hour.

By car

Roads from the rest of the world enter Fairbanks from two directions. The Richardson Highway connects the city east 100 miles to Delta Junction, the end point of the Alaska Highway, and then south to Glennallen and Valdez. The Parks Highway links Fairbanks to Denali National Park, 120 miles away, and then on to Anchorage, 360 miles south. These are all paved, two-lane highways, and you can usually do 65 mph in the summer.

By air

Alaska Airlines (☎ 800-252-7522; www.alaskaair.com) connects Fairbanks to Anchorage. At this writing, a bargain fare is just under $260 round-trip. The airport is a hub for various small carriers to Alaska's Interior and Arctic communities. A cab downtown from the airport is $18 to $20 with **Yellow Cab** (☎ 907-455-5555). **Airlink Shuttle and Tours** (☎ 907-452-3337) charges $3.50, with a three-person minimum and $1 fee per bag, for a ride from the airport to anywhere in town.

By train

The **Alaska Railroad** (☎ 800-544-0552; www.alaskarailroad.com) links Fairbanks with Denali National Park and Anchorage. Tour commentary is provided on the nicely appointed full-service trains. The high season, one-way fare is $64 from Denali and $210 from Anchorage (more than twice the cost of flying between the cities). First-class Gold Star service costs $149 and $320 one-way, respectively.

Orienting Yourself in Fairbanks

The **downtown** area and **College,** which once was a separate town and is the site of the University of Alaska campus, are the two original sections of Fairbanks. The downtown area sits in a bend in the Chena River, which bisects Fairbanks. You won't find an awful lot there, but you can spend a couple hours walking around (see the "More cool things to see and do" section and the "Downtown Fairbanks" map, later in this chapter). College is to the west. The airport and the Parks Highway (the road to Anchorage) are both near College. The two areas are linked by Airport Way, which is a major commercial strip and a kind of spine through the city, and by the Johansen Expressway (part of an outsize road network that makes getting around very speedy). From the east side of downtown, the Steese Highway leads north to several important places, including Chena Hot Springs Road and the suburban area of Fox.

Getting around by car

Fairbanks is designed for cars, and they're the practical way to get around. Without one, you'll be restricted to downtown the whole time and leave with a low opinion of the place. The city is too spread out to use taxis much. If you fly or take the train to Fairbanks, you can find many car-rental agencies. At the airport, you can rent from Alamo, Avis, Budget, Dollar, Hertz, National, and Payless; contact information is in the Quick Concierge. See Chapter 7 for agencies that will rent a vehicle you can use on gravel roads such as the Dalton Highway — most car-rental firms don't allow it.

Getting around by bus

If saving money is your primary consideration, you can use the Fairbanks North Star Borough's **MACS bus system** (☎ 907-459-1011; www.co.fairbanks.ak.us). Buses link the university, downtown, the nearby North Pole community, shopping areas, and some hotels. At best, service is every 30 minutes, but it's worse on Saturday and nonexistent on Sunday. Pick up timetables at the visitor center or online. All buses connect at the transit park downtown, at 5th Avenue and Cushman Street. The fare is $1.50 for adults; 75¢ for seniors, children, teens, and people with disabilities; free for kids 4 and under.

Getting information

The folks offering visitor information in Fairbanks have consolidated offerings in the new **Morris Thompson Cultural and Visitors Center** downtown at the corner of Wendell and Dunkel streets. The center houses the **Fairbanks Convention and Visitors Bureau** (☎ 800-327-5774 or 907-456-5774; www.explorefairbanks.com) and the **Alaska Public Lands Information Center** (see later in this section), as well as a nonprofit **Alaska Geographic** book and gift store (☎ 907-459-3710; www.alaskageographic.org), and cultural and educational programs.

The visitors bureau maintains information kiosks in the main lobby of the center, as well as a video nook featuring films about the area and Alaska. The staff and volunteers answer questions and provide useful maps, driving-tour pamphlets, and walking-tour audio players, and can help you find a room with their daily vacancy listing (weekly in winter). Several computers are set up for free e-mail access or to look up travel information, and the building has free Wi-Fi. Visitor bureau hours are May through mid-September daily 8 a.m. to 9 p.m., the rest of the year 8 a.m. to 5 p.m., with shorter hours on holidays. The organization also has information desks at the airport and train depot (staffed summer only) and at Pioneer Park (closed entirely in the off season).

The **Alaska Public Lands Information Center** (☎ 907-456-3730; www. alaskacenters.gov) also has an information counter at the Morris Thompson Cultural and Visitors Center, as well as trip-planning tables where you can spread out maps. This is an indispensable stop for anyone planning to spend time in the outdoors. The staff is remarkably knowledgeable and can tell you about trips and activities based on first-hand experience. The counter is staffed in summer daily from 9 a.m. to 6 p.m., in winter Monday through Saturday from 9 a.m. to 5 p.m.

The Morris Thompson center as a whole also houses exhibits about the state and its people and a theater that features daily free films and naturalist programs. Parking is free and plentiful.

Where to Stay in Fairbanks

Going the bed-and-breakfast route is a smart choice in Fairbanks, where good budget motel rooms are few. In addition to the B&Bs I list in this section, you can find more through the **Fairbanks Association of Bed & Breakfasts,** which lists about ten on its Web site at www. ptialaska.net/~fabb.

All Seasons Bed and Breakfast Inn
$$$–$$$$ Downtown

This charming and comfortable country inn on a pleasant residential street a couple blocks from the downtown core is the creation of Mary Richards, a longtime transplant from the southern United States who retains, along with a slight accent, the gentle hospitality and refined style she brought with her. Each cozy room has its own inspired decorative details in bold colors, and the housekeeping has always been perfect on our many visits. For visiting with Mary or other guests, a series of elegant common rooms connect downstairs, where you'll find a bar with hot drinks and a sun porch with books and games. Shoes are removed at the front door in winter.

See map p. 273. 763 7th Ave., Fairbanks. ☎ 888-451-6649 or 907-451-6649. Fax: 907-474-8448. www.allseasonsinn.com. Rack rates: High season $145–189 double, off season $89–$109 double; extra person $35. Rates include full breakfast. DC, DISC, MC, V.

Aurora Express Bed & Breakfast
$$$ South of Fairbanks

Susan Wilson's late grandmother appeared to her in a dream and told her there would be a train on a bank below her house, on the family's 15 acres high in the hills south of Fairbanks. So, Wilson went out and got a train — a collection that includes a pair of 1956 Pullman sleepers, a dining car, a locomotive, a caboose, and a World War II hospital car — and her husband, Mike, brought it all up the mountain to install below the house, right in the spot indicated. Some cars are close to their original form, and Susan says older guests sometimes weep over the memories they bring back. Others were elaborately remodeled into rooms, some small, some huge, on themes related to Fairbanks history. A full breakfast is served in the dining car, which also houses the common area, TV, and phone (which rooms lack). They're located 6½ miles out of town, so you'll need your own car if you stay here.

See map p. 269. 1540 Chena Ridge Rd., Fairbanks. ☎ *800-221-0073 or 907-474-0949.* www.fairbanksalaskabedandbreakfast.com. *Rack rates: $145–$160 double; extra person $32–$40. Rates include full breakfast. MC, V. Closed mid-Sept to mid-May.*

Grand View Bed and Breakfast
$$ East of Fairbanks

Perched on 10 acres on Chena Ridge, 15 minutes east of town, a big log house overlooks a panorama of the Tanana Valley and Alaska Range, a view shared by each of the four rooms. The house was crafted of local materials by local craftspeople — even the furniture — and the understated décor makes the most of the logs' rich warmth. Owners Dave and Clodagh Thompson settled here after extensive travels (they speak five languages between them) and are raising three young children, whom they keep from underfoot according to guests' preferences. Rooms have their own full bathrooms, but guests share common areas for TV-viewing. Access to the kitchen is open, and guests also have use of the computer center, laundry room, hot tub, Wi-Fi, and sauna.

See map p. 269. 915 Ridge Pointe Dr., Fairbanks. ☎ *907-479-3388. Fax: 907-479-3389.* www.grandview-bb.com. *Rack rates: High season $135 double, off season $100 double; extra person 12 and over $10. Rates include choice of full or continental breakfast. MC, V.*

Minnie Street Bed & Breakfast Inn
$$$ Downtown

Across the river from the downtown center, four buildings around a garden courtyard contain large, clean, brightly decorated rooms with stylish furniture and many amenities. The inn reflects the personality of its serene but exacting hosts, managing to feel both homey and polished. A full breakfast is served in a dining room with a high-vaulted ceiling and continental breakfasts in some rooms. Huge one-bedroom suites have

Fairbanks

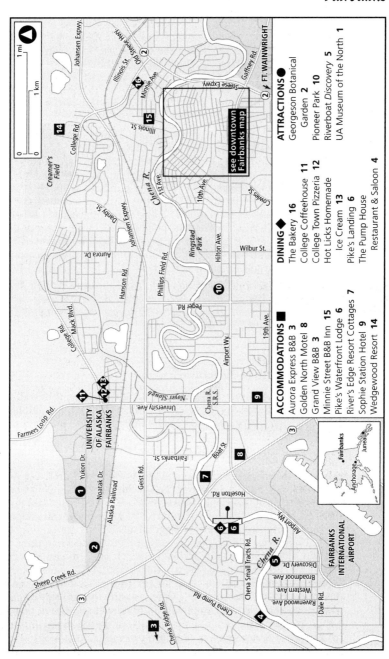

ATTRACTIONS●

Georgeson Botanical
Garden **2**
Pioneer Park **10**
Riverboat *Discovery* **5**
UA Museum of the North **1**

DINING◆

The Bakery **16**
College Coffeehouse **11**
College Town Pizzeria **12**
Hot Licks Homemade
Ice Cream **13**
Pike's Landing **6**
The Pump House
Restaurant & Saloon **4**

ACCOMMODATIONS■

Aurora Express B&B **3**
Golden North Motel **8**
Grand View B&B **3**
Minnie Street B&B Inn **15**
Pike's Waterfront Lodge **6**
River's Edge Resort Cottages **7**
Sophie Station Hotel **9**
Wedgewood Resort **14**

kitchens and extra beds for one or two; all but one have Jacuzzi tubs. A business center and laundry room are available to all guests.

See map p. 269. 345 Minnie St., Fairbanks. ☎ **888-456-1849** *or 907-456-1802. Fax: 907-451-1751. www.minniestreetbandb.com. Rack rates: High season $109–$159 double, $219 suite; off season $69–$99 double, $219 suite; extra person $35. Rates include full breakfast. AE, DISC, MC, V.*

River's Edge Resort
$$$$$ College

An afternoon on a sunny riverbank exemplifies the best of Interior Alaska; this place is built around that knowledge. Trim little cottages stand in a grassy compound along the gentle Chena River, where guests can fish for grayling. Inside, each light, airy cottage is an excellent standard hotel room, with high ceilings and two queen-size beds. Outside, they're like a little village, where guests can sit on the patio, watch the river go by, and socialize. It's perfect for families, as the outdoor areas are safe for playing and noise inside won't bother the neighbors. A large, summer-only restaurant sits at river's edge, with dining on a deck or inside at round, oak tables. Dinner entrees — steak, seafood, and down-home cooking — range up to $30; a burger is $10.

See map p. 269. 4200 Boat St., Fairbanks. Take Sportsman Way off Airport Way to Boat Street. ☎ **800-770-3343** *or 907-474-0286. Fax: 907-474-3665. www.rivers edge.net. Rack rates: High season $205 double, off season $149 double; extra person 13 and over $10. AE, DISC, MC, V.*

Wedgewood Resort
$$$–$$$$ North of Downtown

Off College Road near the Creamer's Field Refuge, this well-kept hotel sprawls across a grassy, 23-acre complex in eight large buildings. Seven of them are three-story apartment buildings converted into suites, regularly refitted, without elevators but with large living rooms, separate dining areas, fully equipped kitchens, air-conditioners, two TVs, balconies, and phones with voicemail in both the living room and the bedroom. The main difference from home is that someone else cleans up after you. Another 157 units are large standard hotel rooms in the three-story Bear Lodge, which has its own lobby; however, those are closed mid-September through mid-May. A scheduled courtesy van runs to the airport and train depot and various tourist sites in the summer. Several attractions are on-site or nearby: a large new antique auto museum, and trails to a pond and Creamer's Field, and the Alaska Bird Observatory research and educational center (see "Hiking and bird-watching," later in this chapter). The same company owns **Sophie Station Hotel,** which is nearer to the airport. It's similar to the Wedgewood but has smaller (although still roomy) suites. The Sophie boasts elevators, is all in one building, and has a very good restaurant.

See map p. 269. 212 Wedgewood Dr., Fairbanks. ☎ **800-528-4916** *reservations or 907-452-1442. Fax: 907-451-8184. www.fountainheadhotels.com. Rack rates:*

High season $170 double, $170–$220 suite for two; off season $95–$120 suite for two, regular double rooms not offered; extra person in suite $10. AE, DC, DISC, MC, V.

Westmark Fairbanks Hotel & Conference Center
$$$$$ Downtown

This Fairbanks landmark, the town's grand meeting place, owned by Holland America Line, fills a city block and includes the city's tallest tower (not exactly a skyscraper, but you don't need to be very high for good views in Fairbanks). The décor in newer rooms is the city's most stylish, with a post-mod pastiche that includes fabrics and lamps out of *The Jetsons* along with colonial woodwork; big, manly furniture; and lots of color. I like it. The rooms are packed with amenities, including, in many, little shelves for the coffeemakers so they're not down with your toothpaste. Downstairs, the hotel has a cafe with a dining room that's a work of art (open summer only) and a comfortable steakhouse. A complimentary breakfast is served in the winter months.

813 Noble St., Fairbanks. ☎ *800-544-0970 reservations, or 907-456-7722. Fax: 907-451-7478.* www.westmarkhotels.com. *Rack rates: Summer $225 double, $240–$500 suite; winter $84 double, $94–$500 suite; extra person 19 and over $15. AE, DC, DISC, MC, V.*

Runner-up accommodations

You'll have no trouble finding chain hotels in Fairbanks. Here are some places with more character, or where you can find a bargain.

Bridgewater Hotel

$$$ Downtown   This older building in a prime downtown location is a great choice for summertime travelers who like staying in a traditional downtown hotel but don't want luxury hotel trappings and rates. *See map p. 273. 723 1st Ave., Fairbanks.* ☎ *800-528-4916, 907-452-6661, or 907-456-3642. Fax: 907-452-6126.* www.fountainheadhotels.com.

Golden North Motel

$ Airport   The Baer family, owners since 1971, keep this two-story motel in good shape and have added nice amenities. The small rooms are an excellent bargain for those who just want a clean, safe place to sleep. *See map p. 269. 4888 Old Airport Way, Fairbanks.* ☎ *800-447-1910 or 907-479-6201. Fax: 907-479-5766.* www.goldennorthmotel.com.

Pike's Waterfront Lodge

$$$$ Airport   The owners packed this riverside hotel with every amenity you can think of, plus some new ones, such as a greenhouse and an ice cream shop with an airplane sticking out of it. *See map p. 269. 1850 Hoselton Rd., Fairbanks.* ☎ *877-774-2400 or 907-456-4500. Fax: 907-456-4515.* www.pikeslodge.com.

Where to Dine in Fairbanks

The Bakery
$–$$ Near Downtown   DINER

You can find an infinite number of old-fashioned coffee shops in and around Fairbanks — the kinds of places where a truck driver or gold miner can find a hearty, down-home meal; a motherly waitress; and a bottomless cup of coffee. This is one of the better versions. The sourdough pancakes are good, the menu is long and inexpensive, portions are huge (sometimes they require two plates), and the service is fast and friendly. You can get breakfast all day (of course). They have no liquor license.

See map p. 269. 69 College Rd., Fairbanks. ☎ **907-456-8600.** *Main courses: $8–$12 lunch, $9–$23 dinner. MC, V. Open: Mon–Thurs 6 a.m.–4 p.m., Fri–Sat 6 a.m.–7 p.m., Sun 7 a.m.–4 p.m.*

Gambardella's Pasta Bella
$$–$$$ Downtown   ITALIAN

This warm, charming restaurant is right in the center of things. The chicken *rustico* (which sits on polenta) is tasty; they serve seafood in interesting ways; and the lasagna — made with sausage, thin noodles, and a rich, dusky tomato sauce — will improve your opinion of this abused dish. Dining rooms are narrow and segmented, so you always seem to be sitting with just a few other people, with elaborate decoration that adds to a pleasingly busy feeling. The restaurant added more space with a second-story dining room and patio while keeping the cozy ambience. Unlike the synthetic ambience of some of Fairbanks's other fine-dining places, Gambardella's feels real, a place where a family shares its cuisine. Perfect, no — but pleasant and satisfying. They serve beer and wine.

See map p. 273. 706 2nd Ave., Fairbanks. ☎ **907-456-3417.** *Main courses: $7–$13 lunch, $14–$28 dinner; 15 percent gratuity added for parties of five or more, or for split checks. AE, MC, V. Open: Mon–Sat 11 a.m.–10 p.m., Sun 4–10 p.m.; closes one hour earlier in the off season.*

Lavelle's Bistro
$$$–$$$$$ Downtown   BISTRO

In a big room of chrome, stone, and glass right downtown (at the base of the Marriott SpringHill Suites), Lavelle's has a grown-up, cosmopolitan feel that is quite welcome when you weary of the Alaskan rustic or gold-rush themes of many of the area's restaurants. It's also got the advantage of consistently superb food, ambitious in conception and fine in execution, and expert service. The cuisine is difficult to categorize, as Southwest and Italian influences may be brought to a single dish, and Northwest, Asian, and French influences turn up variously. Dinner main courses are mostly over $20, but you can dine economically on the ample appetizers and salads, or choose a vegetarian lasagna that, for only $17, comes with

Downtown Fairbanks

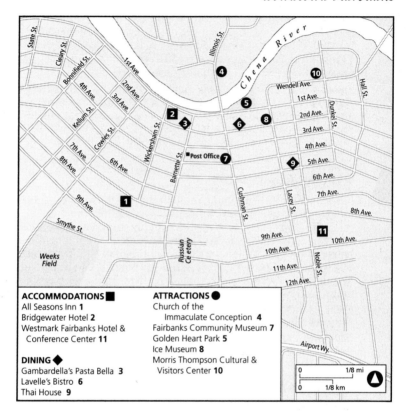

ACCOMMODATIONS ■
All Seasons Inn **1**
Bridgewater Hotel **2**
Westmark Fairbanks Hotel &
   Conference Center **11**

DINING ◆
Gambardella's Pasta Bella **3**
Lavelle's Bistro **6**
Thai House **9**

ATTRACTIONS ●
Church of the
   Immaculate Conception **4**
Fairbanks Community Museum **7**
Golden Heart Park **5**
Ice Museum **8**
Morris Thompson Cultural &
   Visitors Center **10**

soup or a salad and side dishes. The wine list is impressive and the 3,000-bottle cellar is behind glass in the middle of the dining room; the owners are on a mission to educate Fairbanks about wine, as they've already done with food by creating one of Alaska's best restaurants.

See map p. 273. 575 1st Ave., Fairbanks. ☎ *907-450-0555. Reservations recommended. Main courses: $11–$16 lunch, $17–$46 dinner. AE, DC, DISC, MC, V. Open: Summer daily 11 a.m.–2 p.m. and 4:30–10 p.m.; winter Tues–Sat 4:30–10 p.m., Sun–Mon 4:30–9 p.m.*

The Pump House Restaurant & Saloon
$$$$ College   REGIONAL

The historic, rambling, corrugated tin building on the National Register of Historic Places is elaborately decorated and landscaped with authentic gold-rush relics. Sitting on the deck over the Chena, you can watch the riverboat paddle by or a group in canoes stop for appetizers and drinks from the full bar. For dinner, the cuisine is a cut above the area's typical steaks and seafood and includes game you may not have tried, including reindeer and elk. Dishes such as Alaskan bouillabaisse or the seafood chowder — hearty, creamy, and flavorful — make the most of the regional ingredients without trying to get too fancy. Many of the side dishes are a la carte, so, although main courses are generous, it's expensive to order a large meal. Besides, you'll want to save room for one of the exceptional desserts. They serve a big Sunday brunch, too.

See map p. 269. Mile 1.3, Chena Pump Road, Fairbanks. ☎ **907-479-8452.** www. pumphouse.com. *Main courses: $18–$34. AE, DISC, MC, V. Open: Summer Mon–Sat 5–11 p.m., Sun 10 a.m.–2 p.m. and 5–11 p.m.; winter Tues–Sat 5–9 p.m., Sun 10 a.m.–2 p.m. and 5–9 p.m.*

Thai House
$–$$ Downtown   THAI

In a small, brightly lit dining room in the downtown area, this is a simple, family-run restaurant with authentic Thai cuisine. Every time we've dined here, the food came quickly and was deftly seasoned and cooked to a turn. You can rely on the servers, beautifully attired in national costumes, to help you order; just believe that when they say "hot" they really mean it. The first time I ate here, I rechecked the bill because it seemed too small. Thanks to this terrific restaurant and others, Fairbanks has gone a bit Thai crazy, and now, incongruously for such a provincial town, has at least seven Thai restaurants. This one is the most centrally located and among the best, although that debate is part of the fun.

See map p. 273. 412 5th Ave. ☎ **907-452-6123.** *Main courses: $8–$10 lunch, $12–$15 dinner. MC, V. Open: Mon–Sat 11 a.m.–4 p.m. and 5–9:30 p.m.*

The Turtle Club
$$$–$$$$ Fox   STEAK/SEAFOOD

Locals pack into this squat, windowless building, with its vinyl tablecloths and stackable metal chairs, for a menu with just a few famous selections: prime rib, lobster, king crab, and prawns. These are simple, burly meals with friendly, roadhouse-style service; the menu is printed on the place-mat and vegetables are an afterthought from an indifferent salad bar. But when the beef comes, you know it — the middle-sized prime-rib cut is over an inch thick and covers a large plate, an insanely large portion — and the meat is tender and cooked right. The atmosphere is noisy and super-casual; people laugh loud and don't worry about putting their elbows on the table or spilling a little beer. You won't run into many other tourists here, north of the city in Fox, but you do need reservations, and even with them you often wait half an hour in the smoky bar or a narrow corridor. If this doesn't sound like fun, don't go; but if you get it, the place is energizing.

10 Mile Old Steese Hwy., Fox. ☎ **907-457-3883.** *Reservations recommended. Main courses: $21–$37. AE, DISC, MC, V. Open: Mon–Sat 6–10 p.m., Sun 5–9 p.m.*

Runner-up restaurants

College Town Pizzeria

$ **College PIZZA** What would a university be without a top-notch, East Coast–style pizzeria nearby? Find some of Alaska's best pizza at this ultra-casual spot. *See map p. 269. At College and University roads, Fairbanks.* ☎ *907-457-2200.*

Pike's Landing Riverside Dining

$$$$ **Airport STEAK/SEAFOOD** Fairbanks's most formal restaurant (not such a high standard), overlooks the Chena River near the airport. The bar's deck is popular for a casual meal. *See map p. 269. 4438 Airport Way, Fairbanks.* ☎ *907-479-6500.*

Exploring Fairbanks

Some like Fairbanks, some don't. Other than the attractions at the university, the town's tourist offerings can be rather hokey. The major commercial tourist sites, including Gold Dredge Number 8, the Riverboat Discovery, and the El Dorado Gold Mine, are oriented to the cruise lines' escorted-tour trade; independent travelers may not enjoy being part of the herd. Moreover, prices for non-package visitors tend to be too high, and my recommendations here are offered with that proviso. On the other hand, the university's attractions are first-rate, and everything described here can be a lot of fun if you relax and take Fairbanks on its own terms, as an outpost on the unpolished periphery of the known universe.

The top attractions

Pioneer Park
West of Downtown

This city park contains Fairbanks's essence. Created as Alaskaland in 1967 for the centennial of the Alaska purchase, it was renamed in 2002 because town leaders thought the old name promised too much. It's true: This is no theme park. But it is worth your time. The park is relaxing and low-key; entrancing for young children and interesting for adults, if you can give in to its charm. Plan on looking around for at least a couple hours. The centerpiece is the SS *Nenana,* a large stern-wheeler that plied the Yukon and Tanana rivers until 1952, with five decks, two of them endowed with sumptuous mahogany, brass, and white-painted promenades. Additionally, many of Fairbanks's small historic buildings have been moved to the park. And near the park entrance sits President Warren Harding's railcar, from which he stepped to drive the golden spike on the Alaska Railroad.

The **Pioneer Air Museum** is housed in a geodesic dome toward the back of the park. An exhibit called **40 Below Fairbanks** allows visitors to go into a little room and experience the coldest winter weather in the middle of the summer. Other attractions include a gold-rush museum, an illustrated gold-rush show, a dance hall, an Alaska Native museum, and an art gallery. The park also offers canoe, kayak, and bike rentals. And if you have children, you certainly won't escape without a ride on the Crooked Creek and Whiskey Island Railroad that circles the park twice, with a tour guide pointing out the sights. Kids also enjoy the large playground, with equipment for toddlers and older kids, the 36-hole miniature-golf course, and an old-fashioned merry-go-round, the park's only ride. And adults will appreciate the revue and salmon bake (see "Nightlife," later in this chapter).

See map p. 269. At Airport Way and Peger Road, Fairbanks. ☎ *907-459-1087. http:// co.fairbanks.ak.us. Admission: Free to the park; fees for individual attractions are each $6 or less. Open: Attractions Memorial Day to Labor Day daily noon to 8 p.m.; park year-round.*

The Riverboat Discovery
Airport

The *Discovery* belongs to the pioneering Binkley family, which has been in the riverboat business since the Klondike gold rush and has run this attraction since 1950. The *Discovery* is a real stern-wheeler, a 156-ft. steel vessel carrying up to 900 passengers on as many as three trips a day. There's nothing intimate or spontaneous about the 3½-hour ride, which mostly carries package-tour passengers off fleets of buses, but the Binkleys still provide a diverting outing that doesn't feel cheap or phony. After loading at a landing with shops off Dale Road, near the airport, the boat cruises down the Chena and up the Tanana past demonstrations on shore — among others, a bush plane taking off and landing, fish cutting at a Native fish camp, and a musher's dog yard. Finally, the vessel pulls up at the bank for an hour-long tour of a mock Athabascan village.

See map p. 269. 1975 Discovery Dr., Fairbanks. ☎ *866-479-6673 or 907-479-6673. www.riverboatdiscovery.com. Admission: $55 adults, $38 kids 3–12, free for kids 2 and under. Sailings: Mid-May through mid-Sept daily 8:45 a.m. and 2 p.m.*

UA Museum of the North
College

This magnificent on-campus museum of science and art is the most intellectually engaging I've ever visited. Instead of categorizing the content by discipline, curators have thematically combined art, science, anthropology, and natural history to tell Alaska's story and to raise questions in viewers' minds — not only answer them. The building itself is a swooping combination of grand, graceful shapes, recalling moving icebergs, or perhaps the northern lights. The natural history collection is Alaska's best and most scholarly, with information presented at advanced as well as elementary levels, and memorable items such as Blue Babe, the mummified steppe bison; a 5,400-pound copper nugget; and the state's largest public display of gold. In that part of the museum, the mixed cultural and scientific objects are linked by region of Alaska, creating a rich mental map of the state in one room. In a towering newer gallery, the thematic presentation is based more on concepts and issues. This is where you'll find the hypnotic sound and light installation called *The Place Where You Go to Listen,* which *The New Yorker* said confirmed Fairbanks composer John Luther Adams as "one of the most original musical thinkers of the new century." For extra fees, carry an audio tour ($4), or take in a film ($5).

See map p. 269. 907 Yukon Dr., Fairbanks. ☎ **907-474-7505.** www.uaf.edu/ museum. *Admission: $10 adults, $9 seniors 60 and over, $5 kids 7–17, free for kids 6 and under. Open: Summer daily 9 a.m.–9 p.m., winter Mon–Sat 9 a.m.–5 p.m.*

Getting outdoors in Fairbanks

Fairbanks's population is extraordinarily active, making use of an outdoor environment rich in opportunities for exercise and adventure. Most of these activities, however, are not the kind oriented to tourism: Instead of guides taking visitors to easy goals with spectacular vistas, as in coastal Alaska, most outings here are do-it-yourself. Take this opportunity to get out on your own. Also, be sure to take a look at "A Side Trip on Chena Hot Springs Road," later in this chapter.

Canoeing

The Chena River is slow and meandering as it flows through Fairbanks, and you have your pick of restaurants on the bank. To pass wilder shores, go farther upriver. The wilderness section beginning at the Chena Lake Recreation Area, near the town of North Pole, is about 12 to 16 hours from Fairbanks by canoe. You can use various access points along the way to tailor a float to how remote you want to be and how long you want to go, from as little as a couple hours. **Alaska Outdoor Rentals & Guides,** located on the riverbank at Pioneer Park (☎ 907-457-2353; www.akbike.com), rents canoes and offers pickup or drop-off along the river for flat rates. For example, to float from the park to the Pump House restaurant is $37 for the canoe and $19 for pickup. They also offer lessons and drop-offs for longer paddles and expeditions.

Hiking and bird-watching

Creamer's Field, 1300 College Rd. (☎ 907-459-7307; www.creamers field.org), right in Fairbanks, is a 2,000-acre former dairy farm made into a migratory waterfowl refuge by a community fund drive in 1966. The pastures are a prime stopover point for Canada geese, pintails, and golden plovers in the spring and fall. Swans are common in spring. Sandhill cranes, shovelers, and mallards show up all summer. The Friends of Creamer's Field operates a small visitor center in the old farmhouse with displays on birds, wildlife, and history, open mid-May through mid-September daily from 10 a.m. to 5 p.m. They offer guided nature walks in summer Monday, through Friday at 10 a.m., Wednesday at 7 p.m. You don't need a guide, however: During migrations, use the blinds around the edge of the field. Other times, walk 3 miles of trails through forest, field, and wetland. I especially enjoy the boreal forest nature walk, interpreted by signs and an excellent booklet you can pick up at the visitor center or from a kiosk at the trailhead when the visitor center is closed. The **Alaska Bird Observatory** (☎ 907-451-7159;

www.alaskabird.org) conducts research and educational programs on the Creamer's Field refuge, including bird walks and bird-banding that visitors can observe (call for times). It's the farthest north facility of its kind in North America. The organization's building has interpretive displays, a nature store, and a library. Located just west of the refuge on the grounds of the Wedgewood Resort, the observatory can be hard to find — look for the signs.

Other options for hikes are covered elsewhere in this chapter. **Birch Hill Recreation Area,** just north of town on the Steese Highway, has miles of trails in pleasant woods; it's covered in the "Winter recreation" section, later in this chapter. The area's best trail hikes are in the **Chena River State Recreation Area** (see "Getting outside on Chena Hot Springs Road," later in this chapter).

Mountain-biking

Hiking trails around Fairbanks are open to bikes, and the cross-country ski trails described in the following section are fine mountain-bike routes in summer, too. You can get many other good ideas from Larry Katkin, owner of **Alaska Outdoor Rentals & Guides,** whose main bike-rental location is at Pioneer Park (☎ **907-457-2453;** www.akbike.com). He has a large fleet of quality bikes renting for $27 for an eight-hour day in summer. People around here bike year-round: In the cold months, they just use studded tires.

Winter recreation

Fairbanks has real Jack London winters; the visitor bureau guarantees it. Fairbanks is the destination for a growing number of visitors who want to experience deep cold, see the aurora borealis, and ride a dog sled. Chena Hot Springs Resort, covered near the end of this chapter, is a good goal for winter immersion, but you also can have a good time in town, especially in March, when the days lighten up, temperatures become moderate, and the town gets busy with dog-mushing and the ice-carving contest (see Chapter 3).

✔ **Aurora-viewing:** Fairbanks is famous for the northern lights. Some of the world's top scientists studying the phenomenon are at the University of Alaska's Geophysical Institute (check out their predictions at www.gi.alaska.edu). The cold, dark months are the best times to see the aurora, and the best places are away from city lights. Chena Hot Springs Resort specializes in aurora-viewing, but all you really need are warm clothing and someone to wake you up. Many accommodations in town offer aurora wake-up calls.

✔ **Dog-mushing:** The long winters and vast wild lands make the Fairbanks area a center of dog-sledding, both for racers and recreationists. Plenty of people are willing to take you for a lift, an experience not to be missed. **Sun Dog Express Dog Sled Tours** (☎ **907-479-6983;** www.mosquitonet.com/~sleddog) has a good reputation, and charges at little as $15 for a quick spin, with rides up to 11 miles long for $120. A half-day mushing school is $250. The owners also offer summer mushing demonstrations. Or try **Paws for Adventure** (☎ **907-378-3630;** www.pawsforadventure. com), which offers 30-minute rides for $60 up to trips a week long, and it's own $250 half-day mushing school.

✔ **Nordic skiing:** The **Birch Hill Recreation Area,** off the Steese Expressway just north of town (look on the right for the signs and follow them carefully), has about 16 miles of good cross-country ski trails, most groomed for classical or skate skiing, and two warm-up buildings for changing clothes. Several loops of a few miles each offer advanced skiing on the steep southern side of the hill; loops of up to 6¼ miles provide more level terrain to the north. The area has a lighted loop, too. At the **University of Alaska Fairbanks,** a similar but less varied set of trails start, mostly groomed for skate technique. The trailhead is at the west end of campus, near the satellite dishes at the top of Tanana Loop. Rent skis at **Beaver Sports,** 3800 College Rd. (☎ **907-479-2494;** www.beaversports.com).

More cool things to see and do

If you have extra time in Fairbanks, you'll find enough to do to fill several days. I've gathered some additional highlights here:

✔ **Have lunch at Gold Dredge No. 8** (☎ **907-457-6058;** www.gold dredgeno8.com). This is the area's most authentic gold-mining attraction, featuring a 1927 gold dredge standing five stories tall. Visits start with a large group lunch of stew and biscuits, followed by a walk through informational stations on the dredge where perky, well-informed guides explain its workings. Interpretive signs explain the history and workings of the gold dredges as well as the history of gold rushes of Alaska. People usually take about 45 minutes to tour the dredge and buildings, but there is no time limit. The price of $15 for lunch and visiting the historic site is a bargain.

✔ **Walk the historic downtown area.** The town's most interesting buildings are near the Chena River downtown. Across the footbridge from the Morris Thompson Cultural and Visitors Center (see "Getting Information," earlier in this chapter) is the Roman Catholic **Church of the Immaculate Conception.** The white clapboard structure, built in 1904, has gold-rush decoration inside, rare for its authenticity, including a pressed-tin ceiling and stained-glass windows.

✔ **See inside Fairbanks's attic.** A visit to the old city hall, at 410 Cushman St., is a chance to see the town as it sees itself, in the charming **Fairbanks Community Museum** (☎ **907-457-3669**). A series of cramped galleries offer up old photographs, maps, newspapers, and other bric-a-brac, as well as skillfully created explanatory exhibits, mostly focusing on the area's gold-mining history and development. The museum is open Tuesday through Saturday from 10 a.m. to 6 p.m. Admission is free. It's closed in April.

✔ **See ice year-round.** The **Fairbanks Ice Museum,** downtown at 502 2nd Ave. (☎ **907-451-8222;** www.icemuseum.com), shows off the city's legendary annual World Ice Art Championships. Besides a slide show, four expansive freezers with large picture windows contain ice sculptures with an ice artist usually at work. Admission is $12 adults, $11 seniors and military, $6 kids 6 to 12, $2 kids 5 and under. It's open May through September daily 10 a.m. to 8 p.m.

✔ **See the university campus.** A free two-hour walking tour, led by students, meets at Signers Hall June through August Monday through Friday at 1 p.m., except for days around the Independence Day holiday. Call ahead (☎ 907-474-7581) or check www.uaf.edu/visituaf for information. Use that Web site to learn about other things to do on campus, too.

✔ **Walk in a research garden.** The University of Alaska's **Georgeson Botanical Garden,** on West Tanana Drive, at the bottom of the campus (☎ 907-474-1944; http://georgesonbg.org), is a pleasant mix of science and contemplation. Plots laid out to compare seeds and cultivation techniques contain informative posts on the experiment; but at the same time, the flowers and vegetables are spectacular, and there are peaceful memorials and places to picnic here and there. Nearby, the barn of the university's experimental farm is open for visitors to wander through and view the reindeer. A children's garden is slowly being created and includes a fun maze in the form of a five-petal flower. Admission is $2.

✔ **Pan gold at an educational mining tour.** At the **El Dorado Gold Mine,** a train carries visitors (mostly on escorted packages) through an impressively staged tour, including a tunnel through the permafrost. Visitors gather around a sluice to hear the amusing and authentic Dexter and Lynette (also known as Yukon Yonda) Clark and watch a swoosh of water and gold-bearing gravel rush by. You pan the resulting pay dirt, and everyone goes home with enough gold dust to fill a plastic locket — typically $5 to $35 worth. Drive out to the mine after making reservations, or take a $5 shuttle. It's 9 miles north of town, off the Elliot Highway (☎ 866-479-6673 or 907-479-6673; www.eldoradogoldmine.com). Admission is $35 adults, $23 kids 3 to 12, free for kids 2 and under (a bit high, in my opinion).

Spending one, two, or three days in Fairbanks

Here are some ideas for how to organize your time during a stay in Fairbanks. I'm not sure I'd spend three days in Fairbanks if I had only limited time in Alaska (better to add more time somewhere like Denali National Park), but you can certainly have fun if you do. Each element of the following itinerary is reviewed in more detail elsewhere in this chapter.

Day 1 in Fairbanks

Start your day at the **UA Museum of the North.** It's the most interesting place to visit in town, and it provides a good introduction to the region and the whole state. After spending the morning there, take a walk on campus, perhaps strolling through the **Georgeson Botanical Garden.** Eat lunch at **College Town Pizza,** just off campus. In the afternoon, take a cruise on the **Riverboat *Discovery.*** For dinner, dine downtown at **Lavelle's Bistro.**

Day 2 in Fairbanks

Take a morning walk at **Creamer's Field** to see the wildlife and learn about Alaska flora and birds on the wooded trails and at the **Alaska Bird Observatory.** At midday, go to **Pioneer Park** and eat lunch at one of the small restaurants or food booths. Touring the park, be sure to see the stern-wheeler *Nenana* as well as whatever other attractions catch your fancy — it's a good place to wander. Walk to the riverbank and **rent a canoe.** Take your time floating downstream. Finish the paddle at the **Chena Pump House Restaurant,** where you can dine and have the canoe-rental agency pick up you and the canoe for the ride back to your car.

Day 3 in Fairbanks

Here are three options, based on your level of activity:

- ✔ Take a morning stroll around downtown Fairbanks, taking a look at the **Morris Thompson Cultural and Visitors Center,** the **Fairbanks Community Museum,** and the **Fairbanks Ice Museum.** In the afternoon, drive up the Steese Highway to Fox and lunch at **Gold Dredge No. 8,** taking time there to soak in the historic site (you'll also see the Trans-Alaska Pipeline along the road here). After exploring the area, head back to town to dine at the **salmon bake at Pioneer Park** and see the **Golden Heart Revue** there.

- ✔ Spend your morning the same way I outline in the preceding bullet, but in the afternoon head to **Birch Hill Recreation Area** for a hike in the woods, building up an appetite for a big meal at the nearby **Turtle Club.**

- ✔ Pack a picnic and spend the entire day on the magnificent trails in **Chena River State Recreations Area.**

Shopping

Fairbanks isn't a shopping destination by any means, but the town does have some good shops:

- ✔ The **Arctic Traveler's Gift Shop,** 201 Cushman St. (☎ 907-456-7080; www.arctictravelersgiftshop.com), specializes in Native crafts, carrying both valuable art and affordable but authentic Alaska gifts.

- **Big Ray's Store,** 507 2nd Ave. (☎ **907-452-3458;** www.bigrays.com), makes an interesting stop, even if you aren't interested in buying anything. It's known for heavy-duty Arctic wear, camping gear, and work clothes favored by Alaskans who make their living outdoors all over the state.

- **If Only . . . a fine store,** 215 Cushman St. (☎ **907-457-6659;** www.ifonlyalaska.com), is a charming gift and stationery shop with items to hold locals' as well as visitors' interest — not just tourist stuff.

- Near the airport, at 4630 Old Airport Rd., the **Great Alaskan Bowl Company** (☎ **800-770-4222** or 907-474-9663; www.woodbowl.com) makes and sells bowls of native birch — salad bowls, of course, but also for many other purposes. They can carve up to seven nested bowls from one piece of wood and even laser-engrave a photo inside one. Through a glass wall looking into the shop, you can see workers cutting the bowls from raw logs.

Nightlife

To find out what to do, call the 24-hour event recording operated by the **Fairbanks Convention & Visitors Bureau** at ☎ **907-456-4636** or check the bureau's event calendar at www.explorefairbanks.com.

One pleasant way to spend a warm evening is the salmon bake and revue at Pioneer Park. Dinner is served in the evening mid-May to mid-September at the **Alaska Salmon Bake,** in the park's mining valley area (☎ **907-452-7274;** www.akvisit.com). Cost for all-you-can-eat prime rib and fish (halibut, cod, or salmon) is $31 adults, $15 kids 3 to 12, or $6.50 for a child's hot dog plate. Beer and wine are available. The seating area is pleasant, with indoor or outdoor dining. The **Golden Heart Revue** is at the park's Palace Theatre (☎ **907-456-5960;** www.akvisit.com) nightly at 8:15 p.m. during the same months. It covers the story of the founding of Fairbanks with comedy and song in a nightclub setting; admission is $18 adults.

If you want to get away from other visitors for a while, here are some night spots where you'll meet more locals: In the university area, hear local and imported folk music live at the **College Coffeehouse,** 3677 College Rd. (☎ **907-374-0468;** www.collegecoffeehousefairbanks.com); the Web site lists upcoming acts. Three miles southwest of town on the Parks Highway, **The Blue Loon** (☎ **907-457-5666;** www.theblueloon.com) has live music, many beers on tap, and good burgers; they even show movies.

For something a bit wilder, the **Howling Dog Saloon** out in Fox, at 2160 Old Steese Hwy. (☎ **907-456-4695;** http://howlingdogsaloon.alaskansavvy.com), has long been the place to cut loose in the summer. Besides a bar, "The Dog" offers live music Wednesday through Saturday, a cafe, and volleyball out back. It's open May through October.

Fast Facts: Fairbanks

ATMs

Fairbanks has numerous banks with ATMs in the downtown area and along the commercial strips. Key Bank is at 100 Cushman St.

Emergencies

Dial ☎ **911.**

Hospital

Fairbanks Memorial is at 1650 Cowles St. (☎ 907-452-8181).

Information

The Fairbanks Convention & Visitors Bureau is within the Morris Thompson Cultural and Visitors Center at 101 Dunkel St. (☎ 800-327-5774; www.explorefairbanks.com).

Internet Access

You can get online free at the Morris Thompson Cultural and Visitors Center (see "Information," earlier).

Pharmacy

The pharmacy in the Fred Meyer grocery store at 930 Old Steese Hwy. (☎ 907-459-4233) is about a mile from the downtown center.

Police

For non-emergency police business, call the Alaska State Troopers (☎ 907-451-5100) or, within city limits, the Fairbanks Police Department (☎ 907-459-6500).

Post Office

The post office is at 315 Barnette St.

Taxes

Fairbanks has no sales tax. The room tax is 8 percent.

A Side Trip on Chena Hot Springs Road

The 57-mile paved Chena Hot Springs Road traces the Chena River through wooded hills east from Fairbanks. It's an avenue to an enjoyable day trip or a destination for outdoor activities and hot-spring swimming. The road crosses the **Chena River State Recreation Area,** where you'll find spectacular hikes and float trips, and leads to **Chena Hot Springs,** a year-round resort for soaking in hot mineral springs and a useful base for summer or winter outdoor day trips. The resort is most popular in midwinter, when international visitors come for aurora-viewing, but it has many activities, winter or summer, including horseback-riding, hiking, cross-country skiing, and snowmobiling. (The slow seasons are spring and fall.) The owner, a famous and colorful inventor, has built an ice hotel you can tour, offering the chance to sleep on a block of ice overnight. Swimming in the hot-springs water, indoors or outdoors, goes on all year, regardless of the weather. The paved road itself is a pleasant drive, about 1¼ hours each way from Fairbanks, but not particularly scenic.

 As much as I love this area, however, including the hot springs, I must warn that the word *resort* may create some false expectations. Chena Hot Springs is no Club Med. It's locally owned, constantly changing, and full of crazy or interesting new ideas (the ice hotel and geothermal greenhouse, for example). Sometimes the ground may be muddy, or forest fires may be coming through, the road may flood, or bears may be nosing around. Some rooms are rather worn. It's a true slice of Alaska, but don't come expecting the plastic perfection some resorts attain.

Getting there

Chena Hot Springs Road meets the Steese Expressway about 5 miles north of downtown Fairbanks. (Details on renting a car in Fairbanks can be found earlier in this chapter.) The resort offers rides from anywhere in Fairbanks. Summer rates are $115 round-trip for one person, or $75 per person for two or more passengers on the same reservation. Arrange for this at least 72 hours in advance.

Where to stay and dine

The resort is the only place to stay or dine near the hot springs.

Chena Hot Springs Resort
$–$$$$$ Chena Hot Springs

This unsophisticated family resort, set on 440 acres of land in a bowl of mountains, invites a slow pace, with plenty of time spent soaking or in the woods. Swimming and soaking are the main attractions. The hot springs supply an indoor pool, a series of indoor and outdoor hot tubs and spas, and the outdoor hot pond (100–110°F/38–44°C). Kids are limited to the indoor swimming pool, which is kept cool enough to swim, allowing adults to escape from the noise by swimming outside. Winter is the high season, when the aurora-viewing is exceptional, away from city lights, and you can enjoy Nordic skiing groomed for classical or skating techniques, snowmobile tours, dog-sled rides, and more. In the summer, you can go horseback-riding, rafting, canoeing, hiking, fishing, mountain-biking, geo-caching, ATV-riding or flightseeing (for guests only). Many activities are guided and carry extra fees. Some rental equipment is available.

The accommodations range from yurts to large hotel rooms with TVs, phones, and coffeemakers. The newest rooms, in the Moose building, are solidly built and nicely done up, but noise can be a problem on winter nights as guests come and go to look at the aurora. The yurts are basic but adequate if you want inexpensive lodgings and don't mind not having indoor plumbing. The intermediate rooms were cheaply built to start with and are not very good. They have shower stalls, not tubs. The main lodge building contains the restaurant and bar. The menu and staff change fairly frequently and this can affect the quality of service. Overall, this is a good place to have fun in the real Alaska, but be ready for some rough spots.

Mile 56.5, Chena Hot Springs Road, Fairbanks. ☎ *907-451-8104. Fax: 907-451-8151. www.chenahotsprings.com. Rack rates: $189–$249 double, $65 cabins and yurts; extra person $20. AE, DC, DISC, MC, V.*

Getting outside on Chena Hot Springs Road

The best trail hikes in the Fairbanks area are in the Chena River State Recreation Area and the river is a popular waterway for canoeing. The **Alaska Division of Parks and Outdoor Recreation** (☎ 907-451-2708; http://dnr.alaska.gov/parks/units/chena/index.htm) manages Chena River State Recreation Area and produces trail, river, and road guides, which are available at trailhead kiosks, on the Web site, or in a newspaper, *The Chena Trailmarker*, which you can also order online. Or get all that and answers to your questions in Fairbanks at the **Alaska Public Lands Information Center,** in the Morris Thompson Cultural and Visitors Center at 101 Dunkel St. (☎ **907-459-3730;** www.alaskacenters.gov).

- ✔ **Hike the Angel Rocks Trail.** A sometimes steep 4-mile round-trip to huge granite outcroppings, with impressive views of the valley below. Instead of hiking the loop, go into the outcroppings and back, because the far end is poorly maintained. The trailhead is at mile 48.9 of the road.

- ✔ **Backpack or hike the Granite Tors Trail.** This 15-mile loop, starting at mile 39.5 of the road, leads to towering granite tors that stand at random spots on the broad Plain of Monuments. The tors look like a surrealist experiment in perspective, at first confounding the eye's attempts to gauge their distance and size. Water is scarce, so bring along plenty. This is an excellent overnight hike, with the driest ground for camping right around the tors. You'll find a public shelter halfway along. Massive fires in 2004 burned over much of the trail but it remains passable and the Plain of Monuments was practically unscathed.

- ✔ **Swim and soak in the hot springs.** You don't have to stay at the resort to enjoy the pools and outdoor hot pond, all fed naturally by geothermal springs. Swim passes come with your room if you're staying at the resort; for day-trippers, a day pass is $10 adults, $8 seniors 60 and over, $7 kids 6 to 17, free for kids 5 and under. To get there, just drive to the end of the road.

Chapter 18

Driving Alaska's Highways

In This Chapter

▶ Getting acquainted with Alaska's simple road map

▶ Driving the Prince William Sound loop

▶ Driving the Denali/Fairbanks loop

▶ Extending your trip by joining the loops

▶ Taking it to the limit: The Arctic and more

*I*f you're used to a drive being a chore and a highway being an inter-state that looks about the same no matter where you are, prepare for something completely different. Most of Alaska's highways are lonely two-lane roads that string together tiny settlements hundreds of miles apart, with nothing in between but spectacular wild country.

A long drive in Alaska can be a form of wilderness travel. The radio goes dead. You cross great rivers and mountain ranges and see moose and other wildlife, but no people other than the ones who occasionally pass in other vehicles. An hour can pass between buildings. The landscape evolves and storms cross the skies. A winding road slowly unfolds the world, displaying land that belongs to you. Alaska's land is almost all public; you can get out anywhere to walk through the heather, smell the cottonwood trees by a roaring river, or feel the cool air of a bright mid-night on your cheek.

Road trips take a long time around here: You must cover a lot of ground. If you're really ambitious, you'll need a car that you can take over gravel roads. That limits your choice of rental agencies, because only a few allow it (see Chapter 7). On the other hand, you have little need to fear the unknown on an Alaskan road trip during the warm months — you won't be eaten by wild animals. It's a long way between services, but people are friendly and helpful, and if you have a problem, you'll muddle through.

Winter driving on Alaska highways is beautiful (at least during the brief hours of daylight), but undertaking a long winter's drive safely requires some preparation and knowledge. Consider flying or traveling by train instead of driving between cities during the winter. (For winter or summer trips, check out the safety tips in Chapter 7.)

I structure this chapter differently from the others. First, I summarize the qualities of the few main highways. Reviewing this summary with a map in your hand will help you get a fix on the routes and what they're like. Next, I describe some of the best driving itineraries, starting with the loops that most people want to drive, followed by the more extreme, lengthy, and remote drives.

 When planning the itineraries, I link places logically and suggest the most popular activities, but I hope you'll use these driving loops as guides, not plans. For example, suppose you want to see tidewater glaciers and whales in Prince William Sound. You'd need to add to your plan an extra day for a tour-boat ride from Whittier or Valdez. My goal here is to give you a solid foundation; build your trip on this base according to what interests you.

Understanding Alaska's Road Map

Losing your way on Alaska's highways is pretty difficult, because there just aren't enough of them. One leads in and out of the state, another connects Anchorage and Fairbanks, another heads to the Arctic, another to Prince William Sound, and another ends at the Kenai Peninsula. Despite the state's enormous size, a usable highway map can essentially fit on a cocktail coaster, because you need only a few simple lines to show the entire network of roads.

 For planning your trip, you nevertheless need some critical information that's more difficult to come by (but which I'm about to give you): **the drives that really are worth doing.** Alaska has plenty of miles — plenty of 100-mile stretches, in fact — that are as boring as driving through a tunnel of brush can be. So, get out your map (or use the "Alaska Highways" map provided in this chapter) and follow me through this menu, derived from many long road trips across Alaska. Where necessary, I provide cross-references to additional information in other chapters; otherwise, look for more-detailed information later in this chapter. I mention only paved roads here. Remote, gravel highways are covered in the "Driving to the Arctic and Other Extremes" section, later in this chapter.

   ✔ **Alaska Highway (Route 2 from the border to Delta Junction):** Running nearly 1,400 miles from Dawson Creek, British Columbia, to Delta Junction, Alaska, a couple of hours east of Fairbanks on the Richardson Highway, this World War II road is paved and generally easy driving. However, like other northern highways, it's subject to bone-jarring frost heaves and spring potholes. And the 200 miles in Alaska are pretty dull; the prettiest part is on the Canadian side, in the Kluane Lake area.

   ✔ **Glenn Highway (Route 1 from Anchorage to Tok):** From the Alaska Highway, this road is how you get to Southcentral Alaska, including Anchorage, 330 miles southwest of Tok. The northern section, from Tok to Glennallen (sometimes called the Tok Cutoff), borders Wrangell–St. Elias National Park. The park has broad tundra and boreal forest (also known as *taiga*) broken by high, craggy peaks — a pretty drive, but not top-five material by Alaska standards. The section from Glennallen to Anchorage, however, is truly spectacular. The road passes through high alpine terrain frequented by caribou. It then claws its way along the walls of a deep canyon near the Matanuska Glacier and the river that flows from it.

✔ **Parks Highway (Route 3 from Anchorage to Fairbanks):** The George Parks Highway is a straight line from Anchorage to Fairbanks, 360 miles to the north, providing access to Denali National Park (see Chapter 19). Although this highway features some vistas of Mount McKinley from south of the park and nice views on the wide tundra of Broad Pass, it's mostly a transportation route, less scenic than the Richardson or Glenn highways.

✔ **Richardson Highway (Route 4 from Valdez to Delta Junction, Route 2 from Delta Junction to Fairbanks):** Leading 364 miles from tidewater in Valdez to Fairbanks, this route is the most beautiful paved drive in the Interior. I've been hypnotized into awed reverie on this drive; you just can't absorb so much beauty hour after hour. From the south, the road begins with a magnificent climb through Keystone Canyon and steep Thompson Pass, just outside of Valdez, and then passes the huge, distant peaks of southern Wrangell–St. Elias National Park. North of Glennallen, the road climbs into the Alaska Range, snaking along the shores of long alpine lakes and crossing the dizzyingly huge spaces of the tundra slopes, which are good areas for spotting wildlife. The road descends again to the forested area around Delta Junction and meets the Alaska Highway before arriving in Fairbanks (see Chapter 17). The state's first highway, it lost much of its traffic to the Parks Highway, which trims more than 90 miles from the drive between Anchorage and Fairbanks, and to the Glenn Highway, which shaves about 120 miles off the trek from Glennallen to Tok. You'll see few other cars on the Richardson Highway.

✔ **Seward Highway (Route 1 from Anchorage to Tern Lake, Route 9 from Tern Lake to Seward):** The highway leaves Anchorage on the 127-mile drive to Seward following the rocky edge of mountain peaks above a surging ocean fjord. Drivers often slow down to admire the abundant wildlife and unfolding views. (See Chapter 15 for more information about this stretch of highway.) Later, the road climbs through high mountain passes above the tree line, tracing sparkling alpine lakes before descending through forest to Seward (see Chapter 16).

✔ **Sterling Highway (Route 1 from Tern Lake to Homer):** Leading 142 miles from the Seward Highway to the tip of the Kenai Peninsula, the highway has some scenic spots but is mostly a way to get to Kenai, Soldotna, and Homer, places that are discussed in Chapter 16.

Alaska Highways

The Prince William Sound Loop: Anchorage to Whittier to Valdez to Glennallen

Here's a great way to see Prince William Sound, the coastal mountains, and the spectacular Glenn Highway sections from Glennallen to Anchorage, including a trip on the Alaska state ferry from Whittier to Valdez. The loop works equally well in either direction.

Day 1: Anchorage to Valdez

The loop starts with a drive south from Anchorage to Whittier of less than two hours' duration if you don't stop. But making stops on this stretch of road is part of the fun. You can spend a full day in the scenic **Girdwood** and **Portage Glacier** areas (see Chapter 15). Near Portage Glacier, you drive through the unique 2-mile tunnel to Whittier. Important tips about the tunnel's opening times are in Chapter 15.

In Whittier, put your car on the **Alaska Marine Highway ferry** *Chenega* (☎ 800-642-0066 or 907-465-3941; www.ferryalaska.com). The ship shuttles back and forth between Whittier, Valdez, and Cordova daily. Every minute of the ride is scenic and relaxing. Keep an eye out for whales. The fare is $105 for a car up to 15 ft. long, plus $89 per adult passenger (including the driver, so the minimum you'll pay is $194), with kids 6 to 11 half-price and kids 5 and under free. You do need to reserve ahead, but a few weeks usually is sufficient.

In Valdez, check in at the **Best Western Valdez Harbor Inn,** 100 N. Harbor Dr. (☎ 888-222-3440; www.valdezharborinn.com), which sits at the top of the boat harbor entrance, with double rooms for $159 and $169 a night in the high season. A bar and restaurant on-site have a wonderful harbor view, and the restaurant has traditionally been the town's main spot for fine dining.

Day 2: A day in Valdez

Here are some activities for spending the day in Valdez:

✔ **The Valdez Museum & Historical Archive,** 217 Egan Dr. (☎ 907-835-2764; www.valdezmuseum.org), showcases regional history in an engaging and often charming way. An annex contains a detailed model of the town as it looked on another site before it was wiped out by the 1964 earthquake and tsunami.

✔ **Stan Stephens Glacier & Wildlife Cruises** (☎ 866-867-1297 or 907-835-4731; www.stanstephenscruises.com) shows off Prince William Sound on tours daily in the summer. A six-hour tour to the ice-choked waters in front of Columbia Glacier often encounters seals, sea otters, and sea lions, and sometimes whales; it costs $115 adults, half-price for kids 2 to 12.

✔ Take a sea-kayaking outing on Prince William Sound with **Pangaea Adventures** (☎ 800-660-9637 or 907-835-8442; www.alaska summer.com).

✔ Valdez is a great place to **hike or fish.** For information, contact the **Visitor Information Center,** operated by the Valdez Convention & Visitors Bureau, 104 Chenega St., at the corner of Egan Drive (☎ 907-835-4636; www.valdezalaska.org).

Day 3: Valdez to Glennallen

If the weather is clear, the drive north from Valdez on the Richardson Highway will be a highlight of your trip. The road traces the rocky slot of **Keystone Canyon** and then climbs straight up the side of the sheer coastal mountains to high alpine country in **Thompson Pass.** This spot has the distinction of receiving the biggest snowfall ever to occur in Alaska during a 24-hour period (5 ft.) and the most during a season (81 ft.). A glacier that you can walk right up to is located here. A little farther along, you see the silvery Trans-Alaska Pipeline snaking along to the left.

About 100 miles from Valdez, you come to **Copper Center,** a tiny Athabascan community near Wrangell–St. Elias National Park. A remarkable 85-room luxury hotel is here, the **Copper River Princess Lodge** (☎ **800-426-0500** for reservations, or 907-822-4000; www.princess lodges.com/copper_river_lodge.cfm). High-season rates are $119 to $199 double. Stop for lunch at the excellent restaurant, or stay and see the park, making arrangements through the lodge. The mining ghost town of **Kennecott,** within the park, is well worth a visit. Allow two nights for that side trip, because getting to Kennecott takes time and seeing it shouldn't be rushed. (Another lodging option and more details are in the "Edgerton Highway and McCarthy Road" section, later in this chapter.) In any event, check out the National Park Service visitor center in Copper Center to find out about Wrangell–St. Elias, which is by far America's largest and most rugged national park.

Another 15 miles north of Copper Center, you reach the little town of **Glennallen,** which lies at the junction of the Richardson and Glenn Highways. If you want to join the northern Denali/Fairbanks Loop (covered in the next section), bear right (or straight) in Glennallen, taking the next major left, toward Delta and Fairbanks. For that route, skip to "Day 2" under "The Denali Fairbanks Loop: Anchorage to Glennallen to Fairbanks to Denali," later in this chapter. To remain on the Prince William Sound Loop toward Anchorage, turn left in Glennallen onto the Glenn Highway.

 Heading west from Glennallen, the Glenn Highway crosses tundra, swamp, and taiga that are typical of Interior Alaska. The wide and distant vistas are a good place to spot caribou and moose. The road then rises into the craggy peaks of two converging ranges, the Talkeetna and Chugach mountains. Stop about 70 miles beyond Glennallen at either of two welcoming lodges. The **Sheep Mountain Lodge** (☎ **877-645-5121** or 907-745-5121; www.sheepmountain.com) is an authentic mountainside roadhouse where guests eat simply, take saunas or walk on the high tundra trails, and bed down in cute cabins, which rent for $159 double. Across the road, the **Majestic Valley Wilderness Lodge** (☎ **907-746-2930;** www.majesticvalleylodge.com) stands farther from the highway and has impressive common rooms and a first-class cross-country ski-trail network; the rooms range from bargain units for $120 to grander lodge rooms for $165.

Day 4: The road back to Anchorage

Anchorage is only another 115 miles, but you have plenty to do on the way. First comes the enormous **Matanuska Glacier.** See it from the Matanuska Glacier State Recreation Area, which has an overlook and a 1-mile nature trail with explanatory signs at mile 101 of the highway. To get closer to the glacier, you have to take a rough side road and pay a fee to the people who own the land in front of it, who also offer camping and guided hiking under the name **Glacier Park** (☎ **888-253-4480;** www.matanuskaglacier.com). Turn at mile 102. The side road is 3 miles, followed by a 15-minute walk to the glacier's face. The fee for the non-guided hike is $15 adults, $10 seniors and military, and $5 kids 6 to 12.

Even better than walking to the glacier, consider rafting its waters, or taking a glacier hike on the ice itself. An experienced outfit offers these activities, with various difficulty and risk levels: **NOVA,** which is listed in Chapter 14. Call ahead to reserve; NOVA's office is beyond the glacier in Chickaloon.

Charming country development borders the highway as you approach Anchorage. Sutton is a little town left behind by a coal mine that once operated in these mountains. The small historical park is worth a stop to stretch your legs. Next comes Palmer, site of the Alaska State Fair (see Chapter 3). Anchorage is an hour further, but you should also consider stopping along the way at Eklutna Historical Park, Eklutna Lake, or Thunderbird Falls (all described in Chapter 14).

The Denali/Fairbanks Loop: Anchorage to Glennallen to Fairbanks to Denali

Most people who come to Alaska want to see the scenery and wildlife of Denali National Park (see Chapter 19). The cheapest and most convenient way to get there is in a rented car you pick up in Anchorage (see Chapter 13). But after you've got the car, there's far more country to see than just Denali. This loop drive includes the park but also takes you over some of the world's most beautiful terrain on the way — places every bit its equal in their grandeur.

If you have the time, traveling both loops that I describe here makes good sense (see "Linking Up the Loops," later in this chapter). It's also perfectly workable to reverse the direction of this loop.

Day 1: Anchorage to Glennallen

Leave Anchorage northbound on the Glenn Highway (6th Avenue as you depart downtown). This day reverses the Day 4 itinerary of the Prince William Sound Loop, taking you past Palmer, Sutton, and the Matanuska Glacier to the Sheep Mountain Lodge or Majestic Valley Lodge. If you're not ready to stop there (perhaps you're driving through and skipping some sights), go another 70 miles to Glennallen, eat comfort food at the **Caribou Restaurant,** and stay at **The Caribou Hotel** (☎ **800-478-3302** or 907-822-3302; www.caribouhotel.com), where good standard rooms rent for $149 in summer. Be sure to call ahead, however, because they book up fast.

Day 2: Glennallen to Fairbanks

Drive north on the Richardson Highway, turning left at the *T* at the end of the Glenn Highway and bearing left again at the next big *Y*. The next 150-mile stretch passes north through the Alaska Range to Delta Junction. The scenery on this drive is exceptional, even by Alaska standards, and is a primary reason I recommend this loop. The road rises from the forest, past a series of lakes, to an enormous area of alpine tundra, traced topographically by more long alpine lakes. Scan those wide vistas for wildlife. Although sightings of the Trans-Alaska Pipeline are frequent, few other structures interrupt your view along the way, and you can stop and take a walk virtually anywhere you like.

Consider packing a picnic for this drive, because the area has few good places to dine. Or, if you get an early start, you can eat when you arrive in the little farming town of Delta Junction (about three hours from Glennallen); turn left at the junction with the Alaska Highway and stop at the **IGA Food Cache** (☎ 907-895-4653), on the south side of the highway, where you can eat in or carry out. If you need a room at this point, the funky but charming **Kelly's Alaska Country Inn** (☎ 907-895-4667; www.kellysalaskacountryinn.com) is right at the junction, charging $139 double.

Or you can continue 100 miles west to Fairbanks, with one good stop 10 miles along the way at **Rika's Roadhouse & Landing** (☎ 907-895-4201; www.rikas.com), a historic way station from the days when this part of the highway was a dog-sled journey of many days. Rika's is a good indoor and outdoor museum of pioneer life, with a simple restaurant. Nearby, the Alaska pipeline crosses the Tanana River on a suspension bridge, a site that's well worth a look.

In Fairbanks, I often choose the **All Seasons Inn;** it and other accommodations and restaurants are listed in Chapter 17. For a terrific evening meal, dine at **Lavelle's Bistro.**

Day 3: A day in Fairbanks

Spend a day (or more) in Fairbanks. The area offers a wide variety of things to do: the impressive UA Museum of the North, gold-mining sites, hot springs, and other outdoor destinations — there's even an ice museum. A list of ideas is in Chapter 17.

Day 4: Fairbanks to Denali

Driving south from Fairbanks on the Parks Highway, the first worthwhile stop you come to is Nenana, about 60 miles along the way. It's a town straight out of a Mark Twain novel: a sleepy, dusty riverside barge stop. Riverboats, in fact, still load with cargo for villages up and down the Tanana River. Visit the nostalgia-laden **Depot Museum** and explore a little on foot, not missing the riverfront, which is enlivened by a Native craft shop, a gathering place and some old railcars. Stop in at the visitor center on the Parks Highway to find out about the **Nenana Ice Classic** (www.nenanaakiceclassic.com), a contest to guess the exact minute the ice on the Tanana breaks up and starts to go out. The jackpot typically tops $300,000. A big book lists the times of all the guesses.

You should still be able to make Denali National Park for lunch, 120 miles south of Fairbanks. Stop just short of the park in Healy to eat at the **Black Diamond Grill** (☎ 907-683-4653) and check in at the **Motel Nord Haven** (☎ 800-683-4501 or 907-683-4500; www.motelnordhaven. com). In the afternoon, enter the park to get your bearings at the spectacular **Denali Visitor Center.** Take a hike in the front country or go on a river-rafting ride in the Nenana Canyon. In the evening, you can catch a dinner-theater show. All the Denali options are discussed in Chapter 19.

Day 5: A day in Denali

Get up as early as possible to board a shuttle bus into the park. You'll need reservations at least a few weeks in advance and a sack lunch. (These and other preparations are covered in Chapter 19.) Your chances of seeing brown bear, moose, and caribou are excellent, and you may even see wolves, Dall sheep, and other hard-to-find animals. Get off the bus for a walk on the tundra; out of sight of the road, you'll discover how it feels to be all alone in the wilderness. When you're ready, return to the road and catch another bus. Stay out all day and dine in the evening at the **King Salmon Restaurant** in the **Denali Princess Lodge** (☎ 907-683-2282; www.princesslodges.com/denali_lodge.cfm).

Day 6: Denali back to Anchorage

Drive about three hours south of the park to Talkeetna and have lunch at **Talkeetna Alaskan Lodge** (☎ 888-959-9590 or 907-733-9500; www. talkeetnalodge.com) before boarding a bush plane at the Talkeetna Airport for a flight over Mount McKinley and, in season, a landing on one of its glaciers. (Details about the flight are found in Chapter 19.) After the flight, drive two hours south to Anchorage to complete the loop.

Linking Up the Loops

The two loops I describe earlier in this chapter — the Prince William Sound Loop and the Denali/Fairbanks Loop — together form a figure eight over the central part of Alaska. The middle of the eight, where the two loops overlap, is the Glenn Highway from Glennallen to Anchorage. With enough time, connecting these two loops into one long road trip makes good sense, offering everything most visitors come to Alaska to see, including the fjords and forest of Prince William Sound, the high country of the Alaska Range and Denali National Park, and lots of glaciers and wildlife in both places and all along the way.

Here are three ways to connect the loops:

✔ **Do the big loop.** This is the simplest connection, making one big circle. Start with the Prince William Sound Loop, driving south from Anchorage to Whittier, crossing Prince William Sound, and driving north on the Richardson Highway; then join the Denali/Fairbanks Loop by continuing north at Glennallen all the way to Fairbanks, then south to Denali, and back to Anchorage. You won't get to see the beautiful Matanuska Glacier section of the Glenn Highway, between Glennallen and Palmer.

✔ **Complete the figure eight.** If you don't want to miss the amazing vertical scenery of the Glenn Highway as it passes the Matanuska Glacier, do the entire eight: Travel the whole Prince William Sound loop, but when you reach Palmer, turn northward on the Parks Highway to start the Denali/Fairbanks Loop. Complete that loop in reverse order, ending up back on the Glenn Highway (you'll have to cover the middle of the eight twice) before returning to Anchorage.

✔ **Do the Denali Highway.** The unpaved Denali Highway connects the midpoints of the Richardson and Parks highways, running between the tiny towns of Paxson and Cantwell. To drive it with a rental car, you have to rent from one of just a few companies that allow their vehicles to be used on gravel roads (see Chapter 7). The route opens up incomparable high-country scenery along the undeveloped Denali Highway and keeps you off the areas along the southern portion of the Parks Highway that have been spoiled by sprawling development.

Start with the Prince William Sound Loop, but continue north at Glennallen instead of going west toward Anchorage. Drive the Richardson Highway as far as Paxson, and then head west on the Denali Highway to Cantwell, which is just south of Denali National Park. Pick up the Fairbanks Denali Loop there in reverse order, visiting the park and then Fairbanks, and then heading south on the Richardson Highway back to Glennallen. Now turn west, picking up the portion of the Prince William Sound Loop that you missed, and return to Anchorage on the Glenn Highway. Following this loop means you miss Talkeetna and the Denali glacier flight from there and you drive about 70 miles of the Richardson Highway twice (the portion from Glennallen to Paxson). You can find a little more on the Denali Highway in the "Denali Highway (Route 8)" section, later in this chapter.

Driving to the Arctic and Other Extremes

The remote, unpaved highways of the Arctic and Interior offer an opportunity for drivers to venture beyond the beaten path into Alaska's wild country. You won't be as alone as you would if you left the car behind entirely, but you can find many places of extraordinary beauty that are far quieter and more remote than just about anywhere else you can drive in the United States.

However, venturing beyond the beaten path is not for everyone; there's a reason why that other path is so much better beaten. First, you'll have to rent a car from one of only a few agencies that allow their vehicles to be driven on gravel (see Chapter 7). After you have something to drive, you may need to prepare with extra gas, at least one full-size spare, and other emergency equipment (again, see Chapter 7). On the longer routes, you also need food and bedding, because hotels and restaurants can be too far apart to rely on.

When you're on the road, you'll find that conditions are tough and services are crude and infrequent. Even at the end of the highway, there may be little of interest. These roads can be quite scenic, but they don't all go somewhere.

Enough warnings. I personally love driving these remote highways in my own four-wheel-drive vehicle. Doing so is a real adventure, and amazing things sometimes happen. (When I was sleeping in the back of my four-by-four on the side of the Dalton Highway a few years ago, I woke to see a moose mother and calf looking in at me.) If you're prepared and motivated, go for it. The rest of this section provides a preview of what you can expect to see and do on these forgotten highways.

Dalton Highway (Route 11)

Built to haul equipment to the Prudhoe Bay oil fields about 500 miles north of Fairbanks, the Dalton punctures the heart of the wilderness, crossing the Brooks Range and the North Slope to the Arctic Ocean. The scenery is unbearably spectacular, the wildlife is abundant, and the destination is unique. But it takes a full tank of gas between stops, and prudence demands that you take extra gasoline in cans just in case. Services are gritty and rough, and any mishap leaves you far beyond any ordinary kind of assistance. Although the road is excellent in places, it can wash out or become rough and muddy for long stretches.

There are only two substantial stops. Roughly halfway, the **Coldfoot Camp** truck stop at mile 175 (☎ **866-474-3400** or 907-474-3500; www.coldfootcamp.com) has gas pumps, a 24-hour restaurant, and an inn built of leftover construction-camp modular units. The camp also offers minor vehicle repairs, RV hookup, laundry, a post office, a gift shop, and a saloon, and it can help arrange rafting, flightseeing, and shuttles for hiking. Across the road is the **Arctic Interagency Visitor Center** (☎ **907-678-5209** or 907-678-2014), open in the summer daily from 10 a.m. to 10 p.m. The center has exhibits about the North, a theater for nightly educational programs, a trip-planning room, a bookstore, and knowledgeable staff.

Checking road conditions

Sometimes gravel highways are washed out or too rough to use, so checking current conditions on any of the routes described in this chapter before you go is a good idea. Contact the **Alaska Department of Transportation & Public Facilities** at ☎ **511** or visit http://511.alaska.gov. (See Chapter 7 for other important advice.)

The next major stop, another 240 miles up the road, is its end at an oil-field security checkpoint. From here, the only way to the edge of the water, and the true end of the road, is a $37 guided tour offered by the **Arctic Caribou Inn** (☎ **907-659-2368;** www.arcticcaribouinn.com). You need to reserve at least 24 hours in advance to clear security. When you reserve, you must provide your name and an identification number that British Petroleum can use to run a background check before allowing you on the oil field: a driver's license, passport, or Social Security number works.

Denali Highway (Route 8)

I simply couldn't believe my eyes when I first drove this 133-mile gravel road connecting the midpoints of the Parks and Richardson highways. Stunning alpine vistas high in the Alaska Range rival those within Denali National Park, but they're open to all drivers, with a rich network of trails and mountain lakes offering a good chance to see caribou, bear, moose, and waterfowl. The Tangle Lakes area is lovely for canoeing, and there are campgrounds and rough lodges at a few points along the way. The trouble is, the road is not always well-maintained; at best, it's a long, bumpy ride with few services. In winter, the road is not maintained at all and strictly off-limits. For information on outdoor activities on the way, contact the **Bureau of Land Management** Glennallen Field Office (☎ **907-822-3217;** www.blm.gov/ak/st/en/fo/gdo.html).

Edgerton Highway and McCarthy Road (Route 10)

Running east from the Richardson Highway, south of Glennallen, the Edgerton leads to the tiny town of Chitina, where the McCarthy Road, a muddy one-lane route, penetrates Wrangell–St. Elias National Park to historic sites at McCarthy and Kennecott. The road is the rail bed of the Copper River and Northwestern Railroad, which was abandoned in 1938, and it passes over high, narrow trestles. The journey of 93 miles takes 2½ hours, with no services and few views. But the wondrous ghost town of Kennecott is a great destination, with good places to stay and eat. The best choice for lodgings and meals is the **Kennicott Glacier Lodge** (☎ **800-582-5128** or 907-258-2350; www.kennicottlodge.com). If you're not up for the rough drive, the lodge can help you find an easier way to get there, too. See the "Prince William Sound Loop" section, earlier in this chapter, for another lodging and dining option in Copper Center, the jumping-off point for Kennecott.

The Klondike Loop

Following the **Klondike Highway** (Yukon Highway 2), the **Top of the World Highway** (Yukon Route 9), and the **Taylor Highway** (Alaska Route 5), you can make a big detour from the Alaska Highway to see the North's best historic gold-rush treasures in Dawson City and Eagle. Consider this loop when you're driving your own car to Alaska, or when you're in Haines or Skagway and you have a car that you can drive over gravel roads (generally, not allowed with a rental car). From Whitehorse, Yukon, to Tok, Alaska, is 502 miles via the loop, including unpaved roads — that's 127 miles longer than the direct and paved Alaska Highway between the two towns. Completing a circular loop by driving from Skagway to Dawson City to Haines and then taking the Alaska Marine Highway System ferry back to Skagway covers more than 530 miles — a great trip, but if you choose to do it, be prepared to spend a significant amount of your vacation driving.

What you see are historic Dawson City, Yukon, and the fabulous mountain scenery of the Top of the World Highway. Dawson was the destination of the 1898 gold rush; the bed of the nearby Klondike River contained thick veins of gold. The town maintains the look of those bygone days, when it was the second-largest city on the West Coast, after San Francisco. Many buildings were restored by Parks Canada as part of the Klondike National Historic Sites, and there is a lot to learn from the guides and museums. Dawson City also has a nonprofit casino, a center for indigenous culture, and other attractions easily sufficient for two days of touring. The best source of town information is the **Klondike Visitors Association** (☎ 867-993-5575; www.dawsoncity.ca). For information on the historic sites, contact **Parks Canada** (☎ 867-993-7200; http://www.pc.gc.ca/eng/lhn-nhs/yt/dawson/index.aspx). For information on the **Han Nation people** here and their cultural center, call ☎ 867-992-7100.

After passing into the United States on the Top of the World Highway — this border crossing is open only during the day, and only during the summer — a further detour leads north on the Taylor Highway to the forgotten town of Eagle. (Going south on the Taylor leads you back to the Alaska Highway.) The trip to Eagle adds 66 miles each way on a winding, narrow dirt road — allow two hours one-way — but, if you have the time, the destination is more than worth the effort. Eagle is frozen in time, a treasure of a gold-rush river town with many original buildings full of original artifacts from a century ago. It's entirely authentic and noncommercial, with few businesses. The **Eagle Historical Society & Museums** (☎ 907-547-2325; www.eagleak.org) shows off the buildings and several museums of materials. Its three-hour walking tour starts at 9 a.m. daily, Memorial Day through Labor Day, and costs $7. Sadly, a devastating flood in 2009 severely damaged the town and its historic customs house. Huge blocks of ice demolished many buildings and, a year later, the cafe and motel still had not reopened and were unlikely to do so. Even without a motel, you still can camp in Eagle. Call the office of the **Yukon-Charley Rivers National Preserve** (☎ **907-547-2233;** www.nps.gov/yuch) for information on that and other services before your trip.

Steese Highway (Route 6)

The Steese Highway is a mostly unpaved road that climbs the rounded tundra mountains 162 miles east of Fairbanks to the Native village of Circle, on the Yukon River. It's a bumpy route to Bush Alaska, quite scenic, with good hiking trails and river floats along the way. Get details from the **Alaska Public Lands Information Center,** in the Morris Thompson Cultural and Visitors Center, 101 Dunkel St., Fairbanks (☎ **907-459-3730;** www.alaskacenters.gov).

Chapter 19

Denali National Park

. . . .

In This Chapter

▶ Discovering what makes Denali National Park unique
▶ Planning a visit
▶ Going to the park
▶ Getting oriented after you arrive
▶ Riding the shuttle bus into the park's heart
▶ Finding lodging and food

. . . .

Denali National Park is managed the way a park should be: for the animals, not for the cars. That means a visit is different from what you may have experienced at other parks, requiring more planning and plenty of time. You reach the main part of the park by bus, with or without narration from a guide. If you don't want to ride the bus, you shouldn't go to the park. (There are other excellent options *near* the park, covered later in this chapter.) But if you do ride the bus, you stand a good chance of experiencing a remarkable wildlife safari unlike anything else in the national park system.

The brown bears (or grizzlies) here live entirely naturally, but they're used to these buses. I've seen them walk within a yard or two — not like the garbage-eating bears that used to climb on cars in some parks in the Lower 48, but just out of curiosity, like any other wild bear. Elsewhere in Alaska, seeing a bear this way can cost more than $400 per person, because it requires flying out to a remote spot on a small airplane where bears have not been driven away by people. At Denali, it costs around $30. The park handles visitors in a way that prevents them from scaring off the bears. You also have excellent chances of seeing moose, caribou, and Dall sheep, and less often, wolves and beavers.

The shuttle bus has another purpose that is just as important as the scenery and wildlife it enables people to see. It's a mass transportation system to pure wilderness. It allows people without special skills or experience to walk on untracked tundra under an immense sky and to feel what the real world beyond the reach of humanity is like. This is a big step beyond any trail hike. In most of the world, you need plenty of money or muscle to travel to such places. Here, anyone can do it. And when you reach your limit, you merely walk back to the road and catch another bus.

Fair warning for the nervous

Really seeing Denali National Park means taking a long bus ride inside the park. Because the park road is narrow and made of gravel, only lightweight vehicles built on a chassis similar to a school bus's are permitted to drive on it, not highway motor coaches. Different bus types in the park simply have different amenities: The guided tour buses have cloth seats with higher backs and video screens. Despite the extras, however, every bus bounces and rumbles along for a dusty eight hours or more on these trips. Moreover, the buses act like mountain goats on the heights of Polychrome Pass and near Eielson (*aisle*-son) Visitor Center. The road climbs without guardrails and, if you're afraid of heights, this may not be to your liking. If in doubt, I say go: Life is short, and you can put up with a little discomfort to see such a beautiful place. But if you're pretty sure that you wouldn't enjoy it, consider going to Talkeetna instead and seeing the park by air.

The shuttle buses are the secret of Denali National Park, and unfortunately, it remains a real secret. Plenty of visitors leave the park disappointed because they don't get it. They can't separate from their cars, or they don't want to take a long bus ride, or they take a bus but don't understand why. Many gauge their successes purely on whether they see Mount McKinley, a recipe for disappointment, because most days you can't see it from within the park. Some tour companies add to the problem, rushing as many visitors through the park as they can in less than 24 hours — too little time to really appreciate what Denali has to offer.

You need to spend at least two nights at Denali National Park, with one whole, long day devoted to a shuttle-bus outing. Make sure to reserve that bus ticket far in advance and remember that everything else at the park is simply garnish to this main course. Following this advice allows you to have a truly remarkable experience — one you can't have anywhere else.

If the bus doesn't sound like your thing, there are good options in the region besides a traditional visit through the park entrance. South of the park, at Talkeetna, you can do most of the same activities as at the park. The setting is more natural than the ticky-tacky highway strip near the park, you have a better chance of seeing Mount McKinley, and you may even save money. Taking a flight around (or even onto) Mount McKinley with a Talkeetna glacier pilot is an experience not to be missed. Opportunities to view wildlife from the ground and to hike the vast tundra are what you give up by opting to go south of the park.

Planning Ahead

More than at any other national park, making advance reservations is critical to the success of your trip to Denali. That's because the core of the park experience — riding the shuttle bus to see wildlife and access hiking areas — is limited by the number of seats available. For the best bus times, those early in the morning, you must reserve well in advance during the high season. How far in advance varies each year as the number of visitors rises and falls. During some years, reservations have been needed by March for a July visit; other years, a few weeks of advanced planning has been sufficient. Reserving your shuttle tickets and campsites as soon as you know the dates of your visit is safest. The availability of lodgings also tightens in July but isn't as critical. Reserve as far ahead as you can, but don't worry about getting stuck in a dive if you don't get your first choice of rooms or cabins, because there are few really bad places near the park.

To learn more about the park and better plan your visit, contact the **National Park Service** (☎ **907-683-2294;** www.nps.gov/dena).

Reserving shuttle seats and campsites in advance

Sixty-five percent of shuttle-bus seats and all campground sites (except Sanctuary and Igloo) can be booked by phone, fax, or mail; the balance are held back for walk-ins (see the "Reserving when you arrive" section, later in this chapter). Reserve with the park concessionaire, **Doyon/ARAMARK Joint Venture,** 2445 W. Dunlap Ave., Phoenix, AZ 85021 (☎ **800-622-7275** or 907-272-7275; Fax: 907-258-3668; www.reserve denali.com). Reservations open December 1 for the entire upcoming summer. Phone lines are answered daily 7 a.m. to 5 p.m. mountain standard time. (That's two hours later than Alaska standard time, where the hours would be 5 a.m.–3 p.m., and two hours earlier than eastern standard time, where they would be 9 a.m.–7 p.m.)

By using the Internet (www.reservedenali.com), you can reserve any time. You'll need an American Express, Discover Card, MasterCard, or Visa. You also can pay by check if you're reserving by phone, fax, or mail; payment is due within ten days. But this option is not available within 30 days of the date you're arriving. If you use mail or fax, you need to go online or call anyway to get a form.

A **confirmation** will be sent out within two days of your making the reservation. Take it to the reservation desk at the Wilderness Access Center or to the camping check-in desk at the Riley Creek Mercantile, near the Riley Creek Campground, exchanging the confirmation for a camping permit and bus ticket. The center closes at 7 p.m. and the mercantile closes at 11 p.m. If you'll be arriving later, call ☎ **907-683-9274** in advance to avoid losing your site or shuttle seat.

Knowing company names

The main concessionaire at Denali National Park, and your main contact for planning, is **Doyon/ARAMARK Joint Venture,** a partnership of the Doyon Native Corporation of Interior Alaska and ARAMARK, a large national firm. Within the park, Doyon/ARAMARK manages the critical shuttle-bus system, operates most of the tour buses, and takes campground reservations. There are no hotels inside park boundaries. Outside the park, an ARAMARK subsidiary called **Denali Park Resorts** offers river rafting, dinner theater, camping, and several large hotels. You generally have to use Doyon/ARAMARK for services within the park; for services outside the park, you can reserve at the same contact numbers, but you also have many other choices for lodging and activities.

Reserving when you arrive

Internet, mail, and fax orders are not accepted the day before the visit starts (in fact, they're mostly sold out weeks earlier), but walk-in reservations begin two days out, offering the 35 percent of shuttle-bus seats that are held back and any leftover car-camping sites (usually none), and all sites at Sanctuary and Igloo campgrounds. If it's a busy time of year, desirable shuttle reservations are snapped up early in the day. That means you may not get a good reservation for the day of your arrival or even the day after, only the next day after that. That's why it's so critical to reserve in advance.

On the other hand, don't despair if you arrive without reservations — the flow of visitors rises and falls unpredictably. It's perfectly possible that you'll walk into the visitor center and get a shuttle seat on the same day.

Paying entrance fees

Park entrance fees are $20 per vehicle (up to eight passengers) or $10 per person, good for seven days. There is no entrance station to collect the fee, but it's automatically added to your bill when you make shuttle or campground reservations. If you have one of the national passes for senior citizens, those with disabilities, or frequent park users (called the America the Beautiful–National Park and Federal Recreational Lands Pass; see Chapter 11) you can get a refund when you get to the park. Entrance fees are in place year-round and are collected at the Murie Science & Learning Center during winter months.

Reserving rooms

There are no hotels within the park (not counting the remote and expensive wilderness lodges in the Kantishna area), but there are many outside. The park concessionaire operates large hotels outside the park, and you'll find many other choices (see "Where to Stay," later in this chapter).

Packing for the park

The packing advice in Chapter 12 is especially important for a Denali National Park trip. Although it can be warm or even hot, you should prepare for chilly, wet weather at any time of year by taking along waterproof rain gear, fleece jackets, sweaters, and wool socks; a wool hat and gloves can come in handy, too. If you're camping, bring synthetic long underwear and warm sleeping bags. Everyone should bring hiking boots or sturdy walking shoes, binoculars, and insect repellent.

Getting There

For most independent travelers, driving to Denali is the least expensive and most convenient option. However, the train service is famous and you can fly as well.

Driving to the park

A car gives you the greatest flexibility in getting to the park, as well as back and forth to your accommodations, and is the lowest-cost alternative. However, you can only drive 14 miles into the park with a car — not far enough to see much (see "Riding the Shuttle Bus," later in this chapter). The park entrance is 4½ hours (240 miles) from Anchorage, 2½ hours from Fairbanks (120 miles), on a good two-lane road, the George Parks Highway. Talkeetna lies on a 13-mile spur road that branches from the Parks Highway 100 miles north of Anchorage and 140 miles south of the park entrance.

Taking the train

Taking the train to Denali could be a highlight of your trip, a luxurious excursion through unspoiled wilderness fulfilling your fantasies of the golden age of rail. However, it's also a slow and expensive way to go.

The **Alaska Railroad** (☎ **800-544-0552** or 907-265-2494; www.alaska railroad.com) serves Denali daily from both Anchorage and Fairbanks beginning at 8:15 a.m., and arriving at 3:45 p.m. from Anchorage and at 12:15 p.m. from Fairbanks. The two trains cross and arrive back in Anchorage and Fairbanks at 8 p.m. Compared to renting a car and driving, the train adds 70 percent to your travel time and costs far more even for a single passenger. The basic one-way fare from Anchorage to Denali is $146 adults, $73 kids; from Fairbanks to Denali, it's $64 adults, $32 kids. First-class Gold Star seats are $231 and $149, respectively; half-price for kids. The full, daily trains run only from mid-May through mid-September, with somewhat lower fares in the first and last few weeks of the season.

Rail passengers to Denali have extraordinary choices of first-class service. One set of Alaska Railroad locomotives pulls the Alaska Railroad's basic and Gold Star cars, and other sets of cars with full glass domes owned by cruise lines, two of which have seats for independent travelers (although 90 percent or more are filled with their older cruise-ship customers). All passenger seats are assigned on all the cars. You can't walk from one company's cars to another, but you can walk between cars in your own train section.

Princess Tours (☎ 800-426-0500; www.princesslodges.com) has tall, all-dome cars with table seating upstairs and dining rooms downstairs; there's plenty of headroom and large balconies are at the ends of the cars on the lower deck where you can ride outdoors. **Gray Line of Alaska,** part of Holland America (☎ 800-452-1737; www.grayline alaska.com), has newer cars that are even better than Princess's. They're huge and comfortable, with all seats facing forward upstairs — an advantage over table seating — and dining rooms below that are large enough so only two seatings are needed for each meal. (All meals are served at assigned seatings in the cruise-line cars.)

The **Alaska Railroad's** basic service is in traditional railroad cars. They're clean and have big windows and forward-facing seats. Passengers stroll around and dine when and how they please rather than at assigned seatings. Old-fashioned Vista Dome cars provide a limited but adequate number of shared dome seats. The upgrade to Gold Star service buys your own full-dome seat for the entire trip on custom-built double-deck cars like the cruise lines', with a sumptuous white-tablecloth dining room downstairs (eat when you like). These are my favorite cars on the train. They're decorated with original fine art and are very luxurious, but you still know you're on a train, not a cruise ship, and you're not treated as a herd animal. Also, the cars have large outdoor vestibules on the upper deck. The views and open air there are incredible.

If you choose to take the train, especially one of the first-class options, book your accommodations as a package at the same time. This is the only way to get a reasonable price, and it makes the visit much more convenient — the tour operators usually take care of moving you and your luggage around at the park, so you won't need to rent a car or figure out the schedules for the shuttle buses that transport visitors between most of the hotels and the park entrance. Be sure, however, that you allow plenty of time (see the introduction to this chapter). A meaningful visit to Denali is difficult without spending at least two nights and taking an all-day shuttle ride deep into the park.

Taking the bus

Bus and van services bring passengers to Denali and Talkeetna in comfortable vehicles aimed at the tourist market. They're listed in Chapter 7.

Flying to Denali

McKinley Flight Tours (☎ 888-733-2899 or 907-683-2899; www.talkeetna-aero.com) offers the only scheduled air service to Denali from Talkeetna, their base, or from Anchorage, in the summer only. The flights are sold as one-day packages, including flightseeing on the way, a bus tour at the park, a box lunch, and ground transfers. It's the only way to do Denali in a day. The package from Anchorage is $595, from Talkeetna $495, and they go only with at least four passengers.

First to the top

It's the biggest. That's why climbers risk their lives on Mount McKinley. You can see the mountain from Anchorage, more than 100 miles away. On a flight across Alaska, McKinley stands out grandly over waves of other mountains. It's more than a mile taller than the tallest peak in the other 49 states. It's a great white triangle, always covered in snow, tall but also massive and strong.

The first group to try to climb Mount McKinley came in 1903, led by Judge James Wickersham, who also helped explore Washington's Olympic Peninsula before it became a national park. His group made it less than halfway up, but on the trip they found gold in the Kantishna Hills, setting off a small gold rush that led to the first permanent human settlement in the park area. Wickersham later became the Alaska Territory's nonvoting delegate to Congress and introduced the bill that created the national park, but the government was never able to get back land in the Kantishna area from the gold miners. Today that land is the site of wilderness lodges, right in the middle of the park.

On September 27, 1906, renowned world-explorer Dr. Frederick Cook announced to the world by telegraph that he had reached the summit of Mount McKinley after a lightning-fast climb, covering more than 85 miles and 19,000 vertical feet in 13 days with one other man, a blacksmith, at his side. On his return to New York, Cook was lionized as a conquering explorer and published a popular book of his summit diary and photographs.

In 1909, Cook again made history, announcing that he had beat Robert Peary to the North Pole. Both returned to civilization from their competing treks at about the same time. Again, Cook was the toast of the town. His story began to fall apart, however, when his Eskimo companions mentioned that he'd never been out of sight of land. After being paid by Peary to come forward, Cook's McKinley companion also recanted. A year later, Cook's famous summit photograph was re-created — on a peak 19 miles away and 15,000 feet lower than the real summit.

In 1910, disgusted with Cook, four prospectors from Fairbanks took a more Alaskan approach to the task. Without fanfare or special supplies — they carried doughnuts and hot chocolate on their incredible final ascent — they marched up the mountain carrying a large wooden flagpole they could plant on top to prove they'd made it. But on arriving at the summit, they realized that they'd climbed the slightly shorter north peak. Weather closed in, so they set up the pole there and descended without attempting the south peak. Then, when they got back to Fairbanks, no one could see the pole, and they were accused of trying to pull off another hoax.

In 1913, Episcopal archdeacon Hudson Stuck organized the first successful climb to reach the real summit — and reported he saw the pole on the other peak. Harry Karstens led the climb (he would become the park's first superintendent in 1917), and the first person to stand at the summit was an Alaska Native, Walter Harper.

Although McKinley remains one of the world's most difficult climbs, about 10,000 people have made it to the top since Hudson Stuck's party. Since 1980 the number of climbers has boomed. Garbage and human waste disposal are a major problem. One recent June day, 115 climbers made it to the summit. In 1970, only 124 made the attempt all year; now more than 1,200 try to climb the peak each year, with about half making it to the summit. The cold, fast-changing weather is what usually stops people. From late April into early July, climbers fly from the town of Talkeetna to a base camp at an elevation of 7,200 feet on the Kahiltna Glacier. From there, it takes an average of about 18 days to get to the top, through temperatures as cold as –40°F (–40°C).

Climbers lose fingers, toes, and other parts to frostbite, or suffer other, more severe injuries. Some die each year. In 2010, a Belgian climber fell, becoming the 108th to lose his life attempting the mountain. During the season, the park service stations rescue rangers and an emergency medical clinic at the 14,200-foot level of the mountain, and keeps a high-altitude helicopter ready to go after climbers in trouble. In 2002, under pressure from Congress, the park service started charging all climbers a $150-a-head fee, defraying a portion of the rescue costs. The park and the military spend about half a million dollars a year rescuing climbers, and sometimes much more. The cost in lives is high, too. Volunteer rangers and rescuers die as well as climbers. Plane crashes, falls, cold, and altitude all take a toll. Monuments to those who never returned are in the cemetery near the airstrip in Talkeetna.

Getting the Lay of the Land

Denali National Park and Preserve is a huge slice of the Alaska Range that stands like a pivot in the center of Alaska. It encompasses 6 million acres, a roughly triangular polygon about 20 percent larger than Massachusetts. (See the "Denali National Park" map in this chapter.) The Parks Highway provides access to the entrance, which lies at the northeast corner of the park. (Mount McKinley is on the southwest side of the park.) A mile north of the park entrance on the Parks Highway, along a cliff-sided canyon of the Nenana River, hotels and restaurants have developed a seasonal town known locally as **Glitter Gulch,** or for tourism purposes, the **Nenana Canyon Area.** Other services are available at **Carlo Creek,** 14 miles south on the Parks Highway, and in the year-round town of **Healy,** 10 miles north of the park entrance. From the park entrance, a road accessible only by shuttle bus leads west 89 miles through the park, past a series of campgrounds and a visitor center, and ends at the **Kantishna District,** a patch of park-surrounded private land holdings with wilderness lodges. Talkeetna lies well south of the park on the Parks Highway.

Arriving in the Park

Getting situated upon your arrival at Denali depends on whether you go to the park entrance or take the Talkeetna option. I cover each separately.

Arriving at the park's main entrance

On any self-guided trip (as opposed to an escorted tour), your first stop should be the **Wilderness Access Center** on Denali Park Road, a half-mile from the park entrance. At the access center, pick up your previously reserved shuttle tickets and campsite permits, or make new reservations at ticketing desks operated by the concessionaire, Doyon/ARAMARK. Because the park has no entrance station, the center is the place to pick up the park map, a copy of *The Alpenglow* (the park newspaper), and other handouts. The access center is open mid-May through mid-September daily from 5 a.m. to 7 p.m. (reservation desks open at 7 a.m.); it's closed the rest of the year.

The only means of travel into the heart of the park is covered in the "Riding the Shuttle Bus" section, later in this chapter. Getting around the entrance area is easy using your own car or the various free shuttle buses that connect park facilities with nearby hotels. If you choose a hotel that's farther afield, it may have a courtesy van; some are convenient, others are less frequent. Scope out the service when you reserve. Taxis are not a good option because of high rates; however, if you need one, try **Denali Transportation** (☎ 877-683-4765 or 907-683-4765).

Arriving in Talkeetna

The **Denali National Park Talkeetna Ranger Station,** downtown Talkeetna (☎ **907-733-2231;** www.nps.gov/dena), was built to serve climbers — Mount McKinley climbs start with flights from Talkeetna — and it's a fascinating stop for anyone curious about mountaineering. Rangers are on hand to answer questions, too. It's open May through Labor Day daily 8 a.m. to 5:30 p.m.; winter Monday through Friday 8 a.m. to 4:30 p.m. For information about commercial services, stop at the **Talkeetna/Denali Visitors Center,** located in a tiny cabin at Parks Highway and Talkeetna Spur Road and on Main Street (☎ **800-660-2688** or 907-733-2641; www.talkeetnadenali.com). It's open daily 8 a.m. to 8 p.m. in summer and responds to inquiries year-round with free trip-planning help. Keep in mind, though, that it's a business that profits from booking commissions.

You need a car to stay in Talkeetna, far south of the park, unless you're on an escorted tour or staying at a resort lodge that takes care of all your activities and transfers.

Riding the Shuttle Bus

As I explain in the introduction to this chapter, the high point of a trip into Denali National Park is the shuttle-bus ride. It's an inexpensive wildlife safari and an easy way to get to open country for off-trail wilderness hiking — with transportation always close at hand. This section provides tips to help you make the most of your ride.

Denali National Park

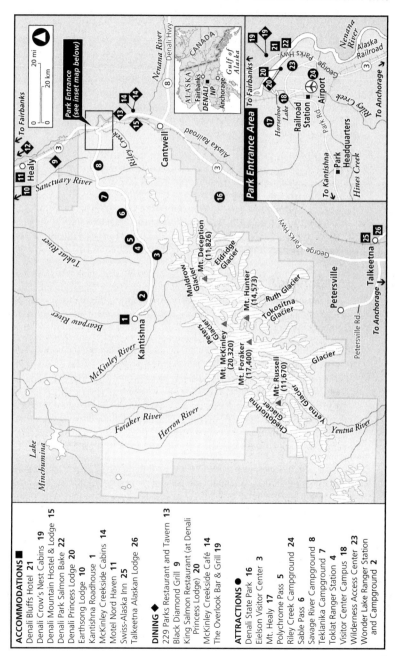

ACCOMMODATIONS ■
Denali Bluffs Hotel **21**
Denali Crow's Nest Cabins **19**
Denali Mountain Hostel & Lodge **15**
Denali Park Salmon Bake **22**
Denali Princess Lodge **20**
Earthsong Lodge **10**
Kantishna Roadhouse **1**
McKinley Creekside Cabins **14**
Motel Nord Haven **11**
Swiss-Alaska Inn **25**
Talkeetna Alaskan Lodge **26**

DINING ◆
229 Parks Restaurant and Tavern **13**
Black Diamond Grill **9**
King Salmon Restaurant (at Denali Princess Lodge) **20**
McKinley Creekside Café **14**
The Overlook Bar & Grill **19**

ATTRACTIONS ●
Denali State Park **16**
Eielson Visitor Center **3**
Mt. Healy **17**
Polychrome Pass **5**
Riley Creek Campground **24**
Sable Pass **6**
Savage River Campground **8**
Teklanika Campground **7**
Toklat Ranger Station **4**
Visitor Center Campus **18**
Wilderness Access Center **23**
Wonder Lake Ranger Station and Campground **2**

McKinley or Denali?

Mount McKinley is so large that Athabascan people speaking different languages had different names for it. The Koyukon, on the north and west, called it Deenaalee, while the Dena'ina and Ahtna on the far side called it Dengadh. In 1839 the name was recorded on a Russian map as Tenada. It often has been translated as "the great one," but a closer translation is the more generic "the high one." The Athabascans never named mountains after people, nor did the Denali area get much use, since fish and game are relatively sparse and the weather extreme, but they did regard high places as spiritually important.

The name McKinley became associated with the mountain in the haphazard way common of the Alaska gold-rush period. A businessman and Princeton graduate named William Dickey was prospecting in the area in 1896, constantly arguing with his traveling companions about the big political issue of the day, the gold monetary standard supported by the Republicans and opposed by the Democrats. The Democratic presidential candidate, William Jennings Bryan, declared at his nomination convention that year, "You shall not crucify mankind upon a cross of gold." It was the gold standard that caused a deflationary economic disaster in those years, which was relieved only by the 1898 Klondike gold rush, which also led to Alaska's settlement. Anyway, when Dickey came out of the Bush, he published a piece about his travels in the *New York Sun* in which he reported his "discovery" and his name for North America's highest mountain—in honor of William McKinley, the Republican candidate who won the White House and was later assassinated. Dickey ultimately admitted he chose the name only to spite his former traveling companions.

Alaskans have long believed McKinley is an irrelevant name for the mountain, especially since it already had a name. In 1975, the state of Alaska petitioned the U.S. Geographic Names Board to change the name back to Denali. In 1980, Congress changed the name of the national park to Denali, but a single congressman from Ohio blocked changing the name of the mountain itself. McKinley was an Ohio governor and congressman before running for president. Rep. Ralph Regula, a Republican who represented McKinley's former seat beginning in 1972, and who even attended William McKinley Law School, found a clever maneuver to keep the name on the mountain. The names board has a policy of taking up no issue that is also being considered by Congress. In each Congress from 1977 onward, Regula introduced a single sentence as a budget amendment or as a standalone bill that states that McKinley is the mountain's permanent name. Although the bill never got so much as a committee hearing, its existence was enough to invoke the board's policy and prevent it from considering the change. In response, Sen. Ted Stevens, R-Alaska, also introduced an annual bill changing the name to Denali, which also went nowhere.

With Regula's retirement and Stevens' defeat in 2008 (he died in a plane crash in 2010), some Alaskans hoped for an end to the stalemate. But a young Ohio Congressman, Rep. Tim Ryan, a Democrat from Niles, Ohio, McKinley's birthplace, took up the cause with the same vigor as the previous generation. Stevens' successor, Democrat Mark Begich, said through staff that he also will keep up the fight. The new blood assures that the issue, entering its fourth decade in Congress, is in no danger of being resolved.

Choosing your bus and destination

Decades ago, when the shuttle-bus system began, the idea was simply to provide inexpensive transportation into the park. That philosophy still prevails on the main shuttle fleet: Basic buses traverse the road and stop for wildlife-viewing, but they don't provide food or formal narration (although some drivers do a terrific job of their own narration). Passengers get on or off wherever they please for hiking or simply to enjoy the countryside. Now, however, options for those who want a tour rather than transportation are also available. The tour buses are more comfortable and have planned narration, but they don't let passengers on and off for hiking.

Shuttle-bus options

Shuttle buses run frequently all day, making wildlife sightings and letting off park visitors along the park road. Shuttle tickets designate the farthest you plan to go, but you don't have to go to the end of the line. Any bus can bring you back. The largest number of buses turns around at the **Eielson Visitor Center,** 66 miles into the park. Other choices are the shorter ride to the **Toklat** (*toe*-klat) **River,** 53 miles into the park, or a longer journey to **Wonder Lake** at 86 miles, or Kantishna, which is farthest from the park entrance at 89 miles.

The Eielson option makes the most sense, balancing a desire to see scenery and wildlife with the need to preserve your rear end from too much sitting, while also saving time to get out and hike. That trip takes about eight hours, and the fare is $31 for adults, $16 for kids 15 to 17, and free for kids 14 and under. No extra fee is charged for getting off the bus at almost any spot of your choosing for a hike or picnic and then flagging down the next bus to travel onward. Bring your own food.

Narrated bus tours

All narrated tours use the same lightweight buses as the shuttles, which are similar to school buses but sized and outfitted for adult riders. However, the Doyon/ARAMARK tour buses have higher-backed cloth seats and those on the Tundra Wildlife Tour include closed-circuit video that allows the driver to zoom in on distant wildlife. However, none of the narrated tours allows you to get off on your own.

- ✔ The **Natural History Tour** ($62 adults, $31 kids 14 and under) travels only 17 miles down the park road, but also includes a film, a history talk at a cabin, and a presentation by an Alaska Native, which could include singing, storytelling, or information about living off the land.

- ✔ The **Tundra Wilderness Tour** ($104 adults, $52 kids 14 and under) travels to Toklat when Mount McKinley is hidden by clouds, and 8 miles farther, to Stony Hill, when McKinley is visible. Programmed commentary provides background on what you're seeing. Food is provided, but you can't get off the bus along the way (that's the fatal flaw, in my opinion).

✔ **Kantishna Wilderness Trails** (☎ 800-230-7275 or 907-683-1475; www.seedenali.com), **Denali Backcountry Tours** (☎ 888-560-2489), and Doyon/ARAMARK's **Kantishna Experience** all cover the entire park road with a 190-mile, 13-hour marathon that includes lunch and activities at the halfway mark at the Kantishna area (private land within the park). The cost is $135 to $169. Doyon/ARAMARK offers a half-off discount for kids, but no kid I know can stay sane on a 13-hour bus ride. The tours differ slightly, so check out each one before making a decision.

Getting ready

Reserve your shuttle ticket for as early as you can stand to get up in the morning. This strategy allows more time for day hikes and enhances your chances of seeing the mountain and wildlife. During peak season, the first bus leaves the visitor center at 5:30 a.m. and then roughly every 15 to 30 minutes in the morning. A few buses leave in the afternoon, mostly to pick up stragglers on the way back, returning late under the midnight sun.

Here's a checklist for preparing the night before you catch your morning shuttle bus:

✔ Lunch (several restaurants pack them) and plenty of water

✔ Sturdy walking shoes and layers of warm and lighter clothing with rain gear packed

✔ Binoculars or a spotting scope

✔ Insect repellent

✔ Camera with long lens (optional)

✔ A copy of the mile-by-mile *Denali Road Guide,* available inexpensively at the park bookstores (optional)

✔ For extensive hiking, a detailed topographic map ($10 at the visitor center) and a compass (not necessary if you're just walking a mile or two off the road)

Spotting wildlife on your way

The shuttle bus has no reserved seats, but if you arrive early, you can find a place on the left side, which has the best views on the way out. Bus passengers often see grizzly bears, caribou, Dall sheep, moose, and occasionally wolves. (It's all up to chance, though — some see no wildlife at all.) Calling out whenever you spot any wildlife is common courtesy on the shuttle bus so that others can see it, too. The driver stops the bus and everyone rushes to your side of the bus. After you've had a look, give someone else a chance to look out your window or to take a picture. Try to be quiet and don't stick anything outside the bus — that may scare away the animals.

Staying sane in the park with kids

Denali can be a challenge for families. Young children tend to go nuts when subjected to an eight-hour bus ride, and they aren't often able to pick out the wildlife. The park isn't like a zoo, and most animals blend in with their surroundings. Likewise, even older kids have a hard time keeping their patience on these trips, as do many adults. The best solution: Get off the bus along the route and turn your trip into a romp in the heather. After you've had a chance to revive, catch the next bus. *Remember:* Just because you buy a ticket to a certain turnaround point doesn't mean that you have to go that far. Keep in mind, too, that if your child normally needs a car seat, you must bring it along on the bus.

Hiking and Backpacking from the Shuttle Bus

Walking away from the road takes a little courage, but doing so may be the best chance you ever have for experiencing a place like this on your own. The major risks of hiking are avoidable. It can get cold and wet in midsummer, so you need to be prepared with layers of warm, water-proof clothing to avoid the spiraling chill of hypothermia. The rivers are dangerous because of their fast-flowing icy-cold water. Experienced backcountry trekkers plan their routes to avoid crossing sizable rivers. (See Chapter 9 for other health and safety tips.)

Day hikes by bus

For a first foray beyond the trails, consider joining one of the hikes guided by a park ranger. One or two daily **Discovery Hikes** take off from spots along the park road. One hike goes well inside the park, toward the Eielson Visitor Center, and the other stays closer to the entrance end of the park. A ranger leads only 11 hikers while teaching about the nature of the surrounding terrain. Plan for a 5- to 11-hour day, including the shuttle ride. Actual hiking time is about four hours. The hikes generally aren't too strenuous for families with school-age kids, but inquiring about how steep the hike will be is wise if you have any doubts. Hikes cost no more than the price of your shuttle ticket. You need to wear hiking shoes or boots and bring food, water, and rain gear. Reserve a place in advance, because hikes fill up in July, and you'll need to know when and where to catch special buses.

Here are some good hiking areas along the park road shuttle-bus ride by milepost. You don't need a permit for any day hike:

- ✔ **Mile 34:** Manageable climbs on Igloo, Cathedral, and Sable mountains take off along the road from Igloo Creek to Sable Pass.

- ✔ **Mile 53:** The bed of the Toklat River is a flat plain of gravel with easy walking. The glaciers that feed the river are 10 miles upstream.

> ✔ **Mile 58:** Highway Pass is the highest point on the road. In good weather, dramatic views of Mount McKinley start here. The alpine tundra from here is inviting for walking, but beware of holes that can turn an ankle.

Backpacking

Imagine backpacking alone in your own area of wilderness, without trails, limits, or the chance of seeing other people. Retracing your route to get back to the bus isn't necessary: Anywhere you meet the 91-mile Denali Park Road, you can catch a bus back to the world of people. Any experienced backpacker should consider a backcountry trek at Denali.

There are planning issues and outdoor risks in this open country that make setting up a trip more challenging than on an ordinary trail. (This section is about **overnight trips,** not day hikes; going for the day requires little planning and no permits.) You need to be able to find your own way without a path, know what hazards to avoid (such as crossing rivers or climbing on slippery, loose rock), and take care of yourself without expecting a lot of other people to come along to help.

Permits for wilderness overnights in the park are issued at the **Backcountry Information Center** near the Wilderness Access Center. Although you can prepare in advance for a trek, you can't choose a backcountry unit to explore before you arrive at the information center and find out what's available. That means you must be flexible about where you're going and what kind of terrain you'll travel.

Information on what's available and a map of the units are posted at the information center. Hikers can reserve permits for overnight backpacking only two days in advance; although you're unlikely to get one for the day you arrive, you can reserve permits for continuation of your trip for up to 14 days at the same time. The first night of a trip is the hard one to get — for one thing, you can reserve only units that are contiguous to the park road for the first night — but after that, each night gets progressively easier. Rangers are available to help you through the process.

Before you go, buy the ***Denali National Park and Preserve* topographical map,** published by Trails Illustrated, available for $12 from Alaska Geographic (☎ **907-274-8440;** www.alaskageographic.org). You'll also want a copy of the book ***Backcountry Companion,*** which describes conditions and routes in each area and is published and sold by Alaska Geographic. You'll find both for sale at the visitor centers.

Great Activities off the Bus

A bus ride into the park is the main event, but that's not the only thing to do at Denali. There are some fun and interesting activities near the park entrance that you can get to without riding on the bus.

Day-hiking near the park entrance

The Park Road is controlled by a checkpoint beyond which only buses and bicycles can travel; short of that point, in the zone known as the entrance area or "frontcountry" you can explore without worrying about schedules or fares. The Savage River Day-Use Area, at mile 14, is just short of the checkpoint. It has a mile-long loop trail and longer informal routes for great alpine tundra hiking. You can drive there or take a free shuttle.

There are several trails near the visitor facilities at the park entrance, mostly weaving through the boreal forest around small lakes. Only one strenuous trail starts there, but it's a gem. The steep and spectacular hike to the **Mount Healy overlook** is a 5-mile round-trip. The trail breaks through the tree line to slopes of tundra and rock outcroppings, where you can see far across the Alaska Range and its foothills in the distance. Several easy nature trails teach about history and natural history of the area. Pick up explanatory materials at the visitor centers.

Flightseeing

Getting a good, close look at Mount McKinley is best accomplished by air. Frequently, you can see McKinley from above the clouds when you can't see it from the ground. These flights take off from the park entrance, from Talkeetna, or from Anchorage (see Chapter 14).

From the park entrance

Small planes and helicopters fly from the park airstrip, private heliports and airstrips along the Parks Highway, and the Healy airstrip. **Denali Air** (☎ 907-683-2261; www.denaliair.com) has an office in Glitter Gulch, and flight operations at mile 229.5 of the Parks Highway. An hour-long flight going within a mile of the mountain costs $350 for adults, $175 for kids ages 2 to 12, free for kids 1 and under. **Era Helicopters** (☎ 800-843-1947 or 907-683-2574; www.eraflightseeing.com) has 50-minute flights for $335, including van pickup from the hotels. Their heli-hikes land for a four-hour walk on a mountain ridgeline, with the degree of difficulty tailored to customers' abilities, for $465. A two-hour outing that includes a 20-minute glacier landing costs $435.

From Talkeetna

McKinley climbs typically begin with flights from Talkeetna to the 7,200-ft. level of the **Kahiltna Glacier.** You can use the same flight services to see the mountain and even land on it, the most dramatic and memorable experience available to the typical tourist in Alaska. Several operators with plenty of experience offer flights. The least expensive excursions cost about $190, approaching McKinley's south face without landing. If possible, however, and if the weather is good, buy an extended tour that circles the entire mountain and flies over its glaciers, for $235 to $375 per person. Best of all, you can arrange a landing on the mountain itself, just as the climbers do. The Don Sheldon Amphitheater on the Ruth

Glacier is a stunning spot high on McKinley; only after you stand there do you realize the incredible scale of what you've seen from above. Landings are usually treated as add-ons to the tours mentioned here, for an additional price of around $75 to $85 per person, plus the $10 park entrance fee.

Try any of these glacier-flight operations that operate out of the Talkeetna airport: **Talkeetna Air Taxi** (☎ 800-533-2219; www.talkeetnaair.com), **McKinley Flight Tours** (☎ 888-733-2899; www.talkeetnaaero.com), or **K2 Aviation** (☎ 800-764-2291 or 907-733-2291; www.flyk2.com). It's wise to reserve at least a couple days ahead and to go early in the morning, before the daily cloud buildup.

Rafting

Rafting on the **Nenana River,** which borders the park along the Parks Highway, is fun and popular. Several commercial guides float two stretches of the river: the upper portion, where the water is smoother and the guides explain passing scenery; and the lower portion, where the river roars through the rock-walled Nenana Canyon, and rafts take on huge splashes of silty, glacial water through class III and IV rapids. Each session takes 2 to 2½ hours, including safety briefings, suiting up, and riding to and from the put-in and takeout points. Prices vary from $82 to $112 for adults, with discounts for kids that range from $10 off to half-price. I've been impressed by **Denali Outdoor Center** (☎ 888-303-1925 or 907-683-1925; www.denalioutdoorcenter.com), which offers rafting trips and instruction in river techniques. It's located 2½ miles north of the park entrance at Otto Lake Road, at mile 247 of the Parks Highway, and also has an office right in Glitter Gulch. Whoever you go with, plan for a shower afterward — the silt in the river water will stick to your skin and hair.

Talkeetna River Guides, on Main Street in Talkeetna (☎ 800-353-2677; www.talkeetnariverguides.com), offers a two-hour wildlife river-rafting tour, without white water, over 9 miles of the Talkeetna River three times a day for $79 adults, $59 kids 10 and under. They also offer longer outfitted expeditions.

Ranger programs

Check the park newspaper, *The Alpenglow,* for ranger talks and slide shows that happen as often as several times a day in the frontcountry area (near the entrance) and at the Riley Creek, Savage River, and Teklanika campgrounds. A daily demonstration of the park's sled-dog teams is a highlight at the kennels. I mention ranger-led hikes in the "Day hikes by bus" section, earlier in this chapter.

Visiting educational centers

The 14,000-sq.-ft. **Denali Visitor Center** introduces the park and its connections to the rest of the world in a spectacular building. Life-size models of cranes overhead lead to an enormous mural, 60 x 28 ft. in size, showing the landscape types found at the park. The carpet simulates a flowing river of gray and brown, making a path to an exhibit area with recreations of Denali wildlife, including a full-scale moose stepping through deep snow. You'll also find exhibits on the Athabascan people, mining, tourism, and scientific research. On the upper floor, a large topographic model of the park demonstrates the arbitrary nature of its boundaries and another exhibit shows the six-continent routes of migratory birds found at Denali. An award-winning orientation film, *Heartbeats of Denali,* lasts 18 minutes. Summer hours are daily 8 a.m. to 6 p.m.; the center is closed in the winter.

Also near the park entrance, the **Murie Science & Learning Center** (**☎ 866-683-1269** or 907-683-1269; www.murieslc.org) supports research and offers programs about the park. It's located about a mile in along the park road on the right side. The lobby houses changing science exhibits. A variety of organizations participate in programming, with evening lectures, morning walk-in science presentations, youth camps, and natural history field seminars for adults and for families with older or younger kids. Three-day courses are around $320 per person. Check topics and register well in advance on the Web site. The center is open in the summer daily 9:30 a.m. to 5 p.m., winter daily 9 a.m. to 4 p.m.

Where to Stay

At Denali, how much you pay for your room depends on how far from the park entrance you stay. The roadside Glitter Gulch area near the park entrance is dominated by large hotels with rack rates well over $200 a night. Most guests don't pay that much, however, because the hotels are owned by cruise lines or their vendors, and generally are filled with guests on escorted package tours. Bargain hunters can sometimes nab discounted rooms or off-season sales at the large hotels, but I prefer to concentrate on smaller, locally owned places catering primarily to independent travelers. These usually have more character and more reliably affordable rates, and most are located 14 miles south of the park in Carlo Creek or 10 miles north in Healy.

In this section, I also include lodgings in Talkeetna, more than two hours south of the park. However, stay there only if you plan to spend all your time in that area and will enter the park itself by air, if at all.

The top hotels and lodges

Denali Crow's Nest
$$$$ Glitter Gulch

Perched in five tiers on the side of Sugarloaf Mountain looking down on Horseshoe Lake and the other, larger hotels, these cabins are roomy and comfortable, especially those on the 100 and 200 level. A log cabin and the warmth of the Crofoot family seem more Alaskan than the modern, standard rooms that have filled the canyon, and the rates are reasonable for the area (believe it or not). They offer a tour desk and courtesy van and there is a hot tub on the deck. You spend a lot of time climbing stairs, however; and the rooms have shower enclosures, not tubs. The restaurant, the **Overlook Bar & Grill,** is recommended separately under "Where to Dine," later in this chapter.

See map p. 309. Mile 238.5, Parks Highway, Denali National Park. ☎ **888-917-8130** *or 907-683-2723. Fax: 907-683-2323. www.denalicrowsnest.com. Rack rates: High season $189 cabin for two; extra person 12 and over $20. MC, V.*

EarthSong Lodge
$$$–$$$$ Healy

These solid-log buildings on the windy open tundra, with sweeping views of the Alaska Range, are well off the beaten path, 17 miles north of Denali National Park and 4 miles down the Stampede Trail Road, but it's worth the trip to stay in an authentically Alaskan lodge hosted by year-round residents Jon and Karin Nierenberg. One- and two-bedroom cabins have quilts on the beds and other cozy features. The lodge common rooms include a library and living room, and there's a coffeehouse, **Henry's,** serving breakfast and dinner and packing sack lunches. In the winter, the lodge operates as the dog-sledding concessionaire for Denali National Park; in the summer, you can tour the kennel.

See map p. 309. Stampede Trail, off the Parks Highway at mile 251, Healy. ☎ **907-683-2863.** *Fax: 907-683-2868. www.earthsonglodge.com. Rack rates: Summer $155–$195 double; $10 each additional person 18 and over, $5 kids 12–17, free for kids 11 and under. MC, V.*

Kantishna Roadhouse
$$$$$ Kantishna

This property of many buildings along Moose Creek in the old Kantishna Mining District trades on both the mining history and outdoor opportunities of the area. Some rooms are large and luxurious, while others are in smaller single cabins with lofts. The log central lodge has an attractive lobby with people coming and going — it's got more of a hotel feel and may be more attractive to an older, less active set or to families than the other lodges in the Kantishna District. It also has a bar. Rates include guided hikes, fishing, interpretive programs, biking, gold panning, and a daily sled-dog demonstration. ***Note:*** They charge a baggage fee of $50 for each piece beyond one checked and one carry-on piece on the bus to the lodge.

See map p. 309. Kantishna District, Denali National Park. ☎ **800-942-7420** *or 907-683-1475. Fax: 907-683-1449 summer, 907-459-2160 winter. www.seedenali.com. Rack rates: $415 per person per night double occupancy, $300 kids 3–11; extra person $330. Rates include all meals, guided activities, and transportation from the park entrance. Two-night minimum. AE, DISC, MC, V.*

McKinley Creekside Cabins
$$$–$$$$ Carlo Creek

These cozy cabins are right by the highway and the pleasant cafe of the same name (covered in "Where to Dine," later in this chapter), but you'd never know it thanks to how they're situated in the woods on the banks of Carlo Creek. The cabins' rustic decoration, in subdued tones, includes log bedposts made by a local craftsman. They have decks and nice private bathrooms, and some have refrigerators and microwaves. Family units sleep up to six, a real money saver. There are communal spots for visiting around barbecues, horseshoes, and fire pits, some at the creek's edge. Cabins have Wi-Fi, but no TV or telephone.

See map p. 309. Mile 224, Parks Highway, Denali National Park. ☎ **888-533-6254** *or 907-683-2277.* www.mckinleycabins.com. *Rack rate: High season $139–$199 cabin for up to four people, off season $99–$149 cabin for up to four people; extra person $10. DISC, MC, V. Closed Oct–Apr.*

Motel Nord Haven
$$$ Healy

This fresh little gray hotel with a red roof has large, immaculate rooms, each with one or two queen-size beds. They're equal to the best standard rooms in the Denali Park area and a lot less expensive. Bill and Patsy Nordmark offer free continental breakfast in the summer, and newspapers, coffee, tea, hot chocolate, free Wi-Fi and a guest computer in a common area, and a sitting room with a collection of Alaska books. The rooms, decorated with Alaska art and oak trim, all have interior entrances and have been smoke-free since their construction. Up to four people can stay in the rooms with two beds for the price of a double. There are three kitchenette units. The Nordmarks pack sack lunches for $10.

See map p. 309. Mile 249.5, Parks Highway, Healy. ☎ **800-683-4501** *or 907-683-4500. Fax: 907-683-4503.* www.motelnordhaven.com. *Rack rates: Summer $138–$164 double, spring and fall $94–$108 double, winter $80–$85 double. AE, DISC, MC, V.*

Talkeetna Alaskan Lodge
$$$$$ Talkeetna

The Cook Inlet Region Native corporation spared no expense building this magnificent hotel of big timbers and river rock 2 miles from Talkeetna, but it's not a gaudy showplace. Trim of regionally harvested birch finishes rooms and hallways in understated geometric designs, hung with Native art. Because the hotel sits atop a high river bluff, views from common rooms and many guest rooms take in a broad-canvas masterpiece of the Alaska Range, with McKinley towering in the center. Rooms in the main building are somewhat larger and have either one king- or two queen-size beds, and the hallways connect to several sumptuous lobbies with reading areas. As much as I like the hotel, however, the rates are high. (A simple, family Talkeetna motel, the Swiss-Alaska Inn, is listed in the "Runner-up accommodations" section, next.)

See map p. 309. Mile 12.5, Talkeetna Spur Road, Talkeetna. ☎ **888-959-9590** *or 907-265-4501 reservations, 907-733-9500 lodge. Fax: 907-733-9545.* www.talkeetna lodge.com. *Rack rates: Summer $279–$309 double, off season $189–$209 double; extra person 11 and over $15. AE, DISC, MC, V. Closed Oct–Apr.*

Runner-up accommodations

Denali Bluffs Hotel

$$$$$ Glitter Gulch Light, tastefully decorated standard rooms overlook the Nenana Canyon from above. *See map p. 309. Mile 238.4, Parks Highway, Glitter Gulch.* ☎ **907-683-8500.** www.denalialaska.com.

Denali Mountain Morning Hostel

$ Carlo Creek Guests in cozy dormitory accommodations and private cabins share a bathhouse and kitchen. Restaurants are nearby and the lodge has a free shuttle to the park. *See map p. 309. Mile 224.1, Parks Highway, Denali National Park.* ☎ **907-683-7503.** www.hostelalaska.com.

Swiss-Alaska Inn

$$ Talkeetna Guests are made to feel like old friends in the simple rooms of this family business. *See map p. 309. F Street, near the boat launch, Talkeetna.* ☎ **907-733-2424.** *Fax: 907-733-2425.* www.swissalaska.com.

Campgrounds

The park has six campgrounds, four of which — Riley Creek, Savage River, Teklanika, and Wonder Lake — have flush toilets and sites you can reserve in advance. Of these four, you can drive to only two: Riley Creek and Savage River. Teklanika and Wonder Lake are in the backcountry, accessible along the park road by the shuttle-bus system. One exception: You can drive to Teklanika if you stay three days and don't move your vehicle during that time. Use the reservation system described in the "Reserving shuttle seats and campsites in advance" section, earlier in this chapter. Two campgrounds don't take reservations, Igloo and Sanctuary River; both are tiny, primitive campgrounds intended primarily for backpackers getting ready for a trek.

Campground fees are $16 to $28 per night for car or RV camping, $14 for walk-in tent camping sites at Riley Creek Campground, and $9 at Sanctuary and Igloo campgrounds. A reservation fee of $4 to $5 is charged for the first night of stays in campgrounds other than Riley Creek and Savage River, and you need a camper bus ticket, for around $30, to get to some campgrounds.

Other than Riley Creek and Savage River, these campgrounds aren't the car-camping you may be used to. You'll be away from any services or even easy communication, so you must bring everything that you need.

✔ **Riley Creek:** This large campground is near the park entrance, with easy access to a store, showers, laundry, and so on. 147 sites.

✔ **Savage River:** A beautiful campground with great tundra views and hiking routes, Savage River is the only one you can readily drive to that's away from the entrance (13 miles, to be exact). 33 sites.

✔ **Teklanika River:** When you wake up here close to the heart of the park, you cut the time you have to spend on the bus on daily explorations. Once you park a vehicle for a three-night minimum stay, you must get around by bus. Teklanika River is 29 miles from the entrance. 53 sites.

✔ **Wonder Lake:** After six hours to cover 85 miles on the bus, you reach this coveted campground by a placid lake near the foot of Mount McKinley. The mosquitoes can be horrendous, but the views are incomparable. Only tents are permitted and no campfires are allowed. 28 sites.

Where to Dine

I list a range of restaurants matching locations with your lodgings (in Talkeetna, try the hotels' own restaurants). If you don't have a car, don't try dining in areas other than the one where you're staying. Except as noted, restaurants are closed during the off season.

Black Diamond Grill
$$–$$$ Healy GRILL

A unique 9-hole golf course lies amid the mountains and rolling taiga north of the park at a center of activities, including all-terrain vehicle tours, GPS treasure hunts, mini-golf, and covered wagon rides with full-service camp-style meals. The associated restaurant produces excellent meals from a menu mostly influenced by northern Italian cookery. For lunch, sandwich choices include a pesto chicken hoagie for $7.50, and for dinner there is halibut in parchment with fresh rosemary and garlic for $20. Although not as perfect as at the best restaurants in Anchorage, the cuisine is memorable and satisfying. The dining room is light and cheery, with pine furniture and flowers on the table.

See map p. 309. Mile 247, Parks Highway, Healy. Take the highway north 10 miles, then turn left at Otto Lake Road. ☎ **907-683-4653.** *Main courses: $7.50–$9 lunch, $14–$24 dinner. AE, DISC, MC, V. Open: Daily 7 a.m.–11 p.m.*

Denali Park Salmon Bake
$–$$$ Glitter Gulch GRILL

You can't miss the homemade highway frontage of this hip nightspot and all-day/all-night eatery. Although extremely casual, the staff is friendly, led by owners who are involved in the community. They'll even come to pick you up and drive you back to your hotel. It's fun and a hot spot for live music as well. Check the Web site for a calendar of who's playing and the amount of the cover charge. The food is tasty and reasonably priced, including Tex-Mex selections, crab cakes, and pulled-pork sandwiches, in addition to the grilled salmon. They also rent inexpensive accommodations.

See map p. 309. Mile 238.5, Parks Highway, Glitter Gulch. ☎ **907-683-2733.** www. denaliparksalmonbake.com. *Main courses: $8–$37. AE, DISC, MC, V. Open: Daily 7 a.m. to midnight.*

King Salmon Restaurant
$$$–$$$$$ Glitter Gulch   SEAFOOD

This is a terrific place for a special night of dining out right near the park. First, there's the waiting area with a cozy fireplace. Next, the dining room, perched on the edge of the Nenana Canyon, where you can watch rafters float by during your meal. Then there's the food and service, which are up to Princess Tours' excellent standards — steak and salmon, the usual choices for Alaska tourists — prepared expertly. For something a bit more casual, the **Basecamp Bistro** (Open: Daily 11 a.m.–11 p.m.) is in the same building.

See map p. 309. In the Denali Princess Lodge, mile 238.5, Parks Highway, Glitter Gulch. ☎ **907-683-2282.** *Reservations recommended. Main courses: $20–$40 dinner. AE, DC, DISC, MC, V. Open: Daily 6–11 a.m., 11:30 a.m.–3 p.m., and 4:30–10 p.m.*

McKinley Creekside Cafe
$–$$$ Carlo Creek   STEAK/SEAFOOD/SANDWICHES

This friendly spot in the Carlo Creek area, south of the park, is a favorite of the locals. You can dine on steak or baked salmon with brown sugar, apples, and toasted almonds for around $20, or order a burger for around $9. The food is consistently good, including breakfast, and craft brews and wine are served. There is a playground outside and a kids' menu. They also pack substantial sack lunches for the park shuttle-bus ride.

See map p. 309. Mile 224, Parks Highway, Carlo Creek. ☎ **888-333-6254** *or 907-683-2277.* www.mckinleycabins.com. *Main courses: $6–$10 lunch, $8–$21 dinner. DISC, MC, V. Open: Daily 6 a.m.–10 p.m.*

Overlook Bar & Grill
$$$–$$$$$ Glitter Gulch   GRILL

This fun, noisy place has the feel of a classic bar and grill, with a vaulted ceiling of rough-cut lumber and a spectacular view of the Nenana Canyon. A huge variety of craft beers is available, with several on tap. There are two dining rooms, one with the bar, and another, behind a glass partition, which is quieter and has tablecloths. Call ☎ **907-683-2723** for courtesy transportation from all area hotels.

See map p. 309. Mile 238.5, Parks Highway (up the hill above the Nenana Canyon area), Glitter Gulch. ☎ **907-683-2641.** *Main courses: $9–$15 lunch, $11–$44 dinner. MC, V. Open: Daily 11 a.m.–11 p.m., bar until 1 a.m.*

Denali dinner theater

Cabin Nite Dinner Theater, at the **McKinley Chalet Resorts** (☎ **800-276-7234** or 907-683-8200), is a professionally produced musical revue about a gold-rush-era woman who ran a roadhouse in Kantishna. You can buy the $62 tickets (half-price for kids 2–12) virtually anywhere in the area. The actors sing throughout the evening, staying in character to serve big platters of food to diners sitting at long tables, and doing a good job of building a rowdy, happy atmosphere for adults and kids. Shows happen daily at 5:30 and 8:30 p.m.

229 Parks Restaurant & Tavern
$$$–$$$$$ **South of the Park   international**

The name comes from the milepost, which puts the restaurant in a quiet area about 8 miles south of the park entrance, where it occupies a beautiful post-and-beam building. Year-round residents Laura and Land Cole own the restaurant — the best in the area. Laura is a professionally trained chef and veteran of Alaska's best dining rooms. Whenever possible, she uses organic ingredients and local produce. The menu changes daily and has included main-course items such as tenderloin filet, lemon pasta with asparagus, venison chops, and, of course, salmon. A sweet-potato soup with king crab meat is fabulous. The appetizer list is long and interesting, including spring rolls second to none. Breakfast is coffeehouse fare, such as quiche, granola, and fruit. Locals keep the place busy even on winter weekends, but the restaurant closes at 1 p.m. on Sundays in the winter so everyone in the community can go play hockey on Deneki Lakes.

See map p. 309. Mile 229, Parks Highway, Denali National Park. ☎ **907-683-2567.** *www.229parks.com. Reservations not accepted. Main courses: $18–$33 dinner. MC, V. Open: Summer Tues–Sun 7–11 a.m. and 5–10 p.m.; winter Fri–Sat 9 a.m.–9 p.m., Sun 9 a.m.–1 p.m. (call ahead in winter for varying closures).*

Part V
Southeast Alaska

The 5th Wave   By Rich Tennant

WHALE-WATCHING IN JUNEAU

@RICHTENNANT

WHALE WATCH CAFE

"Would you like to watch the whale a little longer, sir,
or should I ask him to leave?"

In this part . . .

Southeast Alaska is a world apart, a realm of water and mountains where charming old towns are tucked in wherever they fit among the peaks, bears, and big rain-forest trees. Traveling is made more complicated and yet more interesting by the region's lack of highways — getting from town to town requires you to board a boat or plane. Juneau, the state capital and Alaska's third-largest city, is the hub for this area's transportation network. It's also a delightful place to visit, with excellent access to outdoor activities. Skagway, north of Juneau, is a center of gold-rush history. Sitka is full of charm and the history of Russian America and has a spectacular outdoor setting.

Chapter 20

Juneau

- -

In This Chapter

▶ Basing yourself in Juneau

▶ Getting to the only capital city you can't reach by road

▶ Finding the best places to sleep and eat

▶ Enjoying Juneau's activities — indoors and out

▶ Planning a Juneau itinerary

- -

*J*uneau stands out as a terrific town to visit. You get an inkling of that as your plane glides toward the airport on Gastineau Channel and you spot tall mountains looming above, grassy wetlands and towering conifers below, and a great big glacier nearby that comes right up to a suburban neighborhood. The taxi ride downtown is a scenic treat, traveling at the base of mountains and along a coastal refuge full of eagles. Downtown you'll find steep, narrow streets sheltered by awnings attached to charmingly weathered little buildings. It looks like a thriving old-time downtown straight out of a movie, but in Juneau's case it's real. And at the end of the streets, within walking distance, hiking trails begin, climbing among moss-hung trees.

Few other towns in Alaska can justify a weeklong visit all by themselves, but in Juneau, a long stay makes sense, using the city as a hub for exploring the Southeast region. You'll see plenty in town and on the short road network, and the variety of outdoor activities you can do from here is unmatched anywhere in the state. Next, you can explore the fascinating and splendid options within a day of here: the gold-rush historical sites of Skagway, the whales and glaciers of Glacier Bay National Park or Tracy Arm, or the abundant brown bear of Admiralty Island. Or go dog-mushing at the peak of summer on a glacier high above the city. By the end of your week, Juneau may be one of your favorite places. It's certainly one of mine.

 That's my prediction, anyway, but Juneau has a way of confounding predictions. The climate that produces those lush forests also produces torrential rains, rotten visibility, and canceled flights. When you're unlucky with the weather, a week in Juneau can make you feel like moss is growing between your toes. Even during the summer, it can rain for days, staying as cool and damp as winter in other places. In the fall, the rains here are biblical in proportion. Although rainy days do have a special charm here, especially when the soft light glows on rain-streaked facades and mist drifts among moss-shrouded branches, a little of that goes a long way.

Getting There

Juneau is a transportation hub without any road connection. Air and water are the only ways of getting there.

Arriving by air

Jet service is available only from **Alaska Airlines** (☎ 800-252-7522; www.alaskaair.com), with several daily nonstop flights from Seattle and Anchorage, and from the smaller Southeast Alaska towns. Many of the region's commuter and air-taxi operators also maintain desks at the airport and have flights out of Juneau; these include **Wings of Alaska** (☎ 907-789-0790; www.ichoosewings.com).

Arriving by ferry

All the mainline ferries of Southeast's **Alaska Marine Highway System** (☎ 800-642-0066; www.ferryalaska.com) stop at the terminal in Auke Bay (☎ 907-789-7453 or 907-465-3940 recording), 14 miles from downtown. The run to Haines or Skagway takes five hours. The passenger fare is $37 to Haines, $50 to Skagway. The *Kennicott* connects Juneau to Whittier and points west on the far side of the Gulf of Alaska.

Getting Downtown

The ride downtown from the airport is a long one, and from the ferry dock even longer. At times, airport or ferry-dock shuttles operate, but arrangements change from year to year. For the latest, ask at the visitor information desk in the baggage-claim area or inquire from the purser on the ferry. When selecting your lodgings, keep in mind that if your hotel has a courtesy van, it can save you more than $50 round-trip; in any event, when reserving your room, ask for the best way to get there from the airport.

Navigating by taxi

A taxi is the handiest way for most people to get downtown from the airport or ferry terminal. **Capital Cab** (☎ 907-586-2772) is one company. A cab ride in from the airport will cost you $22; from the ferry dock, $33.

Navigating by bus

An express **Capital Transit** city bus (☎ 907-789-6901) comes to the airport at 11 minutes and 41 minutes past the hour on weekdays from 7:11 a.m. to 6:11 p.m. and costs $1.50; however, your luggage must fit under your seat or at your feet. There is no bus at 7:41 a.m.

"To overhead" — meaning, you're screwed

Juneau's mist-shrouded airport, wedged between ocean and mountain, is a tough place to land in bad weather. That means that sometimes when you think you're flying to Juneau, you end up somewhere else, maybe Anchorage or Seattle, or maybe even some little town that you've never heard of. Landing somewhere other than Juneau is such a common experience that the locals have a special verb for it: *to overhead.* Here's an example of how you may hear it used:

"Why did you miss the fishing trip?"

"I overheaded three times and ended up sleeping in Ketchikan."

When your flight overheads, the airline puts you on the next plane back to Juneau. Even so, you may overhead again. Although people sometimes bounce back and forth like Ping-Pong balls, the airlines won't pay for hotel rooms or give refunds. Your only protection is a relaxed attitude, a loose itinerary that provides you with a chance for making up for lost time, and trip-cancellation insurance (see Chapter 12).

The friendly tourism authorities in Juneau object to my writing about this because, as they rightly point out, improved aviation technology makes it a less common problem, mostly confined to the winter months. But it does still happen occasionally. Passengers can't get into Juneau, or they can't get out because the planes can't get in. If in doubt about whether your plane will leave, you can call ahead, but the airline often says to go to the airport just in case. That's why Juneau residents have the Channel Channel. It's a cable TV channel that silently broadcasts a view of the Gastineau Channel near the airport (hence, the name). Locals can tell from that image whether going to the airport is worth the effort. An example of everyday usage:

"Did you see the Channel Channel? They'll overhead. Let's have another beer."

Navigating by rental car

I often do without a rental car in Juneau because the downtown area is compact and parking can be a headache. Operators of most outdoor activities pick you up at your hotel. On the other hand, you need wheels to visit some attractions, and having a car opens up more choices for dining and lodging and some beautiful drives. Alamo, Avis, Budget, Hertz, and National are based at the airport; national reservation contacts are listed in the Quick Concierge. When contemplating your costs, remember that you can save about $50 by not using taxis to reach the airport. The airport and ferry dock are relatively close together, so when you come by ferry and want to rent a car, do it as soon as you arrive so that you save the cab fare downtown and back.

Orienting Yourself in Juneau

Juneau has three main parts: downtown, the Mendenhall Valley, and Douglas. (Check out the nearby "Greater Juneau" map.) **Downtown Juneau** is a numbered grid of streets (see the "Downtown Juneau" map in this chapter) overlying the uneven topography in the lap of the mountains. As you look at the city from the water, Mount Juneau is on the left and Mount Roberts on the right; Mount Roberts is a few hundred feet taller, at 3,819 ft. When the city outgrew its original site downtown, housing spread to the suburban **Mendenhall Valley,** about a dozen miles north out the Egan Expressway or the parallel, two-lane Glacier Highway. The glacial valley also contains the airport and **Auke Bay** area, where the ferry terminal is located. The road traverses a total of 40 miles to a place known as **"The End of the Road."** Across a bridge over the Gastineau Channel from downtown Juneau is Douglas Island. Turn left for the town of **Douglas,** mostly a bedroom community for Juneau, and turn right for the North Douglas Highway.

Juneau is truly a walking city, but if your feet get tired, taking a cab around downtown is cheap. Try **Capital Cab** (☎ **907-586-2772**). You also can hire a cabby as a personal tour guide for $55 per hour. To go beyond downtown, you need a car.

Getting around by car

Rent a car if you want to stay, dine, or pursue self-guided activities beyond the downtown area. Don't bother if you're happy downtown (by far, the most interesting area) or if you want to take part in only guided outings — the operators usually take care of transfers. Alamo, Avis, Budget, Hertz, and National are based at the airport; national reservation contacts are listed in this book's Quick Concierge.

 If you rent a car, be sure to check with your lodgings about parking arrangements. Finding a place to park in downtown Juneau can be hard amid its narrow, crowded streets, many of which are very steep.

Getting around by bicycle

Strong riders can cover the town with a bike, but you must be able to handle the hills. Separate paths parallel many of the main roads, and downtown traffic is slow. The 24-mile round-trip from downtown to Mendenhall Glacier keeps you on a bike path almost all the way. You can rent bikes at **The Driftwood Lodge,** 435 Willoughby Ave. (☎ **800-544-2239** or 907-586-2280; www.driftwoodalaska.com), for $25 per day.

Where to Stay in Juneau

Hotel rooms are tight in the summer, so don't arrive without a room booked. At the peak of the season, it's a good idea to reserve a month ahead, or longer if you want to be sure of getting into the best places.

Greater Juneau

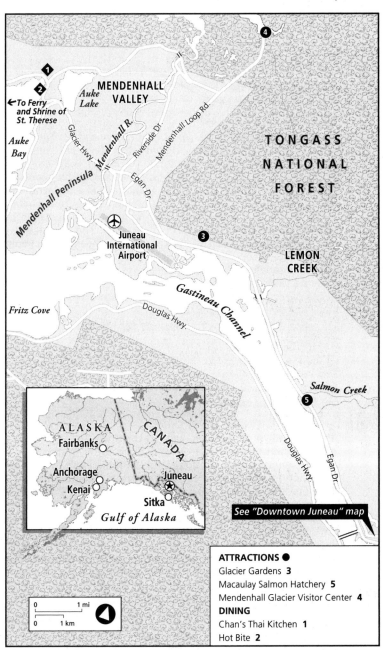

ATTRACTIONS ●
Glacier Gardens **3**
Macaulay Salmon Hatchery **5**
Mendenhall Glacier Visitor Center **4**
DINING
Chan's Thai Kitchen **1**
Hot Bite **2**

Bed-and-breakfasts are a good way to go in Juneau. The Juneau Convention & Visitors Bureau's *Juneau Travel Planner* and Web site contain listings of hotels and B&Bs, with links to their Web sites (☎ 888-581-2201; www.traveljuneau.com).

The top hotels and B&Bs

Alaska's Capital Inn
$$$$–$$$$$ Downtown

This scrupulously restored 1906 mansion offers constant surprises in its fascinating detail: the shining potbellied stove and 1879 pump organ in the parlor, the Persian rugs, the original (electrified) gas lamps, period wallpaper, and even those old-fashioned push-button light switches. It took owners Linda Wendeborn and Mark Thorson three years to bring the house back to this former glory. They poured effort and expense into making details authentic that no one will ever notice. Fortunately, the house was worth it, with many large rooms with high ceilings, good views, fireplaces, claw-foot tubs, and real elegance. The best asset of all, however, may be the warmth and fun of the inn. The common rooms are conducive to socializing, and the hosts love to connect with guests and strive to accommodate their needs. There are some smaller rooms, allowing those on midrange budgets to enjoy the ambience, but the real showplaces carry high luxury rates. An elaborate breakfast is served at 8:30 a.m. They don't take kids 10 or under.

See map p. 333. 113 W. 5th St., Juneau. ☎ *888-588-6507 or 907-586-6507. Fax: 907-586-6508.* www.alaskacapitalinn.com. *Rack rates: High season $259–$339 double, off season $139–$259 double; extra person $25. Rates include full breakfast. AE, DC, DISC, MC, V.*

The Driftwood Lodge
$ Downtown

This downtown motel, next door to the State Museum, is popular with families, and houses legislators and aides in the winter in its apartment-like kitchenette suites. Although the building can't hide its cinderblock construction, old-fashioned motel exterior, small bathrooms, or lack of elevators, the rooms are comfortable and well-kept. The management has held prices low while making improvements, so for a rate that won't get you in the door at most Juneau hotels ($135), you can put four people in a two-bedroom suite with a full kitchen. Don't expect luxury, just a basic, clean motel room for a good price. The round-the-clock courtesy van saves big money to the airport or ferry and the rental bikes will cover your transportation needs downtown. The motel has a laundry room, too.

See map p 333. 435 Willoughby Ave., Juneau. ☎ *800-544-2239 or 907-586-2280. Fax: 907-586-1034.* www.driftwoodalaska.com. *Rack rates: High season $95–$110 double, $120–$135 suite; off season $68 double, $98 suite; extra person $10. AE, DC, DISC, MC, V.*

Downtown Juneau

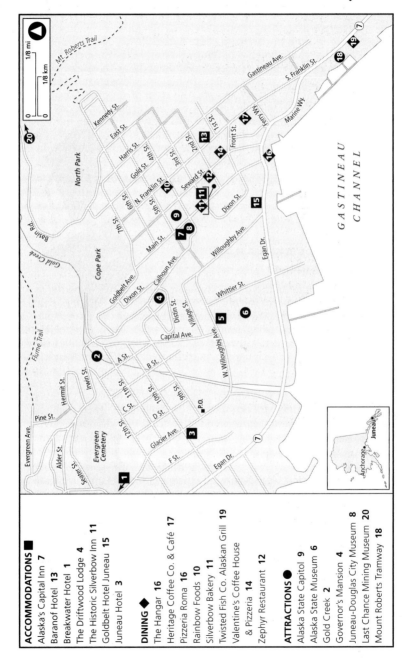

1/8 mi

1/8 km

Mt. Roberts Trail

GASTINEAU CHANNEL

Kennedy St.

East St.

Harris St.

Gold St.

North Park

6th St.

7th St.

N. Franklin St.

Main St.

Cope Park

Gold Creek

Basin Rd.

Flume Trail

Goldbelt Ave.

Dixon St.

Calhoun Ave.

Distin St.

Village St.

Capital Ave.

A St.

B St.

C St.

D St.

Glacier Ave.

F St.

Egan Dr.

Irwin St.

Hermit St.

Pine St.

Evergreen Ave.

Alder St.

Seater St.

Evergreen Cemetery

12th St.

11th St.

10th St.

9th St.

P.O.

4th St.

5th St.

3rd St.

2nd St.

1st St.

Seward St.

Dixon St.

Willoughby Ave.

Whittier St.

W. Willoughby Ave.

Egan Dr.

Gastineau Ave.

S. Franklin St.

Ferry Wy.

Front St.

Marine Wy.

Anchorage • • Juneau

ACCOMMODATIONS ■
Alaska's Capital Inn **7**
Baranof Hotel **13**
Breakwater Hotel **1**
The Driftwood Lodge **4**
The Historic Silverbow Inn **11**
Goldbelt Hotel Juneau **15**
Juneau Hotel **3**

DINING ◆
The Hangar **16**
Heritage Coffee Co. & Café **17**
Pizzeria Roma **16**
Rainbow Foods **10**
Silverbow Bakery **11**
Twisted Fish Co. Alaskan Grill **19**
Valentine's Coffee House & Pizzeria **14**
Zephyr Restaurant **12**

ATTRACTIONS ●
Alaska State Capitol **9**
Alaska State Museum **6**
Gold Creek **2**
Governor's Mansion **4**
Juneau-Douglas City Museum **8**
Last Chance Mining Museum **20**
Mount Roberts Tramway **18**

The Historic Silverbow Inn
$$$–$$$ **Downtown**

There is an oddly pleasing style to this quirky little downtown hotel. The 1914 building, with wood floors, bare brick, and stained glass, is decorated with a stylish, contemporary style that nonetheless captures the warmth of a B&B. The cozy rooms come with extras such as lollipops and popcorn, among other original and considerate touches that show up repeatedly — for example, the shelf of supplies you may have forgotten, the answering machines on the direct-line phones, and the sack breakfast if you have to leave too early for the free full breakfast in the bakery. The proprietors and staff have created a local scene with their popular **Silverbow Bakery,** giving the whole place a hip, community-oriented feel.

See map p. 333. 120 2nd St., Juneau. ☎ *800-586-4146 or 907-586-4146. Fax: 907-586-4242.* www.silverbowinn.com. *Rack rates: High season $149–$208 double, off season $88–$148 double; extra person $20; surcharge of $20 for one-night stays in high season. Rate includes full breakfast. AE, DISC, MC, V.*

Westmark Baranof Hotel
$$$ **Downtown**

The Baranof is the only lodging in Alaska with the pedigree and style to pull off the role of the old-fashioned grand hotel. Built of concrete in 1939, it served for decades as an informal branch of the state capitol. In 2007–08, the hotel's history gained a chapter when a group of legislators, current and former, were convicted of taking bribes from oil-industry executives in Suite 604, which happened to be under FBI surveillance. The structure feels historic, in part, because the concrete construction limits modernization — bathrooms and many bedrooms will always be small. In places, past efforts at renovation have made the most of the classic features, retaining glass doorknobs and pressed-tin hallway ceilings, while most bathrooms were remodeled with period tile and porcelain pedestal sinks and tubs. The upper-floor rooms have great views on the water side. There's a discount on the second floor, which lacks a view, and the rates generally are quite reasonable for this market.

The Art Deco **Gold Room** restaurant is Juneau's most traditional fine-dining establishment, and one of its best. The dining room combines intimacy and grandeur in a showplace of shining brass, frosted glass, and rich wood. Most entrees are over $30.

See map p 333. 127 N. Franklin St., Juneau. ☎ *800-544-0970 or 907-586-2660. Fax: 907-586-8315.* www.westmarkhotels.com/juneau.php. *Rack rates: High season $149–189 double, off season $129–$139 double; $20 each additional person. AE, DC, DISC, MC, V.*

Runner-up accommodations

Breakwater Hotel

$$–$$$ Near Downtown   Good bargains are found in this nondescript building overlooking the boat harbor on the far side of the downtown area from the sights, within a long walking distance. *See map p. 333. 1711 Glacier Ave., Juneau.* ☎ *800-544-2250 or 907-586-6303. Fax: 907-463-4820.*

Goldbelt Hotel Juneau

$$$$ Downtown   Large bedrooms, with many amenities and either two full-size beds or one king-size bed, have bold colors and furniture in a dark cherry finish. They're noticeably quiet and immaculate. *See map p. 333. 51 W. Egan Dr., Juneau.* ☎ *888-478-6909 or 907-586-6900. Fax: 907-463-3567. www. goldbelttours.com/goldbelt-hotel-juneau.*

Juneau Hotel

$$$–$$$$ Downtown   The remarkably comfortable suites in this downtown waterfront hotel offer a terrific bargain for families — rates are for any number of guests in the unit. *See map p. 333. 1200 W. 9th St., Juneau.* ☎ *800-544-2250 or 907-586-5666. www.juneauhotels.net.*

Where to Dine in Juneau

Juneau's best restaurants are within easy walking distance of the downtown hotels.

The Hangar
$$–$$$$ Downtown   GRILL

Situated in a converted airplane hangar on a wooden pier with large windows, this bar and grill has great views and a fun atmosphere; even in the off season, it's packed. It's a fine place to drink beer (with 24 brews on tap), listen to live music, or play at one of the three pool tables. What's surprising is that the food is good, too. The seared ahi sashimi appetizer, raw inside, has a pleasant texture and taste, and the jambalaya, a huge portion for $13, is spicy but balanced. Although the menu's steaks and such range up to $30, plenty of choices are under $15.

See map p. 333. 2 Marine Way, Juneau. ☎ *907-586-5018. Reservations recommended. Main courses: $13–$30. AE, MC, V. Open: Daily 11 a.m.–10 p.m.*

Island Pub
$ Douglas   PIZZA

Across the bridge from Juneau (too far to walk), this is where local people go for a fun night out. The food is good and far from boring — I had a steak salad, which consisted of rare, well-seasoned slices of grilled steak on a bed of lettuce with a load of blue-cheese dressing and onion rings. The specialty is pizza with creative ingredients. The smell of smoke from the wood-fire grill hangs in the air. The dining room, dating from the 1930s, is historic by Alaskan standards and comes by its pub ambience honestly. It looks out on the Gastineau Channel through picture windows; at times customers watch killer whales from the bar. (They have the photos to prove it.) The pub is easy to find. Drive across the bridge to Douglas, turn left, and after entering the town, turn left on E Street.

1102 2nd St., Douglas. ☎ **907-364-1595.** *Main courses: $10–$12, pizza $13–$19. AE, DC, DISC, MC, V. Open: Daily 11:30 a.m.–10 p.m., bar open later.*

Twisted Fish Company Alaskan Grill
$$$–$$$$ **Downtown SEAFOOD**

Overlooking the water at the cruise-ship dock, in the same building as Taku Smokeries, the dining room is magnificent, with high ceilings and an entire wall of windows on the Gastineau Channel, a fireplace of beach rock, lots of hardwood, and, to keep it from being too grand, cartoon-like fish hanging down. The quality and range of the food brings locals to a tourist zone they would otherwise avoid: items like salmon on a cedar plank or in pastry; halibut or salmon tacos; and also little pizzas, burgers, and terrific desserts. The service is fast and attentive, but the dining room makes you want to stay long after you're done eating.

See map p. 333 550 S. Franklin St., Juneau. ☎ **907-463-5033.** *Reservations recommended. Main courses: $7–$15 lunch, $18–$30 dinner. AE, DISC, MC, V. Open: Daily 11 a.m.–10 p.m. Closed Oct–Apr.*

Zyphyr Restaurant
$$–$$$$ **Downtown MEDITERRANEAN**

The dining room, once an old-fashioned grocery store, was remodeled with restraint and a magnificent sense of style, using its wooden floors, very high ceilings, and huge storefront windows to create the illusion of elegance passed down for generations rather than only since late 2006. Tables robed in linen of dark rust are set so far apart that diners feel they're alone; on the winter evening I first ate here, the darkness outside contributed to the velvety intimacy. The food and the service — courteous but world-weary — lived up to the setting. Dishes are from the traditional fine-dining palette of colors: calamari, pasta puttanesca, or veal *osso buco,* for example. On my most recent visit, the day-boat scallops, seared with a soft-cooked egg and romesco sauce, were wonderfully flavored and textured. Desserts are excellent, too. Save this place for a romantic meal or a special treat at the end of the day.

See map p. 333. 200 Seward St. ☎ **907-780-2221.** *Reservations recommended. Main courses: $15–$36. AE, MC, V. Open: Summer Tues–Sun 5–9:30 p.m., winter Tues–Sat 5–9:30 p.m.*

Quick eats and coffee

Sometimes you just want an inexpensive lunch, possibly in a box to take on an outing or a light breakfast in a friendly coffee joint. The **Rainbow Foods** natural food grocery, an organic hangout in a former church at the corner of Franklin and 4th streets (☎ **907-586-6476;** www.rainbow-foods.org), is the best picnic-packing place downtown, making sandwiches and salads at the deli and with a buffet and salad bar; it's also a good place to network with a socially conscious crowd and is a Wi-Fi hotspot. **The Silverbow Bakery,** 120 2nd St. (☎ **907-586-4146;** www.silverbowinn.com), is a happening spot for bagels or hearty sandwiches; it's open long hours every day. **Hot Bite,** at the Auke Bay boat harbor (☎ **907-790-2483**), is a local secret, serving charcoal-broiled hamburgers and halibut burgers and great milkshakes from a run-down little house; take out or sit at one of six indoor tables. **Valentine's Coffee House & Pizzeria,** 111 Seward St. (☎ **907-463-5144;** www.valentinescoffeehouse.com), serves light hot meals in an authentic old-fashioned storefront. **Heritage Cafe,** 174 S. Franklin St. (☎ **907-586-1087;** www.heritagecoffee.com) and 216 2nd St. (☎ **907-586-1752**), has two trendy, comfortable coffeehouses good for watching people; they also road famous coffee. The 2nd Street location has wireless Internet and terminals.

Exploring Juneau

Juneau is like a comfortable, well-loved living room: It's a town where you can settle in and get comfortable, walk around and make your own discoveries, and quickly feel like you belong there. Set aside some time for leisurely walks to enjoy the human-scale surroundings.

Exploring the top attractions

Alaska State Museum
Downtown

The museum contains a large collection of art and historical artifacts, but it doesn't seem like a storehouse at all because the objects' presentation is based on their meaning, not their value. Come here to put the rest of your visit in context. A clan house in the Alaska Native Gallery contains authentic art in the functional places where it would've been used in a memorial potlatch. The Lincoln Totem Pole is here, carved by an artist who used a picture of the president as his model to represent his clan's first encounter with whites. Superb artifacts from Native cultures from around the state are presented to illustrate the lifestyle of those who made them. The ramp to the second floor wraps around the natural history display, with an eagle nesting tree, and at the top a state history gallery uses significant pieces to tell Alaska's story. The children's area is exceptionally fun, with a ship that the kids can play in. In 2009, the museum installed "Science on a Sphere," a huge interactive globe for displaying earth-science concepts, sponsored by the National Oceanic and Atmospheric Administration. Allow at least two hours for the museum; half a day would not be out of line. The shop off the lobby is also well worth a look. Although small, it carries lots of quality Alaska Native art, books, and no junk at all.

See map p 333. 395 Whittier St., Juneau. ☎ **907-465-2901.** www.museums.state. ak.us. *Open: Mid-May to mid-Sept daily 8:30 a.m.–5:30 p.m., mid-Sept to mid-May Tues–Sat 10 a.m.–4 p.m. Admission: $5 adults ($3 off season), free for kids 18 and under.*

Macaulay Salmon Hatchery
Glacier Highway

The hatchery, known by locals as DIPAC (Douglas Island Pink and Chum, Inc.), was ingeniously designed to allow visitors to watch the whole process of harvesting and fertilizing eggs from outdoor decks. From mid-June through October, salmon swim up a 450-ft. fish ladder, visible through a window, into a sorting mechanism, where they're "unzipped" by workers who remove the eggs. Guides and exhibits explain what's happening. During that period, you can often see seals and other wildlife feeding on the returning salmon just offshore from the hatchery. Inside, large and realistic saltwater aquariums and touch tanks show off the area's marine life. The tour is less impressive in May and June, before the fish are running. At that time, visitors see the immature salmon before their release and sometimes get to feed them. The tours don't take long; allow 45 minutes for your entire visit.

See map p 331. 2697 Channel Dr. (3 miles from downtown, turn left at the first group of buildings on Egan Drive). ☎ **877-463-2486** *or 907-463-5114.* www.dipac.net. *Open: May 16–Sept 14 Mon–Fri 10 a.m.–6 p.m., Sat–Sun 10 a.m.–5 p.m.; Sept 15–May 15, call ahead. Admission: $3.50 adults, $2 kids 12 and under.*

Mendenhall Glacier
Mendenhall Valley

At the head of Mendenhall Valley, the glacier glows bluish white, looming above the suburbs like an Ice Age monster that missed the general extinction. Besides being a truly impressive sight, Mendenhall is the most easily accessible glacier in Alaska and the state's third most visited attraction. The parking and an adjacent shelter have a great view across the lake to the glacier's face, and a wheelchair-accessible trail leads close to the water's edge. The land near the parking lot shows signs of the glacier's recent passage, with little topsoil, stunted vegetation, and, in many places, bare rock with scratch marks from the glacier's movement. It's an outdoor science lesson, and kids will enjoy the ability to be themselves while soaking up the fascinating evidence of living geology. Atop a bedrock hill, reached by stairs, a ramp, or an elevator, the Forest Service visitor center contains a glacier museum with excellent explanatory models, computerized displays, spotting scopes, and ranger talks.

Avoiding cruise-ship crowds

On the busiest days of the summer, cruise ships bring more than 10,000 passengers and another 4,000 crew members to the docks on Juneau's Franklin Street. That's simply too many for these narrow old streets; downtown becomes a solid crush of people and attractions are packed, spoiling the experience for everyone. The crush is largely unavoidable, with more than one ship in port every day of the summer, but normally midweek days are busiest and Fridays and Saturdays are quieter, because most cruises begin on the weekend and Juneau is about halfway along their voyage. If you can plan your Juneau sightseeing on the weekend, you may find somewhat less crowding; also, the farther you go from the dock, the less crowding you encounter. You can find a current schedule showing how many ships will be in port each day at www.claalaska. com, the Web site for Cruise Line Agencies of Alaska.

In late summer, the area has the added attraction of being Alaska's most accessible bear-viewing opportunity. Red and silver salmon spawn in **Steep Creek,** just short of the visitor center on the road, an interesting sight in themselves, but even more important as a source of easy bear food. All that fresh salmon attracts many black bears, which visitors easily watch from a trail and platform built for the purpose.

See map p. 331. At the head of Glacier Spur Road (right from Egan Drive on Mendenhall Loop to Glacier Spur), Juneau. ☎ 907-789-0097. Open: Summer daily 8 a.m.–7:30 p.m., winter Thurs–Sun 10 a.m.–4 p.m. Admission: Visitor center $3 adults, free for kids 15 and under.

Mount Roberts Tramway
Downtown

The tram takes only six minutes to whisk passengers from tourist-clogged Franklin Street to the clear air and overwhelming views at the tree line (1,760 ft.), a destination that used to require a day of huffing and puffing. The tram itself can be crowded: It's up on the mountain that the beauty hits you. The Alaska Native owners have done a good job of building a network of paths that take advantage of the views as you pass through a fascinating alpine ecosystem. If you're energetic, you can start a 6-mile round-trip to Mount Roberts's summit (3,819 ft.), or you can hike the 2½ miles back downtown. There's an auditorium at the top tram station showing a film on the Tlingit culture, a shop where Native artisans are often at work, and a bar and grill that serves lunch and dinner. I would choose something else to do on a day when fog or low overcast obscures the view, especially considering the high price; however, I'm told it's sometimes sunny up top while rainy down on Franklin Street — it can't hurt to ask.

See map p 333. 490 S. Franklin St., at the waterfront near the cruise-ship dock, Juneau. ☎ 888-461-8726 or 907-463-3412. Open: Daily 9 a.m.–9 p.m. Admission: All-day pass $27 adults, $14 kids 6 to 12, free for kids 5 and under. Closed Oct–Apr.

More cool things to see and do

These barely-missed-the-top attractions are well worth a visit when you're in Juneau for more than a day or two:

- ✔ **Juneau-Douglas City Museum:** Find out about Juneau at this fun little museum with fascinating history and cultural exhibits and a tiny shop stocked with handy information for your visit, such as walking-tour maps and historic trail guides. The museum is at the corner of 4th and Main streets (☎ 907-586-3572; www.juneau. org/parkrec/museum). Admission is $4 adults (free in winter), free for kids 18 and under. It's open in the summer Monday through Friday 9 a.m. to 5 p.m., Saturday and Sunday 10 a.m. to 5 p.m.; in the winter, Tuesday through Saturday 10 a.m. to 4 p.m.

- ✔ **Last Chance Mining Museum and Historic Park:** Juneau's industrial past survives at these old mining buildings on forested Gold Creek. You can see immense, intact, original equipment before hiking the nearby Perseverance Trail (see "Hiking," later in this chapter). From downtown, take Gold Street to its top, and then join Basin Road, continuing 1 mile up the valley to the end of the road (☎ 907-586-5338). Admission is $4, and the museum is open in summer daily from 9:30 a.m. to 12:30 p.m. and 3:30 to 6:30 p.m.

- ✔ **Glacier Gardens:** For people with mobility problems, this is a chance to see the rain forest as hikers do. A visit starts with a horticultural exhibit in greenhouses and formal gardens, and then visitors board a vehicle similar to a golf cart to ride up a steep trail through woods landscaped with pools and plantings to an overlook. The gardens are about 1 mile from the airport; take Glacier Highway to near the Fred Meyer store (☎ 907-790-3377; www. glaciergardens.com). Admission is $22 adults, $16 kids 6 to 12. It's open in summer daily from 9 a.m. to 6 p.m.

- ✔ **Taking a scenic drive "out the road":** The 40-mile Glacier Highway doesn't go much of anywhere beyond the Mendenhall Valley, but it does go *through* some lovely country with views of islands floating on sun-dappled water. Stop at the moving **Shrine of St. Therese** (☎ 907-780-6112; www.shrineofsainttherese.org), 9 miles beyond the ferry dock, a simple chapel of rounded beach stones on a tiny island reached by a foot-trail causeway. It's also a great place for examining tide pools, and sometimes you can see whales from shore.

Shopping

The most popular shopping district is on the streets surrounding the cruise-ship dock and on South Franklin Street. Many shops that you see here are entirely seasonal, while a few have a local clientele as well. Some worthy of your attention include the **Taku Store,** 550 S. Franklin St. (☎ 800-582-5122 or 907-463-3474; www.takustore.com), a place to buy expensive seafood delicacies and see them made behind glass; and **Decker Gallery,** 233 S. Franklin St. (☎ 907-463-5536), showing Rie Muñoz's charming prints and tapestries on local themes. Her work can also be seen at the **Rie Muñoz Gallery,** 2101 Jordan Ave. (☎ 800-247-3151 or 907-789-7449; www.riemunoz.com).

Walking up the hill a bit, you reach more of the year-round businesses. Check out **Juneau Artists Gallery,** in the Senate Building at 175 S. Franklin St. (☎ 907-586-9891; www.juneauartistsgallery.com), which is an artists' co-op; the shop operated by **Bill Spear,** 174 S. Franklin St. (☎ 907-586-2209; www.wmspear.com), who makes colored enamel pins; and **The Observatory,** 299 N. Franklin St. (☎ 907-586-9676; www.observatory books.com), which specializes in rare maps and books about Alaska. **Annie Kaill's** fine arts and crafts gallery is half a block off Franklin at 244 Front St. (☎ 907-586-2880; www.anniekaills.com).

Nightlife

For a family night out, consider the **Gold Creek Salmon Bake.** It's a 30-year tradition of a picnic with marshmallow roasting, music, and other entertainment. The cost is $39 for adults, $26 for kids. Call ☎ 800-232-5757 or 907-789-0052 to reserve.

I mention **The Hangar** under "Where to Dine in Juneau." Other popular drinking establishments include **The Red Dog Saloon,** 278 S. Franklin St. (☎ 907-463-3658; www.reddogsaloon.com), with a sawdust-strewn floor, frontier atmosphere, and nightly live music. Or join the locals across the street at **The Alaskan Bar,** 167 S. Franklin St. (☎ 907-586-1000), which occupies an authentic gold-rush hotel with a two-story Victorian barroom; boisterous parties and music go on here all year.

Getting Outdoors in Juneau

Juneau has more outdoor activities than anywhere else I can think of. And thanks to the town's role as a top visitor destination, you can do most of it with a guide instead of on your own.

You'll find support for self-guided outings, too. **Alaska Boat & Kayak Shop,** at the Auke Bay Harbor (☎ 907-789-6886; www.juneaukayak.com), rents sea kayaks and camping gear and offers guidance in planning where and how to go.

Bear-viewing

Bears are quite common around Juneau; in fact, they become pests for residents who live near the woods. In late summer, the hot spot to see black bears is the path and platform to **Steep Creek** at Mendenhall Glacier (see "Exploring the top attractions," earlier in this chapter). But to see large numbers of huge brown bears close up in their natural habitat, the best place to go is Admiralty Island and its **Kootznoowoo Wilderness** (*Kootznoowoo* means "fortress of bears" in Tlingit). The island's **Pack Creek Bear-Viewing Area** allows a limited number of visitors to watch bears up close as they feed on salmon spawning in July and August; peak viewing is in the middle of that period. Only 25 miles from Juneau, Pack Creek is so popular that the Forest Service uses a permit system to keep it from being overrun during the day (9 p.m.–9 a.m. no people are allowed). The easiest way to go is with a tour operator who has permits; here are a couple good choices:

- ✔ **Alaska Fly 'N' Fish Charters,** 9604 Kelly Court (☎ **907-790-2120;** www.alaskabyair.com), offers naturalist-guided 5½-hour fly-in visits, which cost $600 per person, and include everything you need.

- ✔ **Mountain Travel Sobek,** 5310 Glacier Hwy. (☎ **800-586-1911;** www.mtsobek.com), offers two-night sea-kayak expeditions camping near the creeks, with ample time to see the bears and other scenery. It costs $995 per person.

Fishing and whale-watching

The closest I ever came to a humpback whale — I almost touched it — was on the way back from king-salmon-fishing out of Juneau on a friend's boat. More than two dozen companies offer charters from Juneau and Auke Bay; you can go to watch whales or fish, or both. Juneau is well-protected behind layers of islands, so the water generally is calm. Many companies offer trips. The Juneau Convention & Visitors Bureau maintains a list of businesses, and its Web site has links to each. **Harv & Marv's Outback Alaska** (☎ **866-909-7288** or 907-209-7288; www.harvandmarvs.com), is run with 6- and 12-passenger boats by a couple of lifelong Juneau residents with decades of experience, each of whom go by their high school nicknames (really they're Jay and Pete), and who are known as characters doing fun, personal whale-watching trips. They charge $149 per person for a half-day, but prices vary by group size. **Orca Enterprises** (☎ **800-733-6722** or 907-789-6801; www.alaskawhalewatching.com) is a larger whale-watching firm, with four good-size vessels, offering 3–1/2-hour tours and free transfers from your hotel. The cost is $114 adults, $84 kids 5 to 12, $54 kids 4 and under.

Flightseeing and dog-mushing

More than 36 major glaciers around Juneau flow from a single ocean of ice behind the mountains, the 1,500-sq.-mile Juneau Ice Field. You can land on it in a helicopter just to touch the ice, or for a nature hike or dog-sled ride. On the flight, you survey the bizarre scenery of long, sinuous strands of flowing glacier ice. Then, when you land, you find yourself transported into winter during the middle of summer, surrounded by blindingly white, crusty snow. **Era Helicopters** (☎ 800-843-1947; www. eraflightseeing.com) is among Alaska's oldest and most respected operators. Its one-hour flight over four glaciers with a 20-minute landing on Norris Glacier costs $279 per person. It also offers a program of **dog-sled rides** on the ice, a chance to try a winter sport in the summer. That excursion includes the same overflight and adds about an hour at a sled-dog camp on a glacier with a ride behind the dogs; it costs $489 per person.

One caveat: Poor or even overcast weather makes seeing the ice difficult, but if you wait for a sunny morning, all seats will likely be booked. Era has a 48-hour cancellation policy, so you must gamble, to some extent, on good viewing conditions.

Hiking

Juneau's superb trail network offers choices ranging from easy strolls to leg-burners up those omnipresent mountains. Here are some highlights, in order of increasing difficulty:

- ✔ **The Treadwell Mine Historic Trail:** This is a fascinating hour's stroll through the ruins of a massive hard-rock mine complex that once employed and housed 2,000 men but was abandoned in 1922. Numbered posts match a historic guide available from the Juneau-Douglas City Museum (see "More cool things to see and do," earlier in this chapter). To find the trailhead, take 3rd Street in Douglas, bearing left onto Savikko Street, which leads to Savikko Park (also known as Sandy Beach Park). The trail starts at the far end.

- ✔ **Outer Point Trail:** This lovely but sometimes crowded trail leads 1⅓ miles on a forest boardwalk to a beach with good tide pools, plenty of eagles, and occasional whale sightings. To get there, drive over the bridge to Douglas, and then go right on North Douglas Highway 12 miles to the trailhead.

- ✔ **Perseverance Trail:** A fairly level 4-mile trail leads from behind downtown up to the Perseverance Mine at the Silverbow Basin, a mining community from 1885 to 1921. The trailhead is about 1½ miles from downtown on Basin Road; check out the Last Chance Mining Museum there (see "More cool things to see and do," earlier in this chapter).

- ✔ **Mount Roberts:** The trailhead is downtown — just follow the stairway from the top of 6th Street. The summit is 4½ miles and 3,819 vertical feet away, but you'll see great views much sooner. At the 1,760-ft. level, you reach the top of the Mount Roberts Tramway, which is mentioned earlier in this chapter. (Of course, taking the tram up and hiking down is easier.)

Choosing glaciers:
Glacier Bay or Tracy Arm

Glacier Bay National Park is awesome — huge glaciers, sheer rock mountains, and whales leaping out of the water — but I don't recommend a visit for land-based visitors with limited time or money. You can see the same kind of sights for less money on a day trip from Juneau to Tracy Arm in the Tongass National Forest. (*Note:* This advice doesn't apply to cruise-ship passengers. Your ship's itinerary will determine if you visit Glacier Bay. If you do, a ranger will come onboard to provide commentary while the ship traverses the bay.)

Glacier Bay is a marine park. To get to the glaciers from the park headquarters, you have to take a boat ride that lasts eight hours and costs $193. And to get to the park headquarters, where the boat ride starts, requires a round-trip flight that costs roughly $200 more. It seems ridiculous to do all that as a marathon day trip, but spending the night at Glacier Bay costs more again. (A double room at the Glacier Bay Lodge is around $200, not including meals and transfers.) On the other hand, an all-day boat trip to Tracy Arm, which includes mile-high mountains that come right out of the sea, calving glaciers, and often whale sightings, costs about $140 and takes eight hours in total, right from the dock in Juneau. One tour is with **Adventure Bound Alaska,** 76 Egan Dr., Juneau (☎ **800-228-3875** or 907-463-2509; www.adventureboundalaska.com); it's a family business operating a 56-ft. single-hull boat with deck space all the way around.

If you do choose Glacier Bay (and I admit that it's awesome), you can book almost everything through the park concessionaire, **Glacier Bay Lodge & Tours** (☎ **888-229-8687** or 907-264-4600; www.visitglacierbay.com). Plan to spend at least one night and include a whale-watching trip in Icy Strait, just outside the park, with waters that offer the most reliable humpback-viewing of anywhere in Alaska. Those cruises are offered by Glacier Bay Lodge & Tours or by **Cross Sound Express** (☎ **888-697-2726** or 907-321-2302; http://taz.gustavus.com).

Sea-kayaking

The protected waters around Juneau call out for sea-kayaking, and the city is a popular hub for trips farther out on the water. Besides the sublime scenery, you'll almost certainly see eagles, seabirds, and seals, and possibly humpback whales. **Alaska Travel Adventures** (☎ 800-323-5757; www.bestofalaskatravel.com), offers 3½-hour kayak trips from an unspoiled spot on the north end of Douglas Island for $89 adults, $59 kids 6 to 12, free for kids 5 and under. The tour includes orientation for beginners, transportation from downtown, and a snack.

Spending One, Two, or Three Days in Juneau

You must go outdoors in Juneau, even if you're only in a car or helicopter. So, these aren't just *seeing* itineraries, they're *doing* itineraries, too. Each element of the following itinerary is reviewed in more detail elsewhere in this chapter.

Day 1 in Juneau

Start the morning by boarding a helicopter bound for the **Juneau Ice Field** to see vast glaciers and the icy plateau they spring from; if you can afford it, add a **dog-sled ride** on the ice. For a lower-budget alternative, take the **Mount Roberts Tramway** for mountain views and a walk. Returning to Juneau, stroll downtown for shopping on **Franklin Street** or to simply explore the town and see the modest public buildings of the state capital. Have lunch at **The Hanger** before going to the **Alaska State Museum** for an orientation to Alaska's history and culture. If the weather's nice, finish the day by eating outdoors while listening to music at the **Gold Creek Salmon Bake.**

Day 2 in Juneau

Rent a car today and pack a picnic at **Rainbow Foods.** Your first stop is the **Mendenhall Glacier,** where you definitely should check out the visitor center, take a hike, and, in season, watch the black bears on Steep Creek. Next, explore the **Glacier Highway** (or go "out the road," in the local parlance) to see the views and visit the lovely **Shrine of St. Therese.** After your picnic, stop on the way back into town at the **Macaulay Salmon Hatchery** for the tour. Cross the bridge to Douglas for a **hike.** You may have time for the historic Treadwell Mine Trail and the natural Outer Beach Trail. Dine at the **Island Pub.**

Day 3 in Juneau

Spend one day on an **all-day outdoor expedition:** taking the boat to Tracy Arm, sea-kayaking in Juneau, or bear-watching on Admiralty Island. Dine at the **Twisted Fish.**

Fast Facts: Juneau

ATMs

Among many other banks and stores, the Wells Fargo Bank, 123 Seward St., has an ATM.

Emergencies

Call ☎ **911.**

Hospital

Bartlett Regional, 3260 Hospital Dr. (☎ 907-796-8900), is 3 miles out the Glacier Highway.

Information

The Juneau Convention & Visitors Bureau has an information center in Centennial

Hall, 101 Egan Dr., near the State Museum
(☎ 888-581-2201 or 907-586-2201; www.
traveljuneau.com).

Internet Access

Try the downtown coffeehouses mentioned
in the "Quick eats and coffee" sidebar,
or go to Copy Express, 230 Seward St.
(☎ 907-586-2174).

Pharmacy

Juneau Drug Company is at 202 Front St.
(☎ 907-586-1233).

Police

You can reach the police, 6255 Alaway Ave.,
at ☎ 907-586-0600 for non-emergencies.

Post Office

You can find post offices downtown in the
federal building, 709 W. 9th St., and in the
Mendenhall Valley at 9491 Vintage Blvd., by
Carr's supermarket. A postal contract sta-
tion handy to the cruise-ship dock is at 145
S. Franklin St.

Taxes

Sales tax is 5 percent. You pay 12 percent
tax on rooms.

Weather Updates

The Alaska Weather Line for Juneau is
☎ 907-790-6850.

Chapter 21

Skagway

- -

In This Chapter

▶ Experiencing Skagway's gold-rush history
▶ Getting to and around Skagway
▶ Finding rest and food
▶ Seeing the gold-rush sites
▶ Exploring the outdoors
▶ Checking out the nightlife

- -

*T*he 1898 Klondike gold rush was the last gasp of the Wild West and the first breath of Alaska's modern history. Skagway was where it hit its wildest. Miners found the gold near Dawson City, Yukon Territory, where Canada's Mounties kept the stampede in relatively good order. But in Skagway, men crazed with greed knew no law at all. They disembarked their boats on Skagway's dock for the tough cross-country trek to Dawson City. One day, the area was wilderness; the next, a city of saloons and brothels. After the men came ashore, they played cards, lifted drinks, spent time (and money) with some very busy women, and got fleeced by the thousands. They settled arguments with guns, and the absence of sanitation caused epidemics, so the cemetery grew fast.

No wonder the governor came to town and asked one of the most popular local citizens to be the territorial marshal, marching with him in the Fourth of July parade. The plan might have worked, too, except that the man he chose, Soapy Smith, was the most dangerous con man and gang leader in town. Four days after the parade, in Skagway's greatest tale, vigilante Frank Reid killed Soapy Smith in a fair fight, standing face-to-face on the docks. Reid later died himself of the wounds he sustained, but not before breaking the grip that Soapy's men had on the town. And then the curtain closed. The rush lasted less than two years, and soon Skagway was an ordinary town, but one with a brief and notorious past.

If that history interests you, Skagway presents it well in the Klondike Gold Rush National Historical Park, a collection of buildings and museums. You can spend a good day there. If you're not interested in the gold rush and the Wild West, however, you can skip Skagway.

Skagway is Alaska's most touristy community, with as many as seven cruise ships pulling into town at a time — that's in a town with fewer than 900 residents. All the cruise-ship passengers make for an awful mob, and they're tough to avoid. Planning sightseeing early and late in the day may help, and weekends appear to be quieter than weekdays. If you arrive with thick crowds (perhaps on a ship yourself), you can avoid some of the crush by renting a bike (see "Orienting Yourself in Skagway," later in this chapter) and riding beyond the central walking area. (For more tips on cruise-ship crowds, see Chapter 20.) And, of course, the city is quieter during the cruising off season (Oct–Apr).

Gold-rush primer

At a big wedding that I attended in Anchorage, most of the wedding party came to Alaska and toured the state together before the festivities. They spent many hours in gold-rush towns, visiting museums and sites devoted to the gold rush. I asked one of the young men what he thought of it. He said he'd enjoyed Alaska and thought all the historic sites were interesting enough. However, he was left with one nagging question: "What's the gold rush?"

Because the gold rush is just about the only big thing that's ever happened in Alaska, we tend to forget that it's not on everyone's mind.

The rush started in 1897 when a group of regular guys got off a boat in Seattle with a ton of gold stuffed in steamer trunks and gunnysacks. A sourdough prospector, George Carmack, and his Native partners, Tagish Charlie and Skookum Jim, had found gold in the Klondike River in Canada's Yukon Territory the year before — gold so plentiful it looked like slabs of cheese in a sandwich. At the time, the nation was in the fourth year of a financial collapse. People were poor, and when the newspapers wrote about a river up north with gold by the ton, they didn't have to be told twice. Some 100,000 — including the mayor of Seattle — quit whatever they were doing and headed north. This rush happened at a time when the total non-Native population of Alaska was counted at 4,000.

The cheapest and most popular route was by boat to Skagway, on foot over the tortuous Chilkoot Pass or White Pass, and then by handmade boat across Lake Bennett and down the ferocious upper Yukon River to the new town of Dawson City. Just to make it alive was impressive. But few who did found any gold — the mining claims had been staked and big companies were soon doing the mining. Some gave up, but others had too much pride or too much greed to go home, or they just liked it here. They populated Alaska, rushing from one gold find to another in a series of gold strikes. That's how many of Alaska's cities, including Fairbanks and Nome, were founded.

Gold fever didn't give out until World War I, and it has never died completely. Big-time companies still mine around Dawson City and Fairbanks. And small-time prospectors still scratch the hills across the state in hopes of a strike as big as the one George Carmack, Tagish Charlie, and Skookum Joe made more than 100 years ago.

Getting There

You can drive, fly, or take a boat to Skagway, but for most visitors, the water is the most practical way.

By boat

Most visitors get to Skagway on a cruise ship (see Chapter 8). The **Alaska Marine Highway System** (☎ **800-642-0066** or 907-983-2941; www. ferryalaska.com) connects Skagway daily with Juneau and Haines. The passenger fare from Juneau is $50; from Haines, $31.

By road

Klondike Highway 2 connects Skagway with Whitehorse, Yukon Territory, 99 miles away over the White Pass. It's a high, rocky, gold-rush route, with views as good as those on the excursion train operating over the pass. The international border is at the top of the pass (a few facts about clearing Customs are in Chapter 6). The highway meets the Alaska Highway and Klondike Highway in Whitehorse for drives to the rest of the state or northward to Dawson City.

By air

Several air-taxi operators serve Skagway. A round-trip from Juneau costs $238 on **Wings of Alaska** (☎ **907-789-0790** reservations, or 907-983-2442; www.ichoosewings.com).

Orienting Yourself in Skagway

Broadway is the main historic street. A simple grid spans a few blocks on either side. The Klondike Highway leads north out of town at the end of the grid. The gold-rush cemetery is just past town on the right.

Walking is the best way to explore. To get to sites on the outskirts, try the **Dyea Dave Shuttle** (☎ **907-612-0290**), which operates like a taxi. Skagway also has a bus, called **SMART** (☎ **907-983-2743**), which runs a circuit around town for $2 per ride, or to sights on the fringes for $5, leaving on the hour from City Hall and 7th Avenue and Spring Street. A bike is fun and practical transportation in Skagway. **Sockeye Cycle,** 381 5th Ave., off Broadway (☎ **877-292-4154** or 907-983-2851; www. cyclealaska.com), rents good mountain bikes for $14 for two hours and leads guided day trips. To go beyond the town or to venture down the highway to the rest of Alaska, rent a car from **Avis,** at 3rd Avenue and Spring Street (☎ **800-230-4898** or 907-983-2247; www.avis.com).

Where to Stay

Skagway has several charming and comfortable places to stay. Accommodations generally have courtesy vans available, but check for exact arrangements when you reserve your room.

At the White House
$$ Skagway

The Tronrud family essentially rebuilt a burned 1902 gable-roofed inn, which has dormer and bow windows and two porticos with small Doric columns. They made the rooms comfortable and modern while retaining the style of the original owner, Lee Guthrie, a successful gambler and saloon owner of the gold-rush years. The inn has hardwood floors and fine woodwork. Bedrooms vary in size; all have quilts and other nice touches and are equipped with TVs, refrigerators, and Wi-Fi.

See map p. 351. 475 8th Ave., at Main Street, Skagway. ☎ *907-983-9000. Fax: 907-983-9010.* www.atthewhitehouse.com. *Rack rates: High season $125 double, off season $85 double; extra person $10. Rates include continental breakfast. AE, DISC, MC, V.*

Chilkoot Trail Outpost
$$$–$$$$ Dyea

These beautifully crafted log cabins contain comfortable, modern lodgings with carpeted floors and log interior walls, some in the form of two-room suites, with many amenities. The hiker's suite consists of two rooms in a duplex with bunk beds that rent for $145 double, including breakfast. The location, in Dyea near the Chilkoot Trail and Taiya River, puts you in quiet, natural surroundings away from the carnival atmosphere created by the crush of tourists in Skagway proper. In good weather, the hosts have a nightly campfire and provide supplies for s'mores. You can also cook your own food at a barbecue and sink in a screened gazebo. Breakfast, served in a remarkable log building with a vaulted ceiling, consists of a buffet with various choices, including one hot selection. The lodge loans bikes to guests; rooms have Wi-Fi but no phones.

Mile 8.5, Dyea Rd., Skagway. ☎ *907-983-3799. Fax: 907-983-3599.* www.chilkoot trailoutpost.com. *Rack rates: $145 double duplex, $175 double-occupancy cabin; extra adult or teen $25, extra kid 2–11 $13. Rates include full breakfast. MC, V. Closed in the off season.*

Sgt. Preston's Lodge
$–$$ Skagway

Four buildings sit on a landscaped lawn just steps off Broadway, Skagway's main historic street, at 6th Avenue and State Street. American, Canadian, and Alaskan flags fly out front, underlining the theme — along with the tan, red, and green paint scheme — of the tidy image of the Royal Canadian

Skagway

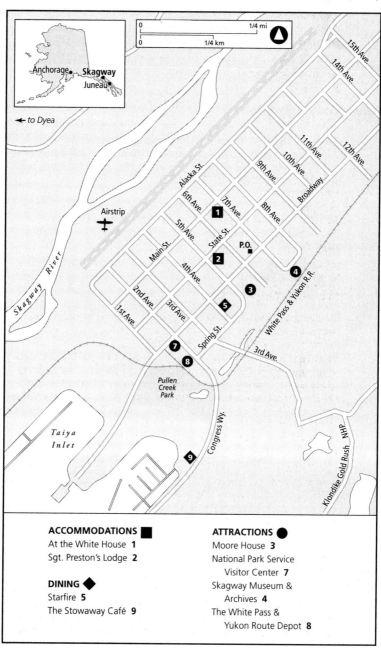

ACCOMMODATIONS ■
At the White House **1**
Sgt. Preston's Lodge **2**

DINING ◆
Starfire **5**
The Stowaway Café **9**

ATTRACTIONS ●
Moore House **3**
National Park Service
  Visitor Center **7**
Skagway Museum &
  Archives **4**
The White Pass &
  Yukon Route Depot **8**

Mounted Police. Once inside, however, you'll find typical modern motel rooms, familiar accommodations for those who simply want a comfortable place to sleep. Ten rooms have only shower stalls — no tubs. The lobby, fixed up in 2010, has a computer station and shelves of books.

See map p. 351. 370 6th Ave., Skagway. ☎ **866-983-2521** *or 907-983-2521. Fax: 907-983-3500.* www.sgtprestonslodge.com. *Rack rates: High season $90–$125 double, off season $90 double; additional person 12 and over $10. AE, DISC, MC, V.*

Where to Dine

Covering the restaurants in this seasonal community is difficult because they change quickly. Ask around for what's new, as something like one-third of the eateries are different each year. The two that follow have been consistent for years.

Starfire
$$ Skagway   THAI

Other menu selections are available, but the specialty here is spicy Thai cuisine — stir fries, curries, soups, and salads. The Pad Thai comes in a large portion with a cabbage salad and is cooked and seasoned just right. But the small, 11-table dining room is the restaurant's most memorable aspect, with dark hues and art that create an intimate and relatively upscale experience, despite the paper napkins and tight quarters. Service is helpful and speedy, and the menu is clearly presented to help those not used to the food to order intelligently.

See map p. 351. 4th Avenue between Spring Street and Broadway, Skagway. ☎ **907-983-3663.** *Main courses: $14–$19. MC, V. Open: Mon–Fri 11 a.m.–10 p.m., Sat–Sun 4–10 p.m. Closed in the off season.*

The Stowaway Café
$$–$$$$ Skagway   SEAFOOD

Housed in a bright blue building overlooking the boat harbor, a five-minute walk from the historic sites, this little restaurant has, for several years, turned out many of Skagway's best meals. Grilled and blackened salmon and halibut anchor the menu, but you also can get either fish with various creative preparations — salmon with a wasabi panko crust or with a green-apple chipotle sauce, or even grilled halibut with Jamaican jerk spice and a cranberry chutney garnish. Another part of the attraction is the restaurant's handmade charm, with a tiny dining room decorated on a mermaid theme that will keep your attention almost as well as the harbor view. The restaurant has a beer and wine license.

See map p. 351. 205 Congress Way, near the small-boat harbor, Skagway. ☎ **907-983-3463.** *Reservations recommended. Main courses: $8–$15 lunch, $16–$29 dinner. V. Open: Daily 10 a.m.–10 p.m. Closed winter.*

Exploring Skagway

Skagway Street Car Tour, 270 2nd Ave. (☎ **907-983-2908;** www.skagway streetcar.com), offers two-hour town tours using antique touring vehicles and costumed guides. The price is $42 for adults, $21 for kids 12 and under; advance reservations are needed.

The top attractions

Klondike Gold Rush National Historical Park

The park encompasses a collection of about 17 restored gold-rush buildings. Start at the **museum** at the park's visitor center, where you can catch one of the frequent ranger-guided walking tours. If you prefer to go alone, a handy brochure is available. Among the highlights are the **Mascot Saloon,** at Broadway and 3rd Avenue, where statues belly up to the bar; the saloon is open daily from 8 a.m. to 6 p.m., and admission is free. Don't miss the 1897 **Moore House,** near 5th Avenue and Spring Street; it's open 10 a.m. to 5 p.m. in the summer, and admission is free. In a brilliant prediction ten years before the gold rush, Captain William Moore homesteaded the land that would become Skagway. But when the rush hit, the stampeders simply ignored his property claims.

2nd Avenue and Broadway, Skagway. ☎ _907-983-2921._ www.nps.gov/klgo. _Open: May–Sept daily 8 a.m.–6 p.m., Oct–Apr Mon–Fri 8 a.m.–5 p.m._

White Pass & Yukon Route

In 1900, after only two years of construction, workers completed this narrow-gauge railroad — an engineering marvel and a fun way to see spectacular, historic scenery. The summer-only excursion uses some cars more than 100 years old, climbing steep tracks chipped out of the mountains' sides. The 40-mile round-trip summit excursion lasts a bit over three hours and costs $110 for adults, $55 for kids 3 to 12, free for kids 2 and under. Other, longer trips are available, too; check the Web site. Go on a nice day — when the pass is socked in by weather, all you see are clouds. Tickets are expensive, and you have to reserve ahead. Take the gamble: Cancellation carries only a $10-per-person penalty, and you can change dates for no charge. Try to go on a weekend, when fewer cruise-ship passengers are in town taking up the seats. You can book weekend trains as little as a week ahead, while midweek reservations can sell out months in advance.

See map p. 351. 231 2nd Ave., Skagway. ☎ **800-343-7373** _or 907-983-2217._ www.wpyr.com. _See Web site for entire fare schedule._

Getting outdoors in Skagway

When you tire of history, there are several ways to get outdoors nearby.

Biking

Sockeye Cycle, 381 5th Ave., off Broadway (☎ **907-983-2851;** www.
cyclealaska.com), leads bike tours, including one that takes clients to
the top of the White Pass in a van and coasts down on bikes; the 2½-hour
trip is $79. Sockeye Cycle also takes riders to Dyea in a van and then
leads a bike tour of the quiet ghost-town site for the same price. Or ride
to Dyea on your own over a scenic, hilly, 10-mile coastal road, with a
rented bike.

Flightseeing

Skagway is a good starting point for flights over Glacier Bay National
Park, just to the west. Operators include Haines-based **Mountain Flying
Service** (☎ **800-954-8747** or 907-766-3007; www.glacierbayflight
seeing.com), known for glacier and beach landings. Prices range from
$159 to $499 per person, and reservations are recommended. **Temsco
Helicopters** (☎ **866-683-2900** or 907-983-2900; www.temscoair.com)
offers 80-minute tours over the Chilkoot Trail, including a 25-minute
landing on a glacier (not in Glacier Bay); those flights cost $289. A heli-
copter and dog-sled tour on Denver Glacier is $479.

Hiking

An easy evening walk starts at the footbridge at the west end of the airport parking lot, crossing the Skagway River to **Yakutania Point Park,**
where pine trees grow from cracks in the rounded granite of the shoreline. Across the park is a shortcut taking a couple miles off the trip to
Dyea and to the **Skyline Trail and A. B. Mountain,** a strenuous climb to
a 5,000-ft. summit with great views. On the southeast side of town,
across the railroad tracks, a network of trails heads up from Spring
Street between 3rd and 4th avenues to a series of mountain lakes, the
closest of which is **Lower Dewey Lake,** less than a mile up the trail. A
Skagway Trail Map is available from the visitor center (see "Fast Facts:
Skagway" at the end of this chapter).

To hike the historic Chilkoot Trail, allow several days and make arrangements for a special permit, gear, and transportation at the other end. For
permit details, contact **Parks Canada** (☎ **800-661-0486** or 867-667-3910;
www.pc.gc.ca/chilkoot). You can rent equipment, get advice,
or even arrange a guided hike with the **Mountain Shop,** 355 4th Ave.
(☎ **907-983-2544;** www.packerexpeditions.com/mountainshop.html).

Other cool things to see and do

The **Skagway Museum and Archives,** at 7th Avenue and Spring Street
(☎ **907-983-2420**), rewards an hour of study in a dignified granite building. Admission is $2 adults, $1 students, free for kids 12 and under. The
museum is open in the summer Monday through Friday 9 a.m. to 5 p.m.
Saturday 10 a.m. to 5 p.m., and Sunday 10 a.m. to 4 p.m.; winter hours
vary, so call ahead.

The graves of Soapy Smith and Frank Reid are the big attractions at the **Gold Rush Cemetery,** but don't miss the short walk up to crashing Reid Falls. The closely spaced dates on many of the cemetery's markers attest to the epidemics that devastated stampeders living in squalid conditions. The cemetery is 1½ miles from town, up State Street.

Nightlife

The *Days of '98 Show* has been staged every year since 1927 in the Fraternal Order of Eagles Hall No. 25, at 6th Avenue and Broadway (☎ 907-983-2545). Actors from all over the United States perform at least two shows a day (10:30 a.m. and 2:30 p.m.), and sometimes as many as four. They include singing, cancan dancing, the story of the shooting of Soapy Smith, and a Robert Service reading. (Service recorded the gold-rush era in his amusing poetry, which he traded for drinks in the saloons.) Daytime shows are $20; evening shows, $22. Kids 12 and under are half-price.

The **Red Onion Saloon,** at 2nd Avenue and Broadway (☎ **907-983-2414;** www.redonion1898.com), celebrates its history as a brothel with waitresses in corsets and a mock madam who offers $5 tours of the rooms upstairs. It's closed in winter.

Fast Facts: Skagway

Bank

Wells Fargo, at Broadway and 6th Avenue, has an ATM.

Emergencies

Dial ☎ **911.**

Hospital

The Dahl Medical Clinic, staffed by an advanced nurse practitioner, can be reached at ☎ 907-983-2255 during business hours.

Information

Contact the Skagway Convention & Visitors Bureau, 245 Broadway, Skagway (☎ 907-983-2854; www.skagway.com). The Web site contains links to hotels and activities; call ☎ 888-762-1898 to have them send you the information on paper.

Internet Access

Free Internet access is available at the Skagway Public Library, 769 State St. (☎ 907-983-2665).

Police

For non-emergency business, call ☎ 907-983-2232. The police station is on State Street, just south of 1st Avenue.

Post Office

The post office is on Broadway between 6th and 7th avenues.

Taxes

Sales tax is 5 percent. The room tax totals 8 percent.

Chapter 22

Sitka

· ·

In This Chapter

▶ Finding Sitka's treasures
▶ Making your way to and around Sitka
▶ Discovering the best spots to stay and dine
▶ Touring the historic sites
▶ Getting outside in Sitka
▶ Going on to Ketchikan

· ·

Sitka has a combination of qualities you can't find anywhere else. It's the center of Russian-American history, with more to investigate from that time than any other town. It's also the site of two great Alaska Native struggles: two centuries ago, a battle against the Russians, and, more recently, a successful fight to keep Tlingit culture alive and accessible. Besides, the town's charm is irresistible and its natural setting spectacular — an island surrounded by islands on waters rich with life. Altogether, Sitka is the best of Alaska. Taking the extra trouble to get there is really worth your while.

Besides the fascinating historic and cultural places to visit, which can easily fill a day or two, make a point of getting outdoors in Sitka. The waters here are full of otters, whales, seabirds, and fish, and the town has some fine hiking trails.

Getting There

Sitka is on the west side of Baranof Island, accessible only by air or water. To get downtown from the airport or ferry dock, **Sitka Tours** (☎ 907-747-8443) charges $8 each way; reservations are not needed. A ride downtown from the ferry dock with **Sitka Cab** (☎ 907-747-5001), one of five cab companies in town, is about $18.

By ferry

The ferries of the **Alaska Marine Highway System** (☎ 800-642-0066; www.ferryalaska.com) serve Sitka from Juneau and Petersburg. Vessels pass through the narrow and scenic Peril Straits to get to Sitka. The fare from Juneau, nine hours by conventional ferry, less than five by fast ferry, is $45. The ferry dock (☎ 907-747-3300) is 7 miles out of town.

Understanding Sitka's place in history

Two crucial historical events took place in Sitka: The Russians took over Southeast Alaska from the Native Tlingit population, and the Americans took over all of Alaska from the Russians. In 1799, the Russians had already conquered the coastal people west of here and were moving eastward in search of new sea-otter hunting grounds (they sold the pelts in China for fabulous sums) when they set up a settlement near present-day Sitka. The Tlingit were a fierce and powerful people, and they didn't accept the invasion: They massacred the occupants of the Russian fort in 1802. In 1804, the Russians counterattacked. The battle lasted six days, but finally the Tlingit withdrew. That battlefield remains the heart of the Sitka National Historical Park, a peaceful and moving place under huge trees and totem poles.

After the battle, Sitka became the capital of Russian America, which at one time stretched all the way to California, and the best remaining buildings from that era are here. But with the near extinction of otters, the colony became a money loser, and in 1867, the Russian czar sold his claim to Alaska to the United States for $7.2 million, or 2¢ an acre. Even at that price, most Americans thought they'd been taken. When the Russian flag came down over Sitka's Castle Hill and the American flag went up, the United States didn't even bother to give the new territory a government. Only decades later, with gold discoveries that provided Alaska with a white population, did the capital move to Juneau and the modern era begin.

By air

Alaska Airlines (☎ 800-252-7522; www.alaskaair.com) links Sitka daily to Juneau and Ketchikan with flights that then continue nonstop to Seattle and Anchorage.

Getting Around Sitka

Sitka is on an island, so you can't drive far (see the nearby "Sitka" map). The **ferry terminal** is 7 miles out, near the end of **Halibut Point Road.** The town faces Sitka Sound. Across Sitka Channel are **Japonski Island** and the **airport.**

You easily can manage Sitka on foot and with a visitor shuttle or taxi, unless you choose lodgings or take hikes out on Halibut Point Road.

By bus

The **Visitor Transit Bus,** operated by the Sitka Tribe, 200 Katlian St. (☎ 888-270-8687 or 907-747-7290; www.sitkatours.com), makes a continuous circuit of the sights May through September when large cruise ships are in town. The fare is $5 for one round-trip loop or $10 all day. Guided town tours of various lengths are offered as well.

By car

If you decide to rent a car for better access to trails or lodgings on Halibut Point Road, you can pick one up at the airport from **Avis** (☎ **800-230-4898** or 907-966-2404; www.avis.com).

By bike

A bicycle can be the most efficient and enjoyable way to get around Sitka. **Yellow Jersey Cycle Shop,** 329 Harbor Dr., right across from the Centennial Hall downtown (☎ **907-747-6317;** www.yellowjersey cycles.com), rents quality bikes for $25 per day.

Where to Stay

The **Sitka Convention & Visitors Bureau** (☎ **907-747-5940;** www. sitka.org) has links to many B&Bs on its Web site and sends out printed lists on request.

Alaska Ocean View Bed and Breakfast Inn
$$$–$$$$ Near Downtown

Ebullient Carole Denkinger and her husband, Bill, have a passion for making their bed-and-breakfast one you'll remember. They've thought of everything — the covered outdoor Jacuzzi where you can watch the eagles, a Wii setup, other toys and games for the kids, a laptop to borrow, an open snack counter, and HEPA air filters in each room for people with allergies, just to name a few items. Rooms are soft and plush and guests are pampered. The exceptional hospitality extends to Carole's big, organic breakfasts, which she cooks to suit guests' dietary preferences — for vegans, dieters, those with special sensitivities, and so on. The couple also strives to reduce the B&B's environmental footprint, which has been certified "green." The house is on a residential street with a view of the water about a mile from the historic district.

See map p. 359. 1101 Edgecumbe Dr., Sitka. ☎ *907-747-8310. Fax: 907-747-3440. www.sitka-alaska-lodging.com. Rack rates: High season $139–$199 double, off season $89–$139 double; extra person $40. Rates include full breakfast. AE, DC, DISC, MC, V.*

Fly-In Fish Inn
$$$–$$$$ Downtown

This is a classy little boutique hotel right on the water a bit off the beaten path north of the town center. The spacious rooms, with entrances off covered walkways, have simple, elegant decoration, in sage, gold, and burgundy. High-quality mattresses are covered with down pillows and cotton comforters. Each unit has a small wet bar with a sink, microwave, and coffee maker, stocked with snacks and supplies. Rooms renting for a $20 premium enjoy wonderful views, as does the beautifully appointed

Sitka

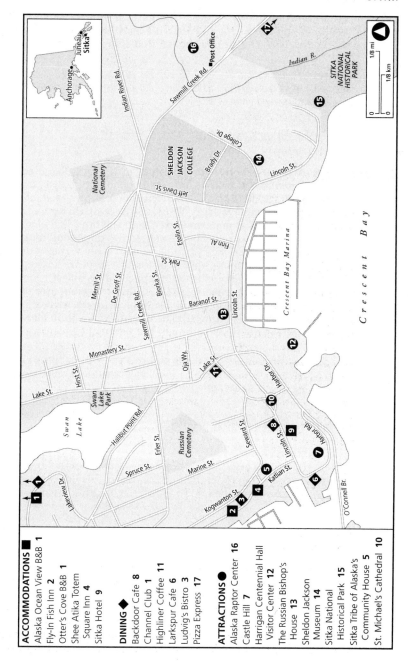

ACCOMMODATIONS ■
Alaska Ocean View B&B **1**
Fly-In Fish Inn **2**
Otter's Cove B&B **1**
Shee Atika Totem
  Square Inn **4**
Sitka Hotel **9**

DINING ◆
Backdoor Cafe **8**
Channel Club **1**
Highliner Coffee **11**
Larkspur Cafe **6**
Ludvig's Bistro **3**
Pizza Express **17**

ATTRACTIONS ●
Alaska Raptor Center **16**
Castle Hill **7**
Harrigan Centennial Hall
  Visitor Center **12**
The Russian Bishop's
  House **13**
Sheldon Jackson
  Museum **14**
Sitka National
  Historical Park **15**
Sitka Tribe of Alaska's
  Community House **5**
St. Michael's Cathedral **10**

waterfront bar downstairs, with a fireplace and a mosaic behind the bar and a deck over the harbor. The included breakfast is served in the bar, cooked to order for each guest. The hotel is only a few years old, and everything has been kept so clean, it's as if you're the first guest. The name comes from the air-taxi service that's on-site and that leaves from the dock.

See map p 359. 485 Katlian St., Sitka. ☎ **907-747-7910.** *www.flyinfishinn.com. Rack rates: High season $159–$179 double, $388 suite; low season $99 double, $199 suite. Extra person no charge. MC, V.*

Shee Atiká Totem Square Inn
$–$$ Downtown

This is the best large hotel in town. Owned by the local Native corporation and standing across the street from the community house, it makes full use of their Tlingit motifs and colors in its decoration — red, black, white, and earth — and employs many Natives on its staff. On both of our recent visits, the service was uniformly excellent; the housekeeping, spotless. The building makes use of the ocean view in two directions, and the rooms are well thought out and nicely equipped, with comfortable beds and large flat-screen TVs. Continuous upgrading for several years has kept it all like new. Common rooms include a light, spacious breakfast room, where a generous continental breakfast is served; fast, free computer terminals in the lobby; and snacks for guests available at all hours. A dock for tour and fishing charter boats is attached. The downtown location allows walking to some of the attractions, although the national historic site is a long walk.

See map p 359. 201 Katlian St., Sitka. ☎ **866-300-1353** *or 907-747-2839. www.totem squareinn.com. Rack rates: High season $139–$179 double, off season $89–$109 double; extra person $15. AE, DC, DISC, MC, V.*

Runner-up accommodations

Otter's Cove Bed & Breakfast
$$–$$$ North of Town With three large, well appointed bedrooms and an attractive common room right on the ocean, this B&B creates an over-all sense of privacy and peace. The hostess cooks full breakfasts. *See map p. 359. 3211 Halibut Point Rd., Sitka.* ☎ **907-747-4529.** *www.ottercovebandb. com.*

Sitka Hotel
$–$$ Downtown This is a budget choice and has its rough edges, including noisy heat, thin walls (it's not for light sleepers), and casual service. The rooms vary, with those in the older section at the front rela-tively small and creaky, and the newer rooms, in the back of the building, larger and with added amenities. *See map p. 359. 118 Lincoln St., Sitka.* ☎ **907-747-3288.** *www.sitkahotel.net.*

Where to Dine

Besides these stand-alone restaurants, note the restaurants described
with the two hotels in the preceding section.

The top restaurants

The Channel Club
$$–$$$$ **Downtown**   STEAK

For five decades, the Channel Club was among Alaska's most famous res-
taurants for its perfectly grilled steaks and unbelievable salad bar, but the
ultra-casual, ultra-masculine formula ultimately wore thin and it closed
several years ago. In its new incarnation, the club has kept the best of the
old restaurant — the rich, various salad bar is still mind-blowing — but
with an updated dining room and improved service that create a lovely,
calming place to eat, enjoy company, and take in the ocean view. Now the
restaurant's look is simple, elegant, and spotless. The menu includes
salmon, halibut, and cod, which is done well, but it's a steakhouse, and the
specialty is seasoned beef grilled right. The location, several miles out of
town, requires that you have a car or take the restaurant's free shuttle.

See map p. 359. 2906 Halibut Point Rd., Sitka. ☎ *907-747-7440. Reservations recom-
mended. Main courses: $16–$48. AE, MC, V. Open: Daily 5–9 p.m.*

Larkspur Cafe
$–$$ **Downtown**   CAFE

Below Sitka's public radio station, KCAW (known as "Raven Radio"), in the
historic cable-house building on the water, this is a happening coffee shop
that also serves sophisticated, handcrafted food. The dining room has a
small collection of funky, mismatched antique tables on a wood floor, and
there's more seating outside with ocean views. That's where you'd go if
you wanted to get away from the live music and the loud voices in the
festive atmosphere inside. The menu changes daily with the availability of
local food, but it includes items such as cold smoked lox on rye toast with
cream cheese and capers, or marinated black cod with brown rice and
baby bok choy. Influences are eclectic, with the common element the
owners' enthusiasm and the positive scene they've created.

See map p. 359. 2 Lincoln St., Sitka. ☎ *907-966-2326. Main courses: $5–$15. MC, V.
Open: Mon–Tues 11 a.m.–3 p.m., Wed–Sun 11 a.m.–10 p.m.*

Ludvig's Bistro
$$$–$$$$ **Downtown**   MEDITERRANEAN

This tiny dining room and its chef-owner, Colette Nelson, offer Sitka first-
rate cuisine, and it's a very pleasant place for a meal. Nelson has taken a
formerly grungy concrete space and filled it with charm and warmth, with
Mediterranean colors, wine bottles, and whimsical art. The restaurant is
too small to serve many meals at night, so each one is carefully crafted,

coming from a changing menu intended to stretch the chef and introduce the small-town clientele to new tastes. A recent menu included grilled marinated lamb chops, a wild mushroom *ragu,* and calamari. For lunch, catch their chowder cart downtown.

See map p. 359. 256 Katlian St., Sitka. ☎ *907-966-3663. Reservations recommended. Main courses: $17–$34. MC, V. Open: Daily 4–10 p.m. Closed Oct–Apr.*

Runner-up restaurants

Backdoor Cafe

$ **Downtown** **COFFEEHOUSE** This spot is a cool hangout for a cold breakfast or for a lunch of soup, sandwiches, or specials. *See map p. 359 104 Barracks St. (back half of the bookstore), Sitka.* ☎ *907-747-8856. Main courses: Under $10. Open: Mon–Fri 6:30 a.m.–5 p.m., Sat 6:30 a.m.–2 p.m.*

Pizza Express

$–$$ **Downtown** **MEXICAN** This is primarily a Mexican place that also serves pizza. Sitka families come here for a filling, inexpensive meal. *See map p. 359. 1321 Sawmill Creek Rd., Sitka.* ☎ *907-966-2428. Main courses: $9–$20. Open: Mon–Sat 11 a.m.–9 p.m., Sun noon to 9 p.m.*

Exploring Sitka

Sitka is Alaska's most historic town and has more high-quality sightseeing than any other. One day may not be enough, if these attractions interest you. Definitely plan for more than a day if you want to see the historic sites and do any of the excellent outdoor activities. The visitor shuttle is covered in the earlier "Getting Around Sitka" section.

Exploring the top attractions

I've arranged these top attractions according to importance, recognizing that you may not have time for everything. I suggest starting at the Sitka National Historical Park, which will put the rest of the sites in context.

Sitka National Historical Park

The park, designated in 1910, preserves the site of the 1804 Battle of Sitka, in which Alaska's Russian invaders defeated the Tlingit and won control of the area (see the "Understanding Sitka's place in history" sidebar, earlier in this chapter). The park contains an extraordinary collection of early totem poles, with reproductions and contemporary originals displayed outside and ancient poles housed indoors in a wonderful 30-ft.-high hall. The visitor center is really a living museum: Besides the fascinating explanatory exhibits, there are workshops in which artisans from the Southeast Alaska Indian Cultural Center create traditional crafts of metal, wood, beads, textiles, and woven grass. Visitors are welcome to come in and ask questions. Don't be shy — striking up a conversation is more polite than just staring. Be sure to walk through the totem park and battle site. A free 12-minute video provides a good historical overview.

See map p. 359. 106 Metlakatla St., Sitka. ☎ **907-747-0110.** www.nps.gov/sitk. *Open: Visitor center daily 8 a.m.–5 p.m; park summer daily 6 a.m.–10 p.m., winter daily 7 a.m.–8 p.m. Admission: $4.*

The Russian Bishop's House

In 1842–43, the Russian America Company retained Finnish shipbuilders to construct this extraordinary house for Bishop Innocent Veniaminov as a residence, school, and chapel. It may have survived many years of neglect in part because its huge beams fit together like those of a ship. Now beautifully restored, the building is the best of only a few surviving from all of Russian America and is Alaska's most interesting historic site. Downstairs is a self-guided museum; upstairs, rangers lead tours of the bishop's quarters, which are furnished with original and period pieces. It's an extraordinary window into an alternate stream of American history, from a time before the founding of Seattle or San Francisco, when Sitka was the most important city on North America's Pacific Coast. The tour concludes with a visit to a beautiful little chapel with many of the original icons that Innocent imported from Russia.

See map p. 359. Lincoln and Monastery streets, Sitka. No phone; call Sitka National Historical Park Visitor Center (☎ **907-747-0110***) for information. Hours depend on staffing. Admission: $4 per person or $15 per family; family admission also covers the visitor center.*

Alaska Raptor Center

This nonprofit center takes in injured birds of prey (mainly bald eagles, but also owls, hawks, and other species) for veterinary treatment and release or, if too badly injured, for placement in a zoo or as part of the collection of 20 that live on-site. Visitors get to see the impressive birds up close in a lecture setting, through the glass wall of the veterinary clinic, and in outdoor enclosures, but the highlight is an extraordinary flight-training center. This enormous aviary is where recuperating birds learn to fly again, and visitors can walk its length behind one-way glass watching them preen, feed, and take to the air in a peaceful setting simulating their natural habitat. Seeing these giant birds fly from so close is awesome. The center's grounds also include a pleasant, disabled-accessible nature trail that leads down to a salmon stream where healthy eagles sometimes can be seen feeding.

See map p. 359. 1000 Raptor Way (off Sawmill Creek Boulevard), Sitka. ☎ **800-643-9425** *or 907-747-8662.* www.alaskaraptor.org. *Open: Summer daily 8 a.m.–4 p.m.; call for hours in winter. Admission: $12 adults, $6 kids 12 and under.*

Sheldon Jackson Museum

Sheldon Jackson, a Presbyterian missionary with powerful friends in Washington, D.C., was Alaska's first General Agent for Education, a paternal guardian of the welfare, schooling, and spiritual lives of Alaska's Natives. On the side, he gathered an omnivorous collection of some 5,000 objects of Native art and culture from 1888 to 1898. That collection, the best in Alaska, has been displayed for more than a century in a concrete building on the campus of a now defunct college bearing Jackson's name. Despite the age of many of the pieces, they appear as if just made. Don't miss Katlian's raven-shaped helmet, which was worn by the Kiksadi clan's war leader in the Battle of Sitka in 1804. It's that rare piece of great history that's also great art. Native artists demonstrate their skills on summer days, and the gift shop offers almost exclusively authentic Native arts and crafts, with prices to match.

See map p. 359. 104 College Dr., Sitka. ☎ *907-747-8981.* www.museums.state. ak.us. *Open: Mid-May to mid-Sept daily 9 a.m.–5 p.m., mid-Sept to mid-May Tues–Sat 10 a.m.–4 p.m. Admission: $4 adults, free for kids 18 and under.*

Getting outdoors in Sitka

No wonder the Russians and the Tlingit fought for this place: It's absolutely gorgeous and full of wildlife and fish. See the historic sites by all means, but also take the time to explore the rich environment that lured those historic figures here — an environment that's still pretty much the way it was in those long-ago days.

Fishing

Many charter boats are available for salmon or halibut. The **Sitka Convention & Visitors Bureau** (☎ 907-747-5940; www.sitka.org) keeps a detailed charter-boat list online. Using the grid view (www.sitka.org/grid.html), you can compare boats, rates, and services, and link to the vessel's own home page. **Alaska Adventures Unlimited** (☎ 907-747-5576) is a long-established booking agent handling many charter boats.

Hiking

Sitka is a great hiking area. A dozen U.S. Forest Service hiking trails are accessible from the roads around town. A beautifully made little book, *Sitka Trails* (Alaska Geographic), covers each trail with a detailed description and fine-scale color topographic map. For additional advice, contact the **Sitka Ranger District**, 204 Siginaka Way, Sitka (☎ 907-747-6671; www.fs.fed.us/r10/tongass/districts/sitka).

Here are some favorites:

> ✔ **Indian River Trail:** From downtown, this is a 4-mile walk (one-way) through the rain forest, rising gradually up the river valley to a small waterfall. Take Indian River Road off Sawmill Creek Road just east of downtown.

- **Gavan Hill–Harbor Mountain Trail:** A steeper mountain-climbing trail to alpine terrain and great views. The trailhead is near the end of Baranof Street, which starts near the Russian Bishop's House. It gains 2,500 ft. over 3 miles to the peak of Gavan Hill and then continues another 3 miles along a ridge to meet Harbor Mountain Road.

- **Starrigavan Recreation Area trails:** The recreation area is at the north end of Halibut Point Road, near the ferry dock, 7½ miles from downtown. On the right, the **Estuary Life Trail** and **Forest Muskeg Trail** total about a mile. Exquisitely developed and accessible to anyone, they circle a grassy estuary rich with birds and fish. The well-built **Mosquito Cove Trail** starts from the far end of the campground loop on the left, loops 1¼ miles along the shore to the secluded gravel beach of the cove, and returns over boardwalk steps through the old-growth forest.

Marine wildlife tours

When sea conditions allow, tour boats visit **St. Lazaria Island,** a bird rookery where you can see puffins, murres, rhinoceros auklets, and other pelagic birds. Volcanic rock drops straight down into deep water, so big boats can pilot in close, but in rough weather even they won't go to the exposed location of St. Lazaria. When you can't get to the island, however, there's still plenty to look at. Humpback whales appear in large groups in fall and often are seen by the half-dozen in summer, and encounters with endearing sea otters are a near certainty.

The largest tour-boat operation, **Allen Marine Tours** (☎ 888-747-8101; www.allenmarinetours.com), has well-trained naturalists aboard to explain the wildlife. A three-hour cruise Tuesday, Wednesday, or Thursday at 1:15 p.m. or on Saturday at 1:30 p.m. costs $119 adults, $79 kids. The boat leaves from the Crescent Harbor Visitors Dock late May through early September. Buy tickets onboard.

Sea Life Discovery Tours (☎ 877-966-2301 or 907-966-2301; www.sealifediscoverytours.com) offers an opportunity to see the rich underwater life in Sitka Sound from an extraordinary boat that has big windows 4 ft. below the waterline; it's really cool. They charge $86 for a two-hour tour; call for times.

Sea-kayaking

Sitka's protected waters and intricate shorelines are perfect for sea-kayaking. You're almost sure to come upon seals, sea otters, sea lions, and eagles, and you may see whales. **Sitka Sound Ocean Adventures** (☎ 907-752-0660; www.kayaksitka.com) offers day paddles of various lengths. A 2½-hour paddle takes kayakers into the islands around Sitka and costs $69 for adults, $49 for kids. A half-day paddle could also go to a historic World War II fort, where you can walk through the abandoned bunkers. That's $149 adults, $109 kids.

What about Ketchikan?

When arriving by boat at the south end of the Southeast Alaska Panhandle, the first place you land is Ketchikan, Alaska's fourth-largest city. Because of the location, Ketchikan is usually first in every Alaska guidebook, but I've neglected to include it at all here. This isn't an oversight. My philosophy in this book is to send you to the best and forget the rest, and that forces me to make some tough choices. I love Ketchikan, but Sitka is unquestionably richer in history and wildlife and is Ketchikan's equal in totem poles and Tlingit culture. Sitka also suffers less from cruise-ship tourism, which tends to create a crowded, carnival atmosphere in the towns where several ships can tie up at once.

If you have time for both communities, or if your itinerary makes Ketchikan easier, by all means go. You'll find plenty to do there, with totem-pole-viewing and fishing topping the list, and also exceptional bear-viewing and flightseeing to Misty Fjords National Monument. I cover it all in my comprehensive Alaska guidebook, *Frommer's Alaska* (Wiley Publishing). Or contact the **Ketchikan Visitors Bureau,** 131 Front St., Ketchikan (☎ **800-770-3300** or 907-225-6166; www.visit-ketchikan.com).

Tide-pooling and shore walks

Halibut Point State Recreation Area, 4½ miles north of town on Halibut Point Road, is a great place for picnics, shore rambles, and tide-pooling. The Mosquito Cove Trail (see "Hiking," earlier in this chapter) is also promising. Check a tide book to find out about the best low tides; the books are available all over town. The best time to go is when the lowest tide is expected, arriving on the shore an hour before the low ebb. To identify the little creatures you'll see, buy a plastic-covered field guide at the National Park Service visitor center or at a bookstore.

More cool things to see and do

Sitka offers so many high-quality attractions that the runners-up here would be the top picks in most Alaska towns:

✓ **Visit a historic Russian Orthodox Church. St. Michael's Cathedral,** at Lincoln and Cathedral streets (☎ **907-747-8120**), was the first in the New World, standing grandly in the middle of Sitka's principal street since 1848 (although today's structure is an exact re-creation of the burned original structure). The cathedral contains several miraculous icons, some dating from the 17th century, as well as a trove of fascinating stories told by knowledgeable guides. The church is open Monday through Friday 9 a.m. to 4 p.m.; call for weekend and winter hours. A $2 donation is requested.

✓ **Attend a traditional Native dance performance.** The Sitka Tribe performs at the community house, 200 Katlian St. (☎ **888-270-8687** or 907-747-7290; www.sitkatours.com), on the north side of the downtown parade ground. Performances last 30 minutes and include dances and a story. It's entirely traditional. You can also sign up for tours and activities in the lobby. Admission is $8 adults, $5 kids; call for times.

Shopping

Most of Sitka's best shops and galleries are on Lincoln and Harbor streets. Several are across the street from St. Michael's Cathedral, on the uphill side.

- ✔ **Fairweather Prints,** 209 Lincoln St. (☎ **907-747-8601**), has a fun, youthful feel. It's large and has a diverse selection, such as wearable art (including T-shirts), watercolors, prints, ceramics, and cute, inexpensive crafts.

- ✔ Continue west on Lincoln to **Old Harbor Books,** 201 Lincoln St. (☎ **907-747-8808**), a good browsing store with an excellent selection of Alaska books and a cozy espresso shop in back, the Backdoor Cafe.

- ✔ In the other direction, near the boat harbor, the **Sitka Rose Gallery** occupies a Victorian house at 419 Lincoln St. (☎ **888-236-1536** or 907-747-3030), featuring higher-end work, mostly local, including sculpture, original paintings, engraving, and jewelry.

- ✔ The **Sheldon Jackson Museum Gift Shop,** 104 College Dr. (☎ **907-747-6233**), is an excellent place to buy Alaska Native arts and crafts, assured of their authenticity.

Fast Facts: Sitka

ATMs

Three banks with ATMs are next to each other downtown, near 300 Lincoln St.

Emergencies

In an emergency, call ☎ 911.

Hospital

Sitka Community is at 209 Moller Dr. (☎ 907-747-3241).

Information

Get visitor information from the Sitka Convention & Visitors Bureau (☎ 907-747-5940; www.sitka.org).

Internet Access

Highliner Coffee on Lake Street near Seward Street offers Internet access.

Police

Call ☎ 907-747-3245 for nonemergency business.

Post Office

The post office is at 338 Lincoln St.

Taxes

Sales tax is 5 percent October through March, 6 percent April through September. The tax on rooms totals 11 percent October through March, 12 percent April through September.

Part VI
The End of the Road and Beyond: Bush Alaska

The 5th Wave   By Rich Tennant

@RICHTENNANT

RUN FOR YOUR LIFE
THE POLAR BEARS ARE
GROUPING FOR AN ATTACK
LODGE

"Martin, is this safe?"

In this part . . .

While reading adventure tales as kids, some people develop an irresistible drive to go to Alaska. That drive has nothing to do with easy-to-reach towns or national parks on roads. They're looking for the Arctic, for remote bear country, for extreme places completely unlike anything they've experienced before. In short, they want to go to the Bush.

In this part, I deal with some of the best Bush destinations — the ones with something to see and reasonable services to get you there and keep you comfortable. Each of these four places — Nome, Barrow, Katmai National Park, and Kodiak Island — offers something unique, exciting, and exotic.

Chapter 23

The Arctic

In This Chapter

▶ Deciding whether you really want to go to the Arctic

▶ Picking an Arctic destination

▶ Taking in the Eskimo culture of Barrow

▶ Joining in the gold-rush fun of Nome

*P*icturing the Arctic in your imagination is easy: in summer, flat green tundra without trees meeting a green ocean; in winter, flat white snow and ocean melding together into one. But you can't imagine the real beauty of the place until you go there. Under diffuse gray light, the land's watercolor tints and hues melt together with its stark shapes and shades. Under the beams of the low midnight sun, rich and yellow, the snow and sky become royal blue. A sense of overwhelming immensity prevails; it can make you feel incredibly tiny and vulnerable but also entirely free for the first time. The Arctic is a remote, unforgiving hell of harsh weather, but it's also a paradise.

All flowery writing aside, however, traveling to the Arctic definitely isn't for everyone. You can't go there cheaply. And, after you're there, you won't find much to do. The Arctic's few communities are tiny. Outdoor activities are rugged and cold. The towns have developed activities for visitors, but they're mostly designed for escorted tour packages and can be scripted and even dreary. If seeing the Arctic isn't a particular interest, you can find better ways to spend your time and money on an Alaskan trip.

If, on the other hand, you feel the drive to go way up north, fulfill your dream now. Just make sure to allow enough time for getting away from the tour bus so that you can have one of those strange, solitary moments that seem to happen only at the top of the world.

In this chapter, I cover in detail the two best towns to visit in the Arctic — Barrow and Nome — because each offers a different flavor to your visit. Although flying is the only way to get to Barrow and Nome, you also can reach the Arctic by driving the Dalton Highway north from Fairbanks. That very ambitious option is covered in Chapter 18.

Discovering the Arctic and Its Major Attractions

Barrow and Nome offer different activities that appeal to different interests. To help you choose, here are the highlights of each.

Barrow

Barrow is the essential Arctic community. It's the farthest north of any mainland town in North America, lying on a point in the Arctic Ocean around which bowhead whales migrate. In a tradition dating back 1,000 years, the Iñupiat Eskimos here hunt whales for sustenance. The town isn't much to look at: Modest plywood houses on pilings sit on flat green tundra along gravel roads. But it's a unique and potentially interesting place to visit, with some of the following highlights:

- The Iñupiat Heritage Center, a living museum of Eskimo culture
- Bird-watching and polar-bear-viewing tours
- Guided tours to discover more about this unusual town

Nome

Nome is a gold-rush town, not a Native community like Barrow, and it isn't technically Arctic, lying just south of the Arctic Circle (although it looks like the Arctic). But in many ways, Nome is a better place for an independent traveler to visit, because you can do more on your own, including some of the following:

- Exploring the network of roads around Nome on your own to see abundant wildlife
- Witnessing a gold-rush town that still rocks, loaded with some of the best stories anywhere in Alaska
- Watching the finish of the Iditarod Trail Sled Dog Race, Alaska's biggest annual event

Beware indoor pollution

Bush Alaska lags behind the rest of the country in many ways, few more startling than the prevalence of smoking in these remote little communities. It seems as if everyone smokes everywhere. Escape can be impossible. Restaurants usually are smoky, and lower-cost hotel rooms tend to smell smoky. If avoiding smoking is a high priority, stick to the most tourist-oriented (and most expensive) establishments.

Going to the Top of the World: Barrow

Barrow is an ancient Iñupiat Native community, founded and still sustained by its access at this farthest-north point to the migrating bowhead whale, which Eskimos hunt from small, open boats. It's also a modern town, rich in North Slope oil revenues, a center of scientific research about the Arctic, and home to Alaska's largest corporation, the Native-owned Arctic Slope Regional Corporation. If these seem like contradictions, they are, but they're like the ones that describe each person you meet here: Corporate leaders also are respected whalers. (Their hunt is not a threat to the bowhead whales' population, which is strong and growing.)

The town's Iñupiat Heritage Center celebrates this cultural mix. There you can view natural and cultural exhibits, see Iñupiat dance, and meet Native people selling their crafts. The bus tour that most visitors take also points out some of the town's interesting points, although it can't be described as a cultural immersion. You also may be able to go out and see polar bears.

Beyond those formal activities, however, you won't find much else to do in Barrow. The town has only one main store and no trails to hike — the tundra tends to be swampy — although walking on the gravel beaches is possible. Most visitors come up just for the day on the escorted package tour offered by Alaska Airline Vacations from Anchorage or Fairbanks; the package is a good deal and gives you the highlights. If you want time on your own, you can spend the night and go back the next day. Few people want to spend more time here than that.

Getting there

The only way to get to Barrow is via **Alaska Airlines** (☎ 800-252-7522; www.alaskaair.com), which flies a couple of times daily from Anchorage and Fairbanks and offers one-day and overnight tour packages. The packages are good deals, competitive in price with stand-alone round-trip tickets from Anchorage, which currently cost $600 to $700. Book through **Alaska Airlines Vacations** (☎ 800-500-5511; www.alaskaair.com/vacations). I explain more about this in "Exploring Barrow," later in this chapter.

Getting around

The Alaska Airlines Vacations package tours provide all transportation. Otherwise, the easiest way to get around Barrow is in a taxi, with competing companies all charging low rates ($6 or $7 per trip in town, $10 beyond the town, plus $1 for each additional passenger). Try **Arcticab** (☎ 907-852-2227).

Where to stay

Barrow has few lodging options, and none I would call cheap. The lowest-cost option is the Alaska Airlines Vacation package, which puts you at the **Top of the World Hotel,** described in this section.

King Eider Inn
$$$$ Barrow

The best rooms in town are found in this clapboard building near the airport. They're crisp and airy, with faux rustic furniture, and kept up well. It surely helps that shoes are not allowed in the hotel — you have to take them off at the front door every time you come in. The halls and rooms are decorated with Native art. A room with a kitchenette is $10 more, and the enormous and luxurious Presidential Suite (where Barrow's honeymooners and visiting celebrities stay) is $297 summer, $269 winter. The lobby is comfortable, with a stone fireplace; free coffee and other hot beverages are offered there around the clock. Bathrooms have large shower stalls, not tubs.

1752 Ahkovak St., Barrow. ☎ *888-303-4337 for reservations, or 907-852-4700. Fax: 907-852-2025.* www.kingeider.net. *Rack rates: Summer $189 double, winter $169 double; extra person $25. AE, MC, V.*

Top of the World Hotel
$$$–$$$$$ Barrow

This is a good hotel with familiar standard rooms, worn in places but perfectly comfortable. The staff works to keep the place clean and quiet. Rooms have light furniture and blue carpet, desks, and refrigerators. Those on the water side have remarkable views of the Arctic Ocean, and it's only a few steps to the beach and the heart of Barrow. The lobby is a place where people pass time, somewhat cluttered with a TV and a stuffed polar bear. The hotel is owned by the Native corporation that also operates Tundra Tours, and you stay here if you come on the package tour.

1200 Agvik St., Barrow. ☎ *907-852-3900.* www.tundratoursinc.com. *Rack rates: Summer $150–$220 double, winter $125–$155 double; extra person $20 AE, DC, DISC, MC, V.*

Where to dine

The sale of alcohol is illegal in Barrow, so you can't buy a glass of wine or beer with your meal in any of the restaurants. Bringing alcohol with you is severely limited; for simplicity's sake, and to avoid breaking the law, don't do it.

You'll find no fine dining in Barrow, but there are plenty of places to eat out where locals go for a pizza or burger.

Most visitors go no further than **Pepe's North of the Border,** 1204 Agvik St. (☎ **907-852-8200**), which adjoins the Top of the World Hotel. It serves large portions of familiar American-style Mexican food, steak, and seafood. On the Alaska Airlines Vacations package, you'll lunch here and likely receive a souvenir from owner Fran Tate, who's locally famous for an appearance she made on the Johnny Carson show decades ago.

The **Northern Lights Restaurant,** 5122 Herman St. (☎ **907-852-3300**), is a comfortable place with a clean dining room and a charming family in charge. The extensive menu features the owner's own Chinese food, plus deli selections and burgers, and the town's top-rated pizza.

Exploring Barrow

For most visitors, the escorted tour is the way to visit Barrow, for reasons I explain in this section. If you're feeling brave, however, you can have an interesting visit without a guide, joining a wildlife-viewing outing and spending time at the Iñupiat Heritage Center and seeing the Iñupiaq dancing there.

Basic Barrow: The Escorted Tour

Even if you hate escorted tours, as I do, they make sense in Barrow. The package offered jointly by Tundra Tours and Alaska Airlines Vacations usually costs little more than an Alaska Airlines plane ticket alone, but includes valuable extras. Barrow is hard to figure out without a guide: It has no downtown, no shops, and few obviously public places. When you take the tour, you'll get a good six-hour orientation and some highlights. Then you can stay overnight to take your own measure of the place. The tour drives around town and out the short roads beyond town, and visits the Iñupiat Heritage Center, described in the next listing, where you watch dancing and a blanket toss and can buy crafts directly from artists. (That presentation is the highlight; if you skip the escorted tour, make sure to visit the Iñupiat Heritage Center anyway.) The day-trip tour is about $500 from Fairbanks; for $600 per person, double occupancy, you can spend one night in Barrow at the Top of the World Hotel, giving you time on your own without the tour group. Both prices include airfare. If you buy the tour separately when you're already in Barrow, it's $105.

Tundra Tours. ☎ **800-882-8478.** *www.tundratoursinc.com.*

The Iñupiat Heritage Center

This is the town's main attraction. It's part museum, part gathering center, and part venue for living culture. Inside is a workshop for craftspeople where hunters build the traditional boats and tools they use and where drummers build their drums; during the summer, an artist is usually in residence for visitors. In the museum area, displays of Iñupiat artifacts change regularly, while a permanent exhibit covers Eskimo whaling and the influence that Yankee whaling has had on it. An added fee of $7 includes Iñupiaq dancing and drumming demonstrations, a blanket toss, games, and a craft sale that happen every afternoon in the summer from

1:30 to 3:30 p.m.; these are the same programs that are the highlight of the escorted tours.

Ahkovak and C streets. ☎ **907-852-0422.** *www.nps.gov/inup. Open: Mon–Fri 8:30 a.m.–5 p.m. (call ahead to see the dancing program on weekends). Admission: $10 adults, $5 students, free for seniors and kids 6 and under.*

Getting outdoors in Barrow

In season, Barrow is a good place to see polar bears. The bears are always around when the ice is in; they're dangerous and people take extreme care to avoid them. Barrow and other North Slope communities have minimized the danger of bears in town by setting up sites outside of the villages to dispose of gut piles and other hunting waste. It's a way of bribing the bears to leave the town alone. In Barrow, heavy equipment hauls the leftovers from fall whale-butchering — bones and a few inedible organs — out to the very end of the point. Polar bears come for an easy meal whenever the pack ice is close to shore, which is October through June. Tours by casual home businesses take visitors out to the point in all-terrain vans or Humvees that can drive on the beach gravel. Arrangements change annually, so you'll have to call ahead to your hotel to line something up. Be sure to get your tour firmly reserved before you go.

Fast Facts: Barrow

Alcohol

The sale of alcohol is illegal in Barrow, and importation for personal use in your luggage is limited and controlled by a permit system. If it's an issue, call ahead to the Barrow Alcohol Distribution (☎ 907-852-3788) or the Office of the Mayor (☎ 907-852-5211, ext. 231). Bootlegging is a serious crime. My advice: Abstain while in Barrow.

ATMs

Wells Fargo, 1078 Kiogak St., has an ATM.

Emergencies

Dial ☎ **911.**

Hospital

Samuel Simmonds Memorial Hospital is at 1296 Agvik St. (☎ 907-852-4611).

Information

To obtain advance visitor information, contact the City of Barrow, Office of the Mayor (☎ 907-852-5211, ext. 231; www.cityof barrow.org), or call one of the hotels listed earlier in this chapter.

Internet Access

You can get online free at the Tuzzy Library at the Iñupiat Heritage Center.

Police

Contact the North Slope Borough Department of Public Safety at 1068 Kiogak St. (☎ 907-852-6111).

Taxes

Barrow has no sales tax. Room tax is 5 percent.

On Your Own in Nome

Compared to Barrow, Nome is not as far north, is not as rich in Alaska Native culture, and doesn't have a sizable museum or polar-bear-viewing tours. But it does have one quality that may trump all those: You don't need a tour guide. Nome has shops, historic sites you can walk to, and, best of all, a long network of roads where you can see wildlife and natural places on your own. That alone may make it a better choice than Barrow.

Nome exploded into existence with gold finds around 1900. The beach sand in front of the community turned out to be full of gold. People poured in by steamship and built a boomtown powered by alcohol and gambling. At the **Board of Trade Saloon,** which still serves drinks on Front Street today, bettors set odds on dog mushers racing across the vast Seward Peninsula, their progress reported by telephone lines set up for the purpose.

The spirit of those days lives on, to some degree. Nome has more strange and funny community events than any other place I know, including the **Bering Sea Ice Golf Classic** in March and the **Polar Bear Swim,** which is scheduled June 21 (late enough for ice to be clear from the ocean). And, of course, Nome has the **Iditarod Trail Sled Dog Race.** The hoopla in March, when mushers arrive at the end of their 1,000-mile dash from Anchorage, is essential Nome.

Getting there

Flying is the only way to get to Nome. **Alaska Airlines (☎ 800-252-7522;** www.alaskaair.com) flies 90 minutes by jet either direct from Anchorage or with a brief hop from Kotzebue. Prices are usually around $500 round-trip. Many visitors come on escorted-tour packages sold by **Alaska Airlines Vacations (☎ 866-500-5511;** www.alaskaair.com/vacations); as a day trip, it costs about $575. But I think Nome is better without an escort, especially if you rent a car or take an independent wildlife-viewing tour.

Getting around

All taxis operate according to a standard price schedule. A ride to town from the airport is $5. Nome has three taxi companies, including **Louie's Cab (☎ 907-443-6000).**

To explore the roads around Nome, you'll need a car. **Stampede Car Rental,** 302 E. Front St. (☎ **800-354-4606** or 907-443-3838), charges $100 to $175 a day for SUVs and vans. The same people operate the Aurora Inn (see "Where to stay," next).

Where to stay

Nome has many lodging options. If you can't find a room at one of these top choices, get a referral from the **Nome Convention & Visitors Bureau,** Front and Division streets (☎ **907-443-6555;** www.visitnome alaska.com). Be sure to get the advice of a real live person, either by phone or e-mail, to avoid stumbling into some of Nome's truly dreadful accommodations.

Aurora Inn & Suites
$$$–$$$$$ **Nome**

Come to this mock country inn on Nome's main street for the best traditional hotel rooms in town. In marked contrast to most of Nome's other rooms, these are nicely furnished and even have some style. Also noteworthy in Nome, you'll find lots of nonsmoking rooms. The same company owns the car-rental operation in town, which is on-site.

302 E. Front St., Nome. ☎ *800-354-4606 or 907-443-3838. Fax: 907-443-6380. www. aurorainnome.com. Rack rates: $150–$250 double; extra person 16 and over $10. AE, MC, V.*

Sweet Dreams B&B
$$$ **Nome**

It's the hosts who make this place special: Erna and Leo Rasmussen, who are deep wells of Nome history and local knowledge. Leo is a former mayor and a personable and funny man. The two-story house has a rustic, old-fashioned feel, with lots of Alaskan memorabilia and a sun room on top. Two rooms share a bathroom while a third has its own, but not attached. A full breakfast is served when Erna has time to prepare it, and they pick up and deliver to the airport.

406 W. 4th St., Nome. ☎ *907-443-2919. Rack rates: $150 double. Rates include full breakfast. MC, V.*

Where to dine

Nome has greasy spoons with typical diner food and ethnic restaurants where the owners serve their own national cuisine, plus that of a few countries. **Milano's Pizzeria,** 503 Front St. (☎ **907-443-2924**), for example, offers Italian and Japanese food and pizza attested to by locals.

Probably the best place to eat in town is **Airport Pizza,** which no longer is at the airport — it's at 406 Bering St. (☎ **907-443-7992;** www.airport pizza.com). The restaurant serves breakfast, sandwiches, and Tex-Mex, as well as pizza, and it brews fancy coffee. It also has 15 microbrews on tap and offers free Wi-Fi. But the delivery service is the biggest claim to fame: They package up pizzas and put them on bush planes out to tiny villages.

Husky Restaurant, 235 Front St. (☎ 907-443-1300), may not look promising from its street frontage, next to a couple liquor stores, but inside the small dining room it's very clean and quiet and the service is friendly and efficient. The specialty is Japanese food, but you can also get a good halibut sandwich or various other American choices.

Twin Dragons, on Front Street near Steadman Street (☎ 907-443-5552), serves Chinese cuisine in a fully decorated dining room, as well as Vietnamese noodles and pizza. The food is good enough to have kept them in business many years.

All restaurants in Nome are open long daily hours, and you can count on them accepting credit cards.

Exploring Nome

It's worth your time to take a walk around Nome to see some of the surviving historic buildings and other sites of interest. Check out the gold-rush-era **Board of Trade Saloon** and a bust of Roald Amundsen, who landed near Nome, in Teller, after crossing the North Pole from Norway in a dirigible in 1926.

Below the library, at Front Street and Lanes Way, the small **Carrie M. McLain Memorial Museum** (☎ 907-443-6630) contains an exhibit dedicated to the town's gold rush. The museum is free; it's open in summer daily from 9:30 a.m. to 5:30 p.m., and in winter Tuesday through Friday from noon to 5:30 p.m.

In good weather, walk or take a taxi to the beach southeast of town, where you may see small-time miners still sifting the sand for gold. You can walk the beach for miles. The gold-digging **Swanberg Dredge** that you can spot from here operated until the 1950s; a large dredge north of town worked into the mid-1990s.

Driving the tundra

Do explore the extraordinary 250-mile road network that provides access to the tundra and mountains beyond the town during your visit to Nome. Nowhere else in Alaska is this kind of wilderness so easy to access. You're likely to see reindeer and musk oxen, and bird-watchers can add many exotic new entries to their life lists.

For information on the three routes around Nome, check with the visitor center on Front Street or your car-rental agency. The best choice may be the **Nome-Council Road,** which heads 72 miles to the east, about half of that on the shoreline, before turning inland at the ghost town of Solomon, an old mining town with an abandoned railroad train known locally as the "Last Train to Nowhere." The engines were originally used on the New York City elevated lines in 1881; they were shipped to Alaska in 1903 to serve the miners along this line to Nome.

Flying over the tundra

Nome is a hub for bush-plane operators. Flightseeing charters are available, or you can fly on one of the scheduled routes out to the villages and spend a couple hours touring. The way to do it is to contact a flight service, explain what you have in mind, and follow their advice. Expect to pay $210 to $350. Don't plan to stay overnight in a village without advance arrangements and don't go in bad weather — you'll see little and may get stuck in a tiny village. **Bering Air** (☎ 800-478-5422 in Alaska only, or 907-443-5464; www.beringair.com) has a long and illustrious reputation and serves 32 villages from Nome and Kotzebue. They offer flightseeing trips by fixed-wing aircraft or helicopter on hourly charter rates (expensive if there are just one or two of you along). Or they'll sell you a seat on a scheduled loop flight that visits various villages, charging the fare only to the closest village on the trip while you enjoy the entire round-trip. They even offer charters across the Bering Strait to the Russian towns of Provideniya and Anadyr.

Shopping

Nome is one of the best towns in Alaska to shop for ivory and other Eskimo artwork, with low prices and a variety of choices, including the following highlights:

- ✔ A legendary collection is assembled in the barroom of the historic **Board of Trade Saloon,** which is attached to a shop at 212 E. Front St. (☎ 907-443-2611).

- ✔ The **Arctic Trading Post,** 302 W. Front St. (☎ 907-443-2686), is more of a traditional gift shop and has a good ivory collection.

- ✔ **Chukotka-Alaska,** 514 Lomen St. (☎ 907-443-4128), is an importer of art and other goods from the Russian Far East and is really worth a look.

Alaska Native art that you find in Nome is likely to be authentic, but you still need to ask; check out the information concerning fake Native art in Chapter 5.

Fast Facts: Nome

Bank

Wells Fargo, with an ATM, is at 250 Front St.

Emergencies

Call **911** in case of an emergency.

Hospital

Norton Sound Regional is at 5th Avenue and Bering Street (☎ 907-443-3311).

Information

Contact the Nome Convention & Visitors Bureau, Front and Division streets (☎ 907-443-6555; www.visitnomealaska.com).

Internet Access

You can access the Internet at the Nome Public Library, 200 Front St. (☎ 907-443-6626).

Police

The police are at Bering Street and 4th Avenue (☎ 907-443-5262).

Post Office

The post office is at Front Street and Federal Way.

Taxes

Sales tax is 5 percent; tax on rooms totals 6 percent.

Chapter 24

Bear Country: Katmai National Park and Kodiak Island

In This Chapter

▶ Finding lots of big bears
▶ Choosing a bear-viewing destination
▶ Traveling to Katmai National Park
▶ Taking in the wonders of Kodiak Island

*W*here the moisture of the North Pacific Ocean runs into the mountains of Kodiak Island and the Alaska Peninsula, frequent snow and rain give rise to rivers full of salmon. During spawning season, brown bears catch as much of that rich, fatty food as they can. When the fish aren't spawning, bears still dine on seafood, using their huge claws to dig clams from the beaches. And to finish the feast, they can find abundant berries on limitless miles of green hills. Inland, the species is called the grizzly bear, growing to a few hundred pounds. But here on the coast, a big bear can weigh three-quarters of a ton and stand 9 ft. tall. The Kodiak brown bear, the world's largest, is an entire subspecies to itself.

The region has other things to do besides looking at bears. **Kodiak** is a fascinating little town on the huge island of the same name, with vestiges of Russian America and the Alaska Native culture that preceded and survived the Russian invasion of 250 years ago. **Katmai National Park** also contains the bizarre and spectacular **Valley of Ten Thousand Smokes,** where one of history's largest volcanic eruptions occurred. You can go salmon-fishing at either place.

Bears are the marquee attraction, and if bears are your main goal, you need to consider your options carefully. The cheapest way to see bears is from a bus at Denali National Park (see Chapter 19), but you won't see the great big ones and you probably won't see them close up. You can't get to big, coastal brown-bear-viewing cheaply, but you may be able to simplify your trip by taking a small plane directly for bear-viewing from Anchorage (see Chapters 14). That may not get you to the absolute best bear-viewing sites, but, in season, you can find brown bears lots of places. Admiralty Island near Juneau also has prodigious bear-viewing; if you reserve well ahead, you can count on seeing bears there in season (see Chapter 20).

Katmai is the ultimate bear-viewing destination, where visitors watch bears feeding from close up, but it's also expensive, and the limited facilities are crowded when bear-viewing is hot. From Kodiak, you can get to bears only by small plane; you see them without crowds when you find them, but you're less likely to see large numbers of bears close up.

Discovering Bear Country and Its Major Attractions

On Kodiak Island and at Katmai National Park, bears rule the landscape. Not only are the bears much larger than the people, but they're also more numerous, the primary reason visitors trek to these remote locales.

Katmai National Park

Katmai is a remote, wilderness park far beyond the road network on the Alaska Peninsula southwest of Anchorage. All accommodations are in tents or expensive wilderness lodges, but you can go for a day trip just to see the bears. The park's main attractions are

- ✓ Watching huge and abundant brown bears feeding in Brooks River
- ✓ Fishing for salmon
- ✓ Hiking in the Valley of Ten Thousand Smokes

Kodiak Island

The nation's second-largest island (after Hawaii's Big Island) is mostly an enormous bear refuge, a kingdom where big bears reign supreme. Besides tiny Alaska Native villages, the town of Kodiak is the only settlement, an unspoiled fishing port with several interesting sites and many outdoor opportunities, including the following:

- ✓ Watching brown bears feeding in areas accessed by floatplane
- ✓ Kayaking in the protected ocean waters of the Kodiak Archipelago
- ✓ Hiking and tide-pooling on little-used trails and shorelines
- ✓ Fishing salmon in some of Alaska's most abundant streams

Bear-Watching at Katmai National Park

Katmai National Park takes in a large section of the Alaska Peninsula, a wild, rugged, and sparsely visited land within which lies a hot ticket: **Brooks Camp,** a former fishing lodge and the site of an extraordinary congregation of large brown bears. When fish are running in the Brooks River, in July and September (but not outside those times), bears come to catch them at a waterfall and feed to their hearts' content. Visitors are led by armed park rangers to elevated viewing platforms, where they can watch the bears in relative safety from quite close up.

The park was set aside in 1918 after the 1912 eruption of Novarupta Volcano, the most destructive volcanic event of the last 3,400 years. A 40-sq.-mile area was buried as deep as 700 ft. in ash. Named the **Valley of Ten Thousand Smokes,** the area continued steaming for decades. Now quiet, it remains a strange, unearthly wasteland, cut by erosion into precipitous gorges. To get to the valley, you first go to Brooks Camp and then take a bus.

Getting a room to stay overnight at Brooks Camp is prohibitively difficult: You must act far, far ahead of time. Even for day-trippers, the viewing platforms are crowded and you have to take turns. And getting there is costly. It's always so with a finite resource that's this desirable: The world's largest protected population of brown bears is here.

Getting there

You have one option to get to Katmai National Park's Brooks Camp: by small plane. Most people first fly by jet from Anchorage to the town of **King Salmon,** which lies just west of the park, on **Alaska Airlines** (☎ 800-252-7522; www.alaskaair.com). Service in summer is about $450 round-trip or more. **Katmai Air,** operated by park concessionaire Katmailand (☎ 800-544-0551 or 907-243-5448; www.katmaiair.com), provides these flights and offers round-trip airfare packages from Anchorage that can save some money (they charge a total of about $620) and add simplicity to your planning.

Every visitor arriving at Brooks Camp is required to attend a 20-minute orientation called "The Brooks Camp School of Bear Etiquette," designed to train visitors (not bears) and keep them out of trouble.

Getting around

Brooks Camp is a place you get around on foot; don't go if you can't walk a mile or more over rough ground. To get to the Valley of Ten Thousand Smokes, you join a bus tour 23 miles by gravel road from the camp. The park concessionaire, **Katmailand,** charges $88 per person, round-trip, for the all-day excursion, plus $8 more for lunch.

Where to stay and dine

Katmai's extreme remoteness means there is only one choice for indoor overnight lodgings at the park's main visitor area, Brooks Camp.

Brooks Lodge
$$$$$ **Brooks Camp**

The park has 16 hotel rooms, and they're all at this lodge. Staying here, you can enjoy the bears close up, perhaps sipping lemonade on the deck while they wander by. Otherwise, they're ordinary rooms with private bathrooms with shower stalls. The problem is, you have to reserve farther ahead than most people can manage. All peak dates (when the bears are around) book up 12 months out or earlier; for your choice, you have to call when the reservation system opens 18 months ahead, or January of the year before your visit. To save money, book the lodge rooms as packages with air travel. The least expensive with airfare is a one-night visit for $931 per person, double occupancy, meals not included; three nights is $1,572. A double room without airfare is $714. Three buffet-style meals are served daily for guests and visitors who aren't staying in the lodge. Breakfast is $15; lunch, $20; and dinner, $35. For food only, they take MasterCard and Visa; everything else, you pay for in advance.

Katmailand, 4125 Aircraft Dr., Anchorage. ☎ **800-544-0551** *or 907-243-5448. Fax: 907-243-0649.* www.katmailand.com/lodging/brooks.html.

Exploring Katmai National Park

You may have been to many national parks, but you've likely never been anywhere that's like Katmai. Read on to prepare for a unique experience.

The bears of the Brooks River

When the fish are running — in July especially, but also in September — 40 to 60 brown bear gather to feed at the falls on the Brooks River, half a mile from Brooks Camp. Visitors sign up for an hour on the viewing platforms and then hike out with park rangers as guides to enjoy their viewing period. Make sure to bring binoculars and warm fleece or wool clothing and rain gear, because the region is cool and damp.

While lodgings at the park are limited to the point of being unavailable to all but a lucky few, as many day-trippers can go as can afford the flights. Permits are not needed and there is no fee for entering the park.

The Valley of Ten Thousand Smokes

If you spend more than one day at Brooks Camp, you can take time to enjoy an outing to the Valley of Ten Thousand Smokes, ground zero of a volcanic eruption ten times more powerful than the 1980 eruption of Mount St. Helens. Although the smokes have stopped smoking, the area remains a dusty desert zone of strange landforms created by the erosion of the thick ash layer. For information about an all-day tour to the area, see "Getting around," earlier in this chapter.

Fishing

Katmai is a prime salmon- and trout-fishing area. **Katmailand** (☎ 800-544-0551; www.katmailand.com) operates two fishing lodges in the park, **Kulik Lodge** (www.katmailand.com/lodging/kulik.html) and **Grosvenor Lodge** (www.katmailand.com/lodging/grosvenor.html).

Fast Facts: Katmai National Park

ATMs

There are no ATMs in the park. A Wells Fargo branch, with an ATM, is in the King Salmon Mall on the Peninsula Highway in King Salmon.

Hospital

There are no hospitals in the park. The Camai Clinic, in Naknek (☎ 907-246-6155), is open during normal business hours; after hours, calls to its number go to emergency dispatchers.

Information

For information, contact the Katmai National Park Headquarters (☎ 907-246-3305; www.nps.gov/katm).

Police

The park has no phones and no cellular service. In King Salmon, call ☎ 907-246-4222; elsewhere, call the Alaska State Troopers at ☎ 907-246-3346 or 907-246-3464.

Crossing to Kodiak Island

I've never seen a place as green as Kodiak. Flying over the island, vivid green hills of brush and meadow rise from intricate shorelines of black rock on green water. Huge spruce trees of dark green cast deep shadows over a forest floor of thick, bright green moss. Frequent rains water the rich landscape, feeding the streams and plants that, in turn, feed animals and fish. The people lucky enough to live here make their living from the fish, and they've built a town that reflects the island, too, with narrow, winding streets, curious old buildings, and constant proximity to the sea.

Another part of Kodiak's charm lies in its undiscovered quality: You see few other tourists, and most businesses are locally owned and supported. The town is one of the oldest in Alaska and still has one of the most important structures left behind by Russian America, in addition to a good museum owned by Alaska Natives still working to recover their culture from the Russian invasion of 250 years ago. But most of the attraction of Kodiak is in the outdoors, with its bear-viewing, sea-kayaking, and fishing.

Getting there

Kodiak is easier to get to than other remote Alaska communities. It's accessible by frequent air service from Anchorage or by ferry from Homer.

The flight by jet from Anchorage to Kodiak is an hour long on **Alaska Airlines** (☎ 800-252-7522; www.alaskaair.com). **Era Alaska** (☎ 800-866-8394; www.flyera.com) also serves the route with prop-driven planes, which can save money. A cab, from **A & B Taxi** (☎ 907-486-4343), runs about $20 from the airport to downtown.

The ferries *Tustumena* and *Kennicott,* of the **Alaska Marine Highway System** (☎ 800-642-0066 or 907-486-3800; www.ferryalaska.com), serve Kodiak from Homer, ten hours away. Traveling by ferry is well worth it if you have the time, but the open ocean is often rough and passengers get seasick. (See tips for avoiding seasickness in Chapter 9.) Booking a cabin is a good idea for an overnight run. The U.S. Fish & Wildlife Service staffs the trips with a naturalist. Without a cabin, the passenger fare is $74 adults, $37 kids 6 to 12, free for kids 5 and under.

Getting around

A rented car helps in Kodiak, because the area has lovely remote roads to explore and the airport isn't close to downtown. You can rent from **Budget** (☎ 800-527-0700 or 907-487-2220; www.budget.com), with offices at the airport and downtown.

Where to stay

Kodiak is a remote small town, but you can find a good room there, either in a substantial hotel or a simple bed-and-breakfast.

Best Western Kodiak Inn
$$$$ Downtown

This is the best hotel in downtown Kodiak, with attractive rooms perched on the hill overlooking the boat harbor, right in the center of things. Rooms in the wooden building vary in size and view, but all are acceptable standard rooms with good amenities, including pillow-top beds with duvets and high-definition TVs with DVD players. On our last visit, some had been recently renovated, while others were a bit worn.

The **Chart Room** restaurant, specializing in seafood and with a great view of the water, is a good choice for a nice dinner out, with main courses in the $15 to $40 range.

236 W. Rezanof Dr., Kodiak. ☎ *888-563-4254 or 907-486-5712. Fax: 907-486-3430. www.kodiakinn.com. Rack rates: High season $170–$259 double, off season $109–$209 double; extra adult $15. AE, DC, DISC, MC, V.*

Kodiak Russian River Lodge
$$–$$$ Downtown

This B&B 12 miles south of town on Women's Bay reflects Kodiak's burly fishing culture, and is a perfect place for anglers. The host, Gus Gustafson, a former Bering Sea crab fisherman, regales guests with stories of high-sea adventures. Bedrooms are around a second-floor common area in the three-story house. A huge deck with grills is on the third floor, along with another common area with TVs, a billiards table, and a small bar with local beer on tap. Alaskan art decorates the rooms and halls. The fish-cleaning and freezing area on the ground floor has commercial-grade equipment. Gus offers free shuttle service to and from the ferry terminal downtown or the airport.

11322 S. Russian Creek Rd., Kodiak. ☎ *907-487-4430. Fax: 907-487-2327. www.kodiakrussianriverlodge.com. Rack rates: High season $115–$165 double, $260 suite; off season $75–$130 double, $200 suite. Rates include continental breakfast. AE, MC, V.*

Where to dine

The restaurant at the Best Western Kodiak Inn (see the preceding section) is among the best conventional restaurants in Kodiak, but another unconventional option is quite good, too: dinner on a 42-ft. yacht, the *Sea Breeze,* from **Galley Gourmet** (☎ **907-486-5079;** www.galleygourmet.biz). The evening starts at 6 p.m. with a one-hour cruise, then a dinner of seafood creations at anchor, and you're back at the dock at 9:30 p.m. The price is $140 per person.

The best restaurant in town is a coffee shop. **Mill Bay Coffee & Pastries,** about 3 miles out of downtown at 3833 Rezanof Dr. (☎ **907-486-4411;** www.millbaycoffee.com). Paris-trained, award-winning chef Joel Chenet, produces wonderful pastries and, at midday, brilliant combinations of local seafood and international seasonings brought to inexpensive sandwiches — the Kodiak sea burger is made of salmon, crab, shrimp, and cream cheese, among other ingredients, and costs only $13.

At the edge of downtown, **The Old Power House Restaurant,** 516 E. Marine Way (☎ **907-481-1088**), is predominantly a sushi restaurant, but excels in other seafood dishes and steak, among other various selections.

Henry's Great Alaskan Restaurant, 512 Marine Way (☎ **907-486-8844**), on the waterfront mall, is a bar and grill where you'll meet many commercial fishermen and other locals. The menu includes daily specials, local seafood, and good halibut sandwiches, as well as steak, pasta, and other items.

Exploring Kodiak

You can easily spend much of a relaxed day of sightseeing in Kodiak between your outdoor sojourns.

Alutiiq Museum

This exceptional museum, governed by Natives, seeks to document and revitalize Kodiak's Alutiiq culture, which the Russians and Americans virtually wiped out in the 19th and 20th centuries. Besides teaching about Alutiiq culture, the museum manages its own archaeological digs, teaches Alutiiq arts and language, and manages collections of over 250,000 artifacts, photographs, and recordings.

215 Mission Rd., Kodiak. ☎ *907-486-7004.* www.alutiiqmuseum.org. *Open: Summer Mon–Fri 9 a.m.–5 p.m., Sat 10 a.m.–5 p.m.; winter Tues–Fri 9 a.m.–5 p.m., Sat 10:30 a.m.–4:30 p.m. Admission: $5 adults, free for kids 15 and under.*

The Baranov Museum

The museum occupies the oldest Russian building of only four left standing in North America, which is Alaska's oldest building of any kind. Alexander Baranof, who ruled Alaska as manager of the Russian American Company, built the log structure in 1808 as a magazine and strong house for valuable sea-otter pelts — the treasure that motivated the Russians' interest here. This was the headquarters for the invasion he extended across Alaska and down the Pacific Northwest coast. The museum stands in a grassy park overlooking the water across from the ferry dock. Inside is a little gallery rich with Russian and early Native artifacts. The guides know a lot of history and show educational photo albums on various topics. The gift store is exceptional, selling antique Russian items and authentic Native crafts.

101 Marine Way, Kodiak. ☎ *907-486-5920.* www.baranovmuseum.org. *Open: Summer Mon–Sat 10 a.m.–4 p.m., Sun noon to 4 p.m.; winter Tues–Sat 10 a.m.–3 p.m. Closed Feb. Admission: $3 adults, free for kids 12 and under.*

Getting outdoors in Kodiak

Kodiak offers more than brown-bear-viewing. You'll also find opportunities for fishing, hiking, and sea-kayaking.

Brown-bear-viewing

Most of the rich bear habitat of Kodiak Island is controlled by the **Kodiak National Wildlife Refuge** (☎ **888-408-3514** or 907-487-2600; http://kodiak.fws.gov). You can learn about the bears at the refuge visitor center at Mission Road and Center Avenue, near the ferry dock, but to count on seeing them you need to get out on a plane or boat and visit at the right time of year. The easiest way is a Kodiak-based floatplane; expect to pay around $475 per person, with a two- or three-person minimum for a half-day trip. Landing on the water, you don rubber boots (provided) and walk up to half an hour to get to where bears congregate. From early July to early August, depending on salmon runs, flights land on Frazer Lake for viewing at Frazer fish pass. A ¾-mile walk on a dirt lane leads to the viewing area. Flights also visit Ayakulik and Karluk rivers when fish are present. At any of these sites, binoculars and telephoto camera lenses are essential, as no responsible guide would crowd Kodiak brown bears so closely that such lenses become unnecessary (although the bears could choose to approach within 50 yards of you). Bears congregate only when salmon are running, so the timing of your visit is critical. From early July to mid-August, you have a good chance of seeing bears fishing in streams on Kodiak, sometimes in numbers. Contact the refuge for more information on timing and bear activity.

Hermits on the homestead

Many years ago, *U.S. News & World Report* did an article about a homesteader on the Kenai Peninsula who was a Vietnam veteran — just one of the many mad hermits from the war who had hidden off in the Alaska woods by themselves, populating the wilderness with human time bombs. The subject of the story, a well-respected member of his little homesteading community, resented the characterization, and the magazine later paid him to settle his libel suit and printed a retraction. Everyone in the area knew the article was a bunch of baloney — Alaska homesteaders are as varied as people in the city. They aren't all crazed veterans any more than they're all victims of unrequited love, although those make the best stories. What they do have in common that's unique is a willingness to invest hard physical labor every day of their lives into the things the rest of us obtain effortlessly by turning a thermostat or a faucet handle.

Alaska's homesteaders came in waves. There were the prospectors from the gold rush who stayed. Then, after World War II, GIs with families looking for new opportunities came north and settled more land. The counterculture movement of the 1960s brought yet another group.

Federal homesteading laws written to open the Great Plains to agriculture in the 19th century made getting land difficult and required Alaska homesteaders to do a lot of anachronistic, absurd work — like clearing large tracts for farming that could never occur. The homesteaders had to survey the land, live on it, clear much of it, and then answer any challenges about their accomplishments at a hearing. If they passed the test, they received a patent to up to 160 acres.

The laws allowing homesteading on federal lands in Alaska were all repealed by 1986, but the state government still sometimes provides remote land to its citizens under various programs. The parcels are very remote and smaller than the old federal homesteads, and the rules still don't make it easy. Some families try, with a Hollywood dream of living in the wilderness, but give up when they learn firsthand of the hardship, privations, and cold. I know from experience that living off the grid can be wonderful, but it means completely reorienting your time and work to basic survival. Homesteading in the wilderness is a big step further, since you also have to build your place from scratch. Homesteaders repair engines below zero; construct houses without heavy equipment, help, or advice; carry their water and firewood; and live poor, largely without an income or any of the things money can buy. You have to be willing to bathe rarely, be cold in winter, be eaten alive by mosquitoes in summer, and end up with land that isn't really worth anything.

Many successful homesteading experiences end with growing children. A couple may make it in the wilderness before having children, and kids don't care if they can take a bath, so long as the parents don't mind washing diapers by hand and being far from medical care. But when children get to a certain age, they need to go to school and be around other children. The families often expect to go back to the homestead someday, but, somehow, they rarely do. I met a couple who moved to town to educate their children; then, after they retired and the kids were through college, they moved back out to their place along the railroad line north of Talkeetna. They didn't last through the winter — they'd forgotten how hard it was. Areas that were thriving little communities of neighbors in the 1950s or 1960s now are deserted, perhaps with one hermit left. Out of Alaska's total land mass of 365 million acres, only about 160,000 acres show any signs of human habitation.

My wife Barbara's parents homesteaded in the 1950s and 1960s. Her father was a World War II veteran. Today the family still has some acreage, and a treasure-trove of great stories — among them the tales of my late father-in-law's feats of strength and endurance, and my wife's memory of playing with dolls as a girl, and looking up to meet the eyes of a bear that had been watching her.

But my favorite is the story of Rose and her lover. They lived in the same area of northern California where Barbara's parents grew up. Everyone in town knew the story of the red-headed beauty who had an affair with an older man. Rose's parents refused to let her marry him and decreed that the couple couldn't see each other anymore. She entered a convent, and he disappeared, never to be seen in the town again. Many years later, after moving to Alaska, Barbara's parents were boating in Kachemak Bay when they got caught by bad weather on the opposite side of the bay from Homer. On their own in an open boat and looking for shelter, they found a cabin on a remote beach of an otherwise uninhabited island. They were taken in and befriended by the hermit who'd homesteaded there for years. After warming up with a cup of coffee, they got to talking about where they'd come from and how they'd ended up in Alaska. When it came time for their host to tell his story, it was about a beautiful young woman he'd loved, named Rose.

When fish aren't running on Kodiak, such as in June or after mid-August, air services fly to the east coast of the Alaska Peninsula, often in Katmai National Park, to watch bears digging clams from the tidal flats and eating grass and greens on the coastal meadows. It's interesting and the flight is spectacular, but the viewing may be from a greater distance than on the streams, and the bears will more likely be on their own. Generally, the flight services charge their standard bear-viewing seat rate regardless of how far they have to fly to find bears; if you charter, it may cost much more, but you'll have the freedom to determine where the plane goes for added sightseeing. Several small flight services offer bear-viewing, including **Sea Hawk Air** (☎ 800-770-4295 or 907-486-8282; www.seahawkair.com), **Island Air** (☎ 800-478-6196; www.kodiak islandair.com), and **Andrew Airways** (☎ 907-487-2566; www.andrewairways.com).

Fishing

The roads leading from the town of Kodiak offer access to terrific salmon- and trout-fishing. You also can seek advice and regulations from the **Alaska Department of Fish and Game**, 211 Mission Rd., Kodiak (☎ 907-486-1880; www.alaska.gov/adfg; click on "Sport Fish," then on the Southcentral region, then on "Kodiak/Aleutians").To fish remote areas, you need to charter a plane, going for a day or staying at a remote cabin or wilderness lodge.

Hiking and tide-pooling

Kodiak has some good, challenging day hikes and a wonderful seaside park with World War II ruins, easy walks, and tide pools for inspection. That's **Fort Abercrombie State Historical Park,** a couple of miles north of town on Rezanof Drive, where concrete ruins sit on coastal cliffs amid huge trees. Paths lead to beaches and tide pools, a swimming lake, and other discoveries. The gun emplacements, bunkers, and other concrete buildings defended against the Japanese, who had seized islands in the outer Aleutians and were expected to come this way. One bunker has a volunteer museum that's open sporadically.

The **Alaska Division of State Parks** manages the area from its Kodiak District Office, 1400 Abercrombie Dr. (☎ 907-486-6339; www.alaska stateparks.org, click on "Individual Parks," then "Kodiak Islands"); stop there for information or a walking-tour brochure. The island's more challenging hikes are cataloged by the town visitor center, at 100 E. Marine Way.

Sea-kayaking

The Kodiak Archipelago, with its many folded, rocky shorelines and abundant marine life, is a perfect place for sea-kayaking. Kayaks were invented here and on the Aleutian Islands to the west. For beginners, it's best to start with a day trip; the waters around the town of Kodiak are lovely for such a paddle. For a half-day, expect to pay around $140 per person; for a full-day, $220. One day-trip guide with a strong environmental ethic is Andy Schroeder, whose business is called **Orcas Unlimited Charters** (☎ 907-539-1979).

Fast Facts: Kodiak Island

ATMs

Several banks downtown have ATMs, including Key Bank and Wells Fargo on the mall at the waterfront.

Emergencies

In an emergency, dial ☎ **911**.

Hospital

Providence Kodiak Island Medical Center is at 1915 E. Rezanof Dr. (☎ 907-486-3281).

Information

For information, check with the Kodiak Island Convention & Visitors Bureau, 100 E. Marine Way, Suite 200 (☎ 800-789-4782 or 907-486-4782; www.kodiak.org).

Internet Access

A. Holmes Johnson Public Library, 319 Lower Mill Bay Rd. (☎ 907-486-8686).

Police

For non-emergencies, contact the Kodiak Police Department at ☎ 907-486-8000.

Post Office

The post office is at 419 Lower Mill Bay Rd., at Hemlock Street.

Taxes

Sales tax is 6 percent within city limits. The room tax inside the Kodiak city limits totals 11 percent, while outside the city it's 5 percent.

Part VII
The Part of Tens

The 5th Wave

By Rich Tennant

"It appears the fierce independent spirit of the Alaskan people is alive and well."

In this part . . .

Gee, going to Alaska on vacation sounds like a lot of effort, doesn't it? All that planning, riding on airplanes, and paddling sea kayaks. . . . Why not just stay at work, instead, and take an extra five minutes in the break room? If you're in any doubt, read this part and become inspired again about the incredible places you'll see, the interesting people you'll meet, and the fascinating things you'll discover in Alaska.

Chapter 25

Ten Great Walks and Hikes in Alaska

In This Chapter

▶ Hiking Alaska's most spectacular trails

▶ Strolling Alaska's most interesting streets

▶ Walking Alaska's prettiest beaches

*F*eet are wonderful things. They don't cost anything to use, and they can take you places no other vehicle can. In Alaska, your feet are especially useful, because hikes and walks can transport you to places of inspiring beauty, often with very little company (except for the occasional moose or eagle).

Hiking information is easy to get. Every town's visitor center has maps, handouts, and trail guidebooks. For strolls around small towns' historic downtown areas, you can frequently find a free walking-tour brochure. Information can enhance beach walks, too; you usually can find out where the tide pools are at Alaska Public Land Information Centers (www.alaskacenters.gov) or bookstores in coastal communities. In this chapter, I supply you with a head start to your information-gathering excursion by outlining ten great walks and hikes.

 Bring good walking or hiking shoes to Alaska. You also need layers of warm clothing, good rain gear, snacks, and water. For beach walks or tide-pool explorations, shin-high rubber boots enhance the experience. You can find a pair for around $15 in any coastal town. While you're in Alaska, wear them everywhere you go and people will think you're a local. When you leave, take the boots home as a souvenir or, if you have no room in your bags, give them away. Guests have left my garage stocked with every size over the years and now it's become a boot lending library for my visiting friends and relatives.

Glen Alps: Stepping from City to Mountain

The Glen Alps Trailhead in Chugach State Park, 2,000 ft. above Anchorage, is a magical portal between two worlds. On one side,

Anchorage spreads out below you like a toy city. From the park, you can see how isolated the city really is — a mere splash of civilization on a much larger background of wild land.

You can hike anywhere and in any style you like. Near the parking lot, take the paved overlook trail. Opposite the trail, climb steep Flattop Mountain. Up the valley, choose one of several trails through the mountains for hikes of up to a few days — you can camp anywhere along the trails. Or don't use a trail at all. Everything is above the tree line, and after you're past the brush near the parking lot, you can walk just about anywhere you want. Enjoy the other world — the total freedom beyond the city's edge. See Chapter 14.

Tony Knowles Coastal Trail: Exploring Urban Wilds

This coastal trail is the best of many paved multiuse trails that network through Anchorage like an alternative circulatory system. It starts downtown. Wander down to Elderberry Park, at the end of 6th Avenue, pass through a tunnel, and you'll find yourself face-to-face with the ocean and mud-flat bird habitat. From there, the trail continues along the shore and in the wooded bluffs above the water for 10 miles to Kincaid Park, the city's crown jewel of forest trails for cross-country skiing or mountain-biking. On the more wooded half of the trail, it's common to see moose and eagles; occasionally, you can spot beluga whales in the nearby Knik Arm from the downtown portion of the trail. The trail is popular at all times of year, good for walking, biking, skiing, and inline-skating. There are many spots to stop for a picnic — by a pond, on an ocean beach, or in a park. See Chapter 14.

Bird Ridge Trail: A Spectacular Cardiac Test

About 25 miles south of Anchorage on the Glenn Highway, this Chugach State Park Trail rises straight up a 3,000-ft. mountain in just a little over a mile, with mind-expanding views all the way. If you don't have the energy to make it to the top, you won't go home feeling disappointed: From near the start, you can see far along Turnagain Arm and into the series of mountains and valleys in the Chugach Range. If you have energy left, the ridge continues as an informal route, even higher and farther into the heart of the mountains. See Chapter 15.

Alaska Center for Coastal Studies: Tide-Pool Adventure

This nonprofit educational center in Homer takes visitors across Kachemak Bay, far beyond the reach of roads, to a lodge in the woods above a lovely, protected cove. From there, well-trained naturalists lead small groups to see the tiny animals in the tide pools of China Poot Bay, to discover the plants along the woodland paths, and to visit an archeological site where an ancient Native family once lived. Back at the lodge, you can use microscopes to inspect the plankton floating around tide-pool water and observe saltwater tanks with creatures you may not have seen in the wild. You don't have to hike more than a mile or two to see it all. See Chapter 16.

Granite Tors Trail: Nature-Carved Monuments

This challenging hike rises to a strange destination called the Plain of Monuments, where big granite monoliths stand up like abstract statues. The 15-mile looping route is in Chena River State Recreation Area, outside of Fairbanks on Chena Hot Springs Road. The trail slowly rises from the partly burned boreal forest to damp tundra, the site of the *tors,* naturally occurring towers of rock, standing at random spots upon the plateau without a sense of scale to orient their size. They were formed when softer material eroded from around granite that had oozed up from below. See Chapter 17.

Denali National Park: Finding Your Measure in the Backcountry

 Denali National Park has few formal trails, and those that do exist have nothing on the places you can explore without a trail, setting out on your own on tundra or on a gravel river plain. Without trees to get in the way, you can walk anywhere you choose, keeping your common sense handy to remember your way back and avoid dangerous situations. One of the best starting points is the Toklat River, reachable on the park's shuttle-bus system. If you don't see wildlife on your hike, you'll likely see animals on the bus ride. Or, if you're not ready to head out on your own, join a ranger-guided Discovery Hike into the backcountry with a small group. See Chapter 19.

Outer Point Trail: Walking to Whale Waters

 This trail, which leads from the North Douglas Highway near Juneau, is an easy walk of just 1⅓ miles. A boardwalk trail leads through mossy rain forest, over sunny wetlands, and out to a rocky beach overlooking islet-dotted Stephens Passage, on the side of Douglas Island opposite the city. Whales frequent these waters. At low tide, you can explore the tide pools on the beach before following the loop trail back through woods so pretty that you have to remind yourself you're not in a botanical garden, but just a small slice of a huge forest. See Chapter 20.

The Streets of Juneau: Finding the Charm of Old Alaska

Start at the capitol building at 4th and Main and walk uphill. You don't need a plan; every street is lined with charming, moss-roofed houses. You do need strong legs, however, as the streets climb insanely, sometimes quitting and becoming stairs, up to the ridge that is 7th Street. Explore in any direction from 7th Street: down the stairs that descend far below to Gold Creek, down Goldbelt Street to the Governor's Mansion, on Calhoun Avenue; or uphill toward the mountains along 7th. You're just steps away from a hike into the rain forest that looms over the city. See Chapter 20.

Sitka National Historical Park: Picturing the War

The battlefield where the Russians and the Native Tlingit settled the ownership of Alaska in 1804 is reached along a quiet, seaside trail lined by big trees and priceless totem poles. The faces on the poles, so dignified and distant, seem laden with memories of the great events that happened here. You can imagine the Russian ship approaching the shore with its cannons blasting. And you can easily picture how the Tlingit warriors felt as they waited for the attack: Listen to the ravens call, watch the waves on the shore, and smell the rain in the cedar trees, and you'll understand why they fought so hard to hold onto this place. See Chapter 22.

Barrow's Arctic Ocean Beach: Standing at the World's Edge

You won't ever mistake the beach of pea-size gravel where the land ends and the Arctic Ocean begins near Barrow for Waikiki, or even Bar Harbor, but it has its own desolate beauty. You're truly at the end of the world, and it feels and looks like it. Huge whale bones left over from Eskimo hunts lie on the beach in several places, especially near the Naval Arctic Research Laboratory (NARL) scientific facilities north of town. In the winter, the beach is a strange place — the frozen sea piles up into miniature mountain ranges. At those times, however, get local advice before walking far to avoid the hazards of polar bears or dangerously cold weather. See Chapter 23.

Chapter 26

Ten Questions to Ask an Alaskan

In This Chapter

▶ Discovering what makes an Alaskan tick
▶ Knowing what makes an Alaskan ticked off
▶ Finding out about an Alaskan's favorite places
▶ Understanding why an Alaskan is an Alaskan

I can say this because I'm an Alaskan and have been all my life: Alaskans tend to think they're better than people from other places. We've either got good self-esteem or delusions of grandeur — you can decide for yourself. One reason for this confidence is the mindset that, because Alaska is such a tough place, the people who live here must be tough, too. That's hooey. Another reason is that Alaska is such a wonderful place that Alaskans must be wonderful, too. More hooey. And yet another reason that actually begins to make a little sense: We love it here. Living here is a conscious decision for most of us, and we want to spread the word. Many Alaskans treat visitors as potential converts. As for you, well maybe, deep underneath, you're an Alaskan, too. You won't know for sure until it's time to get on the plane for home, but some good conversations on the way can give you an inkling. The questions in this chapter can help you get some of those good conversations started.

Where Are You from Originally?

In Alaska, the word *Native* means a member of an indigenous tribe and is always capitalized. Real Alaska Natives comprise about 16 percent of the population. Of the rest of the population, not many qualify to be called "Native," even by the ordinary meaning of the word (someone born in Alaska), because the great majority came from somewhere else. Alaska is a young and growing state. It's still a place people move to for a little adventure, knowing that they'll return to their previous home after a few years. Or at least that's what they *think* they'll do. My own parents came up for what they thought would be only three years. That was in 1966. They're still here.

How Long Have You Lived Here?

When people get up to speak in public meetings in Alaska, they invariably start out by saying how many years they've lived here. Since gold-rush days, it's been a rule that you can judge a resident's wisdom about the North by how many winters he's seen. Although people who don't enjoy winter sports can go stir-crazy, these days it isn't really that tough to get through the winter. Instead, knowing how long a person has been here tells you how much he remembers about the good old days. Alaska changes fast, and no matter how long you've been here, you think the real Alaska is what it was like when you arrived, not the pale copy that's here now.

Would You Tell Me about Your Gun/Boat/Snow Machine?

Save this question for when you have plenty of time to kill. Guns, boats, and snow machines are essential tools for many people who spend time outdoors in Alaska. They're also subjects of intense interest, discussion, and even obsession. People — mostly guys, to be honest — can talk for hours about caliber, horsepower, and track length, discussing what they own, how well it works, and what they dream of owning. Paying attention to the tools upon which your life depends makes sense when you're out in the wilderness. It's also fun to talk about your toys.

What Do You Think of This New Land-Management Plan?

Politics in Alaska — at least the interesting part that isn't just about money — is all about land, water, wildlife, and how they should be used or protected. The two camps — those who would save more, and those who would use more — are both well supplied with organizations, politicians, and lawyers. Because about 85 percent of the land is government-owned (15 percent belongs to Alaska Natives and less than 1 percent is privately owned), almost anything anyone wants to do requires a public debate. Stating your own opinion isn't really a good idea until you find out the views of the person you're talking to. These are the kinds of issues that make people angry.

Is the Legislature Doing a Good Job?

No, the legislature is never doing a good job. In fact, you'll discover that the legislature is a bunch of self-dealing, bone-headed, free-spending buffoons who couldn't be trusted on a cakewalk at a penny carnival.

Alaskans tend to get very worked up about state politics, and elections are often close and acrimonious. The reason for the poor results, despite the high interest, is because the population is a bunch of lazy, spoiled, latte-swilling newcomers (or ignorant, red-necked, pistol-toting old-timers) who want to lock up (or bulldoze) the most beautiful place on Earth. (You'll have to guess which kind of Alaskan I am.)

Why Is the Capital in a City You Can't Drive To?

Many people in Anchorage think the state capital should be in Anchorage, the largest city and the one with the best transportation network. Many people in Fairbanks think the capital shouldn't be in Juneau, but they'd like it even less if it were in Anchorage, a city they view kind of the way Canadians view the United States — big, arrogant, and unaware. In Juneau, everyone knows that keeping the capital means economic survival, and the town fights off the votes that come up every few years to move the capital (or some portion of it) with everything in its power, making many sensible arguments about the costs involved in a move. And that's why the capital is still in Juneau.

Where Do You Like to Go in the Summer?

Never ask, "Where's your favorite place to fish?" That's the best way to stop a conversation, not start one. Alaskans like to think they guard their favorite fishing spots better than the U.S. government guards the gold at Fort Knox. But you'll get the same information whenever you ask for favorite places to camp or to go to a cabin. Cities empty out on long summer weekends. Everyone goes somewhere. Living in Alaska and wasting those precious summer days would be nuts. And the places you go — on the ocean, on a river somewhere, or up in the mountains — are the places where you remember why you live in Alaska and why you enjoy being alive on this Earth. Some people may keep that sort of information to themselves, but most love telling for the sheer joy of talking about their special places. Chances are, in their enthusiasm, they'll end up telling you about their favorite fishing holes, too.

Have You Ever Encountered a Bear?

While dining with my brother's family and his in-laws in New Jersey one evening, I made the mistake of wondering out loud the best way to get to a certain address in Manhattan at rush hour the next morning. The topic stayed alive for 45 minutes. Bringing up the topic of bears at an Alaskan dinner table works about the same way. Two problems with the topic:

✔ Everyone wants to talk, because each thinks he has the best bear story (or five).

✔ After the conversation, you'll be afraid to leave your room for the rest of your trip.

Just remember that the information you receive this way has roughly the same accuracy that you'd expect whenever you ask, "Have you ever lost a really big fish?"

Here's My Itinerary — Do You Have Any Suggestions?

Some of my suggested questions are silly, but this one is a good idea. No matter how much time you spend planning, as a visitor, you'll never be able to know as much as the people who already live here. They'll probably have their own little-known trails, restaurants, and shortcuts to suggest. Besides, many Alaskans are travel experts, whether they want to be or not. When you live here, you get a lot of visitors.

Why Do You Live in Alaska?

In many other places, the answer may be "This is where I was born" or "This is where my job is." But most people who live in Alaska have made a conscious decision to be here. They probably moved here from somewhere else, even though living wherever they came from would've been easier. But they're here, and they know why, and they're likely willing to tell you. They can come out with something as prosaic as "I enjoy hunting" or "I love the snow," or something as eloquent as a gesture toward a grand view of a white mountain range. After you hear those answers and after you see the place for yourself, you may find yourself asking, "Why don't *I* live in Alaska?"

Chapter 27

Ten Ways to Be an Alaska Know-It-All

In This Chapter

▶ Discovering how big Alaska really is

▶ Finding out about mountains, earthquakes, and volcanoes

▶ Puzzling out Alaska's strange government finances

▶ Boning up on fish, fowl, and fur

Commit this chapter to memory and you'll be able to lean over to your fellow passenger on a trip through Alaska and deliver a long stream of informational nuggets that will amaze listeners and make you sound like a resident — or, more likely, make your listener raise a hand and say, "Excuse me, can I switch seats?"

How Big Is It?

Alaska is so big that:

✔ If each of the almost 700,000 residents were spaced evenly through the state, there would be about a mile between each person.

✔ There are a million acres for every day of the year (365 million acres of land).

✔ If it were placed on top of the contiguous 48 states, it would reach from coast to coast (if you include the Aleutian Islands).

✔ The span of north–south latitudes is the same as the distance from Miami, Florida, to Bangor, Maine.

✔ You can fit Germany, France, Italy, and the United Kingdom within its borders, and still have room left over for the state of Maine.

✔ If its shoreline of 34,000 miles were stretched out into a straight line, it would wrap all the way around the world, and then some.

That's a Lot of Park

In 1980, Congress protected a block of Alaskan parks and other conservation lands that, combined, are as large as the state of California, bringing the total protected area to roughly the size of Texas. Alaska contains 69 percent of all the national park lands in the United States, and 85 percent of the wildlife refuges. Alaska has 150 times more protected land than privately owned property. Wrangell–St. Elias National Park is the largest of all at 13.2 million acres, more than six times larger than Yellowstone. East of Wrangell–St. Elias is the Canadian border, where Canada's Kluane National Park begins, covering another 5.5 million acres. Between the two, that's almost as much park as the entire state of Maine. (Why do I keep picking on Maine?) This is why some Alaskans get irritated when people say that the state needs to be protected from development.

Those Mountains Are Really Tall

The top of Mount McKinley is 20,320 ft. above sea level. That's the tallest in Alaska, and about a mile taller than California's Mount Whitney, which is the tallest mountain in all the other states. Moreover, McKinley stands taller from its base to its top than any other mountain in the world. Sure, mountains on other continents are taller in total, but they all start off on higher ground to begin with. That's like my 9-year-old saying she's taller than Daddy when she's standing on a chair. And, although McKinley is Alaska's star center, it also has a deep bench. The fact is that Mount Whitney is only the nation's 17th tallest mountain — the 16 tallest mountains in the United States are in Alaska.

And They're Getting Bigger

You may think that Mount McKinley is big enough, which shows how much you underestimate the strong Alaskan spirit! In fact, McKinley is growing about an inch every three years. The state tourism board would like to take responsibility, but the real reason is that the Pacific *tectonic plate* (a massive slab of the Earth's crust) is constantly crushing itself against Alaska's southern coast. The Alaska Range, of which McKinley is the star attraction, is basically a big dent caused by that massive collision.

The mountains of Southeast Alaska are growing fast, too, but for another reason. There the cause is the melting of immense sheets of ice from the last Ice Age. All that weight lifted off the land is enabling it to spring up like a sofa cushion — about 1½ inches a year in Glacier Bay.

A Whole Lot of Shaking . . .

Alaska averages 50 to 100 earthquakes per *day*. Of course, we don't feel that many (Alaska is very big and most of the earthquakes are small), but we do feel our share. To be precise, Alaska claims

- ✔ Eleven percent of the world's earthquakes
- ✔ Fifty-two percent of all earthquakes in the United States
- ✔ The second and ninth largest earthquakes ever recorded in the world
- ✔ Twelve of the 15 largest earthquakes in U.S. history

It's all thanks to those tectonic plates bashing into each other (see the preceding section), which is also why we have so many volcanoes. But that's another topic — the next one, in fact.

. . . And a Whole Lot of Spewing

Fifty of Alaska's more than 130 volcanoes are active. That's 80 percent of the volcanoes in the United States, and 8 percent of all the above-water volcanoes in the world. A look at a globe tells much of the story. The long arc of the Aleutian Islands, stretching across the North Pacific Ocean to Russia's Kamchatka Peninsula, is the northern edge of the Pacific's *Ring of Fire* (the zone where the collision of tectonic plates causes leaks of the Earth's internal heat in the form of volcanic eruptions). Eruptions are like flares at the site of the collision. Or, maybe, they're bigger than flares. The 1912 eruption that created the Valley of Ten Thousand Smokes in Katmai National Park was the largest in the 20th century and was heard clearly in Juneau, more than 500 miles away. More recently, eruptions of Mount Redoubt and Mount Spur near Anchorage have been costly because of their disruption of aviation and the oil industry.

Free Money Just for Breathing

Yes, it's true: Every man, woman, and child gets a check from the state government just for living through the year. When the Prudhoe Bay oil field was developed in the 1970s (the biggest ever in North America — are you sick of the bragging yet?), it produced so much tax money for the state that, for at least a few years, the politicians in Juneau couldn't spend it fast enough. (You'll be relieved to hear they soon got over that problem.) The voters amended the state constitution and diverted a share of the tax money to a permanent investment account. Half the annual income from that account is passed out in annual checks, called Permanent Fund Dividends, which have risen over $2,000. In 2008, when oil prices went through the roof, the state government again found itself awash in money (thanks, American motorists — here's looking at you). Led by then-Governor Sarah Palin, the legislature voted to send out more free money, adding an additional $1,200 to the $2,000. My family of six, like Palin's, received almost $20,000 in free money. (The seventh member of the Palin family, baby Trig, didn't qualify because he wasn't born by January 1 — you can't give money to just anyone!)

The Most Famous Alaskan

It may come as a surprise to learn that Sarah Palin's popularity in Alaska dropped from over 80 percent to around 60 percent when she rocketed to national fame as John McCain's running mate for the presidency. By 2010, polls showed that the majority of Alaskans didn't like her and a solid 40 percent couldn't stand her. Part of the change may relate to her political personality change: contrary to her national profile, as governor her main allies in the legislature were Democrats and she pursued a moderate program. But an important reason for her popularity decline has got to be sheer embarrassment. Alaskans are used to outsiders asking about cold weather and grizzly bears, questions that allowed us to sound tough and adventurous. Now all anyone asks about is Sarah Palin, and Bristol, and Levi Johnston, and Levi Johnston's body guard, and Levi's views on birth control, and his mother's drug conviction, and so on and so on. We seem to be trapped in tabloid world.

Catching Politically Correct Fish

Alaska's biggest employer is the fishing industry, and the biggest catch is the plentiful wild Pacific salmon. A fact that is universally acknowledged and beyond dispute is that fresh Alaska salmon, properly prepared, is the tastiest and healthiest food on Earth. You'll have plenty of opportunities to agree with that, because people will try to feed you salmon every time you turn around. Unfortunately, the salmon industry is in decline because of competition from fish farmers from other places (fish farming is illegal in Alaska) who pawn off mushy, less flavorful, less pure, captive salmon (at lower prices) as fresh year-round. Wild Alaska salmon is the environmentally sustainable and politically correct choice.

Stating the Facts

If you've read this chapter and you still have someone sitting next to you on the plane after spouting all the knowledge you've gained, don't give up yet. It's time to pull out the heavy artillery:

- ✔ **State bird:** The willow ptarmigan, a grouse so dumb that you can hunt it with a big rock.

- ✔ **State fish:** The king salmon, of which the biggest commercial catch (146 pounds) and biggest sport catch (97 pounds) both came from Alaska.

- ✔ **State flower:** The forget-me-not. Isn't that sweet?

- ✔ **State fossil:** The woolly mammoth. Quick, what's your state's official fossil?

- ✔ **State insect:** The mosquito. No, that would be too honest. The real state insect is some kind of dragonfly (by vote of Alaskan schoolchildren), an insect that at least eats mosquitoes.

- ✔ **State sport:** Dog-mushing. But basketball is even more popular.

Quick Concierge

• •

*T*o simplify the process of finding a particular phone number or fact quickly, I've collected all the details I think you may need and put them here, in this handy directory.

Fast Facts

AAA

For roadside assistance, call ☎ 800-222-4357. AAA is made up of regional affiliates; you can find yours by going to www.aaa.com and typing in your zip code. The Alaska branch is AAA MountainWest (☎ 800-332-6119; www.aaa-mountainwest.com).

Banks and ATMs

You can find banks and ATMs in all but the tiniest towns. In larger towns, every gas station and convenience store has an ATM.

Business Hours

In the larger cities, major grocery stores are open 24 hours a day (or almost 24 hours a day) and carry a wide range of products (even fishing gear) in addition to food.

At a minimum, stores are open Monday through Friday 10 a.m. to 6 p.m. and Saturday afternoon, and they're closed Sunday. But many are open much longer hours, especially during the summer.

Banks may close an hour earlier, and if they're open on Saturday, only in the morning.

Under state law, bars don't have to close until 5 a.m., but many communities have an earlier closing, generally around 2 a.m.

Cellphone Coverage

The most densely populated portion of the state and some of the paved highways have cellphone and data coverage, but it's spotty beyond city limits, so don't bet your life on being able to make a call. In any event, if you plan to use your phone, check with your wireless provider to make sure it will work in Alaska and to find out just how badly you'll be gouged on roaming charges.

Driving

Safety tips for driving on Alaska's rural and seasonally icy highways are found in Chapter 7. For updated road conditions and construction delays, contact the Alaska Department of Transportation & Public Facilities. Call ☎ 511, or go to http://511.alaska.gov.

Emergencies

Generally, you can call ☎ 911 for medical, police, or fire emergencies. Remote highways sometimes have gaps in 911 coverage, but dialing 0 generally connects you with an operator, who can connect you to emergency services.

Citizens Band (CB) channels 9 and 11 are monitored for emergencies on most highways, and so are channels 14 and 19 in some areas.

Holidays

Besides the normal national holidays, banks and state- and local-government offices close on two state holidays: Seward's Day (the last Mon in Mar) and Alaska Day (Oct 18, or the nearest Fri or Mon when the 18th falls on a weekend).

Hospitals

The location of local hospitals is listed in the "Fast Facts" sections in each city chapter or section.

Information

See "Where to Get More Information," later in this Quick Concierge.

Internet Access and Cybercafes

In the cities and even in the Bush, Alaska's population is among the most wired anywhere. Most hotels and even B&Bs have wired or wireless broadband Internet access, or offer public terminals for their guests. Every public library has free Internet access, although there may be a wait for a computer. Internet cafes and business centers are common. I've listed handy places to get online in the "Fast Facts" sections in each city chapter or section.

Liquor Laws

The minimum drinking age in Alaska is 21. Most restaurants sell beer and wine, while a few have full bars that also serve hard liquor. Packaged alcohol, beer, and wine are sold only in licensed stores, not in grocery stores, but these stores are common, and you'll find that they're open long hours everyday, including Sunday.

More than 100 rural communities have laws that prohibit the importation and possession of alcohol (known as being *dry*) or prohibit the sale but not possession of alcohol (known as being *damp*). With a few exceptions, these laws are limited to tiny Bush communities that are off the road network; urban areas are all *wet*. Of the communities featured in this book, Barrow is damp and the rest are wet. Bootlegging is a serious crime and serious bad manners, so before flying into a Native village with any alcohol, ask about the liquor law in that community, or check a list online (go to www.dps.state.ak.us/abc and click on "Dry/Damp Communities").

Maps

You can buy street maps almost anywhere. For the outdoors, I recommend the excellent trail maps published by Trails Illustrated, part of National Geographic (☎ 800-962-1643; http://maps.nationalgeographic.com). They're available in sporting-goods stores and Alaska Public Lands Information Centers.

Post Office

The location of the local post office is listed in the "Fast Facts" sections in each city chapter or section.

Restrooms

Don't expect interstate highway rest stops. When you find the infrequent public restrooms on Alaska's highways, they're usually outhouses. If you require plumbing, you'll have to wait for a roadhouse or town. On unpaved rural highways, you need to be ready to go in the bushes. (Bring toilet paper and a plastic bag in which to carry used paper for proper disposal.)

In the cities, finding a restroom in a hotel lobby, shopping center, or the like is usually easy. Any business that serves food is required to have public restrooms.

Safety

You can find tips about rural highway safety in Chapter 7 and about outdoor safety in Chapter 9.

As for avoiding being a victim of crime, follow the same precautions you'd take anywhere else when traveling. Don't assume that small towns don't have crime. Although mugging is rare in Alaska, rape is much more common than it is nationally, and women need to be careful. Avoid rough bars, and don't go walking alone at night.

Smoking

In rural Alaska, smoking remains quite common and can be hard to get away from. Make a point of asking for an authentically nonsmoking room if you want one in a small town.

Anchorage is more in tune with the times, and smoking isn't allowed in any indoor public place, including bars.

Taxes

Alaska has no state sales tax, but most local governments have a sales tax and a room tax on accommodations. The tax rates are listed in the "Fast Facts" sections in each city chapter or section. The state and local governments and airports also impose high car-rental taxes and fees. In general, they're unavoidable and should be included in your rate quote; however, tips for avoiding some airport fees are covered in Chapter 7.

Telephone

All of Alaska is in area code **907**. In the Yukon Territory, the area code is **867**. When placing a toll call within the state, you must dial 1, the area code, and the number.

Generally, hotels add large surcharges on long-distance calls. You often can pay much less if you use a calling card from your home telephone provider, but make sure to ask about fees anyway. Pay phones often are costly to use with a calling card. Usually, the least expensive and simplest

alternative is to buy a by-the-minute phone card, available in grocery and convenience stores.

Time Zone

Although the state geographically spans five time zones, in the 1980s, Alaska's middle time zone was stretched so that almost the entire state lies in one zone, known as Alaska time. It's one hour earlier than California, four hours earlier than New York. Crossing over the border from Alaska to Canada adds an hour and puts you at the same time as the West Coast of the United States.

As with almost everywhere else in the United States, daylight saving time is in effect from 2 a.m. on the second Sunday in March (turn your clocks ahead 1 hour) until 2 a.m. on the first Sunday in November (turn clocks back again).

Tipping

Follow the same guidelines that you'd use anywhere else in the United States. For information about tipping guides, fishing charters, and wilderness lodges, see Chapter 4.

Weather Updates

The most complete source of weather information is the Web site of the Alaska Region Headquarters of the National Weather Service (NWS) at www.arh.noaa.gov.

The NWS also maintains a system using voicemail technology that enables you to receive forecasts and other weather information (even sea ice conditions) for every part of the state with a telephone call. Within Alaska the toll-free number is ☎ 800-472-0391. From outside Alaska, you have to pay for the call at ☎ 907-266-5145; this is also the local number in Anchorage, where it isn't a toll call.

Where to Get More Information

The following town visitor centers are good sources of information:

- Anchorage Convention & Visitors Bureau, 524 W. 4th Ave. (☎ 907-276-4118; www.anchorage.net)

- City of Barrow (☎ 907-852-5211 ext. 231; www.cityof barrow.org)

- Copper River Visitor Center, Glennallen (☎ 907-822-5555; www.traveltoalaska.com)

- Fairbanks Convention & Visitors Bureau, 101 Dunkel St. (☎ 800-327-5774 or 907-456-5774; www.explorefairbanks.com)

- Homer Chamber of Commerce Visitor Information Center, 201 Sterling Hwy. (☎ 907-235-7740; www.homeralaska.org)

- Juneau Convention & Visitors Bureau, 101 Egan Dr. (☎ 888-581-2201 or 907-586-2201; www.traveljuneau.com)

- Kenai Convention & Visitors Bureau, 11471 Kenai Spur Hwy. (☎ 907-283-1991; www.visitkenai.com)

- Ketchikan Visitors Bureau, 131 Front St. (☎ 800-770-3300 or 907-225-6166; www.visit-ketchikan.com)

- Kodiak Island Convention & Visitors Bureau, 100 Marine Way, Suite 200 (☎ 907-486-4782; www.kodiak.org)

- Nome Convention & Visitors Bureau, 301 Front St. (☎ 907-443-6555; www.visitnomealaska.com)

- Seward Chamber of Commerce and Conference & Visitors Bureau, 2001 Seward Hwy. (☎ 907-224-8051; www.seward.com)

- Sitka Convention & Visitors Bureau, 303 Lincoln St., Suite 4 (☎ 907-747-5940; www.sitka.org)

- Skagway Convention & Visitors Bureau, 245 Broadway (☎ 907-983-2854; www.skagway.com)

- Soldotna Chamber of Commerce & Visitor Information Center, 44790 Sterling Hwy. (☎ 907-262-9814 or 907-262-1337; www.visitsoldotna.com)

- Valdez Convention & Visitors Bureau, 104 Chenega St. (☎ 907-835-4636; www.valdezalaska.org)

For information on outdoor recreation, the **Alaska Public Lands Information Centers** (www.alaskacenters.gov) are centralized sources of information on all government lands, which make up some

85 percent of the state. The centers — in Anchorage, Fairbanks, Ketchikan, and Tok — are operated cooperatively by many land agencies, including the National Park Service and the U.S. Forest Service. The Anchorage center is at 605 W. 4th Ave., Suite 105 (☎ **866-869-6887** or 907-644-3661).

Index

• A •

A & B Taxi, 387
AAA, 410
Access America, 146
accommodations
  Anchorage, 170–175
  Barrow, 374
  budgeting for, 49
  Denali National Park, 317–321
  Fairbanks, 267–271
  Girdwood, 213–214
  Homer, 251–254
  Juneau, 330–335
  Katmai National Park, 385
  Kenai and Soldotna, 243–244
  Kodiak Island, 387–388
  Nome, 378
  one-of-kind lodging, 13–14
  Seward, 230–232
  Sitka, 358–360
  Skagway, 350–352
  Web sites and telephone
    numbers, 414
active-adventure itinerary, 96
activity charges, cruise, 53
Adventure Bound Alaska, 344
Aialik Bay, 238–239
Aialik Glacier, 238–239
Air Canada, 413
air travel
  air service, 70
  airfare, 59–60
  airlines, 58–59, 413
  air-sea program, 95
  to Anchorage, 164
  booking online, 60
  to Bush, 72
  to Denali National Park, 305–307
  to Fairbanks, 265
  flying with bulky outdoor
    equipment, 157–159
  to Homer, 251
  to Juneau, 328

  security measures, 155–157
  to Sitka, 357
  to Skagway, 349
  Southcentral and interior, 71
  Southeast, 71
Alaska Adventures Unlimited, 364
Alaska Airlines
  Barrow, 373
  Bush, 72
  contact information, 413
  in-state transportation, 48
  Juneau, 328
  Katmai National Park, 384
  Kodiak, 387
  Nome, 377
  overview, 59
  Sitka, 357
Alaska Airlines Vacations
  Barrow, 373
  Nome, 377
  package tours, 67
Alaska Boat & Kayak Shop, 341
Alaska Botanical Garden, 191, 196
Alaska Center for Coastal Studies,
    63, 398–399
Alaska Center for Performing
    Arts, 202
Alaska Department of
    Environmental Conservation,
    132
Alaska Department of Fish & Game,
    113, 189, 392
Alaska Department of
    Transportation & Public
    Facilities, 76, 168
Alaska Division of State Parks, 392
Alaska Experience Theater, 199
Alaska Highway Cruises, 67–68
Alaska Law Enforcement Museum,
    195
Alaska Marine Highway System
  cost, 49
  Homer, 251
  Juneau, 328

Alaska Marine Highway System
(*continued*)
  Kodiak, 387
  overview, 61–62, 72–74
  Prince William Sound, 216
  Sitka, 356–357
  Skagway, 349
Alaska Motorhome Rentals, 79
Alaska Mountaineering & Hiking, 187
Alaska Native Arts Foundation
  Gallery, 200
Alaska Native Heritage Center
  (Anchorage), 12, 17, 185
Alaska Natives. *See* Natives
Alaska Public Lands Information
  Center, 167, 193, 416
Alaska Railroad. *See also* trains
  cost, 49, 72
  Kenai Peninsula, 229
  Rail Tours, 67
Alaska Raptor Center, 363
Alaska Sea-Kayakers, 219
Alaska SeaLife Center, 226, 229,
  233–234
Alaska State Council on the Arts, 51
Alaska State Fair, 34, 221
Alaska State Museum (Juneau), 18,
  21, 337–338
Alaska Tour & Travel agency, 63
Alaska Travel Adventures, 344
Alaska Wild Berry Products
  (Anchorage), 201
Alaska Wildland Adventures,
  128, 142
Alaska Wildlife Conservation
  Center, 208
Alaska Yellow Cab, 165, 168
Alaska Zoo, 185–186
Alaskan lingo, 21–22
Alaska.org travel agency, 63
Alaska's Point of View Reservation
  Service, 230
Alaska/Yukon Trails, 75
Albert Loop Trail, 192
alcids, 126–127
alcoholic beverages
  Barrow, 376
  blood alcohol level, 168
  cruises, 93

Aleut people, 16
Allen Marine Tours, 365
Alpenglow (newspaper), 316
Alyeska Resort, 118, 194, 211–212
America the Beautiful–National
  Parks and Federal
  Recreational Lands
  Pass–Senior Pass, 144
American Airlines, 413
American Safari Cruises, 92, 97, 413
American Society of Travel Agents
  (ASTA), 93
Amtrak, 62
Amundsen, Roald, 379
Anchorage. *See also* Girdwood;
  Mat-Su area; Prince William
  Sound
  accommodations, 170–175
  Alaska Native Heritage Center, 185
  Alaska Zoo, 185–186
  Anchorage Museum at Rasmuson
    Center, 186
  arriving by car, 165–166
  arriving by train, 166
  beyond Bowl, 167
  beyond downtown, 196–197
  biking, 169
  Bowl, 166
  bus, 169
  cab, 168
  day trips, 197–198
  downtown, 166, 195
  driving in town, 168
  fast facts, 203–204
  flying in, 164
  guided tour, 197
  information, 167
  midtown, 166–167
  movies, 203
  nightlife, 202–203
  overview, 25–26
  performing arts, 202
  restaurants, 176–183
  road trips from, 4
  shopping, 198–201
  summertime outdoor activities,
    188–193
  wintertime outdoor activities,
    194–195

Anchorage Alaska Bed & Breakfast Association, 170
Anchorage Concert Association, 202
Anchorage Convention & Visitors Bureau, 167, 415
Anchorage Daily News, 152
Anchorage Fur Rendezvous Festival, 32
Anchorage Market, 200
Anchorage Museum at Rasmuson Center, 18, 21, 186
Anchorage Senior Activity Center, 144
Anchorage Symphony Orchestra, 202
Andrew Airways, 391
Annie Kaill's gallery (Juneau), 341
Arctic, 372–380
Arctic Circle, 30
Arctic Outfitters car rental, 76
Arctic Trading Post (Nome), 380
Arcticab, 373
Army Navy Store (Anchorage), 153, 199
Art Shop Gallery (Homer), 261
Artique (Anchorage), 200
ASTA (American Society of Travel Agents), 93
Athabascan people, 16
ATMs
  Alaska, 410
  Anchorage, 203
  availability, 55
  Barrow, 376
  Homer, 262
  Juneau, 345
  Katmai National Park, 386
  Kenai and Soldotna, 249
  Kodiak Island, 392
  Seward, 236
  Sitka, 367
  Ted Stevens Anchorage International Airport, 164
Attu, 20
Auke Bay area, 330
aurora borealis (northern lights), 278
Aurora Fine Arts, 199

• *B* •

B&Bs (bed-and-breakfasts), 49, 136
Backcountry Information Center, 314
backpacking. *See also* hiking
  Denali National Park, 314
  overview, 111
baggage fees, 52
bald eagle, 122
banks
  Nome, 380
  overview, 410
  Skagway, 355
Baranov Museum, Kodiak Island, 389
Barrow
  accommodations, 374
  Arctic Ocean Beach, 400
  bear viewing, 11
  escorted tour, 375
  fast facts, 376
  getting around, 373–374
  Iñupiat Heritage Center, 375–376
  outdoor activities, 376
  overview, 372
  restaurants, 374–375
  transportation to, 373
Battle of Attu, 20
Bay Excursions Water Taxi & Tours, 254
BBB (Better Business Bureau), 67
Bear Glacier, 239
bear-deterrent spray, 130, 157
bear-viewing
  Barrow, 376
  best of, 11
  flightseeing, 190
  Juneau, 341–342
  Katmai National Park, 383–386
  Kodiak Island, 383, 386–393
bed-and-breakfasts (B&Bs), 49, 136
Begich, Nick, 209
Begich-Boggs Visitor Center, 209
Beluga Point, 207
Benson Boulevard, Anchorage, 167
Bering, Vitus, 18
Bering Air, 380

Bering Sea Ice Golf Classic, 377
Better Business Bureau (BBB), 67
Big Ray's Store, 153
biking
  Anchorage, 169
  mountain-biking, 190–193,
      258–259, 278
  off-road, 111–112
  on pavement, 112, 188
  Skagway, 354
Bird Creek, 190, 207
Bird Point, 207
Bird Ridge Trail, 207, 398
bird-watching, 277–278
blood alcohol level, 168
boat tours, 50, 349. *See also* Alaska
      Marine Highway System;
      cruises
Boggs, Hale, 209
booking
  accommodations, 134–138
  air travel through cruise line, 95
  cruises, 91–92
books, recommended, 24
Bread-n-Butter Charters, 219
breakup, defined, 21
Brooks Camp, 384
Brooks River, 385
brown bears
  Kodiak Island, 389–391
  overview, 122–123
budgets
  ATMs and cash, 55
  credit cards, 55–56
  cutting costs, 53–55
  dining, 49
  hidden expenses, 52–53
  lodging, 49
  lost or stolen wallet, 56–57
  nightlife, 52
  shopping, 50–51
  sightseeing and outdoor
      activities, 49–50
  transportation, 48–49
  traveler's checks, 56
budget (economy) season, 94
Bunnell Street Arts Center, 261
bunny boots, 21

bus transportation
  Anchorage, 169
  Denali National Park, 305
  MACS system, 266
  overview, 74–75
  to Prince William Sound, 215
Bush Alaska
  air travel, 70–72
  defined, 21
  overview, 4, 28
business hours, 410

• *C* •

Cabin Fever (Anchorage), 200
Cabin Nite Dinner Theater,
      McKinley Chalet Resorts, 323
cabs, Anchorage, 168
Caines Head (Seward), 13
Caines Head State Recreation
      Area, 235
calendar of events, 32–34
Campbell Creek Science Center, 191
campgrounds, Denali National Park,
      320–321
camping equipment, transporting,
      157
canoeing
  Fairbanks, 277
  Kenai and Soldotna, 247–248
  options overview, 112–113
Capital Cab, 328, 330
Capital Transit city bus, Juneau, 328
car rental, 49, 61–62, 75–78, 165, 414
caribou, 123
Carmack, George, 348
Carnival Cruise Lines
  contact information, 413
  family-friendly, 88
  onboard activities, 89
  overview, 99–100
Carrie M. McLain Memorial
      Museum, 379
Carrs/Safeway Great Alaska
      Shootout, 34
cash, carrying, 55
CDC (Centers for Disease
      Control), 148

Celebrity Cruises, 100–101, 413
cellphone coverage, 155, 410
Center for Alaskan Coastal
    Studies, 260
Centers for Disease Control
    (CDC), 148
CenterTix, 202
Century 16 multiplex, 203
Challenge Alaska center, 212
Channel Channel, Juneau TV, 329
Cheapflights Web site, 60
cheechako, defined, 21
Chena Hot Springs Road, 265,
    283–285
Chena River State Recreation
    Area, 399
children, traveling with, 140–143
Chilkoot Trail, 354
China Airlines, 413
chinook (king) salmon, 23, 115,
    246, 384
Chiswell Islands, 238
Chugach Mountains, 187
Chugach Outdoor Center, 193
Chugach State Park, 26, 186, 193
Chukotka-Alaska (Nome), 380
chum (dog) salmon, 23, 115
City of Barrow, 415
CLIA (Cruise Lines International
    Association), 93
Coal Point Trading Co, 119
coho (silver) salmon, 23, 246–247
collision damage waiver, car-rental
    contract, 78
Coming into the Country
    (McPhee), 24
communicating on road, 154–155
commuter-class airlines, 70
Condor airline, 413
Continental Airlines, 59, 413
contracts, car-rental, 77–78
conventions used in book, 2–3
Cook, James, 208
Copper River Visitor Center, 415
counterfeit Alaska Native art, 51
coupon books, 54
Crackerjack Sportfishing Charters,
    234
credit cards, 55–56

credit-reporting agencies, 56–57
cross-country skiing, 194, 212
Cross Sound Express, 344
Crow Creek Mine, 211
Crow Pass Trail, 192, 213
crowds, avoiding, 339, 348
cruise desk, travel agency, 92
Cruise Lines International
    Association (CLIA), 93
cruise-only agency, 92
cruise specialist, 92
Cruise tours, 84
cruises. *See also specific cruise line
    by name*
    activity charges, 53
    American Safari Cruises, 413
    avoiding crowds, 339, 348
    best ports, 90
    best shore excursions, 90–91
    best tours, 90
    big-ship, 84, 99–109
    booking, 91–92
    booking air travel through cruise
        line, 95
    choosing cabin, 95–96
    cruise line contact information,
        413–414
    deciding when to go, 82–83
    dining, 88
    family-friendly, 88–89
    knowing where to go, 83–84
    luxury, 87–88
    onboard activities, 89
    selecting, 86–87
    small-ship, 85–86, 96–99
    special health and dietary
        concerns, 96
    travel agent, 92–95
    whale-watching, 89–90
Crystal Cruises, 88, 101–102
curbside check-in, 156
Cyrano's Off Center Playhouse, 202

• *D* •

Dall sheep, 124
Dalton Highway (Route 11),
    296–297
David Green Master Furrier, 201

day trips
Anchorage, 197–198
Fairbanks, 280–281
Juneau, 345
day-hiking. *See* hiking
daylight hours, seasonal, 28–30
Days of '98 Show, 355
Deadliest Catch (TV program), 24
Decker Gallery (Juneau), 341
Delta Air Lines, 59, 413
Denali Air, 315
Denali Highway (Route 8), 297
Denali National Park
accommodations, 317–321
backpacking, 314
bear viewing, 11
educational centers, 316–317
entrance fees, 303
flightseeing, 315–316
hiking, 313–315, 399
itinerary, 38–39
main entrance, 308
overview, 27, 300–301
packing for park, 304
rafting, 316
ranger programs, 316
reservations, 302–303
restaurants, 321–323
shuttle bus, 308–313
Talkeetna, 308
transportation to, 304–307
Denali National Park and Preserve
topographical map, 314
Denali Outdoor Center, 114, 316
Denali Visitor Center, 316–317
Denali/Fairbanks Loop, 292–294
Denkinger, Bill, 358
Denkinger, Carole, 358
Department of Natural Resources
Public Information Center, 192
Dew Mound Trail, 192
dimenhydrinate, 133
Dimond Boulevard, Anchorage, 167
dining, 49, 88. *See also* restaurants
DIPAC (Douglas Island Pink and
Chum, Inc.), 338

disabled travelers, 144
discount rates, 54
Disney Cruise Line, 88, 102–103, 413
Division of Parks and Outdoor
Recreation, 245
dog (chum) salmon, 23, 115
dog-mushing, 117, 235–236, 342–343
Dolly Varden char, 247
Don Sheldon Amphitheater, 315
Douglas Island Pink and Chum, Inc.
(DIPAC), 338
downtown
Anchorage, 166, 195
Juneau, 328–329, 330
Downtown Bicycle Rental, 187
The Driftwood Lodge, bike rental,
330
driving. *See also* car rental
to Alaska, 61
to Anchorage, 165–166
in Anchorage, 168
connecting the Loops, 294–295
Dalton Highway (Route 11),
296–297
Denali Highway (Route 8), 297
to Denali National Park, 304
Denali/Fairbanks Loop, 292–294
Edgerton Highway, 297–298
to Fairbanks, 265
to Homer, 250–251
in Homer, 258–259
information, 410
Klondike Loop, 298–299
McCarthy Road (Route 10),
297–298
to Prince William Sound, 216
Prince William Sound Loop,
289–292
renting RV, 78–79
road map, 287–289
safety tips, 79–80
to Seward, 229
to Skagway, 349
Steese Highway (Route 6), 299
dry bags (float bags), 130
Dyea Dave Shuttle, 349

• E •

Eagle River community,
    Anchorage, 167
Eagle River Nature Center, 192
Earthquake Park, 196
economy (budget) season, 94
Edgerton Highway, 297–298
educational centers, Denali
    National Park, 316–317
Eklutna community, Anchorage, 167
Eklutna Lake, 192
Elderberry Park, 188
ElderTreks, 144
emergencies
    Alaska, 410–411
    Anchorage, 203
    Barrow, 376
    Homer, 262
    Juneau, 345
    Kenai and Soldotna, 249
    Kodiak Island, 392
    Nome, 380
    Seward, 236
    Sitka, 367
    Skagway, 355
Equifax, 57
Equinox Wilderness Expeditions,
    113, 114
equipment rental, Anchorage, 187
Era Alaska
    Anchorage, 164
    Homer, 251
    Kenai and Soldotna, 243
    Kodiak, 387
Era Helicopters, 315, 343
Erik Hansen Scout Park, 249
escorted tours
    activity-based, 128
    Barrow, 375
    general discussion, 64–66
Eskimo people, 16–17
Estuary Life Trail, 365
E-tickets, 155
Europ Assistance USA, 148
Europ Assistance's Worldwide
    Healthcare Plan, 148
Exit Glacier (Seward), 10, 226,
    241–242

Expedia, 60, 139
Experian, 57
exposure (hypothermia), 130

• F •

Fairbanks
    accommodations, 267–271
    bird-watching, 277–278
    canoeing, 277
    Chena Hot Springs Road, 283–285
    day trips, 280–281
    fast facts, 283
    getting around in, 265–267
    hiking, 277–278
    mountain-biking, 278
    nightlife, 282
    overview, 12, 27, 264–265
    Pioneer Park, 275
    restaurants, 272–275
    Riverboat Discovery, 275–276
    shopping, 281–282
    transportation, 265
    UA Museum of North College,
        276–277
    winter recreation, 278–279
Fairbanks Convention & Visitors
    Bureau, 152, 266, 415
Fairweather Prints, 367
fall
    Anchorage north, 31
    coastal Alaska, 32
family-friendly activities
    cruises, 88–89
    itineraries, 41–42
    tour packages, 141–142
Far North Bicentennial Park,
    187, 191, 194
fare wars, 59
The Fate of Nature (Wohlforth), 24
ferry travel. *See* Alaska Marine
    Highway System
filters, water, 133
fine art, 201
Fireweed Gallery, 261
The Fish House, 235
fishing
    Anchorage, 189–190
    fly-in, 189

fishing *(continued)*
  general discussion, 113–114
  Homer, 259
  Juneau, 342
  Katmai National Park, 386
  Kenai and Soldotna, 245–247
  Kodiak Island, 392
  Prince William Sound, 218–219
  roadside, 189
  Seward, 234–235
  Sitka, 364
flares, 157
Flattop Mountain, 191
flightseeing
  bear-viewing tour, 190
  cost, 50
  Denali National Park, 315–316
  Juneau, 342–343
  Skagway, 354
float bags (dry bags), 130
flying. *See* air travel
Forest Muskeg Trail, 365
Fort Abercrombie State Historical
    Park, 392
Fox Island, 242
freestyle cruising, 105
Frontier Airlines, 413
furs, 201

• G •

G Street shopping, 199–200
Gavan Hill–Harbor Mountain
    Trail, 365
gay travelers, 145
giardia lamblia protozoan cyst, 133
Girdwood
  accommodations, 213–214
  Crow Creek Mine, 211
  hiking, 212–213
  Mount Alyeska Tram, 211
  overview, 26
  restaurants, 214
  skiing, 211–212
  transportation, 210
Girdwood Chamber of
    Commerce, 210
Glacier Bay Lodge & Tours, 344

Glacier Bay National Park (Juneau),
    10, 344
Glacier City Snowmobile Tours, 194
glacier cruises, 218. *See also*
    cruises
Glacier Gardens, 340
glacier-flight operations, 316
glaciers
  Aialik, 238–239
  Bear, 239
  Exit, 10, 226, 241–242
  Glacier Bay, 344
  Holgate, 238–239
  Kahiltna, 315
  Mendenhall, 11, 338–339
  Northwestern, 238–239
  Portage, 209
  Prince William Sound, 10
  Ruth, 10
  Tracy Arm, 344
Glen Alps Overlook, 188
Glen Alps Trailhead (Anchorage),
    13, 191, 397–398
Glenn Highway, 165, 185, 221
Godwin Glacier Dog Sled Tours, 236
Gold Cord Lake Trail, 220
Gold Mint Trail, 221
gold rush, 19, 348
Gold Rush Cemetery, 355
Golden, Fran Wenograd, 81
Gold-Rush towns, 12
GoNorth car rental, 76
Goose Lake, 188
Granite Tors Trail, 13, 399
gray whale migration, 239
The Great Alaskan TourSaver
    coupon book, 54
Greater Whittier Chamber of
    Commerce, 218–219
grizzly bear. *See* brown bear
Grizzly Man (film), 24
Gulf of Alaska cruises, 83
Guthrie, Lee, 350

• H •

Haggerty, Mako, 254
Haines, 90
halibut, 23, 259

Halibut Cove, 257
Halibut Point State Recreation Area, 366
hard frozen fish, 119
Harding Ice Field, 237, 242
Harv & Marv's Outback Alaska, 342
Hatcher Pass (Mat-Su area), 220–221
Heartbeats of Denali (film), 317
hermits, 390
Herzog, Werner, 24
High Country Car & Truck Rental, 76
highways. *See also* driving
  Dalton Highway (Route 11), 296–297
  Denali Highway (Route 8), 297
  Edgerton, 297–298
  Glenn, 165, 185, 221
  interior, 27
  Klondike Highway 2, 349
  New Seward, 166–167
  Parks, 221
  Seward, 166, 205–209
  Steese, 299
hiking
  Alaska Center for Coastal Studies, 398–399
  Anchorage, 190–193
  Barrow's Arctic Ocean Beach, 400
  Bird Ridge Trail, 398
  day-hiking, 13, 113
  Denali National Park, 313–315, 399
  Fairbanks, 277–278
  Girdwood, 212–213
  Glen Alps, 397–398
  Granite Tors Trail, 399
  Homer, 259–260
  Juneau, 343–344, 400
  Kodiak Island, 392
  Outer Point Trail, 399
  Seward, 235
  Sitka, 364–365
  Sitka National Historical Park, 400
  Skagway, 354
  Tony Knowles Coastal Trail, 398
Hillside, Anchorage, 166, 185
Hilltop Ski Area, 191, 194

history
  1741–1867 (Russian America), 18
  1867–1940 (gold rush), 19
  1940–1968 (United States defense), 19–20
  1968 to present (oil), 20–21
Holgate Glacier, 238–239
holidays, 411
Holland America Line, 66, 90, 103–104, 413
Holy Assumption Russian Orthodox Church, 249
Homer
  accommodations, 251–254
  driving or mountain-biking, 258–259
  fast facts, 262–263
  fishing, 259
  hiking, 259–260
  Islands & Ocean Visitor Center, 257
  natural history tours, 260
  nightlife, 262
  overview, 27, 228
  Pratt Museum, 257–258
  restaurants, 255–257
  sea-kayaking, 260–261
  transportation, 250–251
Homer Brewing Company, 262
Homer Chamber of Commerce Visitor Information Center, 415
Homer Saw and Cycle, 258
Homer Spit, 250
Homestead Trail, 259
homesteading, 390–391
Honey Charters, 218
honeymoon cruises, 103
Hospital Auxiliary Craft Shop, 201
hospitals
  Anchorage, 203
  Barrow, 376
  Homer, 262
  Juneau, 345
  Katmai National Park, 386
  Kenai and Soldotna, 249
  Kodiak Island, 392
  Nome, 380
  Seward, 236
  Sitka, 367
  Skagway, 355

hump (pink) salmon, 23, 115
humpback whales, 124
hypothermia (exposure), 130

• *I* •

icons used in book, 5
IdidaRide company, 236
Iditarod Trail Sled Dog Race,
    33, 377
Imaginarium, 41, 195
Independence Mine State Historical
    Park, 220
Indian River Trail, 364
Indians, 16–17
indigenous culture, 11–12
information services
    Anchorage, 167, 204
    Barrow, 376
    Homer, 262
    Juneau, 345–346
    Katmai National Park, 386
    Kenai and Soldotna, 249–250
    Kodiak Island, 393
    Nome, 380
    Seward, 236
    Sitka, 367
    Skagway, 355
Inlet Charters Across Alaska
    Adventures, 262
InnerSea Discoveries, 92, 98, 413
insect repellent, 157
inside cabin, on cruise, 96
Inside Passage cruises, 83
insurance
    escorted tours, 64
    lost-luggage, 148
    medical, 147–148
    overview, 146
    trip-cancellation, 147
interior air travel, 71
interior highways, 27
International Gallery of
    Contemporary Art, 199
Internet access
    Alaska, 411
    Anchorage, 204
    availability, 154–155
    Barrow, 376

booking flight online, 60
Cybercafes, 411
Homer, 262
Juneau, 346
Kenai and Soldotna, 250
Kodiak Island, 393
Nome, 380
Seward, 237
Sitka, 367
Skagway, 355
Internet service providers (ISPs), 155
Into the Wild (film), 24
Inuit people, 16–17
Iñupiat Heritage Center (Barrow),
    12, 18, 373, 375–376
Iñupiat people, 16
Island Air, 391
Islands & Ocean Visitor Center, 257
ISPs (Internet service providers), 155
itineraries
    family-friendly, 41–42
    National Parks, 38–39
    Southeast Alaska without cruise
        ship, 36–38
    two weeks, 39–41
    winter, 43

• *J* •

Jakolof Bay Dock, 258
Juneau
    accommodations, 330–335
    Alaska State Museum, 337–338
    bear-viewing, 341–342
    by bicycle, 330
    by car, 330
    day trips, 345
    dog-mushing, 342–343
    downtown, 328–329
    fast facts, 345–346
    fishing, 342
    flightseeing, 342–343
    hiking, 343–344, 400
    Macaulay Salmon Hatchery, 338
    Mendenhall Glacier, 338–339
    Mount Roberts Tramway, 339
    nightlife, 341
    overview, 12
    as port of call, 90

restaurants, 335–337
sea-kayaking, 344
shopping, 340–341
transportation, 328
whale-watching, 342
Juneau Artists Gallery, 341
Juneau Convention & Visitors
   Bureau, 152, 415
Juneau-Douglas City Museum, 340
Juneau Ice Field (Juneau), 10

• K •

K2 Aviation, 316
Kachemak Bay, 27, 228
Kachemak Bay Shorebird
   Festival, 33
Kachemak Bay State Park, 259
Kahiltna Glacier, 315
Kantner, Seth, 24
Katmai Air, 384
Katmai National Park
   accommodations, 385
   bear viewing, 11
   Brooks River, 385
   fast facts, 386
   fishing, 386
   getting around, 384
   restaurants, 385
   transportation to, 384
   Valley of Ten Thousand Smokes,
      385–386
Katmailand, 384, 386
Kayak search site, 60
Kenai and Soldotna
   accommodations, 243–244
   canoeing, 247–248
   fast facts, 249–250
   fishing, 245–247
   overview, 27, 226–228, 242
   restaurants, 244–245
   transportation, 243
The Kenai Canoe Trails (Quick), 247
Kenai Convention & Visitors
   Bureau, 415
Kenai Fjords National Park
   Exit Glacier, 241–242
   itinerary, 38–39

overview, 10, 226
park information, 238
tours, 238–241
transportation to, 237–238
Kenai Fjords National Park Visitor
   Center, 238
Kenai Fjords Tours, 239–240
Kenai National Wildlife Refuge, 226,
   242, 247
Kenai Peninsula. See also Homer
   Kenai and Soldotna, 242–249
   Kenai Fjords National Park,
      237–242
   overview, 26–27, 225–226
   Seward, 228–236
Kenai River, 226
Ketchikan, 366
Ketchikan Visitors Bureau, 415
killer whales (orcas), 125–126
Kincaid Park, 187, 190–191, 194
king (chinook) salmon, 23, 115,
   246, 384
Kiska, 20
Klondike Gold Rush National
   Historical Park, 347, 353
Klondike Highway 2, 349
Klondike Loop, 298–299
Kodiak Island
   accommodations, 387–388
   Alutiiq Museum, 389
   Baranov Museum, 389
   bear-viewing, 11, 389–391
   fast facts, 392–393
   fishing, 392
   hiking, 392
   overview, 386
   restaurants, 388
   sea-kayaking, 392
   tide-pooling, 392
   transportation, 387
Kodiak Island Convention &
   Visitors Bureau, 415
Kodiak National Wildlife Refuge,
   389
Kootznoowoo Wilderness, 342
Kumagoro, 182

• L •

Lake Hood, 190
Land's End Resort (Homer), 14, 252
Lanie Fleischer Chester Creek
    Trail, 188
Last Chance Mining Museum and
    Historic Park, 340
lesbian travelers, 145
Lifetime Adventures, 192
lighters, 157
Lincoln Totem Pole, 337
Lindblad Expeditions, 92, 98–99, 413
liquor laws, 411. *See also* alcoholic
    beverages
Little Campbell Lake, 190–191
lodging. *See* accommodations
Log Cabin Visitor Information
    Center, 167
lost-luggage insurance, 148
Louie's Cab, 377
Lowenfels Family Nature Trail, 196
Lower Dewey Lake, 354
luxury cruises, 87–88

• M •

Macaulay Salmon Hatchery, 338
MACS bus system, 266
mail2web service, 155
Majestic America Line/America
    West Steamboat Company, 413
Major Marine Tours, 217, 240
Mako's Water Taxi, 254
maps
    Alaska, 411
    Anchorage, 171, 177, 204
    Denali National Park, 309
    Fairbanks, 269, 273
    Homer, 253
    Juneau, 333
    Kenai Peninsula and Prince
        William Sound, 227
    road map, 287–289
    Seward, 231
    Sitka, 359

Skagway, 351
    wildlife viewing, 120–121
Mariah Tours, 239
marine wildlife tours, Sitka, 365
Matanuska valley, 219–220
matches, 157
Mat-Su area
    accommodations, 221–222
    Glenn Highway, 221
    Hatcher Pass, 220–221
    overview, 219–220
    Parks Highway, 221
    restaurants, 221–222
McCandless, Christopher, 24
McCarthy Road (Route 10), 297–298
McHugh Creek, 207
McKinley Flight Tours, 316
McPhee, John, 24
meclizine, 133
medical insurance, 147–148
MedicAlert, 149
megaships, 84
Mendenhall Glacier (Juneau),
    11, 338–339
Mendenhall Valley, 330
Mezirow, Andrew, 234
Midnight Sun Baseball Game, 33
Miller's Landing water taxi, 235
Minnesota Drive, Anchorage,
    165, 166
money
    budgeting, 47–52
    credit cards, 55–56
    cutting costs, 53–55
    hidden expenses, 52–53
    lost or stolen wallet, 56–57
    traveler's checks, 56
    using ATMs and carrying cash, 55
Moore House (Skagway), 353
moose, 125, 129–130
moraine, 242
Morris Thompson Cultural and
    Visitors Center, 266
Mosquito Cove Trail, 365
mosquitoes, 131
Mount Alyeska Tram, 211

Mount Marathon Race, 33
Mount Marathon Trail, 235
Mount McKinley, 27, 190, 406
Mount Roberts, 343
Mount Roberts Tramway, 339
mountain-biking. *See* biking
Mountain Flying Service, 354
Mountain Shop, 354
Mountain Travel Sobek, 114, 116,
     128, 142, 342
movies, recommended, 24
mud flats, 208
Mulcahy Stadium, 197
Murie Science & Learning
     Center, 317
Museum of Alaska Transportation
     & Industry, 221
museums
  Alaska Law Enforcement Museum,
     195
  Alaska State Museum, 18, 21,
     337–338
  Baranov Museum, 389
  Carrie M. McLain Memorial
     Museum, 379
  cost, 50
  Juneau-Douglas City Museum, 340
  Pratt Museum, 257–258
  Sheldon Jackson Museum,
     12, 363–364
  Skagway Museum and Archives,
     354
  UA Museum of North College,
     276–277
  UAF Museum of the North
     (Fairbanks), 18
musk ox, 125
Mykel's Restaurant, 245

• *N* •

NARL (Naval Arctic Research
     Laboratory), 400
Nast, Thomas, 19
National Parks, 38–39
National Weather Service (NWS),
     412–413
Native corporation, 22

Natives, 21
  arts and crafts, 200–201
  courtesy, 17
  finding, 17–18
  overview, 15–17
natural history tours, Homer, 260
Naval Arctic Research Laboratory
     (NARL), 400
Nelson, Colette, 361
Nenana River, 316
New Seward Highway, Anchorage,
     166–167
nightlife
  Anchorage, 202–203
  budgeting for, 52
  Fairbanks, 282
  Homer, 262
  Juneau, 341
  Skagway, 355
Nome
  accommodations, 378
  fast facts, 380–381
  overview, 12, 372
  restaurants, 378–379
  shopping, 380
  transportation to, 377
  tundra, 379–380
Nome Convention & Visitors
     Bureau, 378, 415
Nome-Council Road, 379
Nordic Skiing Association of
     Anchorage, 193
Norman Lowell Studio &
     Gallery, 261
Norovirus, 149
North Peninsula Recreation Area
     Nikiski Pool, 249
Northern Exposure (TV program), 24
northern lights (aurora borealis),
     278
Northern Lights Boulevard,
     Anchorage, 167
Northwestern Glacier, 238–239
Norwegian Cruise Line, 88,
     104–105, 414
Nova, 114, 193
NWS (National Weather Service),
     412–413

• O •

The Observatory (Juneau), 341
Ocean Shores, 252–253
Oceania Cruises, 105–106
off-peak travel, 53
oil industry, 20–21
Old City Hall, Anchorage, 195
Old Harbor Books, 367
Old Portage, 208
Olivia Travel, 145
onboard activities, cruises, 89
online travel agencies, 60, 67
Oomingmak Musk Ox Producers'
    Co-operative, 200
oosik, defined, 22
open-jaw itineraries, 60
Opodo Web site, 60
Orbitz, 60, 139
Orca Enterprises, 342
orcas (killer whales), 125–126
Orcas Unlimited Charters, 392
Ordinary Wolves (Kantner), 24
Out in Alaska travel agency, 145
Out North Contemporary Art
    House, 202
outdoor activities. See also wildlife
    viewing
  backpacking, 111
  Barrow, 376
  biking, 111–112
  budgeting for, 49–50
  canoeing, 112–113
  cost, 50
  dangers associated with, 128–133
  day-hiking, 113
  dog-mushing, 117
  fishing, 113–114
  rafting, 114–116
  sea-kayaking, 116
  sedate, 153
  skiing, 117–118
  snowmobiling, 118
  summertime, Anchorage, 188–193
  vigorous, 153
  wintertime, Anchorage, 194–195

Outer Point Trail, 343, 399
outside cabin, cruises, 96
overhead, defined, 329

• P •

Pacific salmon, 23, 115, 246–247, 384
Pack Creek, 11, 342
package tours, 66–68
packing
  Denali National Park, 304
  dressing like local, 154
  summer clothing, 152
  winter clothing, 152–153
Palin, Sarah, 20, 408
Panhandle, 27
paralytic shellfish poisoning
    (PSP), 132
Park Connection, 75
Parks Canada, 354
Parks Highway, 221
passports, 61
peak season, 94
People Mover city bus, 165,
    167, 169
Pepin, Jacques, 88
Permanent Fund Dividend (PFD),
    22, 408
Perseverance Trail (Juneau),
    13, 343
personal identification number
    (PIN), ATM, 55
Peterson Bay area, 260
PFD (Permanent Fund Dividend),
    22, 408
pharmacies
  Anchorage, 204
  Juneau, 346
Phillips Cruises & Tours, 217
Pier One Theatre, 262
PIN (personal identification
    number), ATM, 55
pink (hump) salmon, 23, 115
Pioneer Park, 264, 275
pioneers, 22
PJ's Taxi, 229
Point Woronzof, 189

Polar Bear Swim, 377
polar bears, 126
police
Anchorage, 204
Barrow, 376
Homer, 262
Juneau, 346
Katmai National Park, 386
Kenai and Soldotna, 250
Kodiak Island, 393
Nome, 381
Seward, 237
Sitka, 367
Skagway, 355
pollution, Arctic, 372
port calls, ferry, 74
port charges, 93
Portage Glacier, 209
portages, 248
port-to-port itinerary, 96
post offices
Alaska, 411
Anchorage, 204
Homer, 263
Juneau, 346
Kodiak Island, 393
Nome, 381
Seward, 237
Sitka, 367
Skagway, 355
Potters Marsh, 189, 206
Pratt Museum, 257–258
Priceline Web site, 60
Prince William Sound
fishing, 218–219
glacier cruises, 218
Honey Charters, 218
large tour boats, 217
Major Marine Tours, 217
overview, 214–215
Phillips Cruises & Tours, 217
restaurants, 219
sea-kayaking, 219
small tour boats, 218
Sound Eco Adventures, 218
transportation, 215–216
Whittier, 10
Prince William Sound Kayak
Center, 219

Prince William Sound Loop
Anchorage to Valdez, 289–290
day Valdez, 290
road back to Anchorage, 291–292
Valdez to Glennallen, 290–291
Princess Cruises, 88–90, 106–107,
414
Princess Tours, 66
Prudhoe Bay, 20
PSP (paralytic shellfish
poisoning), 132
Ptarmigan Arts, 261
puffins, 126–127

• **Q** •

qiviut, 200
Quick, Daniel L., 247

• **R** •

Rabbit Lake, 207
rack rates, 137
rafting, 50, 114–116, 193, 316
railroads. *See* trains
Rainbow Tours, 259
rainbow trout, 247
ranger programs, Denali National
Park, 316
red (sockeye) salmon, 23, 115, 246
red-eye flights, 59
Reed Lakes Trail, 220
Regent Seven Seas Cruises,
87, 107–108, 414
Reid, Frank, 347, 355
reservations
activities, 150–151
Denali National Park, 302–303
performing-arts, 151–152
restaurant, 151
respectful tourism, 98
restaurants
Anchorage, 176–183
Barrow, 374–375
Chena Hot Springs Road, 284
Denali National Park, 321–323
Fairbanks, 272–275

restaurants *(continued)*
Girdwood, 214
Homer, 255–257
Juneau, 335–337
Katmai National Park, 385
Kenai and Soldotna, 244–245
Kodiak Island, 388
Nome, 378–379
Prince William Sound, 219
reservations, 151
Seward, 232–233
Sitka, 361–362
Skagway, 352
restrooms, 204, 411–412
Resurrection Bay cruises, 238–239
Rie Muñoz Gallery (Juneau), 341
Riverboat Discovery, 275–276
Road Scholar, 144
roadside fishing, 189
rockfish, 23
Rodak Nature Trail, 192
Route 6 (Steese Highway), 299
Route 8 (Denali Highway), 297
Route 10 (McCarthy Road), 297–298
Route 11 (Dalton Highway),
296–297
Royal Caribbean Cruises
best tours, 90
family-friendly, 88
onboard activities, 89
Royal Caribbean International
Cruises, 108, 414
running, salmon, 115
Running of the Reindeer, 32
Russian America (1741–1867), 18
Russian Bishop's House, 363
Rust's Flying Service, 189
Ruth Glacier (Denali National
Park), 10
RV rentals, 78–79

• *S* •

safety
airline security measures, 155–157
Alaska, 412
Anchorage, 204
bear attacks, 129
bugs, 131
driving tips, 79–80
drowning, 130, 132
exposure, 130–131
getting lost, 131–132
seasickness, 132–133
shellfish, 132
staying healthy, 148–149
tainted water, 133
tips, 412
sailing coast, 72–74
salmon, 23, 115, 246–247, 384
Saltry, 256–257
satellite phones, 131
Savage River Day-Use Area, Denali
National Park, 315
scopolamine skin patch, 132
Sea Hawk Air, 391
Sea Life Discovery Tours, 365
Sea Lion Cove, 254
sea otters, 127
seafood, 22–23
sea-kayaking
Anchorage, 193
cost, 50
Homer, 260–261
Juneau, 344
Kodiak Island, 392
overview, 116
Prince William Sound, 219
Seward, 234
Sitka, 365–366
seasickness, 240
seasons
from Anchorage north, 29–31
coastal Alaska, 31–32
overview, 28–29
Seavey, Mitch, 235
senior citizens
discounts, cruise, 95
overview, 143–144
Seward
accommodations, 230–232
Alaska SeaLife Center, 233–234
fast facts, 236–237
fishing, 234–235
hiking, 235
overview, 26, 226, 228–229
restaurants, 232–233
sea-kayaking, 234

sled-dog mushing, 235–236
transportation, 229
Seward Bike Shop, 229
Seward Chamber of Commerce
and Conference & Visitors
Bureau, 415
Seward Highway, 166, 205–209
Seward, William, 19
Sheldon Jackson Museum,
12, 363–364
shopping
Anchorage, 198–201
budgeting for, 50–51
Fairbanks, 281–282
Juneau, 340–341
Nome, 380
Sitka, 367
shore excursions, 91, 366
shoulder season, 82, 94–95
Shrine of St. Therese, 340
shuttle buses, Denali National Park,
308–313
SideStep search site, 60
silver (coho) salmon, 23, 246–247
Silver Fox Charters, 259
Silversea cruises, 87–88, 109
The Simpsons Movie, 24
Sitka
accommodations, 358–360
Alaska Raptor Center, 363
fast facts, 367
fishing, 364
hiking, 364–365
marine wildlife tours, 365
as port of call, 90
restaurants, 361–362
Russian Bishop's House, 363
sea-kayaking, 365–366
Sheldon Jackson Museum, 363–364
shopping, 367
shore walks, 366
Sitka National Historical Park,
362–363
tide-pooling, 366
Tlingit people, 12
transportation, 356–358
Sitka Cab, 356
Sitka Convention & Visitors Bureau,
358, 364, 415

Sitka National Historical Park, 12,
18, 357, 362–363, 400
Sitka Ranger District, 364
Sitka Rose Gallery, 367
Sitka Sound Ocean Adventures, 365
Sitka Summer Music Festival, 33
Sitka Tours, 356
Skagway
accommodations, 350–352
biking, 354
fast facts, 355
flightseeing, 354
hiking, 354
Klondike Gold Rush National
Historical Park, 353
nightlife, 355
overview, 12, 347–348
as port of call, 90
restaurants, 352
transportation, 349
White Pass & Yukon Route, 353
Skagway Convention & Visitors
Bureau, 415
Skagway Museum and Archives, 354
Skagway Street Car Tour, 353
skiing
cross-country, 194, 212
Girdwood, 211–212
overview, 117–118
Skookum Jim, 348
Skyline Drive, Homer, 258
Sloan, Gene, 81
small-ship cruises, 83
American Safari Cruises, 97
InnerSea Discoveries, 98
itineraries, 96
Lindblad Expeditions, 98–99
overview, 85–86
Smarter Travel Web site, 60
Smith, Soapy, 347, 355
smoking
Alaska, 412
Anchorage, 204
Bush Alaska, 372
snowmobiling, 118
Sockeye Cycle, 349, 354
sockeye (red) salmon, 23, 115, 246
soft-adventure itinerary, 96

Soldotna. *See* Kenai and Soldotna
Soldotna Chamber of Commerce &
  Visitor Information Center, 415
Sound Eco Adventures, 218
Southcentral, air travel, 71
Southeast Alaska
  air travel, 71
  defined, 22
  overview, 4, 27
  touring without cruise ship, 36–38
Spear, Bill, 341
special travel needs, 140–145
Sport Fishing Alaska travel
  agency, 63, 114
Sports Den fishing charter, 246
Sports Express Luggage
  Delivery, 158
spring
  Anchorage north, 31
  coastal Alaska, 32
St. Elias Alpine Guides, 111
St. Lazaria Island, 365
St. Michael's Cathedral (Sitka), 366
Stage Line, 75
Stampede Car Rental, 377
Starrigavan Recreation Area
  trails, 365
Steep Creek, 339
Steese Highway (Route 6), 299
Stolzfus, Karl, 254
Suiter, Sheary, 63
summer. *See also* outdoor activities
  Anchorage north, 29–30
  bear-viewing, 190
  biking, 188, 190–193
  clothing, 152
  coastal Alaska, 31
  driving, 79–80, 188–189
  fishing, 189–190
  flightseeing, 190
  hiking, 190–193
  rafting, 193
  sea-kayaking, 193
  walking, 188
Summer Solstice, 33
Sun Country Airlines, 413
Sun Dog Express Dog Sled
  Tours, 117

Sunny Cove Sea Kayaking, 234, 241
Susitna valley, 219–220
Suzi's Woollies, 200
Swan Lake Canoe Route, 248
Swanberg Dredge, 379
Swanson River, 248

● *T* ●

Tagish Charlie, 348
Taku Store (Juneau), 340–341
Talkeetna
  Denali National Park, 308
  flightseeing, 315–316
Talkeetna Air Taxi, 316
Talkeetna Alaskan Lodge, 319–320
Talkeetna Mountains, 220
Talkeetna River Guides, 316
taxes
  Alaska, 412
  Anchorage, 204
  Barrow, 376
  calculating budget, 52
  cruises, 93
  Homer, 263
  Juneau, 346
  Kenai and Soldotna, 250
  Kodiak Island, 393
  Nome, 381
  Seward, 237
  Sitka, 367
  Skagway, 355
taxis, 53, 204, 229, 254, 387
tectonic plates, 406
Ted Stevens Anchorage
  International Airport, 164
telephones, 54, 131, 155, 410, 412
Temsco Helicopters, 354
Rusty Harpoon (Anchorage), 199
Thorson, Mark, 332
Thunderbird Falls, 192
Ticketmaster, 202
tide-pooling
  Kodiak Island, 392
  Sitka, 366
time zones, 412
tipping, 52, 93, 412
Tlingit people, 12, 16, 357

Toklat River (Denali National Park), 13
Tony Knowles Coastal Trail, 169, 188, 398
tors, 399
tour boats, Prince William Sound, 217–218
tours
  cost, 50
  Kenai Fjords National Park, 238–241
Tracy Arm glacier, 344
Trails Illustrated, 247
trains
  to Alaska, 62
  to Anchorage, 166
  to Denali National Park, 304–305
  to Fairbanks, 265
  overview, 72
  to Prince William Sound, 215–216
  to Seward, 229
transportation. *See also* air travel; bus transportation; driving; train
  to Barrow, 373
  budgeting for, 48–49
  escorted tour, 64–66
  ferry travel, 61–62, 72–74
  to Girdwood, 210
  interior highways, 27
  to Katmai National Park, 384
  Kenai and Soldotna, 243
  to Kenai Fjords National Park, 237–238
  to Kodiak Island, 387
  to Nome, 377
  package tours, 66–68
  travel agents, 62–63
Transportation Inspection Division, 168
Transportation Security Administration (TSA), 130, 156
TransUnion, 57
travel agents, 62–63, 91–95
Travel Guard, 146
travel insurance
  escorted tours, 64
  lost-luggage, 148

  medical, 147–148
  overview, 146
  trip-cancellation, 147
Travel Insured International, 146
Travel Sentry–certified locks, 156
traveler's checks, 56
Traveler's Guide to Alaskan Camping (Church), 78, 141
Travelex Insurance Services, 146
Travelocity, 48, 60, 139
Travelsupermarket, 60
Treadwell, Timothy, 24
Treadwell Mine Historic Trail, 343
trip-cancellation insurance, 147
True North Kayak Adventures, 261
TSA (Transportation Security Administration), 130, 156
tsunami, 22
tundra, 379–380
Turnagain Arm Trail, 206
TV programs, recommended, 24
Twentymile River, 208
Two Spirits Gallery, 199

• *U* •

UA Museum of North College, 276–277
UAF Museum of the North (Fairbanks), 18
United Airlines, 413
United States defense, 19–20
US Airways, 59, 413

• *V* •

Valdez Convention & Visitors Bureau, 415
Valley of Ten Thousand Smokes, 382, 384, 385–386, 407
value/standard season, 94
Van Gilder Hotel, 230–231
Via Rail Canada, 62
Viking Travel, 63, 73
villages, 22
Visitor Transit Bus, Sitka, 357
volcanoes, 407

• W •

walking
  Alaska Center for Coastal Studies, 398–399
  Barrow's Arctic Ocean Beach, 400
  Bird Ridge Trail, 398
  Denali National Park, 399
  Glen Alps Trailhead, 397–398
  Granite Tors Trail, 399
  Juneau, 400
  Outer Point Trail, 399
  on pavement, 188
  Sitka National Historical Park, 400
  Tony Knowles Coastal Trail, 398
wallets, lost or stolen, 56–57
water taxis, 235, 254
weather updates
  Alaska, 412–413
  Anchorage, 204
  Juneau, 346
web sites
  travel agencies, 60
weddings at sea, 103
Wedgewood Resort, 270–271
Wendeborn, Linda, 332
Westchester Lagoon, 188, 194
Western Union, 56
whale-watching
  gray whale migration, 239
  humpback whales, 124
  Juneau, 342
  orcas (killer whales), 125–126
  overview, 89
Whistling Swan Productions, 202
White Pass & Yukon Route, 72, 353
Whittier, 10, 26, 214–219
wildlife viewing
  activity-based escorted tour, 128
  bald eagles, 122
  brown bears (grizzly), 122–123
  caribou, 123
  Dall sheep, 124
  general discussion, 118–122
  gray whale migration, 239
  humpback whales, 124
  moose, 125
  musk ox, 125
  orcas (killer whales), 125–126
  polar bears, 126
  puffins, 126–127
  sea otters, 127
  wolves, 127–128
Windy Point, 207
Wings of Alaska, 328, 349
Winner Creek Trail, 212–213
winter
  Anchorage north, 30–31
  clothing, 152–153
  coastal Alaska, 32
  dog-mushing, 117
  Fairbanks, 278–279
  highway driving, 80
  ice-skating, 194
  skiing, 117–118, 194
  snowmobiling, 118, 194–195
Wohlforth, Charles, 24
wolves, 127–128
World Champion Sled Dog Race, 33
Wrangell–St. Elias National Park, 406
Wynn Nature Center, 260

• Y •

Yakutania Point Park, 354
Yankee Whaler, 201
Yellow Jersey Cycle Shop, 358
Young, Don, 209
Yupik people, 16